The **HUTCHINSON**

ENCYCLOPEDIA
OF THE
RENAISSANCE

General Editor: David Rundle
Mansfield College, Oxford

Helicon

Copyright © Helicon Publishing Ltd 1999

First published in Great Britain in 1999 by

Helicon Publishing Ltd
42 Hythe Bridge Stret
Oxford OX1 2PE
e-mail: admin@helicon.co.uk
Web site: www.helicon.co.uk

First published in paperback 2000

Typeset by TechType, Abingdon, Oxon

Printed and bound in Slovenia
by DELO tiskarna by arrangement
with Korotan Ljubljana

ISBN: 1-85986-332-9

British Library Cataloguing in Publication Data

A catalogue record for this book is available from the British Library.

Papers used by Helicon Publishing Ltd are natural recyclable products
made from wood grown in sustainable forests. The manufacturing
processes of both raw material and paper conform to the
environmental regulations of the country of origin.

Jacket illustration:
Detail from the Sistine Chapel ceiling by
Michelangelo Buonarroti (The Bridgeman Art Library)

Background image Copyright © 1996 PhotoDisc, Inc

CONTENTS

LIST OF MAPS

LIST OF GENEALOGIES

INTRODUCTION

Grand claims have been made for what we have come to call 'the Renaissance.' It was, in many accounts, a thorough-going modernizing movement, when Europeans rediscovered their past and simultaneously found their own individuality: it was, as it were, the age when civilization progressed from monochrome to technicolour. But, defined like this, the Renaissance is an urbane myth. The mélange of cultural changes which occurred over the 15th and 16th centuries can not be reduced to a single term; nor are those centuries reducible to just those changes. The conventional interpretation of 'the Renaissance' underestimates the complexity – and the excitement – of two hundred years of European history.

If the Renaissance has been cursed by exaggeration, that is appropriate enough: grandiloquent assertions were the métier of eloquent writers from Petrarch to Giorgio Vasari. Several scholars defined themselves in relation to a classical past, although that past was itself often ill-defined. While some authors emphasized how their modern world failed to live up to the glories of ancient civilization, others declared that they were in the business of reviving Roman or Greek culture. In the process, they also claimed they were reacting against barbarism, which could mean either other people – early Italian humanists were fond of depicting the far-away English as the quintessential barbarians – or previous generations, thus creating the Middle Ages. It hardly mattered where they found barbarism darkly lurking; these scholars' self-appointed task was to eradicate it in their own particular area of interest. Modesty was not the virtue most in evidence in these claims: their exponents oscillated between self-importance and self-congratulation. The first use of the idea of recreating classical culture applied specifically to Latin literature; the tradition of Florentine letters begun by Petrarch emphasized the overwhelming importance of their enterprise – although their detractors sometimes wondered whether a fascination with the niceties of syntax and orthography was anything more than pedantry. A couple of centuries after Petrarch, Giorgio Vasari cre-

ated a grand sweep of art history, describing how classical art had been gradually revived by generations of Italians (in particular by Vasari's fellow Florentines), culminating in Vasari's own generation. Such descriptions were more about marking out one's position in posterity than about dispassionate analysis of recent history. Yet, subsequent scholars have sometimes treated these claims with a naive faith they do not deserve: even the most self-confident humanist might be surprised to realise how persuasive his arrogant rhetoric has proved to be.

Scholars and artists were given to announcing their activities as great transformations to ensure their voices would be heard. They needed to shout loudly because the avant-garde was consistently in the minority. In the early 15th century, for example, the humanists were small coteries of scholars in various Italian cities. They never defined themselves clearly as 'humanists' – what they shared was a devotion to what some called *studia humanitatis,* by which they meant, in effect, ancient Roman literature and its lessons. However, even between the various coteries, there was not a shared agenda. The circle in Florence, centred on Leonardo Bruni, saw the translation of Greek works into a readable, Ciceronian Latin as one of their main tasks; others, like Pier Candido Decembrio in Milan, questioned whether Aristotle or Plato should be rendered into so different an idiom. Still others, like the north-eastern teacher Gasparino Barzizza, concentrated their attention not on Greek but on Latin texts. Yet others, often based in Rome, turned the new style of Latin writing to the service of patristic studies – a vogue also championed by Bruni's Florentine colleague, Ambrogio Traversari. Again, different groups of humanists drew contrasting lessons from the reading: Bruni might use his classical rhetoric in praise of the active life in a republic like Florence; others, like Guarino da Verona, at the d'Este court of Ferrara, thought the classics taught the preferability of living under a monarchy.

If these were the contrasting, competing interests of the early quattrocento avant-garde, some of these became popularized, if not cheapened, in the later 15th century. In particular, *studia humanitatis* became a much more clearly defined academic curriculum – elements of what had earlier been the exclusive preserve of a few scholars thus became available to a wider public. Yet, at the same time, a new avant-garde created itself, concentrating on the work of editing classical texts or on mastering yet other ancient languages, in particular Hebrew. In other words, as one generation's arcane learning became common knowledge, the ambitious scholar found different ways to demonstrate his special skills. This momentum of fashion also applied to art – as did local variation. In the 14th century, Florentine and Sienese painting had developed in dialogue and in competition; similarly, in the 15th and 16th centuries, Tuscan and Venetian art had contrasting preoccupations. There was no one line of development; there was no one unified 'Renaissance.'

Artistic and literary productions were, of course, not confined to these avant-gardes, nor did those who dubbed themselves the cultural élite exist in isolation. Renaissance motifs provided an inconsistent set of styles, not a whole aesthetic for living. A humanist might, for example, build up a library of recherché classical texts and of writings by his colleagues, but he would not disdain other books as well: even on these shelves room could be found for 'medieval' texts. Similarly, few houses would be crammed only with 'Renaissance' art: rich patrons collected paintings alongside their prized possessions of jewellery or of glass or of more exotic objects. The less well-off might have seen the latest artistic style only in a public place or in a church, but they may still have bought one of the small devotional images commonly available. In other words, just as classicizing architecture had to vie for space in the streets of an Italian city, so avant-garde art and literature lived alongside other cultural styles. Not only were Renaissance motifs too varied to exist in harmony; they also played alongside a range of other fashions, with the result – loud cacophony. If we must have an icon for this period, Breughel's *Tower of Babel* might be more fitting than Leonardo's doodled drawing of 'man as his own creator.'

A dictionary definition of the Renaissance often suggests that it was a movement beginning in Italy in the 15th century and spreading across Europe in the 16th century. We have already seen that the cultural phenomena can hardly be classed together as a 'movement' but the problems do not stop there: the idea of the 'spread' of these fashions is also problematic. For one thing, there was consistently an international aspect to intellectual and cultural life. Christendom was united not only by its religion but by its *lingua franca* of Latin; cultural communication might be as slow as physical links but it certainly existed. So, just as English teachers of logic could find employment in Italy in the late 14th century, so in the early 15th century, members of the small coteries of humanists could find patronage abroad. This did not mean that Italians had to travel across the Alps, though some were attracted by the prospects of foreign courts; many sought patronage by correspondence course, as it were, dispatching letters and copies of their works to unsuspecting 'barbarian' princes. In other words, humanists might often be writing for an exclusive, local audience, but their clientele could also be Europe-wide. Even before the invention of print, books could travel across the continent; on the other hand, paintings, sculptures and buildings are less easy to transport. Engravings, like those of Marcantonio Raimondi, became a method of communicating artistic styles, but the predominant method of 'spreading' motifs was by transporting the artists themselves. Princes from Matthias Corvinus in Hungary to Francis I in France summoned (sometimes unsuccessfully) artists to their courts. Others, like the irascible sculptor Pietro Torrigiano who found employment both in London and Seville, chose a peripatetic lifestyle – or had it forced upon them; whatever the circumstances of their departure from Italy, the effect was the creation of Italianate works in foreign settings.

However, the constant communication of artistic and literary styles across Christendom was not a one-way process: the Italian peninsula itself provided an import market. The rich artistic production of the Netherlands in the 15th century is itself sometimes called a Renaissance, but if it is, it is one which developed independent of Italian fashions. Despite – or perhaps because of – the stylistic contrast, Netherlandish paintings found admirers in Italy, with, for example, Jan van Eyck's art especially admired at the Neapolitan court of Alfonso V. Likewise, the genesis of oil-painting is a confused story but it was certainly a northern technique, already known to Cennino Cennini at the end of the 14th century and perhaps first used in Italy in the early 15th century by Antonello da Messina and Colantonio. The debt of Italian culture to the north was not confined to these artistic skills; fashionable in 15th century Italy, as elsewhere, were tapestries from the Low Countries, Federigo da Montefeltro, duke of Urbino, for example, employing northern craftsman to weave a set of tapestries for his palace *in situ*. For all the Renaissance rhetoric of disparaging barbarians, Italy was happy to enjoy elements of 'medieval' civilization.

Yet, if the 'Renaissance' is recognized as one part of the styles available to the culture of Christendom, discussion of its 'spread' becomes somewhat misplaced. Rather than seeing the Renaissance as some sort of benign virus eventually infecting all of Europe, we might want to talk of cultural interaction as a more equal conversation. Just as between the Italian city-states there were differences of style, across Europe there were various local cultural traditions. Christendom may have shared a cultural language but each area, as it were, spoke its own dialect. The Italian trends of the 15th and 16th centuries could not provide a whole new way of speaking but they did add to the cultural vocabulary, from which phrases could be chosen at will. Some might decide to mimic Italian fashions, but more often particular elements were selected and adapted. So, to give an example, in early 16th-century Portugal in the reign of Manuel I, an architecture developed which has come to be called Manueline. This exuberant style, most characteristically displayed at the monastery of Belem near Lisbon, was certainly no homage to Italian fashions – indeed, only after Manuel's death was there a trend towards aping 'the Roman style.' The architectural patronage and the motifs it used, sculpting stone (for instance) as if it were a ship's ropes, celebrated the recent successful explorations of Portuguese sailors – a development which like the architecture owed little to the Renaissance. Yet, at the same time, the eclectic style of buildings like Belem reflected a range of influences, which, alongside Flemish 'Gothic' elements, also included Italianate motifs. Such a partial deployment of Renaissance styles reflects less a failure to recognise the innate superiority of Italian developments than a self-confident appropriation of those elements which were found useful from the range of styles that constituted European culture.

The Renaissance had little use for encyclopedias. Undeniably, Renaissance writers, like their predecessors, collected together lives of illustrious (and infamous) men, as well as stories, both bawdy and moralizing. An encyclopedia's more comprehensive, alphabetical exposition of knowledge, however, was not conceived of – and we might wonder whether any Renaissance scholar would have found the format congenial. After all, humanists, in their attempt to promote themselves, their friends and their patrons, were willing to present a very partial view of the past and the present. And, considering the bad blood which often existed between ambitious scholars or petulant artists, it is hard to imagine that many would have been found who could agree on who should appear in such an encyclopedia. This is not to suggest that distance makes objectivity any the more possible: what follows does not claim to be more than an attempt to provide a sense of the variety and interest of two hundred years in the European cultural history. In doing so, it does not just discuss those developments which have been privileged with the appellation 'Renaissance'; instead, those productions which have come to symbolize the Renaissance – the lyrics of Petrarch and Thomas Wyatt, the plays of Shakespeare and Lope de Vega, the paintings of Michelangelo and Dürer, the architecture of Brunelleschi and Palladio, the prose of Machiavelli and Erasmus – are placed in their social and cultural context. In the process, it is hoped, something of the complexity of the 'Renaissance' can be reborn.

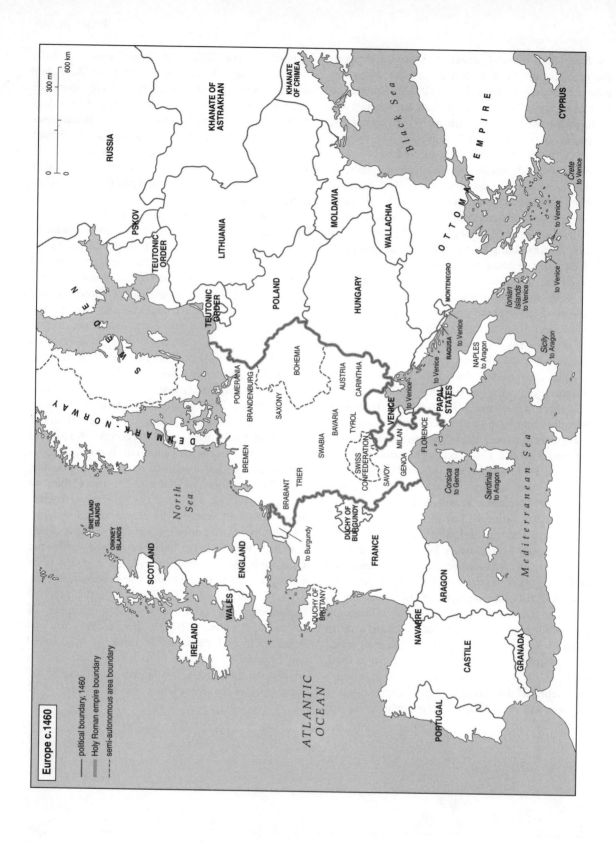

Europe c.1460

— political boundary, 1460
— Holy Roman empire boundary
--- semi-autonomous area boundary

300 mi
600 km

ATLANTIC OCEAN

SCOTLAND
IRELAND
WALES
ENGLAND

North Sea

SHETLAND ISLANDS
ORKNEY ISLANDS

DENMARK-NORWAY

SWEDEN

NORWAY

RUSSIA

PSKOV

TEUTONIC ORDER

TEUTONIC ORDER

LITHUANIA

KHANATE OF ASTRAKHAN

KHANATE OF CRIMEA

POLAND

POMERANIA
BRANDENBURG
SAXONY
BOHEMIA

BREMEN

TRIER

BRABANT

to Burgundy

DUCHY OF BRITTANY

FRANCE

DUCHY OF BURGUNDY

SWABIA
BAVARIA
TYROL
SWISS CONFEDERATION
SAVOY
GENOA
MILAN

AUSTRIA
CARINTHIA

VENICE

FLORENCE
PAPAL STATES

to Venice
to Venice

HUNGARY

MOLDAVIA

WALLACHIA

MONTENEGRO
RAGUSA
to Venice

Black Sea

OTTOMAN EMPIRE

CYPRUS

Crete to Venice

to Venice

to Venice

Ionian Islands to Venice

Sicily to Aragon

NAPLES to Aragon

Mediterranean Sea

Corsica to Genoa

Sardinia to Aragon

NAVARRE
ARAGON
CASTILE
PORTUGAL
GRANADA

Italy c.1454

HOLY ROMAN EMPIRE

SAVOY

VENICE

Bergamo

Padua

Milan

Venice

Turin

HUNGARY

to Venice

MILAN

MANTUA

FRANCE

MONTFERRAT

Ferrara

Modena

FERRARA

GENOA

Genoa

Bologna

Ravenna

MODENA

Rimini

Lucca

to Venice

Florence

LUCCA

FLORENCE

Arezzo

Pisa

Città di Castello

Siena

PAPAL
STATES

SIENA

Spoleto

Ragusa

Viterbo

Corsica
to Genoa

*Adriatic
Sea*

Rome

KINGDOM
OF NAPLES

Sardinia
to Naples

Naples

Salerno

Otranto

*Tyrrhenian
Sea*

M e d i t e r r a n e a n   S e a

Sicily
to Naples

0   100 mi

0   200 km

Aachen, Hans von (1552–1615)

German painter, born in Cologne. He lived in Italy about 1574 to 1588 and returned to Germany, working in Augsburg and Munich mainly on portraits, which showed both Italian and Flemish influences. He was appointed court painter to the Holy Roman Emperor ◊Rudolf II in 1592, a position he also held under Rudolf's successor, Matthias.

Like many German artists of the period – for example, Bartholomeus ◊Spranger, who was later his colleague at the imperial court – von Aachen spent the early part of his career in Italy, living in Venice but also paying extended visits to Rome (where he studied the antiquities) and Florence.

Though he did also paint historical and religious scenes, his output in both Italy and Germany consisted mainly of portraits, being patronized, for example, by the Fugger family. After his appointment to the imperial court (and his eventual move to Prague in 1597, when he married the daughter of Roland di ◊Lassus), he was also called upon to paint mythological and allegorical compositions, such as *The Triumph of Truth* (1598, Alte Pinakothek, Munich).

Abbate, Niccolò dell' (1509–1571)

Italian painter, from Modena. After an early career in Italy, he travelled to France in 1552 and assisted with the decoration of the chateau at ◊Fontainebleau.

Partly trained by his father, Abbate worked first in Modena, producing a series of frescoes based on Virgil's *Aeneid* for the Boiardo castle at nearby Scandiano (*c.* 1540). He then moved to Bologna, where his work included another fresco cycle, this time based on Ludovico ◊Ariosto's *Orlando furioso*, for the Palazzo Zucchini-Solomei (*c.* 1547). His work reflected the influence of recent trends in Italian art, especially as represented by ◊Correggio and ◊Parmigianino. Called to France by ◊Henry II, he worked alongside Francesco ◊Primaticcio at Fontainebleau. Abbate had other French patrons, including Anne, Duke of Montmorency.

Abravanel (Abarbanel), Isaac (1437–1508)

Portuguese Jewish scholar and statesman, born in Lisbon. He was the father of Leone ◊Hebreo. He held high office at the court of ◊Afonso V of Portugal, but was suspected of treason on Afonso's death in 1481 and fled to Toledo, where he wrote Old Testament commentaries. In 1483 he became treasurer to ◊Ferdinand of Aragon, but was forced to leave for Naples when Ferdinand expelled the Jews in 1492 (despite Abravanel's attempts to alter royal policy with an offer of 30,000 ducats). He served Ferrante I and then Alfonso II of Naples; when Alfonso died in Sicily in 1495, Abravanel returned to Italy, settling in Venice. His works include an intellectual analysis of the Kabbala in his *Roshemuna/Principles of the Faith* (1502).

Abravanel wrote throughout his peripatetic life, but only saw two of his works published: his *Sacrificio Pascual/Easter Sacrifice*, written in Naples and printed in 1496, and a commentary on the Book of Daniel, the *Ma'ayenê yesu'ah/Sources of Salvation*, possibly printed in 1497. Many of his other works of biblical commentary were published in Latin and in Hebrew in the second half of the 16th century.

Academia secretorum naturae (Latin 'The Academy of the Secrets of Nature')

A group of scholars with a shared interest in the natural sciences who met at the Neapolitan house of the writer and scientist Giambattista ◊della Porta from 1560. The first true scientific academy in Europe, it was condemned by the Catholic Church in 1580 and closed soon after.

Membership was open to those who had made some contribution to the natural sciences, which members discussed at their meetings. The Church was suspicious of its activities both because science seemed to be threatening its intellectual authority, and also because della Porta's interests often strayed into magic and alchemy.

academy

The term, deriving from the example of Plato's Academy, is applied to two different types of scholarly gatherings. The earliest Renaissance 'academies' were informal meetings of coteries of humanists, often gathering in a patron's house; so, for example, the circle of scholars around Cardinal ◊Bessarion were termed an 'academy' by Niccolò ◊Perotti. In this sense, the term was a *topos* of praise, signifying little that was other than personal. Indeed, in some cases, like that of Aldus Manutius's ◊ *Neakademia*, its claim to exist even in this sense is tenuous.

The second type of academy, however, is institutional and, thus, closer to the modern, formal understanding of the term; indeed, in some cases, they still exist or have been revived, like the Accademia dei Lincei, first founded in 1603, revived in 1795 (remodelled in 1870 as Italy's national academy).

However, having a constitution was not a guarantee of longevity, as the Venetian Academy of the early 16th century discovered: it closed in 1547 following embezzlement of its funds. Indeed, an academy could be a less than convivial organization: Antonio Francesco ◊Grazzini helped found the Accademia degli Umidi in Florence in 1540 but, because of tensions with other members, was expelled. He later founded the Accademia della Crusca in 1582 which aimed to purify and cultivate the Italian language.

At the same time, informality was no bar to influence. There was, for example, a series of Roman Academies, the first gathering around Pomponio ◊Leto in the 1460s, with others following in imitation until the disruption of the ◊Sack of Rome. Indeed, out of personal associations could an institution eventually grow as in the case of the ◊Neapolitan Academy.

Acciaiuoli, Donato (1429–1478)

Florentine politician and humanist. Born into the wealthy ◊Acciaiuoli family, as a youth he was acquainted with the leading scholars in Florence, including Giannozzo ◊Manetti and ◊Poggio Bracciolini. He learnt Greek from Johannes ◊Argyropolous and wrote commentaries on Aristotle's *Ethics* and *Politics* (1472–74), the latter being dedicated (at ◊Vespasiano da Bisticci's suggestion) to ◊Federigo da Montefeltro. He also translated Leonardo ◊Bruni's *History of Florence* into Italian in 1473.

Acciaiuoli was also a trusted member of the Medicean political elite (he was given the honour of delivering the funeral oration for Cosimo de' ◊Medici). He was sent on embassies, for example to France, where he presented Louis XI with a *Vita Carlo Magno/Life of Charlemagne* in 1461, and served on the ◊ *signoria*.

On Acciaiuoli's death, Cristoforo ◊Landino wrote the funeral elegy for him and Vespasiano included him in his *Lives*.

Acciaiuoli family

Family of Italian bankers prominent in the 14th and 15th centuries. Based in Florence, they also had important branches in Rome and Naples. From the 1430s they strongly supported the ruling Medici family in Florence, who rewarded them with political and ecclesiastical positions.

The family moved from Bergamo to Florence in the 12th century, and by the 1340s had created one of the richest banks in Italy, vying with those of the ◊Peruzzi and ◊Bardi. The family business was bankrupted in 1345 by the combination of high Florentine taxation, loss of business in Rome due to strained relations between Florence and the papacy, and (from 1341) the default of Edward III of England on his loan repayments. The Acciaiuoli soon recovered, however, and extended their financial operations: **Ranieri Acciaiuoli** (died 1394) established a branch of the bank in Athens in 1388.

The family also took an increasing part in politics both in Florence and elsewhere. **Niccolò Acciaiuoli** (1310–1365) settled in Naples in 1331, managing the financial affairs of King Robert. After Robert's death he became, as adviser to Joanna I, virtual ruler of Naples. In the early 15th century **Agnolo Acciaiuoli** supported the Medici family and consequently gained when Cosimo de' ◊Medici returned from exile in 1434. In the next decades, other members of the family, such as Donato ◊Acciaiuoli, were trusted Medicean supporters.

Accolti, Benedetto (1415–1464)

Jurist and writer from Arezzo. He taught law at the university of Florence and in 1458 became chancellor of the Florentine republic. He was not, though, in high favour with the Medici, a situation he tried to remedy by dedicating his two major works to members of the family: the *Dialogus*, debating the merits of the ancient world and modern times (dedicated to Cosimo de' ◊Medici in 1462), and *De Bello a Christianis contra Barbaros Gesto pro Christi Sepulchro/ The Christian War Against the Barbarians for Christ's Sepulchre*, a history of the First Crusade (dedicated to Piero di Cosimo de' Medici in 1463–64).

Accolti's history of the crusade was printed in 1532 and translated into Italian in 1543; in this form it was a source for Torquato ◊Tasso's *Gerusalemme liberata* (1574).

Accolti, Bernardo (UNICO ARETINO)
(1458–1535)
Italian writer, the son of Benedetto Accolti. He acquired renown at several Italian courts, notably Mantua and Urbino, as a reciter of impromptu verse. His presence at Urbino gained him a place as one of the main interlocutors in Baldassare ◊Castiglione's *The Courtier*. His comedy *Virginia*, based on a story in ◊Boccaccio's *Decameron*, was first performed in 1494, and printed in 1535.

Accolti family
Italian family from the city of Arezzo (in the Florentine territories) that produced a series of authors and ecclesiastics.

Michele Accolti made his money as a lawyer. He could thus afford to have his sons educated well, both in law and in the *studia humanitatis*. Francesco Accolti (1416–*c*. 1484) who, like his elder brother Benedetto ◊Accolti, taught law at university, had sat at the feet of Francesco ◊Filelfo and was considered a scholar in his own right; he produced an Italian translation of Leonardo ◊Bruni's *De Bello Italico versus Gothos* (printed 1528). Among Benedetto's children, Pietro Accolti (1455–1532) rose to become a cardinal in 1511 and was, alongside Domenico ◊Grimani, put in charge of the legal case of Johannes ◊Reuchlin. Benedetto Accolti (1497–1549), the son of Pietro's brother Michele, became a cardinal and wrote poetry.

Achillini, Alessandro (1463–1512)
Italian philosopher and surgeon. In his philosophy he followed the conventional Averroist interpretation of Aristotle; in his study of ◊anatomy he was one of the first to dissect the human body.

In his anatomical writings he described the veins of the arm, the seven bones of the tarsus (instep), the fornix, ventricles, and infundibulum of the brain, and the trochlear nerve. He also described the ducts of the submaxillary gland before Thomas Wharton (1614–1673) to whom the discovery is traditionally ascribed, and two of the three ossicles of the ear, the malleus and incus.

His *Anatomicae annotationes* (printed posthumously, 1520) brought together his various notes on anatomy.

Acosta, José de (*c*. 1539–1600)
Spanish Jesuit missionary and writer. His religious duties took him to Peru (1571–86) and then briefly to Mexico; he returned to Spain in 1587. Using his knowledge of these New World colonies, he wrote a *Historia natural y moral de las Indias/Natural and Moral History of the Indies* (1590), which proved immediately and internationally popular. Although he subsequently travelled to Rome on a diplomatic mission, he never left Europe again. In 1597 he became rector of Salamanca University.

Acosta's knowledge of Peruvian Indian languages coupled with his evangelical zeal led him to compose catechizing works in Quichua and Aimara. His concern for the heathen natives also prompted him to pen *De Procuranda Indorum Salute/On Tending the Health of the Indies* (*c*. 1576). This was published in 1588, with a brief account of Peru and its peoples, *De Natura Novi Orbis/On the Nature of the New World* (written about 1581), and dedicated to ◊Philip II. His 1590 *Historia natural* was an expanded translation of his *De Natura*.

Adagia
collection of Latin proverbs and allusions published by the Dutch humanist ◊Erasmus in 1500. The texts and his commentaries were meant to encourage the use of a correct and elegant Latin style. The book quickly became enormously successful, with numerous editions appearing during the 16th century.

The first version, *Collectanea Adagiorum*, appeared in Paris and was dedicated to Erasmus's English pupil and patron Lord Mountjoy. It contained about 800 entries. By the time of the second edition, *Chiliades Adagiorum*, published by the Aldine Press in Venice 1508, Erasmus had expanded the collection to over 3000 entries, including a number of Greek sayings.

Adamson, Patrick (1537–1592)

Scottish archbishop and writer. He came into conflict with the Presbyterian Party, was sent in 1583 as an ambassador to Queen Elizabeth I of England by James VI, and on his return to Scotland was charged with heresy and excommunicated in 1585. He was afterwards pardoned, but again excommunicated in 1588.

Adamson became minister of Ceres, Fife, in 1563. In 1566 he went to France, where he studied Calvinism, returning in about 1572, when he became minister of Paisley and chaplain to the regent. He was made archbishop of St Andrews in 1576. He was the author of many theological works in Latin, both prose and verse.

Adlington, William (LIVED 16TH CENTURY)

English translator and writer. He is known for his translation of ◊Apuleius' *Golden Ass* (1566).

Little is known of Adlington, except that he dedicated his work to the Earl of Sussex from University College, Oxford. He may have come from a Cheshire family and may be identifiable with the 'W A' who in 1579 published a verse tract, *A Speciall Remedie against the Furious Force of Lawlesse Love*.

Adoration of the Lamb (GHENT ALTARPIECE)

A polyptych altarpiece with 20 separate panels painted for the cathedral of St Bavo, in Ghent, by the Flemish artists Hubert and Jan van ◊Eyck in 1432. Its subject matter is complex. The lower register of the interior features *The Adoration of the Lamb of God by the Elect*; the upper register shows God the Father enthroned between the Virgin and St John the Baptist, angels, and Adam and Eve.

On the lowest level of the exterior, Jodocus Vyd and his wife, the patrons of the altarpiece, kneel in prayer before St John the Baptist and St John the Evangelist. Over these figures is an Annunciation, and, at the top, pictures of the prophets and sibyls who foresaw the Virgin Birth.

Each of the polyptych's 20 panels has the same high finish and extraordinary attention to detail. The

relative contributions of the two brothers van Eyck remain controversial, though Jan is thought to have painted most of the altarpiece.

Adrian VI (HADRIAN), (1459–1523)

Pope 1522–1523. Born Adrian Dedel in Utrecht, the Netherlands. A trusted adviser to the Holy Roman Emperor ◊Charles V, his election as pope was unexpected and his tenure very brief – he was in Rome for less than 13 months.

Educated at Louvain, where he taught and founded a college, he was appointed tutor to the future Charles V in 1507. In Aragon, on Ferdinand II's death in 1516, Charles made him regent alongside Cardinal ◊Ximenes; he was also inquisitor general of Aragon in 1516 and Castile in 1518. At Charles's request, he was created a cardinal in 1517.

There was little that was new in Adrian's hopes of securing Christian peace and a united crusade, or in his talk of reform – but scholars such as ◊Erasmus and Juan Luis ◊Vives believed that, this time, words might be turned into action. The pen, meanwhile, was Adrian's weapon of choice against heresy: he tried to persuade Erasmus to write against Luther. Such plans, however, came to nothing with Adrian's untimely death.

Adriano de Castello

See ◊Castellesi, Adriano.

Adriano Fiorentino (ADRIANO DI GIOVANNI DE' MAESTRI) (*c.* 1450–1499)

Florentine sculptor, military engineer, and medallist. He worked at courts in Italy and also in Germany, where he produced a bronze bust of Elector Frederick (III) the Wise in contemporary costume (Grünes Gewölbe, Dresden).

He is first recorded as a bronze founder in an inscription on the base of the *Bellerophon and Pegasus* (Kunsthistorisches Museum, Vienna), a bronze statuette designed by ◊Bertoldo di Giovanni in Florence during the early 1480s. Adriano then moved to Naples, serving King ◊Ferrante I as military engineer and artillery founder. He also produced medals of members of the house of Aragon and their court poet Giovanni ◊Pontano. In 1495 Adriano was serving Elizabetta Gonzaga, Duchess of Urbino, and then her brother Gianfrancesco Gonzaga, Duke of Mantua. By 1498 he was working in Germany at the court of Elector Frederick.

Among his finest works are two bronze statuettes: *Venus* (Philadelphia Museum of Art) and *Satyr with Pan-Pipes* (Kunsthistorisches Museum, Vienna).

Aertzen, Pieter (*c.* 1509–1575)

Dutch painter. He trained in Antwerp and worked there for a time before returning to his native Amsterdam. As well as conventional religious pieces, Aertzen specialized in genre painting, producing large canvasses often depicting a domestic scene in the foreground and a religious one in the background. An example is *Kitchen Scene with Christ in the House of Martha and Mary* (1553, Museum Boymans van Beuningen, Rotterdam).

His work was influenced by Antwerp artists, such as Jan Sanders van Hemessen, and also by contemporary prints. His pupils included Joachim Beuckelaer.

Afonso V, EL AFRICANO (1432–1481)

King of Portugal 1438–81. His father died in 1438 and, after a turbulent regency under his uncle Pedro, Afonso assumed the government in 1448. He conducted a successful campaign in Morocco against the Moors 1458–71. During his reign the Portuguese explored along the west coast of Africa almost as far as the Equator.

Agostino di Duccio (1418–1481)

Florentine sculptor, who produced in particular marble low reliefs. Among his many commissions were sculptures for the façade of the oratory of San Bernardino in Perugia, central Italy.

Agostino's training is unknown, though his first dated work, four reliefs for Modena Cathedral (1442), suggest he may have studied in Padua. His style, incisive and calligraphic, may also have been inspired by the reliefs of ◊Donatello.

In 1449 and 1454 Agostino appears in documents at Rimini, where he carved marble panels in the interior of the Tempio Malatestiano. His sculptures for the façade of the oratory of San Bernardino in Perugia, carved in 1457–62, are the reliefs *Christ in Majesty*, *The Annunciation*, and *The Saints in Glory*.

After an unsuccessful year in Bologna, Agostino returned to Florence in 1463, joined the guild of sculptors, and received (abortive) commissions for colossal statues on the cathedral (one of which was eventually carved by Michelangelo into his *David*). After carving several Madonna reliefs, one for the Medici (now in the Louvre, Paris), he returned to Perugia, where his talents were more full appreciated, and it was there that he died.

Agostino Veneziano (AGOSTINO DE' MUSI) (*c.* 1490–*c.* 1536)

Venetian engraver. He was active mainly in Rome, and by engraving paintings by well-known artists helped disseminate Italian Renaissance themes and motifs throughout Europe.

Originally active in his native Venice, Agostino was influenced by the engravers Giulio ◊Campagnola and Jacopo de' ◊Barbari. In 1516 he left Venice for Rome, where he became the foremost pupil of Marcantonio ◊Raimondi. ◊Raphael and ◊Giulio Romano were among the artists whose works were made more widely available through Agostino's prints.

Agricola, Alexander (ALEXANDER ACKERMAN) (1446–1506)

Flemish composer. He was one of the most florid continental composers of the late 15th century, writing in a contrapuntal and decorative style. He served at the court of Galeazzo Maria Sforza, Duke of Milan, during the early 1470s, as well as with Lorenzo de' Medici (the Magnificent) in Florence.

After a brief period at Mantua he returned to the Low Countries, and his name appears in the accounts of Cambrai Cathedral for 1475–76. After a second visit to Italy he entered in 1500 the service of ◊Philip the Handsome, Duke of Burgundy, whom he accompanied on journeys to Paris and Spain. During his second visit to Spain Philip died of fever, Agricola apparently dying at the same time. Agricola's epitaph (printed by Rhaw in 1538) states that he died at the age of 60, the date of death being established by his disappearance from Philip's court rolls.

Works include:
Eight Masses, 2 Credos, 25 motets, and 93 secular pieces.

Agricola, Georgius (LATINIZED NAME OF GEORG BAUER) (1490–1555)

German physician and metallurgist. He wrote on a range of topics from Latin grammar (1520) to the plague (*De Pestis*, 1544) via (following Guillaume Budeà example) weights and measures (*De Mensuris et Ponderibus*, 1533). He first published on metallurgy in his *Bermannus Sive de Re Metallica* (1530); he recorded developments in mining technology in his *De Re Metallica/On Metals* (1556), illustrated with woodcuts.

Agricola was born at Glauchau in Saxony and trained as a doctor. Working as a physician in a Bohemian mining town, he quickly made himself an authority on mining, metal extraction, smelting, assaying, and related chemical processes. His *De Natura Fossilium/The Nature of Fossils* (1546) advances a comprehensive classifications of minerals. He went on to explore the origins of rocks, mountains, and volcanoes.

Agricola, Martin (MARTIN SORE) (1486–1556)

German music theorist and composer. His most important treatise was a work in verse on musical instruments, *Musica Instrumentalis Deudsch* (1528, based on Virdung's *Musica getutscht* 1511), and he contributed three pieces to Georg Rhaw's *Newe deudsche geistliche Gesenge* (1544).

Agricola, Rudolphus (1444–1485)

German humanist. After a university education at Erfurt, Cologne, and Louvain, Agricola travelled in Italy in 1468 and became organist to the court of Ferrara. He returned to Germany in 1479 and became town secretary at Groningen. After another brief trip to Italy, he died at the age of 31.

His works included the influential *De Inventione Dialectica*, as well as several writings proclaiming his humanist allegiances: he wrote a life of Petrarch and *De Formando Studio* (1484), defending *studia humanitatis*. His fame in the next generation, however, was probably based most on his credentials as the Greek tutor to Alexander Hegius, who was Erasmus's teacher. Erasmus, who met Agricola once and briefly at that, praised him in his work as effectively Germany's first humanist.

Agrippa von Nettesheim, Heinrich Cornelius (1486–1535)

German theologian, doctor, soldier, and cabbalist. During his varied career he worked for several European rulers, notably for Emperor ◊Maximilian I 1511–18 as both soldier and diplomat. His writings were as varied as his career, including for example a *De Nobilitate et Praecellentia Foemini Sexus Declamatio/Declamation on the Nobility and Excellence of the Female Sex* (1529), but the majority reflect his lifelong interest in the occult which culminated in his *De Occulta Philosophia/The Occult Philosophy* (1533).

Born near Cologne, he studied in Cologne, Paris, and then Pavia in Italy, and briefly went to England in 1510 to study with John ◊Colet. About 1510 he wrote the first draft of *De Occulta Philosophia*, and in 1515 he was back in Pavia teaching occult science. He then moved to Metz in France but opposition forced him to leave and he settled briefly in Geneva, Switzerland.

In 1522 he became a doctor and was appointed physician to Louise of Savoy, queen mother of France, though his duties consisted mainly of casting horoscopes. In 1530 he published *De Vanitate et Incertitudine Scientiarum et Artium/The Vanity and Uncertainty of the Sciences and the Arts*, a sceptical survey of the state of knowledge in which human learning is unfavourably compared with divine revelation. He spent his last years in poverty in Grenoble, France.

Ailly, Pierre d' (1350–1420)

French theologian and philosopher. He taught at the university of Paris, where he was chancellor 1380–95, and wrote logical treatises. At the beginning of the ◊Great Schism, he argued that it could only be resolved by a ◊General Council of the Church. Thirty years later, as a cardinal, he attended the Council of ◊Constance and propounded his ◊conciliarism more fully. Apart from his academic and clerical activities, Ailly also wrote a geographical work *Imago Mundi/Image of the World* (c. 1410).

Despite his early call for a General Council, Ailly followed his monarch's lead and supported the Avignonese antipopes for much of the Schism. However, he attended the Council of Pisa and transferred his allegiance to the popes elected there; he was subsequently made a cardinal by John XXIII. Ailly was also an influential figure at the Council of Constance, where he presented his conciliarist *Tractatus super Reformatione Ecclesiae/Tract on the Reform of the Church* (1416).

He found most of his material for his *Imago Mundi* in the works of Classical writers, and paid little attention to the growing travel literature of his own day. A related work, *Compendium Cosmographiae/Cosmographical Compendium* (1413), did little more than repeat the geography of Ptolemy. However, while Ptolemy had assumed that both land and sea covered about 180° of longitude, Ailly extended the land mass to 225°. The implications of such a framework were not lost on one of Ailly's readers, Christopher ◊Columbus.

Alamanni, Luigi (1495–1556)

Florentine poet who spent much of his life at the French court. Unlike the other Italians patronized by ◊Francis I, Alamanni was not there because he was

invited but because he was a political exile. He wrote in Italian, his works influenced by Greek and Roman classics; they include *La coltivazione/Agriculture* (1546), a lengthy imitation of ◊Virgil's *Georgics*.

In his youth, Alamanni frequented the discussions in the ◊Orti Oricellari (and, because of this, was included as a speaker in Niccolò ◊Machiavelli's *Art of War* (1520)). Like others of the group, he was implicated in the unsuccessful conspiracy of 1522 against Giulio de' Medici (later Pope ◊Clement VII) and was forced to flee to France. He returned to serve in the Florentine republican government of 1527–30, but when the Medici returned he left again, destined to spend the rest of his life in hardly penurious exile, living off the patronage of Francis I, Henry II, and

Alberti Tempio Malatestiano in Rimini, a 14th century church made unique by the limestone casing designed by Leon Battista Alberti, 1450. Alberti's work was commissioned by the local *signore*, Sigismondo Malatesta (1417–1468) but the grandiose plans remained unfinished. *AKG London/Heiner Heine*

Catherine de' Medici. Indeed, this patronage ensured that he did return occasionally to his homeland and could maintain contacts with the likes of Pietro ◊Bembo and Sperone Speroni. Alamanni's poetry ranges across comedy (*Flora* (1549)), tragedy (*Antigone* (1556), endebted to Sophocles), and epic (*Girone il cortese* (1548), commissioned by Francis I, and *Avarchide* (1570), imitating Homer), as well as his Virgilian *La coltivazione*.

Alberti, Gasparo (*c.* 1480–*c.* 1560)

Italian composer, a singer at the Church of S Maria Maggiore, Bergamo, from 1508. He was one of the earliest exponents of the compositional technique known as *cori spezzati* (Italian 'broken choir'), where a body of singers is divided into smaller groups performing alternately and all together.

Works include:
Five Masses, 3 Passions, and other church music.

Alberti, Leon Battista (1404–1472)

Italian Renaissance architect and theorist. He set out the principles of Classical architecture and covered their modification for Renaissance practice, in *De Re Aedificatoria/On Architecture*, which he started in 1452 and worked on until his death (published 1485; translated as *Ten Books on Architecture* 1955).

Alberti's designs for the churches of San Sebastiano, begun 1460, and San Andrea, 1470 (both in Mantua) – the only two extant buildings entirely of his design – are bold in their use of Classical language but to a certain extent anticipate Mannerism. His treatises on painting (1436) and sculpture (*c.* 1464) were the first to examine the theory as well as the technique of the subjects. He also wrote works on mathematics, ethics, religion, and grammar.

Albertinelli, Mariotto (1474–1515)

Italian painter of religious subjects. He followed Fra ◊Bartolommeo in style, though had his own dignified simplicity of grouping. *The Visitation* (1503, Uffizi, Florence) and *Madonna and Child with Saints* (1506, Louvre, Paris) are among his works.

He was a pupil of Cosimo ◊Rosselli and fellow student of Fra Bartolommeo, with whom he collaborated in some works. ◊Franciabigio was one of his many pupils.

Albizzi, Rinaldo degli (1370–1442)

Italian political figure and soldier, unofficial ruler of Florence 1417–34. A leading member of the Albizzi family, which dominated the government of Florence after the revolt of the *Ciompi* in 1378, he came to power when his father, Maso degli Albizzi, died in 1417. He organized an unpopular and unsuccessful expedition against Lucca 1429–33, and exiled his main opponent, Cosimo de' ◊Medici, in 1433. He himself was exiled when Cosimo returned in 1434.

Albuquerque, Afonso de, THE ELDER (1453–1515)

Viceroy of Portuguese India. He accompanied Prince João in the 1471 capture of Moroccan Arzila. On João's accession in 1481 he became chief equerry, but when Manuel became king in 1495 Albuquerque inexplicably departed for Morocco. He returned eight years later, and in 1503 Manuel sent him on his first, brief, visit to India. He became viceroy in 1508 (despite opposition from ◊Almeida), and proved himself a cunning and adept leader, capturing Goa in 1510 and Malacca in 1511. He consolidated Portuguese power in the Indies by building fortresses, imposing coinage on the native barter economies, and encouraged intermarriage (despite criticism that the Portuguese grooms were unsuitable plebians). However, he never fulfilled his plan to turn Egypt into desert by diverting the Nile, nor captured Muhammad's remains and exchanged them for Jerusalem. His dispatches to Manuel I, justifying his activities, are a remarkable historical source which his son Afonso exploited for his father's biography.

Albuquerque, Afonso de, THE YOUNGER (1500–1580)

Portuguese administrator and author. More fortunate than his father, Afonso de ◊Albuquerque, he changed his name from Blas to that of his late father, Afonso, on the insistence of ◊Manuel I, who, to atone for his ungrateful treatment of Albuquerque senior, showered him with honours and posts. His ascendancy continued under João III. In 1557 he published his *Commentarios/Commentaries*, based on his father's correspondence with Manuel I, it was part apology, part glorification of his father's life.

Alciati, Andrea (1492–1550)

Italian humanist lawyer who wrote in particular on civil law. He also found time to produce his *Emblemata* (1531), one of the first and most popular collections of allegorical images, which had a profound influence on the imagery of 16th- and early 17th-century art.

In his *Emblemata* each image is accompanied by a Latin inscription pointing up its moral or spiritual meaning. There were many editions of the book and it was widely translated.

Alciati was probably born in Milan; he began his legal studies there and continued them at Pavia and Bologna. He lived in France 1518–22 and 1527–33, where he was professor of law at Avignon and then at Bourges. On returning to Italy in 1533 he taught in Bologna, Ferrara, and Pavia. His importance as a jurist lies very largely on his ability to apply to ancient legal texts, in particular the compilation of Roman laws known as the *Corpus iuris civilis* or Justinian's Code, the techniques of historical criticism and philology already being employed in other disciplines by humanists. One of his best-known works in this field is his *Paradoxa*. He also published a volume of notes on the historian ◊Tacitus.

Alcock, John (c. 1430–1500)

English cleric. Educated at Cambridge, he was employed by successive kings as ambassador, tutor (to Edward IV's ill-fated son), and, in ◊Henry VII's reign, controller of the king's works. With royal service went ecclesiastical promotion: he was successively bishop of Rochester in 1472, Worcester in 1476, and Ely in 1486. He wrote several devotional tracts and patronized his old university, founding Jesus College in 1496.

Aldegrever, Heinrich (1502–c. 1561)

German print maker and painter. In his early career he produced several small engravings of religious subjects, but his main work was ornamental designs; his style was strongly influenced by the works of ◊Dürer.

Aldegrever was born at Paderborn, and may have studied in Dürer's workshop in Nuremberg. About 1527 he settled at Soest, where he died.

He executed relatively few paintings. His prints – mostly engravings, but also a few woodcuts – include

events from Classical antiquity, genre scenes, and portraits, as well as his many designs for objects such as dagger sheaths.

Though Dürer was the main influence on his style, Aldegrever also studied the works of Italian engravers closely, in particular those of ◊Pollaiuolo and Marcantonio ◊Raimondi.

Aldine Academy

See ◊*Neakademia*.

Aldine Press

See ◊Manutius, Aldus.

Aldrovandi, Ulisse (1522–1605)

Italian naturalist and physician. He travelled extensively throughout Europe, researching on natural history; his findings were published in a series of books printed in 1599–1606. He established the botanical garden at Bologna in 1568 (the fifth of its sort in Italy) and was its first director; he also formed a natural history museum.

Born in Bologna, he took a medical degree there in 1553 and was subsequently professor of botany and natural history at that university.

Aleandro, Girolamo (1480–1542)

Italian humanist cleric. As a gifted youth who learnt Hebrew as well as Greek and Latin, he visited Paris and gave lectures there. When the Luther affair broke, Aleandro – by now in papal employment – took a staunch line against heresy which made him suspicious of even his close friend ◊Erasmus.

Born in Treviso, he studied at Padua and then entered the household of Domenico ◊Grimani in Venice; there he met Aldus ◊Manutius and worked with him on his edition of Plutarch's *Moralia*. In 1508 he went to Paris on the recommendation of Erasmus, and in 1509 began lecturing on Plutarch. He taught in Paris intermittently until 1513. His lectures were popular and influential – sometimes, according to an enthusiastic listener, as many as 1,500 attended (Aleandro's own estimate was nearer 140); his audience included Guillaume ◊Budé. In 1512 Aleandro published *Lexicon Graeco–Latinum*, a Greek–Latin dictionary.

After ill health (or contrition) forced him to give

up teaching, he was employed first as a librarian at the Vatican in 1519, and then as a papal envoy. He represented Pope ◊Leo X at the Diet of Worms, where he clashed with Luther and drafted the edict, issued by Emperor Charles V, that banished Luther. He was made archbishop of Brindisi in 1524 and a cardinal in 1538.

Alemán, Mateo (1547–POST 1615)

Spanish government inspector, author, and inveterate debtor. Born in Seville of Jewish descent, he was frequently jailed for debts and professional misconduct. Although obtaining permission to emigrate to Peru in 1582, he remained in Spain, becoming a government inspector in 1583. He resigned in about 1596 to concentrate on business activities and, most notably, the completion of his *Primera Parte de Guzmán de Alfarache/Guzmán de Alfarache, Part I* (1599). In 1607 he used bribery to obtain renewed permission to emigrate and in 1608 he left for Mexico.

The first part of Alemán's ◊picaresque novel on the life of Guzmán de Alfarache, and its 1604 sequel, *La Segunda Parte de la vida de Guzmán de Alfarache, atalaya de la vida humana/The Second Part of the Life of Guzmán de Alfarache, Sentry of Human Life*, won him instant fame in Europe and the Spanish American colonies. Such was its success that neither the spurious second part of 1602, nor the 1605 publication of Part One of Cervantes's *Don ◊Quixote* dented its popularity. Alemán's remaining œuvre is small: it includes *La vida de San Antonio/The Life of St Anthony* (1604), with a prefatory poem by Lope de Vega, and an *Ortografía castellana/Castilian Orthography* (1609).

Alessi, Galeazzo (1512–1572)

Architect from Perugia, Italy. His style was based on his enthusiasm for both Classical architecture and ◊Michelangelo's work. Among his works are the courtyard of the Palazzo Marino in Milan (1553–58) and the Church of Sta Maria Assunta di Carignano in Genoa, which was begun in 1552.

Alessi's work characteristically combines the dignity of the Classical orders with sumptuous detail, as seen in the Palazzo Marino courtyard. From 1549 onwards he designed a number of buildings in Genoa, among them the church of Sta Maria Assunta di Carignano and some palaces in the Strada Nuova (now the Via Garibaldi), a street he himself may have laid out.

His style was much admired and it influenced buildings as far afield as Spain and Germany, especially after Pieter Paul Rubens published *Palazzi di Genova/The Palaces of Genoa* (1622), a study in which Alessi's works feature prominently.

Other examples of his work include the sarcophagus of Gian Galeazzo ◊Visconti in the Certosa (Carthusian monastery) in Pavia; the upper part of the Loggia in Brescia; the gateway to the Palazzo Communale in Bologna (*c.* 1555); and the main doorway of the cathedral in his home town Perugia (1568).

Alexander VI (BORN RODERIGO BORGIA OR BORJA) (1430 OR 1432–1503)

Pope 1492–1503. Born in Valencia, his fortunes were established when his uncle was elected ◊Calixtus III in 1455: he was created cardinal in 1456. His favour continued under Calixtus's successors, ◊Sixtus IV making him legate to Spain in 1472, but his own elevation to the papacy proved elusive – until he effectively bought it. His pontificate was marked by his own family ambition and that of others. His son, Cesare ◊Borgia, became the leading princeling of Italy, but, at the same time, the French kings began their repeated invasions of the peninsula.

Rodrigo Borgia had arrived in Rome when his uncle was a cardinal, who provided for his education with Gaspare da Verona and then at Bologna. His meteoric rise during his uncle's pontificate was not reversed by Pius II (who considered him 'young in years but old in judgement') or subsequent popes; nor was it done much damage by the rumours of orgies and the existence of illegitimate children – of the eight or nine of these Cesare Borgia and Lucrezia ◊Borgia both were to play an important part under Alexander VI.

As a cardinal, he needed suitable accommodation and set about building a palace (now Palazzo Sforza-Cesarini, Rome). When he became pope, his patronage went less to architecture (he concentrated those efforts – following Nicholas V's example – on the Castel Sant' Angelo) but to art: he commissioned

Pinturicchio to fresco both part of the Castel (now destroyed) and the Vatican apartments which had been built by Nicholas V; in the latter, Pinturicchio's work 1492–94 followed designs suggesting knowledge of contemporary Florentine Neo-Platonist interests. Nor is that necessarily surprising, considering that one of the scholars who sought Alexander's patronage was ◊Pico della Mirandola.

Alfonso II OF NAPLES (1448–1495)

King of Naples 1494–95. He was the son of Ferrante I and Isabella of Naples. Widely regarded as cowardly and cruel, he was highly unpopular. He was involved in various Italian conflicts, defeating Florence at Poggio in 1479 and the Turks at Otranto in 1481. When Charles VIII of France was advancing on Naples in early 1495 Alfonso abdicated in favour of his son, Ferdinand II (1467–96).

Long before succeeding his father, Alfonso was associated with his father's misrule, for it was during his father's reign that Alfonso pursued his military exploits, as Duke of Calabria, fighting not only Florence and the Turks, but also Venice in 1484 and the Neopolital barons in 1486, suppressing them with characteristic cruelty. These engagements in Italian political struggles came about largely through his marriage to Ipolita, the sister of Lodovico ◊Sforza of Milan, and also through his sister's marriage to Ercole d'Este of Ferrara.

Alfonso V, KNOWN AS 'THE MAGNANIMOUS' (1395–1458)

King of Aragon from 1416, King of Naples (as Alfonso I) from 1443. Alfonso's first task as king of Aragon was to secure his Mediterranean possession of Sicily. He did so by 1420, at which point an opportunity arose to expand his power further: Joanna II of Naples (see ◊Anjou dynasty) faced invasion from Louis III of Anjou and, in return for Alfonso's support, declared him heir to her kingdom. She later changed her mind and, at her death in 1435, her heir was officially Louis III's son, ◊René of Anjou. But Alfonso was determined to win the Italian kingdom and, though he faced early setbacks, by 1443 he had himself crowned king of Naples.

Though Alfonso was born Aragonese, and though Castilian was always his first language, he was deter-

mined to appear an Italian monarch. For humanists, meanwhile, he provided that unusual commodity: a king. He sought to give patronage; they were more than willing to receive it. The scholars who stayed at his court included Panormita (Antonio ◊Beccadelli), Bartolomeo ◊Fazio, and Lorenzo ◊Valla. Such writers provided plentiful biographies of Alfonso, fashioning posterity's view of him even before he was dead. Either for their interest or for his own, Alfonso also collected books (◊Vespasiano da Bisticci says that his favourite author was Livy – it was certainly at his court that some of the work on textual emendation occurred).

In art and architecture, Alfonso looked further afield. His major building project was the redesigning of Castelnuovo in Naples, which was undertaken by Spanish architects (for example, the Catalan Guillem Sagrera). In painting, though he was presented with works by Italian artists – Cosimo de' Medici gave him a triptych by Filippo Lippi – he most admired the art of Jan van ◊Eyck, whose paintings he collected. His collection was, of course, not confined to these arts but in other areas as well a northern bias is visible: the prize possession among his tapestries, for example, was a set designed by Roger van der Weyden.

> *Great princes commit great sins.*
>
>
>
> JUAN FERRANDO, Alfonso's confessor, commenting on his master to Vespasiano da Bisticci

Ali, Mustafa (1541–1600)

Historian and writer of the Ottoman Empire. Ali was responsible for much of the myth of the preceding reign of Suleiman (1520–66) as a golden age.

all'antica

Artistic style imitating Classical motifs, especially used in northern Italy in the late quattrocento. The attempt to emulate Classical styles which lay behind the (ironically mistaken) *littera antiqua* script of ◊Poggio Bracciolini and accompanying ◊*bianchi girari* illumination, became a more faithful replication of the antique with the interest in archaeological remains of the mid-15th century. In northeast Italy, this vogue was apparent in the paintings of ◊Mantegna and the statuettes of L' ◊Antico; it was also reflected in manuscripts in the architectural style of illumination and the imitation of the script of Classical inscriptions.

Allen, William (1532–1594)

English cardinal. His Catholicism conflicted with Elizabeth I's ecclesiastical policy and he went into exile in Europe. He lived in Rome from 1585 and his efforts for the reconversion of England to Catholicism became more political from this time. He was created a cardinal in 1587.

Allen founded the Catholic seminary at Douai in 1568 (later transferred to Rheims), which attracted students from English recusant families and soon provided Catholic missionaries to England. He was also instrumental in the founding of an English Jesuit college in Rome in 1579 (run by Jesuits soon after foundation). The translation of the Douai Bible was begun by Allen.

Alleyn, Edward (1566–1626)

London actor. The only actor to rival Richard ◊Burbage, he appeared in Christopher ◊Marlowe's plays. With his father-in-law, theatre manager Philip Henslowe, he built the Fortune Theatre in 1600 and was also part owner of the Rose Theatre. With the money he had made from his career he founded Dulwich College in 1619.

He retired to Dulwich in 1604. His second wife was the daughter of the poet John Donne.

Allori, Alessandro (c. 1535–1607)

Florentine painter. His style was strongly influenced both by ◊Bronzino, under whom he studied, and by ◊Michelangelo. Among his best-known works are decorations in the Medici villa at Poggio a Caiano. He was the father of Cristofano Allori (1577–1621).

Allori was born in Florence, where he studied and spent most of his career. A visit to Rome in 1554–56 also brought him under the influence of Michelangelo, an influence visible in his frescoes from the early 1560s in the Church of Santissima Annunziata, Florence.

He was patronized by the Medici, contributing paintings in the manner of Bronzino to Duke Francesco I de' Medici's *studiolo* in the Palazzo Vecchio in Florence, notably *The Pearl Fishers* (*c.*

1570). His later works, among them *Birth of the Virgin* (1602, Santissima Annunziata, Florence) and *The Ascension* (1603, San Michele, Prato), are in a softer, more relaxed style.

His son, **Cristofani Allori**, followed his father's footsteps in his career, but not in style; Cristofani's work reflected the Baroque reaction against earlier trends.

Almeida, Francisco de (c. 1450–1510)

Portuguese nobleman and distinguished soldier, born in Lisbon, first viceroy of Portuguese India 1505–08. He understood the importance of naval power for territorial expansion along the Indian coast, and used this to consolidate Portuguese power in the area. He resisted relinquishing the viceroyship to Afonso de ◊Albuquerque in 1508 until he had avenged the death of his son, killed defending Portuguese trade routes. Having decimated the Egyptian fleet off the Muslim port of Diu in 1509, he set sail for Portugal but was killed by hostile natives near the Cape of Good Hope in March 1510.

Aloysius, St (BORN LUIGI GONZAGA) (1568–1591)

Italian Jesuit. In 1585 he joined the Society of Jesus, despite parental opposition, and died while nursing plague victims. Canonized in 1726, he is the patron saint of youth. Feast day 21 June.

Alpini, Prospero (1553–1616)

Italian botanist and physician, director of the botanical garden at Padua, which was originally developed in order to grow plants for their medicinal uses. He studied plants out of interest in both their therapeutic uses and also their structure.

His *De Medicina Aegyptorium/On Egyptian Medicine* was published in 1591, and his *De Plantis Aegypti Liber/Book of Egyptian Plants* (1592) included the first European descriptions of the coffee bush (coffee arabica) and the banana tree. He also studied the flora of Crete. Such was his reputation as a botanist in the 16th century that Linnaeus named the genus *Alpinia* in his honour.

Alpini was born in Maroshica, Italy, and studied medicine at Padua University, graduating in 1578. In 1580 he went to Cairo for three years as the Venetian consul's physician and then returned to Venice. In 1603 he was made the director of the botanical garden at Padua, the earliest European botanical garden of which there are reliable records. The position was later occupied by his son Alpino. He died in Padua of a kidney infection. Other works include *De Praesagienda Vita et Morte Aegrotontium/The Presages of Life and Death in Diseases* (1601).

altarpiece

A painting (more rarely a sculpture) placed on, behind, or above an altar in a Christian church. Altarpieces vary greatly in size, construction, and number of images (◊diptych, ◊triptych, and polyptych). Some are small and portable; some (known as a **retable** or **reredo** – there is no clear distinction) are fixed.

A typical Italian altarpiece has a large central panel, flanked by subsidiary panels, with a **predella**, or strip of scenes, across the bottom. Spanish altarpieces tend to be architecturally elaborate retables. A popular form in northern Europe was the **winged altarpiece**, in which outer wings are hinged so that they can be closed to cover the centre panel; the backs of the panels are usually painted in a less elaborate fashion.

Altdorfer, Albrecht (*c.* 1480–1538)

German painter, architect, and printmaker. Probably the son of a painter, he was active in Regensburg, Bavaria, where he became town architect in 1526. He was one of the first artists to develop an interest in depicting landscapes for their own sake.

Altdorfer worked in a series of media and genres: as well as his landscape drawings and etchings, he produced religious paintings and woodcuts. His early work in particular reflects the influence of other German artists such as Lucas ◊Cranach; he also seems to have consciously imitated the range of work produced by Albrecht ◊Dürer. He was patronized by the Holy Roman Emperor Maximilian, for whom he worked on the outsize prints of the *Triumphal Arch*, and by William IV, Duke of Bavaria, who commissioned the painting *Battle of Alexander at Issos* (1529, now in the Alte Pinakothek, Munich).

Alva, Ferdinand Alvarez de Toledo, DUKE OF ALVA OR ALBA (1508–1582)

Spanish politician and general. He successfully commanded the Spanish armies of the Holy Roman Emperor ◊Charles V and his son ◊Philip II of Spain. In 1567 he was appointed governor of the Netherlands, where he set up a reign of terror to suppress Protestantism and the revolt of the Netherlands. In 1573 he was recalled at his own request. He later led a successful expedition against Portugal 1580–81.

While in the Netherlands he had a life-size bronze made of himself by Jakob ◊Jonghelinck.

Alvarado, Pedro de (*c.* 1485–1541)

Spanish conquistador, ruler of Guatemala 1524–41. Alvarado joined Hernán ◊Cortés's army in 1519 and became his principal captain during the conquest of New Spain. Left in command at Tenochtitlán, Mexico, he provoked the Aztec rebellion that resulted in the death of ◊Montezuma II in 1520. He conquered Guatemala 1523–24 and was its governor and captain general until his death.

He also attacked Ecuador in 1534 in a bid for a share of the former Inca empire, but was paid off by Francisco ◊Pizarro.

Amadeo, Giovanni Antonio (1447–1522)

Italian sculptor and architect. In collaboration with others, he decorated the Certosa at Pavia from 1466. He also took part in the sculpture of the great octagonal dome of Milan Cathedral. Independently, he sculpted the monument of Bartolommeo ◊Colleoni in the Church of Sta Maria Maggiore, Bergamo.

Amat, Juan Carlos (1572–1642)

Spanish scientist and author. He wrote the earliest known treatise on playing the guitar, *Guitarra española* ..., published probably in 1586.

Amberger, Christoph (*c.* 1500–*c.* 1561)

German painter. He established a considerable reputation as a portrait painter, his style, as in his *Portrait of Christopher Fugger* (1541, Alte Pinakothek, Munich), often reflecting Venetian fashion.

Amberger trained in Augsburg under Hans ◊Burgkmair and Leonhard Beck before visiting Italy about 1525–27. His *Portrait of Charles V* (*c.* 1532, Museum Dahlem Gemäldegalerie, Berlin) shows the influence of the Netherlandish court painter Jan Vermeyen, who was at Augsburg in 1530. Mercantile references to Venetian painters – in particular ◊Palma Vecchio and Paris ◊Bordone – appear in such works as the *Portrait of Christopher Fugger*. In 1548 he met ◊Titian, then visiting Augsburg, and helped repair the latter's portrait of *Charles V at the Battle of Mühlberg*.

He altered his style according to the commission, and in several later works – for example *Portrait of the Cosmographer Sebastian Münster* (*c.* 1552, Museum Dahlem Gemäldegalerie, Berlin) – he rejected the Italianate style of portraiture in favour of a more traditional German style. In his *Virgin and Saints Ulrich and Afra* (1554), painted for Augsburg Cathedral, he combined contemporary Italianate idiom with the late Gothic style of Hans ◊Holbein the Elder, whose altarpiece had been destroyed during the iconoclasm of 1583.

Amboise, Georges d' (1460–1510)

French Catholic cleric and politician. He gained the favour of the Duke of Orleans and through his influence was made archbishop of Narbonne in 1492 and subsequently of Rouen in 1493. On the accession of the Duke of Orleans to the throne as Louis XII, Amboise was made cardinal and chief minister.

His foreign and domestic policies were moderate and beneficial. On the death of Alexander VI he hoped to become pope, but was unsuccessful, and the remainder of his life was occupied with abortive scheming.

Ambrosian Republic

Government of Milan, Italy, 1447–50. Consisting of 24 local dignitaries, it was established when Duke Filippo Maria ◊Visconti died without an heir in 1447. It ended when military leader Francesco Sforza occupied the city in 1450.

Named in honour of St Ambrose, Milan's patron saint, the short-lived republic was beset with difficulties – divisions within the ruling group, discontent from the lower middle classes, rebellion in subject cities, and the hostility of Venice, brought the republic close to collapse. In the autumn of 1449 Francesco Sforza, a *condottiere* formerly in Duke Filippo Maria Visconti's employ and married to the duke's illegitimate daughter, besieged the city. In March 1450 the republic surrendered and Sforza was installed as duke of Milan.

Amerbach, Johannes (1443–1513)

Swiss printer and publisher. After studying in Paris he set up a printing press in Basel in 1478 and specialized in producing high quality texts of the works of the Church Fathers. The intellectual tradition of his printing house was continued by Amerbach's successor, the publisher Johann ◊Froben.

As with other printers, like Aldus ◊Manutius, his workshop became a meeting place for scholars; Sebastian ◊Brant and Johannes ◊Reuchlin were among his collaborators. In 1511 Amerbach employed a Dominican, Johannes Cono of Nuremberg (1463–1513), to instruct his sons and anyone interested in Greek and Hebrew in his own house.

Amman, Jobst (1539–1591)

Swiss-born German printmaker, one of the leading book illustrators of the late 16th century. His output included numerous ornamental and heraldic prints and title pages, as well as many narrative illustrations. He received many commissions from humanists and editors, notably Sigmund Feyerabend (1528–1590) of Frankfurt. Among his finest works is his series *Animals*.

The son of a choirmaster and teacher of rhetoric, Amman worked first as a stained-glass designer in his native Zürich before moving, successively, to Schaffhausen, Basel, and Nuremberg, where he finally settled. In 1574 he married the widow of a Nuremberg goldsmith and became a citizen of his adopted city. Although he is not documented as an assistant of Virgil Solis, he was effectively the latter's successor as the leading book illustrator in Nuremberg. His works include his penetrating portraits *Hans Sachs* and *Wenzel Jamnitzer*, as well as his series *Animals* and his *Allegory of Commerce* (1585).

Because of his commissions he travelled widely: to Augsburg in 1578, Frankfurt and Heidelberg in 1583, Würzburg 1586–87, and Altdorf in 1590.

Ammanati, Bartolommeo (1511–1592)

Italian sculptor and architect. He was influenced by Michelangelo, studied under Andrea ◊Sansovino, and did much work for Pope ◊Julius III. With Giorgio ◊Vasari, he built the pope's residence in Rome, the Villa Giulia. In Florence his works included the Fountain of Neptune in the Piazza della Signoria

(1560–75), the rusticated garden courtyard of the Palazzo Pitti (1560), and the graceful bridge of Santa Trinità, completed in 1570 (destroyed in 1944 but rebuilt in 1957).

Ammerbach (AMERBACH), Elias Nikolaus (1530–1597)

German organist and composer. He was organist at St Thomas, Leipzig, from 1560 and published two books of music in organ tablature, containing important explanations of ornaments and modes of performance.

Amsdorf, Nikolaus von (1483–1565)

German Lutheran theologian. One of the most determined supporters of Martin ◊Luther, he assisted in the translation of the Bible into German and accompanied Luther to the Leipzig conference in 1519 and the Diet of Worms in 1521.

Probably born at Torgau on the Elbe, Amsdorf studied at Wittenberg, where he came to know Luther. He became an evangelical preacher, spreading word of the Reformation at Magdeburg (1524), Goslar (1531), Einbeck (1534), and Schmalkald (1537). In 1542 John Frederick, Elector of Saxony (1503–54), appointed him bishop of Naumburg-Zeitz, a post he held until 1547. In 1548 he helped found the university of Jena, and in the same year actively opposed the Interim of ◊Augsburg. From 1552 until his death he lived at Eisenach, remaining a conservative and influential Lutheran.

Amyot, Jacques (1513–1593)

French cleric, Classical scholar, and translator. He was professor of Latin and Greek at Bourges 1536–c. 1546, where he began translating Classical works, including Plutarch's *Lives*, into French. When his version of the *Lives* was eventually published in 1559, it proved an immediate and influential success.

Amyot was born in Melun and educated at Paris University. After teaching at Bourges, he visited Italy and in 1554 became tutor to the sons of Henry II (the future Charles IX and Henry III). He was made bishop of Auxerre in 1570, where he spent the rest of his life. His translations include *L'Histoire éthiopique/ Ethiopian History* by Heliodorus (1547), *Daphnis et Chloé* by Longus (1559), and Plutarch's *Moralia*

(1572). Though these translations were criticized for inaccuracies, they proved very popular. Michel de ◊Montaigne declared that he would 'award the palm, above all our writers in French, to Jacques Amyot'. The *Lives* were translated into English by Thomas ◊North in 1579 and, in that version, became a source for Shakespeare's Roman plays.

Ana, Francesco d' (1460–1503)

Italian composer. His works include *frottole* (songs) and lamentations. He is known to have been active at St Mark's, Venice, in 1490.

Anabaptist (GREEK 'BAPTIZE AGAIN')

Member of any of various 16th-century radical Protestant sects. They believed in adult rather than child baptism, and sought to establish utopian communities. Anabaptist groups spread rapidly in northern Europe, particularly in Germany, and were widely persecuted.

Notable Anabaptists included those in Moravia (the Hutterites) and Thomas Müntzer (1489–1525), a peasant leader who was executed for fomenting a Peasants' War which culminated in their defeat at Mühlhausen (now Mulhouse in eastern France). In Münster, Germany, Anabaptists controlled the city 1534–35. A number of Anabaptist groups, such as the Mennonites, Amish, and Hutterites, emigrated to North America, where they became known for their simple way of life and pacifism.

anamorphosis

Artistic technique of distortion. Something of a fashion in early 16th-century northern Europe, anamorphosis involved producing an over-long, squashed image which would rectify itself when viewed from a particular side angle. Leonardo da Vinci experimented with it while at the French court, and Hans ◊Holbein the Younger employed the technique for the image of the skull in his double portrait *The Ambassadors* (1533).

anatomy

The science of describing the human body and its parts was not original to the Renaissance. It already existed in medieval Europe, based on the writings of the ancient Greek physician ◊Galen, who remained

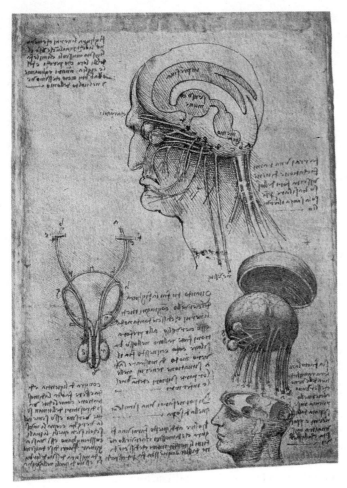

study of the few surviving pieces of ancient sculpture, watching naked people (as practised by Giorgio ◊Vasari), and the process of dissection itself. Antonio del ◊Pollaiuolo is said to have been the first to acquire dead bodies and cut them open; ◊Leonardo da Vinci and ◊Michelangelo left drawings which demonstrate their close study of human remains.

Such researches were private, even – because they often required the purloining of the body in the first place – covert. More official was the university human dissection, for which Vesalius became famous in Padua. The effect of this practice was, in the first place, to build on Galen's knowledge, for example in the discovery by which ◊Falloppio is remembered or in the researches into the structure of the eye which were synthesized in Johannes ◊Kepler's visual theory. It also, however, raised doubts about some of Galen's details and, indeed, about his central theories: dissection, measurements, and reasoning led William Harvey to reject Galen's theory about the movement of blood in the human body.

the standard authority into the late 16th century. However, Galen had based his discussion of human anatomy on his dissections of animals – a method that, as Andreas ◊Vesalius and William ◊Harvey discovered, could lead to erroneous assumptions.

Dissection of humans was not unknown before the 16th century: Mondino di Luzzi's anatomical treatise of 1316 was based on cutting up the bodies of dead men. However, in Christian Europe as in Galen's pagan Greece, such practice was open to the accusation of sacrilege. Despite this, in the late 15th and 16th centuries, human dissection became considered a necessary activity both for professionals and for amateurs (artists).

The 15th-century vogue for lifelike art created an artistic interest in anatomy which took several forms:

Francesco set himself to study nudes from life, and Giorgio with him, in a bath-house near Cardinal Salviati's palace; and afterwards they made some anatomical studies in the graveyard of Campo Santo.

GIORGIO VASARI, *The Lives*, describing the researches of Francesco ÆSalviati and himself into the human form

André, Bernard (*c.* 1450–*c.* 1522)
Blind French poet at the court of ◊Henry VII and Henry VIII of England. Born at Toulouse, he

arrived in England in late 1485. His first English patron may have been Richard ◊Foxe but he was soon employed at the royal court; he was a central figure of what he himself called Henry VII's *grex poetarum* (flock of poets). He wrote mainly in Latin, producing poems on royal occasions, as well as a *Vita Henrici Septimi/Life of Henry VII* about 1502.

Andrea del Sarto (REAL NAME ANDREA D'AGNOLO DI FRANCESCO) (1486–1530)

Florentine painter, who worked in oils and fresco. Del Sarto ('Of the Tailor', from the profession of his father) was a pupil of ◊Piero di Cosimo but his continually evolving style owes most to his private study, especially of the 'modern masters' Michelangelo and Raphael. He worked mainly in Florence but attended the court of ◊Francis I in France in 1518–19.

Much of his fresco work, for example his *Birth of the Virgin* (1514), was done for the convent of Sta Annunziata in the centre of Florence and, further out of the city, for the Convent of S Salvi, where his *Last Supper* (*c.* 1520–25) was considered a masterpiece by his pupil, Giorgio Vasari. He was also employed by the Medici: he painted the *Tribute to Caesar* (replete with a series of exotic animals) at their palace of Poggio a Caiano. His oil paintings attracted Francis I and led to an invitation to the French court 1518–19, where he painted *Charity* (Louvre, Paris). Andrea del Sarto was a product of the cultural cross-fertilization of the period: he himself was influenced by the engravings of Albrecht ◊Dürer's work available in Italy, while in France he influenced native artists such as Jean ◊Clouet.

Andrea del Sarto's relations with Francis I ended less favourably than they began: he requested leave to visit his home town and was dispatched with money to buy artworks for the king. Back in Florence, however, he squandered the money and never fulfilled his promise to return to Paris. Vasari blamed the reversal of del Sarto's fortunes on his wife, Lucrezia.

Andreoli, Giorgio (KNOWN AS AESTRO GIORGIO) (*c.* 1470–1553)

Italian potter. He was born at Intra on Lake Maggiore into a family from Pavia, but is famous for his association with the ◊majolica works of Gubbio, where he was based from 1498. He held a monopoly in a distinctive ruby glaze, which is one of the most characteristic products of the Gubbio potteries.

Andrewes, Lancelot (1555–1626)

English cleric, one of the revisers for the Authorized Version of the Bible. Educated at Merchant Taylor's School (London) and Cambridge, Andrewes was for some time chaplain to Archbishop Whitgift. He was considered for the episcopacy during Elizabeth's reign, but his rise to prominence came under her successor: he was successively bishop of Chichester (1605), Ely (1609), and Winchester (1619). His high view of kingship accorded with James I's view, and his theological bent was equally fashionable at court. His contemporaries admired his preaching but most of his writings were unpublished in his lifetime.

Angeli, Pietro Angelo (PIER ANGELO BARGEO) (1517–1596)

Italian poet from Barga, near Lucca. He wrote in both Italian and Latin; his *Siriade* (1591), a Latin epic on the crusader conquest of Jerusalem, was heavily drawn upon by ◊Tasso in his own epic *Gerusalemme conquistata*.

Besides his Latin verse, Angeli also wrote pastoral poetry in Italian (*Poesie amorose*, 1589) and translated Sophocles' *Oedipus Rex* into Italian.

Angelico, Fra (GUIDO DI PIETRO) (*c.*1400–1455)

Italian painter. He was a monk, active in Florence, and painted religious scenes. His series of frescoes at the monastery of San Marco, Florence, was begun after 1436. He also produced several altarpieces in a style characterized by a delicacy of line and colour.

Fra Angelico joined the Dominican order about 1420. After his novitiate, he resumed a career as a painter of religious images and altarpieces, many of which have small predella scenes beneath them, depicting events in the life of a saint. The central images of the paintings are highly decorated with pure, bright colours and gold-leaf designs, while the predella scenes are often lively and relatively unsophisticated. There is a similar simplicity to his frescoes in the cells at San Marco, which are principally devotional works. Fra Angelico's later fresco sequences,

Scenes from the Life of Christ (Orvieto Cathedral) and *Scenes from the Lives of SS Stephen and Lawrence* (1440s, chapel of Nicholas V, Vatican Palace), are more elaborate.

He became prior of the monastery in Fiesole, near Florence, in 1449, and known as 'il Beato Fra Giovanni Angelico da Fiesole', 'the Blessed Brother John the Angelic of Fiesole'.

Anghiari, Battle of

Battle in 1440 in which Florence defeated a Milanese force. Sixty-two years after the event, Piero ◊Soderini commissioned the rival Florentine artists, Michelangelo and Leonardo, to paint in competition with each other frescoes for the Palazzo Vecchio celebrating Florentine military success. Michelangelo's subject was the 1364 Battle of Cascina, when Florentines took Pisan troops by surprise as they washed in the Arno. Leonardo painted the cavalry engagement of the Battle of Anghiari. Michelangelo's work was left unfinished; Leonardo's fresco soon deteriorated. However, both works were celebrated in the 16th century for their depiction of a mêlée of humans whose reactions are caught at a precise moment.

Anguissola, Sofonisba (1527–*c.* 1623)

Italian portrait painter from Cremona. Alongside Lavinia ◊Fontana, one of the first female Italian artists, she executed several self-portraits. Her best-known work is a family group portrait of her sisters playing chess (1555, Muzeum Narodowe, Poznań, Poland).

The daughter of a Piedmontese nobleman, she was a pupil of Bernardino Campi. In 1559 she moved to

Anghiari Pieter Paul Rubens, drawing of the Battle of Anghiari, after the lost cartoon of Leonardo da Vinci (Louvre, Paris). *e.t. archive*

Spain at the invitation of Philip II, becoming lady-in-waiting and drawing teacher to Philip's wife, Elizabeth of Valois. She stayed in Spain for the next 20 years, and painted many members of the court, though most of these portraits were later destroyed in a fire. She returned to Italy in 1580 and later moved to Palermo in Sicily, where she ran a studio.

Anjou dynasty

Rulers of the Kingdom of Naples until 1435. Charles I of Anjou, brother of Louis IX of France, had become king of Sicily in 1266, a realm which included both the island and the southern part of mainland Italy. After the Sicilian Vespers in 1282, the Anjou dynasty was left only with the mainland lands centring on Naples. From the mid-14th century control of the kingdom was disputed between the various branches of the family. The queen, Joanna I, was heirless and declared as her successor a distant relative, Louis, Duke of Anjou. Louis and his heirs (the second house of Anjou) supported their claim by invasions; the conflict eventually aroused the interest of Alfonso V of Aragon, whose military success brought an end to the dynasty's rule.

Anne of Denmark (1574–1619)

Queen consort of James VI of Scotland (from 1603 James I of England). She was the daughter of Frederick II of Denmark and Norway, and married James in 1589. She bore him five children, two of whom survived: Charles I and Elizabeth of Bohemia. Anne was suspected of Catholic leanings and was notably extravagant but seems to have had little influence on state affairs.

Annio of Viterbo (1432/7–1502)

Antiquarian turned Dominican friar, preacher, astrologer, biblical exegete, epigraphic scholar, and forger. In his *Antiquitates* (1498) Annio turned literary *mimesis* into an art form, using a range of sophisticated scholarly techniques and less subtle smoke screens to create a set of pseudoantique texts in order to back up his theory of ancient history – that the Hebrew patriarch Noah, also known as the Etruscan god Janus, arrived in Italy after the Flood and founded the Vatican and Viterbo as centres of agriculture, piety, and civilization long before the emergence of Greece or Rome.

Annio's main invented 'source', Berosus the Chaldean (a vast embroidery on a figure mentioned briefly by ◊Vitruvius and Josephus), was so outstandingly persuasive an authority that he appears beside Homer and Hesiod in a 17th-century decorative frieze in the Upper Reading Room of Oxford's Bodleian Library.

Annio's lifelong problem was a dearth of adequate patronage. His earlier career as a court astrologer in the north may have been blunted by his prediction in 1476 of a long and happy life (Galeazzo Maria Sforza was assassinated later that year). By then promoting his home town as the capital of ancient Etruria he ensured employment by Viterbo's civic governors. Stressing the importance of Spanish antiquity in the history of the world helped him win the support of Roderigo Borgia, Pope ◊Alexander VI. But this turned out to be, quite literally, a poisoned chalice; Annio was murdered by Roderigo's son Cesare in 1502. None of this, however, should belie Annio's contribution, however oddly warped, to the disciplines of epigraphy and philology, and to the collection of (in particular) Etruscan antiquities in Viterbo which became one of the earliest civic archaeological museums in Italy.

Ansidei Madonna

The painting of the Virgin enthroned by ◊Raphael Sanzio (1506, National Gallery, London). It was executed for the Ansidei family of Perugia, hence its title, and was placed in the Servite Church of S Fiorenzo.

It was painted on panel, dimensions 2 x 1.5 m/82 x 58 in.

Antico, Andrea de (c. 1480–AFTER 1539)

Italian composer and music publisher who worked mainly in Rome and then in Venice during the first half of the 16th century. His publications include *Frottole intabulate da sonar organi* (Rome, 1517), the earliest known printed edition of keyboard music in Italy.

Antico, L' (BORN PIER JACOPO DI ANTONIO ALARI BONACOLSI) (c. 1460–1528)

Mantuan sculptor, bronze-founder, and medallist. He was patronized by the Gonzaga dynasty and by Isabella d' ◊Este. His success was based on his ability to reproduce the style of ancient Greek and Roman sculpture

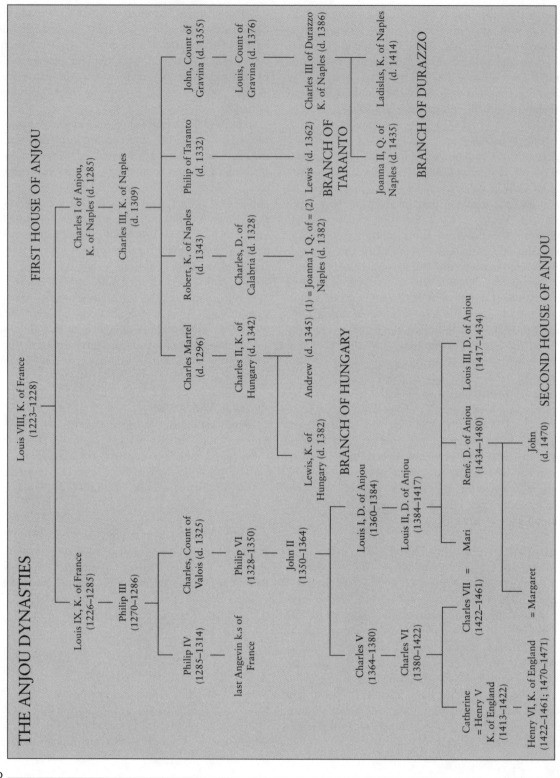

THE ANJOU DYNASTIES

in works like his *Apollo* (1479–98, Ca d'Oro, Venice), imitating the recently refound ◊*Apollo Belvedere*.

He trained as a goldsmith and became one of a group of medallists in Mantua. He was proclaiming himself as L'Antico – the Antique – by, at the latest, 1479, when he used the sobriquet to sign two medals. His style ◊*all'antica* is a sculptural counterpart to the pictorial style of his colleague ◊Mantegna – L'Antico emphasizes the smooth, rounded forms of the human body and contrasts polished surfaces with intricately chiselled details in the hair, drapery, and accoutrements. Details of his sculptures are often gilded and the eyes are sometimes inlaid in silver.

antipope

Claimant to the papal tiara, elected despite the existence already of another pope. The antipopes of the ◊Great Schism resided in Avignon, France, while their rivals held court in Rome, Italy; from 1409 a second line of antipopes was created by the Council of ◊Pisa. Only two decades after the end of the Schism, the Council of ◊Basel elected a further antipope, Felix V.

Antonello da Messina (*c.* 1430–1479)

Italian painter. Along with Colantonio he was a pioneer in his country of the technique of oil painting developed by Flemish artists; he may have acquired his knowledge of it in Naples, or, if Vasari is to be believed, he may have learnt it from Jan van ◊Eyck himself. Flemish influence is reflected in his brushwork, his use of light, and sometimes in his imagery. Surviving works include bust-length portraits and sombre religious paintings.

He visited Venice in the 1470s where his work inspired, among other Venetian painters, the young Giovanni Bellini. His paintings include *St Jerome in His Study* (*c.* 1460, National Gallery, London) and *A Young Man* (1478, Staatliche Museum, Berlin).

Antonino, St (ANTONIO PIEROZZI) (1389–1459)

Florentine cleric. A Dominican friar, he was appointed archbishop of Florence in 1446 by Pope Eugenius IV; he was not (like some other clerics) an absentee bishop – he took his pastoral duties seriously. He was canonized in 1523.

Inspired to join the Dominicans in 1405 by hearing the antihumanist Giovanni ◊Dominici preach, he was, like Dominici, wary of excessive interest in pagan authors. At the same time, he was connected with the early humanists' patron, Cosimo de' ◊Medici: the convent of San Marco, of which Antonino was prior from 1439, benefited from Medicean largesse. His writings are moralistic in a traditional style; although passages in his *Summa Moralis* (1440–59) have sometimes been taken to represent an attitude (like San ◊Bernardino da Siena's) unconventionally positive towards property, they are, in reality, heavily influenced by Thomas Aquinas.

After his canonization, St Antonino was remembered in the convent of San Marco by a series of lunettes by Bernardino Poccetti representing scenes from his life.

Anwykyll, John (DIED 1487)

English schoolmaster and grammarian. He was the first headmaster of William ◊Waynflete's school attached to Magdalen College, Oxford. He produced a grammar book, *Compendium Totius Grammaticae* (printed in Oxford in 1483, reprinted in Deventer, the Netherlands, in 1489 with a preface by the Italian humanist poet Pietro ◊Carmeliano). This work was influenced by the writings of Lorenzo ◊Valla and Niccolò ◊Perotti and suggests that education at the new school included elements of the *studia humanitatis*.

Apel, Nikolas (*c.* 1475–1537)

German compiler of a large manuscript in choirbook form (1494, Leipzig, University Library) containing sacred and secular music of the late 15th and early 16th centuries.

Apelles

Ancient Greek painter, court artist to Alexander the Great. No trace of his work remains, but his reputation survives: he was allegedly so favoured by Alexander that the emperor made a present to him of his concubine. His art was praised by ancient authors, in particular Lucian and Pliny the Elder.

In the 15th and 16th centuries Apelles was considered the archetype of the painter. This was not on the basis of any subtle judgement of his art, but on the claims made for him in ancient literature. In particular, Lucian's ◊ekphrasis of *The Calumny of Apelles* was translated by ◊Guarino (1408) and, among others, Lapo da ◊Castiglionchio (*c.* 1436), Francesco

ANTIQUARIANISM

IN THE TRADITIONAL tale of the Renaissance's progress towards modernity, several key milestones are neatly marked out. When Petrarch climbed Mont Ventoux to enjoy the view, that was supposed to reflect a modern frame of mind. When he and his successors conceived of a break between their present and the classical past, that is said to have invented the very idea of the Middle Ages and, by extension, the modern world. And when the recognition of classical antiquity as a separate society developed into an interest in Roman antiquities and customs, that too is claimed as the origins of a recognizably modern movement. Yet, if by antiquarianism we mean an interest in ancient society as an end in itself – archaeology for archaeology's sake, as it were – the Renaissance had little to do with this. As with other key 'modernizing' events, their purpose for their practitioners was rarely as simple as the traditional narrative has made it seem. For the humanists, 'antiquarianism' was not just an academic exercise: it had extra meaning – just as the import of Petrarch's description of the climb up Mont Ventoux is an allegory of the journey of human life. The weather-worn milestones to modernity are, more often, millstones round historiography's neck.

The interest in the material remains of classical antiquity began early. The so-called Paduan pre-humanist, Lovato ◊Lovati, prided himself in finding the tomb of his city's mythical founder, Antenor.

Similarly, in the 14th century, Petrarch himself claimed that a tomb in the same city inscribed with 'T Livius' must be nothing other than that of the Roman historian, whose writings he had read. Posterity has treated these identifications kindly: it does not matter that they were hopelessly wrong, what is important is that the scholars bothered at all. But why did they bother? In large part, it was because of that element which repeatedly appears in the history of Italy in this period: civic pride. Lovati's Antenor-tomb – and its transferral into a stone ark in 1284 – emphasized the ancient, indeed pre-Roman, founding to Padua. In its own way, it supported the city's claims to an autonomous political existence.

The ruins of classical civilization were paltry elsewhere in Italy, however, when compared to Rome. Petrarch, again, had taken note of some of the monuments (with, once more, an insouciance to factual accuracy). It was, however, in the 15th century that these attracted sustained attention. Poggio ◊Bracciolini, for example, described the ruins of the ancient Forum – but he too had an ulterior motive. In his case, it was less political than moral: for him, the dilapidated grandeur of the once-triumphal arches was a lesson in the omnipotent force of Fortune. 'How are the mighty fallen' was hardly a message novel to the Renaissance, but it was one which continued to hold fascination.

Poggio's archaeological interest was also the result of a circumstance: the permanent return, after the Schism, of the papacy to Rome. The presence of the curia in the city provided an influx of well-educated secretaries to mill around its streets, with time on their hands to take note of the ruins around them. It also provided, in the works of Poggio's colleague, Flavio ◊Biondo, a political reason to describe these remains. In his *Roma Instaurata* (dedicated to Eugenius IV, 1446), Biondo enumerated the monuments and tried to explain the purpose they had in ancient Rome; at the same time, this was an exercise in some ways of appropriating the classical city: for Biondo (as for ◊Augustine), Rome reached its apogee not in the ancient Republic or Empire but under the Christians. In other words, Biondo's archaeology worked in the service of his employer, the revitalized papacy.

It is also Biondo who combines an interest in material remains with an attempt to reconstruct elements of ancient society. This second antiquarian element was not original to him, though: another papal secretary, Andrea ◊Fiocchi, wrote 20 years before Biondo a description of ancient officials. Yet again, however, this was not a simple dispassionate cataloguing: for Fiocchi, born in the Republic of Florence, the significance of his research was to demonstrate that a society had no need of monarchs to work efficiently. His work, that is to say, had an agenda similar to Leonardo ◊Bruni's historical reinterpretation of Florence's origins:

continued

it is civic humanism. And while Fiocchi had a particular outlook, the general tendency – to endow antiquarian researches with a present-centred agenda – continued into the 16th century. For his contemporary readers, for example, one of the delights of Guillaume ◊Budé's *De Asse* was its continual asides, commenting on the politics of the 16th century as much as on ancient weights and measures.

The lessons of Roman antiquarianism could be turned, these scholars realized, to other societies. At the same time, the ancient customs of the different 'nations' of Europe could in their own right become the subject of antiquarian research. Yet, here as well, a present agenda followed closely behind meticulous scholarship. The debates, for example, in early 17th-century England over the 'ancient constitution' and the

Norman yoke were a late instance in a colder climate of a long-accepted truth: antiquarianism was politics carried out by different means.

DAVID RUNDLE

Further Reading
R Weiss, *The Renaissance Discovery of Classical Antiquity* (Oxford, 1969)

Griffolini (1460, who dedicated his version to John ◊Tiptoft), Rudolf Agricola (1479), and Philip Melanchthon (1518). The interest was not merely literary: there were attempts to recreate the picture itself by, for example, Botticelli, Mantegna (in a drawing later engraved by Mocetto), Genga, and Albrecht Dürer.

Apian, Peter (REAL NAME PETER BIENEWITZ) (1495–1552)

German astronomer, cartographer, and instrument-maker. His textbook of astronomy and geography *Cosmographia* (1524) was translated into all the major European languages.

In 1534 he published the first printed table of sines, and in 1540 his illustrated *Astronomicum Caesareum*, in which he included his own observations of five comets and noted that their tails always pointed away from the Sun.

The success of the *Cosmographia*, which included the suggestion that lunar distances might be used to determine longitude, earned him the professorship of mathematics at the University of Ingolstadt, an office he retained till his death.

Apollo Belvedere

Ancient Roman sculpture, unearthed in Rome in the late 15th century. Like the ◊*Laocoon*, it became part of Pope Julius II's collections of antiquities and was similarly studied by artists at the turn of the century, being imitated, for example, in a bronze statuette by L' ◊Antico.

Apostolius, Michael (DIED 1480)

Byzantine scholar. Taught in Constantinople by

Johannes ◊Argyropolous, Apostolius was briefly imprisoned by the Ottomans when they captured the city in 1453. The following year, Apostolius fled to Crete where he spent most of the rest of his career, though he went occasionally to Italy where he met his compatriot, Cardinal ◊Bessarion. Apostolius wrote a defence of Bessarion's old teacher, Plethon, against the strictures of Theodore ◊Gaza, and produced his own funerary oration on the cardinal. Apostolius also composed in Greek a collection of proverbs which his son, Arsenius Apostolius (*c.* 1468–1535) had printed in 1519; it influenced Erasmus's *Adagia*.

Appenzeller, Benedictus (*c.* 1485–AFTER 1558)

Flemish composer. A pupil of ◊Josquin Desprez, he was in the service of Mary of Hungary, dowager regent of the Netherlands.

Works include:
Chansons, church music, a *Nenia* on the death of Josquin, and other pieces.

Appleby, Thomas (1488–*c.* 1562)

English organist and composer of church music. He was appointed organist of Lincoln Cathedral in 1538, and the next year organist at Magdalen College, Oxford. He returned to Lincoln in 1541, and ◊Byrd succeeded him there in 1563.

Apuleius (DIED 2ND CENTURY AD)

Ancient Roman lawyer, philosopher, and writer. He was the author of *The Golden Ass*, or *Metamorphoses*, a prose fantasy.

The source for all later copies of Apuleius's *Golden Ass* is an 11th-century manuscript which was held at Monte Cassino. In the 14th century Zanobi da Strada saw this manuscript (or a copy from it); copies proliferated with Boccaccio and Petrarch both owning one.

In the later 15th century *The Golden Ass* was among the earliest printed books (the driving force behind the first edition being ◊Nicholas of Cusa); it received a full commentary by Filippo ◊Beroaldo the Elder. Apuleius's particular style of Latin enjoyed some sort of vogue; meanwhile, his novel was translated into the *volgare* by Matteo Maria ◊Boiardo. In the following century versions in other vernaculars appeared, including English (William ◊Adlington), French (G Michel, 1522; G Louveau, 1586), and German (J Sieder, 1538). *The Golden Ass* also had artistic influence: the central story of Cupid and Psyche was the subject of frescoes painted by Raphael for Agostino ◊Chigi (Rome, Villa Farnesina).

Aquaviva, Claudius (1543–1615)

Italian theologian, the fifth general of the Jesuits. He helped to strengthen the Society of Jesus when the principles of its founder, Ignatius Loyola, were seriously threatened. He improved its efficiency, membership, missionary work, and also its teaching, commissioning the *Ratio Studiorum/Method of Studies* (1591, revised 1599) which outlined the course of studies to be followed in Jesuit schools.

Having joined the Jesuits in 1567, Aquaviva was elected general in 1581, the youngest in the history of the Society. He was sent on a mission to convert the Mogul emperor Akbar in 1583; this proved unsuccessful. Back in Europe he faced a variety of internal disputes, most importantly the claims of the Spanish Jesuits for special privileges. These he successfully opposed by defeating Spanish demands for an additional commissary-general for Spain. He also resisted demands by the ◊Inquisition to examine the Society's constitution. During his time in office the Society's membership increased from around 5,000 to over 13,000.

Arason, Jón (1484–1550)

Icelandic priest, bishop of the northern diocese in Iceland. He introduced printing there, about 1530, and vigorously opposed the Lutheran Reformation which the Danish king Christian III was forcing upon the country. Because of his resistance he was outlawed, arrested, and beheaded, with which opposition to the Reformation effectively ended.

Arason was also a poet with both devotional and secular works ascribed to him.

Araucana

Epic poem by Alonso de ◊Ercilla y Zúñiga on the struggles between the Spanish and the Araucanian Indians of Chile. Drawing on his own Chilean experiences, Ercilla not only vividly describes battle-scenes, but also provides detailed and sympathetic accounts of the Araucanians, their customs, and their environment.

Unlike ◊Camões's contemporary epic *The Lusiad*, there is little use of the supernatural in the *Araucana* and, where it does appear, it is of no structural importance. Written in the Spanish equivalent of the Italian octave, the *octava real* (introduced by ◊Garcilaso de la Vega), the *Araucana* was soon considered, by foreigners at least, as exemplifying correct Spanish (for example John Minsheu, in his *Spanish Grammar* of 1599).

Arbeau, Thoinot (ANAGRAM OF REAL NAME JEHAN TABOUROT) (1520–1595)

French priest and author. He wrote a book on dancing, *Orchésographie* (1589), which contains a large number of dance tunes current in 16th-century France.

Arcadelt, Jacob (c. 1505–c. 1567)

Dutch or French composer. He wrote masses and motets, but is particularly noted for his Italian madrigals.

He entered the papal chapel in Rome in 1540, and received prebends in 1545 at St Barthélemy and St Pierre, Liège, from Pope Paul III. In 1551 he left papal service to go to France and, in 1554, entered the service of Charles, Duke of Guise, who was eventually appointed archbishop of Rheims. Arcadelt may also have been associated with the royal chapel of France for a time, for he was described as a musician of the king in 1557.

Arcimboldo, Giuseppe (1527–1593)

Milanese painter and designer. His trademark was the composing of fantastical portraits from fruit, plant, and animal details; he also designed tapestries. Much of his career (1562–1587) was spent as portrait painter at the court of ◊Rudolf II in Prague.

Arena Chapel (Scrovegni Chapel)

Chapel in Padua, Italy, with frescoes by Giotto. It was built 1303–05 for the Italian banker Enrico Scrovegni on the site of a 1st-century Roman amphitheatre (arena), the paintings being carried out at the same time.

The main decorative scheme, in three zones along the side walls, depicts the history of the Redemption in scenes from the lives of Mary and Jesus Christ. A fourth zone, below these, has allegorical figures of virtues and vices.

Aretino, Pietro (1492–1556)

Italian poet, prose writer, and consummate slanderer, born in Arezzo. His career began in Rome, where he became notorious for his pasquinades. He moved to Venice after an attempt on his life arranged in 1525 by Giovanni Giberti who failed to see the humorous side of his verses. He wrote in a range of forms, including dialogues (*I Ragionamenti/The Reasonings* (1534 and 1536), a prostitute's advice to her daughter), comedies (*La Cortigiana/The Courtesan* (1525)), newssheets, and letters.

Aretino attracted a string of patrons, sometimes out of fear rather than love of his writing. In Rome he was for some time in the circle of Agostino ◊Chigi; both there and elsewhere he was also patronized by members of the Medici family. In Venice he was protected by Doge Andrea Gritti. Controversy and hatred dogged him throughout his life; in the year of his death, he was the subject of slanders perpetrated by Antonio Francesco Doni.

Here lies the Tuscan poet Aretino
He slandered all but God, Whom he left out
Because, he pleaded, Well, I never knew him.

～

Pietro Aretino's epitaph

Argyll, Archibald Campbell, 5th Earl of Argyll (1530–1573)

Adherent of the Scottish presbyterian John ◊Knox. A supporter of Mary Queen of Scots from 1561, he commanded her forces after her escape from Lochleven Castle in 1568. Following her defeat at Langside, he revised his position, made peace with the regent, James Stuart, Earl of Murray, and became Lord High Chancellor of Scotland in 1572. He succeeded to the earldom in 1558.

Argyropolous, Johannes (1415–1487)

Byzantine scholar. Like ◊Bessarion, Argyropolous attended the Council of ◊Florence, briefly returned to Constantinople but eventually settled in Italy. In Argyropolous's case, his place of residence became Florence, where he continued the tradition Manuel ◊Chrysoloras had begun of teaching Greek at the university; his pupils included Cristoforo Landino and Politian. Argyropolous is credited with a part in the rise of Platonism in late quattrocento Florence, but, though he criticized George of Trebizond's attacks on Plato, his own work was Aristotelian, several of whose writings he translated into Latin.

Ariosto, Ludovico (1474–1533)

Italian poet who served various members of the d'◊Este family. Of his works, which include poems in both the *volgare* and Latin, the one which made his contemporary reputation was his epic ◊*Orlando furioso* (first version 1516).

Ariosto was born in Reggio, and joined the household of Cardinal Ippolito d'Este in 1503. He joined the household of the cardinal's brother, the Duke of Ferrara, in 1518 and was frequently engaged by him on ambassadorial missions. He was governor of Garfagnana (1522–25), a province in the Apennines, where he was mostly occupied in suppressing bandits and enforcing order. After three years he retired to Ferrara to work on the final revision of *Orlando furioso*.

Ariosto's epic was the most successful continuation of Matteo Maria Boiardo's *Orlando innamorato* (1487). As well as his four comedies (*La cassari/The Coffer* (1508), *I suppositi/The Pretenders* (1519), *La lena* (1528), and *Il negromante/The Necromancer* (1529)), Ariosto produced seven satires in the style of Horace, a prose dialogue on the subject of hygiene, *Rime* (sonnets and other poems), and *Cinque canti*, five cantos withheld from *Orlando furioso*.

Armin, Robert (c. 1565–1610)

English comic actor. A pupil of the clown Richard ◊Tarleton, he joined the Lord Chamberlain's (later King's) Men, becoming principal comedian. He adopted the role of Dogberry in *Much Ado About Nothing* and almost certainly created the parts of 'witty fools' such as Feste in *Twelfth Night* and the Fool in *King Lear*.

Arminius, Jacobus (LATINIZED NAME OF JAKOB HARMENSEN) (1560–1609)

Dutch Protestant priest who founded Arminianism, a school of Christian theology opposed to John Calvin's doctrine of predestination. His views were developed by Simon Episcopius (1583–1643). Arminianism is the basis of Wesleyan Methodism.

Arminius was born in southern Holland, ordained in Amsterdam in 1588, and from 1603 was professor of theology at Leiden. He asserted that forgiveness and eternal life are bestowed on all who repent of their sins and sincerely believe in Jesus Christ. He was drawn into many controversies, and his followers were expelled from the church and persecuted.

Arndt, Johann (1555–1621)

Lutheran theologian. He was born at Ballenstadt in Anhalt, and educated at Wittenberg. His principal work, inspired by the mystics St Bernard, Johann Tanler, and Thomas à Kempis, is *Vier Bücher vom wahren Christentum/Four Books on True Christianity* (1606–10, translated 1712). He also wrote *Der Paradiesgartlein/The Garden of Paradise* (1612).

Arrabbiati (ITALIAN 'THE ENRAGED')

Faction hostile to the religious leader Girolamo ◊Savonarola in 15th-century Florence. Its leaders were men of wealth, who, while they did not want Medici rule, detested Savonarola's property tax and other measures against luxury and inequality.

Arran, James Hamilton, 2nd Earl of Arran (c. 1515–1575)

Scottish nobleman, Regent of Scotland during the minority of Mary Stuart. In 1554 he resigned his position as regent to the Queen Mother, Mary of Guise, and went into exile in France. He returned to Scotland in 1569 as a strong supporter of Mary's cause but by 1573 had been forced to acknowledge James VI's authority.

He was created duke of Châtelherault in 1548 by Henry II of France.

ars nova (LATIN 'NEW ART')

Music composed in France and Italy during the 14th century. Originally introduced by Philippe de ◊Vitry, it is distinguished by rhythmic and harmonic variety, and the increased importance of duple time (two beats in a bar) and independent voice parts. Guillaume de ◊Machaut mastered the style in France. In Italy the ◊madrigal grew out of ars nova.

Ascensius, Jodocus Badius

See ◊Bade, Josse.

Ascham, Roger (c. 1515–1568)

English scholar and tutor. His writings included *Toxophilus* (1545), a treatise on archery written in dialogue form, and his educational treatise *The Scholemaster*, published by his widow in 1570. His works could be taken as exemplary of an English Protestant schizophrenia: on the one hand, a mastery of the skills pioneered by the humanists, on the other, a distrust of Italy and all things Italian.

In 1548 Ascham was appointed tutor to Princess Elizabeth. He retained favour under Edward VI and Queen Mary (despite his Protestant views), and returned to Elizabeth's service as her secretary after she became queen.

Ascham was born in Kirby Wiske, near Northallerton, Yorkshire, and adopted by Sir Anthony Wingfield, who had him educated with his own sons. Impressed by Ascham's scholarship, his patron sent him to St John's College, Cambridge, where he proved himself a brilliant Classical student, gained a fellowship, and taught Greek. In 1546 he became public orator of his university.

From 1550 to 1553 he was in the suite of the English ambassador at the court of Charles V, during which time he visited various places in Europe, including a stay (for him, thankfully brief) in Italy. His *Report on the Affairs of Germany* appeared in 1553. During his absence abroad he was appointed Latin secretary to Edward VI, an office which, through Bishop ◊Gardiner's influence, he was able to continue under Queen Mary.

Ashwell, Thomas (OR ASHEWELL, HASHEWELL) (c. 1478–AFTER 1513)

English composer. In 1508 he was *informator choristarum* (choirmaster) at Lincoln Cathedral, and in

1513 held the equivalent post in Durham. His surviving works include four Masses, two (*God save King Harry* and *Sancte Cuthberte*) in a fragmentary state and two (*Ave Maria* and *Jesu Christe*) complete.

Asola, Giammateo (*c.* 1532–1609)

Italian priest and composer. He was *maestro di cappella* successively at Treviso (from 1577) and Vincenza (from 1578). He wrote church music (including 12 books of Masses) and madrigals.

Aspertini, Amico (*c.* 1475–1552)

Bolognese painter and sculptor. Notable works include a series of reredoses and a cycle of frescoes 1508–09 in the Church of San Frediano, in Lucca. As a sculptor he collaborated on the portals of the Church of San Petronio, Bologna.

He was a pupil of Ercole de' Roberti of Ferrara and assistant to both ◊Costa and ◊Francia, with whom he worked on frescoes in the oratory of Santa Cecilia in San Giacomo Maggiore, Bologna, in 1506. Aspertini also visited Rome and Florence and absorbed features of the styles of such painters as ◊Signorelli, ◊Raphael, and Filippino ◊Lippi, whose works he studied in detail. His sketches show his interest in the art of ancient Rome.

Aston, Hugh (*c.* 1480–1558)

English composer. He completed his studies at Oxford in 1510, and was choirmaster at Newarke College, Leicester, 1525–48. His works include six votive antiphons, two Masses, and a 'Hornepype' for keyboard. There are works on a ground bass of his by Whytbroke (for viols) and Byrd (for keyboard).

astrology

Ancient practice of dissecting personality and predicting the future based on the notion that the relative positioning of heavenly bodies determines the course of human events. Astrology was indistinguishable from Albertus Magnus's 'astronomia' until the later 16th century (casting Henry VI's horoscope led to the execution of the 'astronomer'-priest Roger Bolingbroke in 1441). The rediscovery in *c.* 1500 of ancient cosmological and cosmographical texts by, for example, Ptolemy (by whom astrology was treated as the 'applied branch' of astronomy) initially reinforced this elision.

Philosophers such as Pierre d' ◊Ailly faced only limited conflict with the church on the star-gazing front: God's astrological models were used to understand and reveal divine providence. However, beginning in the 15th century, the idea of a new age, the revival of ancient 'pagan' arts, and the accelerated circulation of prophecy (see feature) combined to render astrology as popular both at court and in villages as it had been in Classical antiquity, and, paradoxically, more vehemently attacked by detractors than ever before.

'To believe that God and nature have drawn in the sky lions, dragons, dogs, scorpions, vases, archers, and monsters is a ridiculous thing', proclaimed ◊Savonarola (who elsewhere, nevertheless, foresaw the adventurous young French king ◊Charles VIII as a heaven-sent scourge, and claimed a coming time of change and renewal in the lives of all Florentines). He agreed with Giovanni ◊Pico della Mirandola's vitriolic attack on the impossibility of a relationship between human destiny and astral influence. However, Pico della Mirandola's elder Neo-Platonic peer, Marsilio ◊Ficino, suggested that the stars should always be consulted; Agostino Nifo blamed ◊Borgia wrongdoings on adverse planetary conjunctions; and ◊Leo X, whose machinations against prophesying took years to complete, had a personal horoscope-caster who was also his doctor (physicians, in fact, often combined the practice of astrology and medicine – hence the written career of Girolamo ◊Cardano and the *astrologie judicielle* proposed by ◊Nostradamus). The distinct widening of the gap, by 1500, between scholarly advocates and detractors of astrology had a backlash in popular culture: on the one hand, astrology and astral/cosmological magic proliferated in printed handbooks; on the other, astrological parodies circulated, such as in the following example from Modena (1526):

'The other astrologer lifted up his robe and showed him his rear, and his companion astrologized his rear with the sextant, and he accomplished this task with such grace that the lord governor and all the others took great pleasure in it, except for *misser podestà* because the joke was made on purpose to mock the astrologers and the said *podestà*, whom they had astrologized on the rear end.'

By 1600 the reputable status – though not the popularity – of astrology as a scientific form of prophecy had mainly waned. In its place the less anthropocentric, and essentially descriptive rather than prophetic, computations of astronomy had taken a firm hold on heaven and earth alike.

Atahualpa (c. 1502–1533)

King of Quito who, after winning the civil war against his brother Huáscar, became Inca (emperor) of Peru. Despite commanding vastly superior forces, he was captured at Cajamarca by the newly arrived Castilians, under Francisco ◊Pizarro, in 1532. His people paid a ransom of a roomful of gold, but Atahualpa remained imprisoned. Accused of crimes including polygamy and treason against the king of Spain, he was sentenced to be burned; when he half-heartedly converted to Christianity, the sentence was commuted to strangulation.

Athanasius, St (296–373)

Church Father, bishop of Alexandria from 326. He was, like St ◊Basil, a stern opponent of the Arian heretics.

Athanasius's works, introduced to Western Europe in the early 15th century, were attractive to the Catholics at the Council of ◊Florence: they believed his writings, along with those of other Church Fathers (most notably St Basil), provided patristic support for their view of the Trinity. Several of Athanasius's works were translated by Ambrogio ◊Traversari and also (in England) by Antonio ◊Beccaria; a *Life* of the saint was produced by Giovanni Tortelli. In the mid-15th century his relics were brought from Constantinople to Venice; the event was celebrated in writing by Ermolao ◊Barbaro the Elder who produced another *Life of Athanasius* (based mainly on Eusebius). Around the same time ◊George of Trebizond translated (and dedicated to Pope Nicholas V) Gregory of Nazianus's orations in praise of Athanasius and Basil.

After this spate of interest, Athanasius's popularity seems to have declined. In the Reformation period, his works were less often referred to but he continued to symbolize the protection of the true faith against heresy.

Aubigné, Théodore Agrippa d' (1552–1630)

French soldier and scholar. A Huguenot, he fought for the cause with the pen and the sword. Early in his career he was a companion of Henry of Navare, the future Henry IV, but left his court when Henry converted in 1593. Aubigne's writings comprise mainly histories of France justifying the Huguenot position: the *Histoire universelle* (1560–1601 and 1616–19) and the verse *Les Tragiques* (begun 1577, published 1616). He could also, however, write love poetry (*Printemps* (1571–73)) and satire (for example, his *Confession catholique du Sieur de Sancy* (1598–1600), attacking Protestants who abjure).

Audley, Thomas, BARON AUDLEY OF WALDEN (1488–1544)

Lord Chancellor of England from 1533. In 1529 he became Speaker of the House of Commons. He supported the annulment of Henry VIII's marriage to Catherine of Aragon; presided at the trials of Thomas ◊More and John ◊Fisher; passed judgement on the king's discarded wives Anne Boleyn and Catherine Howard; managed the conviction of Thomas ◊Cromwell; and effected the dissolution of Henry VIII's marriage with Anne of Cleves.

Audley was born in Essex, studied at Cambridge and the Middle Temple, London, and later became a member of the cleric and politician Thomas Wolsey's household. He was created a peer in 1538.

He re-established Buckingham College, Cambridge, as Magdalene College.

Augsburg, Confession of

Statement of the Lutheran faith composed by Philip ◊Melanchthon. Presented to the Holy Roman Emperor Charles V, at the Diet of Augsburg in 1530, it was intended originally as a working document for the negotiations at the Diet aiming at reconciliation between Lutherans and Catholics. It came, however, to be seen as the crucial expression of Lutheran beliefs.

Augsburg, Peace of

Religious settlement following the Diet of Augsburg of 1555, which established the right of princes in the Holy Roman Empire (rather than the emperor himself) to impose a religion on their subjects – later summarized by the maxim *cuius regio, eius religio* ('whose realm it is, his the religion'). The ruler's religion could be either Catholic or Lutheran; the agreement's failure to consider the increasingly important Calvinist movement was one of the difficulties that led to the confessional strife of the early 17th century.

Aurispa, Giovanni (1376–1459)

Sicilian humanist author and searcher for manuscripts of Classical texts. He first travelled to Greece in 1413–14 when he learnt Greek and returned with manuscripts of Homer, Sophocles, and Euripides. He returned to Greece in 1421–23 on a diplomatic mission for Gian Francesco Gonzaga; from this trip, he brought back a veritable horde of manuscripts, including 238 Classical works (several previously unknown in Western Europe). Aurispa's later years were spent alongside ◊Guarino da Verona in Ferrara, Italy, where he was tutor to one of the sons of Niccolò d'Este.

Aurispa's career of manuscript discoveries did not stop when he joined the d'Este household, however; on a journey with his charge through Germany, he discovered Pliny the Younger's *Panegyric*. However, Aurispa's later years were more productive in terms of writing: he translated into Latin texts by, for example, Lucian and Plutarch, as well as making a *volgare* version of Buonaccorso's *De Nobilitate*; he also wrote epigrams and a short satirical dialogue, *De Conquestu Virtutis*.

auto

Term used in both Medieval and Renaissance Castilian and Portuguese to refer to a short, one-act dramatic work of religious or profane theme (for example, Lucas Fernández's *Auto de la Pasión/Auto on the Passion*, or Gil ◊Vicente's *Auto da India/Auto of India*).

Within the all-embracing term *auto* were sub-categories, such as the Castilian *auto sacramental* (sacramental, eucharistic *auto*) which presented allegories of biblical stories or of Catholic dogma (particularly the doctrine of the Eucharist), with markedly didactic intent. It seems to have developed from the processions and tableaux organized for the June festivities of Corpus Christi, and was extremely popular in the late 16th and 17th centuries, when the dramatist Pedro Calderón de la Barca developed and perfected the genre.

Aytoun (AYTON), Robert (1569–1638)

Scottish poet. He was employed by James VI and I and wrote songs and courtly verse. Aytoun was one of the first Scottish poets to write in English rather than in Scots; he also wrote in Latin, Greek, and French.

Aytoun was born in Kinaldie, Fife, and studied at St Andrews University. He remained in the royal service until he died. He was knighted in 1612.

AZULEJOS IN PORTUGAL AND SPAIN

AZULEJOS – THE WORD probably derives from the Arabic *al zuleycha*, 'glazed brick', and is the same in Portuguese and Castilian – are square, glazed, clay tiles. Their function is primarily decorative: they appear set in walls (as a frieze or a whole panel), floors, as wainscoting, between roof-beams, on fountains and altars, though in Arab Spain they were sometimes used to cover the exterior of whole buildings.

Azulejos arrived in the Iberian peninsula with the Moors but in the reconquered Christian territories they gradually evolved into a rather different object. The Arab *azulejo* was a collection of small, many-sided pieces (known as *aliceres*) cut from different-coloured glazed clay plaques and set together to form patterns (usually geometric) within an overall square shape (*alicatado*). It was a slow and expensive procedure, but one which was still frequently used in 15th-century Spain. By the end of that century, though, a new technique known as *cuerda seca* (literally, 'dry rope') was being introduced which produced an *alicatado* effect without the need to laboriously cut out pieces of tile and reassemble them. There were also several other 15th-century techniques for making the tiles: *arista* ('ridge') or *cuenca* ('impression'), for example, in which the design was imprinted upon the damp clay; and *loza decorada* (decorated tiles) where the design was painted on top of a layer of tin oxide and then fired. The most prized *azulejos* of all, though, were those glazed with a golden or coppery sheen using a firing technique learnt from the Arabs.

continued

Commonly known as *manises*, after the Valencian town where much of this type of glaze was produced, the technical term is *ceramica de lustre* (lustreware). In Arab Spain, production of this type of glaze reached its peak at Malaga, during the Nasrid dynasty; production continued in Christian Malaga, spreading to Manises in the 14th century. *Azulejos* glazed in this way tended to be used in a particular, limited fashion as, for example, small panels to face church altars, or as heraldic plaques.

Valencia, Seville, Toledo, and, from the mid-16th century, Talavera, were the main centres of *azulejo* production in the peninsula of the 15th and 16th centuries. Unsurprisingly, it was an industry dominated by Arabs but *azulejos* were also manufactured in some monasteries and convents as a source of revenue, as a 1422 contract drawn up between the Toledo convent of Santo Domingo el Real and a local noblewoman shows. Some centres of production enjoyed royal patronage: in 1575 ◊Philip II placed the industry at Talavera under his protection, and encouraged the establishment of Talavera-style potteries in Mexico. There was, however, little native industry in Portugal during this period – perhaps because it had been completely conquered from the Arabs much earlier than the Spanish kingdoms – and *azulejos* only began to arrive there from Valencia and Seville in the 15th century.

Since workshops did not distinguish the *azulejos* they produced by a particular stamp and since designs were often repeated patterns which were unsigned, identification of *azulejos* from different areas necessarily rests on distinctive features of glaze, colour, and design.

Hence a *manises* glaze is typical of Valencia (it was not used in Seville until the 16th century), while Toledan *azulejos* did not include the colour blue until the 16th century, when the artists began to use a distinctive greyish-blue, obtained from cobalt oxide. By contrast, Talaveran products, first referred to as a distinct group in 1484, were characterized by brilliant yellows, oranges, and emerald greens, and by milky-white backgrounds. *Manises* was never used in Talavera. Meanwhile, the arrival of Fransisco ◊Niculoso 'el Pisano' ('the Pisan') in Seville at the very start of the 16th century signalled a new phase in the style of local production. His approach towards *azulejos* owed much to contemporary Italian trends in painting. Niculoso's *azulejo* panels, with their carefully executed figures and surroundings against a yellow or white background, are given depth by their *chiaroscuro* shading and resemble paintings – albeit ones composed of tens of square sections. Their colouring, too, was innovative: like a painter, he mixed the traditional *azulejo* colours (black, white, green, honey-yellow, blue) to obtain dramatic purples and pinks and, like a painter, he also signed his works. Perhaps his most curious panel is one set in the wall of the Seville church of Santa Ana, to mark the tomb of Iñigo López, buried below (1503). So imitated was Niculoso's œuvre, that *azulejos* painted in this style became known as *pisano*. This did not, however, replace the traditional, Islamic-influenced geometric patterns of *cuerda seca* tiles.

If Portugal did not itself produce *azulejos* in great quantities in the 15th and 16th centuries, it did, however, enthusiastically import them and put them to every conceivable decorative use. ◊Manuel I commissioned *cuerda seca* tiles with his adopted royal symbol, the armillary sphere, from Seville, for his palace at Sintra (*c*.1507). Perhaps the most striking example of Portuguese enthusiasm for *azulejos*, though, is the Old Cathedral ('Sé Velha') at Coimbra. In 1503 the entire interior was lined with geometrically patterned Sevillian *arista*-style *azulejos* which had been commissioned by the Bishop, Jorge d'Almeida. The Portuguese fashion for retrospectively decorating church interiors with *azulejos* was one which continued into the 17th and 18th centuries. Meanwhile, two *azulejo* panels in the Lisbon church of St Roque, decorated with Italianate urns, cornucopi, and grotesques, dated 1584 and signed by Francisco de Matos, testify not only to changing styles of design but also to a modest local industry.

While the Portuguese *azulejo* industry expanded significantly after the 16th century, the Spanish one entered a phase of decline, hastened by Philip III's expulsion of its main practitioners, the *moriscos*, in 1609. Earlier religious intolerance had had more positive results: the *moriscos* who fled Valencia for Italy at the end of the 15th century introduced local craftsmen to the techniques of *manises*. The first Italian lustreware was produced in about 1500 at Deruta (near Perugia).

KIRSTIN KENNEDY

Further Reading

Carlos Cid Priego, *Los azulejos* (Barcelona/Buenos Aires: 1950); Antonio J Morales, *Francisco Niculoso Pisano,* 2nd edn (Seville, 1991)

Bacon, Francis, 1st Baron Verulam and Viscount St Albans (1561–1626)

English philosopher, politician, and writer, a founder of modern scientific research. His works include *Essays* (1597, revised and augmented 1612 and 1625), characterized by pith and brevity; *The Advancement of Learning* (1605), a seminal work discussing scientific method; *Novum Organum* (1620), in which he redefined the task of natural science, seeing it as a means of empirical discovery and a method of increasing human power over nature; and *The New Atlantis* (1626), describing a utopian state in which scientific knowledge is systematically sought and exploited. He was briefly Lord Chancellor in 1618 but lost his post through corruption.

Bacon was born in London, studied law at Cambridge from 1573, was part of the embassy in France until 1579, and became a member of Parliament in 1584. In 1596 he became a Queen's Counsel. He was the nephew of Queen Elizabeth's adviser Lord ◊Burghley, but turned against him when he failed to provide Bacon with patronage and attached himself to Burghley's rival, the Earl of Essex. He subsequently helped secure the execution of the Earl of Essex as a traitor in 1601. Bacon was accused of ingratitude to his patron, but he defended himself in *Apology* (1604), arguing that his first loyalty was to his sovereign. In 1618, having risen to Lord Chancellor, he confessed to bribe-taking, was fined £40,000 (which was later remitted by the king), and spent four days in the Tower of London. From then on he devoted himself to science and writing, in both Latin and English.

Satirist Alexander Pope called Bacon 'the wisest, brightest, and meanest of mankind'. Knighted on the accession of James I in 1603, he became Baron Verulam in 1618 and Viscount St Albans in 1621. His writings helped to inspire the founding of the Royal Society. The **Baconian theory**, originated by James Willmot in 1785, suggesting that the works of Shakespeare were written by Bacon, is not taken seriously by scholars.

He died after catching a cold while stuffing a chicken with snow in an early experiment in refrigeration.

In philosophy, Bacon's work on scientific method has been influential. At Cambridge he had found that the Aristotelian system taught at the time produced only verbal argument but no concrete results. He therefore decided that a new approach must be made to the whole problem of systematizing knowledge. A new instrument of thought, a 'novum organum', must be provided to replace the traditional *organum* (system) of Aristotle. So arose his great plan for the renewal of knowledge, the vast 'Instauratio Scientiarum', which he formed at an early age and sketched out in 1620 in the introduction to his *Novum Organum*. It was a grandiose scheme, of which only parts were completed.

First, there was to be a survey of existing human knowledge; the initial sketch of this was *The Advancement of Learning*, later revised and expanded in the Latin version, *De Augmentis Scientiarum* (1623). Second, there was to be a description of a new method of acquiring knowledge. The outline of this was the *Novum Organum*, which sets out the principles of the Baconian method: to discover the hidden, simple laws of the universe by gathering scientific data, and, by eliminating all its incidental attributes, to arrive at its essential causes. Bacon's scheme was to include a section assembling empirical data, another propounding solutions, and a final section extracting from these a new philosophy. Related to these projections is *The New Atlantis*, which, like Thomas More's *Utopia*, embodies a description of an ideal commonwealth. This makes some remarkable predictions about scientific inventions, including a kind of telephone. *Sylva Sylvarum* (1627), on which Bacon was working at his death, dealt with natural history, and was also part of the 'Instauratio'.

Bade, Josse (JODOCUS BADIUS ASCENSIUS) (1461/2–1535)

Flemish humanist editor and printer, born near Ghent but active in France. While teaching in Lyons,

France, he began to edit works for printing. He moved to Paris in 1499 and set up his own printing house in 1503; he was appointed printer to the University of Paris in 1507. He produced 720 books, many being standard philosophical texts but also among them works by Classical authors and humanists, including his sometime friend Erasmus.

After studying at Ghent, Louvain, and Bologna, Bade settled in Lyons in 1492 and became an editor for the printer Jean Treschel (died 1498); his first work was an edition of the orations of his former teacher, Filippo ◊Beroaldo the Elder, in 1492. He also edited Terence's play *Afer*, which was printed in Venice in 1494. In his first years in Paris, he worked with Jean ◊Petit; his own publishing house became (like that of Froben or Aldus) a centre for intellectual exchange, frequented by Guillaume Budé and Lefèvre d'Etaples, among others. However, in the religious controversy between Lefèvre d'Etaples and John ◊Fisher, he took Fisher's conservative stance; in the 1520s, he printed works attacking the theology not only of Luther but of Erasmus as well.

Bade's son, Conrad, and his son-in-law, Robert ◊Estienne, succeeded him as printers.

Baglioni family

A wealthy and ruthless family who dominated Perugia in Italy during the 15th century. They became notorious for the crimes they committed to maintain their position. Giampaolo Baglioni (1470–1520) seized power in 1500 after murdering several leading members of his family. In 1506 he tried to murder Pope ◊Julius II and much later was himself murdered on the orders of Pope ◊Leo X. Ridolfo Baglioni was defeated and exiled by Pope Paul III in the Salt War.

The Baglioni gained their wealth as *condottieri* (mercenaries) in the 13th century. Their political power was established by Malatesta Baglioni (1389–1427), who was awarded territories by Pope ◊Martin V and who virtually ruled Perugia. From 1488, after killing or exiling their rivals, the Baglioni ruled Perugia unopposed through a council of ten family members.

Baïf, Jean Antoine de (1532–1589)

French poet, born in Venice. A member of the ◊*Pléiade* group of poets, like his colleagues he employed classical themes and was notable for Classical prosody in French verse. His *Le Brave* (1567), for example, adapted ◊Plautus' *Miles Gloriosus*. His poems include *Les Amours* (1552), *Les Amours de Francine* (1555), *Oeuvres en rime* (1572–73), and *Mimes, enseignements et proverbes* (1576).

His brainchild, the Academie de poeàsie et de musique/Academy of Poetry and Music, was founded by royal charter in 1570, with the intention of bringing the two arts closer together. Despite the royal favour, it proved (like so many ◊academies) short-lived, being superseded by the Academie de palais.

Bakfark, Balint Valentin (ALSO KNOWN AS GREFF-BAKFARK) (1507–1576)

Hungarian-born Polish lutenist and composer. He was a great virtuoso, as is reflected by the technical difficulty of his extant works. He published a lute book with Jacques Moderne of Lyon in 1552 (*Intabulatura ...Transilvani Coroniensis Liber Primus*) and a second with Andreae of Kraków (Andrzej z Krakowa) in 1565 (*Pannonii Harmonicarum Musicarum in Usum Testudinis Factarum Tomus Primus*).

He learnt to play the lute while in royal service. He later lived in France, Vienna, and Padua, and was at the Polish court 1549–66.

Balassi, Bálint (1554–1594)

Hungarian poet, born in Bohemia. He produced, for the first time in Hungarian, lyric poetry of great beauty and freshness, as in *A végek dicsérete/In Praise of the Marches* (1589).

Much of Balassi's life was spent fighting the occupying Turks, and in litigation to recover his estates. Couched in a variety of original verse forms, his works treat the themes of love, God, and the military life: his poems include the Julia cycle (1587); the Anna poems (1578); and *Adj má csendességet/Grant Me Peace* (1591).

Baldovinetti, Alesso (1426–1499)

Florentine artist and designer. He was trained in his hometown where formative influences were Domenico ◊Veneziano, Fra ◊Angelico, and Andrea del ◊Castagno. His frescoes are in poor condition because of his experiments with various painting media. He was one of the leading mosaicists of his time and also worked in stained glass.

Works attributed to him are the *Virgin and Child* (*c.* 1460, Louvre, Paris), with its beautiful landscape background; the profile *Portrait of a Lady* (National Gallery, London); *Enthroned Virgin and Child with Saints*; and the *Nativity* (1460), a large fresco in the cloisters of the SS Annunziata in Florence. He was the master of Domenico ◊Ghirlandaio.

Baldung Grien, Hans (1484/85–1545)

German Renaissance painter, engraver, and designer. A prolific and accomplished artist, he designed tapestries and stained glass, produced many graphic works, and painted religious subjects, portraits, and allegories. His works, in which he sometimes employs a dramatic foreshortening, frequently display an interest in the occult, as in *The Bewitched Stableboy*.

He was born in Gmund in Swabia but lived chiefly in Switzerland, near Strasbourg. Early in his career he worked in Albrecht ◊Dürer's workshop in Nürnberg 1503–09; some of Baldung's work reflects Dürer's influence. His principal religious paintings were his altarpiece for the cathedral in Freiburg, *The Adoration of the Kings* (Berlin) and *Crucifixion* (Basel), showing an ornate invention.

His woodcuts are variously signed HB, HBG, and HG.

Bale, John (1495–1563)

English cleric, religious polemicist, and antiquary. He was a vehement supporter of evangelical religion, writing several acerbically anti-Catholic pamphlets; antipapalism is also a theme of his allegorical history play *King John*. At the same time, however, he worked on his scholarly magnum opus *Illustrium Maioris Britanniae Scriptorum Summarium/ Summary of the Illustrious Writers of Great Britain* (1548).

Bale was born in Suffolk and educated at Cambridge. In 1529 he became prior of the Carmelites of Ipswich. Soon after this date he adopted the principles of Lutheranism and wrote in its defence. His outspokenness, however, made it dangerous for him to stay in England and he left for Germany in 1540. Returning on Edward VI's accession, he gained ecclesiastical preferment, being appointed bishop of Ossory in 1552. But on the accession of Mary he was forced to escape, first to Holland and then to Switzerland. On his return to England, he was made a prebendary of Canterbury by Queen Elizabeth. He died in Canterbury and was buried in the cathedral.

Endebted to John ◊Leland's work, the *Summarium* provides listings of the works of every British author whom he knew to have existed (and a few who had not).

ballet de cour

(French 'court dance') an entertainment combining music, spectacle, dancing, song, and drama, developed at the French court during the second half of the 16th century. Light-hearted allegories based on Classical mythology, *ballets de cour* played an important role in the evolution of ballet. One of the best known is the *Ballet comique de la Reine* (1581).

It was the patronage of Catherine de' ◊Medici, who would have seen similar entertainments at the Florentine court in her youth, that encouraged the development of lavish *ballets de cour*. As in a ◊masque the parts were often played by members of the court – in the *Ballet comique de la Reine*, commissioned by Catherine de' Medici to celebrate the marriage of her daughter Marguerite de Lorraine, both she and her daughter had roles.

The costume designs surviving from the early 17th century, especially those by Daniel Rabel (1578– 1637), indicate the grotesque and humorous, as well as the opulent, aspects of these entertainments.

The fashion for hugely expensive and spectacular *ballets de cour* continued in the reigns of Henry IV and Louis XIII.

Banchieri, Adriano (1568–1634)

Italian organist, theorist, and composer. He was a Benedictine monk, and helped to found the Accademia dei Floridi at Bologna in 1615. He wrote theoretical works, especially on figured bass (*L'organo suonarino* 1605). *Cartella musicale* (1614) advises on vocal ornamentation. His sequence of madrigals *La pazzia senile* (1595) has been described as the first comic opera.

A pupil of Gioseffo Guami, in 1596 he became organist at the monastery of San Michele in Bosco

(Monte Oliveto) near Bologna, to which he returned in 1609, remaining there until shortly before his death; from 1600 to 1604 he was organist at Santa Maria in Regola at Imola.

Works include:
Masses; sacred symphonies and concertos; comic intermezzi for the stage; organ works.

Bandello, Matteo (1485–1561)

Lombard author and courtier. He served both Alessandro Bentivoglio and Francesco Gonzaga, Marchese of Mantua; his work took him to France in 1508 and 1537, where he dedicated one of his literary efforts – an Italian translation of Euripides' *Hecuba* – to Margaret of Navarre. In works like his *Canti XI de le lodi de la signora Lucrezia Gonzaga/ Eleven Cantos in Praise of Lucrezia Gonzaga* (1545), he affected an unrequited love for the pre-eminent lady of the court where he was employed. His longest and most successful work, however, was his collection of stories *Novelle/ Tales* (1554), inspired by Boccaccio's *Decameron*.

Many of the stories in Bandello's collection were translated into French by François ◊Belleforest (1559–82) and were in turn soon translated into English. These English translations, by Geoffrey Fenton, Arthur Brooke, and William Painter, provided ◊Shakespeare with the material for several plays, including *Romeo and Juliet* and *Much Ado About Nothing*.

Bandinelli, Baccio (1488–1560)

Florentine sculptor. He often worked on a large scale, his career largely dedicated to trying to equal the sculpture of ◊Michelangelo. His *Hercules and Cacus* (1534), for example, which stands in the Piazza della Signoria in Florence, was specifically intended to rival Michelangelo's *David*.

He was born in Florence and after training under his father, a goldsmith, worked with Rustici, the sculptural associate of ◊Leonardo da Vinci. He later worked on a series of commissions from the Medici family, both in Florence and Rome, and as court sculptor to Duke Cosimo I he was a rival of ◊Cellini.

Among his works are *Laocoon* (1525, Uffizi, Florence), imitating the Classical statue, and his *Prophets* (1555), low reliefs in the choir of Florence Cathedral. He also produced portraits, bronze stat-

uettes, paintings, and drawings, most of which are in Florence.

Barbari, Jacopo de' (1440s–c. 1516)

Italian painter and engraver. In 1500 he went to Nürnberg in the service of the Holy Roman Emperor ◊Maximilian I. After 1504 he worked for Archduke Frederick III of Saxony and Joachim I of Brandenburg under the name of **Jacob Walch.** He became court painter to the regent of the Netherlands, Margaret of Austria, in 1510.

His studies of human proportions turned Albrecht Dürer towards this research, though Barbari seems to have followed Dürer and Lucas Cranach in his later style. Barbari's exquisite still life of a dead bird and pieces of armour (Alte Pinakothek, Munich) is considered one of the earliest still lifes. He also engraved a well-known map of Venice.

Barbaro, Daniele (1513–1570)

Venetian diplomat and art patron. He acted as Venice's ambassador to England 1548–51. He produced several philosophical commentaries and then turned his attention to ◊Vitruvius, publishing an influential Italian edition in 1556. About the same time he commissioned ◊Palladio to design the Villa Barbaro at Maser (built 1560–68), the interior of which was decorated by ◊Veronese.

Being born into the wealthy patrician Barbaro family, he inherited the duty to be active in politics, along with the ability to spend his leisure time in scholarly pursuits. He studied science, philosophy, mathematics, and literature in Padua. In 1545 he founded the botanical garden there and worked as its curator. At the suggestion of the incumbent, Giovanni Grimani, Barbaro was chosen in 1550 as the next patriarch of Aquileia; he attended the later sessions of the Council of ◊Trent and there was talk of him becoming a cardinal, but he never actually entered holy orders. As well as his Italian edition of Vitruvius, Barbaro produced a Latin commentary (1567) and he also published *La pratica della perspettiva/On Perspective* (1569), which contains an early account of the camera obscura. Palladio provided the illustrations to Barbaro's edition of Vitruvius.

Barbaro, Ermolao, THE ELDER (1410–1471)

Venetian cleric and humanist author. Born into the influential Barbaro family, his teachers included (as well as ◊Guarino) his own uncle, Francesco ◊Barbaro. His career was spent in papal service: he was sent, for example, to France in 1460 on a diplomatic mission; he was appointed bishop of Treviso in 1443 and transferred to Verona in 1453.

At the age of 12 he translated some Aesop fables into Latin (dedicating them to Ambrogio ◊Traversari). Antonio ◊Beccaria was his secretary in Verona; they both became involved in a literary dispute on the moral merits of the ancient poets (Barbaro being sceptical they had any). Barbaro also produced a *Life of St Athanasius*, mainly translated from Eusebius (see St ◊Athanasius).

Barbaro, Ermolao, THE YOUNGER (1454–1493)

Venetian humanist teacher and Classical scholar. Born into the influential Barbaro family, his teachers included (as well as Pomponio ◊Leto and Theodore ◊Gazes) his own uncle, also called Ermolao ◊Barbaro. He lectured in Venice on Aristotle and produced a commentary on Pliny the Elder, *Castigiones Plinianae* (1492–93). He was employed by Venice as a diplomat until he fell into disgrace by accepting Pope Innocent VIII's appointment as patriarch of Aquileia in 1491.

Barbaro, Francesco (1390–1454)

Venetian politician and humanist author. In his political career, he became the governor of several Venetian territories and led the defence of Brescia against the Milanese army of Niccolò Piccinino. In his youth, however, he had been educated by Gasparino ◊Barzizza and by ◊Guarino, who taught him Greek; he also spent time with the Florentine humanist coterie and dedicated his *De Re Uxoria/On Wifely Matters* (1416) to a leading Florentine, Lorenzo di Giovanni de' Medici. In later years he acted as patron to Flavio ◊Biondo, among others.

Barbarosa

See ◊Khaired-Din

Barbé, Anton (DIED 1564)

Flemish composer and first of a line of Antwerp musi-cians. He was Kapellmeister at Antwerp Cathedral 1527–62. He published Masses, motets, and chansons, and contributed a Dutch song to Tielman Susato's *Het ierste musyck boexken/The First Music Book* (1551), one of 11 volumes of pieces by composers of the time.

Barclay, Alexander (c. 1475–1552)

Poet, probably Scottish by birth, although most of his life was spent in England. His *The Shyp of Folys* (1509) is a verse adaptation of Sebastian ◊Brant's *Das Narrenschiff/The Ship of Fools* (1494), satirizing the social vices of the age.

His other works are five *Egloges* (written about 1514), the earliest English pastorals; *The Myrrour of Good Maners* (1523); and a translation of the Roman historian Sallust's *Jugurtha*, together with other translations.

Barclay became chaplain of the college of Ottery St Mary, Devon, later a monk at Ely and Canterbury, and then the rector of All Hallows, Lombard Street, London.

Bardi family

Family of Italian bankers prominent in 14th-century Florence. By 1310 they were the wealthiest family in Florence and used their position to secure political dominance. In 1346, however, they were bankrupt and (unlike other Italian banks bankrupted at the same time) failed to regain either their wealth or political influence.

Their downfall came about largely through their involvement with the attempts of Edward III of England to finance the Hundred Years' War. From 1338 they participated in schemes to exploit the English wool trade though monopolistic syndicates, which were intended to repay the large loans they made to the king. These did not work, and in 1341 Edward defaulted on his repayments. It was this, combined with the burden of supporting Florence's war against Lucca, that brought them (and several other Italian banks, such as the ◊Acciaiuoli) to bankruptcy.

The sole surviving evidence of the Bardi fortune can be seen in their gifts to the Church of Santa Croce in Florence. Count **Giovanni Bardi** (1534–1612) was a composer and leading cultural figure in late 16th-century Florence, the patron of musicians, scholars, and poets.

Barends, Dirk (1534–1592)

Dutch painter. He lived in Italy 1555–62, where he spent some time in the studio of ◊Titian in Venice; on his return to Amsterdam he established a career as a portrait painter, in particular producing group portraits such as *Fourteen Guardsmen* (1562). He also painted religious works, which reflect not only Venetian influence but also the influence of Pieter van ◊Aertzen.

Barents, Willem (c. 1550–1597)

Dutch explorer and navigator. He made three expeditions to seek the Northeast Passage; he died on the last voyage. The Barents Sea, part of the Arctic Ocean north of Norway, is named after him.

Barnaba da Modena

Painter from Modena but of Milanese descent, active 1362–83. His works contain elements of the Byzantine tradition of Venice and of the Sienese School and have an enamel-like brilliance of colour, as in the four scenes showing *The Coronation of the Virgin*, *The Trinity*, *Virgin and Child*, and *The Crucifixion* (1374, National Gallery, London).

Barna da Siena (LIVED MID-14TH CENTURY)

Italian painter. Active in Siena, he was a follower of ◊Simone Martini. His principal work is the series of frescoes illustrating the life of Christ in the Collegiata, San Gimignano, which shows great qualities of imaginative design.

Barnes, Barnabe (c. 1569–c. 1609)

English poet and dramatist. Persuaded to write (if Thomas ◊Nashe is to be believed) by Gabriel ◊Harvey, he produced a collection of sonnets, elegies, odes, and madrigals entitled *Parthenophil and Parthenophe* (1593), and *A Divine Century of Spiritual Sonnets* (1595). His tragedy *The Devil's Charter* was printed in 1607 and performed before James I. Barnes was born in Yorkshire, the son of the bishop of Durham, and studied at Oxford. For his style, which is highly elaborate and full of conceits, he has been regarded as a precursor of the ◊metaphysical poets of the 17th century.

Barnfield, Richard (1574–1627)

English poet. His works include *The Affectionate Shepherd* (1594), a pastoral based on ◊Virgil's second eclogue; *Cynthia, with certaine Sonnets and the Legend of Cassandra* (1595); and *The Encomion of Lady Pecunia and other poems* (1598).

The latter contains two of his best-known songs: 'As it fell upon a day' and 'If music and sweet poetry agree'. These were reprinted in *The Passionate Pilgrim* (1599), and for many years were attributed to Shakespeare, whom Barnfield seems to have known.

Barnfield was born in Norbury, Shropshire, and spent most of his life in Stone, Staffordshire.

Barocci, Federico (OR BAROCCIO OR FIORI DA URBINO) (c. 1535–1612)

Artist who came from and worked in Urbino. Many of his pictures, such as his *Holy Family* (c. 1570), show the influence of ◊Raphael (also from Urbino) and ◊Correggio.

In Rome, he decorated the palace of the Cardinal Giulio della Rovere (1533–1575) with frescoes, and at the invitation of Pope Pius IV assisted in the decoration of the Belvedere. He developed a soft and mannered style from the study of Raphael and Correggio but combined it with a sense of theatre as can be seen in his *Madonna del Popolo* (Uffizi, Florence).

His most important patron was the Duke of Urbino, Francesco Maria III della Rovere (1548–1631). Barocci worked in Rome for four years, then returned to Urbino and painted *St Margaret* for the Confraternity of the Holy Sacrament. Returning to Rome in 1560, he began work on the Belvedere, his works being keenly admired by the religious reformer St Philip Neri. His paintings also include an altarpiece of the *Deposition* in the Cathedral of S Lorenzo in Perugia and a picture of the *Last Supper* for the Church of Minerva. He introduced the use of coloured pastels to central Italy, and many of these drawings survive.

Baronius, Cesare (OR CESARE BARONIO) (1538–1607)

Neapolitan historian of the Roman Catholic Church. A cardinal and librarian of the Vatican, Baronius's lifework was his 12-volume *Annales Ecclesiastici/ Annals of the Church* (1588–1607), a history of Christianity meant to counter contemporary Protestant histories and demonstrate the theological legitimacy of the papacy.

Baronius was born at Sora, Naples. He studied law and theology at Naples, and then in Rome, where in 1557 he joined the Oratory, eventually, in 1593, succeeding St Philip Neri as its head. He became confessor to Pope ◊Clement VIII, who made him a cardinal in 1596 and librarian of the Vatican in 1597.

Barros, João de (?1496–1570/71)

Portuguese bureaucrat and author. Although he chronicled the deeds of the Portuguese in India, Barros left Portugal only once: in 1522 King John III sent him to São Jorge da Mina on the Guinea coast. Returning in 1525, Barros became treasurer for the administrative departments (*Casas*) of India, Mina, and Ceuta until 1528, a post which gave him access to documents subsequently incorporated in his chronicles. He was *Feitor* (agent) to the India *Casa* from 1533 until 1567 when he retired to his country retreat at Vermoil (Pombal), debt-ridden because of two failed commercial ventures in Brazil (1535 and 1556).

Barros's œuvre is prolific and didactic, encompassing a chivalric romance on the fictitious emperor Clarimundo (probably published in 1522) and a diatribe against Judaism (1543, unpublished). Entering the linguistic debate of the day, he consciously wrote in Portuguese to demonstrate its dignity and superiority over Castilian. He published the second Portuguese grammar in 1540 (the first had appeared in 1536) accompanied by a *Diálogo em louvor da nossa linguagem/Dialogue in Praise of our Language* and an illustrated reading primer, *Cartinha para aprender a ler*.

Moral issues also preoccupied him. *Rópica pnefma ou mercadoria espiritual/Spiritual Wares* (1532) was written as a moralizing dialogue between the allegorical figures of Time, Reason, and Human Will, but its sense is obscure. Even so, it was banned by the Portuguese Inquisition in 1581. His *Diálogo de Joam de Barros com dous filhos seus sobre preceptos moraes em modo de jogo/Dialogue in the Manner of a Game between João de Barros and Two of his Sons on Moral Teachings* (1540, reprinted 1563) was a clearer and more popular work.

Barros's chronicle on Portuguese deeds and conquests in India, *Asia*, continued his moral preoccupations as he stressed the didactic importance of history. The first part (or *Década*, after the Roman historian Livy's work) appeared in 1552, the second in 1553, and the third in 1563. Barros's reliance on secondary sources rather than first-hand experience drew criticism from the chronicler Fernão Lopes de ◊Castanheda. His unfinished fourth part was completed and published in 1615 by João Batista Lavanha, who claimed authorship for himself. This provoked a legal challenge by Barros's heirs in 1519; the chronicle was officially continued by Diogo do ◊Couto.

Bartas, Guillaume de Saluste du (1544–1590)

French poet. His religious poem *La Semaine, ou Création du monde/The Week, or Creation of the World* (1578), an epic on the Creation, probably inspired by the Italian poet Torquato Tasso's *Sette giornate/Seven Days*, soon went through at least 25 editions and was translated into 6 languages. His *La Seconde Semaine/The Second Week* (1584–1603) was unfinished.

Bartas was a Huguenot and served Henry IV at court and as a soldier. He died from wounds received at the Battle of Ivry.

Bartholomew Fair

Comedy by Ben ◊Jonson (1614). In a satirical panorama of one of Jacobean London's great fairs, the representatives of morality, Justice Overdo and Zeal-of-the-Land Busy, are pitted against the tricksters, traders, and puppeteers of the Fair.

Bartholomew, Massacre of St

See ◊St Bartholomew, Massacre of.

Bartoli, Taddeo (OR TADDEO DI BARTOLO) (1363–1436)

Sienese painter. He worked mainly in fresco in the style of ◊Simone Martini. Examples of his frescoes can be found in the Palazzo Pubblico (town hall) of Siena (1407–14) and the cathedrals of Pisa, Perugia, and Genoa.

His pupils included Stefano di Giovanni ◊Sassetta and his own nephew **Domenico Bartoli** (lived late 14th–early 15th century). Domenico also worked in Siena, producing frescoes for the city's Scala hospital; his style, though still within the Sienese tradition, also shows awareness of the new Florentine interest in perspective.

Bartolommeo, Fra (ALSO CALLED BACCIO DELLA PORTA) (*c.* 1472–1517)

Florentine painter. He was influenced by a visit to Venice in 1508 where he absorbed the Venetian interest in ◊*colore* and by a visit to Rome in 1514–15. His style is one of classic simplicity and order, as in *The Mystical Marriage of St Catherine* (1511, Louvre, Paris).

Greatly affected by the preaching of Girolamo ◊Savonarola, he burned all his nude studies, and on Savonarola's death became a Dominican monk at S Marco. After an interval due to this disturbance he resumed religious painting, and when Raphael visited Florence in 1506 he made Fra Bartolommeo's acquaintance, each artist influencing the other's work.

With Mariotto Albertinelli (1474–1515), whose friend and collaborator he became, he was a pupil of Cosimo ◊Rosselli (1439–1507). Bartolommeo again worked with Albertinelli after 1508 and visited Rome in 1514, when he was impressed by Michelangelo and Leonardo, his *Deposition* (1516, Pitti Palace) showing Leonardo's influence. Among the works in which he collaborated with Albertinelli are the fresco of the *Last Judgement* (1498, Sta Maria Nuova), *Madonna and Saints* (Pitti), and *Assumption* (Berlin). Bartolommeo made use of a life-size wooden lay figure, and to this some attribute the artificialities of pose and lack of real construction beneath the ample draperies of the figures which have also been criticized in Raphael's work. Some of his finest work is in Lucca, including the *Madonna della Misericordia* (1515).

Barzizza, Gasparino (1360–1431)

Humanist educator, grammarian, and Classical commentator from Bergamo. He taught first in his home town in the 1390s, then in Pavia in 1402–07, Padua in 1407–21, and Milan in the 1420s. He was a prolific author of orations in Ciceronian Latin, many of which were intended to be delivered by other people (but which circulated in his name). In humanist circles, he was highly regarded for his Classical learning; he produced commentaries on Roman authors, including Cicero, Seneca, and Pliny. He also wrote tracts on aspects of grammar.

Like ◊Vittorino da Feltre and ◊Guarino da Verona, Barzizza was an influential figure, in part because of his writings but more so for his teaching. Vittorino himself passed through Barzizza's school, and Francesco ◊Filelfo was among his pupils.

> Under Barzizza's guidance and control, Cicero is loved and read and circulates throughout the schools of Italy with the greatest glory.
>
> ∽
>
> GUARINO, in a letter of 1422

Basawan (1556–1605)

Mogul painter. He contributed paintings to many of the albums of miniatures that were a feature of the Mogul courts, in particular the *Akbar-nama*. His works are renowned for their subtle characterization and also show a novel use of perspective and composition, suggesting that he may have been influenced by Western art.

Basel, Confessions of

Two Zwinglian confessions of faith: the Basel Confession of 1534 (sometimes called the Confession of Mühlhausen) and the First Helvetic Confession of 1536 (sometimes called the Second Confession of Basel).

In 1529, under the guidance of Ulrich ◊Zwingli's supporter Oecolampadius, the Swiss city of Basel broke with Rome and joined Zwingli's Christian Civic Alliance. The Basel Confession of 1534 was written by Oswald Myconius (1488–1552) but based on the work of Oecolampadius, and is a confession of moderate Zwinglianism, fully endorsing Zwingli's view of scripture. It held its place in the Church of Basel until 1872.

The First Helvetic Confession was compiled by Heinrich ◊Bullinger and, though also essentially Zwinglian, it has a Lutheran influence.

Basel, Council of

◊General Council of the Church (1431–49), increasingly opposed to the papacy of ◊Eugenius IV. A Council was grudgingly convened in Basel by the popes, fearful of the threat of ◊conciliarism; their worries were borne out by events. In its early years, the Council was concerned with the Hussite heresy in Hungary, but at the same time it attempted to curtail the pope's powers. Such moves increasingly alienated the more moderate clerics present, many of whom were willing to accept Eugenius's decree moving the Council to Ferrara and then ◊Florence. The remaining delegates became more radical, deposing Eugenius in his absence and electing the former Duke of Savoy, Amadeus, as Pope Felix V. Politically, however, the Council was increasingly isolated and eventually dissolved itself.

Basil of Caesarea, St (330–379)

Greek Church Father, founder of the Basilian monks. Born in Caesarea, Cappadocia, he was elected bishop there in 370. Like ◊Athanasius, he was a fierce opponent of the Arian heretics and, like him, produced a series of theological works.

The first humanist translation of a Basil text was the most influential: Leonardo ◊Bruni produced a Latin version of the short tract *On Liberal Studies* in about 1403, and dedicated it to his mentor, Coluccio ◊Salutati. This provided a form of humanist manifesto, since Basil argues that Christians should read pagan texts – the very point which Salutati's critics rejected.

Basil was again used for argumentative purposes at the Council of ◊Florence, when the Catholics referred to a passage in *Against Eunomius* which supported their position on the Trinity. This was enough to convince one of the Orthodox delegates, ◊Bessarion, but others claimed they could not find the relevant passage in their manuscripts. Perplexed by this, after the Council Bessarion returned to Constantinople and did some detective work: he checked the manuscripts and discovered that the text had been tampered with by earlier Byzantine scholars desperate to deny the Catholic position.

Bessarion himself was also a translator of Basil, as were Lorenzo ◊Valla and Niccolò ◊Perotti. Such efforts did not meet with Erasmus's approval in the early 16th century – in his preface to the first printing in Greek of Basil's works in 1532 he complained that the Church Father's works had been badly served by translators.

Bassano, Giovanni (*c.* 1558–*c.* 1617)

Venetian composer and cornet player. He led the instrumental ensemble at St Mark's, Venice, and wrote instrumental music including ornamented transcriptions of vocal works by Gabrieli, Marenzio, and others.

Bassano, Jacopo (JACOPO DA PONTE) (*c.* 1510–1592)

Italian painter. Influenced early in his career by ◊Titian, Bassano's style changed continually but he gradually developed an elegant style of religious painting noted for its rich colour and dramatic handling of light. An example is *Adoration of the Shepherds* (Museo Civico, Bassano).

He also adopted the fashion for graceful attenuation of figures, as in his *Adoration of the Magi* (Kunsthistorisches Museum, Vienna). This painting is one of several in which he displayed his skill (much praised by contemporaries) in depicting animals. He had a keen eye for the world around him and became known for painting biblical scenes with rural settings peopled by sturdy peasants.

The son of the artist Francesco da Ponte the Elder (*c.* 1475–1539), Bassano was born in Bassano (hence his name) and studied first under his father and then under Bonifacio Veneziano (de' Pitati) in nearby Venice. There contact with the paintings of Titian stimulated in him the feeling for colour and light that is characteristic of much of his work. From the 1530s he worked mainly in Bassano.

His four sons included the painters **Francesco the Younger** (1549–1592) and **Leandro** (1557–1622).

Bateson, Thomas (*c.* 1570–1630)

English organist and composer. He was probably organist at Chester Cathedral until 1609, when he became vicar-choral and organist at Christ Church Cathedral, Dublin. Two books of madrigals by him were published in 1604 and 1618.

Báthory, Stephen (1533–1586)

King of Poland, elected by a diet convened in 1575, and crowned in 1576. Báthory succeeded in driving the Russian troops of Ivan the Terrible out of his country. His military successes brought potential conflicts with Sweden, but he died before these developed.

Batten, Adrian (1591–1637)

English organist and composer. He was a chorister at Winchester Cathedral as a boy. In 1614 he went to London as vicar-choral at Westminster Abbey and in 1626 became organist at St Paul's Cathedral. He was probably the copyist of the Batten Organbook.

Works include:
Eleven services, about 50 anthems, and other church music.

Baudart, Willem (1565–1640)

Dutch scholar and Calvinist minister. A leading biblical scholar, he was chosen as one of the translators of the Old Testament for the Dutch Bible commissioned by the Synod of ◊Dort in 1619. He also wrote a history of the Revolt of the Netherlands, and *Morgenwecker* (1610), an attack on the truce negotiated between the Netherlands and Spain in 1609.

He was born at Deinze, near Ghent, but his parents fled from religious persecution to England, and he was educated at Sandwich and Canterbury. In 1577 the family returned to Flanders. Baudart studied at Leyden, Franeker in Friesland, Heidelberg, and Bremen, and became proficient in Hebrew and Greek. He returned to the Netherlands in 1593.

In 1596 he published an index to the Hebrew, Greek, and Latin Bibles. His attack on the truce which ◊Oldenbarneveldt had negotiated with Spain – in full the tract is entitled *Morgenwecker der Vrye Nederlandtsche provinciên/The Dawn of the Free Netherlands Provinces* – was influential and widely read.

Bauldeweyn, Noel (DIED *c.* 1530)

Flemish composer. Maître de chapelle of Notre Dame at Antwerp 1513–18, he composed sacred and secular music including the Mass *Da Pacem* formerly thought to be by Josquin Desprez.

Bay, (BAIUS) Michel de (1514–1589)

Flemish Catholic theologian. Professor of biblical studies at Louvain, he came to prominence for expressing views that might have come from the lips of a Protestant: there is no free will, and spiritual corruption is so intrinsic a part of human nature that salvation depends on faith rather than good works. His views were condemned as false and heretical by Pope Pius V in his bull *Ex Omnibus Afflictionibus* (1567).

Bay was born in Melun and studied theology at Louvain University. In 1522 he became a professor there and in 1563 chancellor. In 1563 he was also a deputy at the Council of ◊Trent.

Published in 1563–64, his views on free will, sinfulness, and justification – inspired by the writings of St Augustine – were openly opposed to the doctrines recognized at the Council of Trent and widely condemned. The Jesuits in particular attacked his works, their main advocate being Robert ◊Bellarmine. This conflict between **Baianism** and the Jesuits during the 16th century anticipated that of the Jansenists and Jesuits during the 17th century.

Bayer, Johann (1572–1625)

German lawyer and amateur astronomer. He practised as a lawyer in Augsburg, and in 1603 published his *Uranometria*, a stellar atlas giving the positions of the brighter naked-eye stars and arranging them by constellation. He identified the individual stars in each constellation by Greek letters, usually assigned in order of brightness.

Beaufort, Lady Margaret (1441–1509)

Countess of Richmond and Derby, English noblewoman, mother of ◊Henry VII, and educational patron. It was through her that the ◊Tudor dynasty gained its claim to the throne. During her son's reign she was a significant political figure. She was also conspicuously devout, and her spiritual adviser John ◊Fisher persuaded her to demonstrate her charity by educational patronage: she endowed professorships in divinity at both Oxford and Cambridge; at the latter she also founded Christ's College in 1505 and, through her legacy, St John's College in 1511.

Beccadelli, Antonio (KNOWN AS 'IL PANOPIMITA') (1394–1471)

Italian poet. He came to fame in 1425 when he published his collection of Latin poems *Hermaphroditus*. Containing poets that explicitly avowed homosexual love, the book was condemned by the Church and copies publicly burnt, though he was widely admired by scholars and patrons and found work at the courts of Pavia and Naples.

He was born in Palermo – in Latin, Panormus, from which he took his pen name – and studied law and Classical poetry in several northern Italian cities 1420–34. His collection *Hermaphroditus* was dedicated to Cosimo de' ◊Medici, who, despite the church's condemnation of the work as immoral, was happy to accept the dedication. Beccadelli's scholarship and literary skill were admired and he was offered a post at the court of Pavia. He then moved to Naples, where he spent the rest of his life in the service of ◊Alfonso (I) the Magnanimous. In 1455 he composed *De Dictis et de Factis Alphonsi Regis/On the Words and Deeds of King Alfonso*, which became a source of the legend of Alfonso's magnanimity.

Beccafumi, Domenico (*c.* 1486–1551)

Sienese painter and mosaicist. His style was characterized by his intense religious scenes crowded with slender, contorted figures and bathed in an eerie light. Among his best-known works are 35 biblical scenes in mosaic for the pavement of Siena Cathedral, and the painting *The Birth of the Virgin* (1543, Pinacoteca, Siena).

The son of a peasant named di Pace, he took the name of his patron, Lorenzo Beccafumi. His studies took place in Siena and Rome. Returning to Siena in 1512, he worked on the decoration of the façade of the Palazzo Borghese and produced a mosaic for the Church of San Bernardino in 1517. In 1541 he went to Genoa where he painted a fresco, now lost, for Andrea ◊Doria, and then moved to Siena, where he spent the rest of his life.

He also produced some sculpture, such as the bronze angels for the cathedral (*c.* 1548).

Beccaria, Antonio (*c.* 1400–1474)

Humanist translator from Verona, who studied under Vittorino da Feltre. He travelled to England and was appointed secretary to Humfrey, Duke of ◊Gloucester, in about 1438. While in England, he translated into Latin works by Plutarch and Athanasius, as well as a Boccaccio tale from the Italian. He also acted as a royal orator. He returned to Italy in about 1446 and entered the service of Ermolao Barbaro, the Elder

Bedford, John, Duke of Bedford (1389–1435)

Third son of Henry IV of England. On the death of his brother Henry V he was appointed regent of English-controlled France. He led the English war effort, at first continuing Henry V's successes. In the early 1430s, the English suffered military reverses which culminated in the collapse of the Burgundian alliance in 1435.

Bedford cultivated a splendid image, befitting his status, and carried out extensive building work on his Paris palace; he requisitioned for himself the French royal library (amassed by Charles V) and attracted dedications from several authors, mainly of medical tracts.

Bedyngham, John (DIED *c.* 1460)

English composer. He wrote Masses, motets, and chansons, possibly including *O rosa bella*, often ascribed to John Dunstable. His music was widely known in continental Europe; one of his two Mass cycles is derived from a ballade by ◊Binchois.

Bekynton, Thomas (*c.* 1393–1465)

English cleric, bishop of Bath and Wells from 1443. He was for a time secretary to Humfrey, Duke of ◊Gloucester; he later served as a royal diplomat and compiled a collection of documents, proving the justice of English claims to the French throne. He was regarded as a potential humanist patron, being presented with copies of works by such diverse characters as Flavio ◊Biondo and John ◊Free.

Belgic Confession

Articles of faith drawn up in 1561 for the reformed churches of the southern Netherlands. A moderate statement of Calvinist doctrine, it was widely influential, and between 1566 and 1581 it was accepted by synods at Antwerp, Wesel, Emden, Dort, and Middelburg, and again by the major Synod of ◊Dort in 1619.

Based on the ◊Gallican Confession of 1559, though less polemical, it was written in French by Guy de Brès and Hadrian à Saravia, and initially intended specifically for the Walloon and Flemish reformed churches. It was soon translated into Dutch, German, English, and Latin.

Bellano, Bartolommeo (c. 1440–c. 1497)

Paduan sculptor. Strongly influenced by ◊Donatello, under whom he studied, he worked in Florence, Perugia, Rome, and Padua, and in 1479–80 accompanied Gentile Bellini on a visit to Sultan Muhammad II (1430–81) in Constantinople. One of his best-known works is a cycle of ten bronze reliefs of Old Testament stories for Padua Cathedral (1484–88).

The son of a goldsmith, Bellano is first documented in 1456 as an assistant to Donatello in Florence. By 1463 he was probably assisting Donatello with the bronze reliefs for the pulpits of San Lorenzo as his style is discernible in the angular chiselling of several panels. In 1467 he was in Perugia, making a statue of Pope Paul II, and the art historian ◊Vasari claims that he served the pope in Rome too, but by 1468 Bellano had settled again in Padua.

During 1469–72 he executed a marble revetment for the reliquary chest of St Anthony of Padua in the sacristy of the cathedral: the panel of the *Miracle of the Mule* is characteristic of his angular and linear style of marble carving.

Bellarmine, Roberto Francesco Romolo (1542–1621)

Italian Roman Catholic theologian and cardinal. He taught at the Jesuit College in Rome and became archbishop of Capua in 1602. His *Disputationes de Controversiis Fidei Christianae* (1581–93) was a major defence of Catholicism in the 16th century.

Belleau, Rémy (c. 1528–1577)

French poet, a member of the ◊Pléiade group. The poems in *Amours et nouveaux eschanges des pierres précieuses/Love Poems and New Exchanges of Precious Stones* (1576) describe the properties of precious stones. Belleau's chief work is *La Bergerie/Pastorale* (1565), a prose and verse pastoral; it includes the poem 'Avril/April'.

Bellechose, Henri (DIED 1444)

Flemish painter, active in Dijon, working for the dukes of Burgundy. The *Crucifixion and Martyrdom of St Denis* (Louvre, Paris) is almost certainly by him.

Bellechose was born in Brabant, and was employed by the dukes of Burgundy in succession to Jean ◊Malouel. Malouel may have begun the *Crucifixion and Martyrdom of St Denis*, though the unity of style suggests it was probably the sole work of Bellechose. Another work attributed to him is the *Trinity* about 1420 (Louvre, Paris).

Belleforest, François de (1530–1583)

French author and courtier. His *Histoires Tragiques/ Tragic Stories* (1559–82) is a collection of tales, most of them translations from the Italian collection *Novelle/Tales* (1554) by the Italian writer Matteo ◊Bandello. He also drew from other sources, notably 12th-century Danish writer Saxo Grammaticus, from whom he took the story of Hamlet.

A number of Belleforest's stories were translated into English by Geoffrey Fenton as *Certaine Tragicall Discourses* (1566). Shakespeare may well have taken several of his plots and incidents from Belleforest's book – notably elements of the plays *Hamlet, Much Ado About Nothing*, and *Twelfth Night*.

Belleforest worked at the court of Queen ◊Marguerite of Navarre, whose collection of tales *The Heptameron* (1559) may have inspired his own literary interests.

Bellegambe, Jean (c. 1470–c. 1535)

Flemish painter, architect, and designer. One of the most successful artists of his day in the Netherlands, he employed a style that combined Flemish and French influences. Among his works is the *Adoration of the Trinity* (c. 1515, Douai Museum, France). He also designed buildings, furniture, picture frames, and embroidery.

Probably a native of Douai, Bellegambe was a follower of the artist Simon ◊Marmion. He may also have been influenced by several other artists of northern Europe, notably Quentin ◊Matsys.

His works include a polyptych in the Church of Notre Dame in Douai (c. 1511); two altar wings depicting the glorification of the Virgin (1526, Notre Dame, Douai); and an *Adoration of Infant Christ* (1528).

Belli, Girolamo (1552–c. 1620)

Italian composer. After studying with Luzzasco

Luzzaschi, he was a singer at the Gonzaga court at Mantua, and was in Rome in 1582. He published several books of madrigals, of which six survive, as well as psalms, *Sacrae Cantiones*, and other church music including Masses.

Belli, Valerio (*c.* 1468–1546)

Italian stone carver, native of Vicenza. He engraved rare stones and semi-precious gems in *intaglio* and relief, often in imitation of Greek and Roman originals which he was considered to have matched if not surpassed. Belli worked extensively in Rome and enjoyed the patronage of ◊Clement VII.

Bellini family

Venetian family of artists influential in defining the Venetian style of painting in the late 15th and early 16th centuries. **Jacopo Bellini** (*c.* 1400–1470/71) worked in Venice, Padua, Verona, and Ferrara. **Gentile Bellini** (*c.* 1429–1507) was probably the elder son of Jacopo and was trained by him. The work of his brother **Giovanni Bellini** (*c.* 1430–1516) marked a striking transformation from the style of his father's workshop.

Jacopo's few surviving paintings are executed in a simple and austere style. He is principally known by the designs for compositions comprising figures, landscape, and architectural perspectives, in his sketchbooks, of which his sons made use (British Museum, London, and Louvre, Paris).

His son Gentile was made count palatine by the emperor Frederick III in 1469, and was chosen in 1479 to go to Constantinople to paint portraits for Sultan Muhammad II (whose much repainted portrait is in the National Gallery, London). In Venice, Gentile painted a series of history pictures for the Doge's Palace in 1474, which were later destroyed, but extant compositions are his paintings of Venetian ceremonies and pageants, in which he gives a fascinating view of the city; for example, *Procession in the Piazza S Marco* (Accademia, Venice). His *St Mark Preaching at Alexandria* (Brera, Milan) was left to be finished by his brother. Gentile's ability in portraiture is shown by the *Man with a Pair of Dividers* (*c.* 1500, National Gallery, London), though the *St Dominic* (*c.* 1500, National Gallery), long attributed to him, is now assigned to Giovanni.

The numerous works attributed to Giovanni, and coming from the workshop where he employed many assistants, show wide variations of style. A sculptural firmness derived from his brother-in-law Andrea

Bellini Jacopo and Giovanni Bellini, *Descent of Jesus into Limbo, c.* 1459 (Civic Museum, Padua). A small predella panel from an altarpiece on which Jacopo and his sons seem to have collaborated. *e.t. archive*

◊Mantegna appears in the impressive early work *The Agony in the Garden* (National Gallery). ◊Antonello da Messina, who visited Venice 1475–76, may have contributed to the development of his oil technique and his consequent emphasis on ◊*colore* (as seen in the portrait of *The Doge Leonardo Loredan*, *c*. 1500, National Gallery).

Giovanni worked to an advanced age on paintings for public buildings and churches in Venice and other cities, including numerous versions of the *Madonna and Child*. Altarpieces for S Pietro Martire, Murano, the Church of the Frari, and the Church of S Zaccaria are notable, as also is a late mythological composition *The Feast of the Gods* (1514, Washington), in which Titian may have had a hand. In its soft fullness of modelling, the *Madonna degli Alberetti* (Accademia, Venice) links Bellini with his pupils Giorgione and Titian.

Belon, Pierre (1517–1564)

French naturalist. He travelled through much of Europe and the Near East 1547–50, and published two major works: a study of sea life (1551) and a study of birds (1555).

Although born into a poor family near Le Mans, Belon was allowed to pursue his education at the university of Paris through the support of his local bishop. He was further enabled to develop his interests in natural history by the patronage of the wealthy Cardinal Tournon and later, King Francis I, who financed his travels, which took him through Europe and to Greece, Asia Minor, Arabia, and Egypt.

In his book on sea life, *La Nature et diversité des poissons*, he described 110 species of marine animals. Like Rondelet, Belon used the term fish to cover virtually all animals found in the sea. His study of birds is entitled *L'Histoire de la nature des oyseaux*.

He was killed by robbers in the Bois de Boulogne while out late at night gathering herbs.

Bembo, Pietro (1470–1547)

Italian scholar, poet, and humanist. He was secretary to Pope ◊Leo X 1513–21 and later official historian of Venice. As a scholar he edited the works of ◊Petrarch and Dante, and played an important role in the development of Italian by suggesting that the works of Petrarch and ◊Boccaccio should be used as

models. His literary reputation was established by his *Gli Asolani/The People of Asolani* (1505), a set of dialogues on love dedicated to Lucrezia ◊Borgia.

Bembo was an important figure in the revival of vernacular poetry, and started a vogue for imitations of Petrarch. He showed a much greater sensitivity to form than did those humanists who concentrated on Classical literature. His *Prose della volgar lingua/Prose in the Vernacular* (1525), in which he cites Petrarch and Boccaccio as models for a vernacular suitable both for literature and for practical discourse, was the first critical history of Italian literature since Dante.

He was also a leading member of the sceptical group of writers and intellectuals that flourished around Leo X, and was patron of the free-thinking philosopher Pietro Pomponazzi.

Born in Venice, he was educated by the scholars Augurello, Ermolao Barbaro, and Donato. He met ◊Politian in 1491 and in the same year travelled to Messina to learn Greek from Constantine Lascaris. In 1493 he returned to Venice and edited Lascaris's Greek grammar for the scholar-publisher ◊Manutius, who also issued Bembo's editions of Petrarch in 1501 and Dante in 1502.

Gli Asolani brought Bembo to Urbino where he is depicted as the advocate of platonic love in Castiglione's *The ◊Courtier* (1528). In 1513 in Rome Bembo published *De Imitatione*, which championed Ciceronianism and led to his appointment as secretary to Pope Leo X, after which he went to Padua.

In 1530 he published *Rime*, a collection of his Italian poetry, and was nominated historian and librarian of the Venetian republic – his *Historia Veneta/History of Venice* is noted for its style rather than its content. In 1539 he was made a cardinal and moved back to Rome, where he died.

Benedetto da Maiano (1442–1497)

Italian sculptor and architect. Training as a sculptor in Florence under Rossellino, he developed an elegant realism typical of 15th-century Florentine sculpture. Among his many works – which include portraits, tombs, monuments and pulpits – the best-known is a series of marble reliefs on the pulpit in the Church of Santa Croce in Florence 1472–75. His architectural projects included the Palazzo Strozzi in Florence, begun about 1490.

A member of a notable artistic family of Florence, Benedetto trained as a stone carver, his early works strongly influenced by his master, Antonio Rossellino. His earliest surviving work is the shrine of San Savino (1472, Faenza Cathedral), on which he worked with his brother, the architect ◊Giuliano da Maiano.

His pulpit reliefs in Santa Croce show a wider range of Florentine influences – ◊Desiderio da Settignano, ◊Donatello, Lorenzo ◊Ghiberti – and also antique pieces. At about the same time he also worked on an altar for Santa Fina in the Collegiata in San Gimignano where he became familiar with the naturalistic style of ◊Ghirlandaio.

His other works include a number of portrait busts, notably of Filippo Strozzi (Louvre, Paris), and of Pietro Mellini (1474, Bargello, Florence), who commissioned the marble reliefs in Santa Croce; and the altar of San Bartolo in the Church of San Agostino in San Gimignano (1494).

Benivieni, Girolamo (1453–1542)

Florentine poet and humanist. One of the many writers who enjoyed the patronage of Lorenzo de' Medici, he became known for his long poem *Canzone d'amore/Song of Love* (*c.* 1487), an adaptation of Plato's *Symposium*. Later he came under the influence of the religious leader ◊Savonarola and wrote religious poetry and translations of the preacher's treatises.

He was born and educated in Florence, where he was strongly influenced by the Neo-Platonism that flourished among the scholars under the patronage of Lorenzo de' Medici – Benivieni's *Canzone d'amore* was based on a translation of and commentary on the *Symposium* by Marcilio ◊Ficino. His reputation was assured when ◊Pico della Mirandola produced an extensive commentary on his poem.

Berchem, Jachet de (*c.* 1505–*c.* 1565)

Flemish composer, not to be confused with Jachet of Mantua. Probably organist to the ducal court at Ferrara in 1555, he wrote church music, madrigals for four and five voices, and French chansons. He is credited with being the first to compose a madrigal cycle; his *Capriccio* is a setting of stories from Ariosto's *Orlando furioso*.

Bermejo, Bartolomé (LIVED 15TH CENTURY)

Spanish painter. He worked in Zaragoza and Barcelona, producing altarpieces influenced by Flemish examples but with an individual realism. Principal works are *St Dominic of Silos Enthroned* (1474–77, Prado, Madrid) and his *Pietà* (1490, Barcelona Cathedral).

Bermudo, Juan (*c.* 1510–*c.* 1565)

Spanish friar and music theorist. He wrote three music treatises, published 1549–55, including the *Declaración* (1555), with the first organ music printed locally.

Bernardino of Siena, St (1380–1444)

Italian Franciscan. He became one of the most popular preachers of his day, his impassioned attacks on corruption and political violence winning wide approval. A keen reformer, he restored the strictness of the early Franciscan rule, and founded the Fratres de Observantia, a branch of the Franciscan order. In 1439 he played an active role in the Council of Florence. He was canonized in 1450.

He was born at Massa di Carrara, between La Spezia and Pisa. During an outbreak of plague in Siena in 1400 he took charge of a hospital there. In 1402 he entered the Franciscan Order and quickly became a popular preacher, travelling widely in Italy; he became vicar-general of the order in 1438. In 1427 he inaugurated the cult of devotion to the sacred name of Jesus, for which he was accused of heresy by the theologians of Bologna University, though he was eventually exonerated. Despite his piety, he accepted conventional beliefs about the guilt of the Jews and the power of witchcraft.

Berni, Francesco (1497–1535)

Florentine poet. Like Pietro ◊Aretino, he made his reputation by poking fun at other people, though his comic verse was less political and less slanderous. He was most noted, however, for a work which was not burlesque: his Tuscan revision of ◊Boiardo's *Orlando innamorato*.

Beroaldo, Filippo, THE ELDER (1453–1505)

Bolognese humanist lecturer and author. From 1472 until his death he was professor of rhetoric at

Bologna University, though this appointment did not stop him spending a few years away from his home town; in particular, he spent a year 1476–77 in Paris and made a great impression on the likes of Robert ◊Gaguin. Nor did his teaching duties prevent him from producing a whole series of editions and commentaries on Classical texts, the most extensive of which was his commentary on Apuleius's *Golden Ass*.

Beroaldo was, according to ◊Pico della Mirandola, a living library; his wide-ranging knowledge was displayed in his discussion of adages, which was imitated by his pupil, Polydore ◊Vergil, and, indirectly, by ◊Erasmus. His Classical commentaries included, besides Apuleius, Aulus Gellius, St Basil, Juvenal, Pliny the Younger, Plutarch, Suetonius, and Vegetius. He also acted as public orator to the Bentivoglio rulers of Bologna.

Beroaldo, Filippo, THE YOUNGER (1472–1518)

Bolognese humanist editor. After being educated by his uncle, Filippo ◊Beroaldo the Elder, he went to Rome and became acquainted with Pietro Bembo. He became secretary to Cardinal Giovanni de' Medici, who, when elected Pope ◊Leo X in 1513, made Beroaldo prefect of the Vatican Library (Biblioteca Apostolica Vaticana). When a codex of the 'lost' first books of ◊Tacitus' *Annals* came into the Pope's possession in about 1508, Beroaldo edited the work and saw it through the printing press in 1515. Beroaldo's other works include epigrams and a translation of Isocrates's *Ad Demonicum*.

Berruguete, Alonso (c. 1488–1561)

Spanish sculptor and painter, the son of Pedro ◊Berruguete. Berruguete completed his training in Italy, copying both Classical (for example, the *Laocoon*) and contemporary (such as Michelangelo's *Battle of Cascina* cartoons) works, before returning to work in Spain. He was appointed court artist to Charles I (the future Holy Roman Emperor Charles V). His career moved from Valladolid to Salamanca to Toledo, in which time he produced mainly a series of sculpted altarpieces, sometimes in collaboration with other artists, including Vasco de la Zarsa and Felipe ◊Vigarny.

Berruguete, Pedro (DIED c. 1503)

Spanish painter, born in Palencia. He may have spent some years working with ◊Justus of Ghent on the frescoes at Federigo da Montefeltro's ducal palace in Urbino, Italy, but most of his work was executed in his homeland, where he became court artist to King Ferdinand and Queen Isabella. His oil paintings, for example his *Life of the Virgin* altarpiece (1482, Sta Eulália, Paredes de Nava), suggest acquaintance with quattrocento Italian work but also with Flemish art in the style of Jan van ◊Eyck.

Bersuire, Pierre (c. 1290–1362)

French scholar. A friend of ◊Petrarch, whom he met at Avignon, he produced a French translation of the Roman historian Livy (1352–56) and a widely read guide to the Bible, *Reductorium Repertorium et Dictionarium Moral Uutriusque Testament* (c. 1340).

Little is known about his life. He was born at St-Pierre-du-Chemin, and was probably a Franciscan monk. He was secretary to King John II, and may have been imprisoned for heresy before becoming prior of St-Eloi in Paris.

Bertaut, Jean (1552–1611)

French court poet under Henry III and Henry IV. He imitated Pierre de ◊Ronsard and Philippe ◊Desportes and wrote both love poetry and religious verse (including paraphrases of the psalms). He became bishop of Sées in 1606.

Bertoldo di Giovanni (c. 1440–1491)

Italian sculptor and medallist. He worked for the Medici family in Florence, one of his most original medals illustrating the assassination of Giuliano de' Medici in Florence Cathedral during the Pazzi conspiracy in 1478. He also sculpted several statuettes of Hercules that are among the finest of the period. His works show the influence of the elderly ◊Donatello.

Of obscure origin, perhaps born in Florence as an illegitimate son of Giovanni di Cosimo de' Medici, Bertoldo worked mainly in the circle of the Medici, especially of Lorenzo the Magnificent, and became curator of the Medici sculpture collection, where his visitors included the young Michelangelo.

His earliest dated piece is a medal of 1469 showing Emperor Frederick III. Among his best-known pieces is the bronze panel *Cavalry Battle* (Bargello, Florence), based on a fragmentary Roman sarcophagus in Pisa. Another well-known piece, cast by ◊Adriano Fiorentino, is the bronze group *Bellerophon and Pegasus* (Kunsthistorisches Museum, Vienna), indebted to the *Horse-tamers* of the Quirinal Hill, Rome.

Bertrand, Antoine de (*c.* 1535–*c.* 1581)

French composer. In some of his settings of Ronsard's 'Amours' he experimented with quarter-tones. Altogether he published three volumes of chansons, and a volume of *Airs spirituels* appeared posthumously in 1582.

Besard, Jean-Baptiste (OR BESARDUS) (*c.* 1567–AFTER 1617)

French lutenist and composer. He first studied law at the University of Dôle, then the lute with Lorenzini in Rome. Later, he lived at Cologne and Augsburg. He published theoretical works and collections of lute music including his own. His *Thesaurus Harmonicus* of 1603 contains more than 400 pieces by various composers and includes a manual on lute playing.

Bessarion, Johannes (*c.* 1403–1472)

Greek-born cleric, patron, and humanist author. He travelled to Italy for the Council of ◊Florence; in recognition of his support of a union of the churches, Pope Eugenius IV made him a cardinal in 1439. He acted as a papal administrator in Bologna 1450–55 and as a diplomat, attempting to persuade the kings of Europe to prepare a crusade; he was even a candidate for the papacy itself. He settled in Rome where his house became an 'academy' (Niccolò ◊Perotti's word) for scholars.

Bessarion was born in Trebizond and taught by Georgios ◊Plethon, who introduced him to Platonism. Later in his career, he felt duty-bound to defend Plato against the writings of one of his own protégés, ◊George of Trebizond: his *In Calumniatorem Platonis/Against a Slanderer of Plato* appeared in both Greek and Latin. Bessarion's other writings included translations from his mother tongue into Latin of Xenophon's *Memorabilia* and Aristotle's *Metaphysics*, as well as shorter works by Basil and Demosthenes. He amassed a large library which he presented to the Republic of Venice in 1468; it became the nucleus of the Biblioteca ◊Marciana.

Beza (PROPERLY DE BÈSZE), Théodore (1519–1605)

French church reformer. He settled in Geneva, Switzerland, where he worked with John Calvin and succeeded him as head of the reformed church there in 1564. He wrote in defence of the burning of Spanish theologian Michael ◊Servetus (1554) and produced a Latin translation of the New Testament. In 1581 he presented a precious 5th-century Graeco-Latin manuscript of the Gospels and the Acts, the so-called *Codex Bezae*, to Cambridge university.

Bianchi Ferrari, Francesco (1460–1510)

Italian painter of the School of Modena. His style is related to that of Andrea ◊Mantegna. He executed church paintings in Modena, as well as mythical scenes such as his *Idyll* (Wallace Collection, London).

He may have been the master of Antonio Correggio.

bianchi girari ('WHITE VINE-STEM')

Style of illumination found in humanist manuscripts. Though an archaizing style, it is, like ◊*littera antiqua*, an imitation not of Classical forms but of a later fashion – in this case, derived from 12th-century Italian manuscripts. The decoration involves a swirl of stems which are left blank (thus white) while the areas between and around them are illuminated in bright colours.

Bible stories in art

The principal subject matter of Rennaissance paintings and sculpture were stories or events taken from the Bible or derived from the lives of saints. While there existed a tremendous number of possible subjects, patrons and artists tended to prefer familiar stories that would be easily recognizable to the spectator. For devotional reasons, the most popular of these subjects were drawn from the life of Christ.

The single most common image in the Renaissance was the Virgin Mary depicted holding the Christ child. This subject was varied frequently with the addition of saints and, more rarely, patrons to the composition. A similar theme was the Adoration of the Christ child in his manger. This took on several forms, the most popular being the Adoration of the Magi, which depicted the three kings paying homage to Christ as the son of God, and bearing the precious gifts of gold, frankincense, and myrrh. Surrounded by the traditional ox and ass, the Christ child was closely watched by the Virgin Mary and Joseph, a scene also known as the Nativity.

Several scenes from Christ's later life were also commonly depicted, including the Baptism of Christ, which shows him being blessed in a river by St John the Baptist who is depicted wearing a hair garment and carrying a staff. Of particular importance to monasteries was the Last Supper, which was generally placed in the refectory. This depicts Christ breaking bread at the centre of a long table together with the 12 apostles, and the traitor Judas generally shown in opposition to the others. Two closely related scenes from the end of Christ's life were commonly depicted in ◊altarpieces. The crucifixion and deposition from the cross show, respectively, Christ dead on the cross with mourners and soldiers below, and the removal of Christ from the

cross with the Virgin Mary below. This latter theme came also to be known in a slightly different form as a *Pietà*, with the Virgin Mary holding the body of Christ in her lap.

Among the common devotional images of the Virgin Mary, the most popular was the Annunciation, depicting the Virgin Mary, reading from a lectern, receiving the message from Archangel Gabriel that she is to bear the son of God. The Virgin Mary was also shown following her death, as in the Assumption and the Coronation. While these scenes were not in the Bible, they were associated with her connection to Christ, and show her being transported into heaven by angels and crowned in heaven by her son surrounded by saints.

The fresco cycles which decorate many churches are often dominated by a single composition, the Last Judgement. This subject was of particular importance

Bible Stories Giovanni Bellini, *The Agony in the Garden* (National Gallery, London). Compare Bellini's treatment with that of Andrea ◊Mantegna. *e.t. archive*

as it was employed to illustrate the rewards or punishments to those who did or did not lead good Christian lives. It depicts Christ seated in heaven and surrounded by his celestial court, blessing the righteous and leading them to paradise, while below, those who are damned are graphically shown being dragged by demons into hell to suffer for eternity.

Saints were another popular subject for paintings.

While they frequently appeared in scenes from the life of Christ such as the Virgin and Child, they were often the subject of fresco cycles in churches attached to monasteries. In particular, images of St Francis were widely depicted throughout Italy. These illustrated the miraculous or significant events from a saint's life and were meant to exemplify the good deeds for which the saint was revered.

BIBLICAL EXEGESIS

ADDRESSING HIMSELF TO his sometime patron, Archbishop Warham, Desiderius ◊Erasmus opened his edition of the letters of St Jerome (c. 345–420) by asking:'Was there ever an individual expert in so many languages? Who ever achieved such familiarity with history, geography, and antiquities? Who ever became so equally and completely at home in all literature, both sacred and profane? If you look to his memory, never was there an author, ancient or modern, who was not at his immediate disposal. Was there a corner of Holy Scripture or anything so recondite or diverse that he could not produce it, as it were, cash down? As for his industry, who ever either read or wrote so many volumes? Who had the whole of Scripture by heart, as he had, drinking it in, digesting it, turning it over and over, pondering upon it?'

The image of Jerome, who had translated the text of the Bible out of the original Hebrew and Greek of the Old and New Testaments to produce the Latin Vulgate text which dominated western perceptions of Scripture thereafter, captivated and inspired humanist scholars of the early 16th century, most notably

Erasmus. Jerome embodied the ideals of the new learning, and had at his disposal all the tools which were needed for the reinterpretation of the Bible, the restoration of the true text of Scripture from the corruptions of time, and the recreation of a true Christianity based upon it. Skill at Latin and Greek, and the diligent comparison of variations in surviving manuscripts (inspired in part by the earlier achievements of Lorenzo ◊Valla), underpinned Erasmus' own edition of the Greek New Testament, the fruit of more than a decade's labour, which was published by the Basle house of Johann ◊Froben, who, in the same year of 1516, issued Erasmus' edition of the letters of Jerome.

Erasmus' Greek New Testament marked a turning point in the understanding of composition of the Bible, and formed the basis for the received text established by the work of further humanist editors, notably Robert ◊Estienne and Theodore ◊Beza, and proclaimed as authoritative by the Elzevier press in 1633. As such it also underlay numerous translations of the Bible, including the English Authorized Version of 1611. Despite this success, Erasmus' editorial work was attacked

by many, and the principle that scholars might reconstruct the original text and its meaning through the application of philological methods proved extremely divisive. Welcomed by heretics, such as the followers of ◊Socinus (who questioned the scriptural authority for the doctrine of the Trinity), it was regarded with ambivalence by both Catholic and Protestant theologians. No scholar completed a critical text of the Hebrew Old Testament to rival Erasmus' Greek New Testament, and many were suspicious of the attempts to increase knowledge of Jewish sources and traditions which formed a necessary preliminary to such an endeavour.

Following ◊Luther, most Protestants of the late 16th century stressed the importance of Scripture as the authoritative source for the doctrine and practice of the Church. They singled out the literal sense of Scripture as conveying its true meaning, in the process revising the fourfold hierarchy of medieval exegesis, in which the literal meaning of the Bible might be subordinated to its allegorical, tropological or anagogical senses. This hierarchy was

continued

explained by the great 14th-century exegete, Nicholas of Lyra, in the following manner:

'Littera gesta docet, Quid credas allegoria, Moralis quid agas, Quo tendas anagogia'.

(This might be paraphrased: 'The literal sense teaches what has happened, the allegorical what you should believe, the moral (or tropological) how you should behave, the anagogical what you may expect.')

In privileging the literal sense of Scripture, Protestants gave special status to a close reading and interpretation of the text as it survived. Consequently, Protestant scholars valued a knowledge of the original languages of Scripture, especially Hebrew and Greek, but were reluctant to accept that these might have changed over time. They were eager to establish the true text of the Bible, not for critical reasons, but in order to know what had been the exact dictation of the Holy Ghost to its authors. However, belief in the divine inspiration of Scripture did not necessarily imply an acceptance of the inerrancy of the literal sense, and many interpreters followed St Augustine's teaching that the Holy Ghost did not expect people to believe things which were contrary to reason. As a result, both Protestant and Catholic divines often read difficult biblical passages, for example those relating to the creation, as allegory or typology. In so doing, they preserved the authority and unity of Scripture, in particular the notion that the Old and New Testaments complemented and expounded one another's teaching.

For everyday purposes, both Catholic and Protestant divines tended to allow Scripture to expound itself, through the comparison of parallel passages. Catholic theologians were supposed, following the formula of the ◊Council of Trent, to interpret the Bible in accordance with the sense of the Fathers of the Church. In their studies of biblical chronology, geography, history, and even zoology, scholars from both confessions applied the skills for which Jerome had been famed. They thus brought to life their faith in the continuity of the human experience of providence, which made the ancient history of Israel relevant for the moral and spiritual life of early modern Western Europe. In part because of better contacts with the Levant, many Catholic scholars, notably those of the Congregatio de Propaganda Fide, eventually developed more wide-ranging linguistic skills than those of most of their Protestant rivals. They tended to use these to cast doubt on the stability of the received text of Scripture, and hence in the service of religious controversy as well as intellectual inquiry. The Catholic Church itself stood by the text of the Vulgate, albeit in the revised version sponsored by Popes ◊Sixtus V and Clement VIII. Catholic scholars were active, however, in the editing of the polyglot editions of the Bible published by Cardinal ◊Ximénes at Alcalá and by Christopher ◊Plantin. These great humanist monuments of biblical scholarship helped to publicize the discoveries of the new learning, which rivalled the achievement of Erasmus and promised one day to eclipse even that of Jerome.

SCOTT MANDELBROTE

Further Reading
Jaroslav Pelikan, Valerie R Hotchkiss, and David Price, *The Reformation of the Bible/The Bible of the Reformation* (New Haven, 1996); James McConica, *Erasmus* (Oxford, 1991)

Binchois, Gilles de Bins (*c.* 1400–1460)

Franco-Flemish composer. Along with the composers Guillaume Dufay (whom he knew) and John Dunstable, Binchois was a major figure in 15th-century music. He composed 28 Mass-movements, 6 Magnificats, and around 30 other liturgical works (motets and hymns) in a severely functional style. His most characteristic works, however, are his chansons.

Binchois was probably born in Binche, near Mons, and was organist at the church of Ste Waldetrude, Mons, 1419–23. He was chaplain to Philip, Duke of Burgundy, from about 1430 until 1453, when he became provost of Saint-Vincent, Soignies.

He wrote around 55 chansons, mostly in three parts and in the form of *rondeaux* or *ballades*, with texts relating to courtly love. They are written in a more pleasing style than his sacred music; most are symmetrical and are set to graceful melodies for one voice and two instruments; they follow closely the form of the poetic text.

Biondi, Gian Francesco (1572–1644)

Italian writer. Introduced to the court of James I in England, he won the king's confidence and later a title. He wrote a *Storia delle guerre civili fra le case di York et di Lancastro/History of the Wars of the Roses* (1637).

Biondo, Flavio (1392–1463)

Cleric and humanist author from Forlì, Italy. In his early career, he seems to have made money as a scribe; in the 1420s, he worked as a secretary for the Venetian Republic (where he was a protégé of Francesco ◊Barbaro). He entered the papal curia in 1432, where his job gave him time for scholarship: he embarked on the ambitious project to write a history of Italy since the fall of Rome – this, his *Decades*, was finally published in *c.* 1453. He also worked simultaneously on other writings, both historical and archaeological.

In the 1430s he was considered an influential figure in the circle of Eugenius IV: it was through him, for example, that eonaelo ◊Bruni presented his translation of Aristotle's *Politics* to the pope in 1436. His influence, however, died with the pope; under Nicholas V, he suffered disfavour and, in his last years, he was also haunted by economic difficulties.

After his death, his *Decades* were seen through the printing press by his son, Gaspare. Biondo's works (unlike those of many other humanists) did not prove a short-term fashion; they continued to be read in the 16th century by, for example, Konrad ◊Celtis.

1435 *De Verbis Romanae Locutionis*
1446 *Roma Instaurata,* an archaeological discussion of the topography of Rome, presented to Eugenius IV
1451 First edition of *Italia Illustrata* presented to Alfonso the Magnanimous
1453 Second edition of *Italia Illustrata* dedicated to Nicholas V
1453 *De Expeditione in Turchos*
1454 *De Origine et Gestis Venetorum* dedicated to Francesco Foscari
1459 *Roma Triumphans,* describing (as Andrea ◊Fiocchi had partially done already) ancient Roman offices and customs, dedicated to Pius II
1460 *Borsus sive de Militia et Iurisprudentia* dedicated to Marchese Borso d'Este
1462 *Additiones ... Italiae Illustratae* dedicated to Pius II

Biringuccio, Vannoccio (1480–c. 1539)

Sienese metallurgist. His *Pirotechnia* was published posthumously in 1540 – a lavishly illustrated book, it gives detailed accounts of such processes as the mining and extraction of ores, the blast furnace, the manufacture of cannon and gunpowder, and the production of glassware.

The son of a Sienese official, Biringuccio began his career in the arsenal of Pandolfo Petrucci, ruler of Siena. After a period of exile during which he worked in Parma, Ferrara, and Venice, he returned to Siena in 1530. In 1538, shortly before his death, he entered the service of Pope ◊Paul III in Rome as superintendent of the papal arsenal.

Bissolo, Francesco (1492–1554)

Italian painter. Active in Venice, he was a follower of Giovanni Bellini. He made frequent use of Bellini's later religious compositions in versions of the Madonna and Child.

Bisticci, Vespasiano da

See Vespasiano da Bisticci.

Blaeu (OR BLAEUW), Willem Janszoon (1571–1638)

Dutch map maker and astronomer. A student of the astronomer Tycho ◊Brahe, he became one of the leading map makers of the early 17th century and founded a major map-publishing house in Amsterdam. His works include a world map issued in 1605, a three-volume sea atlas *Het Licht der Zeevaerdt/The Light of Navigation* (1608–21), and a series of atlases, beginning in 1638.

Born in Alkmaar, Blaeu served a two-year apprenticeship in Amsterdam, then developed his geographical and astronomical skills under the guidance of Tycho Brahe in Denmark. In 1596 he returned to Amsterdam, and established himself as a maker of both globes and scientific instruments. He also founded a publishing house in 1599, specializing in cartography.

Blaeu enjoyed wide acclaim for the quality of his work. His instruments and globes featured unprecedented precision, and he developed a new type of press for mapmaking.

After Blaeu died, his son **Jan Blaeu** (died 1673) continued his work, the 11-volume *Atlas Major* (1662) being the firm's greatest achievement.

Blahoslav, Jan (1523–1571)

Czech theologian. Leader of the ◊Czech Brethren from 1557, he translated the New Testament into

Czech in 1564; he also published a Czech grammar, a book on music (1554), and hundreds of hymns.

His translation of the New Testament was incorporated virtually unaltered into the Kralice Bible of 1588, and his Czech grammar was influential in establishing the language as a literary language. His treatise on music, *Musica*, was also written in Czech. His hymn book, which contains well over 700 tunes, appeared in 1561.

Bles, Herri met de (1480–1550)

Flemish painter, active in Antwerp. He is generally identified with Herri Patinir, nephew of the painter Joachim ◊Patinir, but identification of his work is more difficult. He seems to have specialized, like Joachim Patinir, in religious episodes where most of the panel is taken up with landscape and the characters are relegated to being tiny figures.

His work was known in Italy, where he was nicknamed '*civetta*' from the owl with which he signed his paintings.

Boccaccio, Giovanni (1313–1375)

Florentine merchant's son who trained in commerce and law but became a vernacular poet and later a humanist scholar and friend of ◊Petrarch. His *Decamerone/Decameron* ('Ten Days', ?*c.* 1350–53), containing 100 vernacular tales of adulterous, entrepreneurial, and anticlerical humanity, became extremely popular. Notionally recounted by ten young upper-class fugitives from the Black Death, the *Decameron* defied contemporary literary convention with its imaginative yet worldly narratives. Boccaccio's impact on vernacular composition was inferior only to that of ◊Dante and Petrarch, according to Pietro ◊Bembo (this belief had already become canonical before 1500).

Boccaccio's earliest writings, within the courtly ethos of Angevin Naples, combined Classical literary epic and medieval romance, in an innovatory verse form (*ottava rima*, later refined by ◊Ariosto and ◊Tasso). The *Decameron* linked an elite aesthetic idealism to the vigorous, earthy concerns of trecento urban life – drink, sex, money, and the mockery of pretension. Reinventing himself in middle age with proper humanist *gravitas* – Palmieri was later to say that Boccaccio deserved his name ('nasty little

mouth') – Boccaccio studied Greek and lectured on Dante; he also produced a handbook of mythology (*Genealogia Deorum Gentilium/The Ancestry of the Pagan Gods*, ?*c.* 1350–60s), much valued by Renaissance scholars as an aid to the study of ancient literature.

- *Caccia di Diana* (*c.* 1335)
- *Carmen Bucolicum*
- *Il Parnasso Italiano*
- *Filostrato* (*c.* 1335)
- *Filocolo* (*c.* 1336–38)
- *Teseida* (*c.* 1339–41)
- *Ameto* (*c.* 1342)
- *Amorosa Visione* (*c.* 1342–43)
- *Elegia di Fiammetta* (*c.* 1343–44)
- *Ninfale fiesolano* (*c.* 1344–46)
- *Decamerone* (1350–53)
- *Genealogia Deorum Gentilium* (after 1350)
- *De Casibus Virorum Illustrium*
- *De Claris Mulieribus*
- *Vita di Dante* (1355, revised 1364)
- *Il Corbaccio* (*c.* 1365)
- *Commento alla Divina Commedia* (after 1373)
- *Vita di Petrarca* (after 1374)

Boccalini, Trajano (1556–1613)

Italian satirist and political writer. His *Ragguagli di Parnaso/Dispatches from Parnassus* (1613) deal with contemporary topics and personalities, both private and political.

A similar collection, *La pietra del paragone politico*, was left unfinished at his death.

Bodin, Jean (1530–1596)

French political philosopher whose six-volume *De la République* (1576) is considered the first work on political economy.

Bodin was a lawyer in Paris. He published in 1574 a tract explaining that prevalent high prices were due to the influx of precious metals from the New World. His theory of an ideal government emphasized obedience to a sovereign ruler.

Bodley, Thomas (1545–1613)

English scholar and diplomat, after whom the Bodleian Library in Oxford is named. He was educated at Oxford and then entered royal service. From 1597 he concentrated on restoring the university's library, which was opened as the Bodleian Library in 1602. He was knighted in 1604.

The university's medieval library had been richly endowed with books by ◊Humfrey, Duke of Gloucester, and other benefactors, but this collection had been dispersed in the mid-16th century when intellectual indifference and Protestant zeal combined to take their toll.

Boiardo, Matteo Maria, Count of Scandiano (1434–1494)

Italian translator and poet. He is famed for his *Orlando innamorato/Roland in Love* (1487), a chivalrous epic glorifying military honour, patriotism, and religion. ◊Ariosto's *Orlando furioso* (1516) was conceived as a sequel to this work.

Bol, Hans (1535–1593)

Flemish painter whose landscapes are populated with numerous human figures. In addition to oil paintings he produced watercolours, miniatures, cartoons for tapestry, topographical drawings, and drawings for engravers. He worked in Mechelen, Antwerp, and Holland. His pupils included Georg ◊Hoefnagel.

Boleyn, Anne (c. 1501–1536)

Queen of England 1533–36, as second wife of Henry VIII. The daughter of one of Henry's courtiers, and sister to one of his mistresses, Anne was the woman for whom he divorced his first wife, Catherine of Aragon. However, she did not provide the male heir he required for dynastic security (she only gave birth to a daughter in 1533, the future Elizabeth I). She was arrested, tried on a charge of adultery, and executed on 19 May 1536.

The bare outline of Anne's biography gives little sense of the politics that enveloped her or her significance in them. Anne was educated in the Low Countries (at the court of Margaret of Austria) in 1513 and spent 1514–21 at the French royal court. Her time there made her conversant in humanist fashions; back in England, she presented herself as a champion of these and – more controversially – of evangelical religion. Her influence, alongside that of Cromwell's, helped ensure that the Break with Rome opened the door to religious reform. Her political involvement, however, made her a target for the Catholic aristocracy and when Henry appeared to be tiring of her, they moved to bring about her utter downfall.

Anne appears to have patronized continental artists and poets who, often for religious reasons, had migrated to England: Nicholas ◊Bourbon wrote in praise of her and both Hans ◊Holbein the Younger and Lucas Hornebolte have been connected with her name. It also seems that it was through her influence that several reforming clerics, including Thomas Cranmer, were promoted.

Bologna, Concord(at) of

Agreement reached in 1515–16 that restored papal authority over the French (Gallican) church, but granted the French monarchy a degree of control over church appointments. Signed by Pope ◊Leo X and Francis I, it revoked the Pragmatic Sanction of ◊Bourges of 1438.

The Concord granted the French monarchy a degree of control over French ecclesiastical affairs, allowing the monarch to nominate archbishops, bishops, abbots, and conventual priors. The pope was to confirm the nominations. If two successive royal nominations were found to be invalid, the appointment lapsed to the pope.

Boltraffio (OR BELTRAFFIO), Giovanni Antonio (1467–1516)

Milanese painter. A pupil of Leonardo da Vinci, he painted religious subjects and portraits. The *Casio Madonna* (1500, Louvre, Paris) includes an angel musician which, according to a later tradition, was painted by Leonardo himself.

Boltraffio came from a distinguished Milanese family and for most of his life occupied various civic offices in Milan.

Bombelli, Raffaele (c. 1526–1573)

Italian mathematician. An engineer in the service of the bishop of Melfi, he published his major work, his three-volume *L'algebra/Algebra*, in 1572. This contained important advances in the solution of equations, and in the development of an adequate algebraic symbolism.

The analysis of the cubic equation proposed by ◊Tartaglia had led to a number of cases involving roots of negative numbers. Unsure of how to deal with such problems, Renaissance mathematicians had classified them as irreducible cases and ignored them. Bombelli, however, made the first significant advance in the handling of such problems.

In the field of symbolism he took the step of representing unknown quantities and exponents by special symbols. Though other systems came to be preferred, Bombelli had nonetheless shown the need for such expressions.

Bonfigli, Benedetto (1420–1496)

Italian painter. He worked mainly in Perugia, and was a follower of Benozzo di Lese in style. His main work was a series of frescoes for the Priors' Chapel in the town hall of Perugia, not entirely finished at the time of his death.

Bono da Ferrara (LIVED 15TH CENTURY)

Italian painter. He worked in the studio of Francesco ◊Squarcione in Padua and contributed the fresco *St Christopher Carrying the Infant Christ* to the paintings by Andrea ◊Mantegna and others in the chapel of the Eremitani in Padua (destroyed in World War II).

Bono da Ferrara was a pupil of Pisanello in Verona. There is a signed work by him, *St Jerome in a Landscape*, in the National Gallery, London.

Bonsignori, Francesco (1455–1519)

Italian painter. He produced religious works and portraits. He was court painter to the Gonzagas in Mantua from about 1490, and was influenced by Andrea Mantegna.

Bontemps, Pierre (c. 1507–1568)

French sculptor. He worked on a number of royal monuments, including the tomb of Francis I, Claude de France, and their children (1547–58), in the Church of St Denis in Paris.

He worked as an assistant to ◊Primaticcio at the palace of ◊Fontainebleau, and alongside the French sculptor François Marchand on the tomb of Francis I, which was designed by Philibert Delorme. Bontemps also worked on a monument for the heart of Francis I in the same church. His style, like that of his colleagues, combined indigenous tradition of art with some Italianate elements.

Book of Hours

See ◊Hours, Book of.

Bordone (OR Bordon), Paris (1500–1571)

Italian painter. He was a pupil of Titian, active in Venice. He painted particularly portraits, but also religious, mythological, and allegorical scenes. His *The Fisherman Presenting the Ring of St Mark to the Doge* (c. 1535, Accademia, Venice) has an architectural setting adapted from the Doge's Palace.

Borgia, Cesare (c. 1475–1507)

Italian general, illegitimate son of Pope ◊Alexander VI. Made a cardinal at 17 by his father, he resigned to become captain-general of the papacy, campaigning successfully against the city republics of Italy. Ruthless and treacherous in war, he was an able ruler (a model for Machiavelli's *The Prince*), but his power crumbled on the death of his father. He was a patron of artists, including Leonardo da Vinci.

Borgia, Lucrezia (1480–1519)

Duchess of Ferrara from 1501. She was the illegitimate daughter of Pope ◊Alexander VI and sister of Cesare ◊Borgia. She was married at 12 and again at 13 to further her father's ambitions, both marriages being annulled by him. At 18 she was married again, but her husband was murdered in 1500 on the order of her brother, with whom (as well as with her father) she was said to have committed incest. Her final marriage was to Alfonso d'Este, the heir to the duchy of Ferrara (see Este dynasty). She made the court a centre of culture and was a patron of authors and artists such as Ariosto and Titian.

Borgogne (Bergognone), Ambrogio
(ADOPTED NAME OF Ambrogio di Stefano da Fossano) (DIED 1523)

Italian painter. He was active from 1481 and depicted religious subjects. He spent a number of years working on altarpieces and frescoes for the Certosa, the convent of the Carthusians in Pavia, assisted by his brother Bernadino. On his return to Milan, he painted a series of frescoes for the Church of S Simpliciano.

He was probably the pupil of Vincenzo Foppa. Though a contemporary of Leonardo da Vinci, Borgogne was not influenced by him.

Borromeo, St Carlo (1538–1584)

Italian cardinal. He was instrumental in bringing the Council of ◊Trent (1562–63) to a successful conclusion, and in drawing up the catechism that contained its findings. Feast day 4 November.

Borromeo was born in Arona of a noble Italian family, and was created a cardinal and archbishop of Milan by his uncle Pope Pius IV in 1560. He lived the life of an ascetic, and in 1578 founded the community later called the Oblate Fathers of St Charles. He was canonized in 1610.

Bos, Cornelis (c. 1506–1556)

Dutch engraver. Born in 's-Hertogenbosch, he may have trained in Rome; he certainly produced engravings based on works by Marcantonio ◊Raimondi. On his return to the Netherlands he became known for his engravings of Italian paintings of his day. He also developed grotesque scrollwork, first introduced by Cornelis ◊Floris.

His brother Balthasar (1518–1580) was also an engraver, probably trained by Raimondi.

Boscà i Almogàver, Joan (CASTILIAN JUAN BOSCÁN) (c. 1495–1542)

Catalan diplomat and poet, credited with introducing Italian poetic forms into the Castilian language. From a prosperous merchant family, he served Ferdinand the Catholic in 1514, Charles V, and, in 1532, the Neapolitan viceroy.

Despite his Catalan origins, all except one of Boscà's surviving works are in Castilian. His Spanish and Italian travels introduced him to Italian literary fashions: at Granada, Spain, in 1526 he met the Venetian ambassador and scholar Andrea ◊Navagiero, who encouraged him to attempt Italian poetic metres (such as the Petrarchan hendecasyllable) in Castilian. Boscà's resulting poems (composed 1526–27) appear in Book II (of four) of the anthology of his poetry published posthumously in Barcelona in 1543 (incidentally the first Spanish book to be set in roman, not Gothic, type). Book IV of the anthology contained poems by his friend Garcilaso de la Vega. Although now considered a minor poet, Boscà's anthology was instantly popular; only in 1570 did his works cease to be published with those of the more famous Garcilaso. Boscà's Castilian translation of ◊Castiglione's *Il cortegiano*, entitled *Los quatro libros del cortesano/The Four Books of the Courtier*, made at Garcilasco's suggestion, was printed in 1534 and ran to at least 12 editions in 16th-century Spain.

On the subject of Hieronymus Bosch, I would like to inform the common folk (and some others who are less than common) of an error in their judgement of his paintings. Any monstrosities that they see in painting they attribute to Bosch and so make him the inventor of monsters. I do not deny that he painted strange figures, but he did so because he wanted to portray scenes of Hell and therefore had to depict devils and imagine them in unusual compositions.

FELIPE DE GUEVARA, *Commentarios de la Pintura c.* 1560 explaining the unorthodox nature of Bosch's art

---

Bosch, Hieronymus (JEROEN VAN AKEN) (c. 1460–1516)

Dutch painter, from 's-Hertogenbosch. Born into a family of painters, he developed a style so idiosyncratic and fantastical that it defies easy definition. His work was very popular with 16th-century connoisseurs throughout Europe.

Bosch's paintings take as their subject matter either a religious story or a moralizing scene. In his least intricate works, such as *The Crowning with Thorns* (National Gallery, London) or *Christ Carrying the Cross*, he concentrates on the faces and gestures of the figures; in others, for example *The Adoration of the Kings* triptych (Prado, Madrid), characters are placed before an expansive landscape. In yet others, such as *The Garden of Delights* (Prado, Madrid) or *The Temptations of St Antony* (Museu National de Arte Antiga, Lisbon) – which are sometimes considered his most 'characteristic' work – the canvas is filled with bizarre and hallucinatory allegorical detail.

Bosch's early patrons and admirers ranged from Philip the Fair of Burgundy to Cardinal Domenico ◊Grimani in Venice; in the second half of the 16th century Philip II of Spain was an avid collector, as was his relative the Holy Roman Emperor Rudolf II. It is thanks to such collectors that a wide range of

Bosch's work survives, but their interest also created a market for copies (and engravings) of his works. The influence of Bosch on other original artists is harder to judge, though it can be detected in the paintings, for example, of Pieter ◊Brueghel the Elder. In the end, though, Bosch's style was too individual to be repeatable.

Bostius, Arnoldus (1446–1499)

Flemish Carmelite monk and scholar, born and based in Ghent. He wrote theological and historical works, and was a frequent letter writer. His correspondents included several Italian and Low Countries humanists, such as Ermolao ◊Barbaro the Younger, Cornelio ◊Vitelli, Robert Gaguin, Cornelis Gerard, and Erasmus. Through his epistles and the works that they dedicated or sent to him, he was able to act as a conduit for communication between different coteries of scholars.

Botero, Giovanni (1544–1617)

Italian political theorist. He was briefly secretary to Cardinal (later Saint) Charles Borromeo and later in the service of the dukes of Savoy. He came to prominence with his treatise *Della ragion di stato* (1589), in which, attacking ◊Machiavelli, he argued that effective government could be based on Christian principles.

Botero was born in Cuneo, Piedmont, and was sent to a Jesuit seminary in Palermo, from which he joined the order. While a Jesuit he pursued his studies in a number of centres, including Paris, but in 1580 he left the order to work for cardinal Charles Borromeo.

After the latter's death in 1584, Botero was secretary to Cardinal Federico Borromeo, but from 1599 he was tutor and adviser at the Turin court of Carlo Emanuele I, Duke of Savoy.

Botero's reputation as a political thinker was made by the publication of two works: *Della ragion di stato*, and *Cause della grandezza e magnificenza delle città* (1588), which broke new ground with its analysis of factors determining the growth and prosperity of cities. His *Relazioni universali* (1596) expands his views on population studies, a field in which he often anticipates Malthus.

Botticelli, Sandro (BORN ALESSANDRO FILIPEPI) (1445–1510)

Florentine painter. A highly prolific painter of altarpieces as well as devotional compositions, Botticelli also produced some mythological works, such as the *Birth of Venus* (1482–84, Uffizi, Florence). His adherence to the teachings of Girolamo ◊Savonarola in the 1490s resulted in an emphasis on the production of religious paintings which lasted until the end of his life.

He was born into a large family as Alessandro di Mariano dei Filipepi; the name Botticelli is derived

Botticelli Sandro Botticelli was influenced by those around him: advised by scholars like Politian, he produced pictures representing recondite classical themes; an admirer of Savonarola, he also painted religious allegories like the *Mystic Nativity* (1501, National Gallery, London), topped by a Greek inscription declaring the artist was living through 'the second woe of the Apocalypse' (see colour section). *e.t. archive*

from the nickname of his elder brother Giovanni, who assumed the maintenance of the family. Placed for a brief time with his brother Antonio as a goldsmith's apprentice, Botticelli also studied in the workshop of Filippo ◊Lippi in his early teens, where he gained his first training as a painter. Close association with ◊Verrocchio and the ◊Pollaiuolo brothers in his formative years left a lasting impression on the young painter who, throughout his career, retained a strong interest in the exacting depiction of ornamental details and graceful, elegant figures as can be seen in his *Fortitude* (1470, Uffizi, Florence).

Although closely associated with the ◊Medici family for whom he executed numerous paintings after Classical subjects, he won greater renown in his day for the beauty of his paintings and his skill as a draughtsman. He established his reputation in Florence as a painter of great skill and emotion through public commissions, such as the fresco of Saint Augustine in the Church of the Ognissanti. The mythological subjects painted for the private residences of the Medici and other leading families, such as the *Primavera* in the Uffizi, reflect the taste for secular paintings inspired by elite interest in ◊*studia humanitatis* and Neo-Platonism. He was commissioned, along with other artists, by Pope Sixtus IV in the early 1480s to fresco scenes from the Old Testament on the lower walls of the ◊Sistine Chapel. On his return to Florence, he continued his production of religious and secular paintings, aided by a large and highly skilled workshop. His private devotional paintings, such as the *Madonna of the Pomegranate* (Uffizi, Florence), were in great demand in the late 15th century not only because of the constant popularity of the subject but also because of the high quality of Botticelli's craftsmanship.

The influence of Savonarola from the 1490s was perceptible in the production of an increased number of religious paintings characterized by deep emotionalism. In addition to a continuing production of often mystical and dramatic compositions, such as the *Nativity* (National Gallery, London), he also designed illustrations for ◊Dante's *Inferno* in the 1490s.

Botticini, Francesco (1446–1497)

Italian painter and artisan. A number of works imitating Florentine contemporaries, including Sandro Botticelli, have been attributed to him. His *Assumption of the Virgin* (*c.* 1474, National Gallery, London) illustrates the heretical view expressed in a poem by the donor, Matteo Palmieri, that human souls are the angels who remained neutral when Lucifer fell, a number of saints (having merited salvation) being represented as returned to angelic status.

Bourbon, Charles, 8th Duke of Bourbon (1490–1527)

Constable of France, honoured for his courage at the Battle of Marignano in 1515. Later he served the Holy Roman Emperor Charles V, and helped to drive the French from Italy. In 1526 he was made duke of Milan, and in 1527 he marched on Rome but was killed in the assault (by a shot the artist Benvenuto ◊Cellini claimed to have fired). His troops proceeded to perpetrate the ◊Sack of Rome.

Bourbon, Nicholas (1503–1550)

French humanist poet. His evangelicalism made him powerful enemies and friends. He was imprisoned in Paris for his criticism of the church in *Nugae/Trifles* (1533); after his release he crossed to England in 1534, where he received the protection of Anne ◊Boleyn. He later became acquainted with other evangelicals, including Hans ◊Holbein, the Younger, whom he remembered in the second edition of *Nugae* (1538). This appeared after Boleyn's execution and Bourbon's return to France; he became tutor to ◊Marguerite of Navarre's daughter.

Bourchier, John, Lord Berners (1467–1533)

English politician, soldier, and translator. He served both Henry VII and Henry VIII, for whom he was chancellor of the Exchequer from 1516 and deputy of Calais from 1520, where he eventually died; though dogged by creditors, he lived in a style creditable to his status.

He made translations of various romances (including *The History of Artheur of Lytell Brytaine*), Froissart's *Chronicles*, and Antonio de ◊Guevara's version of Marcus Aurelius' *Meditations* (1533).

BOTANY

THE STUDY OF plants developed dramatically in the 15th and 16th centuries. Whereas previously, herbals were alphabetically ordered reference manuals with limited illustrations, now a large number of different types of herbals were printed, often with lavish pictures. In the Middle Ages, learned physicians or university philosophers who valued their expertise in the theoretical sciences spent little time on studying plants – for them, handling plant specimens smacked of manual labour beneath their dignity. In contrast, during the 16th century the study of plants became a legitimate and learned subject to be pursued in universities, often with a lecturer in botany and a botanical garden. It would be misleading to assume, however, that Renaissance botany was similar to the modern, independent science of the structure, physiology, classification, and distribution of plants.

In the Renaissance, plants were studied mainly for their medicinal properties; that is, they were part of the *materia medica* (medicinal material found in nature). It was, therefore, physicians and those with a medical background who took an interest in the study of plants, mainly as a way to revive the medical knowledge of the ancients. The interest in the study of plants grew as a result of the rediscovery of classical works on plants as well as the classicizing influence of the humanists on learned physicians.

By the beginning of the 16th century, a great many classical texts on plants had been recovered and published. Greek manuscripts of Theophrastus' *Historia plantarum* and *De causis plantarum,* previously unknown to Western Europe, were brought from Constantinople in the 14th century and were printed in the 15th (Greek edition, 1497; Latin translation by Gaza, 1483). Greek texts of Dioscorides' *Materia medica,* previously known mainly through the redactions in the Canon of Avicenna, were sought out and printed (first Greek edition, 1499). Galen's *De simplicibus medicamentorum facultatibus,* previously found in compendia of Arabic origin, was published in new Latin and Greek editions as part of the renewed interest in Galen's works in the 1520s. Another popular, but somewhat controversial source of classical plants was Pliny the Elder's *Historia naturalis* (first printed in 1469), whose merits in confusing names and attributions of classical plants were hotly debated amongst humanists such as Niccolò Leoniceno and Ermolao Barbaro. Humanists applied their philological expertise in analyzing the etymology and attribution in these texts in order to establish borrowing amongst classical authors, the extent of scribal corruption and authorial errors.

Establishing the proper Greek and Latin names of plants and identifying them in contemporary flora was an important part of 16th-century botanical works. Otto Brunfels, for instance, called contemporary plants for which he could not find Latin names 'naked herbs' (*nudae herbae*).

The classics also provided the model of supporting and conducting the study of plants. 16th-century herbals are replete with appeals for support by citing classical precedents of patrons of the study of plants and gardens, such as Achilles, Mithridates, and the Roman emperors. Recommendations for going on field trips to look for plants were found in Galen and Dioscorides who suggested that medical students should travel around, inspecting plants for themselves (*autopsia*) in order to gain knowledge of medicinal material.

In 1530, at the initiative of the Strasburg printer Johannes Schott, Otto Brunfels, and the artist Hans Weiditz, were brought together to produce a pictorial herbal, called the *Herbarum vivae eicones.* In the spirit of Albrecht Dürer's naturalism, Weiditz recorded every single detail of the specimen, its blemishes, insect holes, and withering leaves. Brunfels was to match the description of classical authors with these pictures, though without complete success – sometimes matching classical names could not be found for a pictured plant, and at other times, pictures of a certain plant were not available.

Leonhard Fuchs, who sought to follow a Galenic practice of medicine in his *De Historia Stirpium* (1542), insisted that every different plant should be accompanied by a different picture. He identified classical plants by matching up Dioscorides's description with a picture of a contemporary plant. Such dependence

continued

on pictorial illustration was criticized by contemporaries such as the Zwickau physician, Janus Cornarius. Cornarius himself sought to revive the ancient knowledge of plants, but insisted that one could only use the words of Dioscorides himself. For Cornarius, reviving the ancients was a philological practice, and hence strikingly, his commentary of Dioscorides' *Materia medica* (1557) is devoid of pictures.

Although the status of visual illustrations in learned commentaries of the ancients was controversial, printers understood that pictures sold books. Vernacular editions of learned herbals often contained the word 'counterfeit' or *abconterfeitung* in their titles to imply exact images taken from a prototype. There are also numerous instances of copying and plagiarizing pictures or purchasing blocks to be used for different books, and even with different identification of plants. In one of the most famous legal disputes over botanical pictures, the Frankfurt printer Christian Egnolff defended his plagiarizing of Schott's pictures by pointing out the absurdity of arguing that a counterfeit of a natural thing was the property of a single publisher – Albrecht Dürer may hold privileges for his designs of Adam and Eve, but this cannot prevent others from depicting the same object.

In the 1540s botanical gardens were established at the universities of Padua and Pisa, which were steadily followed by other universities in Europe. Specimens from the New World, Egypt, and Africa were sent to these gardens to be cultivated, whence they were distributed all over Europe. Exchanging bulbs, seeds, and dried specimens became frequent amongst physicians. Such contributions from friends and patrons were meticulously recorded and continuously updated by Pier Andrea Matthioli in the prefaces to his successive editions of his commentary of Dioscorides's *Materia medica*. Lectures in botany were established in the medical faculties: frequently, they were to be carried out in the fields during the summer, alternating with anatomical lectures in the winter.

Luca Ghini, professor of botany at Bologna, is generally credited with disseminating the knowledge to form a 'dried garden' (*hortus siccus*) or herbarium. Matthioli, Ulisse Aldrovandi, Guillaume Rondelet, and Andrea Cesalpino all acknowledge Ghini for teaching them how to dry, press, and gum or sew plants onto paper. Indeed, collecting dried plant specimens as part of forming a natural history cabinet became quite common in the second half of the 16th century. By the end of the 16th century, the

number of plants known to Europeans had increased dramatically, and Andrea Cesalpino suggested that one way to cope with such a large bulk of material was, following Aristotle, to group plants with common features and only describe the differentiating features of sub-groups. In particular, Cesalpino focused on the reproductive organs of plants as a way of differentiation. He considered himself an Aristotelian, and in particular, he followed the groupings of Aristotle's pupil, Theophrastus. Since Cesalpino considered differences of species impossible to depict, he did not include illustrations in his work. Several historians of botany have considered Cesalpino's work a precursor to the classification system devised by Linnaeus (indeed, Linnaeus had read Cesalpino's *De plantis libri xvi*, 1583), but it is in fact a classically inspired work on plants, as many herbals before his were.

SACHIKO KUSUKAWA

Further Reading
Agnes Arber, *Herbals; Their Origin and Evolution: A Chapter in the History of Botany* 1470–1670 (Cambridge 1990, first published 1912); Karen Reeds, 'Renaissance Humanism and Botany', *Annals of Science* 33 (1976), 519–42

Bourdichon, Jean (LIVED LATE 15TH–EARLY 16TH CENTURY)

French painter and miniaturist. He was a follower of Jean ◊Fouquet in style and worked – as Fouquet did – for Louis XI, being appointed in 1481. He was also court painter to Charles VIII, Louis XII, and Francis I. Though he also produced portraits, paintings on wood, and designs for stained glass windows, he was most active as an illuminator of manuscripts such as the Book of Hours (1508) for the wife of Louis XII, Anne of Brittany (Bibliothéque Nationale, Paris).

Bourges, Pragmatic Sanction of

Decree issued by Charles VII of France in 1438 in an attempt to weaken papal influence over the French (Gallican) church. The Sanction gave the monarchy power to nominate bishoprics and other benefices. It was terminated in 1516 by the Concord(at) of ◊Bologna.

Bouts, Dirk (DIERICK) (c. 1420–1475)

Dutch painter. Born in Haarlem, he settled in Louvain, painting portraits and religious scenes influenced by Rogier van der Weyden, Albert van Ouwater, and Petrus Christus. His style was often imitated in the late 15-century in the Netherlands, and he was remembered for his interest in landscape.

Bouts settled in Louvain about 1448. In 1468 he was appointed painter to the town council, and in this year he finished two large panels for Louvain town hall, *The Judgement of the Emperor Otto* (Musée Royal des Beaux-Arts, Brussels), which illustrates a legend of a noblewoman who accused the empress of lying and survived the ordeal by fire, after which the emperor had his wife burnt to death. His only other certain work is an altarpiece commissioned by the Church of St Peter Louvain in 1464, of which the central panel shows *The Last Supper.* Bouts's interest in landscape is exemplified in another triptych, the *Pearl of Brabant* (Alte Pinakothek, Munich), although this is sometimes attributed to either an anonymous artist or his eldest son, Dieric.

Two of his sons, **Dieric Bouts the Younger** (DIED 1490/1) and **Albrecht Bouts** (*c.* 1455–1549), were also painters. Albrecht's work includes copies of his father's paintings, including a *Last Supper* (Musée d'Art Ancien, Brussels).

bowdlerization

Four centuries before Dr Bowdler, the process of purifying texts of unwholesome elements was acceptable practice. Translators of Greek texts, in particular, felt it necessary to remove the more offensive elements of their sources. So, Pier Candido ◊Decembrio, for example, in his version of Plato's *Republic,* waters down the infamous discussion of marital communism. The most severe emendations, however, were often reserved not for such references to wife-swapping but to passages alluding to the Greek penchant of homosexuality.

To give one example: when Leonardo ◊Bruni translated ◊Xenophon's *Hiero,* he came across a passage in which the tyrant, claiming that he can not enjoy love, is mocked: 'What do you say? Passion cannot spring up in a tyrant's heart? Then how do you explain your passion for Dailochus, who's called the prettiest?' Dailochus here is, of course, a boy, but in Bruni's version he becomes a she, Dailocha. Nor was Bruni alone in thus 'improving' the text. When ◊Erasmus a century later retranslated the dialogue,

correcting errors Bruni had made, he too made the same sex change.

At the same time, however, the study of Classical texts could sometimes make their sexual content more apparent rather than less so. Catullus was, of the ancient poets, one least given to blushing modesty – and this may, indeed, explain something of his Renaissance popularity – but there was one set of references whose meaning was usually taken literally, that is, his allusions to his lover's sparrow. Politian, however, pointed out by reference to other Classical poets that the sparrow she held in her lap was, by *double entendre*, Catullus's penis. Some scholars might think it necessary to gloss over obvious sexual references; others delighted in unveiling the 'true' meaning behind less direct sexual allusions.

Boyd, Mark Alexander (1553–1601)

Scottish scholar of law, Latin, and Greek. His *Epistolae Heroides et Hymni*, a collection of Latin poems, was printed in Antwerp in 1592 and dedicated to James VI.

Boyd led a peripatetic lifestyle. Though far from being a model student at Glasgow University, he went to France in 1581 and studied law in Paris, Orléans, and Bourges. In 1587 he served with Henry III against the Huguenots, but having been wounded resumed studying in Toulouse in 1588. In 1595 he returned to Scotland, acting for a time as travelling tutor to the Earl of Cassilis. He died leaving a series of legal and political works unprinted; they passed to the Advocates' Library, Edinburgh.

Bracciolini, Poggio (1380–1459)

See ◊Poggio Bracciolini.

Brahe, Tycho (1546–1601)

Danish astronomer. His accurate observations of the planets enabled German astronomer and mathematician Johannes ◊Kepler to prove that planets orbit the Sun in ellipses. Brahe's discovery and report of the 1572 supernova brought him recognition, and his observations of the comet of 1577 proved that it moved in an orbit among the planets, thus disproving Aristotle's view that comets were in the Earth's atmosphere.

Brahe was a colourful figure who wore a silver nose after his own was cut off in a duel, and who took an interest in alchemy. In 1576 Frederick II of Denmark gave him the island of Hven, where he set up an observatory. Brahe was the greatest observer in the days before telescopes, making the most accurate measurements of the positions of stars and planets. He moved to Prague as imperial mathematician in 1599, where he was joined by Kepler, who inherited his observations when he died.

Brahe was born in Skåne (then under Danish rule). He studied at Copenhagen and in Germany at Wittenberg, Leipzig, and Rostock. His interest was roused by the total eclipse of 25 August 1560, and from that time he took an active interest in astronomy.

He observed the 'new star' that blazed forth in Cassiopeia from November 1572. It was a supernova, which was bright enough to be seen by day, and was visible for over a year. Brahe gave an account of the star in *De Nova Stella* (1573), in which he pointed out that his observations showed it to be further away than the Moon, and thus in those realms where, according to Aristotelian philosophy, no change could take place. He observed the bright comet of 1577, and came to the conclusion that the comet's orbit must be elongated, which conflicted with the belief in planetary spheres. Brahe, the last great astronomer to reject the heliocentric theory of Copernicus, tried to compromise, suggesting that all the planets revolved around the Sun, with the exception of the Earth.

He also became aware that the actual places of the planets did not agree with their places as predicted in the current tables, and saw the need for better tables based on new observations of the motions of the Sun, Moon, and planets. He prepared tables of the motion of the Sun and determined the length of a year to within less than a second, necessitating the 1582 calendar reform. His catalogue giving the positions of about 800 stars was the first completely new one since Ptolemy's and remained in use for over a century. Johann ◊Bayer's famous atlas was plotted from it.

Brahe built Uraniborg, 'the City of the Heavens', on Hven, and with his many assistants observed the Sun, Moon, stars, and planets 1576–96. He was visited there by many notable persons, including James VI of Scotland, later James I of England, who wrote a poem in his honour. Brahe left Denmark in 1597 after he had failed to retain the favour of King Frederick's successors. He found a new patron in Emperor Rudolf II and settled in the emperor's residence in Prague in 1599.

Bramante (ADOPTED NAME OF DONATO DI PASCUCCIO) (1444–1514)

Italian architect and artist. Inspired by classical designs and by the work of ◊Leonardo da Vinci, he was employed by Pope ◊Julius II in rebuilding part of the Vatican and St Peter's in Rome. The circular Tempietto of San Pietro in Montorio, Rome (commissioned in 1502, built about 1510), is possibly his most important completed work.

Bramante was apprenticed to Fra ◊Bartolommeo as a painter, and worked in Milan from about 1480 to 1499, when he moved to Rome. He first appeared as an architect in Milan in 1485. In that year he began the rebuilding of the Church of Santa Maria Presso San Satiro, and in 1492–97 built the apse, transept, crossing, and dome of Santa Maria delle Grazie. In Rome he designed not only the Tempietto, but also the cloister of Santa Maria della Pace (1500). He may have had some share in designing the Cancelleria Palace, finished in 1511.

His remodelling around 1504 of the rambling complex of buildings that formed the Vatican palace and the Belvedere was achieved by creating two long galleries enclosing a court. The design, however, was not finished before the death of either the Pope or Bramante himself. The foundations were defective, and much of the work had to be done again. He completed the designs for his work on St Peter's, and built the four great piers and their arches, besides the cornice and vaulting of this portion. After his death, however, his design was considerably altered.

Bramantino (BORN BARTOLOMMEO SUARDI) (1450–1536)

Italian painter and architect. His religious paintings include the *Holy Family* and *Crucifixion* (both Brera, Milan) and the *Pietà* (Church of San Sepolcro). He was a pupil of Vincenzo Foppa and a follower of Donato ◊Bramante, from whom his name derives.

In 1525 he was made architect and painter to Francesco Sforza II.

Brant (BRANDT), Sebastian (c. 1457–1521)

German humanist and poet. He is best known for his long satirical poem *Das Narrenschiff/The Ship of Fools* (1494), which ridiculed the follies of his age. An immediate popular success – not least because of its outstanding woodcuts – it went into numerous editions and was quickly translated into Latin, French, Dutch, and English (in 1509 and 1517).

Born in Strasbourg, Brant studied in law in Basel (as well as editing texts for printers) before returning to his home town in 1501. There he taught and practised law, publishing several legal treatises, and eventually became city secretary of Strasbourg. His wide-ranging interests expressed themselves in poetry (composed initially in Latin but increasingly in German), translations from Latin and medieval German, historical works, and secular pamphlets and broadsheets.

It was his *Das Narrenschiff*, however, in which he satirizes 110 types of fool (such as the complacent priest and deceitful cook) that brought him fame and that had a lasting impact on the development of German literature. It probably gave ◊Erasmus the inspiration for his satire *In Praise of Folly* (1511). It was first translated into English by Alexander ◊Barclay as *Shyppe of Fooles* in 1509.

Brantôme, Pierre de Bourdeille (ABBÉ ET SEIGNEUR DE) (c. 1540–1614)

French chronicler, soldier, and courtier. Attached to the court of Charles IX and Henry III, he travelled widely in Europe and North Africa as a soldier, and fought on the Catholic side in the French Wars of Religion. In retirement he wrote memoirs that give a vivid account of military and court life in 16th-century France.

He was born in Bourdeilles and spent his early years at the court of Marguerite de Navarre. He then studied in Paris and at the university of Poitiers before embarking on a military career. He fought in French campaigns in Italy, Spain, and Portugal, and in North Africa against the Turks. In the Wars of Religion he supported the Guise faction.

Forced to retire through injury after falling from his horse, he began to write his memoirs, his main claim to fame. These were published posthumously 1665–66 and include: *Les Vies des hommes illustres et des grands capitaines*, an informative account of military life in the 16th century; *Les Vies des dames galantes*, an anecdotal exposé of the scandals of the French court; and *Discours sur les duels*.

Breda, Compromise of

Petition by Dutch noblemen and burghers presented to the Habsburg regent, Margaret of Parma, in 1566. A complaint against the attempts of Philip II of Spain to force Catholicism on the Netherlands, it was rejected by Philip, who called the petitioners 'beggars'. His scornful rejection of the Compromise, and his failure to modify his religious policy, made the Dutch War of Independence (Netherlands) inevitable.

Bregno, Andrea (ANDREA DA MILANO) (1421–1506)

Italian sculptor. Active in Rome from 1465 and later in Siena, he produced monumental decorative sculptures, tombs, and altars in marble, one of his best-known works being the Piccolomini altar in Siena Cathedral (1485).

He was born at Osteno, near Lugano. In Rome he ran a thriving workshop, one of his best-known pupils being Gian Cristoforo Romano. In Rome he is principally noted for his work in the Church of Santa Maria del Popolo. A later work is his tabernacle in Santa Maria della Quercia outside Viterbo (1490).

Breton, Nicholas (c. 1545–c. 1626)

English poet and satirist. A very versatile writer, he produced many works of poetry, including *The Passionate Shepherd* (1604). His prose works include *Wit's Trenchmour* (1597) (about angling) and *Strange News out of Divers Countries* (1622).

Breton was apparently at Oxford in 1577 and spent some time in the Low Countries. From 1592 he enjoyed the patronage of the Countess of Pembroke, Sir Philip Sidney's sister.

Other works of poetry include *A Floorish upon Fancie* (1577), *The Soul's Heavenly Exercise* (1601), and *Pasquil's Madcappe* (1626). His lyrics, eight of which appear in the miscellany *England's Helicon*, show both skill and delicacy. Other prose works include *A Mad World, My Masters* (1603) and *Grimello's Fortunes* (1604).

Brill (BRIL), Matheus (MATTHEW) (1550–1584) AND Paul (1554–1626)

Flemish painter brothers. After training in Antwerp, they both moved to Rome in the mid-1570s and soon received papal commissions, producing landscapes for large frescoes. Matheus's work in the Vatican was completed after his early death by his brother. Paul later produced small landscapes painted on copper which influenced Adam ◊Elsheimer.

The brothers were often commissioned to provide just the landscape of a painting: Mattheus provided the scenery for the *Views of Rome with the Translation of the Remains of St Gregory* cycle in the Galleria Geographica, Vatican (*c.* 1580), while Antonio Tempesta painted the human figures; a similar alliance between Paul and the Alberti brothers (Giovanni and Cherubino) produced the *Martyrdom of St Clement* for the Sala Clementina, Vatican (*c.* 1600–03).

Broederlam, Melchior (*c.* 1355–*c.* 1411)

Netherlandish painter. He was employed from 1385 by Philip the Bold, Duke of Burgundy, and spent some of his time decorating military banners and the rest producing cycles of paintings. His subject matter alternated between the religious, for example the *Infancy of Christ* triptych (Musée des Beaux-Arts, Dijon), and the mythological, as in the (now lost) *Golden Fleece* cycle.

His paintings not only reflect northern fashions but also demonstrate his acquaintance with Italian trends – parts of the *Infancy of Christ* panels echo work by Ambrogio Lorenzetti, while the *Golden Fleece* pictures were inspired by miniatures in Venetian manuscripts.

Bronzino, Agnolo (1503–1572)

Italian painter. One of the premiere Florentine artists of the late 16th century, he became a leading court painter and portraitist to Duke Cosimo de' ◊Medici, as well as receiving acclaim for his public altarpieces in prominent churches.

Born in the Tuscan village of Monticelli d'Ongino, he rose to become one of the leading artists of his day in Florence, in addition to being an accomplished poet. The favourite student of his master ◊Pontormo, he developed a bold style which emphasized the precise articulation of details and strong colour contrasts to convey emotion as well as define compositions. Often associated with the term ◊Mannerism, Bronzino is today known primarily for his extremely lifelike portraits, such as the *Lucrezia Panciatichi* (1540, Uffizi, Florence).

Brueghel (BRUEGEL)

Family of Flemish painters. The pictures of peasant life painted by **Pieter Brueghel the Elder** (*c.* 1525–1569) helped to establish genre painting, and he also popularized works illustrating proverbs, such as *The Blind Leading the Blind* (1568, Museo di Capodimonte, Naples). A contemporary taste for the macabre can be seen in *The Triumph of Death* (1562, Prado, Madrid), which clearly shows the influence of Hieronymus ◊Bosch. One of his best-known works is *Hunters in the Snow* (1565, Kunsthistorisches Museum, Vienna).

The elder Pieter was nicknamed 'Peasant' Brueghel, referring to the subjects of his paintings. Two of his sons were also painters. **Pieter Brueghel the Younger** (1564–1638), called 'Hell' Brueghel, specialized in religious subjects, and another son, **Jan Brueghel** (1568–1625), called 'Velvet' Brueghel, painted flowers, landscapes, and seascapes.

Pieter the Elder was born in a village near Bruges. He became a pupil assistant of Pieter Coecke van Aelst (1502–1578) in Antwerp. During a visit to Italy in 1552 he was more impressed by Alpine landscape than by Italian art. On his return to Antwerp he worked for the engraver Jerome Coecke, designing satirical and allegorical prints. These, and some of his paintings, such as *The Fall of the Rebel Angels* (Brussels), borrow fantasy from Hieronymus Bosch, but between 1558 and 1569 his personal genius was expressed in a series of works depicting peasant life and landscape. They include *The Peasant Dance* and *The Wedding Feast* (Vienna), the *Massacre of the Innocents* (Vienna), and *The Census of Bethlehem* (Brussels) – these two perhaps a covert reference to the Spanish repression in the Netherlands – and the series of the months, of which five remain, including *February* (now known as *Hunters in the Snow*).

Pieter Brueghel the Younger copied many of his father's works in a less polished style, while **Jan**

Brueghel Pieter Brueghel the Younger, *Temptation of St. Antony* (private collection). The influence of Hieronimus ⟳Bosch is apparent not only in the subject but also in the fantastic images of half-beast, half-human forms. *AKG London*

painted still lifes, landscapes, and seascapes with a delicate finish that inspired a number of other artists. He was a friend of Pieter Paul Rubens and collaborated with him on such works as the *Paradise* (Mauritshuis). The sons of Pieter the Younger and Jan were also artists.

Brumel, Antoine (*c.* 1460–*c.* 1515)

French composer. A contemporary of Josquin Desprez, he wrote 15 surviving Masses, including *Et Ecce Terrae Motus* for 12 voices, and *L'homme armé* and *Missa pro Defunctis*, both for 4 voices.

He also wrote sequences, antiphons, motets, chansons, and instrumental music based on popular melodies of the day. He was a singer at Chartres Cathedral in 1483, a canon at Laon in 1497, and from 1498 to 1501 choirmaster at Notre Dame in Paris. In 1506 he went to the court of the Duke of Ferrara, Italy, where he may have died.

Brunelleschi, Filippo (1377–1446)

Florentine architect, goldsmith, and artist. His detailed studies of antique buildings and pioneering use of linear perspective made him the pre-eminent architect of his day. Although involved in the design of numerous palaces and churches throughout Tuscany, he is best known for his completion of the dome for the Cathedral of Florence (1436), a feat deemed impossible by his contemporaries.

Based upon his intimate knowledge of antique buildings in Rome, he was in large part responsible for the articulation of what came later to be known as a Renaissance architectural language, which favoured simple geometries and Classical proportions. Highly influential to his contemporaries, his

Brunelleschi The north transept of the Florentine church of Santo Spirito, designed by Filippo Brunelleschi and begun in 1436 but only completed in 1482. *AKG London/Stefan Drechsel*

buildings, such as the Ospedale degli Innocenti (*c.* 1419), provided an alternative to the medieval architecture which dominated Florence. Responsible for the design of numerous prominent churches, his vision of Classically inspired simplicity and harmony is evident in the Church of Santo Spirito, which was completed following his death.

Brunfels, Otto (1489–1534)

German physician and botanist. His *Herbarum vivae eicones* (1530–36), one of the first printed ◊herbals is particularly interesting for its illustrations – by Hans (II) Weiditz – of plants meticulously drawn from nature rather than from earlier drawings. In contrast to Weiditz's ground-breaking drawings, Brunfels concentrated on the southern European plants familiar to traditional herbalism.

Bruni, Leonardo (*c.* 1370–1444)

Florentine humanist author and translator. One of the – if not the – pre-eminent promoters of *studia humanitatis* in the first decades of the 15th century. His writings, especially his translations of Plutarch and Aristotle, were widely read and helped set a new standard of Ciceronian Latin.

Though Bruni was born in Arezzo (which became part of the territories of Florence in 1385) and though he was known to contemporaries by his place of birth, much of his career and his writing connect him to the Republic of Florence. One of his earliest writings was written in praise of the city (*Laudatio Florentinae Urbis*) and from 1427 he was its chancellor. That post had earlier been held by Coluccio Salutati, who was also Bruni's mentor: it was at Salutati's instigation that Bruni studied Greek at the feet of Manuel ◊Chrysoloras and that he began to translate Greek texts (the first being by Xenophon and St Basil).

Bruni's translations were both successful and controversial. His insistence that Aristotle should be rendered in a Ciceronian style had political implications – it suggested that Rome and the Greek *polis* were similar states – and showed philosophical insensitivity, rejecting as barbarous the vocabulary which had been constructed by the medieval Aristotelian translations. His position was attacked (in what is called the 'Ethics controversy') by Alonso de Cartagena and by Pier Candido Decembrio, both of whom insisted that the traditional terms, often transliterated straight from the Greek, should remain. Bruni remained adamant, although his 1430s translation of the *Politics* did perpetuate some of the quirks of the earlier 13th-century rendition.

Bruni's writings were not confined, however, to translations. His other works ranged over a series of genres but, in particular, out of his interest in Plutarch grew an interest in biography and history. His histories, in particular, set out a style of writing different from the prevalent chronicle tradition which was taken up by later Florentine writers, including Niccolò Machiavelli.

c. **1403** *Laudatio Florentinae Urbis/Praise of the City of Florence*
c. **1406** *Dialogi ad Petrum Paulum Histrum*
1415 *Cicero Novus/Cicero Anew*
1416 Translation of Aristotle's *Ethics*
c. **1418** *History of the Florentine People*
1421 *De Militia/On Knighthood* (dedicated to Rinaldo degli Albizzi)
The First Punic War
1424 *On the Study of Literature* (addressed to Battista Malatesta da Montefeltro)
c. **1424** *On the Correct Way to Translate Isagogicon*
1428 *Oration for the Funeral of Nanni Strozzi*
Vita Aristotelis/Life of Aristotle (dedicated to Cardinal Albergati)
1436 Lives of Dante and Petrarch
Translation of Aristotle's *Politics* (dedicated to Eugenius IV)
1439 Commentary on the *Hellenica*
On the Constitution of the Florentines (written in Greek, perhaps for circulation at the Council of ◊Florence)
1441 *Italian War against the Goths*

Bruno, Giordano (1548–1600)

Dominican friar and priest before excommunication as a heretic, Lutheran convert (then excommunicated), and finally a Calvinist, Bruno was also, crucially, a radical cosmographer and student of natural philosophy. Bruno's strange and fascinating writings combine magic, memory, the Classical Epicurean natural physics of ◊Lucretius, and the planetary theories of ◊Copernicus. Advocating a synchretic and tolerant spiritual knowledge of God, far from the dogmatic and persecuting church he delineated, Bruno was captured and in 1600 burned publicly in Rome.

Bucer, Martin (1491–1551)

German Protestant reformer who was instrumental in introducing his own brand of Lutheranism to the city of Strasbourg 1523–24. He gained an international reputation second only to that of Luther himself: a symptom of the high regard in which he was held was the invitation of the English government early in Edward VI's minority for him to help bring about reform in England. He accepted, becoming professor of divinity at Cambridge University, England, from 1549. In his theology he tried to reconcile the views of his fellow Protestants Martin Luther and Ulrich Zwingli with the significance of the eucharist.

Buchanan, George (1506–1582)

Scottish humanist. He wrote *Rerum Scoticarum Historia/A History of Scotland* (1582), which was biased against Mary Queen of Scots.

Forced to flee to France in 1539 owing to his satirical verses on the Franciscans, Buchanan returned to Scotland in about 1562 as tutor to Mary Queen of Scots. He became principal of St Leonard's College, St Andrews, in 1566.

Buchner, Johann (HANS VON CONSTANTZ) (1483–1538)

German composer. He wrote sacred and secular songs, and organ pieces. His *Fundamentum* is a didactic (self-taught) work incorporating organ music for the liturgical year.

He was probably a pupil of Paul Hofhaimer. He worked at Konstanz Cathedral, but left in 1526, because of its growing Protestantism, and went to Überlingen.

Budaeus

Latin form of Guillaume ◊Budé.

Budé, Guillaume (1468–1540)

French royal administrator and gentleman scholar. Born of a family made rich (and noble) by royal service, Budé himself served Charles VIII as secretary and Francis I as master of requests from 1522 and, later, as the first royal librarian. He was not, however, born to a life of scholarship: his interest in letters, by his own reckoning, came to him relatively late and very suddenly in 1491. In subsequent decades, his publications, in particular *De Asse/On the Pound* (1515), gained him a reputation as France's leading scholar.

Budé's scholarly interests began with his teaching himself Greek; his main works had Roman legal or antiquarian subject matter: for example, his *De Asse* took as its point of departure one particular Roman law and built from that an exhaustive discussion of ancient coinage and measures, littered on the way with *obiter dicta*. Budé's services to letters were not, though, merely a matter of writings: he used his position at court to promote the idea of a Collège de France to rival humanist establishments such as the Trilingual College of Louvain, Flanders.

Budé, like his sometime correspondent ◊Erasmus, was concerned to construct an international image for himself. It was, in part, through his exchange of epistles with men such as Erasmus and Thomas More that he was accorded the unofficial position of France's leading scholar. This became something of a self-fulfilling prophecy as Francis I gave Budé positions at his court which both reflected and increased his standing. If, though, there are similarities with Erasmus, the two humanists also had their differences which finally led to a breakdown in communication between them.

1503	Latin translations of two Plutarch essays
1505	Latin translations of two more Plutarch essays and a letter of St Basil
1508	A philological discussion of Roman law, *Annotationes in Quattuor et Viginti Pandectarum Libros* printed
1515	*De Asse et Partibus Eius*
1519	A manuscript 'mirror-for-princes', *L'Institution du prince,* presented to Francis I (only printed after Budé's death)
1520	*De Contemptu Rerum Fortuitarum*
1526	*Annotationes Posteriores* printed as sequel to his 1508 legal work
1529	*Commentarii Linguae Graecae,* with preface to Francis I
1532	*De Philologia* and *De Studio Literarum*
c. **1533**	*De Canonica Sodalitate,* a discussion of the virtues of monastic life written but never published
1535	*De Transitu Hellenismi ad Christianismum*
incomplete	*Forensia,* a glossary of ancient legal terms, left unfinished at death

Bugenhagen, Johannes (1485–1558)

German Lutheran theologian. He was one of the closest friends of Martin ◊Luther, serving as his confessor and assisting him in his New Testament translations. He played a major role in spreading Lutheranism to northern German states and to Denmark, where he lived 1537–39, and was one of the signatories of the Saxon Confession.

After a career as a canon at Treptow in his native Pomerania, Bugenhagen became an early convert to the Reformation through a reading of Luther's *De Captivitate Babylonica Ecclesiae/The Babylonian Captivity of the Church.* In 1521 he abandoned his post as rector of the city school in Treptow and enrolled as a theology student in Wittenberg, where he was appointed minister of the town church in 1523 and professor in 1535.

Although Bugenhagen remained in Wittenberg until his death, his most important work was undertaken in missions away from the city, particularly in northern Germany and Denmark, where he was the architect of numerous church orders, notably Hamburg in 1529, Lübeck in 1531, and Denmark in 1537. His contribution to the Danish Reformation was particularly important.

He was responsible for the production of a Low German edition of Luther's Bible.

Bullant, Jean (*c.* 1520–1578)

French architect. He studied in Italy, developing a style that combined Classical styles (largely derived from his study of monuments in Rome) and aspects of contemporary fashions. He became architect to the French court, his projects mainly comprising royal residences (many of them lost).

Born at Amiens, Bullant studied in Rome 1540–45, where he was strongly influenced by Classical architecture. On his return to France he entered the service of Constable Anne de ◊Montmorency, for whom he worked on the Château d'Ecouen about 1555, and became the first French architect to make use of the colossal order by modelling his work on the Pantheon in Rome.

Subsequent works included the Petit Château (Capitainerie) at Chantilly about 1561 and a bridge and gallery combining ancient Roman and Mannerist elements at Fére-en-Tardenois 1552–62.

In 1570 Bullant succeeded ◊de l'Orme as architect to ◊Catherine de' Medici, for whom he executed work at the Chapelle des Valois and the Tuileries and drew up plans for the enlargement of the châteaux of St-Maur and Chenonceau and for the Hôtel de Soissons.

He was also the author of a treatise on architecture, *La Règle générale d'architecture, étude des cinq ordres de colonnes* (1564), which became a textbook for French architects of the following generation.

Bullinger, Johann Heinrich (1504–1575)

Swiss reformer and theologian. A supporter of

◊Zwingli, Bullinger succeeded him as pastor of Zürich in 1531. He played a very active role in the Reformation, signing the Zürich Agreement with Calvin in 1549 and drawing up the second Helvetic Confession in 1566. He had an international reputation, and in 1570, when ◊Elizabeth I of England was excommunicated by Pope ◊Pius V, he helped her to draw up her reply.

Born in Bremgarten, the son of a parish priest, Bullinger studied in Germany and accompanied Zwingli to the Bern Conference in 1528. The following year, having married an ex-nun, he returned to Bremgarten as its pastor. In 1531 he was appointed minister in Zürich in succession to ◊Zwingli, where his resolute defence of the Zürich church preserved it through the many difficulties which followed Zwingli's death. In the eucharistic controversy Bullinger defended the Zwinglian position, but he also associated himself with ◊Bucer in attempts to reconcile the German and Swiss churches. In 1549 he and Calvin made the important Zürich Agreement (Consensus Tigurinus), which defined a common sacramental doctrine for the Zürich and Geneva churches.

By this time Bullinger enjoyed a considerable international influence, largely through his enormous correspondence (12,000 surviving pieces). A prolific writer, he wrote sermons (published as the *Sermonorum Decades Quinque*) that had an enduring popularity, particularly in England where his reputation rivalled that of Calvin.

Bullinger was also the architect of the second Helvetic Confession in 1566 and the author of a history of the Reformation down to 1532.

Buon, Bartolommeo (BARTOLOMMEO BON) (c. 1374–c. 1467)

Venetian architectural sculptor. He is best known for his work on the Porta della Carta (one of the main doorways of the ducal palace in Venice), with its famous *Lion of St Mark*, and its statue of *Justice* and other figures.

Trained by his father Giovanni, Bartolommeo is first recorded collaborating with him on the façade of the Church of Santa Maria dell'Orto in his native Venice in 1392. They next appear in 1422 working, with others, on the Ca d'Oro, where their work continued until 1437. The large well head in its courtyard, adorned with allegorical figures, is documented to Bartolommeo in 1427.

From the late 1430s date a lunette over the entrance to the Scuola di San Marco and the Porta della Carta of the ducal palace. Another important carving is the lunette of the *Madonna of Mercy* (now Victoria and Albert Museum, London) from the façade of the Misericordia, a charitable brotherhood.

Buon's style, with its emphasis on luxuriant foliage and heraldry, is essentially Gothic and has an attractive boldness, owing to the relatively hard local stones he used, Verona red marble and Istrian limestone.

Buonamente, Giovanni Battista (DIED 1642)

Italian violinist and composer. He was an imperial court musician from 1622, and maestro di cappella at the Franciscan monastery of Assisi from 1633. He wrote sonatas for two violins and bass, and music for mixed teams of instruments.

Buonconsiglio, Giovanni, (KNOWN AS IL MARESCALCO) (DIED c. 1536)

Painter from Vicenza, influenced by Bartolommeo ◊Montagna. He worked both in Vicenza and in Venice, where he decorated a number of churches in association with ◊Antonello da Messina.

Burbage, Richard (c. 1567–1619)

English actor. He is thought to have been Shakespeare's original Hamlet, Othello, and Lear. He also appeared in first productions of works by Ben ◊Jonson, Thomas ◊Kyd, and John ◊Webster. His father **James Burbage** (c. 1530–1597) built the first English playhouse, known as 'the Theatre'; his brother **Cuthbert Burbage** (c. 1566–1636) built the original Globe Theatre in London in 1599.

Burchard, Johannes (DIED 1506)

German cleric at the papal curia, the only man with such a surname who deserves a mention in this encyclopedia. Born near Strasburg and educated in law, Burchard travelled to Rome in 1481 in the hope of employment at the curia. He was appointed papal master of ceremonies in 1483, in which position he attended to the managing of papal events and procession (in ◊Alexander VI's pontificate fighting a losing battle for traditional protocol against the pope's taste for the extravagant). He kept a diary recording ceremonial details and, increasingly, gossip. Made bishop of Orto in 1503, he died still hoping for a cardinal's hat.

Burchiello, Domenico (ORIGINALLY DOMENICO DI GIOVANNI) (c. 1404–1449)

Florentine poet. A barber by profession, poetry was a pasttime; he wrote mostly sonnets of the burlesque type and often licentious which had great contemporary popularity.

Opposed to the Medici, he was forced into exile when they returned to Florence in 1434. His poems, which reflect a vernacular tradition, include an attack on Cosimo de' Medici ('O humil popul/O humble people'); though he was no Medicean and no humanist, the collectors of his works included Lorenzo de' Medici 'the Magnificent'.

Burghley, William Cecil, 1st Baron Burghley (1520–1598)

English politician, chief adviser to Elizabeth I as secretary of state from 1558 and Lord High Treasurer from 1572. He was largely responsible for the religious settlement of 1559, and took a leading role in the events preceding the execution of Mary Queen of Scots in 1587.

One of Edward VI's secretaries, he lost office under Queen Mary, but on Queen Elizabeth's succession became one of her most trusted ministers. He carefully avoided a premature breach with Spain in the difficult period leading up to the attack by the Spanish Armada in 1588, and did a great deal towards abolishing monopolies and opening up trade.

Bürgi, Jost (1552–1632)

Swiss-born clockmaker and mathematician. One of the first clockmakers to use second hands, Bürgi also introduced a mechanism for providing the escapement with a constant driving force. In mathematics, he developed a comprehensive system of logarithms (about 30 years before ◊Napier), but his work has been largely ignored.

In 1579 he became court clockmaker to William IV of Hesse-Kassel, and in 1603 moved to a similar post at the Prague court of Emperor Rudolf II.

His work in mathematics remained unknown until 1620 when he published his *Arithmetische und Geometrische Progress-Tabulen*. By this time the glory had gone to Napier, and Bürgi's own role remained unrecognized until relatively recent times.

Burgkmair, Hans (1473–1531)

German painter and wood engraver. His woodcuts – nearly 700 in all – are remarkable both for their dramatic strength and for their faithful presentation of contemporary life. He worked for the Holy Roman Emperor ◊Maximilian I, in particular on the *Triumph of Maximilian* series (1517).

Born in Augsburg, he was a pupil of Martin ◊Schongauer, friend and colleague of Albrecht ◊Dürer, and father-in-law of Hans ◊Holbein the Elder.

As a painter he enriched his colour by the study of the Venetians, and his *Esther in the House of Ahasuerus* (Alte Pinakothek, Munich) is an elaborate attempt to adapt an Italian type of composition, with profuse Renaissance detail of architecture and ornament.

He also illustrated a German translation of Petrarch's *De Remediis Utriusque Fortunae*.

Burmeister, Joachim (1564–1629)

German music theorist. In treatises published in 1599, 1601, and 1606 he codified as *figurae* the various technical and expressive devices used by 16th-century composers.

Burton, Avery (c. 1470–c. 1543)

English composer. He is known as the composer of a Mass, *Ut re mi fa sol la*, in the Forrest-Heyther part-books (this is probably not the Mass of 1494) and of a Te Deum for organ.

In November 1494 he was paid 20 shillings by Henry VII for composing a Mass; in 1509 he became a gentleman of the Chapel Royal. In 1513 he went to France with the Chapel Royal, a Te Deum of his being sung after Mass at Tournai in September; in June 1520 he was present at the historic meeting between Henry VIII of England and Francis I of France, known as the Field of the Cloth of Gold. His name disappears from the records of the Chapel Royal after 1542.

Bury, the Monk of

Another name for the English medieval Benedictine monk and poet John ◊Lydgate.

Busnois, Antoine (c. 1430–1492)

French composer. He was a pupil of Okeghem and was in the service of the Burgundian court until 1482, when he became music director at the Church of Saint-Sauveur at Bruges.

Works include:

Two Masses, Magnificat, hymns, 61 songs for three or four voices; motets, including *Fortunata desperata*, used later by Josquin Desprez.

Butinone, Bernardino (DIED 1507)

Painter working in Milan. Active from 1484, he was associated with Bernardo ◊Zenale in painting frescoes in S Pietro in Gessate, Milan, and an altarpiece in Treviglio. He appears to have been a pupil of Vincenzo ◊Foppa.

Buus, Jacques (c. 1500–1565)

Flemish composer and organist. He first published some work in France, but went to Italy and in 1541 became organist at St Mark's in Venice, succeeding Baldassare da Imola. He went to Vienna on leave in 1550, but never returned and became organist at the court of Ferdinand I.

Works include:

Motets, madrigals, French chansons, ricercari for organ.

Buxtorf, Johannes (I) (1564–1629)

German Hebrew scholar. Professor of Hebrew at Basel 1591–1629, he brought a new discipline and depth to Hebrew studies, largely by drawing on rabbinical scholarship. His published works include grammars, dictionaries, and biblical commentaries.

The son of a Protestant minister, Buxtorf was born in Marburg. He studied there and in Geneva and then Basel, where he met Théodore ◊Beza. He occupied the chair of Hebrew at Basel for 38 years, rejecting attractive offers from the universities of Saumur and Leyden.

To the study of Hebrew Buxtorf brought rabbinical learning acquired from the many scholarly Jews whom he befriended. His main works had an educational purpose: a number of elementary grammars and readers, a Hebrew-Chaldee *Lexicon* (1607), and a Hebrew reference grammar (1609). He also produced an edition of the Bible with rabbinic commentary, and the Chaldean paraphrases 1618–19.

His son **Johannes II** (1599–1664), followed him as professor of Hebrew at Basel and completed his father's *Lexicon Chaldaicum Talmudicum et Rabbinicum* (1639), which provided a scientific basis for the study of post-biblical Jewish writings.

Byrd, William (1543–1623)

English composer. His sacred and secular choral music, including over 200 motets and Masses for three, four, and five voices, exemplifies the English polyphonic style.

Probably born in Lincoln, Byrd studied under Thomas ◊Tallis as one of the children of the Chapel Royal in London. He became organist at Lincoln Cathedral in 1563. He married Juliana Birley there in 1568, and was elected a Gentleman of the Chapel Royal in 1569, but continued his duties at Lincoln until 1572, when he became organist of Queen Elizabeth's Chapel Royal jointly with Tallis. In 1575 Queen Elizabeth granted Byrd and Tallis an exclusive licence for printing and selling music and they dedicated to her their *Cantiones Sacrae* published that year.

Byrd married for the second time in about 1587. In 1593 he bought Stondon Place near Stapleford-Abbott, Essex, where he remained for the rest of his life, as far as his duties in London would let him. He was frequently involved in litigation and was several times prosecuted for recusancy as a Roman Catholic, but remained in favour with the Queen.

Byrd's popular reputation rests with his three great Masses, in three, four, and five parts, in which his contrapuntal mastery is most fully displayed. Other aspects of his genius are found in the ornate *Cantiones Sacrae* and the large body of consort songs and instrumental music.

Works include:

Three Masses; 17 Latin motets in the *Cantiones Sacrae* by Tallis and Byrd; 61 Latin motets in two books of *Cantiones Sacrae*; 99 Latin motets in two books of *Gradualia*; about 50 motets in manuscript form; 4

Anglican services; about 61 anthems; some miscellaneous English church music; *Psalmes, Sonets and Songs* (18 nos.); *Songs of Sundrie Natures* (47 nos.); *Psalmes, Songs and Sonnets* (32 nos.); 4 separate madrigals (others are in those three books); consort songs, canons; rounds; fantasies for strings, 7 *In Nomines* for strings, 10 pieces for strings on plainsong tunes, some miscellaneous music for strings; about 100 virginal pieces, among them fantasias, preludes, grounds, variations, pavanes and galliards, and other dances.

Byzantine novel

A style of narrative, Greek in origin, in which two lovers, separated by a series of seemingly insurmountable obstacles, yet always remaining faithful to one another, are finally reunited. The 1534 discovery and first edition of Heliodorus' novel *Teágenes and Caricela* began a vogue for this type of work, praised for its morality and ingenious narrative. Both Lope de ◊Vega and ◊Cervantes produced a work in this style.

Cabezón, Antonio de (1510–1566)

Spanish organist and composer. Although blind from early childhood, he studied with Tomás Gómez at Palencia and became chamber organist and harpsichordist to Charles V, remaining at court under Philip II, and accompanying him to England on his marriage to Mary I. He composed music for organ, vihuela, and other instruments.

Cabot, Sebastian (1474–1557)

Italian navigator and cartographer, the second son of Giovanni ◊Caboto. He explored the Brazilian coast and the Rio de la Plata for the Holy Roman Emperor Charles V in 1526–30.

Cabot was also employed by Henry VIII, Edward VI, and Ferdinand of Spain. He planned a voyage to China by way of the Northeast Passage, the sea route along the north Eurasian coast, encouraged the formation of the Company of Merchant Adventurers of London in 1551, and in 1553 and 1556 directed the company's expeditions to Russia, where he opened British trade.

Caboto, Giovanni (JOHN CABOT) (c. 1450–c. 1498)

Italian navigator. Commissioned, with his three sons, by Henry VII of England to discover unknown lands, he arrived at Cape Breton Island on 24 June 1497, thus becoming the first European to reach the North American mainland (he thought he was in northeast Asia). In 1498 he sailed again, touching Greenland, and probably died on the voyage.

Cabral, Pedro Alvares (1460–1526)

Portuguese explorer who made Brazil a Portuguese possession in 1500 and negotiated the first commercial treaty between Portugal and India.

Cabral set sail from Lisbon for the East Indies in March 1500, and accidentally reached Brazil by taking a course too far west. He claimed the country for Portugal on 25 April, since Spain had not followed up the landing by Vicente Pinzón (c. 1460–1523) there earlier in the year. Continuing around Africa, he lost 7 of his fleet of 13 ships (the explorer Bartolomeu ◊Diaz was one of those drowned), and landed in Mozambique. Proceeding to India, he negotiated the first Indo-Portuguese treaties for trade, and returned to Lisbon in July 1501.

Caccini, Giulio (c. 1545–1618)

Italian singer, lutenist, and composer. He wrote short vocal pieces in recitative style and sang them to the theorbo, which led to larger essays of the kind, set to scenes by Count Giovanni Bardi, and eventually to Rinuccini's libretto for the opera *Euridice*, first set by Jacopo Peri and immediately afterwards by Caccini in 1602. In 1604–05 he visited Paris with his daughter, **Francesca Caccini** (1587–c. 1640), who was herself a composer as well as a singer.

Caccini was born in Tivoli or Rome, and was taken to Florence by Cosimo I de' Medici around 1565. He was successful as a singer there, and became known throughout Italy. He used to attend Count Bardi's salon in Florence, and was credited with the invention of a new style of song, the *stile recitativo*, which developed there. The first mention of Caccini as a composer dates from 1589, when he composed music for the marriage of Grand Duke Ferdinando I. In 1600 he was appointed musical director at the court of the Medici family, and remained in their service until his death.

His two songbooks, *Le nuove musiche*, published in 1602 and 1614, contain pieces for solo voice and figured bass. The first has a preface on the new style of singing and composition adopted by Caccini, and embellishments in the music that were usually improvised are written out in full.

Works include:
The operas *Euridice* and *Il rapimento di Cefalo* (both 1602); *Nuove musiche* containing madrigals and arias for voice and continuo.

Caius, John (JOHN KAYE OR KEYS) (1510–1573)

English physician and humanist. He was educated at Gonville Hall, Cambridge, and at the University of

Padua, Italy, where he studied medicine under ◊Vesalius. On his return to England he taught anatomy in London and in 1547 became a member of the College of Physicians. He was physician royal to Edward VI, Mary Tudor, and Queen Elizabeth I. In 1557 he refounded his old college at Cambridge, which was renamed Gonville and Caius.

He was born in Norwich. He became a fellow of Gonville Hall in 1529 and received his MD from Padua in 1541. After lecturing on anatomy in London, he practised medicine in Shrewsbury and Norwich. He was president of the College of Physicians nine times.

In 1557 he received permission to elevate his college, providing it with a new court and three fine gates, which he designed himself – some of the earliest examples of English architecture inspired by the Italian Renaissance. He became master of the college in 1559. His period in office was difficult, for as a Catholic he met opposition from the Protestant college fellows – he had two of them put in the stock for burning his vestments, and became involved in protracted lawsuits. A pioneer of anatomy studies, he obtained permission for Caius College to obtain two bodies of criminals a year for dissection.

Much of his own time was spent editing a number of texts by Hippocrates and ◊Galen. He also wrote *A Boke or Counseill against the Sweatyng Sicknesse* (1552), an account of the mysterious epidemic which swept through 16th-century Britain. He also became involved in controversies over the pronunciation of Greek, and the relative antiquity of Oxford and Cambridge.

Cajetan, Jacopo (TOMMASO DE VIO) (1469–1534)

Italian Dominican theologian. A committed opponent of the Reformation, he played an active role in the international politics of his age, being involved in the elections of Emperor ◊Charles V and Pope Adrian VI. He also disputed with Martin ◊Luther and strongly opposed the divorce of ◊Henry VIII from Catherine of Aragon.

He entered the Dominican Order in 1484 and studied at Naples, Padua, and Ferrara. He taught philosophy and theology at Brescia, Pavia, Paris, and Rome. He was general of the Dominican Order

1508–18, and spoke in favour of reform of the church at the Fifth Lateran Council of 1512–17. He was appointed a cardinal in 1517 and in 1518 bishop of Gaeta (Caieta, hence his name). In 1517 Pope ◊Leo X sent him as papal legate to Germany, where he was to urge Emperor Maximilian and the Scandinavian kings to form a league against the Ottoman Turks. He was also to bring Luther back into the Church, and in 1518 argued the Church's case with Luther in Wittenberg. In 1523 he was appointed papal legate to Hungary. He was a prolific writer, and from 1507–22 published a commentary on the *Summa theologica* of St Thomas Aquinas that remains an important contribution to Thomist philosophy.

Calcar, Jan Steven van (ALSO KNOWN AS GIOVANNI FIAMMINGO) (1499–c. 1550)

German painter and woodcut designer. Perhaps first trained in the Netherlands, he moved to Venice in 1536, where he became a disciple – or, at least, fell under the influence – of ◊Titian. He provided the illustrations for ◊Vesalius' anatomy book *De Humani Corporis Fabrica/On the Construction of the Human Body* (1543).

His illustrations for *De Fabrica* – which, Vasari claimed, 'must do him honour for all time' – show dissected cadavers in dramatic action, reproducing the gestures and poses of living beings.

His paintings are often confused with those of Titian, but one of the best documented examples of his style is his *Portrait of Melchior von Brauweiler of Cologne* (1540, Louvre, Paris). In 1545 ◊Vasari met him in Naples, where Calcar died.

Calderini, Domizio (1446–1478)

Humanist commentator on Classical texts, born near Lake Garda, Italy. Educated in Verona and Venice, he went to Rome in about 1466–67 and entered the scholarly circle round Cardinal ◊Bessarion. Calderini was appointed to teach rhetoric and Greek at the University of Rome in 1470; he also became a papal secretary to Sixtus IV in 1471. He worked on several Classical commentaries which suffered the usual ignominy of scathing remarks from fellow scholars. His commentary on Martial, dedicated in 1473 to Lorenzo de' Medici, caused a dispute with another

Bessarion protégé Niccolò ◊Perotti. Giorgio ◊Merula launched another attack on this commentary in 1478; Calderini was posthumously defended by Cornelio ◊Vitelli.

Calepino, Ambrogio (c. 1440–c. 1510)

Italian monk and lexicographer, born in Bergamo. He compiled a Latin–Italian dictionary (1502).

Calixtus III (BORN ALONSO BORGIA) (1378–1458)

Pope 1455–58. He was born in Aragon and trained there as a canon lawyer; he entered the service of ◊Alfonso V in 1417, and followed him to Italy in 1432. He was made bishop of Valencia in 1429 and a cardinal in 1444, after having arranged a reconciliation between Alfonso and Pope Eugenius IV. His pontificate was dominated by attempts to organize a crusade, bringing him into conflict with his former employer, Alfonso.

The aged and bedridden candidate who emerged from the 1455 conclave as Calixtus III was very much a compromise choice; other candidates, such as ◊Bessarion, aroused strong support but also strong opposition. If, though, he began his pontificate without many enemies, Calixtus subsequently alienated influential figures. The arrival of Catalans at the Roman curia caused consternation and accusations of nepotism, which only increased when Rodrigo Borgia, Calixtus's nephew, was created a cardinal. What is more, humanists became all too aware that the halcyon days of Nicholas V's cultural patronage were over – Calixtus considered the money better spent on crusading.

Calvaert, Denis (1540–1619)

Flemish painter. He established a school in Bologna, Italy, in rivalry with that of the Carracci. Domenichino, Guido Reni, and Francesco Albani were for a time his pupils.

Calvin, John (ALSO KNOWN AS CAUVIN OR CHAUVIN) (1509–1564)

French-born Swiss Protestant church reformer and theologian. He was a leader of the Reformation in Geneva and set up a strict religious community there. His theological system is known as Calvinism, and his church government as Presbyterianism. Calvin wrote (in Latin) *Institutes of the Christian Religion* (1536) and commentaries on the New Testament and much of the Old Testament.

Calvin, born in Noyon, Picardie, studied theology and then law, and about 1533 became prominent in Paris as an evangelical preacher. In 1534 he was obliged to leave Paris and retired to Basel, where he studied Hebrew. In 1536 he accepted an invitation to go to Geneva, Switzerland, and assist in the Reformation, but was expelled in 1538 because of public resentment against the numerous and too drastic changes he introduced. He returned to Geneva in 1541 and, in the face of strong opposition, established a rigorous theocracy (government by priests). In 1553 he had the Spanish theologian Servetus burned for heresy. He supported the ◊Huguenots in their struggle in France and the English Protestants persecuted by Queen Mary I.

Calvisius, Seth (1556–1615)

German scholar and musician. He was cantor of St Thomas's School, Leipzig, and music director of its church from 1594. In addition to writing several learned books on music, he compiled collections of vocal music and composed motets, hymns, and other pieces.

Cambiaso, Luca (1527–1585)

Genoese painter. He travelled widely in Italy and absorbed a variety of Renaissance influences. In 1583 he went with Pellegrino Tibaldi (1527–1596) and Federigo Zuccaro to Spain, where they were commissioned by Philip II to execute extensive frescoes in the ◊Escorial. Cambiaso's dramatic use of light and shadow anticipated the style of Michelangelo Merisi Caravaggio.

Cambiaso was born in Moneglia and studied with his father and a painter from Bergamo, G B Castello. At 15 he helped his father to paint subjects from Ovid's *Metamorphoses* on the front of a house in Genoa.

Cambrai, League of

An alliance formed at Cambrai in northern France in December 1508 by European powers hostile to Venice. The stated aim of Emperor ◊Maximilian I,

◊Louis XII of France, and Ferdinand II of Aragon was to fight the Ottoman Turks, but the real aim was to dismember the Venetian empire. They were joined by Pope ◊Julius II and the dukes of Mantua and Ferrara, all of whom had territorial disputes with Venice. After some initial successes, beginning with the Battle of Agnadello in 1509, the League began to collapse in 1510, owing to the defection of the pope and Ferdinand. By 1517 Venice had won back virtually all the territory it had lost.

Camden, William (1551–1623)

English antiquary and teacher. Educated at St Paul's School and at Oxford, his early profession was teaching (at Westminster School, where he became headmaster in 1593) but he was then appointed a herald in 1597. Both careers allowed him time (if not much money) to carry out the researches for which he became famous among a select but international group of scholars. His main works are his topographical survey *Britannia* (1586), dedicated to William Cecil, Lord ◊Burghley (supplemented by *Remains*, 1605, dedicated to his friend Sir Robert ◊Cotton) and his *Annales*, a history of Elizabeth's reign to 1588, published in 1615.

Camerarius, Joachim (1500–1574)

German scholar, theologian, and diplomat. A leading figure in the Reformation, he was a close friend of ◊Luther and ◊Melanchthon. He took part in drawing up the Confession of ◊Augsburg in 1530 and later attempted, in negotiations with Emperor ◊Maximilian II, to reconcile the Lutheran and Catholic churches. He made many translations from Latin and Greek, notably the first complete edition of the plays of ◊Plautus (1552).

He was born Joachim Liebhard in Bamberg. As his family had long held the office of chamberlain at the court of the bishops of Bamberg, he changed his name to Camerarius, the Latin form of the German word *Kämmerer* (chamberlain).

He studied Greek at Leipzig, then went to Wittenberg, attracted by the reputations of Luther and Melanchthon – he was later Melanchthon's biographer. In 1524 he published a Latin translation of Demosthenes' first *Olynthiac Oration*. The following year his commentary on Cicero's *Tusculan disputations*

brought him into contact with ◊Erasmus.

In 1526 Melanchthon made him professor of Greek and Latin at the new Protestant college in Nuremberg. In 1530 he attended the Diet of Augsburg and collaborated on the formulation of the Augsburg Confession. A moderate voice in Lutheranism, even as late as 1568 he was discussing with Emperor Maximilian II the possibility of a reconciliation between the Catholic and Protestant churches. In 1535 he moved to Tübingen and in 1541 to Leipzig, where he eventually died.

Camões, Luis Vaz de (1524/25–1580)

Portuguese soldier and poet. Although his epic poem ◊*The Lusiads/Os Lusíadas* and his lyric poetry are familiar, details about his life remain obscure. Probably born in Lisbon, he served as a soldier in Ceuta, where he may have lost an eye. Back in Lisbon, he was imprisoned for brawling. Leaving for India in 1553, his first known work, a poem prefacing Garcia da ◊Orta's 1563 medical treatise, was published at Goa, while his play, *Auto do Filodemo/ Filodemo* was probably performed in 1555 to celebrate the appointment (if not the assumption) of the governor of Chaul. He returned to Lisbon in *c.* 1570, perhaps with Diogo do ◊Couto, and *The Lusiads* appeared in 1572. The same year King Sebastião recognized his literary talents and awarded him a modest pension.

There is no evidence to suggest Camões was ever a gallant courtier, exiled to India for indiscreet love affairs. Nor is there much support for claims that he saved his *The Lusiads* manuscript but lost his Chinese mistress when shipwrecked at the mouth of the river Mekong (Vietnam). The four surviving letters penned by him reveal little of his persona, although one, written in India, reveals a nostalgic preference for Portuguese women.

Aside from *The Lusiads*, only four of Camões's lyric poems were published during his lifetime (three of these were laudatory book-prefaces). His poetry was, though, collected in manuscript ◊*cancioneiros*, such as the one compiled by Cristóvão Borges in 1578. Despite the difficulty that few of Camões's lyrics existed in autograph manuscripts, his collected poems, entitled *Rythmas/Rhymes*, were published in 1595. Most of these were sonnets, an Italian form originally introduced into Portugal by the Marques de ◊Santillana but which had been popularized by ◊Sá de Miranda. The compilation was soon reprinted (1598) and a third edition appeared in 1607.

His three plays were also published posthumously and seem not to have enjoyed as wide a circulation as his poetry. The *Auto do Filodemo and Anfitriões/ Amphitrion* (based on Plautus' *Amphitruo*) appeared in the first part of Antonio Prestes's *Autos e Comedias Portuguesas/Portuguese Plays and Comedies* (1587), while *El Rey Seleuco/King Seleuco*, inspired by Plutarch's *Parallel Lives*, appeared in the second volume of his collected works, published by Paulo Craesbeck in 1645.

Campagnola, Giulio (*c.* 1482–*c.* 1518)

Italian engraver. Trained by Andrea ◊Mantegna, he is remembered for popularizing the works of such artists as ◊Dürer (whose popularity in Italy derived in part from Campagnola's etchings), and ◊Giorgione, who influenced his style. His technique anticipated later schools of engraving.

He was born in Padua. By 1499 he was executing work for the court in Ferrara, and by 1509 he was working in Venice. His pupils included his adopted son **Domenico Campagnola** (*c.* 1484–*c.* 1563).

Campana, Pedro de (PIETER DE KEMPENEER) (1503–1580)

Flemish artist. Although born in Brussels, he spent several years in Italy, where he worked at Bologna, Venice, and elsewhere. By 1537 he had moved to Seville in Spain, where he painted religious scenes for the cathedral, notably the *Descent from the Cross* (1547). Having done much to popularize Italian fashion in Andalusia, he returned to Brussels, where he worked as a tapestry designer.

Campanella, Tommaso (1568–1639)

Italian philosopher. Born in Calabria, he was implicated in the Calabrian revolt against their Spanish ruler and was imprisoned 1599–1626. He wrote many books in prison, the best known being his utopian fantasy *La città del sole/The City of the Sun* (written about 1602).

Campanella was born at Silo. Like Giordano ◊Bruno, he began his career by joining the Dominican Order in 1582. In 1591 he published *Philosophia*

Sensibus Demonstrata/Philosophy Demonstrated by the Senses, in which, rejecting Aristotelianism, he insisted that knowledge should be based on a close observation of the natural world. His *De Monarcha Christianorum/ Christian Monarchy* (1593) set out his ideas on the reform of the church and society.

The church found his views, which were strongly influenced by Bernardino Telesio, deeply suspect. After trials in Naples in 1592 and Padua in 1593 on charges of heresy and blasphemy, he moved to Rome and then, in 1598, back to Calabria during a revolt against Spanish rule. The revolt quickly collapsed and he was arrested (on little or no evidence) and imprisoned in Naples. Frequently tortured, he was finally sentenced to life imprisonment. When finally released in 1626, he returned to Rome and was imprisoned again, this time by the Holy Office (Inquisition). He finally fled Italy in 1634 and settled in Paris, where he had the support of Louis XIII and Cardinal Richelieu.

His *La città del sole*, inspired by Plato's *Republic*, was first published in Frankfurt in 1623 in a Latin version, *Civitas Solis*. The books describes an ideal world in which religion, science, and occult knowledge are the moral, intellectual, and spiritual guides. In the City of the Sun the 'Solarians' regulate their lives by astrological principles; hermetic influences are also identifiable among them, and they admire Copernicus and reject Aristotle. All things are shared in a kind of communist state, though it is ruled by a moral and intellectual elite who are able to interpret God's design for the world (see also Thomas ◊More and Francis ◊Bacon).

Campanella also wrote an *Apologia pro Galileo/ Defence of Galileo* (1622) and *De Sensu Rerum et Magia/On the Sense in Things and on Magic* (1620), both of which had also to be published by his disciple Tobias Adami in Frankfurt.

Campin, Robert (ALSO KNOWN AS THE MASTER OF FLÉMALLE) (*c.* 1378–1444)

Early Netherlandish painter, active in Tournai from 1406. Few works are attributable to him, but those that are suggest an interest in naturalistic depiction comparable to that of his contemporary, Jan ◊van Eyck.

Campin's outstanding work is the *Mérode Altarpiece*

Campion was born in Witham, Essex. Educated at Cambridge and other European universities, he then studied law, but left this profession and practised medicine in London.

He published a first collection of airs to the lute with Philip Rosseter in 1601 and four more followed between about 1613 and 1617, all the words of the songs being his own. He composed masques that are among the best of their kind, and produced many fine lyrics notable for their metrical finish. His songs are verbally delicate, and he composed most of his own settings for them; the balance between the lyrics and the music is sensitive and satisfying. The best known are 'There is a Garden in her Face' and 'My Sweetest Lesbia, Let Us Live and Love', a translation from Catullus.

In 1613 he published a book on counterpoint, and wrote the poetry for *Songs of Mourning* on the death of Prince Henry, set by Coprario. His poem 'Neptune's Empire' was set for chorus and orchestra by Ernest Walker.

Works include:
Five books of airs to the lute (over 100) and three separate earlier songs; songs for the production of four masques, 1607–13, including *The Mask of Flowers*.

(*c.* 1425, Metropolitan Museum of Art, New York), which shows a characteristic blend of naturalism and elaborate symbolism, together with a subtlety of modelling and a grasp of pictorial space. Other works include the *Sitting Madonna* (*c.* 1435, National Gallery, London), the *Werl Altar* (Prado, Madrid), and his two portraits of a man and woman (*c.* 1430, National Gallery, London).

Campion, Thomas (1567–1620)

English poet and musician. He was the author of the critical *Art of English Poesie* (1602) and four books of *Ayres* (1601–17), for which he composed both words and music.

The *Art of English Poesie* is an attack on the use of rhyme and a plea for the adoption of unrhymed metres formed on Classical models, such as are used in Campion's own 'Rose-cheeked Laura, Come'. He also wrote *Poemata* (1595), in Latin, containing poems, elegies, and epigrams.

cancionero, or *cancioneiro*

Song book. Castilian *cancioneros* or Portuguese *cancioneiros* were books of lyric poetry (sometimes accompanied by music) gathered and arranged according to the personal criteria of the compiler. Thus a *cancione(i)ro* could consist of a single author's works (which could have also been compiled by the author) or it could be a collection of verse texts by sundry poets on diverse themes which, for the general editor at least, would have had some unifying factor. Popular in the 13th century, the assorted *cancione(i)ros* of more contemporary poets were equally popular in the 15th and 16th centuries.

The 15th-century fashion for *cancione(i)ros* appears

to have originated in Castile, with Juan Alfonso de Baena's (*c.* 1375–*c.* 1474) eponymous *Cancionero de Baena*, dedicated in *c.* 1430 to Juan II and his wife, Maria of Aragon. With poems mostly in Castilian rather than in Galician-Portuguese, the main lyric language of the 13th and 14th centuries, Baena's *Cancionero* represented a break with medieval troubadour traditions. It did not, however, contain the poetry of his contemporaries (nor even Juan II's own verses): fossilized in Baena's collection were the works of late 14th-century poets. Another notable Castilian *cancionero* was Hernando del Castillo's *Cancionero General* (1511), an erratically organized collection of poems from the time of Juan de ◊Mena to the early 16th century. It ran to five editions, but not in its original form. The second edition of 1514 represented a somewhat altered version (as in, for example, the addition of three poems by Joan ◊Boscà) and subsequent reprints were taken from this edition. Castillo's *Cancionero* inspired a Portuguese equivalent: Garcia de Resende's (1470–1536) *Cancioneiro Geral* (1516). Dedicated to the future João III, it haphazardly assembled poems from the 1440s to 1516, and included twelve by Bernadim Ribeiro as well as the first known published lines by Gil ◊Vicente. Resende's aim, set out in his prologue, was to create a monument to the greatness of the Portuguese (although not necessarily to the Portuguese language, as it included numerous Castilian poems by Portuguese poets). In keeping with this patriotism, several lyrics dealt with historical events, such as the rounding of Cape Bojador (1434), but the *Cancioneiro's* sheer monumentality coupled with the trivial subject matter of many of its poems (such as Luis de Silveira's composition to 'a lady who threw a stone at him') made it the target of criticisms even in the 16th century. Criticism which did not prevent it being plundered for copies of its more popular poems, however. The Portuguese ◊Inquisition banned it in 1624 (because it contained anticlerical satire), while a second edition did not appear until the 19th century. All these *cancione(i)ros* are very different from those copied during the same period by Angelo ◊Colocci.

Cane, Facino (*c.* 1350–1412)

Italian ◊*condottiere*. From 1397 he was employed by the ◊Visconti of Milan and, under the rule of the weak Giovanni Maria Visconti (1402–12), became so powerful that he seemed to be on the point of ousting the ◊Visconti family. When Filippo Maria Visconti came to power in 1412 he married Cane's sister, Beatrice, whom he put to death on a false charge of adultery in 1418.

Piedmontese by birth, Cane led mercenary forces there and in Savoy from his youth and established a reputation as a ruthless and efficient *condottiere*. The Genoese gave him a major command in 1394, and he entered the employ of Giangaleazzo Visconti in 1397.

Canis, Corneille (CORNELIS DE HOND) (*c.* 1510/20–1561)

Flemish composer. He was choirmaster of Charles V's imperial chapel in the Netherlands from 1548, and later became chaplain to the Holy Roman Emperor Ferdinand in Prague. He wrote church music, chansons, and other pieces.

Cano, Juan Sebastian del (*c.* 1476–1526)

Spanish voyager. It is claimed that he was the first sea captain to sail around the world. He sailed with Ferdinand ◊Magellan in 1519 and, after the latter's death in the Philippines, brought the *Victoria* safely home to Spain.

Cano, Melchior (1509–1560)

Spanish theologian. A Dominican friar at Salamanca from 1523, he taught at Valladolid from 1533, and in 1543 became the first professor of theology at Alcalá. He came to prominence when he defended ◊Philip II of Spain in his political conflict with Pope ◊Paul IV.

His doctrine of marriage – that the priestly blessing was the essential form of the sacrament – was controversial. His principal theological work was his *De Locis Theologicis* (1563).

cantus firmus (LATIN 'FIXED SONG')

In music, any familiar melody employed in counterpoint as a reference for the invention of an accompanying melody.

In early music, multiple parts were composed one at a time, each referring to the cantus firmus, but not to any other, with sometimes strange harmonic results, for example the final cadence E minor–G major–F major.

Caravaggio, Polidoro Caldara da (c. 1495–1543)

Italian painter. An assistant to ◊Raphael, he became famous for his monochrome fresco decoration of Roman history subjects on palace façades. Of these, only his work at the Palazzo Ricci, dating from about 1524, survives. One of his best-known paintings is *Christ Bearing the Cross* (Naples).

He was born in Caravaggio, northern Italy. First employed by Raphael as a plasterer in the Vatican Loggie, he later participated in painting narrative frescoes there. After Raphael's death, he worked for ◊Giulio Romano in the Vatican and in the Villa Lante. His landscapes with figures in the series *Lives of the Magdalen* and *St Catherine of Siena* anticipate later 17th-century developments in landscape. (Examples are in Rome, S Silvestro a Quirinale.) After the sack of Rome he fled to Naples and then to Messina where he amassed a large fortune. He was robbed and murdered at Messina.

Cardano, Girolamo (1501–1576)

Italian physician, mathematician, philosopher, astrologer, and gambler. He is remembered for his theory of chance, his use of algebra, and many medical publications, notably the first clinical description of typhus fever.

Born in Pavia, he became professor of medicine there in 1543, and wrote two works on physics and natural science, *De Subtilitate Rerum* (1551) and *De Varietate Rerum* (1557).

Carlo Emanuele I (1562–1630)

Duke of Savoy 1580–1630, the son of Emanuel Philibert (duke 1553–80). Carlo Emanuele pursued his father's ambitions to make Savoy a major Italian power and involved the duchy in frequent wars. He gained some territory, but constant warfare strained the duchy's finances. He did, however, successfully promote commercial development and made his court at Turin a centre of culture and learning.

Among his many enterprises, he took advantage of the conflict between France and Spain in Italy to make some gains for Savoy, but then failed in his attack on Geneva in 1602.

Carlton, Richard (c. 1558–c. 1638)

English composer. He was educated at Cambridge, and later became vicar at St Stephen's Church, Norwich, and a minor canon at the cathedral. He published a book of madrigals in 1601 and contributed to *The Triumphes of Oriana*.

Carmeliano, Pietro (1451–1527)

Humanist poet, born in Brescia, Italy. His career was spent in England, where he arrived in 1481. He dedicated poems to Edward IV, Edward's son (*De Vere/ On Spring*, 1482), and Richard III. But he found no difficulty in changing with the times after 1485; he produced several poems celebrating Henry VII's rule. He received royal patronage and was appointed royal secretary in about 1495. As with Polydore ◊Vergil and Bernard ◊André, the succession of Henry VIII in 1509 made patronage less secure, but Carmeliano remained in England, continuing to produce poems.

Caro, Annibale (1507–1566)

Italian poet. He translated into the *volgare* Virgil's *Aeneid* (in blank verse, 1581) and Longus' *Daphnis and Chloé*.

Other works include a comedy, *Gli straccioni*, written about 1544. He frequently favoured the burlesque.

Carpaccio, Vittore (1450/60–1525/26)

Venetian painter. His fresco series *The Legend of St Ursula* (1490–98, Accademia, Venice) inventively refreshed the traditional story by placing it against a backdrop of Venetian life, with detailed portrayals of its townscape.

His real name was Scarpazza, and he probably came from a family established in the Venetian islands. He is said to have been a pupil of Lorenzo Bastiani, but was evidently influenced by Gentile ◊Bellini, with whom he vied in depicting the aspect and ceremony of Venice. He was much employed by the *scuole* or confraternities of Venice and his charm and narrative gift are beautifully displayed in his cycles of the Life of St Ursula (1490–95) painted for the Scuola di Sant' Orsola and now in the Accademia, Venice, and the Life of St George and other saints for the Scuola di San Giorgio degli Schiavoni (1502–07). *The Miracle of the Cross at Rialto* (Accademia), like his rival Bellini's *Miracle of the Cross on San Lorenzo Bridge*, also pays close attention to the Venetian townscape. He also produced the (perhaps misleadingly titled) *Courtesans* (Correr Museum, Venice).

Cartier, Jacques (1491–1557)

French navigator who, while seeking a northwest passage to China, was the first European to sail up the St Lawrence River, in 1534. He named the site of Montréal.

cartoon

The base design for a large fresco, mosaic, or tapestry, transferred to a wall or canvas by tracing or pricking out the design on the cartoon and then dabbing with powdered charcoal to create a faint reproduction. Surviving examples include Leonardo da Vinci's *Virgin and St Anne* (National Gallery, London).

Carver, Robert (*c.* 1490–AFTER 1546)

Scottish monk and composer. He was a canon of Scone Abbey. His work was influenced by such major Flemish contemporaries as ◊Josquin Desprez and Henricus ◊Isaac.

Works include:
Masses (one in 10 parts), motets (one in 19 parts), and other church music.

Casa, Giovanni della (1503–1556)

Italian writer and cleric. His treatise on courtly manners *Galateo*, written 1551–55, printed in 1558, was attempted to follow the success of Baldassare Castiglione's *The ◊Courtier* by providing would-be social climbers with an easy guide to etiquette and modern manners.

He was appointed archbishop of Benevento and nuncio (papal ambassador) to Venice in 1544 by Pope Paul III, and was entrusted with much delicate diplomacy.

Casaubon, Isaac (1559–1614)

Swiss-born French Classical scholar. He published editions of numerous ancient writers, including Aristotle, Theophrastus, Polybius, Theocritus, Persius, and Suetonius. His own works include the treatises *De Satirica Graecorum Poësi et Romanorum*

Satira/On Greek and Roman Satire (1605) and *De Libertate Ecclesiastica/On the Liberty – or Free Estate – of the Church* (1607).

His *Correspondence*, in Latin, and his diary, *Ephemerides*, were published posthumously.

Casaubon was born in Geneva, where he became professor of Greek in 1583. In 1596 he accepted the Greek professorship at Montpellier, France, and from 1600 to 1610 he was in Paris, pre-eminent among French scholars. Henry IV gave him a pension with a promise of the royal librarianship when it became vacant, which was not until 1604. After Henry's assassination, Casaubon was forced to move to London because of his Protestant religion, where he was made a prebendary of Canterbury.

Cascina, Battle of

See ◊Anghiari, Battle of.

Caserta, Anthonello (Marotus) da (*c.* 1365–AFTER 1410)

Italian composer. His works include eight French songs, several in the most complex three-voice style of the *ars subtilior*, and eight simpler Italian songs, mostly in two voices.

Caserta, Philipottus da (*c.* 1350–AFTER 1390)

Italian composer and theorist. He composed works for the papal court of Clement VII (1378–94) and for the Milanese court of Bernabò Visconti (1354–85), and probably taught Johannes Ciconia. His works include one Credo, six French ballades (several in the most complex *ars subtilior* style), and three treatises on music.

Cassander, Georg (1513–1566)

Dutch theologian and humanist. A Catholic, Cassander devoted his career to reconciling the Protestant and Catholic churches, though this met with fierce attacks from entrenched positions on both sides. In 1564 he was an advisor to Emperor ◊Ferdinand I, who was searching for a way of uniting Protestants and Catholics.

After early study in his native Bruges and in Ghent, Cassander went to Cologne with the intention of finding some means of reconciling the orthodox

Catholic and reforming positions. In 1561 he anonymously published *De Officio Pii ac Publicae Tranquillitatis in Hoc Religionis Dissidio/On the Duty of Pious and Public Peace in the Present Dispute of Religion*. His eagerness for unity sometimes led him to adopt views that were doctrinally suspect but he remained faithful to the authority of the Church.

As well as his voluminous theological writings Cassander produced treatises on antiquarian subjects. He died in Cologne.

cassone (PLURAL *CASSONI*)

In Renaissance Italy, a wooden marriage chest used for storing garments, documents, and valuables. Pairs of *cassoni* were made for bridal trousseaux, with one bearing the husband's armorial and the other that of the bride. Richly adorned and often painted, some are among the finest examples of Renaissance craftsmanship.

Early examples have painted panels depicting Roman triumphs and battles, and, in northern Italy, religious subjects. Others had gilded carving and intarsia decoration. More intricate 16th-century designs included carved and polished wood versions of antique sarcophagi on lion-paw supports.

A variant on the cassone was the *casapanca*, to which a back and arms were added, enabling the piece to double as a storage chest and a seat.

Castagno, Andrea del (ADOPTED NAME OF ANDREA DI BARTOLO DE BARGILLA) (*c.* 1421–1457)

Italian painter, active in Florence. His work, for example his *David* (*c.* 1450–57, National Gallery, Washington, DC), which develops from that of ◊Masaccio, is powerful and sculptural in effect, showing clear outlines and an interest in foreshortening.

He was called Castagno after Castagno San Godenzo, the town where he spent his early life. He attracted the notice of Bernardetto de' Medici (1393–1465), who took him to Florence, where he mainly worked, though he stayed in Venice for a time and painted frescoes at San Zaccaria. The Convent of Sant'Apollonia, now a Castagno museum, has major works in fresco including his *Last Supper,* a *Crucifixion*, and the series of famous men and women, in which the writers Dante, Petrarch, and Boccaccio figure (originally a decoration for the Villa Carducci Pandalfini at Legnaia). In these frescoes he followed Masaccio's lead in adapting the pictorial space, with its carefully constructed linear perspective, to the architectural framework of the building. The figures have a sculptural quality and grandeur that derives in part from ◊Donatello. Castagno died of the plague in Florence. Despite his short life, he was widely influential.

Among his few other works are the equestrian portrait of Nicolò da Tolentino in the Cathedral of Florence, an *Assumption* (Berlin), a *Crucifixion* (National Gallery, London), and stained glass in Florence Cathedral.

Castanheda, Fernão Lopes de (*c.* 1500–1559)

Portuguese chronicler. Castanheda was born in Santarém, Portugal. His studies were interrupted in 1528 when he accompanied his father, a magistrate, to Goa, India. He remained there for ten years, collecting both oral and documentary material for a projected history of India. Returning to Portugal in 1538, he completed his studies at Coimbra, where he remained as a beadle and archivist due to family financial circumstances. He became involved in university intellectual life; one of his academic friends, Nicolau de Grouchy, translated his chronicle of the Portuguese in India into French in 1553.

Castanheda *História do descobrimento e conquista da India pelos portugueses/History of the Discovery and Conquest of India by the Portuguese* ran to ten volumes, although only I to VIII (1551–61) were published during his lifetime, IX and X remaining unpublished because of political sensitivities. The first work of its kind, it was immensely popular and was translated into French, Castilian, Italian, and (in 1582) English. Castanheda stressed his narrative was drawn from personal experience, not hearsay (a veiled reference to João de ◊Barros's chronicle), which drew praise from Barros's successor Diogo do ◊Couto.

Castellesi, Adriano (*c.* 1461–1521)

Tuscan cleric and ineffectual plotter. After a time in England where he was papal collector of taxes from 1489, he found favour with Pope Alexander VI, who made him bishop of Hereford in 1502 (he was translated to Bath and Wells in 1504) and cardinal in 1503.

After Alexander's papacy, he was suspected of slandering Julius II and plotting the assassination of Leo X (the Petrucci conspiracy). He twice fled Rome for Venice, and was murdered on a return journey.

Castellesi was also something of a poet; more significantly, he was a defender of Johannes ◊Reuchlin, who dedicated to him *De Accentibus et Orthographia* (1518).

Castellio, Sebastian (SEBASTIEN CHÂTEILLON) (1515–1563)

French teacher and translator. He was an early follower of the reformer John ◊Calvin, but they later quarrelled over doctrinal issues and Castellio's humanist sympathies. Calvin's support for the execution of ◊Servetus in 1553 led Castellio to write his best-known work, *De Haereticis/On Heresy*, a defence of religious toleration. He translated the Bible into French and into Latin.

Born at St Martin de Fresne, near Nantua in Savoy, Castellio was educated at Lyons and kept a school there. After reading Calvin's *Institutio* he went to Strasbourg in 1540 and, having met Calvin, he was converted to the reformed religion and accompanied Calvin to Geneva.

He was appointed rector of the college at Geneva, but his humanism later brought him into conflict with Calvin and in 1544 he was forced to move to Basel. In 1552 he was appointed professor of Greek at Basel. He deplored the execution of Servetus and broke entirely with Calvin and Beza after the publication of his plea for religious tolerance.

Castellio's Latin Bible, a version noted for its Classical elegance, appeared 1546–51 and was dedicated to Edward VI of England. His French version was published in 1555. He was also a translator of Greek and Latin classics. His work on predestination was not published until 1578 and his answer to Calvin's criticisms appeared in 1612.

Castelvetro, Lodovico (1505–1571)

Italian scholar and critic. One of the leading linguists of his day, he wrote on the evolution of Italian, and commentaries on ◊Dante and ◊Petrarch. He also translated Aristotle's *Poetics* and published an influential commentary on it in 1570.

He was born in Modena. His grasp of the histori-

cal evolution of Italian is demonstrated in his *Giunta fatta al ragionamento di Messer Pietro Bembo* (1563) and in his commentaries on Petrarch's *Rime/Poems* and on the first part of Dante's *Inferno*. From 1560 he spent some years in exile after the Inquisition had condemned him for doctrinal irregularities, and he died at Chiavenna, north of Lake Como.

Castiglionchio, Lapo da (1406–1438)

Florentine humanist author. Educated by Alberti and Filelfo, he found employment in several cardinals' households. In his short career, he produced two tracts written in humanist Latin, *Comparatio inter Rem Militarem et Studia Litterarum/A Comparison of Arms and Letters* and *De Curiae Commodis/On the Benefits of Court*. He was a respected and prolific translator from Greek, producing versions of works by Plutarch, Lucian, and Isocrates, among others.

Castiglionchio dedicated his works to a range of leading figures, including ◊Alfonso V, Cosimo de' ◊Medici, and Humfrey, Duke of ◊Gloucester. However, his ◊dedications outnumbered his works since he indulged in the practice of dedicating a text to more than one patron. For example, he presented one of his Plutarch translations to Pope Eugenius IV but he also dedicated the work to Cardinal Giordano Orsini.

Castiglione, Baldassare (1478–1529)

Italian writer and diplomat, from Mantua. He served the courts of Milan 1492–99, Mantua 1500–04 and 1516–24, and Urbino 1504–15. He idealized the court of Urbino in his one extended piece of writing, *Il cortegiano/The ◊Courtier* (1528). He demonstrated the cultural accomplishments befitting a courtier by producing poems in both Latin and Italian (including an elegy on Raphael in 1520); with Cesare Gonzaga, he wrote a dramatic eclogue *Tirsi* (1506), in which he also acted.

Castiglione's career took him across Europe. For Guidobaldo, Duke of Urbino, he visited the court of Henry VII of England in 1506. From 1524 he was papal nuncio to the court of the Holy Roman Emperor Charles V (Charles I of Spain). He was made bishop of Avila, Spain, in 1528 and died in Spain the following year.

Castillejo, Cristóbal de (c. 1491–1550)

Castilian poet. He served Charles V's brother, Archduke (later, King) Ferdinand of Austria at intervals throughout his life, but derived little material benefit from his efforts. In 1515 he entered the Cistercian Order. A competent poet, he rendered passages from Ovid into lively Castilian, as well as Catullus' 'Vivamus, mea Lesbia'. Around 1540 he entered the fray of poetic debate with an attack on the new Italian-style verse forms recently introduced by ◊Boscà and ◊Garcilaso: *Contra los que dejan los metros castellanos y siguen los italianos/Against those who Abandon Castilian Metres and Follow Italian Ones.* Part of his grievance was that Italianate poetry was annoying to read and, rhythmically, was ploddingly slow. Castillejo saw only two of his works published (a burlesque poem, 1542, and a dialogue on women, 1544); these were included in his *Obras/Collected Works* which appeared, pettily censored by the Inquisition, in 1573.

Castro y Bellvís, Guillén de (1569–1631)

Valencian dramatist, sometime captain of the Aragonese coastguard and governor of Scigliano (1607). He was a prolific writer whose main skill lay in his exploitation of 14th- and 15th-century Castilian ballads for dramatic ends.

Among his 43 surviving plays is the two-act *Las mocedades del Cid/The Young Cid* (published in the authorized edition of Part I of his works, 1618), which inspired Corneille's 1636 *Le Cid.* He composed three stage adaptations of ◊Cervantes' works, among these a version based on an episode from *Don ◊Quixote.* Bellvís was a member of the Valencian *Academia de los nocturnos* (Academy of the nightowls), under the suitably nocturnal pseudonym of 'Secreto' ('Secret'). The Academy folded in 1594, but in 1616 Bellvís revived it, renaming it *Montañeses del Parnaso/Parnassian Dwellers.*

Catherine de' Medici (1519–1589)

French queen consort of Henry II, whom she married in 1533; daughter of Lorenzo de' Medici, Duke of Urbino; and mother of Francis II, Charles IX, and Henry III. At first outshone by Henry's mistress Diane de Poitiers (1490–1566), she became regent 1560–63 for Charles IX and remained in power until his death in 1574.

During the religious wars of 1562–69, she first supported the Protestant ◊Huguenots against the Roman Catholic Guises to ensure her own position as ruler; she later opposed them, and has been tradionally implicated in the Massacre of ◊St Bartholomew of 1572.

Catherine of Genoa, St (BORN CATERINA FIESCHI) (1447–1510)

Italian mystic who devoted herself to the sick and to meditation. Her feast day is 15 September.

Catherine of Siena (BORN CATERINA BENICASA) (1347–1380)

Italian mystic, born in Siena. In 1375 she is said to have received on her body the stigmata, the impression of Jesus' wounds. The fame of this miracle forced her to become a public figure and she acted as an emissary for both Florence and the pope. She also wrote a mystical book *Dialogue.* Her feast day is 29 April. She was canonized in 1461.

Her life was painted several times in the 15th century (for example, by ◊Giovanni di Paolo) despite a papal interdict on images of her receiving the stigmata.

Cavalieri, Emilio de' (c. 1550–1602)

Italian composer. He was long in the service of Ferdinando de' Medici at Florence. He was in close touch with the group of professional and amateur musicians known as the camerata, and with them worked towards the evolution of opera; in 1600 he produced *Euridice,* with text by Ottavio Rinuccini and music by Giulio Caccini and Jacopo Peri, the first opera of which the music is extant.

Cavalieri was born in Rome, where he was organist at the Oratorio del Crocifisso 1578–84. In 1589 he oversaw the production of a lavish series of *intermedi* ('interludes'), to celebrate the marriage of Ferdinando to Christine of Lorraine. His own works were still dramatic pieces to be performed in concert form. They include the following, all set to words by Lelio Guidiccioni: *Il satiro, La disperazione di Fileno,* and *Il giuoco della cieca* (all lost), and *La rappresentatione di Anima, et di Corpo,* an allegory produced in 1600 and the first play set throughout to music.

Cavazzoni, Marco Antonio (*c.* 1490–*c.* 1560)

Italian composer, father of Girolamo Cavazzoni. The two *ricercari* from his *Recerchari, Motetti, Canzoni* for organ, published in Venice in 1523, are toccata-like pieces designed as preludes to the two motet arrangements; the *Canzoni* are arrangements of French chansons and the forerunners of the Italian instrumental canzone.

Caxton, William (*c.* 1422–1491)

English printer. He learned the art of printing in Cologne, Germany, in 1471 and set up a press in Belgium where he produced the first book printed in English, his own version of a French romance, *Recuyell of the Historyes of Troye* (1474). Returning to England in 1476, he established himself in London, where he produced the first book printed in England, *Dictes or Sayengis of the Philosophres* (1477).

Caxton, born in Kent, was apprenticed to a London cloth dealer in 1438, and set up his own business in Bruges 1441–70; he became governor of the English merchants there, negotiating on their behalf with the dukes of Burgundy. In 1471 he went to Cologne, where he learned the art of printing, and then set up his own press in Bruges in partnership with Colard Mansion, a calligrapher. The books from Caxton's press in Westminster included editions of the poets Chaucer, John Gower, and John Lydgate (*c.* 1370–1449). He translated many texts from French and Latin and revised some English ones, such as Malory's *Morte d'Arthur.* Altogether he printed about 100 books.

Cecil, Robert (1563–1612)

1st Earl of Salisbury, Secretary of state to Elizabeth I of England, succeeding his father, Lord Burghley; he was afterwards chief minister to James I (James VI of Scotland) whose accession to the English throne he secured. He discovered the Gunpowder Plot, the conspiracy to blow up the king and Parliament in 1605. James I created him Earl of Salisbury in 1605. He was knighted in 1591, and made a baron in 1603 and viscount in 1604.

Cecil, William

See ◊Burghley, William Cecil, 1st Baron Burghley

Celestina, La

Popular Spanish literary character of the 15th and 16th centuries, the 'old bearded woman' (*una vieja barbuda*) of the *Comedia o Tragicomedia de Calisto y Melibea/Comedy or Tragicomedy of Calisto and Melibea.* She was created by the anonymous author of the incomplete *Comedia de Calisto y Melibea/Comedy of Calisto and Melibea,* and her character was retained and elaborated by the Castilian author Fernando de ◊Rojas in his continuation of the work and his subsequent expansion of it into the *Tragicomedia/ Tragicomedy.* Celestina, though, is not the central character in the plot: she is the bawd and sorceress who the lovesick Calisto employs at the suggestion of his servant Sempronio to bring him into (sexual) contact with Melibea. Intertwining with and influencing this plot is the account of relations between Calisto's two servants and Celestina's servant and her cousin. Celestina successfully arranges a meeting between Calisto and Melibea, but is stabbed to death when she refuses Calisto's servants' demands that she reward them for their part in this meeting. The two servants are themselves then promptly killed: leaping from a window they are executed by a passing patrol. Meanwhile, Calisto has climbed into Melibea's garden, satisfied his passion, and then falls to his own death. Melibea, after confessing all to her father, commits suicide by leaping from a tower; the work closes with her father's lament.

The anonymous inspiration for Rojas's expansions of the original work and his *Comedia* (?1499) and *Tragicomedia* (*c.* 1520) are structured as a prose dialogue between the characters. All versions are too long to be classified as theatre, despite Rojas's division of them into ◊autos (acts) and scenes. Instead, scholars have suggested that *La Celestina,* as the work came to be known, was intended to be read aloud by one person to a small group and that the model for this dialogue structure was adapted from 15th-century Latin humanistic comedies. The dialogue form allowed Rojas (and the first author) to present his characters in an ambiguous way – for example, Pármeno and Sempronio observe that Celestina's false ways are the result of her impoverished circumstances. Rojas explained in a new prologue to his expanded version that he had added five acts in the middle of act 14 in response to readers' requests that

Calisto and Melibea's pleasure be prolonged; moreover he had changed the title from the original author's *Comedia* to *Tragicomedia* because the comic opening gives way to a sorry ending.

Printers added Celestina's name to the title page early in the work's history, as, for example, in the 1518 Seville edition of the *Tragicomedia*, the *Libro de Calixto y Melibea y de la puta vieja Celestina/Book of Calisto and Melibea and the Old Whore Celestina*. Juan Luis ◊Vives and Alfonso de ◊Valdés, writing in the 1520s and 1530s, both refer to it as *La Celestina*, and the first French translation (1527) is entitled simply *Celestine*.

Rojas's first version, the 16-act *Comedia*, had probably already circulated in manuscript form before its publication. At least a further 3 editions were published (which, unlike the first one, contained acrostic verses naming Rojas as coauthor) before the 21-act *Tragicomedia* appeared. The earliest extant version is a 1506 Italian translation – in itself testimony to the work's extraordinary popularity – and there were a further 18 Italian editions and 24 French ones. A 22nd act, explicitly not attributed to Rojas, was added in 1526, and this version enjoyed at least 6 editions (the latest dated 1560).

A year before Rojas's death the *Tragicomedia* was versified by another lawyer and author, Juan Sedeño, while its canonical status was confirmed not only by numerous imitations (such as Sancho de Muñón's 1542 *Tragicomedia de Lisandro y Roselia/Tragicomedy of Lisander and Roselia*) but by the appearance of a corrected, scholarly edition published in Salamanca, Spain, in 1570.

I fell acquainted with an old bearded woman called Celestina, a witch, subtle as the devil, and well practised in all the rogueries and villainies that the world can afford [...] she will move hard rocks if she list, and at her pleasure provoke them to luxury.

～

SEMPRONIO on Celestina, Act I, transl. James Mabbe (1631)

Cellini, Benvenuto (1500–1571)

Italian sculptor and goldsmith. Among his works are a graceful bronze *Perseus* (1545–54, Loggia dei Lanzi, Florence) and a gold salt cellar made for Francis I of France (1540–43, Kunsthistorisches Museum, Vienna), topped by nude reclining figures. He wrote an autobiography (begun 1558), which was both frank and boastful (he claimed, for example, to be the man who killed Charles, Duke of ◊Bourbon, at the Sack of Rome).

Cellini was born in Florence and apprenticed to a goldsmith. In 1519 he went to Rome, later worked for the papal mint, and was once imprisoned on a charge of having embezzled pontifical jewels. He worked for some time in France at the court of Francis I, but finally returned to Florence in 1545.

Celtis, Konrad (1459–1508)

German humanist and poet. He taught classics and literature at a number of German universities, wrote plays and poetry, rediscovered German literary works, established a number of debating societies, and edited Latin classics, notably Tacitus' *Germania* in 1500. In 1487 he became the first German ◊poet laureate.

Born into a peasant family near Würzburg, Celtis ran away at 18 to study. He spent the next 20 years studying and teaching at a succession of universities – Cologne, Heidelberg, Erfurt, Rostock, Leipzig, Cracow, Nuremberg, Ingolstadt – before settling at Vienna University in 1497 to teach poetry and rhetoric.

His travels included two years in Italy (1487–89), where he met many Italian humanists. Although generally disillusioned by Italy, he was inspired by the academy of ◊Leto in Rome to start similar societies in Germany where humanists could meet and work together – most notably the 'Sodalitas danubiana' in Vienna. Peutinger and ◊Pirckheimer were among his friends and correspondents.

Celtis's own studies of Greek and Hebrew, his editions of Latin authors, and his Latin dramas were important in the humanist movement, as were his introduction of literary studies to various universities and his ideas on education. Resenting Italian cultural domination, he passionately wanted to revive German culture. Significant here was his discovery in 1492–93 at Regensburg of six Latin dramas by Hrosvitha von Gandersheim, a 10th-century German nun, and his edition of Tacitus' *Germania*.

His great ambition was to write the first comprehensive geographical and historical survey of Germany, although only a few preparatory studies were completed. He was a gifted poet, as seen especially from his *Quattuor Libri Amorum* (1502), a semi-autobiographical verse narrative of four love affairs. He died in Vienna of syphilis.

Cennini, Cennino (*c.* 1370–*c.* 1440)

Italian painter and writer, who wrote a practical manual on painting *Il libro dell'arte/The Book of Art* (*c.* 1390), an important source of information on the workshops of the early Renaissance. None of his paintings survives.

Born in Colle di Val d'Elsa, near Siena, he went to Florence to be a pupil of Agnolo ◊Gaddi, who worked in the tradition of Giotto. The *Book of Art* explains in detail a range of techniques for panel painting and for fresco painting. While, as reflected in contemporary Italian practice, much of the discussion is taken up with painting in *tempera*, he also mentions oil painting as a German practice.

Cennini's work was copied and remained in circulation into the 16th century, when Giorgio Vasari saw a copy.

Centuriators of Magdeburg

The collective name for the authors of *Historia ecclesiae Christi/History of the Church of Christ* (1559–74), a Protestant history of the church century by century until 1400. The book's main aim was to show that papal authority was groundless. A Catholic reply was written by Cesare ◊Baronius.

Among the Centuriators were Matthias Flacius (Vlacic), Nicolaus von Amsdorf, Johann Wigand, Nicolaus Gallus (Hahn), and Matthäus Judex (Richter). The work was begun about 1550 at Magdeburg and continued from 1562 at Regensburg (Ratisbon); it was published in Basle. Broad in conception, but often inaccurate in detail, it was cogently attacked by Baronius.

Certon, Pierre (DIED 1572)

French composer. He was in the Sainte-Chapelle in Paris in 1532, and became choirmaster there before 1542 and chaplain in 1548. As a canon of Notre Dame at Melun he founded an annual service there.

Works include:
Masses, about 50 motets, psalms, canticles, about 200 chansons.

Cervantes Saavedra, Miguel de (1547–1616)

Castilian author, soldier, and sometime civil servant. Born at Alcalá de Henares, of humble origins, he studied in Madrid under the humanist scholar Juan López de Hoyos (*c.* 1566–67), who in 1569 was responsible for publishing Cervantes's first writings (funerary poems on the late Queen Isabel). Cervantes may have left Madrid 1567–68; he may also have been charged with assault in 1569. Later that year he was in Italy, in Cardinal Claudio Acquaviva's entourage, but soon joined the army, fighting at Lepanto (1571) where he lost his left hand. Held captive in Algiers for five years, despite four escape attempts, Cervantes was ransomed by his family and returned to Madrid in 1580. He twice requested, and was twice refused, permission to emigrate to America (1582, 1590), instead obtaining minor government posts in Andalusia. In addition to these jobs, and despite a seven month spell in Seville jail for debts (he never became a rich man) Cervantes wrote constantly – and successfully – from 1580 until his death.

Cervantes's literary output was as varied as it was vast. Although only two of his plays from the 1580s have survived, in 1585 he published *La Galatea/Galatea*, a work which may in fact have been drafted years earlier. *Galatea* was a ◊pastoral novel, composed in the wake of ◊Montemayor's popular *La Diana*. The 'second part' promised by Cervantes never, however, materialized. Although it seems he continued to write in the following decades (in a 1592 contract Cervantes exempts his patron from payment if he judges his six plays anything less than the best ever seen in Spain) he published nothing until 1605, the year in which part I of *El Ingenioso Hidalgo Don Quixote de la Mancha/The Ingenious Knight ◊Don Quixote of La Mancha* appeared. 1613 saw the publication of his *Novelas ejemplares/Exemplary Novels*, 12 stories of diverse and original content without any clear literary precedents. The second part of *Don Quixote* appeared in 1615, as did a collection of short plays (in part a response to the works of Lope de ◊Vega), the *Ocho comedias y ocho entremeses nunca representados/Eight Comedies and Eight Farcical Interludes, Never Before Performed*.

Cervantes's final work, *Los trabajos de Persiles y Sigismunda. Historia septentrional/The Labours of Persiles and Sigismunda: A Northern Tale* (1617), with its labyrinthine plot and simple characterization, drew on the traditions of the ◊Byzantine novel.

Cesalpino, Andrea (1519–1603)
Italian botanist who showed in his *De plantis* (1583) that plants could be classified in Aristotelian fashion by their anatomy and structure. Before this plants were classed by their location – for example marsh plants, moorland plants, and even foreign plants. (See ◊Botany.)

Cesariano, Cesare (c. 1477–1553)
Italian architect and painter, mainly active in Milan. He considered ◊Bramante, whom he met at the Milanese court, his main teacher. His early works were frescoes in Reggio Emilia and Parma; he had returned to Milan by 1513 where he was employed over the next years on work at Milan Cathedral and fortifications at the Castello Sforza. At the same time he produced a translation and commentary on ◊Vitruvius (printed 1521), with woodcuts developed from those already produced by ◊Giocondo.

Céspedes, Pablo de (1548–1608)
Spanish painter, sculptor, and architect. He studied under the brothers ◊Zuccaro in Rome, where he copied Michelangelo and Raphael Sanzio, returning to Spain in 1575. He produced crowded religious pictures influenced by the Italians' style, as in his *Last Supper* (Museo de Bellas Artes, Seville).

chambers of rhetoric
Amateur literary societies in the Netherlands and France during the 15th and 16th centuries. The members were mainly middle-class townspeople who formed associations similar to guilds in order to promote their love of poetry and drama. The chambers of rhetoric often organized public celebrations.

They were usually very traditional in their literary interests, but in the Netherlands (where they were called *rederijkers*) they did play an important role in the development of secular drama and then poetry. The leading Dutch writers to emerge from the *rederijker* tradition were Dirck ◊Coornheert and Henrick Spiegel.

The chambers of rhetoric were the literary equivalent of ◊*Meistergesang* guilds in Germany. They were not usually innovative in their literary enterprises or particularly quick to respond to Renaissance ideas. In the Netherlands they did, however, encourage the development of an increasingly self-conscious and ambitious national literature. An example is the play *Elckerlijk* (c. 1495), the probable source for the English morality play *Everyman*.

Significant Dutch writers associated with the *rederijker* tradition include: Cornelis Everaert (c. 1480–1556), playwright and member of De Drie Santinnen chamber in Bruges; Matthijs de Castelein (1485–1550), author of the first Dutch treatise on poetry, *De Const van Rhetoriken* (1548); Colijn van Rijssele, the 15th-century author of the middle-class drama cycle *De Spiegel der Minnen/The Mirror of Love*; and Anna Bijns (1493–1575), a schoolmistress in Antwerp.

Chambord, Château de
Royal château near Blois in the Loire Valley, central France. Begun by ◊Francis I in 1519 and completed in about 1540, it was probably designed by Domenico da Cortona, although it may also reflect the inspiration of Leonardo da Vinci (who died in France the year it was begun). It incorporated Renaissance features, in particular, the Greek cross layout of the keep probably imitating the Medici villa at Poggio a Caiano, but also contained a double spiral staircase. At the same time, there are many elements characteristic of recent French and Burgundian architecture – the most clearly seen are hundreds of chimneys, turrets, gables, and pinnacles that crowd the skyline.

It was built on the site of a royal hunting lodge on the banks of the River Cosson, a tributary of the Loire, east of Blois. The construction was carried out by French builders and designers, including Jacques Sourdeau, Pierre Neveu, and Denis Sourdeau. Despite the layout of the keep, the basic plan is that of a medieval castle, while its 440 rooms were decorated in Italian classicizing style.

Champlain, Samuel de (1567–1635)
French pioneer, soldier, and explorer in Canada. Having served in the army of Henry IV and on an expedition to the West Indies, he began his exploration

of Canada in 1603. In a third expedition in 1608 he founded and named Quebec, and was appointed lieutenant governor of French Canada in 1612.

Chapman, George (c. 1559–1634)

English poet and dramatist. His translations of the Greek epics of Homer (completed 1616) were the earliest in England; his plays include the comedy *Eastward Ho* (with Ben ◊Jonson and John ◊Marston, 1605) and the tragedy *Bussy d'Ambois* (1607).

Chapman's translations of Homer are among the most faithful to the original in English verse. Of his plays, *All Fools* (1605) and *The Widow's Tears* (1612) are among his better comedies, whereas *Bussy d'Ambois* is a tragedy written in the tradition of the Roman writer Lucius Seneca. Chapman also published several other translations and various poetical works.

Chapman was born in Hitchin, Hertfordshire. He is said to have been educated at Oxford, which he left for London about 1576. There he settled at once to a literary career, was patronized by Thomas Walsingham, Henry, Prince of Wales, and powerful noblemen including Robert Carr, Earl of Somerset, and became friendly with the writers Shakespeare, Edmund Spenser, Samuel Daniel, Christopher Marlowe, Ben Jonson, and the architect Inigo Jones.

Charles (VI) the Mad (OR THE WELL-BELOVED) (1368–1422)

King of France from 1380, succeeding his father Charles V; he was under the regency of his uncles until 1388. He became mentally unstable in 1392, and civil war broke out between the dukes of Orléans and Burgundy. Henry V of England invaded France in 1415, conquering Normandy, and in 1420 forced Charles to sign the Treaty of Troyes, recognizing Henry as his successor.

Charles VII (1403–1461)

King of France from 1429. Son of Charles VI, he was excluded from the succession by the Treaty of Troyes, but recognized by the south of France. In 1429 Joan of Arc raised the siege of Orléans and had him crowned at Reims. He organized France's first standing army and by 1453 had expelled the English from all of France except Calais.

Charles VIII (1470–1498)

King of France from 1483, when he succeeded his father, Louis XI. In 1494 he unsuccessfully tried to claim the Neapolitan crown, and when he entered Naples in 1495 he was forced to withdraw by a coalition of Milan, Venice, Spain, and the Holy Roman Empire. He defeated them at Fornovo, but lost Naples. He died while preparing a second expedition.

Charles V (1500–1558)

Holy Roman Emperor 1519–56. Son of Philip of Burgundy and Joanna of Castile, he inherited vast possessions, which led to rivalry from Francis I of France, whose alliance with the Ottoman Empire brought Vienna under siege in 1529 and 1532. Charles was also in conflict with the Protestants in Germany until the Treaty of Passau of 1552, which allowed the Lutherans religious liberty.

Charles was born in Ghent and received the Netherlands from his father in 1506; Spain, Naples, Sicily, Sardinia, and the Spanish dominions in North Africa and the Americas on the death of his maternal grandfather, Ferdinand V of Castile (1452–1516); and from his paternal grandfather, Maximilian I, the Habsburg dominions in 1519, when he was elected emperor. He was crowned in Aachen in 1520. From 1517 the empire was split by the rise of Lutheranism, Charles making unsuccessful attempts to reach a settlement at Augsburg in 1530 (see Confession of ◊Augsburg), and being forced by the Treaty of Passau to yield most of the Protestant demands. Worn out, he abdicated in favour of his son Philip II in the Netherlands in 1555 and Spain in 1556. He yielded the imperial crown to his brother Ferdinand I, and retired to the monastery of Yuste, Spain.

Charles VIII (1408–1470)

King of Sweden from 1448. He was elected regent of Sweden in 1438, when Sweden broke away from Denmark and Norway. He stepped down in 1441 when Christopher III of Bavaria (1418–1448) was elected king, but after his death became king. He was twice expelled by the Danes and twice restored.

Charles the Bold, Duke of Burgundy (1433–1477)

Son of Philip the Good, he inherited Burgundy and

the Low Countries from him in 1465. He waged wars attempting to free the duchy from dependence on France and restore it as a kingdom. He was killed in battle.

Charles's ambition was to create a kingdom stretching from the mouth of the Rhine to the mouth of the Rhône. He formed the League of the Public Weal against Louis XI of France, invaded France in 1471, and conquered the country as far as Rouen. The Holy Roman Emperor, the Swiss, and Lorraine united against him; he captured Nancy, but was defeated at Granson and again at Morat in 1476. Nancy was lost, and he was killed while attempting to recapture it. His possessions in the Netherlands passed to the Habsburgs by the marriage of his daughter Mary to Maximilian I of Austria.

Charonton (QUARTON), Enguerrand (LIVED MID-15TH CENTURY)

French painter active in Avignon where he created the altarpiece *The Coronation of the Virgin* (1453, Hospice of Villeneuve-lès-Avignon). The contract for this work survives, making both authorship and date precise.

Another document of 1454 shows that he painted the *Madonna of Mercy* (Musée Condé, Chantilly) in collaboration with Pierre Vilatte of Limoges. Charonton was at one time identified with the Master of Avignon, but this suggestion has since been discarded.

Charron, Pierre (1541–1603)

French writer and preacher. He was a close friend of ◊Montaigne, whose *Essais* influenced his own neostoic *De la Sagesse/Wisdom* (1601), in which he argued for religious tolerance. The book's sceptical claim that it is impossible to know anything for certain was severely censured by the Sorbonne and leading figures in the Catholic Church.

Born in Paris, the son of a bookseller, he was one of a family of 25 children. After studying law at Orléans and Bourges he practised as an advocate, but became disenchanted with the profession. He turned to the church and enjoyed a distinguished career as a preacher, becoming chaplain-in-ordinary to Margaret of Valois, first wife of Henry of Navarre. In 1588 he returned to Paris determined to join a religious order,

but, when none would accept him because of his age, he retired to Bordeaux where he became a close friend of Montaigne.

Charron's earlier writings were less than tolerant: he published anonymously the treatise *Les Trois vérités/The Three Truths* (1593), which combined an apology for Catholicism with an attack on the Protestant religious leader Philippe ◊du Plessis-Mornay.

Chastellain, Georges (c. 1404–1475)

Burgundian poet and chronicler. Employed by both ◊Philip the Good and ◊Charles the Bold, he wrote *Chronique des ducs de Bourgogne/Chronicle of the Dukes of Burgundy* and other similar chronicles, and a number of epitaphs, rondeaux, and ballades.

Chaucer, Geoffrey (c. 1340–1400)

English poet. *The Canterbury Tales*, a collection of stories told by a group of pilgrims on their way to Canterbury, reveals his knowledge of human nature and his stylistic variety, from urbane and ironic to simple and bawdy. His early work shows formal French influence, as in the dream-poem *The Book of the Duchess* and his adaptation of the French allegorical poem on courtly love, *The Romaunt of the Rose*. More mature works reflect the influence of Italian realism, as in *Troilus and Criseyde*, a substantial narrative poem about the tragic betrayal of an idealized courtly love, adapted from ◊Boccaccio. In *The Canterbury Tales* he shows his own genius for metre and characterization. Chaucer was the most influential English poet of the Middle Ages.

He was born in London, the son of a vintner. Taken prisoner in the French wars, he had to be ransomed by Edward III in 1360. In 1366 he married Philippa Roet, sister of Katherine Swynford, the mistress and later third wife of John of Gaunt, Duke of Lancaster. Payments during the period 1367–74 indicate a rising fortune and show that Chaucer made several journeys abroad, both on military service and public business. He was sent to Italy (where he may have met Boccaccio and ◊Petrarch), France, and Flanders. He was controller of wool customs 1374–86, and of petty customs 1382–86. He became justice of the peace for Kent in 1385 and knight of the shire in 1386. In 1389 he was made clerk of the king's works, and superintended undertakings at Woolwich and Smithfield. In 1391 he gave up the clerkship and accepted the position of deputy forester of North Petherton, Somerset. Late in 1399 he moved to Westminster and died the following year; he was buried in the Poets' Corner of Westminster Abbey.

The first of his poems that can be dated with certainty, *The Book of the Duchess*, was written as an elegy on the Duke of Lancaster's first wife, Blanche, who died in 1369. This was one of four allegorical dream-poems; he also wrote several love complaints, a group of moral and personal ballades, and another (unfinished) collection of tales, *The Legend of Good Women*. Many of his works cannot be dated exactly but the list of works in the first *Prologue to The Legend of Good Women* (1385–86) gives evidence of earlier writings, while topical references and dedications often help with dating in general. His dream-poem *The Parliament of Fowls*, in which birds debate a dispute of love, is usually dated 1382 from its connection with Richard II's marriage. The translation of Boethius's *De Consolatione Philosophiae* as well as *Troilus and Criseyde* and *The Knight's Tale* probably also belong to the first half of the 1380s.

Though the *Prologue* and the general plan of *The Canterbury Tales* are thought to be later work, the tales themselves probably incorporated a good deal of earlier material. In the envoy to *The Complaint to his Empty Purse*, Chaucer implores Henry IV for increased payments, suggesting 1399 as the date. *A Treatise on the Astrolabe* (an introductory manual on the construction and use of the astronomical instrument) as well as the revised version of the *Prologue to The Legend of Good Women* belong to the 1390s. *The Canterbury Tales* were left unfinished at his death. Difficult to date are *Anelida and Arcite* and the unfinished dream-poem *The House of Fame*.

Though Chaucer's themes are rarely his own invention, there is a recurring and profound originality in his handling of them. Much of his poetry is concerned with varying concepts of love – human, divine, and philosophical – and in order to show their various aspects he sets them in a dramatic context beside marriage, tyranny, lust, ill fortune, faithlessness, and death. The contrasting demands of human love and rationality is also a favourite theme, and *Troilus and Criseyde* may owe something of its time-less appeal to the conflict found in it between idealizing human love and the values of eternal life.

With similar versatility and through his use of critical and ironic undertones Chaucer also produces refreshing variations on an accepted literary style. The dream-allegory as well as the love narrative show new possibilities under his treatment, while the technique in *The Canterbury Tales* of ascribing each of the stories to a character introduced in a prologue produces a many-layered interest. Chaucer's profound insight into character and situation and the final values that emerge are based firmly on a deeply Christian view of life. The Canterbury pilgrims have an animation and a solidarity that makes them immediately sympathetic to a modern reader, and the element of appraisal surrounding this colourful gathering adds greatly to the flavour with which each individual emerges: the Wife of Bath, the Pardoner, the Knight, Madam Eglantine, and Chaucer himself. As in all his work, warmth and humour soften the portrayal of vice and wretchedness, and they are presented together with more wholesome joys and sorrows in a positive universal picture of humanity.

Cheke, John (1514–1557)

English Classical scholar. The first regius professor of Greek at Cambridge 1540–51, he translated several Greek texts into Latin and was largely responsible for introducing the Erasmian pronunciation of Greek. Though he published little in English, he was an advocate of the English language as a mode of literary expression, deploring the introduction of foreign terms and preferring phrases derived from earlier English usage.

A Protestant, Cheke was appointed tutor to Edward, Prince of Wales, in 1544; sat as member of Parliament for Bletchingley in 1547 and 1553; and was appointed provost of King's College in 1548. He was ordained a cleric before 1549. On Edward VI's death, Cheke supported the attempt to stop Mary's succession; she imprisoned him in 1553–54. He then retired to Basel, Switzerland, travelled in Italy, and taught Greek for a living in Strasbourg. Arrested by order of Philip II of Spain while returning from a visit to Brussels in 1556, he was sent to London, imprisoned in the Tower, and compelled by threat of torture to abjure Protestantism.

Chelčický, Petr (c. 1390–c. 1460)

Czech writer and theologian. The most influential writer of the Hussite religious reformation movement, he composed a number of Bible commentaries and treatises, written in a vigorous, popular style, among them *The Net of Faith*.

Chelčický was a believer in nonviolence, and held that true Christians should refrain from the pursuit of riches and power.

Chenonceau, Château de

A château in central France, 28 km/17 mi southwest of Paris, bridging the River Cher. It was begun in 1513 by Thomas Bohier, the financial minister of Normandy, but was subsequently confiscated by Francis I and became a royal residence in 1535. It was inherited by Henry II who presented it to his mistress ◊Diane de Poitiers.

Incorporating a single tower from an earlier building of the 15th century, the château is noted for its combination of Gothic and Renaissance features. Diane de Poitiers added an arched bridge spanning the Cher, designed by the leading architect Philibert ◊De l'Orme. When the château passed to Catherine de' Medici this wing was enlarged 1570–78 by Jean ◊Bullant as the Grande Galerie.

Chettle, Henry (c. 1560–c. 1607)

English dramatist and pamphleteer. In 1595 he published the romance story *Piers Plainnes Seaven Yeres Prentisship*, and between then and 1603 he wrote or collaborated on over 40 plays. Of his own plays, written for Philip ◊Henslowe's Rose Theatre, London, *The Tragedy of Hoffman* was the only one to be printed (1631) and the only one to survive. He also wrote the poem *England's Mourning Garment* (1603), an elegy on Queen Elizabeth I.

Chettle was born in London and became apprenticed to a stationer. In 1592 he published Robert ◊Greene's *A Groat's-Worth of Wit* and in 1593 found it necessary to produce his own *Kind Hart's Dream*, apologizing to three people abused in Greene's work, of whom Shakespeare appears to have been one. Chettle's own plays include *Troyes Revenge* and the tragedy *Polefeme*. In *The Pleasant Comodie of Patient Grissill* (1603) he collaborated with Thomas Dekker and William Haughton, and in

The Death of Robert, Earle of Huntingdon (1601) with Anthony Munday.

chiaroscuro (ITALIAN 'LIGHT-DARK')

In painting and graphic art, the balanced use of light and shade, particularly where contrasting luminous and opaque materials are represented, for example, glinting metal and dark velvet.

Chigi, Agostino, KNOWN AS 'IL MAGNIFICO' (1465–1520)

Italian banker and patron of the arts. He founded his bank in Rome in 1485 where he became in effect the pope's banker. His Villa Farnesina near Rome was built by the architect ◊Peruzzi (1508–11) and decorated with a cycle of frescoes by ◊Raphael (c. 1518).

Chigi was a member of a noted Sienese family. In 1500 he became lessor of the papal alum mines and church treasurer. His position enabled him to exert financial influence in several European countries and also allowed him to patronize the leading artists and architects of his day, notably Peruzzi, Perugino, Sebastiano del Piombo, and Raphael, who designed a private chapel for him in the Church of Santa Maria del Popolo.

Chigi was also a patron of scholarship and literature, and with his support the Cretan-born publisher Zacharias Calliergis (c. 1473–c. 1524) set up the first Greek press in Rome and published an important edition of Pindar in 1515.

chivalry

That most 'medieval' of concepts – the forms and conventions of aristocratic warrior lifestyle – enjoyed, in truth, a heyday during the period called 'the Renaissance'. This was not just a matter of literary subject matter, with epics like the works of Torquato ◊Tasso and ◊Spenser's *Faerie Queene*, providing grand expositions of chivalric themes. The occasion which inspired Politian's *Stanze* was a joust which occurred in Medicean Florence in 1475. And that was by no means an isolated occasion: the extravagance of chivalric events like tournaments was a fashionable display of magnificence for rulers (and popular, blood-thirsty days out for the spectators) throughout these two centuries.

The allusiveness, the symbolism, of such occasions

may have become more recondite, with increasing use at tournaments and at royal ceremonies of Classical references, although it remains a moot point how appreciated such allusions were by their audience. However, behind that addition of extra mythical figures to be invoked and compared to living characters, the substance of such occasions was constant: the identification of an exclusive group of people, united by bonds of loyalty and hierarchy. At the same time, chivalric displays also spoke, as they had always done, an international language. Indeed, diplomacy was often executed with a chivalric veneer, both at 'summit meetings' like the Field of the Cloth of Gold when Henry VIII and Francis I vied to present the more resplendent pavilion, and at the celebrations which often greeted the (often short-lived) peace treaties: it was at one such joust that ◊Henry II of France was hit in the eye by a lance and died a few days later.

Alongside such events, there were the institutions of the chivalric orders. The first of these was the Order of the Band of Alfonso XI of Castile (1330), soon followed by the Order of the Garter, founded by Edward III of England in 1348. But if a chivalric order was a 14th-century invention, they enjoyed a heyday during the 15th. The Order of the Golden Fleece (replete with its inapposite Classical allusion) was founded by Philip the Good of Burgundy in 1431; this was preceded by the Emperor ◊Sigismund's Order of the Dragon (*c.* 1413) and followed by orders founded by, for example, ◊René of Anjou and Louis XI of France. These orders, which met once a year for a religious service and a feast, were not just a method of a ruler celebrating the physical prowess of his leading knights; they were also used as a tool of international relations, with foreign princes elected to an order. So, for example, Philip the Good had Alfonso V of Aragon elected as one of the first members of the Order of the Golden Fleece in 1445 – and, to make this a reciprocal arrangement, was elected in turn to Alfonso's own chivalric order. Again, when Baldassare ◊Castiglione visited Henry VII's England it was in order to receive the Garter on behalf of his lord, Guidobaldo da Montefeltro.

If chivalry did eventually become less potent, it was not because of the classicizing ideals called 'Renaissance' but because of technology. The long

'military revolution' stretched from the introduction of gunpowder to the 17th-century professionalization of armies. While the early changes in weaponry may have affected fortifications and death rates more than they did the perception of war, the later transformations in military organization made the idea of the knight on horseback outdated. And, yet, the 17th century still did not see the death of chivalric orders: they were too important simply to be pensioned off when circumstances changed.

Christian I (1426–1481)

King of Denmark from 1448, and founder of the Oldenburg dynasty. In 1450 he established the union of Denmark and Norway that lasted until 1814. He was king of Sweden 1457–64 and 1465–67.

Christian II (1481–1559)

King of Denmark and Norway 1513–23, and Sweden 1520–23. He was hated by the nobility in Denmark and Norway for his system of taxation. Jutland (Denmark) revolted and gave the Danish crown to Frederick I in 1523. Christian fled to the Netherlands, but attempted to regain his throne in 1531 by invading Norway. He was captured by Danish forces in 1532 and imprisoned until his death.

Christian was the son of King John II of Norway and Denmark and Christina of Saxony, and he married Isabella of Burgundy. The Swedes refused to accept him on his accession and held out against him for some time, but were defeated near Stockholm in 1520. After the heads of the nation had sworn loyalty, Christian gave a banquet and had most of his guests seized and imprisoned. About 82 people were executed or drowned by his order the following day (the 'Stockholm Bloodbath'). In 1523 Sweden successfully broke away under King Gustav I Vasa. Norway remained under the Danish crown.

Christian III (1503–1559)

King of Denmark and Norway from 1534. During his reign the Reformation was introduced.

Christine de Pisan (1364–*c.* 1430)

French poet and historian. Her works include love lyrics, philosophical poems, a poem in praise of Joan of Arc, a history of Charles V of France, and various defences of women, including *La Cité des dames/The City of Ladies* (1405).

She championed her sex against the satire of Jean de Meun (who completed the *Roman de la Rose*) in *Epitre du dieu d'amour/Epistle of the God of Love* (1399), as also in *Dit de la rose/Tale of the Rose* (1402).

Born in Venice, she was brought to France as a child when her father entered the service of Charles V. In 1389, after the death of her husband, the Picardian nobleman Etienne Castel, she began writing to support herself and her family. She tells her own story in *La Vision/The Vision* (1405). *Livre des trois vertus/The Book of Three Virtues* (1407) provides a description of the domestic life of the time.

Christus, Petrus (*c.* 1410–1472/73)

Flemish painter. He was a citizen of Bruges from 1444 and follower of Jan van ◊Eyck (some of whose paintings he may have completed after the master's death). His *Madonna with Two Saints* (1457, Städel, Frankfurt) is an early example of the use of perspective in northern European art.

His portraits, such as *Portrait of a Young Woman* (*c.* 1450, Staatliche Museum, Berlin), have a gentle sensuality and inward gaze unlike the starker realism of his contemporaries. His two major works are the *Legend of St Eloi* with its minute detailing of jewel and metal, texture, and reflection; and the *Lamentation* (*c.* 1457, Brussels), exquisite in its play of line and detail.

Chrysoloras, Manuel (*c.* 1350–1415)

Byzantine diplomat and Greek teacher from Constantinople. He was sent to Italy by Emperor Manuel II Palaeologus in 1394 to seek support for the Byzantine Empire against the Turks. Some of his hosts proved more interested in his educational skills than his political message: ◊Salutati probably had him invited to Florence to teach Greek; he took up his post in 1397. However, he moved to Pavia, the university of Florence's enemy, Milan, in 1400. His later career involved diplomatic missions for the Byzantine emperor across Europe; he died at the Council of ◊Constance.

Chrysoloras can be described, with little exaggeration, as the well spring of Florentine interest in Greek. His pupils in Florence included Leonardo ◊Bruni, Pier Paolo ◊Vergerio, Palla Strozzi, and Roberto Rossi. When Chrysoloras returned to Constantinople in 1403 he was followed by ◊Guarino, who himself became an influential teacher of Greek.

Chrysoloras's writings include *Erotemata/Questions*, which proved an accessible and popular textbook of Greek grammar. He also, with the help of Uberto Decembrio (a colleague from his Milanese days), produced a translation of the first books of Plato's *Republic*, which later inspired another translation by Uberto's son Pier Candido ◊Decembrio.

Churchyard, Thomas (*c.* 1520–1604)

English poet. He produced a number of broadsheet ballads including *Shore's Wife* (1563), *Churchyard's Chips* (1575), and *The Worthiness of Wales* (1587).

He was born in Shrewsbury, Shropshire. He began his career as a page to the Earl of Surrey, served as a soldier in various wars, and was given a pension by Elizabeth I.

Cigoli, Lodovico Cardi da (1559–1613)

Italian painter. Nearly all of his paintings are fervent treatments of religious subjects, usually saints, such as his *St Peter Healing the Lame Man at the Beautiful Gate of the Temple* for St Peter's in Rome. He also wrote treatises on perspective and on ◊colore.

Born at Cigoli in Tuscany, he was a pupil of Alessandro ◊Allori and Santi di Tito but was more influenced by the works of ◊Michelangelo, ◊Pontormo, and ◊Andrea del Sarto. His works include *The Conversion of St Paul* in the Church of San Paolo fuori le Mure and the fresco *The Story of Psyche* in the Villa Borghese.

After travelling in Lombardy he returned to Florence, where he executed paintings for the Palazzo Pitti at the request of the grand duke, and also frescoes in the Church of Santa Maria Novella (1581–84). He died in Rome.

Cima, Giovanni (ALSO KNOWN AS CIMA DA CONEGLIANO) Battista, (*c.* 1459–*c.* 1517)

Venetian painter. His use of colour was distinctive and he often set his Madonnas against a landscape: his *Virgin and Child* used his native town and its castle as the background. His work resembles that of

Giovanni Bellini, whose studio foreman he is said to have been.

Cima was a prolific artist, and there are paintings by him in various churches in Venice and a number of galleries, including Milan, Munich, Dresden, the Louvre, and the National Gallery, London.

Cincius Romanus

Romanized name of the humanist translator Cencio de' ◊Rustici.

cire perdue (OR LOST-WAX TECHNIQUE)

Bronze-casting method. A model is made of wax and enclosed in an envelope of clay and plaster, with a small hole in the bottom.

When heat is applied, the wax melts and runs away through the hole, and the clay and plaster becomes a hard mould. Molten bronze is poured in and allowed to cool; then the clay envelope is cut away.

The result is a bronze cast that exactly reproduces the original and is formed in a single piece. The bronze will be hollow if the original wax model was made around a core of burnt clay.

Civitali, Matteo (1436–1501)

Italian architect and sculptor. He was born and died in Lucca, and most of his work remains in and around the city. The cathedral there contains tombs by Civitali, a pulpit (1494–98), and the Tempietto del Volto Santo (1484), an octagonal marble shrine housing a wooden image of Christ traditionally believed to have been the work of the biblical figure Nicodemus.

Outside Lucca, Civitali has a lectern and candelabra in the cathedral at Pisa and statues of Old Testament figures in Genoa Cathedral. Civitali was also the original architect of Lucca's Palazzo Pretorio (1492).

Clanvowe, John (c. 1341–1391)

English poet and courtier. His poem *The Cuckoo and the Nightingale* was once attributed to Geoffrey Chaucer and later associated with his nephew Thomas Clanvowe, but it is now ascribed, together with a religious treatise in prose, *The Two Ways*, to the elder Clanvowe.

Clavius, Christopher (CHRISTOPH KLAU) (1537–1612)

German mathematician and astronomer. A leading Jesuit and professor of mathematics at the College of Rome, he was frequently consulted by the Vatican on controversial scientific matters. The best-known case was his defence of the Copernican system against the theories of Galileo. His books on mathematics were among the most widely used mathematics textbooks in the 17th century.

Between 1588 and 1603 he wrote no fewer than five separate works defending the calendar reforms of Pope Gregory XIII in 1582. He was again called upon in 1611 to advise the Vatican authorities upon the reliability and significance of Galileo's telescopic observations of the Moon. While responding sympathetically to Galileo's work, he advised, nonetheless, that the observations did not constitute a convincing proof of tne Copernican system. He argued that the lunar mountains described by Galileo – which indicated that the celestial system was not unchanging – were covered with a smooth but transparent crystalline surface.

His widely used textbooks were *Epitome Arithmeticae* (1583) and *Algebra* (1608). He also published a major treatise on gnomonics in 1581, and in 1612 he wrote a treatise on the construction and use of sundials.

Clemens non Papa (ALTERNATIVE NAME OF JACQUES CLÉMENT) (c. 1510–c. 1556)

Franco-Flemish composer. Clemens was a prolific composer known chiefly for his sacred works, especially his settings of *souterliedekens*, the Dutch psalms. He produced over 400 works, including Masses, motets, psalms in Flemish, and chansons.

The reason for the *non Papa* ('not the pope') in his name is uncertain, though it was probably coined as a joke, for Pope Clement VII died in 1534, and the name was not used in a publication until 1545.

He was succentor at Bruges Cathedral 1544–45, and in late 1550 was at 's-Hertogenbosch. He also spent some time in Ypres, and had links with Leyden and Dort. His three-voice psalms were the first polyphonic settings of the psalms in Dutch, with the use of popular song melodies as cantus firmi. All but one of his Mass settings are parody settings on chansons and motets by contemporary composers.

THE REDISCOVERY OF CLASSICAL LITERATURE

Late in 1416, three secretaries played truant from the Council of Constance. They absented themselves in order to search out a book which they had heard was at the nearby monastery of St Gall. Their trip was a success, as one of their number, Poggio Bracciolini, described:

'amid a tremendous quantity of books, we found Quintilian safe and sound, though filthy with mould and dust. For these books were in a foul and gloomy dungeon at the bottom of one of the towers, where not even men convicted of a capital offence would have been confined.'

Poggio's discovery of the full text of Quintilian's rhetorical textbook became a celebrated moment among the humanist coteries scattered across Italy. For them, it exemplified the revival of classical learning after centuries of neglect. For us, it can provide a window on their rhetorical claims.

First of all, the image of a barbarian past is, of course, exaggerated. Western Europe before the 15th century was by no means bereft of classical texts, nor – at least since the Aristotelian revolution of the 13th century – was their utter ignorance of Greek learning. Indeed, Quintilian himself was not a complete stranger to scholars pre-1416: his work did circulate, albeit in fragments. It was, in fact, this acquaintance that partly explains the excitement occasioned by Poggio's find. In this, as in other cases, what interested the humanists was learning more about a known figure – they were attracted by the lure of the big name.

Nor were these Italian detectives necessarily the first to get hold of a manuscript. Poggio suggests he and his colleagues visited St Gall already knowing Quintilian was kept prisoner there; one wonders how they came to learn this. Certainly, on another occasion, a 'discovery' by Poggio was less original than he claimed: in 1415, he found two Cicero speeches which were new to him but had already been noticed and copied by the French scholar, Nicholas de ◊Clamanges. Similarly, 70 years earlier, Poggio's fellow Florentine, Petrarch, announced that he had found Cicero's *Letters to Atticus*. The manuscript, in Verona Cathedral, showed signs of having been previously studied, but none of those earlier readers had cared to boast of their knowledge of the *Letters* as Petrarch did. In other words, what was unusual in the actions of a Petrarch or a Poggio was not their reading of rare classical texts but their advertising and circulating their 'discoveries'.

It was Petrarch and his disciple Boccaccio who in the mid-14th century set the precedent: their excitement about manuscript-searches was both vociferous and infectious; among the next generations of Florentine scholars who held Petrarch in high esteem, the hunt for classical texts became a fashion. In a couple of significant ways, however, circumstances were more propitious for Poggio's generation than they had been for Petrarch.

For one thing, it is significant that Poggio made his Quintilian discovery during the Council of Constance; this cosmopolitan rendezvous of rich clerics and educated secretaries gave him not only the opportunity to go searching but also a forum in which to announce his successes: a Council of the Church (and there were several in the early quattrocento) could act as catalyst for textual circulation. So, when in 1433, Giovanni ◊Aurispa arrived at the Council of Basel with a copy of Pliny the Younger's previously unknown *Panegyricus,* he found not just eager readers but a scholar, Tommaso Parentucelli (the future Nicholas V), who was able to correct the text. Aurispa's most celebrated manuscript discoveries, however, were not made in western Europe but in Greece. The introduction into Italy of Greek texts – both classical and patristic – is the other part of the 'revival of learning' and it reflects the second favourable circumstance: the dire situation in which the Byzantine Empire found itself. With the Ottomans advancing towards Constantinople, the Greeks were keen to increase diplomatic contact with the West; they were even willing to consider a union of their Orthodox church with the papacy, a proposal which brought Byzantine delegates to another of those international conferences, the Council of Florence. And with the interchange of emissaries, books also travelled.

Even a selective list of works which the humanists made better known

continued

makes impressive reading: in the 14th century, Apuleius' *Golden Ass* began to circulate, as did Catullus, as well as parts of Tacitus. In the early 15th century, besides Quintilian and Cicero speeches, Poggio unearthed a copy of Lucretius, a better text of Vitruvius than previously known, and fragments of Petronius. Gerardo Landriani substantially added to knowledge of Cicero by finding the complete text of *De Oratore*. Nicholas of Cusa more than doubled the number of Plautus' plays which circulated. The discoveries continued in the late 15th century: a more accurate text of Terence was found, for example, as were the first books of Tacitus' *Annals*. In terms of Greek works, the 15th-century knowledge-boom was even greater: writers from Xenophon to St Basil, from Isocrates to Diogenes Laertius

were read and translated for the first time.

Yet, despite these achievements, there remained something impermanent about the 'rediscovery' of classical texts. At times, humanist enthusiasm actually aided time's destructive habits: Landriani's copy of Cicero's *De Oratore* was so eagerly passed from hand to hand that it quickly deteriorated. A prototype might disappear but, of course, copies would remain – but these were likely to include accidental errors or unmarked 'corrections' to the text. It might be concluded that a manuscript was safer left in its monastic captivity, but (even discounting Poggio's description of mouldy dungeons) it could die there of neglect. An incident involving Poggio is probably unusual: in 1417, he saw a codex of Tacitus'

minor works, but neither copied nor stole the manuscript; the works did not circulate until, in the 1450s, Enoch of Ascoli revisited the library and took the copy back to Italy. In other cases, the outcome might not have been as positive: humanist claims about what they saw (and did not copy) on their travels often seem unlikely, but if even a fraction of their boasts are true, they tell of a whole series of texts that, unlike Quintilian, must have remained languishing in their prison until they perished.

DAVID RUNDLE

Further Reading

L D Reynolds (ed), *Texts and Transmission* (Oxford, 1983); N G Wilson, *From Byzantium to Italy* (London, 1992)

Pieter Brueghel the Elder, *The Tower of Babel*, c. 1567–8 (Museum Boymans-van Beuningen, Rotterdam). Brueghel's depiction of Babel appears to reflect his own studies of the Colosseum in Rome. (see ◊Brueghel) *AKG London*

Clement VII (BORN GRIULIO DE' MEDICI) (1478–1534)

Pope from 1523. The illegitimate and posthumous son of Giuliano de' Medici, he was brought up by Lorenzo de' ◊Medici and later entered the circle of his cousin, the future ◊Leo X. In Leo's first months as pope, he was elected to the cardinalate and became an influential figure both in Rome and, by being appointed papal legate there, in Florence. After Adrian VI's brief pontificate, he became the second Medici pope at an inauspicious time. Faced with both the Lutheran Reformation and the advances of the Ottomans, Clement could not even rely on the support of Charles V: his troops perpetrated the ◊Sack of Rome. The complications of European politics also meant that it was impossible successfully to resolve the issue of Henry VIII's divorce, leading eventually to England's break from Rome.

The future Clement VII was concerned to appear a generous patron when he was a cardinal, commissioning paintings from both ◊Sebastiano del Piombo and ◊Raphael; the latter is also thought to have provided the design for Clement's palace (Villa Madama, Rome) which was built by Antonio da Sangallo the Elder and Giulio Romano. He also showed interest in learning and was instrumental in Niccolò ◊Machiavelli's commission to write the *Florentine Histories*, which were dedicated to him as pope. He also used his power to act as a protector, albeit at a distance, to Erasmus. Culturally, however, his pontificate is better remembered for one negative factor – the Sack of Rome of 1527 – than for his continuing patronage of, for example, del Piombo who painted his portrait twice (1526: Pinacoteca, Naples, and post-1527: Pinacoteca, Parma). Outside Rome, Clement commissioned the design of the Florentine Biblioteca Laurenziana from ◊Michelangelo, as well as the tombs of Lorenzo de' Medici, Duke of Urbino (1492–1519) and Giuliano de' Medici, Duke of Nemours (1478–1516).

Clement VIII (BORN IPPOLITO ALDOBRANDINI) (1536–1605)

Pope 1592–1605. A fervent supporter of the ◊Counter-Reformation, he issued a new edition of the *Index prohibitorum* and supported the execution of Giordano ◊Bruno. In 1598 he annexed Ferrara to the Papal States, after the death of the last duke without legitimate heirs.

He was born in Fano, near Pesaro, and studied law at Padua, Perugia, and Bologna. He held numerous offices in the Roman curia, became a cardinal in 1585, and pope in 1592. One of his advisors was St Philip Neri.

He reduced Spanish influence in the college of cardinals, and recognized Henry IV as king of France in 1593. He arranged the Treaty of Vervins between France and Spain in 1598, and tried to resolve a controversy between the Jesuits and Dominicans concerning grace and free will. He was also responsible for a new standard edition of the Vulgate (the Sistine-Clementine version) and for revisions of the missal, breviary, and pontifical.

Cleve, Joos van (der Beke) (1464–1540)

Flemish painter. He has been identified with the ◊Master of the Death of the Virgin. He painted religious subjects and portraits in which the trace of various masters' styles has been detected, though a main influence on his work was that of Quentin ◊Matsys.

Perhaps born in Cleve, he worked in Antwerp but also travelled in Italy, Germany, and England.

Clouet

French portrait painters and draughtsmen of the 16th century, father and son. The father, **Jean** (or **Janet**) (*c.* 1485–1541), is assumed to have been of Flemish origin. He became painter and *valet de chambre* to Francis I in 1516. His son, **François** (*c.* 1520–1572), succeeded his father in Francis I's service in 1541 and worked also under Henry II, Francis II, and Charles IX.

Jean Clouet was possibly the son of the painter Jehan Cloêt, who was working at Brussels in 1475 and is mentioned in the account books of the Duke of Burgundy. At the court of Francis I, there was a fashion for portrait drawings in black or red chalk in which Clouet excelled, his work including 127 such portraits, mostly at the Musée Condé, Chantilly, comparable with those of Holbein, though distinct and freer in style.

François's portrait of a Parisian apothecary, Pierre Quthe, 1562, and that of Elizabeth of Austria, 1571, attributed to him, reflect Italian influence. His draw-

CLIMATE CHANGE

How far climate change may determine the fate of societies or regimes, as and when these are critically poised for other reasons, is now widely appreciated. Less evident to many would be its influence on the broader transformations of culture.

But let us take pre-Renaissance Europe. Oft-remarked among specialists is a concurrence in the period 1150–1300 between (a) a gradual peaking out of several centuries of warming across much of Europe and (b) the zenith, in various respects, of medieval civilization. Warming will have then been benign because it connoted (a) longer growing seasons and (b) less bitter winters. Nor will the associated shifts in rainfall patterns have been, in the main, too acute. After all, the net warming was one degree Celsius in 500 years: a rate of change not a tenth of the mean trend predicted for this next century if the 'greenhouse effect' goes unchecked.

Less easy is relating the 'Renaissance' to the similarly slow and uneven cooling by then under way across the continent and, indeed, the world. It may be, however, that less clement conditions can help explain why the period 1400–1600 saw so much violence. Certainly a largely agrarian social order came under stress as the extensive margins of arable and of forestry receded. In northern and central Europe, both the tree line and the upper limit of cultivation typically fell 75–100 metres between 1300 and 1500. Climate deterioration was a fundamental cause.

What the evidence from Europe (well corroborated by Chinese imperial records) also reveals is a tendency for the weather to become more erratic: maybe, for instance, more floods and yet also more droughts occurred than had been the case before. This tendency, one hardly conducive to social stability, may be linked with a general extension of pack ice, the actual limits of which fluctuate markedly from year to year. Iceland, which experienced the cooling trend a century or so ahead of western Europe proper, found pack ice to be increasing around her northern coasts as early as 1200. Perhaps as early as the 1470s, Bristol fishermen were visiting the Newfoundland Banks because the fisheries of the north-east Atlantic/Norwegian Sea were declining as sea temperatures fell. John Cabot decided to base himself in Bristol not long afterwards.

Another way climate change may have influenced the Renaissance was by strengthening ecologically its core area, the western Mediterranean. Other things being equal, climatic belts tend to move towards the poles during eras of warming but towards the equator during those of cooling.

Let us again start from medieval warming. In 1935, Henri Pirenne, the Belgian medievalist asked how, under such rulers as Charlemagne and Offa of Mercia, much of northwest Europe had thrived so from 750 to 850 or thereabouts. His own thesis, that the Mediterranean's commercial life was severely curtailed by the Arab-Islamic conquests, has now all but been demolished, leaving an explanatory vacuum that might best be filled by climate change. Maybe zonal displacement made northwest Europe agreeably drier while leaving the western Mediterranean more droughty. What this could have meant more specifically is that the Azores belt of high pressure would ridge strongly across Europe even in winter while the Siberian High, a wintertime feature, would generally have been less in evidence.

To this there could be a corollary. It is that, as long-term cooling resumed, zonal displacement towards the equator could have made the western Mediterranean moister again. A Siberian dimension in such a reversal seems confirmed by more droughts and winter cold on the Russian plain from 1300 onwards. However, what little data there thus far is does not support this interpretation for the Iberia-Maghreb sector. On the other hand, a study of lake levels in Italy north of 43°N shows them to have been generally high from 1300 onwards. But overall there was erraticism, especially as regards seasonal rains.

Analysis of the causes of climate change is the key to comprehending the course it took. Heavy deforestation had occurred through the early Middle Ages in Europe and China. This will initially have been conducive to atmospheric warming as carbon dioxide exuded from dead wood. Yet eventually, this scaling

continued

down of the carbon cycle will have favoured cooling. Meanwhile, long-term cycles in the Earth's revolution and rotation relative to the Sun were, on balance, working towards cooling. Also one must consider fluctuations in solar activity *per se* and in volcano behaviour. Sunspots are quite a good indication of how energetic the Sun is at a given time. So one might expect the pronounced Sporer Minimum in sunspot sightings from 1450 to 1534 to be associated with accentuated global cooling though maybe, too, with more serene weather. Yet through the first half of the 16th century it was, in fact, a little warmer across much of Europe. Then dust veils produced by volcanic explosions supervened. Two severe eruptions in the 1550s were to be followed by more extensive vulcanism as the turn of the century approached. This best explains not only pronounced cooling from its middle years but also the storminess that struck the Atlantic

seaboard in its last decade or so. Witness the fate of the Spanish Armada of 1588 and of follow-up attempts by Madrid to invade England.

When assessing the influence of climate change, it is always salutary to compare it with that of other ambient factors such as currency circulation, disease transmission, or technical advance. In the Renaissance the vagaries of the elements surely affect societal development less profoundly than printing presses or bullion inflow. Correspondingly, the weather and climate seem not to enter the consciousness of the age the way they were to as the Little Ice Age approached its nadir around 1700.

That was certainly true of the visual arts. In February 1565, the Flemish artist, Peter Brueghel the Elder, painted *Hunters in the Snow* in awestruck celebration of a most savage winter then in progress. Yet it was nearly a century later that people

like Hendrick Avercamp (1585–1635) developed more fully the Netherlands school of winter landscapes. Nor did atmospheric science advance during the Renaissance the way astronomy and some aspects of biology did. Still, one spin-off from astronomy was that, by 1600, comets were known to transit outside the Moon. Their exclusion thus from meteorology gave that subject sharper delineation; and served, above all, to separate it from astrology. To that extent, the stage was set for the big advances in instrumentation and physical principles the century ahead was to witness.

NEVILLE BROWN

Further Reading

Raymond S Bradley and Philip D Jones (eds), *Climate Since* AD *1500* (London, 1995); Jean M Grove, *The Little Ice Age* (London: Methuen, 1988); H H Lamb, *Climate, History and the Modern World* (London, 1995)

---

ings are less robust than those of Jean, but his fame was even greater (though both were renowned), Ronsard calling François 'honneur de notre temps' ('the pride of our age'). The name of a third Clouet (de Navarre) appears in records, and a number of other artists worked in a closely related style.

Clovio, Giulio (JURE CLOVIĆ) (1498–1578)

Croatian-born painter. He worked in Italy, establishing a reputation as one of the leading miniaturists of his day. His works include illustrations of the victories of Emperor Charles V (British Library, London) and a *Pietà* (1553, Uffizi, Florence).

Clovio was born in Grizane, but lived in Italy after 1516 and probably studied under ◊Giulio Romano in Rome. After the ◊Sack of Rome in 1527, during which he was captured, Clovio escaped and took holy orders. His abilities as a miniaturist are seen in his illustrations of the victories of Charles V and in a manuscript life of Federico, Duke of Urbino (Vatican

Library, Rome). Other commissions included decorations in the Palazzo ◊Farnese in Rome.

Clovio also helped and encouraged the young El ◊Greco on his arrival in Rome.

Cobbold, William (1560–1639)

English organist and composer. He was organist at Norwich Cathedral 1599–1608, and was one of the ten musicians who harmonized the tunes in East's Psalter of 1592. In 1601 he contributed a madrigal to *The Triumphes of Oriana*. Among his other few surviving works are 11 consort songs.

Cochlaeus, Johannes (JOHANN DOBNECK) (1479–1552)

German humanist and fervent opponent of ◊Luther. He strenuously opposed the marriage of ◊Henry VIII of England to Anne Boleyn, and in 1525 also opposed the printing (in Cologne) of a translation of the New Testament by the English reformer ◊Tyndale. In 1549 he published a commentary on the words and deeds of Luther in the period 1517–46.

He was born at Wendelstein, near Schwabach, and studied philosophy in Nuremberg, where he was a protégé of Willibald ◊Pirckheimer, and in Cologne. About 1518 he was ordained priest in Rome. In 1526 he was a canon of Mainz, transferring to Meissen around 1535 and then to Breslau (Wrocław, now in Poland) in 1539. He was a member of the Catholic delegation at both the Regensburg Colloquy in 1546 and the drawing up of the Interim of Augsburg in 1548.

His attack on the marriage of Henry VIII to Anne Boleyn is contained in his *De Matrimonio Regis Anglicae* (1535) and *Scopa in Araneas Ricardi Morysini Angli* (1538). His book on Luther is *Commentaria de Actis et Scriptis Lutheris*; a translation from Latin into German appeared in 1580. Among his books is a 12-volume history of the Hussites, published as *Historia Hussitorum* in 1549.

Coclico (Coclicus) (ADRIANUS PETIT) (1499 OR 1500–1592)

Flemish composer. He became a Protestant and went to Wittenberg in 1545. After holding various posts in Germany he went to the Danish court at Copenhagen. He published a treatise entitled *Compendium Musices* and a collection of psalm settings entitled *Consolationes Piae*.

Codussi, Mauro (CODUCCI) (c. 1440–1504)

Venetian architect. Influenced by the Renaissance architecture of Florence, he imitated the style in his Church of San Michele in Isola (1469–79). His San Giovanni Crisostomo (c. 1500) is the first centrally planned church in Venice.

Although he was born near Bergamo, Codussi was active from 1469 in Venice, where he developed a distinctive style based upon the architecture of Florence and central Italy. The influence of the architectural principles of ◊Alberti are evident in many of his works, notably the Torre dell' Orologio (1496–99) and the Procurazie Vecchie (begun 1496) on the Piazza San Marco.

Other major projects include the churches of Santa Maria Formosa (rebuilt 1492–1502) and the Scuola Grande di San Giovanni Evangelista (1498), with its famous double staircase. The Palazzo Corner-Spinelli (c. 1490) and Palazzo Vendramin-Calerghi (1501–09) are both Lombardesque in style, but incorporate innovatory features, such as the free-standing Classical orders on the façade of the latter palace. The churches of San Zaccaria (1483) and the Scuola Grande di San Marco (1485–95) are notable for their façades.

Coecke van Aelst, Pieter (1502–1550)

Dutch painter, print publisher, and designer. He ran a busy workshop in Brussels, producing not only prints and paintings, but also designs for tapestries and stained-glass windows. He is remembered not for his own works – many of which have been lost – but for helping to spread knowledge of the Italian Renaissance fashions to northern Europe through his many prints. His printmaker's included Pieter ◊Brueghel.

Also influential was his own summary of the major architectural treatise *De Architectura/On Architecture* by the Roman architect Vitruvius. His wife, Meyken Verhulst, was also an artist.

Coecke was born in Aelst and is believed to have studied under Bernard van ◊Orley. He is recorded as a master at Antwerp in 1527. He visited Italy about 1530 and Constantinople in 1533; in 1535 he may have accompanied Emperor Charles V on his Tunis campaign. He was still at Antwerp in 1544, but subsequently moved to Brussels, where he died.

No surviving paintings of Coecke's can be identified with absolute certainty. His most famous composition, the *Last Supper* (c. 1527), is loosely based upon Leonardo da Vinci's famous fresco; it exists in several versions, all possibly replicas of a lost original.

Coello, Alonso Sánchez (1532–1588)

Spanish portrait painter. He became court painter to Philip II, of whom he painted a number of likenesses. The *Portrait of a Young Man* (probably Alessandro Farnese) (National Gallery of Ireland, Dublin) is a good example of his work.

He was the pupil of Anthonis Mor. As keeper of the royal collection, he had works by Titian under his care, and utilized Titian's portrait accessories in his own painting, devoting much meticulous attention to rich detail of costume.

He was the master of Juan Pantoja de la Cruz.

Coeur, Jacques (c. 1395–1456)

French merchant and financier. He was the master of the mint under Charles VII, and from 1436 was in charge of the French royal finances. With the fortune that he amassed he founded colleges in Paris, Montpellier, and Bourges.

Unfounded allegations of poisoning and fraud led to the confiscation of his fortune in 1451, and Coeur went into exile.

Colet, John (1467–1519)

London humanist theologian, dean of St Paul's from 1505. After an English university education, Colet travelled in France and Italy where, though he might not have met Marsilio ◊Ficino, he certainly became acquainted with his Platonist works. On his return to England, his sermons and writings were marked by Christian Platonism. He was an advocate for reform within the church and in education; he founded St Paul's School in 1512 for the teaching of boys 'good manners and literature ... both Latin and Greek'. In this project, he enlisted the help of William ◊Lily and ◊Erasmus in producing textbooks.

I never met a more fertile mind and for this reason he took especial delight in minds like his own ... He would find a moral in everything if ever he relaxed under the charm of story-telling.

Erasmus on Colet

Coligny, Gaspard de (1519–1572)

French admiral and soldier, and prominent ◊Huguenot. About 1557 he joined the Protestant party, helping to lead the Huguenot forces during the Wars of Religion. After the Treaty of St Germain of 1570, he became a favourite of the young king Charles IX, but was killed on the first night of the Massacre of ◊St Bartholomew.

Colleoni, Bartolommeo (1400–1475)

Italian mercenary soldier. He fought for both sides in the wars between the Milanese and Venetians 1423–54, and was imprisoned as a spy by Filippo Visconti, Duke of Milan, in 1446. In 1451 he joined the Venetian army and became *generalissimo* of the Venetian state.

He is the subject of an equestrian statue in Venice by Andrea del ◊Verrocchio, and a monument in Bergano by Giovanni Antonio ◊Amadeo.

Colocci, Angelo (1474–1547)

Italian cleric, poet, and humanist. He combined an interest in Greek and Roman literature with a lively involvement in vernacular poetry, particularly the study of the origins of Italian poetry in Provence. He was himself a poet in both Latin and Italian and his house in Rome was a centre for the discussion of literary theory and scholarship.

Colocci was born at Iesi and from 1497 was a papal secretary, first to ◊Leo X and then to ◊Clement VII. In 1537 he was made bishop of Nocera Umbra.

He collected many manuscripts and inscriptions, but his collections suffered in the Sack of Rome in 1527.

Colombe, Michel (c. 1430–c. 1515)

French sculptor. He is remembered chiefly for two major sculptures, both showing a blend of Gothic and Italian Renaissance styles. The first is the tomb of Francis II of Brittany and Marguerite de Foix in Nantes, with allegorical figures (sculpted 1502–07). The second is the marble relief of St George and the dragon for the altarpiece of the Château de Gaillon (1508–09), now in the Louvre in Paris.

The tomb of Francis II of Brittany was designed by the sculptor Jean Perréal and also worked on by Girolamo da Fiesole.

Born in Brittany, Colombe belonged to a family of artists and was the brother of the miniaturist Michel Colombe. Little is known of his early years, from which no works survive.

Colombo, Matteo Realdo (c. 1516–1559)

Italian anatomist who discovered pulmonary circulation, the process of blood circulating from the heart to the lungs and back.

This showed that ◊Galen's teachings were wrong, and was of help to William ◊Harvey in his work on the heart and circulation. Colombo was a pupil of Andreas ◊Vesalius and became his successor at the University of Padua. Colombo is also remembered for his 'discovery' of the clitoris.

Colonna, Francesco (*c.* 1433–*c.* 1527)

Venetian writer. He wrote a mysterious allegorical romance, *Hypernotomachia Poliphili*, which would probably have been forgotten but for the sumptuous illustrated edition published in 1499 by Aldus ◊Manutius. An abbreviated version of the romance was published by Richard Dallington in 1592 as *The Strife of Love in a Dream*.

Colonna, Pompeo (*c.* 1479–1532)

Italian cardinal, member of the illustrious Colonna family. As bishop of Rieti, he incited the people to revolt against Pope Julius II and was removed from office, but he was pardoned by Pope Leo X and created cardinal in 1517. He helped the Holy Roman Emperor Charles V in his attack on Rome in 1527 to punish pope Clement VII for breaking their alliance, but the pope pardoned him and he was made viceroy of Naples.

He was the nephew of Prospero ◊Colonna.

Colonna, Prospero (1452–1523)

Italian ◊condottiere and member of the famous Colonna family. He offered to help Charles VIII of France when he invaded Italy 1494–95 and later entered the service of the pope. Among his many victories were those of Vicenza in 1513, against the Venetians, and Bicocca in 1522, against the Franco-German forces under Odet de Foix, Vicomte de Lautrec.

Colonna, Vittoria (*c.* 1492–1547)

Italian noblewoman and poetess. Unlike her fellow women poets Gaspara Stampa (1523–1554) and Veronica ◊Franco, she led a blameless – and leisured – life. Born from the union of the illustrious Roman Colonna family and the Montefeltro of Urbino, Vittoria Colonna was destined from the age of four for a marriage with Fernando Francesco d'Avalos, Marchese of Pescara. She gathered around herself a circle of poets and theologians, which included Pietro ◊Bembo and the artist ◊Michelangelo (who addressed her repeatedly in his poems), as well as Cardinal Pole. On her husband's death in 1525, she wrote poems lamenting his loss in the established Petrarchan style. Her *Canzoniere/Songbook* (1544) collected together poems on the death of her husband and other religious poems.

> Now in a short breath,
>
> Even in an instant, The Lord
>
> Has recaptured her from the unwary world
>
> And taken her from our eyes.
>
> But it can not cast into darkness,
>
> Though her body may be dead,
>
> Her sweet, graceful and sacred writings.
>
> ❧
>
> MICHELANGELO on the death of Vittoria Colonna

colore (ITALIAN 'COLOUR')

Term that came to be associated primarily in Venice in the 16th century with the predilection for defining compositions through the juxtaposition of colours rather than contour line. *Colore* was viewed in contrast to ◊*disegno*, for which a fierce debate raged amongst artists and humanists, including Ludovico ◊Dolce in *Il dialogo della pittura intitolato l'aretino/The Dialogue on Painting Known as the Aretine* (1557).

Columbus, Christopher (SPANISH CRISTÓBAL COLÓN) (1451–1506)

Italian navigator and explorer who made four voyages to the New World: 1492 to San Salvador Island, Cuba, and Haiti; 1493–96 to Guadaloupe, Montserrat, Antigua, Puerto Rico, and Jamaica; 1498 to Trinidad and the mainland of South America; 1502–04 to Honduras and Nicaragua.

Believing that Asia could be reached by sailing westwards, he eventually won the support of King Ferdinand and Queen Isabella of Spain and set off on his first voyage from Palos on 3 August 1492 with three small ships, the *Niña*, the *Pinta*, and his flagship the *Santa Maria*. Land was sighted on 12 October, probably Watling Island (now San Salvador Island), and within a few weeks he reached Cuba and Haiti, returning to Spain in March 1493.

Born in Genoa, Columbus went to sea at an early age, and settled in Portugal in 1478. After his third voyage in 1498, he became involved in quarrels among the colonists sent to Haiti, and in 1500 the governor sent him back to Spain in chains. Released and compensated by the king, he made his last voyage 1502–04, during which he hoped to find a strait leading to India. He died in poverty in Valladolid and is buried in Seville Cathedral. In 1968 the site of the wreck of the *Santa Maria*, sunk off Hispaniola on 25 December 1492, was located.

Comines, Philippe de (*c.* 1445–1511)
French diplomat in the service of Charles the Bold, Louis XI, and Charles VIII; author of *Mémoires* (1489–98).

commedia erudita (ITALIAN 'ERUDITE COMEDY')
Italian vernacular comedy of the 16th century, modelled on the Latin comedies of the Roman dramatists ◊Plautus and Terence. While the action, construction, and certain stock characters were derived from the Roman models, and the unities of time (a single day) and place were observed, the settings were contemporary Italian urban ones. A well-known example is *La mandragola/The Mandrake Root* (1518) by ◊Machiavelli.

The action involved several plots and these drew on a wealth of post-Classical stories and novellas as well as on the Latin sources. Typically the problems faced by lovers are finally resolved in marriage after much intrigue and trickery involving mistaken identities and disguises, conniving servants and other clever, shady, or gullible comic types.

Important examples of the *commedia erudita* are *La cassaria/The Coffer* (1508) by ◊Ariosto; *La calandria/The Follies of Calandro* (1513) by Bibbiena; and *La triunizia* and *I lucidi* (both 1549) by ◊Firenzuola.

Later examples tend to have more intricate plots, to develop moral and romantic elements, and to show the increasing influence of the *commedia dell'arte*. Among the many writers of this later type are Anton Francesco ◊Grazzini, Giovanni Maria Cecchi (1518–87), Pietro ◊Aretino, Annibale ◊Caro, and Giambattista della ◊Porta. Francesco d'Ambra (1499–1558) wrote the prose play *Il furto* (acted 1544), and the verse plays and *I Bernardi* and *La cofanaria* (acted 1547/65).

Common Life
Brothers and Sisters of the followers of the Christian mystic Gerard Groote (1340–1384), a widely travelled Carthusian monk based in Holland. The Brethren of the Common Life were a semi-monastic order of laymen and clergy dedicated to the cultivation of inner spirituality and good works. The spirituality they practised was known as the ◊*devotio moderna*.

The brethren's emphasis on inner spirituality greatly influenced Christian humanists and some of the reformers. Both ◊Erasmus and ◊Luther were educated by members of the movement, which was at its peak during the second half of the 15th century.

The classic statement of their belief is the *Imitatio Christi/The Imitation of Christ* by ◊Thomas à Kempis, which became the most widely read work of Christian mysticism.

Common Prayer, Book of
Defining act of the process of Reformation in England was the production of a service book in English in Edward VI's reign. At the same time, it is a reflection of the inconstant, fast-moving flow of events that there were two Books of Common Prayer within three years of each other.

Both were written under the guidance of Thomas ◊Cranmer but demonstrate the development of religious attitudes in the mid-century. The first, of 1549, condemned some Catholic practices but in many ways avoided controversy and had an Erasmian tinge. The second, of 1552, was more strident in its Zwinglian condemnation of the Catholic Mass and its doctrine of transubstantiation but it still fell short of a Calvinist position. When Elizabeth reintroduced Protestantism in 1559, it was the second *Prayer Book* which was employed but with some additions from the 1549 *Book*, which softened the denial of transubstantiation.

communications
In Renaissance Europe, communications were slow and erratic. Certainly, the 15th-century invention of print constituted an information technology revolution but this accelerated the circulation of books by speeding up their production. The structures of communication – road networks, shipping routes, postal systems – saw no renaissance. Ideas could spread only as fast as these structures could carry them.

Governments sometimes employed messengers to

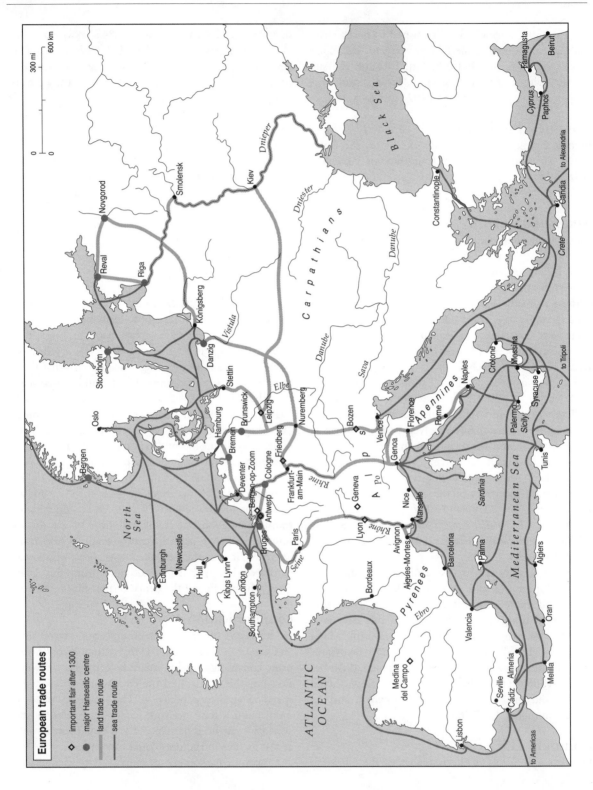

European trade routes

◇ important fair after 1300
● major Hanseatic centre
land trade route
sea trade route

600 km
300 mi

Novgorod
Reval
Riga
Stockholm
Oslo
Bergen
Smolensk
Kiev
Königsberg
Danzig
Stettin
Hamburg
Bremen
Brunswick
Leipzig
Nuremberg
Deventer
Bergen-op-Zoom
Cologne
Friedberg
Antwerp
Bruges
Frankfurt-am-Main
Paris
Geneva
Lyon
Nice
Avignon
Aigues-Mortes
Barcelona
Bordeaux
Edinburgh
Newcastle
Hull
Kings Lynn
London
Southampton
Bozen
Venice
Genoa
Florence
Rome
Naples
Crotone
Messina
Syracuse
Palermo
Tunis
Algiers
Oran
Melilla
Valencia
Palma
Almeria
Seville
Cádiz
Lisbon
Medina del Campo
Constantinople
Famagusta
Beirut
Paphos
Candia
to Alexandria
to Tripoli
to Americas

Dnieper
Dniester
Danube
Sava
Vistula
Elbe
Rhine
Rhône
Seine
Po
Ebro

Black Sea
North Sea
ATLANTIC OCEAN
Mediterranean Sea
Carpathians
Apennines
Alps
Pyrenees
Sardinia
Sicily
Crete
Cyprus

carry written correspondence not only within a country but also to other powers. As in so many matters, the most advanced bureaucracy was that of the papacy which had a system of 'runners' or *cursores* who travelled across Europe with papal bulls: when necessity required, this system could be surprisingly efficient, with news of the Union of the Churches at the Council of ◊Florence reaching England in two weeks. This, though, was exceptional; communication was more often achieved by sending a letter or parcel with merchants. In other words, the main lines of communication across Europe followed the major trade routes. So, for example, the Baltic Hansa league had their own postal system, as later did the German bankers, the Fuggers. Italian firms with branches across Europe like the Borromei or the Medici could be used to transport parcels.

Many of the trade routes were by sea rather than land – a potentially quicker and safer way of ensuring communications. Correspondents sometimes bemoaned the loss of letters when their messenger was robbed or murdered on his travels (or, alternatively, simply played truant). On the other hand, letters also provide testimony to the problems of getting an international firm to take a parcel by ship: unless you had enough goods to warrant chartering a ship for yourself, you would have to wait for the company to arrange its next consignment, which could be weeks or even months. In other words, in a humanist culture that prized so much the art of letter writing, there was little certainty that the epistles would actually be read.

Compenius, Heinrich, THE ELDER (*c.* 1525–1611)
German music theorist and composer, the eldest member of a family of organ builders who also worked in Denmark. His son **Esaias Compenius** (died 1617) built the organ at Frederiksborg Castle and was coauthor with Michael Praetorius of *Orgeln Verdingnis* (*Organographia*). Esaias's brother **Heinrich Compenius the Younger** (died 1631) built the organ at Magdeburg Cathedral. Heinrich's nephew **Johann Heinrich Compenius** (died 1642) built the organ at St Mauritius, Halle, for Samuel Scheidt.

Compère, Loyset (*c.* 1445–1518)
French composer. He started as a chorister at Saint-Quentin Cathedral, later became a canon, and was eventually appointed its chancellor.

Works include:
Masses, magnificats, and other church music; also many secular songs with French and Italian words.

Complutensian Polyglot
Monumental multilingual edition of the Bible published in Spain in 1520. Begun in 1502, under the patronage of Cardinal Francisco Ximénes de Cisneros, it made the Bible text available for the first time in parallel columns of Greek, Latin, and Hebrew. The project employed leading Spanish scholars, including Antonio ◊Nebrija – but he resigned from the work because of what he considered to be the conservatism of the editing, which preferred to keep Vulgate mistranslations than question orthodoxy. Nebrija's own desire for a philologically more accurate Latin version of the Bible was preempted by Erasmus' *Novum Instrumentum* (1516).

Ximénes de Cisneros, the confessor to Queen Isabella, was the founder of the university of Alcalá (Latin name: Complutum), the town after which this Bible is known.

concetto (ITALIAN 'CONCEPT' OR 'IDEA')
In Renaissance literary criticism, an elaborate or striking metaphor drawing a parallel between two very unlike objects, qualities, or experiences. Gaining currency in the 17th century, it was used in particular of two schools of literature: that of the imitators of the ◊Petrarch, and the English metaphysical poets.

The **Petrarchan conceit**, as employed by Petrarch in his love poems, became more exaggerated by his imitators, notably ◊Tasso and the French and Elizabethan sonneteers. The Petrarchan conceit typically compares the beloved's beauty (or the lover's emotions) to very dissimilar concrete objects, often greatly exaggerated. In many of Petrarch's imitators, this amounts to nothing more than the trite and conventional love imagery which Shakespeare deflates in his sonnet beginning 'My mistress' eyes are nothing like the sun'.

The **metaphysical conceit** is especially associated with the English metaphysical poets, such as John ◊Donne.

conciliarism

Theory of Catholic Church government developed in the late 14th and early 15th centuries, during and after the ◊Great Schism (1378–1417, when rival popes had seats in Rome and Avignon), claiming that ultimate authority should lie with the ◊General Councils of the Church. Conciliarism provided justification for the increasingly radical acts of the Councils, in particular that at ◊Basel (1431–49).

Attempts, theoretical and practical, to limit the power of the papacy were nothing new; to mention only the most recent example, an early 14th-century dispute between pope and claimant to the Holy Roman Empire had inspired antipapal writings by Marsilius of Padua and William of Ockham. It was, indeed, a commonplace of canon law that, in certain circumstances, a pope could be deposed by a General Council. However, the beginning of the Great Schism, made the issue of conciliar power topical. In the immediate wake of the election of an antipope, some writers, for example Pierre d'◊Ailly, argued that the only legitimate method of ending the crisis was through a General Council. In the early 15th century, when General Councils were the means used to heal the Schism, clerics such as Jean ◊Gerson and Francesco ◊Zabarella developed theories to explain why a General Council should have authority not only in exceptional circumstances but also as a matter of course. Their writings were backed up by the decrees of the Council of ◊Constance (1414–18), with the decree *Frequens* (1417) demanding that General Councils should be frequently held. At Basel, the claims of conciliar theory were stretched further: some of this generation, including ◊Nicholas of Cusa, Juan de Segovia, and Panormitanus, argued that General Councils could convene themselves and could take over functions which, as they put it, had been delegated to the papacy.

Conciliarism, however, was not a single worked-out doctrine; there were differences between the various theorists on issues such as the source of ecclesiastical authority and the balance of authority between pope and council. This was, in part, a natural consequence of the continually changing political circumstances which created the intellectual debate. It had the effect, though, that as some theorists became more radical, more moderate opinion became alienated and a General Council which claimed to represent the whole church found it was losing support to the papacy.

Though some conciliarists drew parallels with secular authority in constructing their arguments and though their arguments were potentially applicable beyond the confines of Church government, 15th-century conciliarism remained an ecclesiastical issue. And it was one which lost its topicality in the second half of that century; but this did not mean that the writings were merely filed away and lost from view. There was a brief revival of conciliarism in the early 16th century, in particular, in the writings of the Scottish theologian and historian John Mair (*c.* 1470–1550). More influentially, however, the store of ideas first created in discussions of Catholic Church government were deployed in a rather different context – by proponents of Calvinist resistance theory.

Concord, Formula of

A formulation of Lutheran belief drawn up by six Lutheran divines in March 1577. The Concord rejected the views on the Eucharist put forward by Melanchthon, and also the views on predestination expressed by ◊Calvin. It proved only a partial settlement of the Lutheran debate, and was rejected by many Lutherans, especially outside Germany. For this reason the Formula never possessed the authority of the Confession of ◊Augsburg.

Its original inspiration lay in a series of articles by the German divine Jakob Andreae (1528–90) that had resulted in the Swabian-Saxon Formula of Concord in 1575, and the Torgau Book of 1576.

Condé, Louis I de Bourbon, Prince of Condé (1530–1569)

Prominent French ◊Huguenot leader, founder of the house of Condé and uncle of Henry IV of France. He fought in the wars between Henry II and the Holy Roman Emperor Charles V, including the defence of Metz.

Condé, Henri I de Bourbon, 2nd Prince of Condé (1552–1588)

French ◊Huguenot leader. He fought for Henry of Navarre under Gaspard de Coligny, against the Catholic nobles in the French Wars of Religion. He embraced the Catholic faith to save his life after the Massacre of ◊St Bartholomew in 1572, but on the death of King Charles IX in 1574 he recanted and went to Germany, where he raised an army and in 1575 joined the leader of the moderate Catholics, François d'Anjou, Duke of Alençon (1554–84). He was eventually taken prisoner.

He was the son of Louis I de Bourbon, Prince of Condé.

Condivi, Ascanio (1525–1574)

Italian painter and biographer. There are a few religious paintings of his which survive (for example, *The Mysteries of the Virgin*, 1554, in the Church of S Domenico in his home town of Ripatransone); his immortality rests rather on his *Vita di Michelagnolo Buonarroti/Life of Michelangelo* (1553).

Condivi went to Rome in *c.* 1550 and became a pupil of Michelangelo's. He wrote his *Life* under Michelangelo's supervision and, in part, as the result of the artist's desire to correct errors in the recently printed biography of him in Giorgio ◊Vasari's *Lives*. The work provides a detailed, if at times fictitious, account of the artist's life. It influenced Vasari's own rewritten life of Michelangelo, in his second edition of the *Lives* (1568), and became a central text in the mythology surrounding the artist.

condottiere

Italian mercenary commander. Soldiers who received a short-term contract (*condotta*) to raise a force and fight for a particular lord or city first appeared in Italy in the 13th century but increasing use was made of them in the late 14th and 15th centuries. The prestige that a *condottiere* could receive could be impressive, if often posthumous: witness Uccello's memorial monument to Sir John Hawkwood in Florence Cathedral or Donatello's equestrian statue to Il ◊Gattamelata. It was rare, however, to win a princedom through such a career; Francesco Sforza won Milan by a combination of martial and marital success, while ◊Federigo da Montefeltro, who hired himself out as a *condottiere*,

simply secured and augmented his patrimony of Urbino.

Though a *condottiere* could win reputation and (moderate) rewards, he was also open to vituperation. The mercenaries were often noted for disloyalty and accused of destroying the peace of Italy. On the second charge, it could be retorted that it was the employers, not the soldiers, who created the wars and rumours of wars. Repeated changing of sides, however, was certainly something of a lifestyle for the *condottieri*. A city or prince could not expect enduring support from a *condottiere*, unless they could continually provide them with the appropriate income. The response of the Florentine humanists was that mercenaries should not be used at all: from ◊Leonardo Bruni to Niccolò ◊Machiavelli, the solution to military difficulties was said to be the raising of a citizen

condottiere Paolo Uccello, monumental fresco in the Duomo, Florence commemorating the English *condottiere*, Sir John Hawkwood (d. 1394). See ◊Uccello. *Bridgeman Art Library*

militia – one which, when it was tried under Piero Soderini, must be said to have been ineffective.

Coninxloo, Gillis van (1544–1607)

Flemish landscape painter and engraver. The most prominent of a large family of painters, he settled in Amsterdam in 1595, becoming the leader of a group of landscape painters. His son, of the same name, was a flower painter.

Coninxloo the elder was born in Antwerp. He combined elements of Brueghel and Brill, producing fanciful compositions which progressively became more naturalistic in their treatment of detail.

Constable, Henry (1562–1613)

English poet. His *Diana* (1592) is a series of 23 sonnets, praised by Ben Jonson and others. He also wrote 16 *Sprituall Sonnettes to the Honour of God and hys Sayntes* and *The Shepheard's Song of Venus and Adonis*.

Constable was educated at Cambridge. He became a Roman Catholic, and spent much of his time in Paris. In 1598 he tried to form a new English Catholic college there. He went to London in 1603, and was confined in the Tower for about a year because of his involvement in pro-Catholic publications. In 1610 he returned to Paris. He was a friend of the writers Philip Sidney and John Harington.

Constance, Council of

◊General Council of the Church held in Constance, Germany, 1414–18 that ended the ◊Great Schism. Brought about by the diplomacy and cajoling of the Holy Roman Emperor Sigismund, it deposed the antipope John XXIII in 1415 and the Avignonese pope Benedict XIII in 1417 (although the latter, having moved to Aragon, continued to style himself pope until his death); the Roman pope Gregory XII resigned in 1415. Oddone Colonna was subsequently elected Pope Martin V.

In addition to ending the Great Schism, the Council was also set the goals of dealing with Hussite heresy and reforming the church. The Hussite leader John (or Jan) Huss was called to the Council and was arrested, tried, and executed in 1415, as was his ally, Jerome of Prague. The next years were to show, however, that killing heretical leaders did not destroy a heresy. As to reform, the issue was how to improve the central institutions of the church. Constance produced two conciliarist decrees: *Haec Santa* (1415), which claimed that popes were answerable to a General Council, and *Frequens* (1417), which demanded that a General Council should be held at regular intervals. These decrees laid the basic foundation for the 1430s conflict between the Council of ◊Basel and Pope Eugenius IV.

The Council of Constance was not simply an event of international political moment; it was also a talking shop for scholars. In the entourages of the high clerics were several secretaries interested in the *studia humanitatis*. The Council gave them an opportunity to exchange books (some of Leonardo ◊Bruni's writings circulated there, for example), to try out their rhetoric (◊Poggio Bracciolini, for instance, gave a funeral sermon in classicizing style on the death of Cardinal Zabarella), and to travel to nearby monasteries in search of Classical texts (see feature on the rediscovery of Classical literature). It also provided possibilities for patronage (two English bishops commissioned a Latin translation of Dante's *Divine Comedy*) and for employment (Poggio left Constance in the entourage of another English bishop). The Council of Constance was thus the first international conference for humanists.

contrapposto

In the visual arts, a pose in which one part of the body twists away from another part, the weight of the body being balanced on one leg rather than two. First achieved in ancient Greek sculpture contrapposto was revived in the free-standing statues of the Renaissance, notably Donatello's *David* (1430s, Bargello, Florence) and Michelangelo's *David* (1504, Accademia, Florence).

converso

In Spanish history, a Jew who had converted to Christianity. Despite their conversion, and the fact that many of them rose to positions of power in the 14th and 15th century, *conversos* and their descendants suffered at the hands of the ◊Inquisition. Insincere converts who continued to practise Judaism in secret, branded *marranos* (pigs), and particularly ran the risk of persecution.

COPERNICANISM

DESPITE MODERN-DAY estimations of Nicholas Copernicus' *De Revolutionibus Orbium Coelestium* (1543) as a revolutionary work, there is in fact scant evidence for the spread of Copernicanism, the belief in the theory of Copernicus, in the 16th century. Copernicus' own preface to the *De Revolutionibus* was far from a revolutionary manifesto for overthrowing Ptolemaic astronomy. It was written in the language of a clerical humanist, seeking astronomical reform by appealing to the aesthetics of symmetry and decorum prevalent in the ecclesiastic court of the pope. It was a language very similar to that of an earlier work on planetary ordering by Girolamo Fracastro, *Homocentrica, Sive de Stellis* (1538), also dedicated to Paul III. Hence 16th-century readers of the *De Revolutionibus* seldom read it as a revolutionary program of astronomical reform.

Contemporary reactions to Nicholas Copernicus' *De Revolutionibus* were indeed mixed. On the one hand, few took on wholeheartedly Copernicus' physical theory of a heliocentric universe – that all the planets, including the Earth, orbited around the Sun and that in addition the Earth was spinning on its own axis. On the other hand, as an advanced treatise on mathematical astronomy, the *De Revolutionibus* was studied closely by several of his contemporaries and his parameters were adopted by many others. Reading the *De Revolutionibus* for its technical and mathematical

improvements, but not for its physical, heliocentric claims, was a response typical of the time. It is an attitude that could also be found in the anonymous preface to the *De Revolutionibus* (soon identified as written by by Andreas Osiander, the Lutheran pastor at Nuremberg). In it, Osiander pleaded for a fair hearing of what might seem like a confusion of disciplinary boundaries. In terms of contemporary categories of learning, astronomy was considered a mathematical discipline and was regarded as having no claim to establishing physical reality. That was the domain of natural philosophy. A treatise of mathematical astronomy could not, therefore, establish the truth of a physical system.

Moreover, Copernicus' heliocentric system implied anomalies which could not be explained within the physical explanations available in contemporary Aristotelian philosophy. Why, for instance, could a stone thrown up come straight down to the same place if the Earth were spinning rapidly? The claim of a moving Earth also contradicted passages in the Bible. Whilst Copernicus' heliocentric claims were quietly glossed over or dismissed out of hand, the *De Revolutionibus* was not necessarily consigned to oblivion as an absurd book. By 1535, Copernicus had an established reputation for his accurate computations, and many of his contemporary astronomers had eagerly awaited the book which they hoped would correct the errors in existing astronomical tables.

Reading the *De Revolutionibus* for its mathematical content rather than its physical claim became widespread among the teachers and students at the Lutheran University of Wittenberg. The reformer, humanist, and professor of Greek at Wittenberg, Philip Melanchthon (1497–1560), incorporated Copernicus' improved parameters for astronomical prediction in his textbook, *Initia Doctriniae Physicae* (1549), while dismissing the heliocentric claim. It was the lecturer in mathematics at Wittenberg, Georg Joachim Rheticus (1514–76), who sought out Copernicus and persuaded him to publish the *De Revolutionibus* in the first place. Although Rheticus believed in Copernicus' heliocentric theory, he also reported it in the language of astrology – the changing fortunes of the kingdom of the world, according to Rheticus, depended on the changing eccentricity of the Sun. Another lecturer in mathematics at Wittenberg, Erasmus Reinhold (1511–1553), re-calculated the parameters from the tables in the *De Revolutonibus* and published a new set of astronomical tables, the *Prussian Tables* (1552), with additional guides for those who were accustomed to the older, but faulty Alfonsine tables. Although the improvement in predictive precision using Copernican tables was small, the *Prussian Tables* became popular in German-speaking countries for nationalistic and confessional reasons. It became the basis for many other tables – for instance, the *Tabulae*

continued

Bergenses by Johannes Stadius (1566) and the *Ephemerides* of Michael Maestlin (1580). It is through the prefaces of these tables that Copernicus' reputation was established as a skilled mathematician or an astronomer on a par with Ptolemy, without reference to his heliocentric claims. German vernacular calendars in the second half of the 16th century similarly boast their uses of Copernicus' calculations, without mentioning his physical claims. The reception of Copernicus' *De Revolutionibus* and the reputation of Copernicus himself, then, can hardly be described as revolutionary during the 16th century. Amongst the readers of his *De Revolutionibus,* his physical claims were largely ignored and it was his mathematical and technical competence in computational astronomy that established his authority: he was often cited as an authority on a par with Ptolemy, rather than one who replaced the ancient astronomer. Towards the end of the 16th century, however, there were serious attempts to grapple with Copernicus' model of the physical

universe. Thomas Digges (c.1545–c.1595) translated most of Book I of the *De Revolutionibus* in his *A Perfit Description of the Coelestiall Orbes* (1576). Digges abandoned the idea of the sphere of fixed stars and placed Copernicus' heliocentric model in an infinite universe of stars. Tycho Brahe devised a 'compromise' model – the Moon and the Sun went around the Earth, but the other planets orbited around the Sun. A stationary Earth meant that Aristotelian physics could be maintained. This model became popular with early 17th-century astronomers. Tycho Brahe's assistant, Johannes Kepler, believed in a heliocentric universe, though he diverged considerably from Copernicus' insistence on perfect circles by adopting elliptic orbits of planets. It is debatable whether Giordano Bruno (1548–1600) should be considered a 'martyr' to the new science, since his views were heavily steeped in neo-Platonic mysticism and he lacked competence in mathematical astronomy. It was Galileo Galilei, in the 17th century, in his *Dialogues Concerning Two New*

Sciences (1638) spelt out a new system of physics which was consistent with his heliocentric world-view.

It was not until the Galileo affair (1616), when heliocentric views came to be regarded as directly contradicting Biblical truth, that the *De Revolutionibus* was placed on the *Index of Prohibited Books,* and requisite corrections were spelt out in 1620. It seems that 60% of the copies in Italy (and hardly any in Spain or Portugal) were censored. The *De Revolutionibus* was taken off the Index in 1758.

SACHIKO KUSUKAWA

Further Reading

Robert S Westman, 'The Melanchthon Circle, Rheticus and the Wittenberg Interpretation of the Copernican Theory', *Isis* 56 (1975), 165–93; Owen Gingerich, *The Copernicus Census,* forthcoming; Owen Gingerich, 'Copernicus' *De revolutionibus:* an example of Renaissance scientific printing' in G R Tyson and S S Wagonheim (eds), *Print and Culture in the Renaissance: Essays on the Advent of Printing in Europe* (London) pp. 55–73.

Curiously, some of the most zealous persecutors of the Jews were themselves of *converso* stock – the antipope Benedict XIII (Pedro de Luna; died 1423) and Torquemada are two well-known examples.

Coornheert, Dirck Volckertszoon
(1522–1590)

Dutch humanist, scholar, and engraver. From 1566 he was a keen supporter of ◊William the Silent in the political struggle against Spain, and had to withdraw into exile in 1568, acting as the prince's political agent in Cleves, in France. A Catholic, he argued in favour of religious toleration, and his views on free will strongly influenced the development of Arminianism. His own writings, as well as his transla-

tions of ◊Boccaccio, Homer, and Latin authors, played an important role in the development of Dutch literature.

He drew up the manifesto of William the Silent, and in 1568 he was imprisoned in The Hague by the Spanish. He escaped to Cleves, where he was taught engraving by Goltzius. He returned from exile in 1572 and from 1577 he was a notary at Haarlem; he later moved to Delft and finally, in 1588, to Gouda.

On his return to the Netherlands he became embroiled in a serious theological controversy with orthodox Calvinists, largely because of his views on free will. His writings influenced the young Arminius (appointed to refute Coornheert but in large measure persuaded by him), and he is consequently seen as one of the forebears of Arminianism. His humanist-inspired defence of religious toleration found little favour with either Catholics or Calvinists.

In his writings – he wrote poetry, plays, and treatises, many of them polemics against the Calvinists – he strove to improve the literary quality of Dutch. *Zedekunst* (1586) is modelled on the ethical treatises of the ancient stoics. He also began, but left incomplete, a Dutch version of the New Testament (from the Latin of ◊Erasmus).

Coornheert was also an engraver and book illustrator, illustrating *Das Buch Extasis* (1576) by Noot. He translated works by Cicero, Boethius, and Seneca, Homer's *Odyssey*, various tales from Boccaccio's *Decameron*, and Boethius.

Coperario, John (ADOPTED NAME OF JOHN COOPER) (c. 1570–1626)

English lutenist, viol player, and composer. He studied in Italy and on his return, about 1604, adopted the Italianized name of Coperario or Coprario. He taught the children of James I and was the master of William and Henry Lawes. In 1625 he was appointed composer-in-ordinary to Charles I.

Works include:

The Masque of the Inner Temple and Gray's Inn (F Beaumont), *The Masque of Flowers*; *Funeral Teares* on the death of the Earl of Devonshire, *Songs of Mourning* on the death of Prince Henry (words by Campion); anthems; works for viols and for viols and organ; fancies for the organ based on Italian madrigals; lute music; songs and other pieces.

Copernicus, Nicolaus (LATINIZED FORM OF MIKOŁAJ KOPERNIK) (1473–1543)

Polish astronomer who believed that the Sun, not the Earth, is at the centre of the Solar System, thus defying the Christian Church doctrine of the time. For 30 years, he worked on the hypothesis that the rotation and the orbital motion of the Earth are responsible for the apparent movement of the heavenly bodies. His great work *De Revolutionibus Orbium Coelestium/On the Revolutions of the Heavenly Spheres* was the important first step to the more accurate picture of the Solar System built up by Tycho ◊Brahe, ◊Kepler, ◊Galileo, and later astronomers.

Copernicus proposed replacing Ptolemy's ideas with a model in which the planets (including the Earth) orbited a centrally situated Sun. He proposed that the Earth described one full orbit of the Sun in a year, whereas the Moon orbited the Earth. The Earth rotated daily about its axis (which was inclined at 23.5° to the plane of orbit), thus accounting for the apparent daily rotation of the sphere of the fixed stars.

This model was a distinct improvement on the Ptolemaic system for a number of reasons. It explained why the planets Mercury and Venus displayed only 'limited motion'; their orbits were inside that of the Earth's. Similarly, it explained that the planets Mars, Jupiter, and Saturn displayed such curious patterns in their movements ('retrograde motion', loops, and kinks) because they travel in outer orbits at a slower pace than the Earth. The movement of the Earth on its axis accounted for the precession of the equinoxes, previously discovered by Hipparchus.

Copernicus's model represents a complete reformation of astronomy by replacing the **anthropocentric** view of the universe with the **heliocentric** viewpoint. Unable to free himself from the constraints of Classical thinking, however, Copernicus was able to imagine only circular planetary orbits. This forced him to retain the system of epicycles, with the Earth revolving around a centre that revolved around another centre, which in turn orbited the Sun. Kepler rescued the model by introducing the concept of elliptical orbits. Copernicus also held to the notion of spheres, in which the planets were supposed to travel. It was Brahe who finally rid astronomy of that concept.

Copernicus was born in Toruń, on the River Vistula, Poland. After the death of his father in 1483, he was adopted by his uncle, Lucas Watzelrode, afterwards bishop of Ermland. He studied mathematics, astronomy, classics, law, philosophy, and medicine at Kraków and various universities in Italy. In 1500 he lectured in mathematics in Rome with great success. On his return to Poland in 1506 he became physician to his uncle, the bishop of Varmia, at the castle of Heilsberg. His uncle had also secured for him the post of canon at Frombork, enabling him to intersperse astronomical work with the duties of various civil offices.

Copernicus began to make astronomical observations in 1497, although he relied mainly on data accumulated by others. Where observational facts failed he found them himself, but he was essentially a thinker rather than an observer. In about 1513 he wrote a brief, anonymous text entitled *Commentariolus*, outlining the material he later discussed in *De Revolutionibus*. He had been at work for more than 30 years before at last agreeing to the publication of his major work. This was not, as is often supposed, because he feared that it would be seen as heretical, but because his idea was at that time so incredible that only those with an intimate knowledge of astronomy could be expected to consider it.

Copernicus was at last persuaded to publish by friends and by his young pupil Rheticus, who issued an account of the new system under the title *Narratio Prima de Libris Revolutionum*. This was the first printed work on the theory, and as it was received with less ridicule than Copernicus had feared, he consented to the publication of his own work. Pope Paul III accepted the dedication of the work to himself. Andreas Osiander, a Lutheran minister, oversaw the publication and inserted a preface (without permission) stating that the theory was intended merely as an aid to the calculation of planetary positions, not as a statement of reality. This served to compromise the value of the text in the eyes of many astronomers, but it also saved the book from instant condemnation by the Roman Catholic Church.

The book's immediate effects in the sphere of philosophy and theology were not conspicuous. The reaction was favourable among Roman Catholics but antagonistic among Lutherans. There was no question of persecution, and it was only when new philosophies began to develop from it that *De Revolutionibus* was denounced by ◊Luther. It was placed on the index of forbidden books in 1616, and was removed in 1835.

Cornaro, Caterina (1454–1510)

Queen of Cyprus 1473–89. A Venetian noblewoman, she married James II, King of Cyprus, in 1472. She was left a widow in 1473 and governed for her son, James III, until his death in 1475. She was browbeaten into abdicating in favour of the Venetian republic in 1489.

She retired to the castle of Asolo, near Venice, where she lived until her death, surrounded by poets and artists. Pietro ◊Bembo set his *Gli Asolani* at her

residence; she was painted by many artists, including Palma Vecchio, Gentile Bellini, and Titian.

Cornaro, Luigi (1475–1566)

Italian dietician. After a period of serious ill health, he devised an austere diet, largely through trial and error, and published several treatises explaining his theories on the relationship between food and health. Some of the first systematic accounts of diet, they enjoyed a wide popularity, largely because he himself lived to the age of 91. His *Discorsi sulla vita sobria/Discourse on the Sober Life* (1558) was widely translated.

A member of the powerful Cornaro family of Venice, he spent the first 40 years of his life indulging his passion for food and drink. Threatened by his physician with death if he continued to indulge himself, Cornaro resolved to restrict his diet drastically. Initially it was reduced to a daily intake of a modest amount of food and wine, but eventually it was reduced to a single egg a day.

Corneille de Lyon (CORNEILLE DE LA HAYE) (DIED 1574)

Dutch-born French painter. He became a naturalized French subject in 1547 and was court painter to Henry II and Charles IX, working in Lyon 1541–74. He is known to have painted small portraits, though no works are attributed to him with certainty.

A number of paintings, distinguishable from those of his contemporary François ◊Clouet (and, unlike them, apparently not based on preliminary drawings), are considered as being in his style.

Cornelisz., Cornelis (CORNELIS VAN HAARLEM) (1562–1638)

Dutch historical and portrait painter. He created large historical pictures filled with contorted, life-size nudes and group portraits, for example his *Banquet of the Archers Guild* (1583, Haarlem).

A pupil in Haarlem of Pieter ◊Aertzen, he also studied in Rouen, France, and Antwerp.

Cornelisz., Lucas (1495–1552)

Dutch subject and portrait painter. Probably trained by his father, Cornelisz Engelbrechtsz, he moved to England around 1527 and became one of Henry

VIII's court painters. He was later employed in Ferrara, Italy.

Cornelisz. (van Oostzanen), Jakob (1477–1533)

Dutch painter. His style was modelled on that of the south Netherlands but added to it a hard precision, as in the *Christ Appearing to Mary Magdalene* (Staatliche Kunstsammlungen, Kassel, Germany). He was the master of Jan Scorel.

Cornyshe, William (DIED 1523)

English composer. He was attached to the courts of Henry VII and Henry VIII, not only as a musician, but also as an actor and producer of interludes and pageants. He was made a Gentleman of the Chapel Royal in about 1496, and succeeded William Newark as Master of the Children in 1509. He wrote music for the court banquets and masques and officiated in France at the Field of the Cloth of Gold in 1520.

Several other musicians of the period also had the surname Cornyshe, including a **William Cornyshe senior** (died *c.* 1502), who was the first recorded master of the choristers at Westminster Abbey, about 1480–90.

Works include:

Motets, Magnificats, *Ave Maria*; secular songs, some with satirical words, for instruments and voices, including a setting of Skelton's *Hoyda, Jolly Rutterkin*.

Coronado, Francisco Vásquez de (*c.* 1510–1554)

Spanish explorer who sailed to the New World in 1535 in search of gold. In 1540 he set out with several hundred men from the Gulf of California on an exploration of what are today the Southern states. Although he failed to discover any gold, his expedition came across the impressive Grand Canyon of the Colorado and introduced the use of the horse to the indigenous Indians.

Correggio (ASSUMED NAME OF **ANTONIO ALLEGRI**) (*c.* 1494–1534)

Italian painter. Active primarily in Parma, his style reflects his studies of ◊Leonardo da Vinci and ◊Titian, while anticipating the Baroque in its emphasis on movement, softer forms, and contrasts of light and shade.

In his youth Correggio studied with Bianchi Ferrari at Modena and later in Mantua with ◊Mantegna, although he appears to have been most deeply influenced by Leonardo as can be seen in his subtly gradated ◊*chiaroscuro*. It is presumed that he visited Rome to study the paintings of ◊Michelangelo and ◊Raphael, which inspired him with a new vigour and boldness, particularly evident in his frescoes following his return to Parma, such as in the Camera di San Paolo in the monastery of Saint Lodovico (1518). Although he received his greatest contemporary praise from ◊Titian for the dramatic fresco of the *Assumption of the Virgin* (1526–30) for the cathedral of Parma, Correggio was also a prolific oil painter of both religious and mythological subjects. He employed a rich technique characterized by warm colours defined by *chiaroscuro,* such as in the Dresden *Nativity* and the London *Cupid and Psyche*.

Corsi, Jacopo (1561–1602)

Italian nobleman and amateur composer. He was involved in the initiation of opera at Florence. Peri's *Dafne* was produced at his house in 1598 and he took some share in its composition.

Corteccia, (Pier) Francesco di Bernardo (1502–1571)

Italian organist and composer. He made a substantial contribution to the development of the madrigal; many of those he wrote were for particular occasions, the most famous being those composed for the wedding of Duke Cosimo I de' Medici to Eleonora of Toledo in 1539. He also wrote a considerable amount of liturgical music, though this is more conservative in style than his secular compositions.

From 1515 he served the Church of S Giovanni Battista, Florence, in various capacities and was organist there 1535–39. In 1531 he was appointed organist at the Church of San Lorenzo, Florence, and from 1539 was maestro di cappella to Duke Cosimo I. For the marriage of Cosimo's son Francesco to Joanna of Austria in 1565 he collaborated with the elder Alessandro Striggio on music for Giovanni Battista Cini's intermezzo *Psiche ed Amore*. Corteccia also wrote a prologue, five *intermedii*, and an epilogue for Antonio Landi's comedy *Il comodo*, which was performed at the wedding banquet. The *intermedii* were written for solo singers, ensemble, and varying combinations of instruments to depict different times of the day; they were published in Corteccia's madrigal collection of 1547.

Works include:
Hymns in four parts, canticles and responses, madrigals; pieces for four to eight voices and instruments.

Cortegiano, Il

See ◊*Courtier, The*.

Cortés, Hernán Ferdinand (1485–1547)

Spanish conquistador. He conquered the Aztec empire 1519–21, and secured Mexico for Spain.

Cortés went to the West Indies as a young man and in 1518 was given command of an expedition to Mexico. Landing with only 600 men, he was at first received as a god by the Aztec emperor ◊Montezuma II but was expelled from Tenochtitlán (Mexico City) when he was found not to be 'divine'. With the aid of Indian allies he recaptured the city in 1521, and overthrew the Aztec empire. His conquests eventually included most of Mexico and northern Central America.

cortigiana onesta (ITALIAN 'HONEST COURTESAN')

High-class prostitute; an 'honest courtesan' was educated, worked from home (rather than in a brothel), was expensive and selective in her clients. You were most likely to find her in Rome or Venice. An 'honest courtesan' like Veronica ◊Franco could gain an international reputation – Franco was visited by Henry III of France when he passed through Venice in 1574. She could also present her own pretensions to learning, as did Tullia D'Aragona (died 1558) – known as the courtesan of the academicians because of the scholarly elements in her clientele – who published her own *Rime* (1547).

Coryate, Thomas (c. 1577–1617)

English traveller, writer, and eccentric. In 1608 he travelled through France and Italy to Venice, returning via Switzerland, Germany, and the Netherlands. His account of this tour, *Coryate's Crudities* (1611), was prefaced with verses by many eminent contemporaries. In 1612 he set out on extensive travels through Asia, and visited the court of the Great Mogul at Ajmer, India.

In 1612 he went by sea to Constantinople, spending nearly a year there before visiting Palestine. From Aleppo, Syria, he travelled through Persia (Iran) and Afghanistan to Ajmer. After over two years in India he died at Surat.

He was born at Odcombe, Somerset, where his father was rector. Educated at Winchester College and Oxford University, he then entered the household of Prince Henry, eldest son of James I of England, where he earned a reputation for fooling. He was an accomplished wit, scholar, and linguist. Most of Coryate's notes on his eastern travels have been lost, but some fragments and five letters from India were published.

Cossa, Francesco (1435–1477)

Italian painter. He worked at the court of Ferrara and also in Bologna, where he painted altarpieces. He was largely responsible for a series of frescoes of *The Months* at the Schifanoia Palace, Ferrara (completed in 1470).

Cossa was born in Ferrara and was probably the pupil of Cosimo Tura; he was also influenced by Andrea Mantegna and Piero della Francesca. In the early 1470s he left Ferrara for Bologna, where he produced a number of church paintings, including his altarpiece *The Madonna Enthroned*. He was the master of Lorenzo ◊Costa.

Costa, Lorenzo (1460–1535)

Italian painter, active in Bologna. An early work is his *Madonna Enthroned with the Bentivoglio Family* (1487) in the Bentivoglio Chapel of S Giacomo Maggiore, Bologna. He succeeded Andrea Mantegna as court painter to the Gonzagas in Mantua in 1509.

Born in Ferrara, he probably studied under Cosimo Tura and Francesco Cossa. In Bologna his work was influenced by the softer style of Francesco Francia, with whom he worked in 1506. The two allegories in the Louvre, Paris, the *Gateway of Comus* and the *Garden of Harmony*, were painted for the *studiolo* of Isabella d'Este.

His two sons **Ippolito** and **Girolamo** were also painters.

Costanzo, Angelo di (1507–1591)

Italian historian and poet, born in Naples. His most important work was *Historia del Regno di Napoli, 1250–1489* (published 1581–82), which occupied him for over 30 years.

Coster, Laurens Janszoon (*c.* 1370–1440)

Dutch printer. According to some sources, he invented movable type, but after his death an apprentice ran off to Mainz with the blocks and, taking Johann ◊Gutenberg into his confidence, began a printing business with him.

Cotton, Robert Bruce (1571–1631)

English antiquary. At his home in Westminster he built up a fine collection of historical manuscripts and coins, many of which derived from the dissolution of the monasteries. His son **Thomas Cotton** (1594–1662) added to the library (which eventually became the Cottonian Collection of the British Library, London).

During his lifetime, Cotton acquired a great reputation as an antiquary. He was referred to by Queen Elizabeth I regarding a question of precedence between England and Spain, and similar requests were made by members of her government. Under King James VI and I he rapidly gained royal favour, being employed on several antiquarian researches.

Cotton was first elected to Parliament in 1604, but after the accession of Charles I his influence was used in opposition to the crown on constitutional grounds, and he strongly opposed the suggested debasement of the coinage. Cotton's written criticisms of royalty led to his exclusion in 1629 from his library, which was not restored to the family until after his death.

Cotton was particularly concerned to collect manuscripts relating to English history – sometimes so keen that he helped books wander from other libraries to his own. He ordered his collection in a series of cupboards above which there were busts of Roman emperors; these shelf marks are still used.

Council, General, of the Church

See ◊General Council of the Church.

Council of Ten

Italian *Consiglio dei Dieci*, the highest decision-making body in the Venetian Republic. It was mainly responsible for state security. Established in 1310, it consisted of 10 (sometimes 16) senior figures in the Venetian government. In time it became the most powerful body in Venetian affairs, its aims being to protect the interests of Venice (from both internal and external threats) and to investigate serious crime. It employed spies, conducted secret diplomacy, and sometimes ordered assassinations. It was abolished in 1797, when Venice fell to Napoleon.

It was created after the defeat in 1310 of the revolt, led by Baiamonte Tiepolo, against the increasing power of Venice's aristocratic families. The Council consisted of the Doge and his six councillors, together with members elected from the Great Council and the Supreme Court, the selection being made by the Great Council. Usually, members were elected for one year and could not serve consecutive terms.

After the appointment of three inquisitors of state in 1539 for the secret investigation and punishment of crimes, the council was widely perceived as a sinister organization.

counterpoint

In music, the art of combining different forms of an original melody with apparent freedom while preserving a harmonious effect. Giovanni Palestrina was a master of counterpoint.

Counter-Reformation

Name given since the 19th century to a series of measures taken by the Catholic Church to counter the Protestant Reformations. These measures included the reaffirmation of traditional doctrine and simultaneous reorganization of the Church at the Council of Trent; the repression of heresy through increased use of the Inquisition and the censorship of the *Index Librorum Prohibitorum*; and the use of new clerical orders, in particular the Jesuits, as missionaries to reconvert the lost souls.

The term is problematic, however, as it assumes the

Catholic Church was merely reactive to the Lutheran threat. However, there was a tradition of proactive reform within the Church. The Jesuits of Ignatius Loyola, for example, were a late instance of a new order: they were preceded by, among others, the Theatines of 1524 who themselves developed out of the Oratory of Divine Love in Rome that included in its number Matteo Giberti (1495–1543) and ◊Cajetan and Gian Pietro Carafa (the future ◊Paul IV). Again, while the Catholic Church might have been increasingly concerned to monitor and improve lay piety, there was no lack of fervent commitment to the church before the Luther affair, reflected in bequests to local churches and the organization of lay confraternities. Some of these popular habits, like the veneration of relics, came under attack from humanists within the Church, but their calls for reform were, in effect, another sign of its vitality and variety, rather than a symptom of a thirst for drastic change which could only be quenched by Luther. See also ◊reform and ◊Refomation.

Courtier, The (ITALIAN *IL CORTEGIANO*)

Dialogue by the Italian writer Baldassare ◊Castiglione, first written between 1508 and 1515, redrafted in 1521–24, and printed in 1528, a year before the author died. The four books record an imaginary conversation supposed to have taken place on consecutive evenings at the court of Urbino, Italy, in March 1507. The ladies and gentlemen of the court entertain themselves with witty and improving talk on various topics, all related to the subject of the ideal courtier.

The speakers, who include Bernardo ◊Accolti ('L'Unico Aretino'), Pietro ◊Bembo, and Giuliano de' Medici, construct an image of a courtier whose aim is to advise his prince frankly by winning his friendship and admiration; to do this, the courtier must master all the arts of war and peace and display them with an effortless superiority called *sprezzatura*.

The Courtier began to circulate before it was printed, with manuscripts being read in Italian court circles (much to Castiglione's annoyance, Vittoria ◊Colonna had a copy made). Its printing made it available beyond the courts of the peninsula and its international circulation was assisted by Castiglione's own circumstances: he had copies imported to Spain

and sent at least one copy to Portugal – the dedicatee was the aristocratic bishop Dom Miguel de Silva. The first translation of the work was made in Spain, by Joan ◊Boscà i Almogàver, and printed in 1534; versions in French, English (by Thomas ◊Hoby), German, and Latin followed.

In rendering the text into their vernacular, each translator had to deal with the new term *sprezzatura*, and many did so with uncertainty. Thomas Hoby, for example, was characteristic in trying out two terms – 'recklessness' and (a term that had pejorative overtones) 'disgracing'. One of the French translators chose to render the noun as 'nonchalance' (a solution which, since the 18th century, has also found favour in English), though others thought that word, too, needed glossing.

If translators often had difficulty with the terminology, the practice of the ideal behaviour described in *The Courtier* proved even more challenging. Few, if any, ever achieved this ideal – and some thought it unwise even to attempt it: the long-standing anti-court tradition (to which Pope ◊Pius II and Ulrich von ◊Hutten had contributed) did not wilt before the nonchalant courtier. Even some of the praise of *The Courtier* was guarded: Roger ◊Ascham advised young gentlemen to study Castiglione's book, but mainly because it saved them from the dangers of having to travel to Italy.

However, *The Courtier* was read, praised, and imitated, in part because it, along with works such as Henry Peacham's *The Compleat Gentleman* (1622), provided the aspirant with what were effectively self-help books on 'how to be a courtier'. Yet, however many strained to achieve effortlessness, *The Courtier* had another use as well: it provided an easy reference point for flattering praise. A Philip ◊Sidney, say, may not have been courtly perfection made flesh, but his admirers could build a myth around him by claiming that he was the ideal of which Castiglione wrote.

Cousin, Jean (1490–c. 1560)

French painter influenced by the style employed in the decoration at ◊Fontainebleau. He produced the first important French painting of a nude, *Eva Prima Pandora* (Louvre, Paris), a work influenced by the Venetian painters Titian and Giorgione.

His son **Jean Cousin the Younger** (*c*. 1520–

*c.*1592) was a painter, goldsmith, miniaturist, sculptor, and engraver. He painted in oils a *Last Judgement* (Louvre, Paris) with a multitude of nude figures.

Couto, Diogo do (1542–1616)

Portuguese adventurer, archivist, and author. He left John III's court for India in 1559 to defend Portuguese interests. Arriving in Mozambique in 1567/68, he encountered his impoverished friend ◊Camões, who encouraged him to write a commentary on *The Lusiads.* The pair arrived in Lisbon in 1570 but Couto returned to India in 1571, settling in Goa. Seeking royal patronage, he wrote a chronicle of recent events in India (*Década X/Decade X*). In 1595 Philip II appointed him archivist at Goa and successor to João de ◊Barros.

Couto's manuscripts suffered numerous vicissitudes. His *Commentários/Commentaries* on *The Lusiads* (apparently never completed) are known only from a reference in book eight of his *Décadas da Asia/Asian Decades.* Couto's fourth *Decade* was published in 1602; he was forced to rewrite books VIII and IXafter they were stolen, and all six *Decades* were only published as a set 1778–88. The fragmentary survival of *Decade X* may be due to Couto's critical accounts of Portuguese activities, a tone also adopted in the second version of his *Diálogo do soldado prático que trata dos enganos e desenganos da India/The Experienced Soldier's Dialogue, Concerning the Illusions and Disillusions of India* (1612). His original version, equally critical, was stolen and circulated widely but anonymously in Lisbon; both works were published together for the first time in 1790.

Covarrubias, Alonso de (*c.* 1488–1564)

Spanish architect and sculptor. His works, which were increasingly influenced by Italian fashions, include the chapel of the New Kings (1531–34) in Toledo Cathedral. As architect to the royal castles he also oversaw the rebuilding of the Alcázar at Toledo (1537–53) for Emperor ◊Charles V. Many of his works are good examples of the ◊plateresque style.

Covarrubias was evidently trained in the Gothic tradition and, as one of nine consultants on Salamanca Cathedral, had an opportunity at an early age to practise in an essentially Gothic style. However, his subsequent works were executed in a manner influenced by contemporary Italian trends. Many of his most important works were executed in Toledo, where from 1504 he worked on the hospital of Santa Cruz with the late Gothic architect Enrique ◊Egas; on Egas's death (1534) Covarrubias succeeded him as master mason at Toledo Cathedral.

Other works included the Church of the Piedad at Guadalajara (1526), a fine staircase at the archbishop's palace at Alcalá (*c.* 1530), and the rebuilding of the Bisagra Neuva gate at Toledo (1559).

Coverdale, Miles (1488–1568)

English Protestant priest whose translation of the Bible (1535) was the first complete version to be printed in English. His translation of the psalms was used in the Book of Common Prayer.

Coverdale, born in Yorkshire, became a Catholic priest, but turned to Lutheranism and in 1528 went to the continent to avoid persecution. In 1539 he edited the Great Bible which was ordered to be placed in churches. After some years in Germany, he returned to England in 1548, and in 1551 was made bishop of Exeter. During the reign of Mary I he left the country.

Cowper, Robert (*c.* 1474–BETWEEN 1535 AND 1540)

English composer. He was clerk of King's College, Cambridge, 1493–95, and wrote sacred pieces and carols, notably those in *XX Songs* (1530).

Coxcie (COXCYEN), Michiel van (1499–1592)

Flemish painter and engraver. After a visit to Rome he based his style on that of ◊Raphael Sanzio, painting religious works such as *St Sebastian* and *Triumph of Christ* (both Musée Royal des Beaux-Arts, Antwerp).

Coxcie was born in Mechelen, and became a pupil of Bernard van Orley. On his return from Italy, he worked in Brussels and Antwerp. He also copied the van Eyck brothers' *Adoration of the Lamb* for Philip II of Spain.

Cranach, Lucas, THE ELDER (ORIGINALLY LUCAS MÜLLER) (1472–1553)

German painter, etcher, and woodcut artist. He painted religious scenes, allegories (many featuring full-length nudes), and precise and polished portraits, such as *Martin Luther* (1521, Uffizi, Florence).

He was born in Kronach, Bavaria, and settled in Wittenberg in 1504 to work for the elector of Saxony. He is associated with the artists Albrecht Dürer and Albrecht Altdorfer and was a close friend of the religious reformer Martin Luther, whose portrait he painted several times. *The Flight into Egypt* (1504, Staatliche Museum, Berlin) is typical in its combination of religious subject and sensitive landscape. His work shows the effect of the Reformation in changes of artistic direction, religious compositions gradually giving place to portraits of the Lutheran circle and to allegories from Classical mythology, in which the sensuality of women is freely expressed.

His second son, **Lucas Cranach the Younger** (1515–1586), succeeded him as director of the Cranach workshop.

Cranmer, Thomas (1489–1556)

English cleric, archbishop of Canterbury from 1533. A Protestant convert, he helped to shape the doctrines of the Church of England under Edward VI. He was responsible for the issue of the Prayer Books of 1549 and 1552, and supported the succession of Lady Jane Grey in 1553.

Condemned for heresy under the Catholic Mary Tudor, he at first recanted, but when his life was not spared, resumed his position and was burned at the stake, first holding to the fire the hand which had signed his recantation.

Cranmer suggested in 1529 that the question of Henry VIII's marriage to Catherine of Aragon should be referred to the universities of Europe rather than to the pope, and in 1533 he declared it null and void.

Credi, Lorenzo di (1458–1537)

Italian painter. In his sensitive Madonnas and other decorous religious paintings, his fondness for painting children appears. An example is *Madonna and Child* (Louvre, Paris).

A fellow pupil with Leonardo da Vinci under Andrea del ◊Verrocchio, he remained Verrocchio's assistant until the latter's death in 1488, and among his works is a portrait of Verrocchio (Uffizi, Florence). His work reflects the influence of the young Leonardo. He burnt some of his pictures during the 'bonfire of vanities' in 1497 led by the religious reformer ◊Savonarola.

Credi's works include *The Nativity* (Accademia, Florence); *The Virgin and Child* (National Gallery, London); and *The Holy Family* (National Gallery of Scotland, Edinburgh).

Crillon, Louis des Balbes de Berton de (c. 1541–1615)

French soldier, called *'le Brave'*. His valour at the siege of Calais in 1558 and the taking of Guines became almost legendary. At Dreux in 1562 and Montcontour in 1569 he again distinguished himself, fighting against the Huguenots, and at the Battle of Lepanto, in spite of wounds, he was chosen to bear the tidings of victory to the king.

Crivelli, Carlo (c. 1435–c. 1495)

Italian painter in the early Renaissance style. He was active in Venice and painted extremely detailed, decorated religious works, often festooned with garlands of fruit. The *Annunciation* (1486, National Gallery, London) is his best-known work.

His work, linear and wiry in style and full of rich and sometimes bizarre details, is highly personal and is outside the mainstream of art in Venice. He painted only religious subjects and, until the 1480s, employed the then outmoded device of raised plaster details in his work, which shows exquisite and sumptuous colour and decorative effects.

The National Gallery, London, has the finest collection of his work, including the richly embellished Demidoff altarpiece and the magnificent *Annunciation*. In addition to its formal splendour the latter includes a famous detail, the little girl peeping round a doorway, depicted with sympathetic humour.

He seems to have left Venice under a cloud after 1457 and thereafter worked mainly at Ascoli Piceno. He was knighted by Ferdinand II of Naples in 1490, after that date adding to his signature, 'Carolus Crivellus Venetus', the title 'Miles' ('knight').

Vittorio Crivelli was possibly a younger brother and painted in a similar style.

Crocus, Cornelius (c. 1500–1550)

Dutch educationalist and playwright. One of the first Jesuits, he became known for his school textbooks and for his Latin plays written for performance in schools. Of these the *Coemedia Sacra Joseph* (1535) was the most successful, achieving over 20 editions and being imitated as far afield as Poland (see ◊Rej, Mikołaj).

Crocus was born in Amsterdam and after studying at Louvain was ordained a priest. In 1528 he then became a headmaster in Amsterdam, a post which he held until the year before his death, when he resigned it in order to travel on foot to Rome, where he was received by Ignatius Loyola into the Jesuits. He engaged in religious controversy against ◊Luther and the ◊Anabaptists, wrote a popular textbook to assist children to form a correct Latin style (1536), as well as his play for schools.

Croll, Oswald (*c.* 1560–1609)

German chemist and physician. He is best known for his treatise *Basilica Chymica/Royal Chemistry* (1609), a highly influential text that did much to spread the ideas of ◊Paracelsus throughout Europe. This work also contained his treatise *De Signaturis*, an account of the widely held doctrine of signatures.

The son of the mayor of Wetter, near Marburg, Croll studied at a number of German universities, then spent several years travelling throughout Europe. Thereafter he practised medicine and in about 1602 entered the service of Prince Christian of Anhalt-Bernberg. He is also reported to have served subsequently as a councillor to Emperor Rudolf II.

Cromwell, Thomas (*c.* 1485–1540)

Earl of Essex, English politician who drafted the legislation that made the Church of England independent of Rome. Originally in Lord Chancellor Wolsey's service, he became secretary to ◊Henry VIII in 1534 and the real director of government policy; he was executed for treason. He was created a baron in 1536.

Cromwell had Henry divorced from Catherine of Aragon by a series of acts that proclaimed him head of the church. From 1536 to 1540 Cromwell suppressed the monasteries, ruthlessly crushed all opposition, and favoured Lutheranism. His mistake in arranging Henry's marriage to Anne of Cleves (to cement an alliance with the German Protestant princes against France and the Holy Roman Empire) led to his being accused of treason and beheaded.

Cronaca, Simone, Il (SIMONE DEL POLLAIUOLO) (1457–1508)

Florentine architect. Most of his works are in Florence, though he did spend the years 1475–85 in Rome, where he gained an understanding of Classical architecture. His Church of San Salvatore al Monte, near Florence, which he built at the end of his life, is a model of Classical simplicity and restraint, and was praised by Michelangelo.

Cronaca was born in Florence. In 1495 he built the Sala del Consiglio (now Sala dei Cinquecento) of the Palazzo Vecchio to accommodate the council instituted by ◊Savonarola on the lines of the Venetian ◊Maggior Consiglio. He continued the work of ◊Benedetto da Maiano on the Palazzo Strozzi; probably designed the Palazzo Guadagni; and executed the design by Giuliano da ◊Sangallo for the vestibule and sacristy of the Church of Santo Spirito in Florence.

Cueva, Juan de la (1543–1610)

Sevillian playwright, he left for Mexico in 1574, but soon returned to Spain, where he published his first play in 1579. His use of Spanish history and popular ballads for dramatic inspiration anticipates more skilled playwrights, such as Lope de ◊Vega; he also drew on classical themes and contemporary events (even writing a play on the 1527 ◊Sack of Rome). Unusually for the period, he took great pains to publish these works: his *Primera parte de las comedias y tragedias/Comedies and Tragedies, Part I* appeared in 1583, with a second edition in 1588. His claim that he was the first to have used Italianate metres in dramatic dialogue (made in his *Egemplar poético/Poetic Exempla*, unpublished until 1770) is perforce unprovable because of his contemporaries' casual attitude towards publication. Among his erotic and historically inspired poems (also diligently published) is the amusingly titled burlesque 'Batalla entre ranas y ratones/Battle between the frogs and the mice'.

culteranismo

Literary term which seems to have been first used by Luis Carrillo y Sotomayor in his *Libro de la erudición poética/Book of Poetic Knowledge*, published as part of his collected works in 1611. It referred, in positive terms, to the elliptical metaphors and Latinate language and syntax of ◊Góngora and his followers. Thus, the definite article was often omitted, Castilian words of Latin origin were used in their original, Latin, sense (for example, 'cándido' meant 'white', not 'frank') and metaphor substituted reference to the actual object: hence maidens had pearls, not teeth, and tablecloths were 'spun snow'. In time, *'culteranismo'* (or 'gongorismo', after its leading exponent) came to be a term of abuse. In Góngora's day it was attacked by Quevedo's *conceptismo* which advocated linguistic games of free association to achieve different levels of meaning; so, for example, the untranslatable *conceptista* 'Con dados se hacen condados' ('With dice, counties are made'), in which the conflation of words leads to a completely different meaning.

Cymbeline

Play by ◊Shakespeare, first acted about 1610 and printed in 1623. It combines various sources to tell the story of Imogen (derived from Ginevra in ◊Boccaccio's *Decameron*), the daughter of the legendary British king Cymbeline, who proves her virtue and constancy after several ordeals.

Cyriac of Ancona (CIRIACO DE' PIZZICOLLI) (1391–1452)

Italian merchant and antiquarian. Having a keen interest in Classical Greece, he travelled in Italy, Egypt, Greece, and the Near East, drawing monuments, copying inscriptions, and collecting manuscripts, statuettes, and medallions. His notebooks and collection, although not published until the mid-18th century, proved valuable to archaeologists and Classical scholars.

Czech Brethren (OR BOHEMIAN BRETHREN)

Followers of the religious reformer Jan ◊Huss in Bohemia. They were the radical but peaceful side of the Hussite church of Bohemia. After the suppression of the militant Taborites in 1434, the Czech Brethren became the group most closely associated with the evangelical and social views of the early Hussites. During the 16th century they played a leading role in Bohemian life but after the battle of the White Mountain in 1620 they fled Bohemia to escape persecution. One of their leading figures was Jan ◊Blahoslav.

Although possessing a sectarian tendency in their discipline and organization, they did demonstrate a desire for Protestant unity. Connections were established between Wittenberg and the brethren and it was for them that Luther wrote his *Adoration of the Sacrament* (1523). Under the leadership of Jan Augusta in 1532, they endeavoured to create greater unity through negotiation with Luther, Calvin, and Bucer, but this bore little fruit.

They won the freedom of worship under the Compacts of Prague in 1436, but they suffered persecution between 1548 and 1552 and many fled to Poland and Prussia. In 1575 Emperor ◊Maximilian II granted the Czech Brethren freedom to practise their religion, and under Rudolf II they played a leading role in education. Dispersed after the Battle of the White Mountain they eventually merged with other groups.

Daddi, Bernardo (DIED 1350)

Italian painter, active in Florence. Although he was influenced by Giotto – who was probably his teacher – his work leans towards the charm of colour and delicacy of line of Sienese painting. An example is his *Madonna and Child* (Accademia, Florence).

He was one of the founders of the artists' Guild of St Luke in Florence in 1339. Frescoes of the lives of St Stephen and St Lawrence in the Church of Sta Croce, Florence, are attributed to him.

Dalmau, Luis (DIED 1460)

Spanish painter of Catalan origin. He was court painter to ◊Alfonso V of Aragon. He assimilated the style of Netherlandish painting (visiting Bruges in 1431), being particularly influenced by Jan van Eyck. His single known work is the *Virgin and the Councillors* (1445, Museu d'Art Catalunya, Barcelona).

Although closely following Netherlandish style in symmetrical arrangement, architectural setting, and landscape distance, in portraiture and total effect this work has its own distinct Spanish character.

Damett, Thomas (1389 OR 1390–c. 1437)

English composer. He was at the Chapel Royal 1413–31, and was canon of Windsor from 1431 until his death. Works of his are included in the Old Hall manuscript.

Daniel, Samuel (1562–1619)

English poet. His works include the sonnet sequence *Delia* (1592) and several masques for the court (1604–14), such as *The Vision of the Twelve Goddesses* (1604), *The Queen's Arcadia* (1605), and *Hymen's Triumph* (1614).

Daniel went to Magdalen Hall, Oxford, in 1579, and then served as a tutor in several noble families. When *Delia* appeared in 1592 it was accompanied by a narrative poem, 'The Complaint of Rosamund'. Daniel's work also includes Senecan tragedies such as *Cleopatra* (1594) and *Philotas* (1605), a play about a favourite of Alexander the Great which, appearing to resemble too closely the circumstances of the fall of the Earl of Essex in 1601, got Daniel into some trouble at court; a number of masques and entertainments for King James I; treatises on poetry including *A Defence of Ryme* (against attempts to introduce Latin and Greek metres into English poetry); and the *Civil Wars*, an epic poem on English history. Ben Jonson cuttingly described him as 'a good honest Man ... but no poet'.

Daniele (Ricciarelli) da Volterra (1509–1566)

Italian painter and sculptor. His style notably transformed over the years from being influenced by his teacher Il ◊Sodoma (in the fresco of *Justice* (c. 1530) in the Palazzo dei Priori, Volterra) and Baldassare ◊Peruzzi (in frescoes in the villa of Cardinal Agostino Trivulzio, Rome), to one heavily endebted to Raphael and Michelangelo. This change was brought about by his long residence in Rome (from the mid-1530s) and is exemplified by his fresco of the *Deposition from the Cross* (1541) in the Orsini Chapel of Santa Trinità dei Monti.

Da Volterra also produced a bronze portrait bust of ◊Michelangelo (c. 1564, Bargello, Florence, and Louvre, Paris). At the very end of his life he was employed by Pope Pius IV to paint over the genitalia that cropped up all too often in Michelangelo's *Last Judgement* in the ◊Sistine Chapel. Though he made as few changes as possible and died leaving the work unfinished, he gained the nickname 'Il Braghettone' ('the breeches-maker').

Dante Alighieri (1265–1321)

Florentine-born poet and politician, exiled in 1302, with a remarkable and powerful range of intellectual, philosophical, visionary, and political expression. His writings mapped autobiographical experience and local political agitation onto universal theological speculation about the nature of God and the medieval conventions of temporal authority. This led to the condemnation of his political treatise *De Monarchia/Monarchy* (?*c*.1310-14) as heretical; the unique nature of Dante's work nevertheless ensured a lasting audience for his complex description of the afterworld, *La divina commedia/Divine Comedy* (written about 1304–19, first printed 1472).

Dante may have taken part as a knight in the Battle of Campaldino in 1289 against Arezzo. Suspicious of papal intervention in Florentine affairs even during his political career (*c*. 1295–1302), he became disgusted by the displacement of the pope to Avignon in 1309 and came to advocate the claims of the ◊Holy Roman Emperor. His political allegiances were complex and shifted according to circumstances; he composed many of his works while moving his base from city to city before his death in Ravenna in 1321.

oeuvre Dante was a profoundly expressive poet and imaginative visionary, though neither a great Latin prose stylist nor original political philosopher: his *terza rima* poetry was extremely influential in the development of the Tuscan vernacular which ultimately became normative in Italian Renaissance literature. Dante's early writings owed much to contemporary exponents of the fashionable, lyrical, emotionally intense courtly love poetry, adapted from an older Provençal tradition into an Italian civic context. It was Dante who gave this new literary convention the name ◊*dolce stil nuovo* ('sweet new style') and whose early poetic pieces (for example *Donne ch'avete intelletto d'amore/Ladies who Comprehend Love*) refined its grace and finesse. It was also Dante who rewrote the canon *La vita nuova/New Life* (a collection of poems dating from about 1293), shifting this vivid courtly language of unrequited passion into a Stoic philosophical sublimation of his love for Beatrice Portinari. After his exile Dante resumed his musings (the order of composition is not known and the dates suggested below are speculative). In *Convivio/The Banquet* (*c*. 1304–08) he revealed in retrospect the influence on *Vita nuova* of the *De amicitia/On Friendship* of Cicero and of *De consolatu philosophiae/The Consolation of Philosophy* of Boethius. *Convivio*, written in Tuscan dialect, is a series of philosophical treatises on language, love, and humanity: it elaborates the theme of *De Vulgari Eloquen-* *tia/On Vernacular Eloquence* (*c*. 1303–04) (Dante's defence, paradoxically in Latin, of the nobility of his dialect). *Convivio* also incorporates a distillation of contemporary Aristotelian 'scientific' learning, and at the same time anticipates neo-Platonic models of love and light later used to invoke images of the structure of the universe, of the near apotheosis of Beatrice, and of the immanent nature of the Godhead in *Paradiso/Paradise* (*c*. 1315–19), the third section of the *Divina commedia/Divine Comedy*.

In the initial decade of the trecento Dante also wrote at least the first part (*Inferno/Hell*, about 1304–08) and started the second (*Purgatorio/Purgatory*, *c*. 1308–14) of the *Divina commedia*. Set notionally at Easter in the first ever Jubilee Year, 1300, it records Dante's highly individual vision of his journey through a civic Hell, a rural, mountainous Purgatory, and a mystical astral Paradise. In *Inferno* and *Purgatorio*, the political events of the time inspired Dante to criticize with vehemence the corrupt nature of papal worldly authority and to advocate, prophetically, a secular saviour figure.

This theme was all the more enthusiastic and politically explicit in *De Monarchia/Monarchy* (?*c*. 1310–14), which encouraged the quixotic Italian adventures of the German Holy Roman Emperor Henry VII. According to Dante's argument – an elaboration of medieval pope–emperor dualism, with a new emphasis on renewal linked to the city of Rome itself – God and the law both rendered the Roman Empire the only justifiable instrument for world government. Dante also claimed, in tune with most late medieval prophecy, that the renewal of imperial power would herald a new spiritual age; *Monarchy* openly condemned the temporal ambitions and moral bankruptcy of the papacy (and was itself later condemned by the Avignon curia).

Paradiso, composed in the years before Dante's death, was just as politically strident at base, but less overtly concerned with secular salvation. Here the sacro-political element was eclipsed by the historical, theological, and cosmological web of Dante's speculations on divine providence, the Roman Empire, his own personal destiny, and the physical dimensions of an entirely idiosyncratic heaven.

Dante in the Renaissance In the course of the next three centuries, the *Divine Comedy* achieved sufficient fame among and beyond a literary elite that it could be referred to merely as *Il Dante*. Hundreds of manuscript copies of the poems, plus numerous scholarly commentaries, were made and it was printed as early as 1472, with nearly 50 editions appearing before 1600. Dante was rightly claimed by his trecento successors (including ◊Petrarch and ◊Boccaccio, the first to lecture on and write a biography of Dante) as the inaugurator of the powerful vernacular *stilnovismo*. What ◊Vasari did for ◊Giotto (see feature on the History of Art) was already in hand for Dante within years of his death. In some circles Dante's status (the first writer of a new Golden Age of literature) developed a *topos* of self-conscious revival. Similar encomia, though also criticism of his unclassical stylistic traits, continued after 1400 in the writings of ◊Bruni, ◊Filelfo, Palmieri, ◊Manetti, ◊Politian, ◊Ficino, ◊Landino, and Giovanni ◊Pico della Mirandola, and in the sophisticated analyses of Pietro ◊Bembo.

But Dante was not a 'typical' Renaissance poet. His verse, while sublimely lyrical, is often closer in comprehensibility to the obscure quatrains of ◊Nostradamus than to the clear and measured stanzas of ◊Tasso. The Florence that Dante evokes was a rich, growing, medieval mercantile entity with a measure of dominance over other Tuscan cities but with few pretensions – as yet – to be the centre of the cultural universe. His acquaintance with Cicero, ◊Virgil, Brutus, and Caesar, Cato, Trajan, Constantine, and Justinian is packaged uniquely in the *Divine Comedy*, but has more in common with the teachings of medieval rhetoricians than with the exchange of ideas among a humanist scholarly elite. His emphasis on Rome is distinct, and sincere, but owed as much to factors beyond the beginning of the revival of letters, such as the medieval heritage of papal–imperial claims to universal authority, and the fact that the 'exile' the papacy in Avignon focused attention on Rome as the 'proper' centre of power. Dante 'the first Renaisssance poet' was therefore a construction of the Renaissance period itself. Dante's own participation in soldiery and politics had more to do with ◊duecento than ◊quattrocento conceptions of the ideal citizenry of the republic, but this Classical ideal helped create Dante's 'Renaissance man' image. The same is true of Dante's use of Platonic as well as Aristotelian metaphysics: he was heir to the scientific language of Aquinas and Albertus Magnus, rather than the prophet of ◊Ficino or ◊Galileo.

On the other hand, there is no doubt that Dante's *Divine Comedy* was a unique creation; it is less morally, theologically, and historically conventional than many other Renaissance autobiographical, political, or metaphysical accounts. The combined humility and arrogance alone of Dante, subject-object of his poem, places it beyond literary category. Its perceived audience, to the dignified dismay of some humanist commentators, embraced the commercial *hoi polloi* as well as the *cognoscenti*. The *Divine Comedy* was a formal anomaly deliberately created in a precise chronological context; it was not a timeless, seamless, model Renaissance epic. Its vernacular linguistic subtlety and conceptual originality, nonetheless, undoubtedly provided inspiration for the generations of writers and thinkers who contributed to the acceleration of European literary culture in the 15th and 16th centuries.

Danti, Ignazio (1536–1586 OR 1587)

Perugian Dominican friar, scholar, papal cartographer, cosmographer, and astronomer, mathematician, amateur artist, architect, and distinguished mechanical engineer who designed the Vatican Galleria delle Carte Geographiche (Corridor of the Maps) in the later 1570s and helped provide 'scientific' support for pope ◊Gregory XIII's calendar reform of 1582.

Danti also constructed an enormous ceiling dial in the 1579–80 Torre dei Venti (Tower of the Winds), within the Vatican palace, to indicate the direction of the wind, connected by rods and gears to a vane high on the roof; this was roughly based on Vitruvius' description of the eponymous tower in ancient Athens. Danti's treatise of 1581, with its precise line-drawn diagrams and calculation of the meridian line (proving the Julian calendar inaccurate), still survives.

Danti, Vincenzo (1530–1576)

Italian goldsmith and sculptor. He worked mostly in Florence, producing for example a bronze group in the baptistery there, the *Beheading of St John the Baptist* (1571). These figures, as is characteristic of his work, are gracefully elongated and set in balletic poses. His sculpture has a delicacy of detail and an elegance of line reminiscent of the works of other goldsmiths-turned-sculptor, such as ◊Ghiberti and ◊Cellini.

He was born in Perugia and his earliest sculpture was a monumental bronze figure, *Pope Julius III Enthroned* (1553–56), set up outside Perugia Cathedral. From 1557 until 1573 Danti worked as a court sculptor to Duke ◊Cosimo I de' Medici. For the Medici he cast in bronze a large narrative relief of *Moses and the Brazen Serpent* for the altar frontal of a chapel, and a cupboard door (1561, both now in the Bargello, Florence), as well as a statuette of *Venus Anadyomene* for the *studiolo* of Francesco I in the Palazzo Vecchio (*c.* 1573).

Danti also carved marble statuary during the 1560s, examples being *Honour Triumphant over Falsehood* and *Duke Cosimo I* (both in the Bargello).

In 1567 he published a treatise on proportion. About 1573 he retired to Perugia, where he was appointed public architect and was a founder member of the Accademia del Disegno.

Datini, Francesco di Marco, 'THE MERCHANT OF PRATO' (*c.* 1335–1410),

Italian merchant. From his home town of Prato, near Florence, he built up a trading empire in northern Italy, Avignon, Aragon, and Majorca. After 1378 he settled in Florence, joined the silk guild there, and used his surplus wealth to embark on banking. His letters and account books have survived, affording an unparalleled insight into the life and values of a wealthy middle-class merchant in 14th-century Italy.

Daucher, Hans (*c.* 1485–1538)

German sculptor. Active in Augsburg, Hans was the son of the sculptor Adolf Daucher (*c.* 1460/65–1523/24) and executed a number of works for Emperor ◊Charles V and the dukes of Württemberg. Noted for his small decorative bronze figures, he also produced the influential group *Christ with the Virgin and St John* for the altar of the chapel of the Fugger family in Augsburg.

David Gerard David, *Ecce Homo*, (Fine Arts Museum, Bilbao). *e.t. archive*

David, Gerard (*c.* 1450–*c.* 1523)

Netherlandish painter. He was active chiefly in Bruges from about 1484. His style follows that of Rogier van der ◊Weyden, but he was also influenced by the taste in Antwerp for Italianate ornament. *The Marriage at Cana* (*c.* 1503, Louvre, Paris) is an example of his work.

Born in Holland, in a village near Gouda, he arrived in Bruges in 1482, married, in 1501, Cornelia Cnoop, daughter of the dean of the Goldsmiths' Guild and a miniaturist, and apart from a short stay at Antwerp, about 1515, when he was admitted to the Painters' Guild, spent his working life in that decaying but still wealthy city. Tranquil and highly detailed, his art takes elements from van ◊Eyck, van der Weyden, and ◊Memling, late works also suggesting the influence of Quinten ◊Massys. Famous paint-

ings are the panels ordered by the magistrates of Bruges for the Hall of Justice depicting the arrest and punishment of the corrupt judge Sisamnes (Bruges, Musée Communal) and the *Baptism of Christ*, also in Bruges. Some miniatures are attributed to him.

Davies (DAVIS), John ((1569–1626)

English poet and lawyer. In his *Orchestra* (1596), the world is exhibited as a dance; *Hymns to Astraea* (1599) consists of 26 acrostic poems addressed to Queen Elizabeth; and *Nosce Teipsum* (1599) is a didactic poem on the vanity of human learning and the immortality of the soul.

Born in Tisbury, Wiltshire, and educated at Oxford University, Davies became a barrister in 1595. He had a reputation for wit, and wrote many epigrams as well as poems. James I made him solicitor general of Ireland in 1603, and three years later attorney general. He was appointed lord chief justice shortly before his sudden death.

His *Discovery of the True Causes why Ireland Was Never Entirely Subdued* (1612) is a revealing account of the Irish question. In conjunction with Robert ◊Cotton, he founded the Society of Antiquaries.

Davis, John (c. 1550–1605)

English navigator and explorer. He sailed in search of the Northwest Passage through the Canadian Arctic to the Pacific Ocean in 1585, and in 1587 sailed to Baffin Bay through the straits named after him. He was the first European to see the Falkland Islands, in 1592.

Davy, Richard (c. 1467–c. 1507)

English composer. He was educated at Magdalen College, Oxford, where he was organist and choirmaster 1490–92. He later became chaplain to Anne Boleyn's grandfather and father 1501–15. He wrote motets, Passion music for Palm Sunday, part songs, and other pieces.

Day, John (c. 1574–1640)

English dramatist. He wrote an allegorical play, *The Parliament of Bees*, which probably appeared in 1607 and in which all the characters are bees. He collabo-

rated successfully with Thomas Dekker and others 1598–1608.

Decameron, The

Collection of tales by the Italian writer Giovanni Boccaccio, brought together 1348–53. Ten young people, fleeing plague-stricken Florence, amuse their fellow travellers by each telling a story on the ten days they spend together. The work had a great influence on English literature, particularly on Chaucer's *Canterbury Tales*.

Decembrio, Angelo (1415–AFTER 1467)

Italian humanist author, born in Milan but employed for much of his life in Ferrara. Educated first by Gasparino ◊Barzizza, he moved to Ferrara to finish his education with Battista ◊Guarino. He entered the intellectual circle around Leonello d' ◊Este in Ferrara and described (or rather mythologized) it in his *De Politia Litteraria/On The Lettered Republic* (1462). After Leonello's death he moved first to Naples and then to Spain in about 1458, but eventually returned to Ferrara.

Angelo was the younger brother of Pier Candido ◊Decembrio, but this was not a fact of which he was proud. Sometime early in Angelo's adult life, the two Decembrio brothers became permanently estranged. In part, this may have been because Angelo considered his brother's translation of Plato's *Republic* merely a crib of their father's version. In Angelo's eyes, Pier Candido was 'a most abominable man' who was attempting to appropriate the honour that should have been their father's.

Decembrio, Pier Candido (1399–1477)

Milanese humanist author and administrator. The son of Uberto (c. 1350–1427), who himself combined scholarly interests with an administrative career, Decembrio entered the service of Filippo Maria ◊Visconti in 1419. He acted as his secretary and diplomat, but found time to produce Latin and Italian translations, as well as a large collection of humanist epistles. After Visconti's death Decembrio was forced to wander Italy seeking a patron; he entered papal service, then the court of ◊Alfonso V and ended his career in the service of the d'Este of Ferrara.

Decembrio's writings impressed (according to his detractors) more by quantity than quality. Self-taught in Greek, he translated works into Latin, most notably Plato's *Republic* (which his father had already translated – a factor which brought criticism on Pier Candido from his own brother, Angelo ◊Decembrio); he presented this to Humfrey, Duke of ◊Gloucester. He also, for Visconti's benefit, translated Latin texts into Italian, both Classical (for example, Caesar) and humanist (Tito Livio ◊Frulovisi's biography of Henry V). His original works included a life of Visconti, as well as a *Panegyric* of Milan (*c.* 1436).

The *Panegyric* was written to rival Leonardo ◊Bruni's praises of Florence. Indeed, much of Decembrio's early career was spent trying to present himself as the equal of Bruni. In part, this was a matter of personal ambition, but it was also a reflection of politics: Milan and Florence were rivals, sometimes foes; the literary quarrels between these humanists continued the conflict by other means.

Decius, Nikolaus (*c.* 1485–AFTER 1546)

German Lutheran pastor and theologian. He wrote the words and composed or adapted the music of three chorales, anticipating even Martin Luther in this field.

Dedekind, Friedrich (*c.* 1525–1598)

German satirist and Protestant pastor. While a student at Wittenberg, he wrote *Grobianus Sive de Morum Simplicitate Libri Duo* (1549), a book of anecdotes in Latin verse which lampoons boorish, selfish behaviour (particularly table manners) by ironically praising it. It was freely translated into German in 1551, both versions becoming immensely popular during the second half of the 16th century and throughout the 17th century.

His satire was strongly influenced by the *Narrenschiff* of Brant.

dedication

A letter or verse prefacing a literary work and presenting it to a particular person. Humanists, like other writers, often published works with a dedication; dedicatees were usually leading clerics or secular politicians, sometimes fellow scholars. The advantage of

writing a dedication was threefold: it was a crucial method of seeking patronage; it associated the text with a respected figure; and it provided an opportunity for the author to introduce or explain his work. Sometimes, this explanation occupied a separate prefatory letter or verse, usually addressed to a friend. Whatever the particular arrangement, this introductory material was an integral part of the published work.

The scholar's expectation was that by dedicating a work to an influential figure, the dedicatee would feel bound to demonstrate his largesse in return. As, therefore, dedications were potentially lucrative, the more money-conscious humanists developed ways of maximizing that potential. For example, if a work consisted of several books or sections, each part could be dedicated separately to a different patron. So, in 1506 Thomas ◊More and ◊Erasmus produced a series of Lucian translations, and while More made a single dedication of all his work, Erasmus dedicated each of his translations separately, to, for example, Richard ◊Foxe and Christopher Urswick. Erasmus also used the technique of the double dedication; that is, one work was dedicated to one potential patron and then rededicated to another. Erasmus was not the first to do this; it was frequently practised in the 1430s by Lapo da ◊Castiglionchio.

The problem, however, with such ruses was that potential patrons became suspicious of humanists. Erasmus tells of an occasion when a dedication to Archbishop Warham attracted paltry recompense; Erasmus complained to his friend William Grocyn who explained that Warham suspected Erasmus was merely rededicating the work; for, after all, Grocyn said, 'It is the sort of thing you people do'.

de Dominis, Marc Antonio (1566–1624)

Dalmatian churchman. A brilliant student and teacher and member of the Jesuits, de Dominis left the order in 1596 and six years later became archbishop of Spalato. Deeply critical of the papacy, he relinquished his archbishopric in 1616 and fled to England. Warmly received by James I, he was made dean of Windsor and published an indictment of Rome, *De Republica Ecclesiastica* (1617). He later returned to Rome.

His period in England was made difficult by personal conflicts and political considerations, and in

1622 he left England and attempted a reconciliation with the church in Rome. In 1623 he published a vehement attack on the Anglican Church. He died in Rome, a captive of the Inquisition.

Dee, John (1527–1608)

English alchemist, astrologer, and mathematician who claimed to have transmuted metals into gold, although he died in poverty. He long enjoyed the favour of Elizabeth I, and was employed as a diplomatic agent.

He exported his brand of occult to Europe, making several extended journeys in the 1560s and 1580s; on the latter trip he spent some years in Poland and in Prague (at the court of the Holy Roman Emperor ◊Rudolf II).

Dee had a European-wide reputation as a learned man. His library, which impressed contemporaries, passed into the hands of Sir Kenelm Digby and eventually to the Bodleian Library, Oxford.

Dekker, Thomas (c. 1572–c. 1632)

English dramatist and pamphleteer. He wrote mainly in collaboration with others. His play *The Shoemaker's Holiday* (1600) was followed by collaborations with Thomas ◊Middleton, John ◊Webster, Philip Massinger, and others. His pamphlets include *The Gull's Hornbook* (1609), a lively satire on the fashions of the day.

Dekker's plays include *The Honest Whore* (1604–05) and *The Roaring Girl* (1611; both with Middleton), *Famous History of Sir Thomas Wyat* (1607, with Webster), *Virgin Martyr* (1622, with Massinger), and *The Witch of Edmonton* (1621, with John Ford and William Rowley).

della Porta, Giacomo (c. 1537–1602)

Italian architect working in Rome during the late 16th century, he completed several works by ◊Michelangelo. These include the Palazzo dei Conservatori on the Capitol and, most notably, the dome of St Peter's Cathedral (1586–90), though both he and Domenico ◊Fontana made a number of alterations to Michelangelo's designs.

Born in Rome, della Porta trained under Michelangelo and was later influenced by ◊Vignola,

developing a style based upon academic Mannerism. Sometime after 1572 he completed the façade for Vignola's Gesù, the mother church of the Jesuit order, He then incorporated features of Vignola's design into several of his own churches in Rome, including Santa Maria dei Monti (1580–81), S Atanasio (1580–83), and San Andrea della Valle (1591).

della Porta, Guglielmo (c. 1500–1577)

Italian sculptor. In 1537 he went to Rome, where he became the principal sculptor to Pope ◊Paul III. He was appointed to the office of the papal seal (*piombatore*) in 1547 and executed busts of the pope in bronze and marble as well as his monument to Paul III, central to which is a bronze seated portrait of the pope, in St Peter's in Rome.

Born in Milan, Guglielmo is first recorded working with other, older members of his sculptor family at Genoa in 1534. He was an admirer of Michelangelo, until their dispute over the nature and location of a monument to Paul III in St Peter's, of which Michelangelo was architect: this was Guglielmo's major work and now stands to the left of the high altar, though he had initially hoped that it would stand free under the dome. This work is a major contribution to a series of portraits of popes in St Peter's, the others including Pope Innocent VIII by ◊Pollaiuolo and the Baroque portraits by Bernini and Algardi.

Della Porta was a prolific draughtsman and also produced many smaller statuettes and reliefs of religious subjects in gold, silver, or bronze.

Del Monte, Pietro (c. 1400–1457)

Venetian cleric, author of papalist, legal, and humanist works. During the Council of ◊Basel, he wrote in support of papal power. Pope ◊Eugenius IV employed him as a diplomat, sending him to England 1435–40 and France 1442–45, and appointed him bishop of Brescia in 1442. In England, Del Monte dedicated to Humfrey, Duke of ◊Gloucester a humanist dialogue, *De Vitiorum Differencia* (mainly copied from ◊Poggio's *De Avaritia*). In his later years he produced a voluminous *Repertorium* of canon and civil law.

Deloney, Thomas (c. 1543–1600)

English novelist and poet. His works portray the everyday life of middle-class citizens and artisans. The narratives are episodic in structure, but they employ humour and irony and often have a dramatic immediacy. *Jack of Newberie* (1597) tells of weavers, *The Gentle Craft* (1598) of shoemakers, and *Thomas of Reading* (1600) of clothiers.

Deloney worked as a silk weaver in Norwich and wrote pamphlets and popular ballads, one of which, on the scarcity of corn in 1596, led him into trouble with the authorities. After this he turned to writing prose fiction.

Collections of his verse are *Strange Histories* (1602) and *The Garland of Good Will* (1618).

de l'Orme, Philibert (c. 1505/10–1570)

French architect. He is remembered principally as the author of two important architectural treatises, *Nouvelles Intentions* (1561) and *Architecture* (1567). His building work includes the tomb of Francis I in St Denis, begun in 1547, and extensions to the Château of Chenonceaux in the Loire Valley (1556–59), including the first storey of the picturesque covered bridge.

Born in Lyons, he was trained by his father as a builder, studied in Italy 1533–36, and returned to France about 1540. He was given charge of the work at Fontainebleau in 1548; extended the palace of the Tuileries (1565), with Jean Bullant (died 1578); and also designed the chateaux of St Maur-des-Fosses (*c.* 1540) and Anet (1547–56).

deposition from the cross

A depiction of the body of Christ being taken down from the cross as, for example, van der Weyden's *Deposition* (*c.* 1430, Prado, Madrid).

Dering (DEERING), Richard (c. 1580–1630)

English organist and composer. He became a Catholic and went to Brussels in 1617 as organist to the convent of English nuns, but returned to England to become organist to Henrietta Maria on her marriage to Charles I in 1625.

Works include:

Cantiones Sacrae for several voices, motets, anthems; canzonets for three and four voices, quodlibets on street cries; fancies and other pieces for viols.

Desiderio da Settignano (c. 1430–1464)

Italian sculptor. Desiderio was a successful imitator of the shallow-relief carvings (*rilievo schiacciato*) of ◊Donatello. One of his most important commissions was the altar of the sacrament (completed in 1461) in the Church of San Lorenzo in Florence.

Few facts are known about this precocious but short-lived sculptor. Born in the stone-quarrying village of Settignano, near Florence, he probably learned to carve from his family and later collaborated closely with Antonio ◊Rossellino. He was strongly influenced by Donatello, but cannot have been trained by him, for the master was in Padua during the relevant decade.

Among his other important works is the Marsuppini monument in the Church of Santa Croce in Florence (*c.* 1453), which was an elaboration on the theme of the Bruni monument by Bernardo Rossellino.

de Soto, Hernando (c. 1496–1542)

Spanish explorer who sailed with Pedro Arias de Ávila (*c.* 1440–1531) to Darien, Central America, in 1519, explored the Yucatán Peninsula in 1528, and travelled with Francisco Pizarro in Peru 1530–35. In 1538 he was made governor of Cuba and Florida. In his expedition of 1539 he explored Florida, Georgia, and the Mississippi River.

Des Périers, Bonaventure (c. 1510–c. 1544)

French writer and humanist. He is remembered for two works: his controversial *Cymbalum Mundi* (1537), a satirical attack on Christianity in the form of four allegorical dialogues, which was banned soon after publication, and *Nouvelles récréations et joyeux devis*, a collection of short stories providing a lively picture of 16th-century society, published posthumously in 1558.

He was born at Arnay-le-Duc and after collaborating with Olivetan on his translation of the Bible and with ◊Dolet on the *Commentarii Linguae Latinae*, Des Périers became *valet de chambre* and secretary to Marguerite de Navarre, whom he assisted with the transcription of her *Heptaméron*.

He is believed to have committed suicide in 1544.

Desportes, Philippe (1546–1606)

French poet. He was court poet to Henry III. His poems include *Premières oeuvres/First Works* (1573) and metrical versions of the Psalms. His love poetry, harmonious though conventional, reflects a revival of the style of the Italian poet ◊Petrarch.

Deutsch, Niklaus Manuel (c. 1484–1530)

Swiss artist, writer, and religious reformer. Many of his works dwell on the morbid subjects of ghosts and death, as in *The Dance of Death*, painted for the Dominican monastery at Berne (destroyed in 1660, it is now known only through copies). Having spent time in Italy, his work also reflects Italianate influence. He was an active supporter of the Reformation and wrote songs, plays, and treatises in its support.

Born in Berne, he studied painting in Colmar, and then in Venice under Titian. On his return to Berne he was commissioned to paint a series of pictures for a monastery there. This work, his *Dance of Death*, was in the style of Holbein. His other works include *The Judgment of Paris*, *Pyramus and Thisbe*, and *Beheading of John the Baptist*.

Deutsch was also an active member of the Berne city councils, and author of such satires on ecclesiastical affairs as *Der Ablasskrämer* (1525) and *Testament der Messe* (1528).

devotio moderna

A movement of revived religious spirituality which emerged in the Netherlands at the end of the 14th century and spread into the rest of Western Europe. Its emphasis was on individual, rather than communal, devotion, including the private reading of religious works.

The movement's followers were drawn from the laity, including women, and the clergy. Lay followers formed themselves into associations known as ◊Brethren of the Common Life. Among the followers of *devotio moderna* was ◊Thomas à Kempis, author of *De Imitatio Christi/Imitation of Christ*.

De Vries, Adriaen (c. 1545–1626)

Dutch sculptor. He was a pupil of ◊Giambologna in Florence, Italy. Most of his work was executed in Augsburg, where he designed a series of fountains, and in Prague, at the court of the Holy Roman Emperor ◊Rudolf II. For the emperor he produced two heroic busts, as well as mythological group statues, including *Mercury and Psyche* (1593, Louvre, Paris), and allegorical bronze reliefs, for example *Rudolf II as Patron of the Arts* (1609, Windsor Castle, England).

Diana, La

Beloved central character in Jorge de ◊Montemayor's *Los siete libros de la Diana/The seven books of Diana*, published at Valencia around 1559. The main plot is a study in frustrated love. Sireno and Diana love one another, but Diana marries Delio. Sireno, grief-stricken, visits the enchantress Felicia seeking a potion to turn his love for Diana to indifference. He is accompanied by other unhappy lovers, whose stories are weaved into the principal narrative. The potion has its effect; meanwhile, Diana remains trapped in an unhappy marriage. Montemayor's promised sequel never appeared; instead, it was continued by Gaspar Gil Polo. His *Los cinco libros de la Diana enamorada/The Five Books of Diana in Love*, in which Diana finally marries Sireno, appeared in 1564.

Although not the first ◊pastoral novel to have appeared in Castilian, *La Diana* was a phenomenal success (by 1581 it had run to 15 editions) and inspired numerous imitations, such as ◊Cervantes's *La Galatea*.

Diane de Poitiers (1499–1566)

Mistress of ◊Henry II of France. She exercised almost unlimited power over the king, who made her Duchess of Valentinois. When he died she was expelled from court by his widow, Catherine de' Medici.

Diaz, Bartholomeu (c. 1450–1500)

Portuguese explorer, the first European to reach the Cape of Good Hope, in 1488, and to establish a route around Africa. He drowned during an expedition with Pedro ◊Cabral.

Díaz del Castillo, Bernal (c. 1492–c. 1581)

Spanish soldier and chronicler. He arrived in the New World in 1514 with conquistador Pedro Arias de

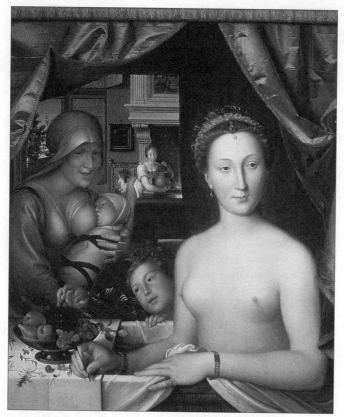

Diane de Poitiers Francois Clouet, *Lady in her Bath,* a portrait of a royal mistress, either Diane de Poitiers (Henri II's) or Marie Touchet (Charles IX's) (National Gallery of Art, Washington). *AKG London*

that this diverged from Classical usage. In humanist Latin therefore, the diphthongs were reintroduced – and the failure to mark the diphthong was regarded as a sign of barbarism. An example: if there were a humanist around today, he or she would insist that this book is an *Encyclopædia* and would brand as medieval barbarism the spelling *Encyclopedia*.

diptych

Painting or sculpture (usually in ivory) consisting of two panels hinged together, most often employed as a portable altar or ◊altarpiece.

Discourses on the First Ten Books of Livy (*Discorsi sopra La Prima Deca di Tito Livio*)

Italian Political tract by Niccolò Machiavelli, ostensibly a commentary on the first books of Livy's history of Rome. It contrasts the success of the ancient republic with the failures of the latterday government of Florence. The work seems to have arisen from discussions held in the ◊Orti Oricellari and was probably, in some form, read to members of that group; certainly, it was dedicated to Cosimo ◊Rucellai, who owned the gardens, and Zanobi Buondelmonti, who was also involved in the discussions there. Written probably between 1515 and 1519, it circulated in manuscript in Machiavelli's lifetime; it was printed in 1531.

Machiavelli's 'commentary' does not follow Livy word by word or even section by section. Instead, the present-day purpose of his work is reflected by its structure, selecting tales from Livy and demonstrating their immediate relevance; moreover, his discussion of a particular ancient event is often partial, allowing him to draw his desired conclusions. Nor is Livy Machiavelli's only source; indeed, in its cynicism the work is rather unlike Livy and much closer to a later Roman historian, ◊Tacitus.

Ávila (*c.* 1440–1531) and took part in the exploration of the Gulf coast of Mexico in 1517 and 1518. He served as a common soldier under Pedro de ◊Alvarado during the conquest of Mexico, and is known for his *Historia verdadera de la conquista de la Nueva España/True Account of the History of New Spain.*

Diaz de Solís, Juan (*c.* 1471–*c.* 1516)

Spanish explorer in South America who reached the estuary of the Río de la Plata, and was killed and reputedly eaten by cannibals.

diphthong

Two consecutive vowels creating one vowel sound in a word; a true Renaissance rediscovery. In medieval Latin, diphthongs such as 'ae' and 'oe' had been reduced to a mere 'e'. This caused consternation to the early practitioners of *studia humanitatis* (see feature) such as Niccolò ◊Niccoli when they realized

Machiavelli's concern in the *Discourses* is to discuss how a republic can be established and maintained so that it can achieve glory. Crucial are two factors: that the constitution be correctly arranged and that the people should have *virtù*. In both of these, Florence is severely lacking. The idea of *virtù* is central to Machiavelli's analysis; it is a concept by no means original to him but his definition subverts the humanist, Ciceronian tradition which believed what was proper and what was beneficial always coincided. In *The Prince*, Machiavelli put forward an exaggerated analysis that defined *virtù* as just the opposite of the conventional litany of virtues, like generosity, clemency, and the rest. In the *Discourses*, he stands by some of what he had said, insisting that *virtù* is what achieves success – for the sake of the republic. The founders of a city can help to sustain a people's *virtù*, for example, by arranging a civic-centred religion (Machiavelli does not exactly reject Christianity, just the lily-livered type practised in Christendom). But, if a people loses its *virtù*, it is set on the long path towards its own destruction – a pessimistic assessment for his own Florence.

Despite the notoriety of *The Prince*, the *Discourses* was Machiavelli's more substantial work. Indeed, the developed republicanism of this work suggests that his brief parody of the mirror for princes tradition was intended more in the spirit of irony than of honest counsel. There was certainly much which was objectionable to a Christian society in Machiavelli's *Discourses* but there was also much in his analysis that a few, in the 17th century, came to admire.

disegno (ITALIAN 'DESIGN')

Study of form and in particular figures through the practice of drawing live subjects, generally with chalk or pen on prepared paper. It was stressed by ◊Ghiberti and later ◊Vasari as the single most important skill for an artist to learn, and which aspiring youths were first taught. Although practised universally, the term came to be associated primarily with Florentine artists, who placed emphasis on its importance and contrasted it with Venetian emphasis on ◊*colore*.

dissection

See ◊anatomy.

Dissolution of the Monasteries

The closing down of English monasteries by royal order in the reign of ◊Henry VIII. A policy of taking the property of the church into crown hands was not unique to England; princes in Germany and Christian III in Denmark found this to be a singularly lucrative policy. They, though, introduced it (in their smaller states) along with Lutheranism, which advocated such moves. No such consistency occurred in England.

In 1535 Thomas Cromwell instituted a census of all ecclesiastical lands – the *Valor Ecclesiasticus*. On the basis of this and of reports of the dissolute life in some monasteries, a dissolution of the smaller houses was announced in 1536. At this point, it was claimed that the larger monasteries would remain but in the following year a creeping process of closing these institutions as well began and was complete by 1540. The resources which came to the crown through this process were not all pocketed or used for patronage; Henry had a plan to endow new bishoprics, for example at Oxford and Chester, and to attach to the cathedral an educational establishment: in Oxford's case, the prototype already existed in Wolsey's Cardinal College which became the double foundation of Christ Church and the city's cathedral in 1546.

The Dissolution did not go by without facing opposition: the large-scale revolt, the Pilgrimage of Grace in 1536, had as one of its main complaints the destruction of these established parts of the community. The policy, however, was carried through and was irreversible: as often former church lands were given by Henry to newly ennobled courtiers, his daughter ◊Mary's attempt to return to the previous status quo in the 1550s was forced to accept the permanent loss of these lands to the Church.

Dodoens, Rembert (1517–1585)

Flemish physician and botanist. His *Cruydeboeck* (1554) owes much to the herbal by Leonhart Fuchs, including its illustrations. The French botanist l'Ecluse translated it into French in 1557, a version used by Henry Lyte for his *Niewe Herball* (1578). Lyte's translation and Dodoens's last book, *Stirpium Historiae Pemptades Sex* (1583), were among the sources ◊Gerard used for his *Herball*.

Dolce, Lodovico (1508–1568)

Italian writer. He worked for the publishing house of Giolito in his native Venice. Besides translating or paraphrasing the classics, he produced (among other original pieces) *L'Aretino* (1557), a dialogue on painting.

dolce stil nuovo (ITALIAN 'SWEET NEW STYLE')

A style of Italian lyric verse written between about 1250 and 1300. It was characterized by musicality, the spiritualization of courtly love, and a mystical and philosophical strain in the analysis of love. It was expressed in sonnets, *canzoni*, and ballads. The style was developed by Guido Guinizelli (*c.* 1240–1276), Guido Cavalcanti (*c.* 1255–1300), Gino da Pistoia (*c.* 1265–*c.* 1336), and above all Dante, in his *Vita nuova*. It greatly influenced ◊Petrarch and through him many later Italian poets.

The term was coined by Dante in *Purgatorio* XXIV 57.

Dolet, Etienne (1509–1546)

French Renaissance scholar and printer. He set up a printing press in 1542 and was arrested several times for publishing heretical works, eventually being burned for heresy.

Domenico da Cortona (LE BOCCADOR) (1470–1549)

Italian architect and woodcarver. Domenico executed most of his best-known works in France, where he arrived in 1495 at the summons of Charles VIII. Responsible for the furthering of many Italian ideas in France, he probably designed the wooden model for the Château de ◊Chambord, which was begun in 1519. A development of the designs of Giuliano da Sangallo, the model included such novel features as a double central staircase and had a profound influence upon subsequent architects in France.

Other works included the design of the Hôtel de Ville in Paris (1532).

Domenico Veneziano (*c.* 1400–1461)

Italian painter. He was active in Florence. His few surviving frescoes and altarpieces show a remarkably subtle use of colour and light (which recurs in the work of Piero della Francesca, who worked with him).

He worked in Sta Egidio, Florence, on frescoes now lost. Remaining works include the *Carnesecchi Madonna and Two Saints* (National Gallery, London) and the *St Lucy Altarpiece*, now divided between Florence (Uffizi), Berlin (Staatliche Museen), Cambridge (Fitzwilliam), and Washington, DC (National Gallery).

Dominici, Giovanni (1357–1419)

Florentine cleric and opponent of Coluccio ◊Salutati's humanist circle. A Dominican friar and prior of San Marco, Florence, he played a part in trying to bring the ◊Great Schism to an end. He attempted to persuade Pope Gregory XII to negotiate with the antipope, but subsequently decided to support him; Gregory made him a cardinal in 1408. Dominici's apparent volte-face attracted the mockery of ◊Poggio Bracciolini in his *Contra Hypocritas* – but, then, Poggio had little time for the man who had also attacked the enterprise of *studia humanitatis*.

In 1405 Dominici wrote *Lucula Noctis/The Firefly* (1405), a diatribe against the Classical reading habits of Salutati and his followers. Dominici (himself demonstrating knowledge of Classical literature) argued that ancient pagan authors could only confuse, not enlighten, a Christian, who would better spend his time tilling the soil than reading such books. Dominici did not accept the humanists' defence: that their interest in the Classical world was compatible with, and an assistance to, their understanding of Christianity. In insulting them as pagans, Dominici launched a myth that has endured a thousand repetitions.

The writings of pagans are bound in silk, decorated with gold and silver, read as precious things, and all the schools of Christians – Christians in name only – resound day and night ... with the words of pagans.

∼

GIOVANNI DOMINICI, *Lucula Noctis*, 1405, on Salutati and his circle

---

Donatello (DONATO DI NICCOLO BARDI)
(c. 1386–1466)

Florentine sculptor. His detailed study of antique sculpture and linear perspective was instrumental in the reform of Florentine art in the quattrocento. His advances in the portrayal of free-standing as well as relief sculpture were widely influential to his contemporaries, such as in the marble *David* of 1408 (Florence).

Considered by his contemporaries to have been avant-garde in his understanding of forms and the use of perspective, he was also praised for his technical virtuosity as a sculptor. Highly proficient in both the carving of marble and the casting of bronze figures, his works were influential to his contemporaries for their striking expressiveness, such as the *Saint George* (*c.* 1415, Florence). He made important advances in relief sculpture by introducing figures into a coherent perspectival space, such as in the *Saint George and the Dragon* (*c.* 1415, Florence).

Studies in Rome between 1430–32 further broadened his knowledge of antique sculpture, which he employed in his best-known work, the bronze *David* of 1430–32 (Florence). In his later work in both free-standing and relief sculpture, such as in the aged *Mary Magdalene* (*c.* 1456) in the Baptistery of Florence, he explored the emotional possibilities of forms through a dynamic and often roughly finished figural style.

Donatello Bronze relief of 'St. Antony of Padua and the Miser's Heart' 1447/50 (Basilica di Sant' Antonio, Padua). *AKG London*

Donne, John (1572–1631)

English metaphysical poet. His work consists of love poems, religious poems, verse satires, and sermons. His sermons rank him with the century's greatest orators, and his fervent poems of love and hate, violent, tender, or abusive, give him a unique position among English poets. A Roman Catholic in his youth, he converted to the Church of England and finally became dean of St Paul's Cathedral, London.

His earliest poetry consisted of the 'conceited verses' (using elaborate metaphors to link seemingly dissimilar subjects) passed round in manuscript among his friends at the Inns of Court (finally published in the 1633 *Poems*). Most of these were apparently written in the 1590s. They record a series of actual or fictitious love affairs, in which the lover woos, not by praising his mistress's beauty, but by arguing, cajoling, and plunging off into philosophical speculation and flights of fancy. They show a strange blend of the conversational (most of these poems open with a phrase that might come straight from colloquial speech) with the involved, and of the outspokenly erotic with theoretical questions apparently having little to do with the experience of love. His religious poems show the same passion and ingenuity as his love poetry.

Common to all the poems is the imaginative power of their imagery, which ransacks the intellectual world for symbols, curious and sometimes far-fetched, but always compellingly apt. The sermons, in an elegant prose style less rugged and harsh than that of the poems, show the same preoccupation with humanity's place in the universe and its approaching end.

Donne was brought up in the Roman Catholic faith and matriculated early at Oxford to avoid taking the compulsory oath of supremacy at the age of 16. Before becoming a law student at Lincoln's Inn in 1592, he travelled in Europe. During his four years at the law courts he was notorious for his wit and reckless living, and it was probably around this time that he renounced Catholicism. In 1596 he sailed as a volunteer in an expedition against Spain with the Earl of Essex and Walter Raleigh, and on his return became private secretary to Sir Thomas Egerton (*c.* 1540–1617), Keeper of the Seal. This appointment was ended by his secret marriage in 1601 to Ann More (died 1617), niece of Egerton's wife. They endured many years of poverty, made worse by the births, in rapid succession, of twelve children (of whom seven survived childhood).

With the accession of James I, Donne's fortune changed. In 1610 he made a bid for royal patronage with the prose work *Pseudo-Martyr* (a contribution to the disputes about the oath of supremacy and allegiance), and in 1611–13 with *Ignatius his Conclave* (an attack on the Jesuits), an *Elegy on Prince Henry*, and an *Epithalamium* for the marriage of Princess Elizabeth. In 1611 he travelled in Europe with Robert Drury, whose daughter he had already eulogized in the *First Anniversary*. In 1615 he was ordained in the Church of England, urged on by the King. In 1616 he became divinity reader of Lincoln's Inn with the responsibility of preaching there. From 1621 to his death he was dean of St Paul's, where he often preached before Charles I. He died of consumption and was buried in St Paul's.

One principle which unifies the divergent elements of his work is the desire to isolate and analyse a particular psychological state and relate it to the outside world. The *Anniversaries* on the death of Elizabeth Drury (1611 and 1612) link the direct expression of grief, 'She, she is dead', with an exploration of the emptiness of the world; in the *Divine Poems* the introspective dissection of the experience of love is replaced by that of the fear of death. His verse was long out of favour, but he is now recognized as one of the greatest English poets.

Dorat (DAURAT), Jean (1508–1588)

French poet and Classical scholar. He was the teacher of several members of *La ◊Pléiade* and is sometimes counted a member of the group himself. As director of the Collège de Coqueret and professor at the Collège de France, he played an important part in stimulating the young humanists and introducing such writers as Pierre de ◊Ronsard and Joachim ◊Du Bellay to Classical literature.

Doria, Andrea (1466–1560)

Genoese ◊condottiere. When the French took Genoa, he accepted a contract to fight for Francis I and continued in his pay until 1528. At that point, dissatisfied with French rewards, he transferred his services to the

Doria, Andrea Agnolo ◊Bronzino, portrait of Andrea Doria, depicting the admiral as Neptune, c. 1533 (Brera, Milan). *AKG London*

political issues, the assembly clarified the central precepts of Calvinism and led to the suppression of moderate Calvinism – the scholar Grotius was imprisoned and the statesman ◊Oldenbarneveldt, a supporter of the Arminianists, beheaded.

Dossi (Dosso) (*c*. 1479–*c*. 1542)

Adopted name of **Giovanni Luteri** and **Battista Luteri**, Italian painter brothers. They excelled in fanciful composition, a somewhat romantic landscape background often being enveloped in a strange coppery light. Battista was the landscape painter while Dossi painted the figures. Both worked for the Duke of Ferrara, for whom they painted frescoes, religious scenes, and portraits.

They were pupils of Lorenzo ◊Costa. Both spent time in Venice, where they were influenced by ◊Giorgione and ◊Titian, and also worked in Mantua, but mainly in Ferrara and Modena. They were also in Rome, where Battista worked in ◊Raphael Sanzio's studio. Versions of *Circe* (Borghese, Rome; National Gallery, Washington) and *Muse inspiring a Court Poet* (National Gallery, London) are among their principal works. Their work is original and has beautiful colouring.

The painters were friends of the poet Ludovico ◊Ariosto, who mentions them in *Orlando furioso*, from which they took subjects.

Douglas, Gavin (GAWIN) (*c*. 1475–1522)

Scottish poet. He translated into Scots ◊Virgil's *Aeneid* (1513), including the thirteenth book added by Maffeo Vegio. He wrote the allegorical *The Palace of Honour* (*c*. 1501).

Douglas was born at Tantallon Castle, North Berwick, the son of the 5th Earl of Angus, and educated at St Andrews University. He was made provost of St Giles, Edinburgh, in 1501; an attempt was made in 1514 to promote him to the archbishopric of St Andrews but this was fought off by other contenders. He was, however, named bishop of Dunkeld

Holy Roman Emperor Charles V. He expelled the French garrison from Genoa and ruled the city on republican lines. Charles later made him Prince of Melfi. He was very active against the Turkish pirates in the Mediterranean.

Doria was keen to celebrate his success in art. His palace in Rome (now the Palazzo Doria-Pamphili) was decorated under the guidance of ◊Perino del Vaga, with frescoes by him and by Domenico Beccafumi. They alluded to Doria's successes, to the extent of comparing him with Jupiter. Doria also had his portrait painted by Sebastiano del Piombo in 1526.

Dort, Synod of

An assembly of Dutch Calvinists 1618–19 in Dordrecht (Dort), Holland. The main purpose of the assembly was to formulate a response to Arminianism, which it condemned. A victory for strict Calinists (Gomarists) in both religious and

in 1515 and, after a year's imprisonment, was confirmed in the see. In 1520 he was again expelled, and two years later died of the plague in London.

Dowland, John (*c.* 1563–*c.* 1626)

English composer of lute songs. He introduced daring expressive refinements of harmony and ornamentation to English Renaissance style in the service of an elevated aesthetic of melancholy, as in the masterly *Lachrymae* (1605).

Drake, Francis (*c.* 1540–1596)

English buccaneer and explorer. Having enriched himself as a pirate against Spanish interests in the Caribbean 1567–72, he was sponsored by Elizabeth I for an expedition to the Pacific, sailing round the world 1577–80 in the *Golden Hind*, robbing Spanish ships as he went. This was the second circumnavigation of the globe (the first was by the Portuguese explorer Ferdinand Magellan). Drake also helped to defeat the Spanish Armada in 1588 as a vice admiral in the *Revenge*.

Drayton, Michael (1563–1631)

English poet. He wrote historical poems, including *England's Heroical Epistles* (1597), and graceful pastorals and sonnets, including the sonnet sequence *Love's Idea*. His longest poetical work was the topographical survey of Great Britain, *Poly-Olbion* (1612–22), in 30 books.

Drayton was born in Hartshill, Warwickshire. He became a page in a wealthy household and went to London in 1590. His volume of poems *The Harmony of the Church* (1591), containing metrical versions of scripture passages, was destroyed by order of the archbishop of Canterbury. His first pastorals include *Idea, the Shepherd's Garland* (1593) and his first sonnets *Idea's Mirror, Amours in Quatorzains* (1594). Between 1597 and 1602 he undertook theatrical hackwork for Philip ◊Henslowe and among his associates were Thomas ◊Dekker and Anthony Munday (1560–1633) and, somewhat later, John ◊Webster and Thomas ◊Middleton.

Drayton's historical poems began with the *Legends* of the historical figures Piers Gaveston (1593), Matilda (1594), and Robert, Duke of Normandy,

(1596). In the heroic poem *Mortimeriados* (1596) his theme was the political troubles of Edward II's reign. This, his first poem of length and importance, appeared as *The Barons' War* in the revised edition of 1603. The inequalities and harshness of style disappear in *England's Heroical Epistles*, historical poems written on the model of the Roman poet Ovid's *Heroides* and containing some of his very finest lines. Equally national in spirit is his 'Ballad of Agincourt', first published with his odes in *Poems Lyric and Pastoral* (1606). 'Fair Stood the Wind for France' also appeared in this volume.

Drayton described the ponderous *Poly-Olbion*, begun in 1598, as a 'Herculean toil', for in it he undertook a 'chorographical description', in alexandrine couplets, of everything of antiquarian and topographical interest throughout Great Britain. In contrast, he was able to produce poetry of grace and charm, such as *Nymphidia* (1627), a mock-heroic fairy poem; the pastorals *The Shepherd's Sirena* and *The Quest of Cynthia*, love idylls; and the sonnet, 'Since there's no help, come let us kiss and part'. Among his last poems were *The Muses' Elizium* (1630) and a few *Divine Poems* on Old Testament themes.

Drebbel, Cornelis (1572–1633)

Dutch inventor and alchemist. In the early 1600s he moved to England, where he tried to attract the patronage of James I by presenting him with a supposed *perpetuum mobile*. Drebbel was later involved in plans to drain fenland in East Anglia, and was famous as the inventor of a scarlet dye that he and his sons-in-law exploited at their dyeworks in Bow, London. Among his many inventions was a submarine, which he demonstrated in the River Thames.

A native of Alkmaar, Drebbel trained as an engraver under his brother-in-law Hendrick Goltzius, but subsequently turned his hand to hydraulic engineering.

Duarte (1391–1438)

King of Portugal from 1433. Eldest son of João I, he seems to have visited the English court in *c.* 1405. He took part in the 1415 conquest of Ceuta and played a significant role in government before acceding to the throne. A monarch of literary inclinations, he drew up an inventory of the 80 or so books in his library, and appointed Fernão ◊Lopes as royal chronicler. Shortly before his death he edited a compilation of his jottings – the *Leal conselheiro/Loyal Councillor*, together with a hunting treatise – in response to his wife's request.

du Bellay, Joachim (*c.* 1522–1560)

French poet and prose writer. He published the great manifesto of the new school of French poetry, the ◊*Pléiade*: *Défense et illustration de la langue française/Defence and Illustration of the French Language* (1549). He also wrote sonnets inspired by the Italian poet Petrarch and his meditations on the vanished glories of Rome, *Antiquités de Rome/ Roman Antiquities* (1558), influenced English writers such as Edmund Spenser who translated some of his work. *Les Regrets/Regrets* (1558), a collection of sonnets, is his most characteristic work.

The *Défense* advocated the use of French with an enriched vocabulary, and also a loftier status for poetry, following Classical models. *L'Olive/The Olive*, a collection of Petrarchan love sonnets, appeared the same year. From 1553 to 1557 du Bellay was in Rome as secretary to his cousin, the ambassador Jean du Bellay. On his return he published *Antiquités de Rome* and *Les Regrets*, satirizing the corruption of contemporary Rome. His poems suggest a melancholy mind concerned with the flight of time and the passing of human greatness, together with a talent for lively observation.

Dubroeucq, Jacques (*c.* 1500–1584)

Flemish sculptor and architect. He is best known for a series of carvings for the Cathedral of Sainte Waldetrude at Mons (1535–48) – although much of this decoration was destroyed during the French Revolution. As architect to ◊Mary of Hungary, he built and decorated the castles of Binche and Mariemont. His works show his first-hand knowledge of Italian sculpture and architecture. He is also notable as the teacher of the sculptor ◊Giambologna.

He was born near Mons, and became acquainted with the ideals of the Italian Renaissance while travelling in Italy sometime before 1535. There he studied the works of Ghiberti, Michelangelo, Sansovino, and others. In 1545 he became 'master artist of the emperor' (Charles V).

Duccio di Buoninsegna (BEFORE 1278–1318/19)

Sienese artist who developed a visual equivalent of his contemporary ◊Dante's ◊*dolce stil nuovo*. Duccio's *Maestà* (a panel genre depicting the enthroned Virgin and Child, dated before 1308–11), with its huge architectural frame (over 4×2 m/13×6.5 ft) and its 57 separate elements, was, deliberately, the most ambitious and influential altarpiece conceived to date; an achievement in visual narrative certainly equivalent to ◊Giotto's frescoes. Duccio's innovatory solutions, however (both to the structural impositions of the panel format and the attendant narrative problems), consistently refused to privilege form over content.

Duccio is usually compared unfavourably with Giotto, whose pictorial techniques were undeniably more typical of trends throughout the next 200 years. But in fact Duccio's works provided deeper emotional content and much greater pictorial delicacy. This influenced Duccio's Sienese successors, Simone ◊Martini, the Lorenzetti brothers (Pietro and Ambrogio), and both the conservative, deliberately archaic 15th-century Siena School (for example ◊Giovanni di Paolo); it also helped inspire the gorgeous colour and detail of the so-called International ◊Gothic style.

Duccio's life is difficult to reconstruct outside his interaction with the government of Siena, and this is perhaps appropriate to the civic culture of Italy around 1300. Duccio was urban Siena's artist *par excellence* – though it should be immediately recalled that he, and not Cimabue, Giotto's master, was commissioned in about 1285 to produce the *Rucellai Madonna* in the economic rival city of Florence (for the high altar of Sta Maria Novella). Naturally, Duccio never worked in Florence again, because the *Maestà* was commissioned by the Sienese government precisely to celebrate the city's military defeat of their Florentine neighbours. The day of its installation on the high altar of the cathedral in 1311 (a description survives) was declared a public holiday and treated with the same excitement as the annual Palio (the terrifying Sienese horse race round the city's centre).

Duccio's pride, temper, and financial woes were

also matters of public document in the civic annals of Siena: fines (for debt, for refusing a call-up to fight, for contravening building regulations) often ate into the funds due him from commissions. Duccio's work was the first Sienese artistic expression of a powerful civic ideology, though the hubristic self-proclaimed 'city of the Virgin' (and heir of ancient Rome) was brought down a peg or two with the failure of plans for the baptistery and its façade, and the collapse (almost literally) of a scheme after 1339 to convert the pre-existing cathedral into the known world's largest edifice. This, and the downturn, relative to rival Florence, in Siena's economic growth in the later trecento, gradually dragged Duccio's work out of fashion; the *Maestà* was replaced, and later broken up and sold off as examples of so-called 'naïve' painting. Most of the sections have now been reassembled in the Sienese cathedral museum, but individual panels still lurk as shamefully far afield as London and New York.

Oeuvre (for other minor works dating and attribution is tentative):
- *Crevole Madonna* (*c.* 1280)
- *Rucellai Madonna* (*c.* 1284)
- *Madonna of the Franciscans* (mid-1290s)
- London triptych (*c.* 1300)
- Boston triptych (*c.* 1300)
- *Maestà* (before 1308–11)

Dufay, Guillaume (*c.* 1400–1474)

Flemish composer. He wrote secular songs and sacred music, including 84 songs and 8 masses. His work marks a transition from the style of the Middle Ages to the expressive melodies and rich harmonies of the Renaissance.

Dunbar, William (*c.* 1460–*c.* 1520)

Scottish poet at the court of James IV. His poems include a political allegory, *The Thrissil and the Rois*, written in 1503, celebrating James IV's marriage with Margaret Tudor, and the lament with the refrain 'Timor mortis conturbat me' ('Fear of death confounds me'), printed in 1508.

He was probably born in East Lothian and educated at St Andrews, but practically nothing is known of his early years, and little of his later life except that he entered the Franciscan order of monks, giving this

up for employment by James IV in court and political business.

His chief poems include *The Dance of the Sevin Deidly Synnis*, an allegory written before 1508; *The Goldyn Targe* (1508), another allegory; and various lyrics of which the most notable is *The Lament for the Makaris* (poets of Scotland and England), written about 1507. In his allegorical poems Dunbar follows ◊Chaucer in his setting, and is thus more or less imitative and conventional: in his satirical pieces and lyrics he shows his individual power. Of his comic poems, the best is *The Twa Marriit Wemen and the Wedo*, a satire on bourgeois marriage. Other works are *The Merle and the Nightingale* and *The Flyting of Dunbar and Kennedie*.

Dunstaple (DUNSTABLE), John (*c.* 1385–1453)

English composer of songs and anthems who enjoyed a reputation across Europe for his new style of harmony.

Duperron, Jacques Davy (1556–1618)

Swiss-born French churchman and statesman. A convert to Catholicism, he played an important role in defending Catholicism in the French religious conflicts of the late 16th century. He was a friend of Henry III and after the king's death in 1589 he supported first Cardinal de Bourbon, and then the Protestant ◊Henry IV. In 1593 he brought about Henry IV's conversion to Catholicism, and in 1595 obtained papal absolution for him.

Duperron was born in Berne, the son of French Huguenot refugees. In 1573 he went to Paris, and studied the Fathers of the Church, the schoolmen, and Roman Catholic theologians. He was received into the Roman Church by the Jesuits about 1578.

In 1591 he became bishop of Evreux, and was made cardinal in 1604 (when he went to Rome as the king's *chargé d'affaires*) and archbishop of Sens in 1606. In 1607 he reconciled Pope Paul V and the Venetians, whom the pope had placed under an interdict on account of their defiant assertion of secular control in matters affecting the property and buildings of the church.

Duperron took part in the conference at Nantes, and in 1600 he had the advantage in a theological disputation with the Protestant ◊du Plessis-Mornay. Duperron was a defender of ultramontanism, and corresponded with James I of England on the question of the true church.

du Plessis-Mornay, Philippe (1549–1623)

French churchman and statesman. A Protestant, he played a leading role in trying to reconcile the Catholic and Protestant (Huguenot) factions during the French religious conflicts of the late 16th century. An adviser to Henry of Navarre (later ◊Henry IV), he acted as mediator between the Huguenots and the king, being instrumental in the promulgation of the Edict of ◊Nantes.

Born at Buhi in the Vexin into one of France's most distinguished families, he was converted by his mother to Calvinism and after study in Germany became attached to Coligny. The Massacre of St Bartholomew forced him to take refuge in England. Returning to France, he became an advisor to Henry of Navarre. He wrote extensively in favour of the Huguenots and religious toleration, his best-known work being *Traité de la vérité de la religion chrétienne/Treatise on the Truth of the Christian Religion* (1581). Henry employed him in many official roles, including ambassador to Spain and Flanders, and governor of Saumur.

He lost favour after the publication of his treatise *De l'institution, usage, et doctrine du saint sacrement de l'eucharistie en l'Eglise ancienne/The Sacrament of the Eucharist in the Early Church* (1598), and in 1611 he published an overt attack on the Catholic Church. Marie de' Medici restored him to favour because of his efforts to avert religious war after Henry IV's death but, following the Huguenot uprising of 1620, he fell once more from grace.

Du Plessis-Mornay is also a possible author of the anonymous *Vindiciae contra Tyrannos*, a justification of a subject's right to resist his or her (Catholic) monarch, which was produced in 1579.

Dürer, Albrecht (1471–1528)

German painter, printmaker, and art theorist, born in Nuremberg. He was a prolific engraver and artist, celebrated in Germany and Italy in his lifetime and very popular throughout Europe in the late 16th century.

The attraction of his work was his mastery as a draughtsman, evident both in his prints and his portraits, as well as his style, derived from Italian fashions but developed to become distinctively his own.

For much of his life Dürer was based in Nuremberg, though he made several trips out of Germany. The details of his career are unusually well recorded; they can be constructed from his own notebooks, his letters to friends and his habit of dating his work, as well as from the early biographies.

He was apprenticed to Michael Wolfgemut for three years, 1486–89. From 1492 to 1494 he worked in Basel, providing woodcuts for printed books, including Sebastian ◊Brant's *Ship of Fools* (1494). In 1494 he married Agnes Fey (1475–1539) and the following year made his first trip to Italy, visiting Venice. He then established himself in Nuremberg, concentrating at first on printmaking; an example is *The Apocalypse* series (1498). From about 1500 he increasingly took on commissions for paintings, for example *The Adoration of the Magi* (1504, Uffizi, Florence).

Between 1505 and 1507 he made a second trip to Italy, again visiting Venice – where he met Giovanni ◊Bellini and the young ◊Giorgione – and also travelling to Bologna. Returning to Nuremberg in 1507, he painted two panels of *Adam* and *Eve* (Prado, Madrid). In 1512 he was appointed artist to the Holy Roman Emperor ◊Maximilian I; in this capacity, together with other artists, he produced the *Triumphal Arch* (1515), a set of 192 woodcuts. His *Master Engravings* (1514) included *Melancholia I*.

In about 1519 he became a follower of Martin Luther's teachings, and in 1520–21 travelled to the Netherlands, to the court of the Holy Roman Emperor Charles V, who continued his imperial stipend. Back in Nuremberg in 1521, Dürer was increasingly in demand for portraits. In 1526 he produced engravings of ◊Erasmus, Philip ◊Melanchthon, and Willibald ◊Pirckheimer; he also produced the *Four Apostles* panels (complete with quotations from Luther's translation of the Bible) for the Nuremberg town council. Dürer's writings include a treatise on geometry, *Underweysung der Messung* (1525), and one on proportion, *Vier Bücher menschlicher Proportion* (1528).

In part, Dürer achieved renown because of the

media he used: his engravings were easily exportable. Johann Cochläus claimed in 1512 that merchants from across Europe bought these and took them back for the artists of their own countries to imitate. At the same time, Dürer's success was entwined with that of his friends. Willibald Pirckheimer (to whom he sent letters from Italy) may have secured his position in the emperor Maximilian's entourage; his connection with Erasmus, the master of self-presentation, enhanced both men's reputations.

Dürer's international status was reflected by the frequent references made to this 'most marvellous painter' in Giorgio ◊Vasari's *Lives*. Vasari talked in particular about the mutual respect between Dürer and ◊Raphael and about the influence of Dürer's engravings on Marcantonio ◊Raimondi and Jacopo da ◊Pontormo. In the second half of the 16th century, Dürer's art was hailed by the Catholic Church (apparently not realizing that his last years were spent as a Lutheran) and was particularly prized by the Holy Roman Emperor ◊Rudolf II. This period of immense popularity of his work has been called the 'Dürer Renaissance'.

1486–89 Apprenticed to Michael Wolfgemut
1492–94 In Basel, providing woodcuts for printed books, including Sebastian ◊Brant's *Ship of Fools* (1494)
1494 Marries Agnes Fey (1475–1539)
1495 First trip to Italy, going to Venice; returns to Nuremberg and establishes himself there, concentrating on printmaking (for example, *The Apocalypse* series 1498) but later (from *c*. 1500) increasingly takes on commissions for paintings, including *The Adoration of the Magi* (1504, Uffizi, Florence)
1505–07 Second trip to Italy, staying in Venice (where he meets Giovanni ◊Bellini and the young ◊Giorgione) and travelling to Bologna
1507 Back in Nuremberg, paints two panels of *Adam and Eve* (Prado, Madrid)
1512 Appointed artist to ◊Maximilian I: with other artists produces *Triumphal Arch* (1515), a set of 192 woodcuts
1514 Produces the *Master Engravings*, including *Melancholia I*

c. **1519** Becomes a follower of Martin ◊Luther's teachings
1520–21 Travels to the Netherlands, to the court of Charles V, who continues his imperial stipend
1521 Returns to Nuremberg where he is increasingly in demand for portraits
1525 His *Underweysung der Messung*, a treatise on geometry, printed
1526 Produces engravings of ◊Erasmus, Philip ◊Melanchthon, and Willibald ◊Pirckheimer; also produces the *Four Apostles* panels (complete with quotations from Luther's translation of the Bible) for Nuremberg town council
1528 His *Vier Bücher menschlicher Proportion*, a treatise on proportion, printed

du Vair, Guillaume (1556–1621)

French statesman and philosopher. A supporter of Henry of Navarre (later ◊Henry IV), he made his name as an orator with such speeches as *Exhortation à la paix*/*An Exhortation to Peace* (1592). He served in a number of important government posts, and in 1616 became lord chancellor and bishop of Lisieux. His influential treatises on religion and philosophy were strongly influenced by stoicism.

His writings include the treatises *De la Sainte Philosophie*/*Sacred Philosophy* and *De la Philosophie morale des Stoïques*/*The Moral Philosophy of the Stoics*, translations of Epictetus and Demosthenes, and the *Traité de la constance et consolation ès calamités publiques* (1593; translated into English as *A Buckler against Adversitie* in 1622), which applies the philosophy of Stoicism to the Christian faith.

Du Vair's influence can be traced in the poems of his contemporary ◊Malherbe and in the works of the French philosophers of the 17th century.

Dyer, Edward (1543–1607)

English poet and courtier. Edmund ◊Spenser speaks highly of Dyer as a poet but only one of his songs is now generally remembered, 'My mind to me a kingdom is'.

Born at Sharpham Park, Somerset, after studying at Oxford Dyer went to court, and Elizabeth I employed him on several embassies.

East, Michael (c. 1580–1648)

English composer. He was apparently in the service of Lady Hatton in London early in the 17th century and from 1618 was organist of Lichfield Cathedral.

Works include:

Evening Service, anthems; six books of madrigals (some with anthems) and a madrigal contributed to *The Triumphes of Oriana*; music for viols.

Eccard, Johann (1553–1611)

German composer. His works were chiefly choral pieces. As a Lutheran composer, Eccard made much use of the chorale melodies in his works. The collection of sacred pieces which he published in 1597 contains simple harmonizations, but in other volumes he developed the complex chorale motet, of which he was one of the major exponents.

He was a pupil of David Köler in the choir school attached to the Weimar court chapel, 1567–71, and then of Orlande de Lassus in the Hofkapelle at Munich. From the late 1570s he was in the service of Jacob Fugger at Augsburg, and in 1579 joined the Chapel of the Margrave of Brandenburg-Ansbach at Königsberg; he was assistant Kapellmeister there until 1604 when he succeeded to the senior post. In 1608 the new Elector Joachim Friedrich of Brandenburg in Berlin appointed Eccard Kapellmeister at his Berlin court, and Eccard continued to serve his successor, Johann Sigismund. His music was still printed 30 years after his death.

Works include:

Motets, chorales (some harmonized, some newly composed by him); sacred songs; secular German songs for several voices, wedding songs, odes, festival songs.

Eck, Johann (Johann Maier of Eck, or Egg) (1486–1543)

German Catholic theologian and polemicist. He was an early and determined critic of Martin ◊Luther, engaging in public disputations with Luther and other reformers. His attacks, including the claim that Luther was associated with Jan ◊Huss, forced Luther to define his position concerning the authority of the Bible, the character of Christ's Church, and the papacy and church hierarchy.

Eck helped draw up the *Confutatio* declaring Emperor Charles V's total rejection of Protestant principles that was read at the Diet of ◊Augsburg in 1530. He was one of the three Catholic advocates in the debates at the Colloquy of Regensburg in 1541. In 1537 he published his German translation of the New Testament.

Born in Egg, in Swabia, he was professor of theology 1510–43 and then chancellor at the university of Ingolstadt in Bavaria. His attack on the reformers was initially launched against Luther's supporter, Andreas Carlstadt (c. 1480–1541), which led to a formal disputation at Leipzig in June and July 1519.

Edward IV (1442–1483)

King of England 1461–70 and from 1471. When his father Richard, Duke of York, died in battle in 1460, Edward became the Yorkist claimant to the throne (see Wars of the ◊Roses); in four months he took London and was declared king. However, opposition from forces loyal to Henry VI continued until 1465. In 1470, with the support of the disaffected Earl of Warwick, Lancastrian forces invaded England, forcing Edward to flee to Burgundy. He returned the following year, defeated his enemies, and thus ended the wars (for the time being).

Politically, Edward (like ◊Henry V) relied on a Burgundian alliance: his sister Margaret married ◊Charles the Bold in 1468. Culturally, Edward emulated – perhaps even surpassed – the splendour of the Burgundian court. He collected manuscripts illuminated in the Burgundian style; his library may also have included some of William ◊Caxton's printed books. His main patronage, however, was architectural: most notably, in the 1470s, he commissioned both the Great Hall of Eltham Palace in Kent and St

George's Chapel, Windsor (probably designed by Henry ◊Janyns).

Edward VI (1537–1553)

King of England from 1547, only son of Henry VIII and his third wife, Jane Seymour. The government was entrusted to his uncle the Duke of Somerset (who fell from power in 1549), and then to the Earl of Warwick, later created Duke of Northumberland. He was succeeded by his sister Mary I.

Edward became a staunch Protestant, and during his reign the Reformation progressed. He died of tuberculosis, and his will, probably prepared by Northumberland, set aside that of his father so as to exclude his half-sisters, Mary and Elizabeth, from the succession. He nominated Lady Jane Grey, a granddaughter of Henry VII, who had recently married Northumberland's son. Technically Jane reigned for nine days, and was deposed by Mary I.

Edwards, Richard (c. 1523–1566)

English poet, musician, and dramatist. He was highly regarded for his comedies, madrigals, and interludes. His *Palamon and Arcite* was acted before Elizabeth I in Oxford in 1566, but *Damon and Pythias* (1564), a tragedy with scenes of low farce, is his only extant play. He compiled the anthology *The Paradise of Dainty Devices* (1576), which contains many of his own poems.

Born in Somerset and educated at Oxford, Edwards trained as a lawyer in London but apparently never practised law.

Egas, Enrique de (c. 1445–c. 1534)

Spanish architect. He was cathedral architect at Toledo about 1498 before moving to Granada, where he designed the chapel royal (1506) and the cathedral (1521), although the latter was remodelled and completed by Diego de Siloe. His works are mainly in the ◊plateresque style, with some sign of knowledge of Italian Renaissance trends.

He was probably born at Toledo, where his father Egas (died 1495) and uncle Hanequin (died c. 1475) were associated with work on the cathedral. Although Enrique and his brother Anton adopted the name of their father as their family name, it seems likely that the family was an offshoot of a well-known Brussels family of masons called Coeman.

He also designed buildings in Valladolid and Santiago de Compostela, his cruciform hospital plan for the latter in 1501 being copied for the Santa Cruz hospital in Toledo (1504) and then in Granada (1511).

Egidio of Viterbo (c. 1469–1532)

Scholar, theologian and reformer, Platonic philosopher, papal diplomat, prophetic preacher and orator, vernacular poet, and biblical exegete of the early 16th-century Roman curia. Before his elevation to cardinal in 1517, Egidio had been a reluctant but determined minister general of the Augustinian friars – and thus Luther's superior. Personally modest, he nonetheless enjoyed the patronage of popes Julius II, Leo X, and Clement VII. Egidio's letters and sermons expose the literary and antiquarian tastes, the prevailing apocalyptic tensions, and the intrigue of Roman papal circles.

Egidio's most ambitious philosophical and historical-prophetic works remain unpublished. Partly following the work of ◊Annio of Viterbo, Egidio also favoured the mythical importance of the role of Etruscan civilization within sacred history. As a Christian cabbalist and supporter of the heretic cabbalist Johan Reuchlin, Egidio worked hard to legitimize and, indeed, to privilege Hebrew studies alongside the linguistic revival of Greek and Latin; he helped establish, in Rome, the first Hebrew press.

Eight Saints, War of the

A war between Florence and the papacy over the secular power of the papacy in central Italy, fought 1375–78. The war ended in compromise, set out in the Peace of Tivoli, in 1378. The threat the war posed to the security of Rome prompted Gregory XI to end the papacy's 70-year exile in Avignon, and so helped ended the Babylonian Captivity.

The 'saints' referred to were the eight officials who exacted war taxes from the clergy, here confused with the Eight of War (*otto della guerra*), who conducted Florence's military operations.

ekphrasis

Vivid literary description of a work of art, a popular rhetorical exercise in late Antiquity. Several were written by the Greek writer Lucian. These, in particular his descriptions of ◊Apelles' *Calumny* and ◊Zeuxis' *Centaur Family*, were influential in the Renaissance as the only surviving evidence of ancient paintings. On the basis of these descriptions, artists such as Botticelli, Mantegna, and Albrecht Dürer tried to recreate the works of art.

Elizabeth I (1533–1603)

Queen of England from 1558. The daughter of ◊Henry VIII by Anne ◊Boleyn, Elizabeth was, like her mother, evangelical in her religion. This put her, in the reign of her sister, Mary, under suspicion as a potential focus for radical discontent. When she herself succeeded on Mary's death, she attempted a second reimposition of Protestantism on England, which was successful although it faced criticism from both English Catholics and Puritans. The more 'forward' Protestants urged her to support the Calvinist Netherlands against their Spanish overlords, which led to a war against Philip II. Despite the victory of the English (and, more importantly, of the weather) over the Armada, it was a war with few successes. In Elizabeth's last decade, a deteriorating economic situation and uncertainty over the succession helped create increasing disillusion with her government.

The rule of a woman, either as widow and regent (like Catherine de' Medici) or as a married queen (like Mary), was not unusual in 16th-century Europe. Elizabeth, however, remained unmarried through her reign – although this was not for want of looking for a husband. Robert Dudley, Earl of Leicester, was talked of as a suitor; a more prestigious match, and one which was seriously considered in 1579–80, was to the Duke of Anjou (the former Duke of Alençon, one of Henry II's younger sons). The idea of marriage to a Catholic prince shocked the more committed Protestants; Elizabeth eventually, and without explanation, failed to pursue the case. This created a different problem: uncertainty over who would succeed the ageing queen. There were several contenders, who included Mary, Queen of Scots, in exile in England from 1568 and the focus of Catholic plots against Elizabeth until she was executed in 1587. The

Stewart claim then passed to her son, James VI of Scotland and, despite being a foreigner and the son of a traitor, it was he who succeeded on Elizabeth's death.

The cultural advantage of female rule was that it allowed authors to celebrate their monarch with underused imagery of Classical heroines. The so-called 'cult of Elizabeth' developed fairly late in her reign (the complex of allusion and illusion reached its height when there was increasing disquiet); it had various manifestations. The progresses Elizabeth made around the country allowed for an unprecedented level of pageantry focused upon the queen. The tradition of court portraiture (established by Hans ◊Holbein the Younger) was continued but also somewhat formalized: particular images of the queen were authorized and then copied for the delectation of her loyal subjects. At the same time, there were literary expressions of Elizabeth's glory, although, as in Edmund ◊Spenser's *Faerie Queene*, these could be attempts to direct and advise the monarch under the guise of praise.

In fact, much of the cultural vitality at the end of the 16th century – the explosion of printed literary works, the rise of the London theatres (see feature) – was merely coincidental to Elizabeth's reign. It also continued after her death: in 1603, the same metaphors of virtuous female rule were churned out in epitaphs to her, but a large number of poems also revived the images of male monarchy to celebrate the succession of the new king, James I.

Elsheimer, Adam (1578–1610)

German painter and etcher. He was active in Rome from 1600. His small paintings, nearly all on copper, depict landscapes darkened by storm or night, with figures picked out by beams of light, as in *The Rest on the Flight into Egypt* (1609) (Alte Pinakothek, Munich).

Elsheimer studied at Frankfurt under a minor landscape artist, Philip Uffenbach, leaving the city about 1598 to work at Munich and in Venice with Johann Rottenhammer. He settled in 1600 in Rome, where he was known as 'Adamo Tedesco', and began to produce small pictures, painted, like Rottenhammer's, on copper, which had a great influence on the development of 17th-century landscape.

Landscape played a principal part in these works, ostensibly biblical or mythological in subject, and in its treatment Elsheimer seems to have drawn suggestions from a variety of sources, such as Tintoretto, the Carracci, Caravaggio, and the Flemish painter Paul Bril. He is noted for the effective contrast between different sources of light in the same picture, for example the firelight, torchlight, and moonlight in his *Rest on the Flight into Egypt*, which may well have inspired Rembrandt's *Flight into Egypt* (Dublin). Effects of this kind delighted and influenced Rubens, who bought works by him. He also made a study of the country round Rome, and his sketches in the Campagna foreshadow the 'Classical' landscape with ruins that Claude was to perfect.

Elyot, Thomas (*c.* 1490–1546)

English diplomat and scholar. In 1531 he published *The Governour*, the first treatise on education in English. He published the first Latin-English dictionary in 1538.

Elyot was born in Wiltshire. He was clerk of the Privy Council (1523–30), and a friend of the political thinker Thomas ◊More.

Elzevir Press

Dutch publishing house founded in Leiden in 1593 by the printer and bookseller Louis Elzevir (1546–1617). Establishing a high reputation for classic texts that were both well edited and inexpensive, the Elzevir press continued as a family business, opening branches in The Hague, Amsterdam, and Utrecht. The first contemporary author published by the Elzevirs was Grotius. It remained a family business until 1712.

The founder of the dynasty, **Louis Elzevir**, born in Louvain, worked for Plantin in Antwerp, and settled in Leiden in 1580 as a binder and bookseller. His publishing started with an edition of Eutropius, and Classical authors continued to be the main stock of the firm.

Louis's son Bonaventura (1583–1652) and grandsons Abraham (1592–1652), and Izaak (1596–1651) – the offspring of Louis's oldest son, Matthias – began the series of pocket classics in 1629, providing accurate texts for a large market.

These little thirty-twomos, with their narrow margins and solid slabs of type, often with engraved title pages, became the family's most famous product. Izaak, who had established a press of his own in 1616, became printer to the university of Leyden in 1620, and his successors retained the office.

The Amsterdam branch was established by Louis III (1604–70) in 1639, and concentrated on modern books in Dutch, German, English, and French until the death of Daniel Elzevir (1626–80), Bonaventura's son, when it was wound up. The Leyden branch lasted a little longer, under the control of Abraham's grandson, Abraham II (1653–1712).

The Elzevirs, from Louis I on, sold new or second-hand books throughout Europe, an activity just as important as their printing and publishing.

Encina, Juan del (1468–1529)

Spanish poet, playwright, and composer. He cultivated especially the villancico, a form resembling the French virelai. Over 60 of his songs are contained in a manuscript at Madrid, the *Cancionero Musical de Palacio*.

Encina studied at Salamanca University and entered the service of the Duke of Alba at Toledo. His poems were published at Salamanca in 1496. In 1498 he went to Rome, where he held a post at the court of the Spanish pope. While there he produced the *Farsa de Placida e Vittoriano* and composed many songs for his own plays. He was archdeacon of Málaga Cathedral from 1508–19, and of León Cathedral from 1519 until his death.

Enoch of Ascoli (*c.* 1400–*c.* 1457)

Humanist teacher and searcher for Classical texts, born near Piceno, Italy. Himself educated by Francesco Filelfo, he became tutor to the sons of Filelfo's enemy, Cosimo de' ◊Medici. In the 1440s, Enoch lectured first in Perugia, then in Rome, where the pope, ◊Nicholas V, was probably already an acquaintance. Nicholas entrusted to Enoch investigations for Classical manuscripts, first in the Middle East and then in northern Europe (Denmark, Norway, and Germany). Among the prizes he brought back was the only known copy of ◊Tacitus' minor works.

Enzinas, Francisco de (FRANCIS DRYANDER) (c. 1520–1570)

Spanish scholar, translator, and religious reformer. He produced the first translation of the New Testament into Spanish, which was published at Antwerp in 1543. His sympathy for ◊Luther earned him the suspicion of the Catholic Church and of Emperor ◊Charles V, and in 1546 he fled to England, where he became a professor of Greek at Cambridge. He later translated Latin and Greek classics.

Enzinas was born at Burgos and studied at Wittenberg, where he was influenced by Luther's teaching. This translation of the Bible incurred the displeasure of Charles V because it was based on the Greek text of Erasmus and because of Enzinas's marginalia, which expressed unorthodox opinions. He also printed in capitals the verses of *Romans* iii which provided one of the main supports for those who endorsed justification by faith. Enzinas was therefore imprisoned in 1543 at Brussels but managed to escape to Antwerp two years later. After several years travelling, he settled in England, but had to leave when Mary Tudor came to power.

He even travelled as far as Constantinople, founding a Protestant colony there. His works included a history of religion in Spain and Spanish translations of Lucian (1550) and Plutarch (1551). He also wrote memoirs in Latin that remained in manuscript until the 19th century.

Equicola, Mario (c. 1470–1525)

Italian humanist and courtier. He was secretary to Isabella d' ◊Este, and his letters and accounts of his travels with her give a valuable insight into Italian court life in the early 16th century. His treatise *De Natura de Amore/ On the Nature of Love* (1525) shows the influence of Renaissance neo-Platonism derived from ◊Ficino.

Born at Alvito, Calabria, Equicola was mainly associated with the house of Este. As early as 1505 he composed a treatise on the phrase 'Nec spe nec metu'

('neither in hope nor in fear'), which was Isabella d'Este's favourite motto, and in 1519 she appointed him her secretary. In this capacity he travelled with her on a pilgrimage to St Mary Magdalene at Sainte-Beaune; his account of the trip still survives. He also became involved in the quarrel between Isabella and her son Federico d'Este. He died in Mantua.

Erasmus, Desiderius (c. 1469–1536)

Dutch humanist. He was the prolific, self-promoting, often controversial, towering figure of intellectual life in the first decades of the 16th century. His career – perhaps as much by accident as design – was what might be called that of a 'professional' author. He sometimes received pensions from rulers, took short-term posts at universities, often sought pieces of patronage, but, for the most part, was employed on his own enterprises. His publications included dialogues, educational treatises, editions of Classical and patristic authors, translations of Greek texts, grammatical works, and his voluminous correspondence.

Erasmus, the child of unmarried parents, was born in Rotterdam and educated at Alexander ◊Hegius's school in Deventer; on his parents' deaths about 1484, he was sent to another school at 's-Hertogenbosch and was taken into the care of the Brethren of the Common Life who (to his later regret) did not send him to university but instead

Erasmus Medal of Erasmus of Rotterdam by Quentin Massys, 1519 (Bibliothèque Nationale de France, Paris). An example, like that of Isabella ◊d'Este, of the popularity of medals – and also of the prestige of Erasmus. *AKG London/Erich Lessing*

guided him into taking monastic orders about 1487. He was ordained as a priest in 1492 and became Latin secretary to Hendrik van Bergen, bishop of Cambrai; under his auspices, he eventually went to university, entering the theology faculty at Paris in 1495.

In print he was always 'Erasmus of Rotterdam', but he spent relatively little of his adult life in the Low Countries. He was based there before the 1520s, but went on extended trips to, for example, England (1499, 1509–14) and Italy (1506–09); these travels were undertaken in the hope of patronage or for the sake of assisting with the printing of his works. In the 1520s, however, another factor entered his calculations: the Luther affair. At first sympathetic to Luther's criticisms of the church, Erasmus was not keen to join (as the Holy Roman Emperor ◊Charles V and Pope ◊Adrian VI hoped and expected that he would) the condemnations of the heretic emanating from Louvain and Paris. At the same time, reticence was dangerous since some conservative opinion, remembering for example his emendations to the Vulgate, questioned his own orthodoxy. So, in an attempt to move away from the controversy, he decamped in 1521 to Basel; there he wrote his considered riposte to Luther, on the issue of free will. However, Basel itself was overtaken by evangelical reform and Erasmus moved again, to Freiburg in 1529, only to return to Basel in 1535.

Some humanists before Erasmus had been polymaths, with their work ranging from translations to theological studies to grammatical and literary discussions; the figure of Lorenzo ◊Valla comes to mind, who was in some ways an inspiration to Erasmus. Erasmus's reputation and popularity was, however, surely unprecedented. In part, it was a result of the sort of works he produced; some of the best-selling – his adages, for example, or his *Paraphrases* of the Gospels – were useful handbooks, providing easy access to knowledge. At the same time, some of Erasmus's writings aroused, and sometimes courted, controversy: from, in his later years, his *Ciceronianus*, an attack on other humanists whom he considered were slavish in their imitation of Cicero, to the more serious dispute which surrounded his *Novum Instrumentum*. This work, demonstrating errors in St Jerome's Vulgate transla-

tion of the Bible, questioned some accepted teachings of the church – causing an unsurprising backlash from conservative opinion. Such controversies could at times become uncomfortable for Erasmus but they also ensured his fame, or notoriety. Yet, beyond these factors, the 'secret' of Erasmus's success was probably a lucky concurrence of personal inclination and technology.

Humanists before Erasmus had been concerned to construct for themselves a persona through their publications and their correspondence. Erasmus, however, could take these techniques further thanks to the new medium of print. In the workshops of Aldus ◊Manutius or Johannes Froben, the printing of a work was often a scholarly exercise and Erasmus was willing to take part in those activities. This meant that he was able to oversee the appearance as well as the content of these relatively mass-produced copies. Certainly, poor or pirated editions did appear but Erasmus achieved unusual control over the image of him that was projected through these printings. In particular, he could control the dissemination of his letters. Since the time of the poet ◊Petrarch, who was himself imitating Cicero, the compiling of a correspondence was a crucial part of creating a scholarly identity. It was not, of course, a persona in isolation: for correspondence to exist, there needed to be correspondents and Erasmus's letter collections often included letters to him as well as from him. The result was twofold: first, it created a sense of Erasmus as the centre of an international circle of scholars, a sort of prince in the republic of letters. Second, at the same time, it encouraged others to write to him, in the hope that they might be included in future collections. In other words, the image was self-fulfilling: Erasmus became the centre of an ever-increasing circle which his printed works had originally drawn around him.

Selective list of Erasmus's works
The following list for the most part excludes Erasmus's many translations, commentaries, and editions of Classical texts, and the various collections of his letters that appeared throughout his life.

1493	*Antibarbar/Against the Barbarians* (revised 1495, 1520)
1500	*Adagiorum Collectanea* (dedicated to Lord Mountjoy)

1503	*Enchiridion Militis Christiani/Handbook of the Christian Soldier*
1504	*Panegyricus/Panegyric* to Philip the Fair
1508	*Adagiorum Chiliades,* an expanded version of his adages (further revised 1515)
1511	*Moriae Encomium/Praise of Folly*
1512	*De Copia/On the Copious Style* (an earlier version had been written 1499); *De Ratione Studii/On The Method of Study*
1515	Edition of Jerome's letters published (revised edition 1526)
1516	*Institutio Principis Christiani/Education of the Christian Prince* (dedicated to Charles V, printed with the *Panegyricus* and translations from Isocrates and Plutarch; copies sent to Francis I and Henry VIII) *Querela Pacis/Complaint of Peace Novum Instrumentum* printed with *Annotationes* – the Greek text of the New Testament with Erasmus's own translation and comments on the Vulgate
1517	*Julius Exclusus/Pope Julius II Barred from Heaven*
1518	*Colloquia* (expanded 1523, 1524, 1526, 1527) *Epigrammata/Epigrams* printed with those of Thomas ◊More (in an edition also including More's ◊*Utopia*)
1519	Revised edition of the *Novum Instrumentum* printed as *Novum Testamentum*
1521	*De Conscribendis Epistolis/How to Write Letters* (first written 1498, revised 1509 for Robert ◊Fisher)
1522–24	*Paraphrases of the Four Gospels*
1524	*De Libero Animo/On Free Will*
1528	*Ciceronianus*

Erastianism

Belief that the church should be subordinated to the state. The name is derived from Thomas Erastus (1534–1583), a German-Swiss theologian and opponent of Calvinism, who maintained in his writings that the church should not have the power of excluding people as a punishment for sin.

Ercilla y Zúñiga, Alonso de (1533–1593)

Spanish nobleman and author, he had travelled to England in the future ◊Philip II's entourage when in 1554 he was summoned to Chile to help quell the native Araucanian Indians. There he combined arms with letters, beginning his epic, *Araucana*. Ercilla returned to Spain in 1563 but continued to travel: this time around Europe, on royal and military missions, including the successful 1580 campaign to unite Spain and Portugal. The first part of his *Araucana* appeared in 1569, the second and third parts in 1578, and all three were published together in 1590, shortly before his death.

Bar a few poems, the *Araucana* was Ercilla's only work. It was, however, a very successful one in the Hispanic world: twice published in his lifetime, continued in 1597 by Diego de Santistevan Ossorio (who added parts four and five), by the mid-17th century there had been 18 editions. It also inspired a series of other 'American' poems, such as Pedro de Oña's 'Arauco domado/Arauco tamed' (1596). However, the earliest translation was a Dutch one in 1619: it was left to Voltaire in 1726 to introduce the *Araucana* to a wider European audience.

Escobar, Pedro (c. 1465–AFTER 1535)

Portuguese composer. He spent much of his life in Spain, where he was maestro de capilla at Seville early in the 16th century. He composed church music and secular pieces for three and four voices.

Escorial, El

Monastery and palace standing over 900 m/2953 ft above sea level on a southeastern slope of the Sierra de Guadarrama, 42 km/26 mi northwest of Madrid, Spain. El Escorial was built (1563–84) for Philip II. It was designed by Juan Bautista de Toledo (assistant to Michelangelo at St Peter's, Rome (1546–48)) and Juan de Herrera (c. 1530–97).

It was dedicated to St Lawrence, on whose day in 1557 the Spaniards defeated Henry II of France at St Quentin. The immense structure, built of granite and measuring 207 m/679 ft by 161 m/528 ft, is shaped to resemble the gridiron on which St Lawrence was martyred.

This austere monastry-cum-palace became the favoured dwelling of Philip II. It was here that he gathered together his collection of paintings (including, in particular, works by Hieronymus ◊Bosch) and artists (like El ◊Greco).

Esquivel Barahona, Juan de (*c.* 1565–AFTER 1613)

Spanish composer. He was maestro de capilla at Salamanca Cathedral in 1608 and at Ciudad-Rodrigo (1611–13). His Masses and motets were published in two volumes in 1608, and a volume of miscellaneous sacred works in 1613. An *Officium pro defunctis/ Mass for the dead* survives in manuscript form.

Essex, Robert Devereux, 2nd Earl of Essex (1566–1601)

English soldier and politician. Having taken part in the Dutch fight against Spain, he became a favourite with Queen Elizabeth I in 1587, but fell from grace because of his policies in Ireland, where he was Lieutenant from 1599, and was executed.

Son of Walter Devereaux, 1st Earl of Essex, and stepson to Robert Dudley, Earl of Leicester, he succeeded to the earldom in 1576. Essex fought in the Netherlands (1585–86), supporting their war of liberation from Spain, and distinguished himself at the Battle of Zutphen. In 1596 he jointly commanded a force that seized and sacked Cádiz. In 1599 he became Lieutenant of Ireland and led an army against Irish rebels under the Earl of Tyrone in Ulster, but was unsuccessful, made an unauthorized truce with Tyrone, and returned without permission to England. He was forbidden to return to court, and when he marched into the City of London at the head of a body of supporters, he was promptly arrested, tried for treason, and beheaded on Tower Green.

Este, Isabella d' (1474–1539)

Italian noblewoman, a leading member of the powerful d'◊Este family. In 1490 she married Gianfrancesco II Gonzaga, Marquess of Mantua. A skilled diplomat, she protected the interests of Mantua and Ferrara during his frequent absences on military campaigns, and after his death in 1519 was a trusted counsellor to her eldest son, Federico II (1500–40). She is best remembered as one of the leading Renaissance patrons, notably of artists such as ◊Leonardo da Vinci and ◊Raphael, and the writer ◊Castiglione.

She was the daughter of Ercole I d'Este (1431–1505), Duke of Ferrara. He ensured that she received a thorough humanistic education – Battista ◊Guarino was among her tutors – and she is chiefly

Este, Isabella Giovanni Cristoforo Romano's portrait medal of Isabella d'Este. While medals were a fashionable art-form from Pisanello onwards, this one was extravagant in its added gems, spelling out Isabela (Kunsthistorisches Museum, Vienna). *AKG London/Erich Lessing*

remembered for the extraordinary cultural flowering she brought about in Mantua. Both she and her husband were keenly interested in choral and organ music, and Isabella's music room survives in the Reggia de' Gonzaga, Mantua, decorated with wooden inlays of musical motifs by Tullio ◊Lombardo. Among those to whom she gave patronage were the artists ◊Mantegna, ◊Titian, ◊Giulio Romano, ◊Francia, and ◊Perugino. The writers included ◊Ariosto, ◊Trissino, Mantovano (Battista Spagnoli), and ◊Bandello.

Este dynasty

Family who ruled Ferrara and Modena in northern Italy from the 13th century to the end of the 16th. Allied to other important families such as the Gonzaga, they played an important role in the political and cultural life of Renaissance Italy, founding the university of Ferrara and making their courts major centres of literature and the arts. One of the leading members of the family was Isabella d' ◊Este.

THE ESTE DYNASTY OF FERRARA

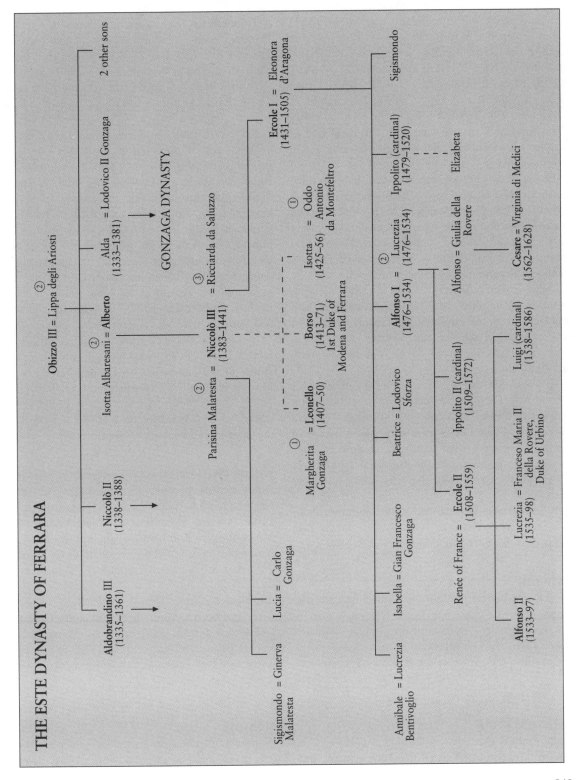

The dynasty was established when **Obizzo II** became perpetual lord of Ferrara in 1264, despite papal claims to the title. Este power was considerably extended by **Niccolò III d'Este** (lord 1393–1441), and by **Borso d'Este** (lord 1450–71), who became Duke of Modena and Reggio in 1452 and Duke of Ferrara in 1471. **Ercole I d'Este** (Duke 1471–1505), allied his family by marriage with the royal line of Naples and with the Bentivoglio, Gonzaga, and ◊Sforza families.

Ercole I encouraged the arts and he beautified Ferrara. His daughters by Eleonora of Aragon, Isabella d' ◊Este and **Beatrice** (1475–1497), carried the Ferrarese enthusiasm for music, art, and literature to their husbands' courts, Isabella to Mantua and Beatrice to Milan. Other Este patrons of the arts included **Niccolò II** (lord 1361–88), who built the Castello Estense; **Alberto V** (lord 1388–93), who founded the university of Ferrara; and **Leonello** (lord 1441–50), who was educated by ◊Guarino da Verona and encouraged scholars and artists, among them ◊Alberti, ◊Pisanello, Jacopo Bellini, van der ◊Weyden, and ◊Mantegna.

In 1502 **Alfonso I** (duke 1505–34) married his second wife Lucrezia ◊Borgia, their court becoming renowned for its brilliance. His brother Cardinal **Ippolito I d'Este** (1479–1520) was also a patron of the poet ◊Ariosto, who dedicated his epic *Orlando furioso* to him. Alfonso's son, **Cardinal Ippolito II d'Este** (1509–1572) built the Villa d'Este at Tivoli, near Rome.

When **Alfonso II** (duke 1559–97) died without an heir the papacy recovered Ferrara, but a junior Este branch continued to rule Modena and Reggio.

Estienne, Charles (1504–1564)

French scholar and publisher, a leading figure in the family firm, the ◊Estienne Press. He was a man of extensive learning, compiler of the popular *Praedium Rusticum* in 1554 (a collection of agricultural tracts). He was also the author of the first French encyclopedia (1553) and of the important anatomical textbook *De Dissectione* (1548).

Estienne Press

French publishing house in Paris (1502–1674). The leading French publishers of the 16th century, they were noted for their scholarly editions of Greek and Roman classics. A family business, it was founded by Henry I Estienne (died 1520), whose widow married his partner, Simon de Colines. He in turn trained his stepson Robert (1503–59) who took over the press in 1526, later receiving the royal appointment to Francis I. In the 1550s a branch was established in Geneva.

Robert Estienne's Latin thesaurus 1531 (an enlarged edition appeared in 1543) was followed by several bilingual dictionaries, while his editions of the Bible, including a Greek-Latin New Testament (1551) (the first to divide the chapters into numbered verses), combined his scholarship and his firm Christian beliefs. Robert's Calvinist sympathies took him to Geneva in 1550, while his brother ◊Charles continued printing in Paris, his outstanding works being the first French encyclopedia (1553) and a textbook on anatomy. He was followed by his nephew **Robert II** (1530–71), who also became a royal printer in 1564.

In Geneva Robert I was succeeded by his sons **Henry II** (1528–98), who brought out a Greek thesaurus (1572) to match his father's Latin one, and **Francis** (1537–82). Robert's grandson **Paul** (1567–1627), son of Henry II, eventually returned to Paris, where his son **Antoine** (died 1674) was the last of the dynasty and another royal printer.

Estius (WILLEM HESSELS VAN EST) (1542–1613)

Dutch scholar and polemicist. His history of the martyrs of Gorcum (killed by Protestants) appeared in 1603. He was the author of commentaries on the works of Peter Lombard and the epistles of St Paul. A Roman Catholic, he also made notes for an edition of St Augustine. His zeal against the Protestants was such that it led him to defend the murder of ◊William the Silent, Prince of Orange, in 1584.

He was born at Gorinchem (Gorcum), educated at Utrecht, and from 1561 studied at Louvain under Michel Baius (Baianism). From 1582 he was professor of theology at Douai, becoming chancellor of the university in 1595.

etching

Printmaking technique in which a metal plate (usually copper or zinc) is covered with a waxy overlayer (ground) and then drawn on with an etching needle. The exposed areas are then 'etched', or bitten into, by a corrosive agent (acid), so that they will hold ink for printing.

The earliest dated etching is by Urs Graf (1513). Albrecht ◊Dürer was also a pioneer, with his *The Cannon*, etched on iron.

Eton College

School founded near Windsor, England, in 1440, in Henry VI's name. Established as part of a twin foundation with King's College, Cambridge, Eton consisted of a chantry chapel (where masses for the king's soul were to be sung), the school, and an almshouse. The college's statutes bear little sign of the influence of *studia humanitatis* but several of the clerics involved in the founding, such as Thomas ◊Bekynton and William ◊Waynflete, had humanist interests.

Through the 1440s the plans for Eton became increasingly grandiose, but they were never fulfilled. The chapel, built in Henry's reign in Perpendicular style, was half its intended size. In the late 1470s Flemish-influenced wall paintings were added to the chapel; this was after Edward IV had briefly considered abolishing the college 1463–67.

Eugenius IV (BORN GABRIELE CONDULMER) (1383–1447)

Pope 1431–47. From a Venetian patrician family, Eugenius owed his election to the fact that he was not related to his predecessor ◊Martin V. The backlash against the Colonna family of Martin V was bloody, and Eugenius had to flee Rome in disguise amid rioting in 1434. He settled in Florence until 1443, bringing prestige to that city before returning to Rome. His pontificate was dominated by the issue of conciliarism.

The Council of ◊Basel opened soon after Eugenius was elected; Eugenius was keen to dissolve it but the pressure for it to continue (partly because the Holy Roman Emperor ◊Sigismund was concerned about the threat of the Hussite heresy) was too great. The Council, however, was determined to limit the pope's authority. In response, Eugenius had two weapons: a diplomatic offensive to persuade secular rulers to abandon the Council, and the attempt to unite the Eastern Orthodox churches with the Catholic Church. In pursuing the latter, he announced that the General Council would meet at Ferrara (and, later, ◊Florence). These moves did not stop the conciliarists at Basel declaring Eugenius deposed and electing an antipope, nor did they prevent secular rulers such as Charles VII of France from taking advantage of the situation; however, they did ensure that secular and religious opinion was increasingly on the side of the pope.

Eugenius's pontificate could be characterized as dominated by intellectuals. The threat of Basel, whatever its political impact, was based in (and developed) theories of ◊conciliarism; Eugenius's response similarly tapped into the Greek interests of Florentine humanists like Ambrogio ◊Traversari. Like Martin V, his curia was increasingly manned by scholars with interests in *studia humanitatis*. Despite his long absence from Rome, he showed a concern for the fabric of the papal city; he patronized the rebuilding of churches there and of the Pantheon, and decreed that stone should not be stolen from the Colosseum. Such steps foreshadowed the grand projects which his successor Nicholas V pursued with greater personal involvement.

euphuism

Affected style of writing full of high-flown language and far-fetched metaphors, especially in imitation of English playwright John ◊Lyly's *Euphues: The Anatomy of Wit* (1578) and *Euphues and his England* (1580).

Euphuism aimed to be artificial and affected in its desire for refinement. It was fashionable towards the end of Queen Elizabeth I's reign. Lyly, in addressing his writings chiefly to women, said he would rather see his works 'lie shut in a lady's casket than open in a scholar's study'. His idea was not to improve, but to amuse.

Some commentators on Shakespeare have suggested that in *Love's Labour's Lost* he was satirizing the euphuists in the character of Don Adriano de Armado.

Eustachio, Bartolommeo (1520–1574)

Italian anatomist, the discoverer of the Eustachian tube, leading from the middle ear to the pharynx, and of the Eustachian valve in the right auricles of the heart.

Everyman

Popular English ◊morality play of the early 16th century, probably derived from an earlier Dutch play, *Elckerlijc*. Summoned by Death, Everyman is forsaken by his former friends – allegorical abstractions such as Fellowship and Kindred – and is saved only by Good Deeds, who accompanies him to the grave.

Eworth, Hans (HANS EWOUTSZOON) (*c.* 1515–*c.* 1574)

Flemish-born English portrait and minature painter. Arriving in England in the late 1540s, he worked for the court. About 35 portraits can either definitely or probably be attributed to him, many of them of Roman Catholic notables in the circle of Mary I. One of the best-known is the allegorical *Portrait of Sir John Luttrell* (1550, Courtauld Institute, London).

His works show the influence of both Hans ◊Holbein the Younger (whose style remained fashionable at the English court) and Holbein's French counterpart, Jean ◊Clouet.

Eworth was born in Antwerp and may possibly be identified with the 'Jan Euworts' mentioned as a freeman of the St Luke guild in that city in 1540. His fame, however, dates from his arrival in England, where he spent the rest of his life. The earliest of his dated paintings, signed with his monogram 'HE', is from the year 1549. He was also a painter and designer for court fêtes.

Among his finest works is the double portrait traditionally identified as Frances Brandon, Duchess of Suffolk, and her second husband and former secretary, Adrian Stokes (1559) (private collection). A more plausible theory is that they are Mary, Baroness Dacre, and her son Gregory, 10th Baron Dacre.

exploration

The medieval tradition of exploration gained increased momentum in the 15th century and, ultimately, transformed the European conception of the map of the world. The Portuguese taking of Ceuta (Moroccan Africa) in 1415 was the first success in a long-held ambition to carve out a Christian kingdom beyond the Mediterranean. Further progress down the coast of Africa was fuelled by both the ambitions of Prince Henry 'the Navigator' and, more practically, the increasing difficulties of the spice trade in the Eastern Mediterranean. The Portuguese enterprise, then, turned into an economic venture with its final goal reaching the source of the spice trade (with Vasco da ◊Gama finally reaching India in 1498).

Only a few years later (if not earlier), a Portuguese ship bound for India went magnificently off course and touched the coast of what became known as Brazil. This, though, was not the first time that the continents (which, perversely, were named the Americas after one of the less successful explorers, Amerigo ◊Vespucci) had encountered European interest. Christopher ◊Columbus had finally gained patronage for his plan to reach the spice islands by a westerly route from Isabella of Castile: celebrating the capture of Moorish Granada in 1492, the queen announced two ventures, the first to expel the Jews from the new Christian Spain and the second to send Columbus across the Atlantic. Columbus' landfall was in a set of islands which became known as the West Indies. He made further trips across the Atlantic but was increasingly discredited. In the early 16th century, Spanish interest concentrated on the conquest of lands in South America, with expeditions led by *conquistadores* such as Francisco ◊Pizarro and Hernán ◊Cortés.

Despite the coincidence of timing, it is difficult to draw connections between the Renaissance and the age of exploration. Some specific links have been proposed but they are tenuous. For example, it is suggested that Christopher Columbus' calculations of the world's circumference were influenced by the Classical writings of Strabo, whose work may have been recommended to a possible correspondent of Columbus, Paolo Toscanelli (1397–1482), by Gemistus ◊Plethon. Perhaps this line of communication did exist, though, even if it did, it tells us little more than that one explorer, Columbus, shared some contemporaries' interest in ancient geographical accounts. And this being so, it marks Columbus out from other explorers: he may have combined bookish learning with practical skills – and some of the patrons of exploration may have had humanist interests (Prince Henry 'the Navigator', for example, was

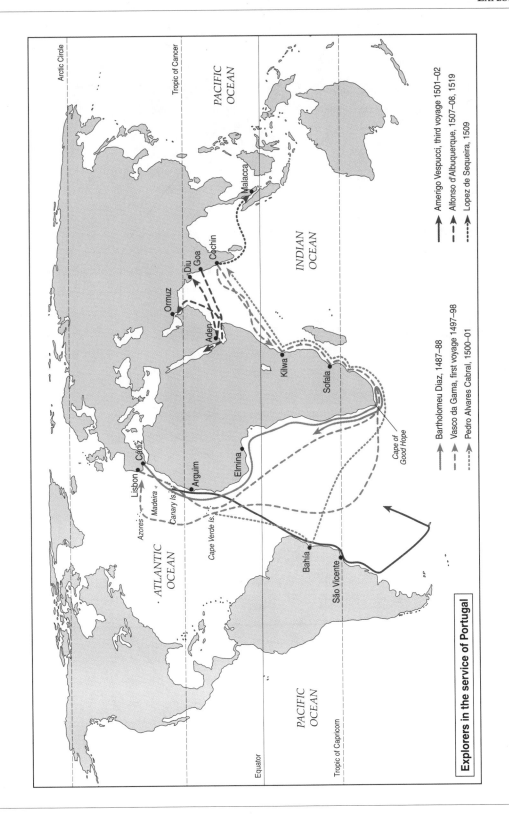

Explorers in the service of Portugal

Bartholomeu Diaz, 1487–88
Vasco da Gama, first voyage 1497–98
Pedro Alvares Cabral, 1500–01

Amerigo Vespucci, third voyage 1501–02
Alfonso d'Albuquerque, 1507–08, 1519
Lopez de Sequeira, 1509

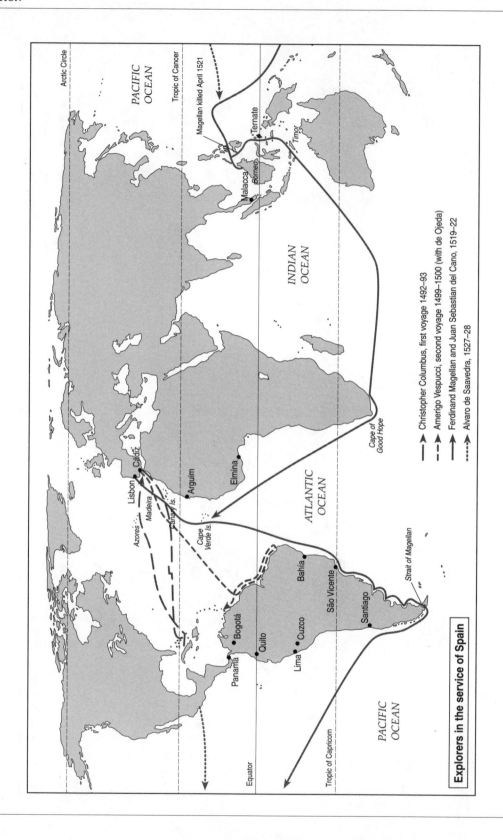

Explorers in the service of Spain

Christopher Columbus, first voyage 1492–93
Amerigo Vespucci, second voyage 1499–1500 (with de Ojeda)
Ferdinand Magellan and Juan Sebastian del Cano, 1519–22
Alvaro de Saavedra, 1527–28

in contact with ◊Poggio Bracciolini) – but most explorers and *conquistadores* were rarely conversant with esoteric intellectual fashions. Indeed, someone like Francisco Pizarro may have been an accomplished seaman and soldier but he had limited reading skills. Even, then, a 'Renaissance mentality' or that chimera, a shared 'spirit of inquiry', can not explain the voyages of 'discovery'.

Yet, at the same time, there is no denying that the voyages of exploration had a impact on Renaissance Europe. Conceptually, coming to comprehend the significance of the discovery of the Americas was a slow process but the idea of discovering new worlds became a fashionable reference in learned works. It provided, for example, a backdrop to Thomas ◊More's *Utopia*, while, contemporaneously, Niccolò ◊Machiavelli used it as a metaphor for the humanist enterprise of discovering the Classical world. Practically, however, the results of the discoveries were more tangible, introducing to Europe new plants, new animals (including other humans) and a new disease: ◊syphilis.

Eyck, Jan van (*c.* 1390–1441)

Netherlandish painter, who gained in his lifetime a Europe-wide reputation. One of the first painters to use oil paint effectively, he is noted for his meticulous detail and his brilliance of colour and finish. He painted religious scenes like the altarpiece, *The Adoration of the Lamb* (1432) (St Bavo Cathedral, Ghent), and portraits, including *The Arnolfini Wedding* (1434, National Gallery, London), which records the betrothal of the Bruges-based Lucchese cloth merchant Giovanni Arnolfini to Giovanna Cenami.

Unlike his presumed elder brother **Hubert van Eyck** (died 1426), Jan is a clearly defined historical figure. He worked as a miniaturist 1422–25 in The Hague for John, Duke of Bavaria and Count of Holland (died 1425), and then entered the service of ◊Philip the Good, Duke of Burgundy, as court painter and *valet de chambre*. Philip employed him not only in Burgundy but also abroad: van Eyck was sent with the embassy to Portugal in 1428 to paint the portrait of Joao I's daughter Isabella, whom Philip subsequently married. He settled in Bruges about 1430, still working for the duke, but employed also by the wealthy burgesses of Bruges and the Italian merchants who resided in this international seat of trade. Among his portraits are *Madonna with Chancellor Rolin* (1435/37, Louvre, Paris), *Madonna with Canon van der Paele* (1436, Groningen Museum, Bruges), and *Man with a Turban* (1433, National Gallery, London), thought by some to be a self-portrait. He and his brother may also have illuminated the Turin-Milan Book of Hours (destroyed in the 20th century).

Jan (and perhaps his brother) improved on the already existing technique of oil painting, which allowed subtler effects of tone, colour, and detail than the egg-tempera technique then in common use. However, the brilliance of colour and perfection of enamel-like surface attained by Jan must be attributed also to his superbly skilled and methodical handling of paint, skills acquired as an illuminator.

Jan van ◊Eyck's works were influential not only in the Low Countries where they were often copied by artists like Grard ◊David, but in Germany, Spain, and Italy. ◊Alfonso V was one of the early collectors of his paintings but examples of his work also soon entered the collections of the Medici in Florence (*St Jerome in his study*) and the d'Este in Ferrara. Elements of his works were imitated by Italian artists like ◊Piero della Francesca, Sandro ◊Botticelli, and Andrea ◊Mantegna.

Faber, Heinrich (BEFORE 1500–1552)

German theorist and composer. He was the author of a music textbook for beginners, *Compendiolum Musicae pro Incipientibus*, which was first published at Brunswick in 1548 and ran into numerous editions. There is some church music to Latin and German texts.

Faber, Johann (1478–1541)

German Catholic theologian and diplomat. A close friend to ◊Erasmus, Faber at first sympathized with those wishing to reform the Catholic Church, but later became a staunch supporter of the established church order. His treatise *Malleus in Haeresiam Lutheranam/Hammer of Lutheran Heresy* (1524) earned him the nickname of 'hammer of the heretics'.

He was born at Leutkirch near Memmingen and studied at Tübingen and Fribourg. In 1518 he joined the diocesan bureaucracy of the bishop of Constance. His knowledge of philosophy and science was valuable to his side in the debate. Among his diplomatic missions was the occasion when the future Emperor Ferdinand I sent him to England to enlist the support of Henry VIII against the Turks. From 1530 Faber was bishop of Vienna.

Fabricius, David (1564–1617)

Dutch clergyman, who discovered the first variable star, Omicron Ceti or Mira, in 1596.

Fabricius, Geronimo (LATINIZED NAME OF GIROLAMO FABRIZIO) (1537–1619)

Italian anatomist and embryologist. He made a detailed study of the veins and discovered the valves that direct the blood flow towards the heart. He also studied the development of chick embryos.

Fabricius also investigated the mechanics of respiration, the action of muscles, the anatomy of the larynx (about which he was the first to give a full description) and the eye (he was the first to correctly describe the location of the lens and the first to demonstrate that the pupil changes size).

Fabricius was born in Aquapendente, near Orvieto, and studied at Padua, where he was taught by anatomist Gabriel ◊Fallopius. In 1565 he succeeded Fallopius as professor and remained at Padua for the rest of his career. Fabricius built up an international reputation that attracted students from many countries, including William ◊Harvey.

Fabricius publicly demonstrated the valves in the veins of the limbs in 1579, and in 1603 published the first accurate description, with detailed illustrations, of these valves in *De Venarum Ostiolis/On the Valves of the Veins*. He mistakenly believed, however, that the valves' function was to retard the flow of blood to enable the tissues to absorb nutriment.

In his treatise *De Formato Foetu/On the Formation of the Fetus* (1600) – the first work of its kind – he compared the late fetal stages of different animals and gave the first detailed description of the placenta. In *De Formatione Ovi et Pulli/On the Development of the Egg and the Chick* (1612) he made some erroneous assumptions; for example, that the sperm did not enter the ovum, but stimulated the generative process from a distance.

facetiae

Latin collections of humorous (often bawdy) stories. Perhaps the most popular was that made by ◊Poggio Bracciolini, made late in his life, and which circulated in manuscript and, from 1470, in print. Some of his tales entered into vernacular collections, like the 16th-century English jestbooks.

A friar was preaching at Tivoli with too little consideration of his audience: he condemned and with many words deplored adultery, saying that it was so grave a sin that he would prefer to have ten virgins than a single married woman. With this many in his audience heartily concurred.

～

POGGIO BRACCIOLINI, *Facetia 44*

Poggio's collection includes not just ribald stories: some of his tales are recollections of his friends demonstrating their wit. In other cases, he records rumours of monstrous births or unusual events. But, alongside these, there are jokes poking fun at a whole range of individuals and types of people, in particular Poggio's particular *bête noire*, the preaching friars.

Faerie Queene, The

Epic poem by Edmund ◊Spenser, published in 1590–96, dedicated to Elizabeth I. Drawing on the traditions of chivalry and courtly love, the poem was planned as an epic in 12 books, following the adventures of 12 knights, each representing a different chivalric virtue, beginning with the Red Cross Knight of holiness. Only six books were completed; part of a seventh (*The Mutabilitie Cantos*) also survives.

The general end of all the book is to fashion a gentleman

in virtuous and gentle discipline … In which I have

followed all the antiques Poets historical, first Homer, then

Virgil; after him Ariosto and lately Tasso …

◇

SPENSER, letter to Sir Walter Ralegh prefacing *The Faerie Queene*

Falconetto, Giovanni Maria (1468–1535)

Veronese architect and painter. Working chiefly around Padua, Falconetto designed a number of buildings based on Classical forms, notably the loggia and odeon in Padua in 1524, which later became part of the Palazzo Giustiniani. A fresco of the *Annunciation* (1514, San Pietro Martire) and architectural frescoes painted in 1503 (cathedral) survive in his native Verona.

He was also responsible for the town gates in Padua, the Porta San Giovanni (1528) and the Porta Savonarola (1530).

Fallopius, Gabriel (LATINIZED NAME OF GABRIELE FALLOPPIO) (1523–1562)

Italian anatomist who discovered the Fallopian tubes, which he described as 'trumpets of the uterus', and named the vagina. As well as the reproductive system, he studied the anatomy of the brain and eyes, and gave the first accurate description of the inner ear.

Fallopius, born in Modena, studied at Padua under Andreas ◊Vesalius, becoming professor of anatomy at Pisa in 1548 and Padua in 1551. He was the teacher of Geronimo ◊Fabricius.

Fallopius extended Vesalius's work and corrected its details. He was the first to describe the clitoris (previously brought to man's attention by Matteo Realdo ◊Colombo), and the tubes leading from the ovary to the uterus, which were subsequently named after him. He failed, however, to grasp the function of the Fallopian tubes. He also carried out investigations on the larynx, muscular action, and respiration.

Family of Love (LATIN '*FAMILIA CARITATIS*')

An obscure branch of ◊Anabaptists founded about 1540 by Hendrick Niclaes (*c.* 1502–*c.* 1580) in the Netherlands. It became best established in England during the second half of the 16th century through to the end of the 17th. An antinomian sect, the Familists, as they were also known, were persecuted by Elizabeth I during the 1580s but survived and spread, enjoying a revival of popularity in the mid-17th century.

Fancelli, Domenico, (ALSO KNOWN AS DOMENICO DE ALEXANDRE) (1469–1519)

Italian sculptor, born at Settignano. Patronized by the Spanish nobility and royal family, the tombs he designed at their request introduced Renaissance forms into Spanish sculpture.

Initially he carried out his commissions in Genoa, travelling to Spain only to assemble the completed monument. Thus he arrived in Seville in 1510 to erect Diego ◊Hurtado de Mendoza's tomb (commissioned 1508), and at Avila in 1513 with Prince Juan's sepulchre (modelled on Pollaiuolo's Vatican tomb for Sixtus IV and unprecedented in Spain). Remaining in Spain, he completed the tombs of ◊Ferdinand and ◊Isabella in 1517, but death prevented him finishing ◊Ximénes de Cisneros's tomb, eventually completed by Bartolomé Ordoñez.

Farnaby, Giles (*c.* 1563–1640)

English composer. He wrote madrigals, psalms for the *Whole Booke of Psalms* (1621), edited by Thomas

Ravencroft (1582–1633), and music for the virginal (an early keyboard instrument), over 50 pieces being represented in the 17th-century manuscript collection the *Fitzwilliam Virginal Book*.

He lived in London, where he married in 1587, and took a degree in music at Oxford University in 1592.

Works include:
Twenty canzonets for four and 1 for eight voices, madrigals, psalm tunes set for four voices in East's Psalter; over 50 virginal pieces.

Farnese, Palazzo

A Roman palace near the Campo dei Fiori. It was commissioned by Cardinal Alessandro Farnese (later Pope ◊Paul III) and designed in the Florentine style by the architect Antonio da ◊Sangallo the Younger, who began work in 1517. After Sangallo's death in 1546 ◊Michelangelo became the chief architect, introducing a number of alterations. At the end of the 16th century, the interior of the palace was decorated with frescoes by Annibale Carracci, notably the Galleria, which was decorated with mythological scenes.

Also involved in the building of the palace was the architect ◊Vignola, who was in charge from the 1560s until his death in 1573, when Giacomo ◊della Porta took over, completing the building in 1589.

Farrant, Richard (*c.* 1530–1580)

English organist and composer. He was a Gentleman of the Chapel Royal in London until 1564, when he became organist and choirmaster at St George's Chapel, Windsor. He also wrote music for the Blackfriar's Theatre, London.

Works include:
Service in A minor (usually sung in G minor), anthems 'Call to Remembrance' and 'Hide not Thou Thy Face', and other church music, songs for plays produced by him with the choirboys before Queen Elizabeth; keyboard pieces in the Mulliner Book.

Fastnachtspiel (GERMAN 'SHROVETIDE PLAY')

Carnival play that emerged in the 15th century as Germany's first truly secular form of drama, surviving until the end of the 16th century. It combined popular farce and elements from religious drama and was usually performed by amateurs.

Hans Sachs was the leading writer of *Fastnachtspiele* in the 16th century.

Fauchet, Claude (1530–1601)

French critic and historian. He was historiographer ('official historian') of France under Henry IV. He wrote *Antiquités gauloises et françaises jusqu'à Clovis* (1579–99) and *Recueil de l'origine de la langue et poésie française* (1581), by which he may be considered to be the first French historian of literature.

Fayrfax, Robert (1464–1521)

English composer. He was a Gentleman of the Chapel Royal on the accession of Henry VIII, with whom he attended the Field of the Cloth of Gold in 1520.

He became organist and choirmaster at St Albans Cathedral before 1502. He gained a degree in music at Cambridge University in 1501 (for his Mass *O quam glorifica*) and a doctorate in 1504; he received a doctorate from Oxford in 1511.

Works include:
Six cyclic Masses, motets, two Magnificats, *Stabat Mater*, songs for several voices, and other pieces.

Fedé, Jehen (*c.* 1415–*c.* 1477)

French composer. He was well known in his day as a writer of sacred and secular music, but only six pieces believed to be by him have survived.

He was vicar of Douai (1439–40), a papal singer (1443–45); at the Sainte Chapelle in 1449; at the court of Charles VII (1452–53); at St Peter's, Rome in 1466; and a member of Louis XI's chapel (1473–74).

Federigo da Montefeltro (1422–1482)

Signore (from 1444) and ultimately Duke (from 1474) of Urbino. Federigo, the illegitimate offspring of Urbino's ruling dynasty, chose for himself the career of a ◊condottiere. He learnt his military craft at the side of Niccolò Piccinino and turned his training to the advantage of whoever proved the highest bidder. This was often the papacy and it was ◊Sixtus IV who finally endowed him with the title of Duke.

Montefeltro Piero della Francesca, *Triumphal procession of Federigo da Montefeltro, Duke of Urbino, c.* 1460/75 (Uffizi, Florence). The *condottiere*-duke, with his distinctive hooked nose, sits on the chariot in this fashionably classicizing image. *AKG London/Erich Lessing*

Federigo had taken charge of Urbino 30 years earlier, on the death of his half-brother, and continually used campaigns fought in others' names to increase his own patrimony.

Federigo was concerned not to appear just another sanguineous mercenary. He had been educated at the feet of ◊Vittorino da Feltre and was keen to show that he had learnt something at school. He involved himself in the design of his palace in the ducal city, for which the architects were Francesco ◊Laurana and ◊Francesco di Giorgio Martini. In this work he employed the best-reputed craftsmen; and this did not mean just Italians. The large halls of the palace were decked with Low Countries tapestries, and Federigo's private *studiolo* was decorated with paintings by ◊Justus of Ghent. While the main sign of his magnificence was his building project, he also spent lavishly on building up an impressive library. His book dealer was, most often, ◊Vespasiano da Bisticci, who claimed that the collection he had supplied was beyond comparison throughout Europe.

In this library all the books are superlatively good and written in pen; had there been one printed volume it would have been ashamed in such company. They were beautifully illuminated and written on parchment. This library is remarkable amongst all others in that, taking the works of all writers, sacred and profane, original and translated, there will be found not a single imperfect folio.

VESPASIANO DA BISTICCI'S rhetorical praise for the library of Federigo da Montefeltro which he, in large part, supplied

Feliciano, Felice (1433–*c.* 1479)

Italian epigraphist, antiquary, and calligrapher. During the 1460s he devised a way to carve Roman capital letters on mathematical rules derived from the study of ancient inscriptions at Rome, Ravenna, and elsewhere. The effect of these studies can be seen in inscriptions on many Renaissance commemorative statues. He also wrote a number of calligraphic manuscripts in a hand which exercised a considerable influence over later manuals of penmanship.

He also wrote poetry in the vernacular, and his interests included printing and alchemy, the latter causing him to spend much time and money on the search for the philosopher's stone.

Feragut, Beltrame (BERTRAND) (*c.* 1385–*c.* 1450)

French composer who travelled in France and Italy. His motet *Excelsa civitas Vincencia* was written in honour of a new bishop of Vicenza, Francesco Malipiero, in 1433. A few other sacred works survive.

Ferdinand I (1503–1564)

Holy Roman Emperor who succeeded his brother Charles V in 1556; King of Bohemia and Hungary from 1526, King of the Germans from 1531. He reformed the German monetary system and reorganized the judicial Aulic council (*Reichshofrat*). He was the son of Philip the Handsome and grandson of Maximilian I.

Ferdinand II (1452–1516)

King-consort of Castile from 1474 (as **Ferdinand V**), King of Aragon from 1479, and **Ferdinand III** of Naples from 1504. In 1469 he married his cousin ◊Isabella I, who succeeded to the throne of Castile in 1474; they were known as **the Catholic Monarchs** because they completed the *reconquista* (reconquest) of the Spanish peninsula from the Muslims by taking the last Moorish kingdom, Granada, in 1492. To celebrate this success they expelled the Jews, and financed Christopher ◊Columbus's expedition to the Americas in 1492.

Ferdinand conquered Naples (1500–03) and Navarre (1512). On his wife's death, the crown of Castile passed to his daughter Joanna and her husband, ◊Philip the Handsome of Burgundy in 1506. However, on Philip's death and Joanna's subsequent decline into madness, Ferdinand was recognized as ruler of Castile, establishing the rule of one man for all the kingdoms which became permanent under his grandson, Charles I of Spain (later Emperor Charles V).

Fernández, Juan (*c.* 1536–*c.* 1604)

Spanish explorer and navigator. As a pilot on the Pacific coast of South America in 1563, he reached the islands off the coast of Chile that now bear his name. Alexander Selkirk was later marooned on one of these islands, and his life story formed the basis of Daniel Defoe's *Robinson Crusoe*.

Fernández de Avellaneda, Alonso (LIVED 17TH CENTURY)

Spanish novelist who in 1614 published a sequel to Miguel de Cervantes's *Don Quixote*, entitled *Segundo tomo del ingenioso hidalgo don Quijote de la Mancha*. He wrote under this pseudonym, and his real name is unknown.

Fernández de Navarrete, Juan (*c.* 1526–1579)

Spanish painter, known as 'El Mudo' because he was a deaf-mute. Fernández was born in Logroño, studied in Italy under ◊Titian, and became painter to King Philip II in 1568. From 1576 he also helped in the decoration of the Escorial near Madrid, producing a series of altarpieces for the church there, among them a striking *Burial of St Lawrence* (1579).

Fernandez de Quirós, Pedro (1565–1614)

Spanish navigator, one of the first Europeans to search for the great southern continent that Ferdinand ◊Magellan believed lay to the south of the Magellan Strait. Despite a series of disastrous expeditions, he took part in the discovery of the Marquesas Islands and the main island of Espíritu Santo in the New Hebrides.

Fernel, Jean François (1497–1558)

French physician who introduced the terms 'physiology' and 'pathology' into medicine.

Ferrabosco, Alfonso (1543–1588)

Italian composer, active in England. He wrote madrigals, lute pieces, and motets. Many of his works appear in *Musica Transalpina*.

He was born at Bologna, son of the singer and composer Domenico Ferrabosco (1513–1574). He settled in London before 1562; left the service of Queen Elizabeth I in 1569, after becoming involved in a murder case, and returned to Italy on leave, which he extended until 1572. In 1578 he left England for good and entered the service of the Duke of Savoy at Turin, leaving his children in England. One of these, Alfonso Ferrabosco (*c.* 1575–1628), later became court musician to James I.

Works include:
Motets, madrigals, and other pieces.

Ferrante I (FERDINAND) (1423–1494)

King of Naples (1458–94). The illegitimate son of Alfonso V of Aragon, his reign was dominated by attempts to secure his kingdom against external opposition. His authoritarian rule provoked several baronial revolts, including major ones in 1462 and 1485. All the same, he was able to act as a major player on the Italian stage, allying (for example) with Sixtus IV against Lorenzo de' Medici following the Pazzi conspiracy. He promoted learning (inheriting some scholars, like Giovanni ◊Pontano, from his father's court) as well as the arts (or at least the more militarily useful of them – Fra ◊Giocondo was for a time in his service). His hold on his territories was weak. He fought a series of campaigns against the French and Turks to retain his dominions, but the French invaded soon after his death.

Ferrari, Gaudenzio (1484–1546)

Lombard painter and sculptor. Among his works, which combine Italian and German styles, is a *Crucifixion* (Sanctuary of Sacro Monte, Varallo), a fresco with 26 life-size terracotta figures.

Ferreira, António (1528–1569)

Portuguese poet and magistrate who, while a canon law student at Coimbra, composed two prose comedies, one of which, *O cioso/The Jealous Man*, was the first European comedy to rely for its humour upon characters rather than situations. After a brief spell teaching at his *alma mater*, he was appointed chief magistrate in Lisbon. An admirer of ◊Sá de Miranda, he was a fervent supporter of the Portuguese language over Castilian and, unlike his contemporaries, wrote solely in Portuguese. His most important works appeared in print posthumously. His son published his collected poems as *Poemas Lusitanos/ Lusitanian [Portuguese] Poems* in 1598; in 1587 his dramatization of the doomed love between Pedro I of Portugal and his mistress, Inês de Castro, had been published. The first dramatic treatment of the subject, it was reprinted in 1598 and provided a source of inspiration for contemporary and later dramatists and poets, including ◊Camões.

Feuillants

Reformed order of Cistercians. They were named after Les-Feuillans, near Toulouse, where their order was founded in 1577 by Abbot Jean de la Barrière (1544–1600). Encouraged by Henry III, the Feuillants were established in Paris. By the time they were given status as an independent order (1589), the Feuillants had spread to Italy, where they were known as Bernardines.

Fiammingo, Giovanni

See ◊Calcar, Jan Steven van.

Ficino, Marsilio (1433–1499)

Florentine cleric and Platonic philosopher. The leading light of the Platonic Academy of Florence (see feature), Ficino's teachings, translations, and Platonic interpretations formed the basis of a thriving literary and aesthetic culture which formed a pillar of European thought over subsequent ages. Ficino both translated the complete works of Plato from Greek into Latin (begun in 1462 and published in 1484) and produced commentaries on Plato and the Platonists (in particular the *De Amore* on Plato's *Symposium*). In 1492 Ficino published the first complete translation of Plotinus, together with commentaries which interpreted his mystical sayings in the light of Christian revelation.

While his own father commended Ficino to the study of medicine, Ficino's 'soul father', Cosimo de' ◊Medici, commended him to Plato, whom he regarded as a doctor of the soul. Ficino's interest in 'spritual medicine' is a recurring theme throughout his work, apparent in his numerous letters to friends and in his *Three Books on Life* (1491). It was with the intention of becoming himself a doctor of the soul that, in 1462, Ficino set to work on translating the Platonic dialogues as well as the *Corpus Hermeticum*. For most of his life, Ficino enjoyed the support of the Medici. Ficino first appeared in literature as a speaker in Cristoforo ◊Landino's *Disputationes Camaldulenses* where he praised the life of contemplative ascent in the eremitic Camaldolese setting.

Ficino's most influential work was his *De Amore*, or commentary on Plato's *Symposium*. Itself written as a Platonic dialogue given in honour of Plato's feast day, here Ficino revives the idea of love as the desire for beauty, and beauty as the splendour of divinity. Ordained priest in 1473, Ficino dedicated the *De Christiana Religione* to Lorenzo de' Medici. Here Ficino describes Christianity as the fulfilment of both Hebrew prophecy and of all that was true in ancient

Greek philosophy. Ficino was a speaker in Lorenzo de' Medici's Altercazione, where he defends the primacy of the intellect over the will; in a later letter by Ficino on happiness, however, Ficino emphasized the primacy of the will, whereby love could be expressed in virtuous action. At the end of his life Ficino sought to reconcile these views in a letter to the Camaldolese philosopher Paolo Orlandini, where he described the ascent of the intellect as a natural process, but the ascent of the will as supernatural, and attributable only to the grace of God. Though often portrayed as a pagan or apostate, Ficino remained a loyal Christian throughout his life.

Chronological List of Ficino's Published Works:

- *De Amore*, commentary on Plato's *Symposium*; wide MS circulation from 1469
- Hermes Trismegistus, *Pimander*, tr. lat. (Treviso, 1471) dedicated to Cosimo de' Medici
- *Della Christiana religione* (Florence, 1474) dedicated to Girolamo Rossi
- *De Christiana religione* (Florence, 1476)
- *Consilio contro la pestilenzia* (Florence, 1481)
- *Theologia platonica* (Florence, 1482)
- Plato, *Opera Omnia*, tr. lat. (Florence, 1484, revised Venice, 1491) dedicated to Lorenzo de' Medici
- *De Triplici vita* (Florence, 1489) dedicated to Lorenzo de' Medici
- Plotinus, *Enneads*, tr. lat. and commentary (Florence, 1492) dedicated to Lorenzo de' Medici
- *De sole et lumine* (Florence, 1493) dedicated to Piero de' Medici
- *Epistolae* (Venice, 1495) dedicated to Niccolo Valori
- *Commentaria in Platonem* (Florence, 1496) dedicated to Niccolo Valori, commentaries on Plato's *Timaeus, Parmenides, Sophist, Philebus, Republic, Phaedrus*
- Dionysius the Areopagite, *De Mystica Theologia, De Divinis Nominibus*, tr. lat. (Florence, *c.* 1496)
- Xenocrates, *De Morte*, Plato (attr.) *Axiochum*, Anaxagoras, *De Resurrectione*, (Paris, 1498)

Fidei Defensor (LATIN 'DEFENDER OF THE FAITH') Title conferred by Pope Leo X on Henry VIII of England in 1521 to reward his writing of the *Assertio Septum Sacramentum/ Assertion of the Seven Sacraments* refuting the doctrines of Martin Luther. Henry was assisted (at least) in the work by scholars at his court, including Thomas ◊More.

Figueroa, Francisco de (1536–1617) Soldier and poet, born at Alcalá. Praised for his poetry by ◊Cervantes in his 1585 ◊pastoral novel *La Galatea*, his sobriquet 'el Divino' ('the divine one') testifies to his literary fame while alive. On his death, he ordered his love poems burned, but a number of his works survived to be published in Lisbon (1625). A new edition which included a further six poems appeared in 1626. Figueroa, who wrote both in Castilian and Italian, drew his inspiration from ◊Horace, ◊Petrarch (writing Petrarchan sonnets), and ◊Garcilaso's pastoral eclogues.

Filarete (BORN ANTONIO AVERLINO) (*c.* 1400–1469) Florentine architect, sculptor, and author. He may have worked first as an assistant to Ghiberti on the baptistery doors in Florence; if so, this was an apprenticeship for one of his most celebrated works – the huge west door of St Peter's, Rome, commissioned by Pope ◊Eugenius IV in about 1445. After that, much of his career was spent in the pay of the Sforza in Milan, where he built the Ospedale Maggiore (1456–65), in which Lombard ornamented brickwork is combined with the classicizing style of Brunelleschi.

In this period, he also wrote his *Tratto d'architettura/Treatise on Architecture*, a dialogue discussing the building of an ideal city (to be called Sforzinda). When relations worsened with his Milanese patron, he rededicated his *Treatise* to Piero de' Medici in 1465. In the same year, he presented to Piero a bronze statuette in imitation of the ancient Roman statue of Marcus Aurelius.

Filelfo, Francesco (1398–1481) Italian scholar, teacher, and rhetorician. Born at Tolentino, he studied at Padua, where he was appointed professor at the age of 18. In 1419 he travelled to Constantinople to learn the language and acquire Greek manuscripts. There he married Theodora, daughter of his teacher John ◊Chrysoloras. He returned to Venice in 1427 with over 40 manuscripts, and during the next 50 years established a reputation as one of the finest Greek scholars of his age.

He returned to Venice in 1427 but was dissatisfied with his reception and moved on, first to Bologna, then to Florence. He quarrelled with the Florentine humanists and Cosimo de' ◊Medici and in 1434 had to leave the city for Siena. Eventually he reached Milan in 1440, where he remained, apart from a visit to Rome in 1475, for the rest of his life. In 1481 he was invited back to Florence, but died there soon afterwards.

Finck, Hermann (1527–1558)

German composer and theorist. He wrote a theoretical book, *Practica Musica,* in five volumes. Works include motets, sacred songs, and wedding songs for several voices.

He studied at the University of Wittenberg, where he taught music from 1554. In 1557 he was appointed organist in Wittenberg, but died the following year at the age of 31.

Finiguerra, Maso (1426–1464)

Italian goldsmith, designer, and engraver. He is best known for his work in *niello,* a type of decorative metalwork in which incisions in the metal are filled with a black metallic compound. Although he did not actually invent the process of copper engraving (as ◊Vasari claimed), he was instrumental in developing its use as an extension of *niello* work.

Born in Florence, Maso was praised by Vasari and Benvenuto ◊Cellini as a printmaker and a master of *niello* work. As a young man he may have assisted ◊Ghiberti on the east door of the baptistery in Florence and he was later associated with Antonio ◊Pollaiuolo, several of whose paintings he may have reproduced in a series of copperplate engravings (1459–64). Few works by Maso survive. Among those that are often attributed to him are the Thewalt cross (*c.* 1464, Metropolitan Museum of Art, New York) and a series of engravings called the *Seven Planets.*

Fiocchi, Andrea (DIED 1452)

Italian cleric and humanist author, born in Florence. His career was spent in the papal curia, where he wrote his one work, *De Potestatibus Romanorum* (*c.* 1424), a discussion of the religious and secular officials of ancient Rome, which he dedicated to cardinal Branda Castiglioni. Its ◊antiquarianism antedated that of Fiocchi's colleague Flavio ◊Biondo. His contemporaries liked the work so much they did it the dubious honour of attributing a shortened version of it to the ancient historian Lucius Fenestella.

Fioravanti, Aristotele (*c.* 1415–*c.* 1485)

Italian architect and engineer. He worked in Italy and Hungary, and in 1475 was summoned to Russia to build the Cathedral of the Assumption (Uspenskii Sobor) in the Kremlin in Moscow. His design combined elements of conventional Russian church architecture with features of Renaissance design. He died in Moscow.

Born in Bologna into a family of architects, Fioravanti helped to spread Renaissance styles throughout Europe in the course of his travels. After work in Rome, Bologna, and Milan, and other major Italian artistic centres, Fioravanti was invited to Hungary in 1467, where he worked for a short time for King ◊Matthias Corvinus, before finally moving to Russia.

Firenzuola, Agnolo (1493–1543)

Florentine monk and author. He translated works both from Latin (the *Golden Ass* of ◊Apuleius and, in the *Discorsi degli Animali* (written 1541, printed 1548), from a Spanish collection of Indian animal stories. Other writings include a *Dialogo delle bellezze delle donne/Dialogue on the Beauties of Women* (printed 1558).

Fisher, John (1459–1535)

English cleric, bishop of Rochester from 1504. He was educated at Cambridge and became chancellor of the university in 1504. His early career was closely linked with Lady Margaret ◊Beaufort. After her death, he executed her will in founding St John's College, Cambridge, and himself endowed lectureships in Greek and Hebrew. In the 1520s, like Erasmus, he was repelled by the break in the Catholic Church created by the Lutherans, and in the 1530s, like Thomas More, he refused to countenance Henry VIII's claim to head the English church. He shared More's fate and was executed on 22 June 1535.

It was Fisher who secured for ◊Erasmus the position of reader in theology at Cambridge in succession to himself in 1511. Erasmus did not remain in England long, but the contact between the two scholars continued. In the late 1510s and 1520s Fisher became embroiled in religious controversy, first against ◊Lefèvre d'Étaples (defending the contemporary – erroneous – belief that Mary Magdalen was the sister of Lazarus) and then against Luther. At the end of the decade he turned his attention to the issue of the royal divorce, writing several tracts against Henry VIII's actions, until, in September 1533, he called upon Charles V to invade England and help depose Henry.

Flecha, Mateo (1481–c. 1553)

Spanish monk and composer. He was a pupil of Juan Castelló at Barcelona, and became maestro de capilla to the Infantas of Castile, the daughters of Charles V. He later became a Carmelite and settled in the monastery of Poblet.

Flecha, Mateo (1530–1604)

Spanish monk and composer. He was taught by his uncle Mateo ◊Flecha. Works by the two Flechas (not always distinguishable) include church music, madrigals, *ensaladas* (burlesque madrigals), and other pieces. A stage work of his, *El Parnaso*, is believed to have been performed at Madrid in 1561.

He was in the service of the Emperor Charles V until 1558 and of Philip II. He then went to Prague in the service of the Emperor Maximilian, and after the emperor's death in 1576 he remained there until 1599. After this he joined the abbey of Solsona as a Franciscan monk.

Fletcher, Giles, THE ELDER (1546–1611)

English lawyer, diplomat, and writer. He was sent on a diplomatic mission to Russia in 1588, where, despite a hostile reception from the tsar, he secured important concessions for English merchants. His frank and colourful account of Russia in *The Russe Commonwealth* (1591) was suppressed on publication on account of the English traders' fears that it would antagonize the Russians.

Born in Watford and educated at Eton and Cambridge, Fletcher gained his doctorate in law in 1581. From 1587 to 1605 he was Remembrancer of the City of London. A diplomatic mission to Scotland

in 1586 was followed by one to Germany and then his trip to Russia. He also wrote a cycle of sonnets entitled *Licia* (1593) and a quantity of Latin verse. His sons Giles and Phineas were also poets.

Fletcher, John (1579–1625)

English dramatist. He is remarkable for his range, which included tragicomedy and pastoral dramas, in addition to comedy and tragedy. He collaborated with Francis Beaumont in some 12 plays, producing, most notably, the tragicomedy *Philaster* (1610) and *The Maid's Tragedy* (c. 1611). He is alleged to have collaborated with ◊Shakespeare on *The Two Noble Kinsmen* and *Henry VIII* (1613).

Among some 16 plays credited to Fletcher alone are the pastoral drama *The Faithful Shepherdess* (1610), the tragedy *Bonduca* (c. 1613–14), *The Chances* (1617), the tragedy *Valentinian* (1618), the comedy *The Humorous Lieutenant* (1619), and the comedies *The Pilgrim* and *The Wild-Goose Chase* (both 1621).

Fletcher was born in Rye, Sussex, and was educated at Benet College, Cambridge, but little is known of his life. Other plays resulting from the collaboration with Beaumont include *The Scornful Lady* (1610), *A King and No King* (c. 1611), and *Thierry and Theodoret* (1616), but the pair were credited with a great many more as publishers found that their names on the title page made a good selling line. Of the two, Fletcher is generally reckoned the more fluent and creative, and had a keener sense of 'theatre'.

He also collaborated with Philip Massinger in several plays, and probably with William Rowley and Thomas Middleton in others. He died of the plague.

Florence, Council of

◊General Council of the Church held in Florence, Italy, 1437–39 that negotiated union between the Catholic and Orthodox churches. It was the result of Pope Eugenius IV's decree transferring the Council from Basel to Ferrara and subsequently (for fear of the plague) to Florence. The discussions at Florence revolved around the theological issue of the Holy Trinity and around the more practical issue of papal authority. The Council culminated in the Acts of Union of 6 July 1439, uniting the Orthodox churches to the Catholic communion, but the agreement proved short-lived.

The personnel of the Council was what might be called a star-studded cast. The Greek delegation, led by the Byzantine emperor John VIII Palaeologus and the patriarch of Constantinople Joseph II, included Gemistus ◊Plethon and ◊Bessarion. The representatives on the papal side included Ambrogio ◊Traversari, ◊Nicholas of Cusa, and ◊George of Trebizond.

The debate often centred around the reading of texts of the Greek Church Fathers, in particular St ◊Basil and St ◊Athanasius. For a long time the Catholics found their Orthodox guests intransigent. However, the patriarch Joseph II retired one night, died in his bed, and the next morning a note was found declaring his final acceptance of the Catholic stance. This mysterious change of heart may have had less impact on the delegation than political realities: the Byzantine emperor needed Western support against the Ottomans and he knew he would only receive it if an agreement was reached. As it turned out, the expected military support did not materialize and the union floundered.

Culturally, the Council has been credited with an increased interest in ancient Greek ideas, in particular Platonism. But, of course, knowledge of Greek texts did precede the Council and, indeed, was in some senses a prerequisite of it. The Council did, however, assist Greek studies in three ways: the Byzantine delegation brought with them manuscripts which could then be circulated in the West; it also introduced intellectuals, in particular Bessarion, who were subsequently to become influential; and, least tangibly but no less importantly, it made Greek learning seem both fashionable and relevant.

Florio, John (c. 1553–1625)

English author and translator. His writings include his Italian–English dictionary *A World of Words* (1598) and his translation of ◊Montaigne's essays (1603), dedicated to Lucy, Countess of Bedford.

Florio was born in London, the son of refugee Italian Protestants. His father acted as tutor to the ill-fated Lady Jane Grey. John Florio became acquainted with the circle around Sir Philip ◊Sidney and with Samuel ◊David. He taught at Oxford, and in 1603 was appointed reader in Italian to James I's wife, Queen Anne, being made groom of the chamber the following year. He also taught James's son, Henry, Prince of Wales.

Floris, Cornelis (CORNELIS DE VRIENDT) (c. 1514–1575)

Netherlands sculptor and architect. He executed numerous tombs, church screens, and other ecclesiastical furnishings in the Netherlands, and as far afield as north Germany and Scandinavia. His most famous work was the new town hall at Antwerp (1561–66).

A native of Antwerp and brother of Frans ◊Floris, Cornelis seems to have received his initial training from one of the early Netherlands Italianist artists, possibly Pieter ◊Coecke van Aelst. In 1538 he was in Rome, returning to Antwerp the following year. He published two volumes of engravings: one, with various adaptations of grotesque ornament, was published in 1556 and the other, with numerous designs for funeral monuments, in 1557.

His principal student was Hans Vredeman de Vries.

Floris, Frans (FLORIS DE VRIENDT) (1516–1570)

Flemish painter. He visited Italy, where he was strongly influenced by the works of ◊Michelangelo. Among his finest works are *The Last Judgement* (Musée des Beaux-Arts, Brussels) and *The Fall of Rebellious Angels* (1554, Musée Royal des Beaux-Arts, Antwerp).

Floris was born in Antwerp. He began as a sculptor under his father, and later went to Liège, where he studied painting under Lambert Lombard. He travelled to Rome with his brother, the architect and sculptor ◊Cornelis Floris, whose chief work was the town hall in Antwerp. Frans's large and successful family workshop in Antwerp later helped to popularize the contemporary Italian artistic style in the Netherlands.

Fogliano, Ludovico (DIED AFTER 1538)

Italian music theorist and composer, brother of Giacomo Fogliano. He sang in the papal chapel and was choirmaster at Modena Cathedral. His *Musica Theorica* was published in 1529, and a single *frottola* was included in Ottaviano Petrucci's ninth book, published in 1508.

Folengo, Teofilo (1491–1544)

Italian poet. His pseudonym was Merlin Cocaio and he wrote mainly in macaronic Latin, a mixture of normal Latin and Italian words with Latinized endings. His first publication was *Il Baldus* (1517), a humorous epic; this proved a success and was followed by *Orlandino*, and an account of his roamings called *Caos del Triperuno*.

Folengo was born at Cipada, near Mantua. He became a Benedictine monk, but in 1542 sought to be released from his vows, only to return again to the monastic life some years later.

Fontainebleau

French royal palace southwest of Paris. A royal residence since the 12th century, ◊Francis I undertook major rebuilding work, which was continued by Henry II and revived by Henry IV.

The 1528 designs of Francis's architect, Gilles Le Breton (*c.* 1500–1552) reflected the classicizing style of contemporary Italy: the new gatehouse, for example, imitated the entrance to ◊Federigo da Montefeltro's palace at Urbino. On the interior decoration, Francis employed Italian artists: Rosso Fiorentino from 1530, Francesco Primaticcio from 1532. They worked with groups of assistants, who included artists like Antoine Caron (1521–1599) who himself became an established court artist. The work continued under Henry II, when Niccolò dell' ◊Abbate became yet another Italian on the royal payroll. These artists' style of frescoes and stucco relief, with its fashionably elongated figures and its often mythological subject matter, has been called (since the 19th century) the **First Fontainebleau School;** the work at the palace was certainly distinctive in mid-15th-century France and influenced indigenous artists like Jean Cousin the Elder.

During the Wars of Religion, the work at Fontainebleau was in abeyance. However, Henry IV, emphasizing the return to normality, revived the project, commissioning a group of artists like Toussaint Dubreuil (1561–1602) who employed a style consciously echoing that of the earlier generation (and thus sometimes dubbed the **Second Fontainebleau School).**

Fontana, Domenico (1543–1607)

Italian architect, born in Melide, Canton Tizino. In 1563 he went to Rome where Cardinal Felice Peretti became his patron. Under his auspices Fontana built a chapel in the Church of Santa Maria Maggiore in 1581 and the Villa Montalto in 1578. When Peretti was elected pope as Sixtus V, Fontana was appointed papal architect and undertook various important commissions in Rome, notably the Lateran Palace (1586–88), the Quirinal, and the Vatican library (1587–90). He also assisted in the completion of the dome of St Peter's (1587–90).

The engineering achievement for which he gained renown was the removal of the Egyptian obelisk (brought to Rome in the time of Caligula) from Nero's circus (now Piazza Pia) to the Piazza of St Peter's (1586); of this event he published an account (*Della Trasportatione dell obeliso vaticano/On the Transportation of the Vatican Obelisk*). When Clement VIII became pope, Fontana was dismissed and went to Naples, where he became architect to the viceroy, the Count of Miranda, and built the Royal Palace (1600–02).

Fontana, Lavinia (1552–1614)

Italian painter, from Bologna; the daughter of Prospero Fontana. Along with Sophonisba ◊Anguisciola, Fontana was one of the few female Italian artists of the 16th century. She produced portraits and also religious paintings, including an altarpiece of the *Holy Family with Sleeping Christ Child* (1589, El Escorial, Spain) for Anguisciola's patron, Philip II of Spain. (See Picture Gallery)

Fontana, Niccolò

See ◊Tartaglia.

Foppa, Vincenzo (*c.* 1427–1515)

Italian painter, who worked mainly in Milan and nearby Pavia. He was their leading artist until the arrival of Leonardo da Vinci in the 1480s. His works include *Crucifixion* (1456, Bergamo), strongly influenced by Jacopo Bellini, from whom Foppa derived his interest in colour and light, and *Boy Reading Cicero* (Wallace Collection, London), the only part of a fresco cycle for the Medici bank in Milan which survives.

RENAISSANCE FORGERY: IMITATION OR FRAUD?

THE NEW FASHION for antiquities from the 14th century onwards and the collection of *objets* had an automatic corollary in the refinement of pre-existing arts of forgery. ◊Annio of Viterbo (*c*.1469–1502), the first full-scale forger of the Renaissance, produced a supposedly 9th-century decree, previously 'lost' fragments of Babylonian, Egyptian, Greek, Roman, and Jewish authors' work (his 'big names' included Cato the Elder and Philo of Alexandria), and a handful of ancient inscriptions in pseudo-Etruscan, pseudo-Egyptian hieroglyphics, and in Latin and Greek. A successful Dominican apocalyptic commentator (and less successful astrologer), Annio also produced new inscriptions for genuine Etruscan statues (uncovered during a staged archeological 'discovery'), working on the premise that as no one else in the late 15th century understood Etruscan script, its invention and interpretation was up for grabs. His agendum was complex: cynically, Annio sought (and received) preferment in the curia by flattering the Spanish origins of the ◊Borgia dynasty. Patriotically, he attempted to boost the ancient importance of the Etruscans and their capital city (according to Annio), Viterbo (his home town). More sincerely, however, Annio genuinely sought the preservation of antiquities (albeit under his own paid supervision) and began a collection in Viterbo – perhaps the earliest civic museum of the western tradition. A number of scholars (◊Crinito, ◊Raffaele Volterrano, the Spanish

scholars Agustn and Barreiros, Vincenzo Borghini, Joseph ◊Scaliger, Johann Funck) all debunked Annio's enormous collection of 1498, the *Antiquitates*: nevertheless, many other scholars (◊Egidio of Viterbo, ◊Postel, ◊Bodin), were fascinated and generally convinced. The *Antiquitates* were reprinted in whole or in summary numerous times over the next two centuries and were still occasionally treated as authoritative in the later 18th century.

Annio's example illustrates the multivalent nature of imitation, restoration, and reproduction in an era enthralled by remains: a range which the anachronistic and perjorative term 'forgery' has insufficient scope to convey. ◊Ciriaco d'Ancona, and Bartolomeo ◊Fontius (1445–1513), though otherwise admirable and ground-breaking scholars, also both, technically, forged antique work. The notorious 16th-century forger Alfonso Ceccarelli produced numerous bogus genealogies and medieval statutes. The scholar Carlo Sigonio 'discovered' new texts of Cicero, which he had written himself, in the 1580s; he lost his reputation over them. ◊Erasmus' faith was unquestionable, his desire for authenticity was unmatched, his attacks on the hypocrisy of scholarly deceit appeared constantly, and his philological standards were exacting. Nevertheless, he wrote a short pseudo-patristic 'hoax' treatise on martyrdom which chimed remarkably well with his own views on death and suffering. In his defence, it could be that Erasmus was attempting to reveal, in disgust, the gullibility of

fellow-scholars (interestingly, Erasmus rejected the chronologies but accepted other sections of Annio's forged *Antiquitates*). Meanwhile, should the replacement of the arms, noses and genitalia of mutilated ancient statues be considered forgery? Surely not; but the fabricators of these parts were also quite capable of producing whole statues (or other 'antique'-style coins, vases, frescoes, and furniture) to order; ◊Vasari talks of ◊Francis I adorning his new chateau at Fontainebleau with 125 bronze copies of ancient *or* remoulded marble statues. By the 15th century artists already employed sophisticated 'distressing' techniques to reproduce the appearance of age: ◊Lorenzo de' Medici suggested ◊Michaelangelo bury one of his cupids to give it a 'truly antique patina'. Annio incorporated accurate archaic linguistic usages in his *Antiquitates* to invoke the aura of the past (he also made some mistakes, which sharp-eyed scholars noted). The medieval ◊prophecy of Joachim of Fiore, already much embroidered since the abbot's death in 1202, received another new section 'rediscovered' in about 1500: a writer with a classicizing humanist hand attempted to reproduce a 'medieval' script.

Indeed, it is worth remembering that the Shroud of Turin was produced, probably in the south of France, in the 1320s, using authentically Eastern linen and image-rendering techniques which baffled scientists until the late 1980s. By inserting genuinely ancient

continued

elements into a production at least a part of it is rendered authentic; perhaps a sufficiently substantive part to allow the 'artist' to consider the work perfectly genuine. At least, the whole becomes plausible, if not entirely convincing. The scholars of the Florentine ◊Academy thoroughly believed in the distant antiquity of the *Corpus Hermeticum,* though in fact these Neoplatonic writings date from the late Antiquity, and are thus a thousand years 'younger' than claimed and certainly not the works of Hermes or Orpheus. But the claim was sincere; the gaps between imitation (*passim*), false or 'wishful' attribution *pseudepigrapha* (including falsified inscriptions – 'I, Caesar crossed the Rubicon *here*'), literary mimesis, comic parody, and forgery 'proper' were relatively narrow in the Renaissance period.

The proximity of these different forms of restoration, in spite of the Renaissance scholarly drive towards the genuine, critically more perfect text owed much to an inherited relationship between authenticity and perceived authority; it is this which renders the modern concept of forgery anachronistic. Of course, the

motivation to forge was mixed, as Annio's example demonstrates. But to manufacture texts and images in sincere pursuance of a religious belief – so-called *pia fraus* – was age-old and even more readily justifiable. It was particularly rife within the medieval Christian tradition – bogus relic-collecting is a notorious example (Erasmus once commented that there was enough wood of the True Cross floating around Christendom to construct a ship). The classical heritage of the Renaissance was mapped over Christian values, to the extent that the sincere ideological conviction of the moral and cultural superiority of certain ancient civilizations was more than an aesthetic: it had near-sacral connotations, as Annio's creations demonstrate. *Pia fraus* not only continued unabated into the 16th century, but extended its boundaries to incorporate 'antique' sacred cows. Certainly the sacred nature of 'the word' and the philological refinements of the early Renaissance are woven closely together (the fashion for the Hebrew mystical exegesis of Kabbalah, around 1500, was the logical progression of this combination), and

with that came the ambivalence around 'reproduction'. While deception of the flock could be condemned if too overt, a lie which was designed to calm and comfort, or even an embroidery on the Scriptures which satisfied religious longings; the popular 14th-century handbook, *Meditations on the* (almost entirely imaginary) *Life of Christ* fits this category. Such writings were not considered in 1400 to be the perversion of biblical intention and historic truth which Protestant scholars such as ◊Casaubon later condemned – though even ◊Luther permitted a textual lie to reveal a deeper truth. An ironic marker of how closely connected scholarly criticism and religiosity remained – even as *pia fraus* became increasingly discredited in the later 16th century – may be seen in Scaliger's comment that God needs no lies to proclaim his message; nevertheless, *mundus vult decipi* ('the world longs to be deceived').

AMANDA COLLINS

Further Reading
A Grafton, *Forgers and Critics: Creativity and Duplicity in Western Scholarship* (Princeton, 1990)

Born near Brescia, Foppa probably trained in Padua, possibly as a pupil of Squarcione. While his early works show the influence of Bellini, later works also bear the influence of Provençal and Flemish art. There is also the influence of the paintings of ◊Bramante, as seen in Foppa's frescoes in Milan of the life of St Peter Martyr (1466–68) and the martyrdom of St Sebastian (1485).

Formé, Nicolas (1567–1638)
French composer. He was a clerk and singer in the Sainte-Chapelle in Paris from 1587–92, then became a countertenor in the royal chapel and succeeded Eustache du Caurroy as choirmaster and composer

there in 1609. Although almost dismissed from the Sainte-Chapelle for not conforming to the ecclesiastical rules, he returned there in 1626 and, as a favourite musician of Louis XIII, enjoyed special privileges. Only his church music survives.

Works include:
Masses, motets, Magnificat, and other church music.

Forster, Georg (*c.* 1510–1568)
German music publisher and composer. He published five sets of German songs, the *Frische Teutsche Liedlein* (1539–56), some of which he wrote himself; he also composed sacred and Latin works.

Fossa, Johannes de (*c.* 1540–1603)

German or Flemish composer. He wrote six Masses and other sacred works. He succeeded Roland de Lassus as Kapellmeister at the Munich court in 1594.

Fouquet (FOUCQUET), Jean (*c.* 1420–*c.* 1481)

French painter and manuscript illuminator. He was active at the French court from the 1450s at the latest, painting portraits of Charles VII and leading figures at his court, and later working for his son Louis XI. In some of his illuminations and paintings, in particular the *Melun Diptych* (*c.* 1453, Musées Royaux, Antwerp, and Gemäldegalerie, Berlin), Fouquet demonstrated his mastery of recent Italian innovations in artistic technique.

Little is known about his life: he may have trained in Bourges or Paris. It is unclear why he went to Italy, but he was certainly there between 1446 and 1448, when he painted a portrait of Pope ◊Eugenius IV that was noted by his contemporaries, including Antonio ◊Filarete. Returning to France, he worked on both paintings and manuscript illuminations. Some of the latter show an interest in perspective (for example, MS Gall 6, a French translation of Boccaccio, Städtsbibliothek, Munich), and some of the capital letters imitate humanist ◊*littera antiqua* (for example, MS 10475, a French translation of Frontius, Bibliothèque Royale, Brussels). In portraits such as that of *Guillaume Jouvenel des Ursins* (*c.* 1460–65) he reflected his Italian contemporaries' fascination with both classicizing architectural detail and lifelike representation of human features.

For one of his patrons, Etienne Chevalier, Charles VII's treasurer, he produced both the miniatures of a Book of Hours (MS 71, Musée Condé, Chantilly) and the *Melun Diptych*. Formerly in Melun Cathedral but now dispersed, one panel represents Chevalier and St Stephen (Brussels) and the other the Virgin and Child (Antwerp). In the latter, the Virgin is traditionally said to be an idealized portrait of the mistress of Charles VII, Agnes Sorel (of whose will Chevalier was executor).

Foxe, John (1516–1587)

English Protestant propagandist. He became a canon of Salisbury in 1563. His *Book of Martyrs* (1563) (originally titled *Actes and Monuments*) luridly described persecutions under Queen Mary, attempting to incite popular hatred of Roman Catholicism.

Foxe, Richard (*c.* 1448–1528)

English cleric, bishop of Winchester from 1501. Foxe joined the future ◊Henry VII while he was in exile in France; when Henry claimed the English throne, Foxe became a close adviser to the king and was appointed Lord Privy Seal 1487–1516. Foxe's political influence declined during the reign of Henry VIII, but it was in these years that he founded Corpus Christi College, Oxford (1517), as a centre for teaching *studia humanitatis*. The foundation included a lecturer in Greek and attracted the Spanish humanist Juan Luis ◊Vives as one of its first teachers (paid for by Thomas ◊Wolsey).

Foxe was well acquainted with humanists, including ◊Erasmus, to whom he acted as patron in 1506, and Thomas ◊Linacre, who presented him with a copy of his Galen translation. Foxe was also an architectural patron, rebuilding part of Winchester Cathedral in Renaissance style.

Fracastoro, Girolamo (*c.* 1478–1553)

Veronese physician. He wrote two medical books: *Syphilis Sive Morbus Gallicus/Syphilis or the French Disease* (1530) was written in verse and was one of the earliest texts on syphilis, a disease Fracastoro named; in *De contagione/On Contagion* (1546), he argued that diseases were spread by 'seeds of contagion'.

Francesco Canova da Milano (1497–1543)

Italian lutenist and composer. Known as *Il divino* ('the divine'), he was the finest composer of lute music before John Dowland. He was in the service first of the Duke of Mantua, about 1510, and then of Pope Paul III from 1535. He was a prolific composer, publishing and contributing to several books of lute pieces.

Francesco di Giorgio Martini (1439–1502)

Sienese painter, sculptor, architect, engineer, and bronze-caster. He worked mainly in his hometown, though also in Naples and elsewhere in Italy, and had a studio for a time with his brother-in-law ◊Neroccio di Bartolommeo Landi. Trained as a painter and sculptor in the workshop of ◊Vecchietta in his native Siena, Francesco subsequently turned to architecture and military engineering.

In his capacity as military engineer, Francesco travelled to Milan, Naples, and Urbino, pioneering a design for the angled bastion, and in 1477 he succeeded Luciano ◊Laurana as architect to ◊Federigo da Montefeltro. Moving to Urbino, he probably continued construction of the Palazzo Ducale there and provided plans for the ducal palace in Gubbio, as well as building many fortresses in the Marches.

His architectural work is poorly documented, but his singular style makes attribution fairly secure. His hallmarks include the use of arches supported on piers and capitals with flat fluting, evidenced in the Palazzo Ducale, Urbino, and the Palazzo Communale, Iesi (1486–98); superimposed pilasters whose capitals are formed by the stringcourse, executed in the churches of San Bernadino in Urbino (1482–90), and Santa Maria del Calcinaio, just outside Cortona (completed 1516); and the deployment of classical lettering in the courtyards of the ducal palaces of Urbino and Gubbio.

Having maintained professional links with Siena throughout his career, Francesco returned there in 1497, after a six-year stay in Naples, to advise on military fortifications.

Francesco was also a painter – his only signed work being a *Nativity* (Pinacoteca, Siena) – a sculptor, and a writer. Over his career, he produced a collection of manuscripts, now grouped under the title *Trattati dell 'architettura civile e militare/Treatises on Civil and Military Architecture*, which include, for example, his own translation of ◊Vitruvius.

Francia, Francesco (Raibolini) (1450–1517)

Bolognese goldsmith and painter. His painting was much influenced by ◊Perugino and ◊Raphael Sanzio as well as by Lorenzo ◊Costa, with whom he worked; his eclectic style can be seen in paintings like *Virgin and Child and St Anne* and *Pietà* (National Gallery, London).

Originally a goldsmith and engraver of dies for medals (becoming mint master in Bologna), Francia

took up painting in middle age when he made the acquaintance of Andrea ◊Mantegna. He was patronised by the humanist Bartolommeo Bianchini whose portrait he painted (*c.* 1485, National Gallery, London) and the ruling Bentivoglio family for whom he produced *Virgin Enthroned with Augustine and Five Other Saints* (Bologna Gallery), *St Peter Martyr* (Borghese Gallery, Rome), and frescoes in the Church of St Cecilia, Bologna (where Costa also worked). When the Bentivoglio fell in 1506, some of Francia's works were destroyed and he sought work elsewhere, in Modena and Parma. He eventually returned to Bologna, however, and died there.

Franciabigio (ADOPTED NAME OF FRANCESCO DI CRISTOFANI BIGI) (1482–1525)

Florentine painter. His work includes portraits such as *Portrait of a Young Man* (1514, National Gallery, London). He collaborated with ◊Andrea del Sarto on frescoes in the Church of SS Annunziata, Florence (1512), and in decorating the Medici palace at Poggio a Caiano.

He studied under Mariotto ◊Albertinelli and ◊Piero di Cosimo.

Francis I (1494–1547)

King of France from 1515. A cousin of his predecessor, Louis XII, he succeeded when Louis died childless. Combined with the succession of Charles (later Charles V) to the Spanish crowns in the following year, Francis's accession marked a new generation taking over the leading thrones of Europe. Though the personnel changed, however, the politics did not: Francis's reign was dominated, like his immediate predecessors, with wars in Italy.

It all started gloriously with Francis's victory at the Battle of Marignano in 1515 which won him Milan. In the following years, however, it proved difficult to hold on to gains with the continually shifting loyalties of the Italian cities and the repeated intervention of Charles V as heir to the Aragonese claims. The nadir for Francis was 1525 and his capture at the Battle of ◊Pavia. Despite this event and later attempts at a peaceful settlement, conflict continued and was increasingly directed against the lands of France: the Emperor and Henry VIII of England repeated an ear-

Francis I Jean Clouet, *Francis I, c.* 1535 (Louvre, Paris). *AKG London*

lier manoeuvre and launched an invasion in 1544. At the same time, Francis's court in the 1540s was ridden with faction, with the king and his heir, the future Henry II, divided.

Whatever the realities of politics in Francis's reign, he was concerned to give the appearance of greatness. Like many Renaissance patrons, Francis's patronage was primarily directed to the most visible signs of wealth: buildings. On his orders, restoration work was done at the Paris palace of the Louvre and late in his reign part of it was demolished in preparation for a new wing (built under his son, Henry II). In the environs of the capital, Francis had built the Château of Madrid, begun 1528 (at the Bois de Boulogne, now destroyed), and the year after began one of his two largest-scale architectural projects: the palace of ◊Fontainebleau. The other grandiose plan was the building of ◊Chambord near Blois – a project which began early in Francis's reign.

Francis, however, was not only concerned to give an appearance to the outside world of cultural leader-

ship; he also wanted his court to be comparable with the splendour of, say, Gonzaga Mantua, or Medici Florence. Indeed, he attempted to attract to his court Italian artists, including the former employee of the Ludovico 'il Moro' Sfoza, ◊Leonardo da Vinci. Among others who visited Paris were ◊Andrea del Sarto, Benvenuto ◊Cellini, and, to work at Fontainebleau, Rosso Fiorentino and Francesco ◊Primaticcio. His court, however, was not devoid of homegrown talent; for example, the fashionable portraitist was Jean ◊Clouet.

Nor were Francis's interests confined to the arts: he also recognized the importance of patronizing scholars and, in return, receiving their praise. In particular, the royal positions held by Guillaume ◊Budé provided a link with the international circles of avantgarde humanists. However, as in so many cases, the disturbing effects of the Reformation were felt at Francis's court. At first tolerant of those leaning towards a heresy that could appear close to the reforming but orthodox views of, for example, Jacques ◊Lefèvre d'Etaples, Francis's attitude was changed by the Day of ◊Placards in 1534. In its aftermath, those who became suspected of heresy included court figures like the poet Clément ◊Marot.

Francis II (1544–1560)

King of France from 1559 when he succeeded his father, Henri II. He married Mary Queen of Scots in 1558. He was completely under the influence of his mother, ◊Catherine de' Medici.

Franco, Veronica (1546–1591)

Venetian prostitute and poet, a so-called ◊*cortigiana onesta*, for whom sex was work and poetry pleasure. She was a member of the literary circle around Domenico Venier, who assisted her with her *Terze Rime* (1575). Denounced by the Inquisition in 1580, she retired, denounced her former occupation (she included in her *Lettere familiari* (1580) a riposte to Pietro ◊Aretino's *La cortigiana)* and set up an asylum for other 'fallen women'.

Fraunce, Abraham (*c.* 1558–*c.* 1633)

English poet. His works include *The Lamentations of Amintas for the Death of Phillis* (1585) and a series of translations reprinted in 1591 as *The Countess of Pembroke's Ivychurch*, followed by *The Countess of Pembroke's Emanuel* (1591) and *Amintas Dale* (1592).

Fraunce also wrote *Victoria*, a Latin comedy, and two prose treatises: *The Arcadian Rhetoric* (1584) and *The Lawyer's Logic* (1588). He was among the group of writers who advocated the use in English poetry of Classical metres; all his own poems are in hexameters.

He was born in Shropshire and educated at St John's College, Cambridge, of which he became a fellow in 1580. He was later called to the Bar at Gray's Inn. He enjoyed the patronage of Philip ◊Sidney and of his sister, the Countess of ◊Pembroke, and was a close friend of Edmund ◊Spenser.

Frederick III, 'THE WISE' (1463–1525)

Elector of Saxony from 1486, when he succeeded his father Ernest. He exercised an enormous influence on German politics of the 16th century. He founded the University of Wittenberg in 1502, making Martin ◊Luther and Philip ◊Melanchthon professors, and protecting them even after they were declared heretics.

Free, John (*c.* 1430–1465)

English humanist author from Bristol. At the expense of William ◊Gray, he went to Ferrara, Italy, in 1456, to study with the humanist scholar ◊Guarino da Verona. He then travelled to Padua where he met John ◊Tiptoft, future constable of England, to whom he dedicated a Latin translation of a minor Greek work, Synesius' *Laus Calvitii/In Praise of Baldness* (1461). He translated another piece by Synesius and presented it in 1464 to Pope ◊Paul II (who, it is said, wanted to make Free a bishop). Free died in Rome the following year.

fresco

Mural painting technique using water-based paint on wet plaster that has been freshly applied to the wall (*fresco* is Italian for fresh). The technique is ancient and widespread; some of the earliest examples (*c.* 1750–1400 BC) were found in Knossos, Crete (now preserved in the Archaelogical Museum at Heraklion). However, fresco reached its finest expression in Italy from the 13th to the 17th centuries.

The advantage of fresco over other wall-painting methods is that it produces an exceptionally permanent result. The colours become incorporated with the substance of the plaster, and if the process is properly carried out, are as lasting as the plaster itself. It is suitable only for dry climates, as damp causes the plaster to crumble. For this reason, fresco was never as popular in watery Venice as it was in other major Italian art centres such as Florence and Rome.

technique The plaster is applied to a brick or stone wall in two basic coatings, the first (*arriccio*), half an inch thick, to the whole wall at once; the second, finer coating (*intonaco*) only to that portion of the wall which it is intended to paint in any one day so that it may not be dry before receiving the pigments. In drying, a crystal surface of carbonate of lime forms over the plaster, and it is essential that the pigments should be there ready to receive this coating, which is protective to them and gives them clearness. The artist would earlier have made a full-scale drawing of the picture (called a cartoon) and this was transferred to the *intonaco* by holding it against the wall and either running a stylus around the outlines, indenting the plaster beneath, or dusting charcoal through a series of pin pricks along the outlines (a process known as pouncing). The cartoon was usually cut into sections of varying size, so that each could be used for a day's work. As the joins of each section of plaster remain fairly clearly perceptible, it is possible for art historians to calculate the number of days the artist spent painting the whole work. The colours, principally earths or minerals, which best resist the chemical action of the lime, are ground and mixed with pure water and applied thinly and transparently, rather darker than the desired effect because they become paler in drying. The painter must be skilled enough to work with the utmost decision and certainty, and the whole work must be previously planned with great thoroughness. If the artist made a mistake the only way to make changes was to chip away an area of plaster, replaster it and start again. *Buon fresco,* the true method, is distinguished from *fresco secco* ('dry fresco'), painted on dry plaster. The result of the latter method was far less durable, though *fresco secco* was sometimes employed to add final touches to work carried out in true fresco.

Frescobaldi, Girolamo (1583–1643)

Italian composer and virtuoso keyboard player. He was organist at St Peter's, Rome (1608–28). His compositions included various forms of both instrumental and vocal music, and his fame rests on numerous keyboard toccatas, fugues, ricercari, and capriccios in which he advanced keyboard technique and exploited ingenious and daring modulations of key.

He studied at Ferrara under the cathedral organist Luzzasco Luzzaschi, and first gained a reputation as a singer. It was reported that 20,000 people came to hear his first recital at St Peter's in Rome. He was given leave of absence (1628–33), during which time he served as organist to Ferdinand II, Duke of Tuscany. He also worked in Brussels, Mantua, and Florence. Johann Froberger was among his pupils. Bach owned a copy of his *Fiori musicali* (1635); it contains various pieces for use in the Mass.

Works include:

Two Masses, a Magnificat, motets and madrigals; ricercari, canzoni, toccatas, and other pieces for organ and for harpsichord; fantasies for instruments in four parts; madrigals.

Froben, Johann (c. 1460–1527)

Printer based in Basel. Born near Würzburg, Froben learned his trade first in Nuremberg and then in the workshop of Johannes ◊Amerbach in Basel. He had established himself separately by 1491, but often collaborated with Amerbach, and worked with a partner, Wofgang Lachner. In the 1510s Froben's press began printing Erasmus's works and the success of these – and of the other volumes Erasmus forwarded to them, like the second edition of Thomas More's *Utopia* – helped him gain an international reputation.

On his death, the business passed to his son **Hieronymus Froben** (1501–1563) who, unlike his father, involved himself in the scholarly editing of his publications.

Frobisher, Martin (c. 1535–1594)

English navigator. He made his first voyage to Guinea, West Africa, in 1554. In 1576 he set out in search of the Northwest Passage, and visited Labrador and Frobisher Bay, Baffin Island. Second and third expeditions sailed in 1577 and 1578. Knighted in 1588.

He was vice admiral in Drake's West Indian expedition in 1585. In 1588 he was knighted for helping to defeat the Armada. He was mortally wounded in 1594 fighting against the Spanish off the coast of France.

Froissart, Jean (1338–1401)

French historian and poet. He was secretary to Queen Philippa, wife of Edward III of England. He travelled in Scotland and Brittany, went with Edward the Black Prince to Aquitaine, and in 1368 was in Milan at the same time as the writers Chaucer and Petrarch. He recorded in his *Chroniques/Chronicles* events of 1326–1400, often at first hand. Later he entered the church and in 1385 became a canon at Chimay (in what is now southern Belgium), where he died.

His *Chronicles* are one of the most important sources of information about the Hundred Years' War and recount events in France, England (including the Peasants' Revolt of 1381), Scotland, Spain, the Low Countries, and elsewhere. The early part of the *Chronicles* is drawn largely, sometimes almost word for word, from the chronicle of Jean le Bel. Froissart's own work begins with the Battle of Poitiers (1356). He draws widely on his own experiences and on the accounts of eyewitnesses. He twice revised the text of the first of his four books, the later versions being less pro-English than the earliest.

Froissart also wrote a long verse romance, *Méliador,* and much other poetry of no great literary value.

Froment, Nicolas (c. 1430–c. 1484)

French artist, active in Avignon. Two documented works by Froment survive, both important altarpieces: *The Resurrection of Lazarus* (1461, Uffizi, Florence) painted for ◊René of Anjou and *Mary in the Burning Bush* (1475–76, Cathedral of St-Sauveur, Aix-en-Provence). These works demonstrate an awareness of trends in both Flemish and Italian art.

Originally from Uzès in Languedoc, Froment was active chiefly in Avignon where he and Enguerrand ◊Charonton developed a distinctive style of painting during the 1450s.

The Resurrection of Lazarus includes portraits of his patron René of Anjou and Renés wife.

Frueauf, Rueland, THE ELDER (*c.* 1445–1507)

Austrian painter. Active in his native Salzburg from about 1478, Frueauf worked at first largely for the Benedictine monks there. His style (that of the Flemish painters of the period) was influenced by the work of Konrad ◊Laib, who had painted in Salzburg a few decades earlier. Like Laib, Frueauf paid much attention to the expressive power of his figures, which he set in carefully observed landscapes.

He died in Passau, to which he had moved in 1497. His son, **Rueland Frueauf the Younger** (died after 1534), worked in Passau, following his father's style.

Frulovisi, Tito Livio (LIVED 1430S)

Italian humanist author from Ferrara. Educated in Venice by ◊Guarino da Verona, his first writings were Latin comedies in the style of ◊Plautus. He dedicated a Ciceronian dialogue, *De Republica*, to Leonello d' Este (*c.* 1435). Travelling to England in 1436, he became 'poet and orator' to Humfrey, Duke of ◊Gloucester, and dedicated to Henry VI of England a life of his father, *Vita Henrici Quinti* (*c.* 1438). He soon returned to the Continent and, lacking patronage, changed career later life he was a doctor.

Frundsberg, Georg von (1473–1528)

German soldier. He was the leader of the *Landsknechte* (a group of mercenary soldiers) during the Italian wars of the Holy Roman Emperors ◊Maximilian I and ◊Charles V.

He fought for Maximilian against the Swiss in 1499, and in 1504 took part in the war against the Netherlands. In 1509 he won fame in the war against Venice, and in 1513 and 1514 was again occupied with the French and Venetians. He gained a victory at Bicocca in Italy in 1522, was partly responsible for the defeat of the French at the Battle of ◊Pavia in 1525, and suppressed a peasant revolt in Germany the same year.

Fulda, Adam of (*c.* 1445–1505)

German monk, music theorist, and composer. He wrote a tract on music and composed motets and other pieces.

Gabrieli, Andrea (*c.* 1533–1585)

Italian composer. He was organist at St Mark's, Venice, from 1566, and his music, for example *Concerti* (1587), makes much use of the spatial effects possible within St Mark's, with vocal and instrumental groups separated in contrasting ensembles.

He was a member of a Venetian school which cultivated an antiphonal style suited to the two choir galleries and two organs of St Mark's Church. He became second organist at St Mark's, Venice, in 1566 and first organist in 1584. He was a famous teacher and had many distinguished pupils, Italian and foreign, including his nephew Giovanni ◊Gabrieli and the Germans Hans Hassler and Gregor Aichinger.

Works include:

Masses, motets, and other church music with instruments; spiritual songs; madrigals, and other pieces for several voices; choruses for Sophocles' *Oedipus Tyrannus*; ricercari for organ.

Gabrieli, Giovanni (*c.* 1555–1612)

Italian composer. He succeeded his uncle Andrea Gabrieli (*c.* 1533–1585) as organist of St Mark's, Venice. His sacred and secular works include numerous madrigals, motets, and the antiphonal *Sacrae Symphoniae* (1597), sacred canzonas and sonatas for brass choirs, strings, and organ, in spatial counterpoint.

Gaddi

Italian family of artists. **Gaddo** (*c.* 1260–1332) was a painter and mosaic worker, a friend of Cimabue, whose influence has been perceived in the *Coronation of the Virgin with Saints and Angels*, a mosaic in the cathedral at Florence attributed to Gaddo. Other works attributed to him are the mosaics in Santa Maria Maggiore and those of the choir of the old St Peter's, Rome. His son, **Taddeo** (*c.* 1300–1366) was

a pupil of ◊Giotto and is considered one of his most important followers. His paintings include the frescoes *Virgin and Child between Four Prophets* and other scenes from the life of the Virgin in the Baroncelli Chapel in Santa Croce at Florence (1332), as well as works at Pisa, Pistoia and in various galleries. The son of Taddeo, **Agnolo** (died 1396), perhaps trained by his father, was placed on the latter's death in the care of Jacopo del Casentino and Giovanni da Milano. He worked in the Vatican in 1369, probably with his brother Giovanni. Frescoes in Santa Croce depicting the legend of the Cross, and in the cathedral of Prato (1392–95), representing the legends of the Virgin and the Sacred Girdle, are attributed to him. He died while working on an altarpiece for San Miniato. He employed a number of assistants, and Cennino ◊Cennini was among his pupils, embodying the methods of the followers of Giotto in his treatise on art.

Gafori, Franchino (1451–1522)

Italian priest, theorist, and composer. He wrote several theoretical books, including *Theorica Musicae* (1492) and *Practica Musicae* (1496), and also composed Masses and other church music. Leonardo da Vinci was among his friends.

He was maestro di cappella at Monticello and Bergamo, and from 1484 was attached to Milan Cathedral.

Gagliano, Marco da (REAL NAME ZENOBI) (1582–1643)

Italian composer, brother of Giovanni Battista da Gagliano. In 1607 he founded the Accademia dell' Elevati for the cultivation of music. His opera *Dafne* (1608), a setting of Rinuccini's libretto, followed Monteverdi's epoch-making *Orfeo* by one year; it also developed early operatic form, to include airs and choruses as well as recitative.

He studied organ and theorbo under Luca Bati at the Church of San Lorenzo, Florence, where he was a priest. He became instructor there in 1602 and maestro di cappella in 1608. About 1610 he was appointed maestro di cappella to the Grand Duke of Tuscany. He was in touch with the ducal family of Gonzaga at Mantua, where *Dafne* was produced in

1608. He also wrote music for the wedding of the Duke's son.

Works include:
The operas *Dafne*, *La Flora*, *Il Medoro* (music lost); oratorio *La regina Santa Orsola* (1624, music lost); Masses, Offices for the Dead, *Sacrae Cantiones*; madrigals.

Gaguin, Robert (*c.* 1423–1501)

French monk and humanist. Elected general of his order in 1473, he was sent on several missions across Europe under both their auspisces and those of the French king. On one of these trips, his willingness to praise his own king to the extent of damning others, caused controversy: on his visit to England in 1491, certain injudicious comments about Henry VII led to stinging responses from his group of poets, who included Bernard André.

Gaguin's own scholarly productions included translations into the vernacular of Caesar and Livy; he also wrote a chronicle, *Compendium de Origine et Gestis Francorum*, first printed in 1497 and repeatedly revised up to his death.

Galen (*c.* 129–*c.* 200)

Greek philosopher and anatomist. Central to his thinking was the theory of the ◊humours. He also demonstrated, by dissection, that blood rather than air (as previous writers had claimed) flowed through the arteries; he believed that the blood seeped into the heart through a thin membrane.

At least some of Galen's anatomical work was known in Western Europe from the 14th century, when *On the Use of the Parts* was translated into Latin by Niccolò da Reggio (1322). Though he thus became a standard author, interest in Galen's writings became fashionable in the late 15th and early 16th centuries: translations were made by Niccolò ◊Leoniceno, Thomas Linacre (1523), and Guinther of Andernach (1531), and Aldus Manutius printed a Greek edition of his complete works (1525).

At the same time, however, Galen's popularity led to questioning of his description of human ◊anatomy. Because the dismembering of human bodies was a religious taboo in ancient Greece, Galen worked from animal dissections, assuming that the human body was formed like that of animals so, for example, the

right kidney was said to be higher than the left. This assumption remained current even in ◊Vesalius's work, although his human dissections, as those of the Italian anatomist Gabriele ◊Falloppio and others, disproved some of Galen's statements. Following their example, William Harvey made the more fundamental discovery that, despite what Galen said, blood circulated through the heart.

Galilei, Vincenzo (*c.* 1520–1591)

Italian composer, theorist, and lutenist. He took part in the discussions which, after his death, helped transform the Florentine camerata into opera; he also wrote theoretical books. Galilei upheld Greek drama against the contemporary madrigal, becoming involved in controversy with his teacher, Gioseffo Zarlino. He was the father of the astronomer ◊Galileo Galilei.

Works include:
Cantata *Il Conte Ugolino* from Dante, a setting of the Lamentations of Jeremiah (both lost, and both among the earliest music for a single voice with accompaniment); two books of madrigals; pieces for two viols; a lute book in tablature; *Dialogo della musica antica et della moderna* (1581).

Galileo (PROPERLY GALILEO GALILEI) (1564–1642)

Italian mathematician, astronomer, and physicist. He developed the astronomical telescope and was the first to see sunspots, the four main satellites of Jupiter, and the appearance of Venus going through phases, thus proving it was orbiting the Sun. Galileo discovered that freely falling bodies, heavy or light, have the same, constant acceleration and that this acceleration is due to gravity. He also determined that a body moving on a perfectly smooth horizontal surface would neither speed up nor slow down. He invented a thermometer, a hydrostatic balance, and a compass, and discovered that the path of a projectile is a parabola.

Galileo's work founded the modern scientific method of deducing laws to explain the results of observation and experiment, although the story of his dropping cannonballs from the Leaning Tower of Pisa is questionable. His observations were an unwelcome refutation of the Aristotleian ideas taught at the universities, largely because they made plausible for the first time the Sun-centred theory of Polish astronomer Nicolaus ◊Copernicus. Galileo's persuasive *Dialogo sopra i due massimi sistemi del mondo/ Dialogues on the Two Chief Systems of the World* (1632) was banned by the church authorities in Rome and he was made to recant by the Inquisition.

astronomy and the invention of the telescope In July 1609, hearing that a Dutch scientist had made a telescope, Galileo worked out the principles involved and made a number of telescopes. He compiled fairly accurate tables of the orbits of four of Jupiter's satellites and proposed that their frequent eclipses could serve as a means of determining longitude on land and at sea. His observations on sunspots and Venus going through phases supported Copernicus's theory that the Earth rotated and orbited the Sun. Galileo's results published in *Sidereus Nuncius/The Starry Messenger* (1610) were revolutionary.

He believed, however – following both Greek and medieval tradition – that orbits must be circular, not elliptical, in order to maintain the fabric of the cosmos in a state of perfection. This preconception prevented him from deriving a full formulation of the law of inertia, which was later to be attributed to the contemporary French mathematician René Descartes.

the pendulum Galileo made several fundamental contributions to mechanics. He rejected the impetus theory that a force or push is required to sustain motion. While watching swinging lamps in Pisa Cathedral, Galileo determined that each oscillation of a pendulum takes the same amount of time despite the difference in amplitude, and recognized the potential importance of this observation to timekeeping. In a later publication, he presented his derivation that the square of the period of a pendulum varies with its length (and is independent of the mass of the pendulum bob).

mechanics and the law of falling bodes Galileo discovered before Newton that two objects of different weights – an apple and a melon, for instance – falling from the same height would hit the ground at the same time. He realized that gravity not only causes a body to fall, but also determines the motion of rising bodies and, furthermore, that gravity extends to the centre of the Earth. Galileo then showed that the motion of a projectile is made up of two components:

one component consists of uniform motion in a horizontal direction, and the other component is vertical motion under acceleration or deceleration due to gravity.

Galileo used this explanation to refute objections to Copernicus. It had been argued against Copernicus that a turning Earth would not carry along birds and clouds. Galileo explained that the motion of a bird, like a projectile, has a horizontal component that is provided by the motion of the Earth and that this horizontal component of motion always exists to keep such objects in position even though they are not attached to the ground.

Galileo came to an understanding of uniform velocity and uniform acceleration by measuring the time it takes for bodies to move various distances. He had the brilliant idea of slowing vertical motion by measuring the movement of balls rolling down inclined planes, realizing that the vertical component of this motion is a uniform acceleration due to gravity. It took Galileo many years to arrive at the correct expression of the law of falling bodies, which he presented in *Discorsi e dimostrazioni matematiche intorno a due nove scienze/Discourses and Mathematical Discoveries Concerning Two New Sciences* (1638) as: $s = 1/2 \ at^2$ where s is speed, a is the acceleration due to gravity, and t is time. He found that the distance travelled by a falling body is proportional to the square of the time of descent.

A summation of his life's work, *Discourses* also included the facts that the trajectory of a projectile is a parabola, and that the law of falling bodies is perfectly obeyed only in a vacuum, and that air resistance always causes a uniform terminal velocity to be reached.

engineering The other new science of Galileo's masterwork was engineering, particularly the science of structures. His main contribution was to point out that the dimensions of a structure are important to its stability: a small structure will stand whereas a larger structure of the same relative dimensions may collapse. Using the laws of levers, Galileo went on to examine the strengths of the materials necessary to support structures.

thermometer Galileo's other achievements include the invention of the thermometer in 1593. This device consisted of a bulb of air that expanded or contracted as the temperature changed, causing the level of a column of water to rise or fall. Galileo's thermometer was very inaccurate because it neglected the effect of atmospheric pressure, but it is historically important as one of the first measuring instruments in science.

life Galileo was born and educated in Pisa, and in 1589 became professor of mathematics at the university there. In 1592 he accepted a position as professor at Padua, as his revolutionary discoveries had made him many enemies at Pisa. At Padua he wrote a treatise on the specific gravities of solid bodies, and experimented with falling bodies to determine the laws governing their motions. He worked at Padua until 1610, when he was appointed chief mathematician to the grand duke of Tuscany, Ferdinand II, to whom he dedicated his *Dialogo*.

Galileo's attempts to explain biblical texts in the light of his theory were against the accepted opinion, and he was compelled by the Roman Inquisition not to assert 'what seemed to contradict Scripture' in 1616. He was tried for heresy in 1633, and, forced to abjure his belief that the Earth moves around the Sun, Galileo is reputed to have muttered: '*Eppur si muove*' ('Yet it does move'). He was to recite the seven Penitential Psalms once a week for three years, and was put under house arrest for his last years.

Gallican Confession (LATIN 'CONFESSIO GALLICANA')

French Calvinist confession of faith drawn up at the first national synod of Protestants in Paris in 1559. The synod, called out of fear of persecution by Henry II, lasted four days and confessed adherence to the doctrines of ◊Calvin as revised by the French theologian Antoine de la Roche Chandieu (1534–91).

This confession, written in French and comprising 35 articles, was confirmed, in modified form, by the synod of La Rochelle in 1571.

Galvão, Antonio (*c.* 1490–1557)

Portuguese historian. Galvão was the first major historian to marshal a comprehensive knowledge of the voyages of all the leading Renaissance explorers, regardless of nationality. His works remain among the most accurate and thorough of the period, especially *Livro dos descobrimentos das Antilhase India*, which was published in Lisbon in 1563 and translated into English by ◊Hakluyt in 1601.

Galvão went to India in 1527 and rose to become governor of the Moluccas (1536–40), before his abilities led him to be offered the throne of Ternate, which he declined. On his return to Portugal in 1540 he found he was out of favour and lived the rest of his life in anonymity and poverty, dying in Lisbon.

Gama, Vasco da (*c.* 1469–1524)

Portuguese navigator. He commanded an expedition in 1497 to discover the route to India around the Cape of Good Hope (in modern South Africa). On Christmas Day 1497 he reached land, which he named Natal. He then crossed the Indian Ocean, arriving at Calicut (now Kozhikode in Kerala) in May 1498, and returned to Portugal in September 1499.

Da Gama was born in Sines, southwest Portugal, and was chosen by King Manoel I for his 1497 expedition. In 1502 he founded a Portuguese colony in Mozambique. In the same year he attacked and plundered Calicut in revenge for the murder of some Portuguese sailors. After 20 years of retirement, he was dispatched to India again as Portuguese viceroy in 1524, but died two months after his arrival in Goa.

Garcilaso de la Vega (?1501–1536)

Toledo-born poet and soldier. Of noble birth, he spent most of his life in the Emperor Charles V's service. In 1522 he met his lifelong friend ◊Boscà while fighting on the unsuccessful campaign to relieve Rhodes. He married in 1525, but in 1526 fell in love with the Portuguese Isabel Freyre, to whom he dedicated numerous love poems. Her death, in childbirth, in 1534, inspired his haunting and reflective 'First Eclogue' (1534/35). He fell briefly from favour at court in 1532 for witnessing a marriage opposed by Charles, who sent him to serve the Neapolitan governor. There he met ◊Tasso and Juan de ◊Valdés. Restored to favour, he fought at Tunis in 1535 and just survived, only to die the following year after sustaining a fatal head injury during Charles's invasion of France, apparently because he forgot to wear a helmet.

Garcilaso's skilful use of Italian verse forms such as the sonnet, *canzione* ('song'), and *versi sciolti* ('free verse') had a significant impact on the poetry of his day, and inspired many imitators. His surviving oeuvre, edited and published by Boscà's widow in 1543, is small. Of his elegies, *canzioni*, sonnets, and eclogues, perhaps the most influential were his eclogues, of which three survive. 'Eclogue I', in which the shepherd characters reflect the poet himself, is a response to the death of his beloved, while 'Eclogue II' (1533), inspired by ◊Ariosto's *Orlando furioso* is a lengthy meditation on accepting frustrated love set mostly as a dialogue. 'Eclogue III' (1536) is a metaphorical meditation on amorous sorrow of the past. Garcilaso was the subject of a laudatory poem by ◊Sá de Miranda, and his works achieved canonical status with Francisco Sánchez de las Brozas's critical edition in 1574. They were also edited – with some critical comments – by Fernando de ◊Herrera, in 1580.

Garcilaso de la Vega (KNOWN AS 'EL INCA') (1539–1616)

Peruvian soldier, author, and priest, Cuzco-born Garcilaso was the son of an Inca princess and related by his Spanish conquistador father to the poet ◊Garcilaso. On his father's death in 1560, he travelled to Spain, where he made an unsuccessful claim for his inheritance and then became a soldier. In the 1570s he entered the priesthood, settling in Córdoba. In 1590 he translated Leone ◊Hebreo's *Dialoghi* (later censored by the Inquisition); in 1609 he drew on his childhood experiences to write the first part of his *Comentarios reales/Royal commentaries*, on the Inca peoples of Peru. Part II, an account of the Spanish conquest, was published posthumously in 1617.

Gardiner, Stephen (c. 1493–1555)

English priest and politician. After being secretary to Cardinal Wolsey, he became bishop of Winchester in 1531. An opponent of Protestantism, he was imprisoned under Edward VI, and as Lord Chancellor (1553–55) under Queen Mary he tried to restore Roman Catholicism.

Gargantua and Pantagruel

Cycle of four (or five) satirical novels by the French writer François ◊Rabelais, published 1532–64. The novels are written in mock-heroic style and reveal the extent of Rabelais's learning in the fields of medicine, theology, and law. Often bawdy, they satirize a variety of institutions, notably universities and the church: the intensification of these attacks in the third and forth volumes led to their condemnation by the university in Paris.

The first volume written, *Gargantua*, deals with the birth and childhood of the giant Gargantua, son of Grandgousier; his education in Paris (an opportunity for a satirical attack on the university); and the foundation of the infamous abbey of Thélème, the motto of which is *Fay ce que vouldras* ('Do what you will'). The remaining volumes, the *Pantagruel* books, tell the story of Gargantua's son, a giant of enormous strength and appetite, his friendship with the cunning rogue Panurge, and his conquest of the kingdom of the Dipsodes.

The books are a continuation of a medieval tradition of bawdy stories that employ gross exaggeration and unlikely adventures, though their immediate inspiration was the successful anonymous chapbook *Les Grandes et Inestimables Chroniques du grand et énorme géant Gargantua/The Great and Inestimable Chronicles of the Great and Enormous Giant Gargantua* (1532).

The full titles of the books are: *La Vie inestimable du grand Gargantua, père de Pantagruel/The Inestimable Life of the Great Gargantua, Father of Pantagruel*, the first to be written, but published in 1534, two years after *Les Horribles et Epouvantables Faits et prouesses du très renommé Pantagruel/The Horrible and Dreadful Deeds and Prowess of the Very Renowned Pantagruel* (1532).

Le Tiers Livre des faits et dits héroïques du noble Pantagruel/The Third Book of the Deeds and Words of the Noble Pantagruel and *Le Quart Livre de Pantagruel/The Fourth Book* appeared in 1546 and 1552.

The *Cinquième Livre/Fifth Book* (1564), which continues the story of Pantagruel in the style of Rabelais, is of doubtful authenticity.

Garnier, Robert (c. 1545–1590)

French dramatist and poet. Following the example of Etienne ◊Jodelle, he wrote Classically styled tragedies (in particular following the example of Seneca). These include: *Porcie* (1568), *Hippolyte* (1573), *Antigone* (1580), and *Les Juives* (1583), which was based on the Bible story of Nebuchadnezzar's persecution of the Jews. He also wrote a tragicomedy *Bradamante* (1582) based on Ludivico ◊Ariosto's *Orlando furioso*.

Garofalo (ADOPTED NAME OF **BENVENUTO TISIO**) (1481–1559)

Italian painter, active in Ferrara. He was an eclectic artist, much influenced by ◊Raphael Sanzio, whom he met in Rome in 1509. Works by ◊Garofalo can be seen in churches in Ferrara, including the Church of S Niccolo, for which he painted a *Virgin Mary and Infant Jesus* (1520).

Gascoigne, George (1525–1577)

English poet and dramatist. He is the author of *Supposes* (1573), a translation of *I suppositi* by Ludovico ◊Ariosto, and the earliest extant comedy in English prose; *Jocasta* (1573), a version of the *Phoenissae* of Euripides, the second earliest tragedy in blank verse; an original comedy *The Glasse of Government* (1575); and a verse narrative *The Complaynte of Phylomene* (1587). His satire in blank verse, *The Steele Glas*, appeared in 1576.

Gascoigne was born in Cardington, Bedfordshire, and educated at Canterbury and Trinity College, Cambridge. In 1555 he was entered at Gray's Inn, and was member of Parliament for Bedford 1557–59. Owing to his prodigality he was disinherited by his father, and fled from his creditors to Holland, where he took service under the Prince of Orange against the Spaniards 1572–75. On his return he accompanied Queen Elizabeth on one of her royal progresses, and to celebrate the event wrote a masque entitled *The Princely Pleasures, at the Courte at Kenelwoorth* (1576). He also wrote a prose romance, *The Pleasant Fable of Ferdinando Jeronimi* (1587), and *Dan Bartholomew of Bath* (1573), a kind of novelette in verse. His *Certayne Notes of Instruction concerning the Making of Verse or Rhyme in English* (1575) is said to be the first attempt at a treatise on prosody in the language. He is, however, much more entertaining in undisguised verse narrative of his own experiences, as in *The Voyage into Holland* (1573) and *Dulce Bellum Inexpertis* (1575), the latter giving a vivid picture of his experiences in Flanders.

Gattamelata, Il (ERASMO DA NARNI) (1370–1443)

Condottiere from Padua whose name in Italian means 'honeyed cat'. He learnt his trade with Braccio da Montone and Niccolò Piccinino (1386–1444). He was first employed by the Florentine and papal armies, and then in 1434 entered the service of Venice. During the Venetian republic's wars with the ◊Visconti of Milan, he developed a reputation for determined resourcefulness; he rose to become captain-general of the city. A celebrated equestrian statue of him by ◊Donatello stands outside the Church of the Santo in Padua. His funerary monument was designed by Bartolommeo ◊Bellano.

Gazes (GAZA), Theodore (c. 1400–1475)

Greek scholar and teacher. A leading figure in the development of Renaissance Greek studies, he wrote a Greek grammar, printed in Venice in 1495, that long remained a standard textbook. He also translated many Greek authors into Latin, including Aristotle, Theophrastus, and John Chrysostom.

Born at Thessalonica, he came to Italy in 1430 and lived at Mantua, supporting himself by giving Greek lessons and copying manuscripts while learning Latin from ◊Vittorino da Feltre. He was made professor of Greek at Ferrara in 1447 but in 1450 went to Rome at the invitation of Pope ◊Nicholas V. In 1456 he moved to Naples and in 1459 to Calabria, where he died.

Geertgen, tot Sint Jans (c. 1460–c. 1490)

Dutch painter. His name means 'Little Gerard of (the Order of) St John', but little is known about him. Of the few works firmly attributed to him, two best exhibit his characteristic charm and delicacy: *The Nativity* (National Gallery, London), a night scene lit solely by the radiance of the infant Jesus, and *St John in the Wilderness* (Staatliche Museum, Berlin), which shows a subtle mastery of landscape (both dated around the 1480s).

Gemma Frisius (GEMMA REGNIER) (1508–1555)

Dutch mathematician, astronomer, and geographer. He is best known for improving mapmaking and for showing (before it was feasible to carry out) how to calculate longitude using portable clocks. He also wrote a mathematics textbook that was widely used in the 17th century, and was well known as a maker of globes, astrolabes, and other mathematical and astronomical instruments.

Born at Dockum, East Friesland, he became a pupil of Peter ◊Apian and was educated at the university of Louvain, where he was appointed professor of medicine in 1541. In his *Libellus de Locorum Describendorum Ratione/Little Book on a Method for Delineating Places*, incorporated in his 1533 edition of Apian's *Cosmographia*, Frisius published the first clear description of how maps could be constructed more accurately using triangulation.

Less immediate in its application (on account of the lack of sufficiently reliable timepieces) was his proposal in *De Principiis Astronomiae et Cosmographiae/The Principle of Astronomy and Cosmography* (1530) that longitude at sea and elsewhere could be determined with the aid of portable clocks. His mathematics text book, *Arithmeticae Practicae Methodus Facilis* was published in 1540 and went through 59 editions.

General Council of the Church

In the early Christian church, gatherings of the clergy had debated and decided major issues of doctrine. In Catholic Western Europe, both General (or ecumenical) Councils and Lateran Councils (a meeting of the cardinals in the Lateran, Rome) were called fitfully by the popes. At the turn of the 15th century, however, there were two pressing needs for a General Council: to resolve the ◊Great Schism and to deal with the new threat of Huss's heresy. At the same time, the problems of the papacy raised questions about the institution itself: ◊conciliarism, advocating the supremacy of General Councils, challenged the pope's authority.

There was a tension, then, between the Catholic Church's need to appoint a single pope through a General Council and the inevitable concern of the elected pope to avoid further Councils and their conciliarist threat. The Council of Constance (1414–18) both ended the Great Schism and also decreed that General Councils should be held at regular intervals. Popes Martin V and Eugenius IV, under pressure from secular rulers keen to avoid the papacy regaining too much power, reluctantly abided by this decree, but the Council of Basel (1431–49) increasingly became a showdown between papalists and conciliarists, to the point that a return to schism was threatened. The strength of the papacy, however, was that it was an established bureaucratic institution: only a General Council with firm international support could hope to challenge the traditional power structure. And Basel increasingly lacked such support. After Basel, successive popes avoided calling a General Council in the second half of the 15th century.

In the early 16th century there was an abortive attempt to call a General Council in defiance of Pope Julius II – the 'schismatic' Council of Pisa (1511). The pope's response was to convene his own Lateran Council in 1512. However, the success of the Lutheran and evangelical movements in the 1520s made the calling of a General Council a matter of urgency, despite being an unattractive prospect both to reformers (perhaps mindful of what had happened to the Hussite leader John Huss at Constance) and popes (mindful of conciliarism and the emperor's power). Eventually a Council was called, the Council of Trent (1545–63); although it did little to heal the heretical schism within Western Christendom, it did help define and reorganize the Catholic Church.

- General Council of ◊Pisa (not recognized by either pope, each calling a rival Council), 1409
- General Council of ◊Constance, 1414–18
- General Council of Pavia (transferred to Siena), 1423–24
- General Council of ◊Basel (transferred to Lausanne), 1431–49
- Council of Basel was transferred by pope to Ferrara and then to ◊Florence, 1437–39
- 'Schismatic' Council of Pisa, 1511
- Fifth Lateran Council, 1512
- General Council of ◊Trent, 1545–63

Genet, Elzéar (Carpentras) (*c.* 1470–1548)

French composer. He wrote secular works to both Italian and French texts, and numerous Masses, motets, hymns, and Magnificats. He was a papal singer to Julius II in 1508 and maestro di cappella under Pope Leo X (1513–21), as well as being at the court of King Louis XII some time between those dates.

Genevan Academy

College in Geneva, Switzerland, founded by the religious reformer ◊Calvin in 1559 (opened in 1564). It was of great importance in the spread of Calvinism. Calvin's main intention was that his academy would prepare ministers to preach the gospel. Its outstanding academic reputation and brilliant teachers – including ◊Beza, the first rector, and Jacob Arminius (1560–1609) – attracted Protestant students from all over Europe.

Genga, Girolamo (1472–1551)

Italian painter and architect. Genga was born in Urbino and worked for much of his life there. He collaborated with his master ◊Signorelli before going with ◊Perugino to Florence in 1502. Back in Urbino he completed the top storey of the ducal palace about 1536. He also restored and decorated the Villa Imperiale near Pesaro for the Duke of Urbino, decorating it with fine wall-paintings, stuccoed ceilings, and majolica tiled floors.

Gennadius (GEORGE SCHOLARIUS) (c. 1400–c. 1468)

Greek scholar and theologian. He attended the Council of ◊Florence as a representative of the Eastern Church and at first supported the reconciliation of the Eastern and Western Churches, but later became a firm opponent of the union. In 1453, when Constantinople fell to the Ottoman Turks, Sultan Mehmet II made him patriarch of Constantinople.

Perhaps born in Constantinople (the details of his early life are obscure), he came to Italy in 1438 as counsellor to Emperor John Palaeologus at the Council of Florence. Here he wrote works attacking the philosopher ◊Plethon on both theological and philosophical grounds. On the schism between Eastern and Western Churches, Scholarius advocated compromise and drew up a form of agreement ambiguous enough to be accepted by both, but on his return to Greece, he completely changed his position.

In 1448 he became a monk and took the name

Gennadius. When made patriarch of Constantinople in 1453 he composed an exposition of Christian belief for the sultan's use, but eventually found the strain of being patriarch of a Muslim city too much and retired to Serrae in Macedonia where he died.

Gentile, da Fabriano (BORN NICCOLO DI GIOVANNI DI MASSIO) (c. 1370–c. 1427)

Italian painter of frescoes and altarpieces who worked in a gothic style uninfluenced by the fashions of contemporary Florence. Gentile was active in Venice, Florence, Siena, Orvieto, and Rome and collaborated with the artists Pisanello and Jacopo Bellini. His *Adoration of the Magi* (1423, Uffizi, Florence) painted for the church of Santa Trinità in Florence is typically rich in detail and colour.

He worked in Venice 1408–14 on frescoes for the Doge's Palace and was the master of Jacopo Bellini. Other notable works are the altarpiece of the Quaratesi family (1425), of which the centre panel, *Madonna and Child*, is in the British Royal Collection and the wings and other panels in the Uffizi and Vatican galleries; and a *Madonna with Saints* (Berlin). His last work was a series of frescoes (since destroyed) for S Giovanni in Laterano, Rome. These were finished by ◊Pisanello, who was influenced by Gentile's Gothic manner.

Gentili, Alberico (1552–1608)

Italian jurist. He practised law in Italy but having adopted Protestantism was compelled to flee to England, where he lectured on Roman law in Oxford. His publications, such as *De Jure Belli/On the Law of War* (1598), made him the first true international law writer and scholar.

George of Trebizond (GEORGE TRAPEZUNTIUS) (1396–c. 1472)

Cretan humanist translator and despiser of Plato. Educated by ◊Guarino and ◊Vittorino da Feltre, he converted from Orthodoxy to Catholicism in about 1426 and spent most of his career from 1440 in the papal curia. His life was punctuated by disputes which, in the case of a clash with ◊Poggio in 1452, became physical and landed him in gaol. His most controversial work was the *Comparatio Platonis et Aristotelis/Comparison of Plato and Aristotle* (1458), which angered Cardinal ◊Bessarion.

His early works include the *Rhetoricorum libri quinque/Five Books of Rhetoric* and a logical textbook, *Isagoge Dialectica*. He translated Plato's *Laws* (1450–51) and *Parmenides* (1458–59) but this was not out of sympathy with the work's original author. His real assessment of Plato was virulently expressed in the *Comparatio*: for him, Plato was the epitome of evil, an incompetent philosopher, a pagan polytheist, and an apologist for sexual depravity.

Gerard, John (1545–1612)

English herbalist and gardener. In 1596 he published a catalogue of plants in his garden in Holborn, London, and the following year his *Herball*, the woodcut illustrations provided by a printer in Frankfurt.

Born in Nantwich, Gerard travelled abroad before settling in Holborn to pursue his medical career as a barber-surgeon and to keep a large physic garden. In 1607 he became master of the Company of Barber-Surgeons.

His catalogue, *Catalogus Arborum Fruticum ac Plantarum ... in Horto Joannis Gerardi.../Catalogue of the Fruiting Trees and Plants ... in the Garden of John Gerard...*, listed over 1100 varieties. His *Herball, or Generall Historie of Plantes* owes a great deal to ◊Dodoens.

Gerhaert van Leyden, Nicolaus (c. 1430–1473)

Dutch sculptor. He worked mostly in Germany and brought a new degree of naturalism to German sculpture. His best-known works are a sandstone crucifix (1467) in Baden-Baden parish church, and his astonishingly realistic and expressive *Head of a Man* (Musée de l'Oeuvre Notre-Dame, Strasbourg), widely thought to be a self-portrait.

Gerhaert's works possess an entirely novel dynamism and expansiveness combined with profound characterization. The widespread diffusion of his style was stimulated both by his extensive travels, from Holland to Austria, and by numerous prints influenced by his work.

Born at Leyden, Gerhaert was first documented in 1462 as executing the vigorously carved tomb of Archbishop von Sierck in Trier. Between 1463 and 1467 he was in Strasbourg, after which he moved to Wiener Neustadt, where he died.

An assessment of Gerhaert's development is difficult because of the destruction both of his early sculptures in the Netherlands and also of his chief work, the high altarpiece of Constance Cathedral (1465–67). The latter, in particular, had a deep influence on south German sculptors. Only three fragments survive from his sandstone portal (c. 1464) for the new chancellery in Strasbourg (one of them being his presumed self-portrait). His last years were spent working on the flamboyant and expressive red marble tomb effigy of Frederick III in Vienna Cathedral.

Gerhard, Hubert (c. 1545–1620)

Dutch sculptor. Trained in Italy, he imported to northern Europe the so-called Mannerist style of sculpture. He worked for several important patrons, including the Fugger banking family in Augsburg and Duke Wilhelm V of Bavaria in Munich. In Augsburg he created the Augustus fountain, the first major work of monumental German sculpture to incorporate the latest Italian fashions.

He worked in Augburg for the Fuggers from 1581, and his commissions included figures and fittings for Hans Fugger's new castle at Kirchheim (1583–95) as well as the courtyard fountain showing Mars and Venus embracing. His Augustus fountain in Augsburg was erected in 1594 to celebrate the city's centenary.

From 1584 he worked for the Duke Wilhelm V of Bavaria in Munich. The first sculptor of note to work in Munich for many years, he made sculptures for Wilhelm's palace there (the Residenz) and for the Church of St Michael which Wilhelm was building for the Jesuits. After Wilhelm abdicated in 1597, Gerhard moved to the court of his successor, Archduke Maximilian I, at Innsbruck.

Gerson, Jean Charlier de (1363–1429)

French theologian. He was educated in Paris under Pierre d' ◊Ailly, whom he succeeded as chancellor of the university in 1395. He was, like his master, a proponent of ◊conciliarism, although differences between them appeared at the Council of ◊Constance; at that gathering, Gerson presented his *De Ecclesiastica Potestate/On Ecclesiastical Power* (1417). Gerson's writings, however, were not confined to discussions of church government. He also produced a series of popular devotional tracts in Latin, the *Dialogus de Perfectione Cordis/Dialogue on the Perfection of the Soul* (1417), and in the vernacular, *La Montagne de Contemplation* (1400).

Gerusalemme liberata/Jerusalem Delivered

Epic poem by the Italian poet Torquato ◊Tasso, published in 1581. Its subject is the climax of the First Crusade, the siege and conquest of Jerusalem in 1099 by the army of Godfrey of Boulogne. The Christians defeat the many stratagems of the Saracens and the poem concludes as Godfrey leads the triumphant crusaders to the Holy Sepulchre. These historical events provide the framework for the adventures of the central character, Rinaldo, a Christian knight.

To the historical participants – Godfrey, Baldwin, Tancred, Raymond of Toulouse, Bohemond, Peter the Hermit, and Solyman, Sultan of Nicaea – Tasso added fictional characters: Rinaldo (introduced as the ancestor of the d' ◊Este family), the enchantress Armida, and also several women, notably Clorinda and Erminia, who are romantically involved with Tancred.

It was translated into English in 1594 and 1600 and influenced parts of Spenser's *Faerie Queene*.

Although he had completed his epic by 1575, Tasso remained dissatisfied and the poem underwent several revisions after its first publication. Retitled *Gerusalemme conquistata/Jerusalem Retaken*, the last of these revisions appeared in 1593.

Like ◊Boiardo and ◊Ariosto, his predecessors at the Este court in Ferrara, Tasso wrote in *ottava rima*, aiming to produce a Christian epic founded in history without, however, abandoning the appeal of the chivalric and marvellous elements (*materia cavalleresca*) of earlier romances based on the legends of King Arthur, Charlemagne, and Roland.

Gese, Bartholomäus (BARTHEL GÖSS) (1555 OR 1562–1613)

German theologian and composer whose works were important in the development of the Protestant Passion. He was cantor at the Marienkirche, Frankfurt, from 1593 until his death.

Works include:

Masses (one on themes by Lassus), motets, psalms, hymns, sacred songs, and other pieces, all for the Lutheran Church; Passion according to St John; wedding and funeral music.

Gesner, Konrad von (1516–1565)

Swiss naturalist. He produced an encyclopedia of the animal world, the five-volume *Historia animalium* (1551–58). He began a similar project on plants that was incomplete at the time of his death. He is considered the founder of zoology.

Gesner was born in Zürich, Switzerland, and was the godson of the Protestant reformer Ulrich Zwingli. He studied theology at Carolinum in Zürich and then at the Fraumünster seminary. He went to Strasbourg Academy in 1532 to study Hebrew and then studied medicine in Bourges, Paris, and Basel. He was the professor of Greek at Lausanne Academy 1537–40 and obtained his doctorate in 1541. After a spell in Montpellier studying botany, he returned to Zürich to become a physician. He travelled widely in Europe and worked on *Opera Botanica*, which was completed and published after his death by C Schmiedel. He died in Zürich on 13 March.

gesso

Italian 'gypsum', in painting and gilding, an absorbent white ground made of a mixture of plaster and size (a gluey mixture). *Gesso* was used as a preparatory base for panels and canvases, especially in ◊tempera painting.

Gesta Romanorum/Deeds of the Romans

Title given to a collection of short, didactic Latin stories for the use of preachers. It was made, probably about 1300 (first printed about 1473), by an English Franciscan from Latin and Greek sources, and was gradually expanded with other Eastern and European material. It proved endearingly popular, despite being by humanist standards, a 'barbarian' text; in the age of print, it was among the earliest printed books (Utrecht, *c.* 1473) and an English version was printed by Wynkyn de Worde around 1510.

It recorded stories which were originally transmitted orally, and in the analogues it contains are some of the narratives which appear in the works of Chaucer, John Gower, and Shakespeare, among others. For example, it holds Chaucer's *Man of Lawes Tale*, the main outlines of Shakespeare's *King Lear* and *Pericles*, and Longfellow's *King Robert of Sicily*.

Gesualdo, Carlo (*c.* 1561–1613)

Prince of Venosa, Italian composer and lutenist. His compositions, which comprise sacred and secular vocal music, and some instrumental pieces, are noted for their complex (modern-sounding) harmonic structure, most unlike the work of his contemporaries. His highly chromatic madrigals (in six books, 1594–1611), set to emotional, passionate texts, have been admired in the 20th century by Igor Stravinsky, among others.

In 1590 he had his wife and her lover murdered; he married Leonora d'Este of Ferrara in 1593, and lived at the court in Ferrara until 1596.

Gesualdo took his music studies seriously in his youth and became a very accomplished lutenist. He married his first cousin Maria d'Avalos, a Neapolitan noblewoman, in 1586. Though only 21, she had already been married twice and had children. She bore him a son, but became the lover of Fabrizio Caraffa, 3rd Duke of Andria; Gesualdo had them both murdered on the night of 16 October 1590. In 1594 he went to the court of Ferrara and married Leonora d'Este there, but returned to his estate at Naples in 1596, where he spent the rest of his life in a state of profound depression.

His work is notable for its expressive power and chromatic harmony. In 1960 Stravinsky orchestrated three of Gesualdo's madrigals, to mark the 400th anniversary of his birth. He is the subject of Alfred Schnittke's second opera, *Gesualdo*.

Works include:
Seven books of madrigals (the last posthumously published of pieces composed in 1594); two books of *Sacrae cantiones*, responds for six voices.

Ghiberti Story of Joseph, son of Jacob, from a panel of the Baptistery doors, Florence, designed by Lorenzo Ghiberti (Museo dell'opera del Duomo, Florence). *e.t. archive*

Gherardello da Firenze (*c.* 1320/25–1362/63)

Italian composer. He wrote sacred works, madrigals, and other pieces, but is famous especially for his caccia (canonic hunting song) 'Tosto che l'alba del bel giorno appare'.

Ghiberti, Lorenzo (1378–1455)

Italian sculptor and goldsmith. His career was dominated by the prestigious commission to provide a pair of elaborate gilded bronze doors for the baptistery of Florence Cathedral (1425–52). He was admired in his time particularly for his skill in casting and finishing bronze sculpture. Around 1450 he wrote the *Commentarii/Commentaries*, the earliest surviving autobiography of an Italian artist and an invaluable source of information on 14th-century artists.

Although he trained as a goldsmith in Florence, he established his reputation largely on the two sets of doors that he supplied for the baptistery. He gained the commission based on the success of a trial scene depicting the Sacrifice of Isaac, which was considered superior artistically as well as technically to other competitors such as ◊Brunelleschi. The first set of doors, known as the North Doors, was completed

over a 20-year period beginning in 1402, and it consists of 28 scenes from the New Testament. While demonstrating a sophisticated understanding of bronze relief techniques, the scenes also illustrate the difficulties that Ghiberti faced artistically in challenging the conventional design of the doors through the introduction of a more elaborate conception of space and a stronger interaction of forms. Based on the success of the project, Ghiberti began work on the East Doors, which were also of gilded bronze and consisted of ten much larger panels of Old Testament scenes. In them he was able to elaborate more cohesive and dynamic compositions through the use of a finely gradated relief technique inspired by the art of ◊Donatello.

He also produced numerous other sculptures, including a series of larger than life-sized sculptures of saints for the Church of Orsanmichele, such as the *St John the Baptist* (*c.* 1415).

It was ◊Michelangelo who called the East Gates the 'gates of paradise', by which they are most commonly known. In producing the doors, Ghiberti created an extensive workshop which employed many of the leading artists of the early 15th century in Florence.

Ghirlandaio, Domenico (ADOPTED NAME OF DOMENICO DI TOMMASO BIGORDI) (*c.* 1449–1494)

Italian fresco painter. He was the head of a large and prosperous workshop in Florence. His fresco cycle (1486–90) in Sta Maria Novella, Florence, includes portraits of many Florentines and much contemporary domestic detail. He also worked in Pisa, Rome, and San Gimignano, and painted many portraits.

He was styled Il Ghirlandaio or Grillandaio (garland-maker) after his father Tommaso, who was a goldsmith. He studied under Baldovinetti and his style was influenced by Castagno, Masaccio, and Verrocchio. His first major work was the *Life of St Fina* in the Cappella Fina, 1475, and his frescoes in Florence include those for the Sassetti Chapel in Santa Trinità, 1485, and for the choir of Santa Maria Novella (the *Life of St Francis*, 1485, and the scenes from the life of St John the Baptist and the Virgin, his masterpiece, 1486–90). A prolific painter with a flourishing studio, Ghirlandaio produced not only

frescoes and mosaics but many religious subjects on panel and portraits. Of the two frescoes he contributed to the Sistine Chapel to the order of Sixtus IV, 1481, the *Calling of St Andrew and St Peter* remains. His altarpiece from Santa Maria Novella is at Munich. Among his pupils was ◊Michelangelo.

Ghirlandaio was assisted by his brothers, **Davide** (1452–1525) and **Benedetto** (1458–1497). Davide helped in the mosaic of the *Annunciation* over the north portal of Florence Cathedral and executed others at Orvieto, Florence, and Siena. The son of Domenico, **Ridolfo** (1483–1561), was also a painter and was a friend of Raphael. He too had a busy studio and was employed by the Signoria of Florence and the Medici. There are paintings by him in galleries at Berlin, Paris (Louvre), and Florence (Uffizi and Pitti).

Ghiselin, Jean (VERBONNET) (*c.* 1455–*c.* 1511)

Flemish composer. He was active especially in Ferrara. The music printer Ottaviano Petrucci of Venice published several of his works between 1501 and 1507. He composed Masses (a volume was published in 1503), motets, songs, and other pieces.

Giambologna (GIOVANNI DA BOLOGNA OR JEAN DE BOULOGNE) (1529–1608)

Flemish-born sculptor who settled in Florence, Italy, about 1552, where he became court sculptor to the Medici. He produced a series of monumental statues for the Medici, including *The Rape of the Sabine Women* (1583) placed in the Loggia dei Lanzi, Florence. He also worked in bronze, producing for example the equestrian monument to *Cosimo I, Grand Duke of Tuscany* (1587–93, Piazza della Signoria, Florence).

His work was not solely for the Medici: for the city of Bologna, he sculpted a large-scale *Neptune* (1566). Moreover, his bronze works were often copied in his workshop – in particular, his *Mercury* – and used by the Medici as diplomatic gifts. This naturally assisted the spread of Giambologna's renown, as did the numerous sculptors who passed through his studio as part of their training (for example, Adriaen ◊De Vries and Pietro Tacca, his eventual successor as Medici sculptor).

Gibbons, Orlando (1583–1625)

English composer. He wrote sacred anthems, instrumental fantasias, and madrigals including *The Silver Swan* for five voices (1612). From a family of musicians, he became organist at Westminster Abbey, London, in 1623.

Gibbons was brought up at Cambridge, where he took a degree in music in 1606. He was a singer at the Chapel Royal from 1603 and organist there from about 1615 until his death. Oxford awarded him an honorary doctorate in 1622, and the following year he was appointed organist at Westminster Abbey. He died suddenly at Canterbury while waiting to officiate at Charles I's marriage service, for which he had written music.

Works include:
Anglican church music (5 services, about 13 full anthems, and about 25 verse anthems); 20 madrigals; *Cries of London* for voices and strings, 30 fantasies for strings, 4 *In Nomine* for strings, 2 pavans and 2 galliards for strings; 16 keyboard fantasies, 6 sets of variations for keyboard, and other keyboard pieces.

Gilbert, Humfrey (c. 1539–1583)

English soldier and navigator who claimed Newfoundland (landing at St John's) for Elizabeth I in 1583. He died when his ship sank on the return voyage. Knighted in 1570.

Gilbert, William (1540–1603)

English scientist who studied magnetism and static electricity, deducing that the Earth's magnetic field behaves as if a bar magnet joined the North and South poles. His book on magnets, published in 1600, is the first printed scientific book based wholly on experimentation and observation.

Gilbert was the first English scientist to accept Nicolas Copernicus's idea that the Earth rotates on its axis and revolves around the Sun. He also believed that the stars are at different distances from the Earth and might be orbited by habitable planets, but erroneously thought that the planets were held in their orbits by magnetic forces.

Gilbert was born in Colchester, Essex, and educated at Cambridge. In about 1573, he settled in London, where he established a medical practice. He was appointed physician to Queen Elizabeth I in 1600 and later briefly to James I.

Gilbert discovered many important facts about magnetism, such as the laws of attraction and repulsion and magnetic dip. He also investigated static electricity and differentiated between magnetic attraction and electric attraction (as he called the ability of an electrostatically charged body to attract light objects). This is described in his book *De Magnete, Magneticisque Corporibus, et de Magno Magnete Tellure/Concerning Magnetism, Magnetic Bodies, and the Great Magnet Earth* (1600).

Giles, Nathaniel (c. 1558–1634)

English organist and composer. He was organist of Worcester Cathedral (1581–85), and then became organist and choirmaster of St George's Chapel, Windsor. In 1596 he became organist and choirmaster of the Chapel Royal in London, and took the official titles of Gentleman and Master of the Children on the death of William Hunnis in 1597. He collaborated with the playwright Ben Jonson at Blackfriars Theatre, London, from 1600.

He received a doctorate in music from Oxford University in 1622.

Works include:
Services, anthems, motets; madrigal 'Cease now, vain thoughts'.

Gintzler, Simon (c. 1500–AFTER 1550)

German composer. His collection of lute music was published in Venice in 1547, and he also contributed to Hans Gerle's *Eyn Newes ... Lautenbuch*, published in Nuremberg in 1552.

Giocondo, Giovanni (KNOWN AS FRA GIOCONDO) (c. 1433–1515)

Italian friar, architect, engineer, and humanist editor, born in Verona. His early interest was in Latin inscriptions; his collection of about 2,000 was dedicated to Lorenzo de' ◊Medici 'the Magnificent' in c. 1489. He emigrated to France in 1495, where he was employed as royal military engineer. While in Paris, he may have designed the Pont Notre-Dame; he certainly discovered a complete copy of the ancient Roman administrator ◊Pliny the Younger's letters and lectured on the Roman architect ◊Vitruvius.

His interest in Vitruvius continued after his return to Italy in the mid-1500s; he produced an edition of Vitruvius' treatise on architecture, complete with his own woodcuts, and dedicated it to Pope ◊Julius II in 1511. Julius's successor, ◊Leo X, called Giocondo to Rome to assist with the building of St Peter's basilica in 1514.

Giorgione, da Castelfranco (GIORGIO BARBARELLI) (1475–1510)

Venetian painter. He is regarded as the leading innovator in Venetian painting of the late 15th century because of his inspired use of oil paint. Much of his life remains unclear owing to a lack of specific contemporary or documentary testimony. Although fierce debate surrounds the attribution of many paintings to his hand, he is credited with the popularizing of intimate landscapes characterized by rich colour and soft forms diffused by light.

Giorgio Barbarelli, Zorzi da Castelfranco, called Giorgione after his death, appears to have been the pupil of Giovanni ◊Bellini in Venice, and together with ◊Titian he achieved early success there. He decorated the façades of several Venetian palaces, working with Titian on the now ruined façade of the Fondaco dei Tedeschi when it was rebuilt in 1504. He is credited for his virtuoso technique as an oil painter, and for establishing a particularly Venetian interest in the effect of light on harmonizing the relationship between figures and landscape. The poetic and enigmatic beauty of paintings such as the so-called *Tempest* of 1508 (Venice) included subjects independent of a particular position or function and proved immensely influential to later artists, in particular ◊Sebastiano del Piombo and Titian.

Apart from *The Tempest*, relatively few pictures are generally accepted as unquestionably by his hand, including the Castelfranceo Altarpiece in the Cathedral of Castelfranco, the *Three Philosophers*, and the *Portrait of a Lady* (Vienna).

Giorgione *Venus Resting* (Gemeldegalerie, Dresden) by Giorgione, completed after his death by Titian. *AKG London*

Giotto di Bondone (?1267/77–1337)

Florentine artist whose fresco cycles in Padua and Florence were claimed to have influenced the entire course of Italian Renaissance art. Giotto's work predates the introduction of mathematical perspective and *chiaroscuro* in the depiction of landscape. Most other aspects of Renaissance painting are, however, anticipated: the effective spatial distribution and three-dimensional delineation of architectonic elements; the representation of light and its sources; the naturalistic portrayal of human figures with convincing volume and expression; and a focus and intensity never previously achieved on plaster or panel.

Giotto's reputation as 'first Renaissance artist' owes much to ◊Vasari, but the myth started within his own lifetime and was elaborated throughout the next century: ◊Dante noted that Giotto eclipsed all predecessors, while ◊Petrarch praised Giotto alongside ◊Simone Martini. Giotto's monumental style remained normative in Florence until ◊Masolino and ◊Masaccio; his work was still being used as a model by ◊Raphael and ◊Michelangelo. A witty Giotto stars in anecdotes retailed by ◊Boccaccio and Franco Sacchetti; he was also an entrepreneur (for example, he hired out weaving equipment).

The dating of Giotto's surviving oeuvre is problematic, as is the course of his career up and down the Italian peninsula. The dramatic fresco cycle of lives of the Virgin and of Christ – thirty-eight scenes on three tiers and two end walls, brilliantly designed in both the spatial sense, and in iconographic terms (to atone for the patron's father's usurious career) in the Arena Chapel in Padua – was executed at the peak of his career. Late in life (in 1334) he was employed to construct and decorate the cathedral *campanile* (bell tower) in Florence. His early career included commissions to the Angevin court at Naples and in the atrium of the Constantinian basilica of St Peter in Rome, but only fragments or copies of these works remain. Even more widely contested is the question of the attribution of the narratives on the walls of the Upper Basilica at Assisi. Giotto's employment of less talented assistants, obvious in his panel paintings (including the *Ognissanti Madonna*, now in the Uffizi, Florence; the *Stigmatization of St Francis*, now in the Louvre, Paris; and the Baroncelli Altarpiece in Sta Croce, Florence), makes it possible that he oversaw the scheme at Assisi; stylistic factors, however, suggest strongly that he was not responsible for the execution of individual scenes.

Oeuvre:
- *Navicella*, St Peter's, Rome (after 1300)
- *Apocalypse* cycle (fragments), Naples (after 1300)
- *Stigmatization of St Francis* (after 1300)
- *Lives of the Madonna and Christ*, Arena Chapel, Padua (1304–13)
- *Ognissanti Madonna* (c. 1310–15)
- *Life of St Francis*, Bardi Chapel, Sta Croce, Florence (c. 1315–20)
- *Lives of the Evangelist and the Baptist*, Peruzzi Chapel, Sta Croce, (c. 1315–mid 1320s)
- Stefaneschi altarpiece (late 1320s–30s)

Giovannelli, Ruggiero (c. 1560–1625)

Italian composer. After holding various church apointments in Rome, he succeeded Palestrina as maestro di cappella at St Peter's in 1594, and was maestro di cappella of the Sistine Chapel (1614–24). At the request of Pope Paul V he contributed to a new edition of the Gradual.

Works include:

Masses, Miserere, and other church music; six books of madrigals, one of canzonette and villanelle.

Giovanni di Paolo (1403–1482)

Sienese painter. He ranks with ◊Stefano di Sassetta, by whom he was influenced, as the leading Sienese painter of the 14th century. Six scenes from the life of John the Baptist from a dismembered polyptych (Chicago and National Gallery, London) are among his most striking works.

He is also known as **Giovanni del Poggio**, from the district of Siena where he lived. His work is individual in its imaginative simplification, and fantastic in effect, as in his *Miracle of St Nicholas of Bari* (Philadelphia Museum of Art).

Giovio, Paolo (1483–1552)

Italian historian and biographer. He spent most of his life at the papal court, where he acquired an intimate knowledge of its workings. His major work, *Historiae Sui Temporis/History of Our Times* (1550–52), covers

Italian affairs during the years 1494–1547. He also wrote biographies (of Pope ◊Leo X and others), and encouraged ◊Vasari to write his famous lives of artists.

Educated as a doctor, Giovio left his native Como to become a servant of the papacy under Leo X in 1513. In 1528 Pope Clement VII made him bishop of Nocera. He withdrew from Rome in 1549, having failed to become a cardinal under Paul III, and spent the last few years of his life in Florence. He also wrote a commentary on Turkish affairs in 1531, and a work on heraldry.

Giraldi, Giambattista Cinzio (CYNTHIUS) (1504–1573)

Ferrarese author. He held various academic posts at Ferrara and elsewhere, and wrote nine tragedies, the best known of which is *Orbecche* (1541). *Gli hecatommiti* (1565) is a famous volume of tales, from which Shakespeare borrowed his plots for *Measure for Measure* and *Othello*.

Giuliano da Maiano (1432–1490)

Florentine architect. A member of an established artistic family, Giuliano trained with his brother, the sculptor ◊Benedetto da Maiano, as a stone-carver and later collaborated with him on a number of projects, including the shrine of San Savino (1472, Faenza Cathedral) and a chapel for Santa Fina in the Collegiata at San Gimignano in 1468. He designed Faenza Cathedral (1474–86).

Following in the artistic footsteps of ◊Brunelleschi and ◊Michelozzo, Giuliano worked on the Palazzo Pazzi in Florence 1460–72; on the vaulting of the nave in the Cathedral of Loreto (after 1481); and on a royal villa in Naples, the Poggio Reale (1484–90), now destroyed. He also executed several notable carvings in wood.

Giulio Romano (ADOPTED NAME OF GIULIO PIPPI DE GIANNUZZI) (c. 1499–1546)

Roman painter and architect. As assistant to ◊Raphael, he developed a style, characterized by its exaggerated movement and rich colours, as seen in the frescoes in the Palazzo del ◊Tè, Mantua.

Having studied under Raphael, Giulio became his chief assistant on the Sala del Incendio frescoes in the Vatican. He succeeded Raphael as head of his Rome workshop, together with Giovanni Francesco Penni (c. 1488–c. 1528), completing the Sala di Costantino frescoes and other works, including the *Transfiguration* (Vatican). In 1524 he entered the service of Federico Gonzaga, Duke of Mantua, and in 1526 he built the Palazzo del Tè, a Mannerist building of capricious design with Giulio's frescoes inside, which range from the extremes of illusionism in the Sala di Psyche/Psyche's Room to the grotesque in the Sala dei Giganti/Room of the Giants. Later he designed the façade of the Church of S Petronio in Bologna.

Two works of his in Hampton Court, London, and one in the National Gallery, London, are thought to have belonged to Gonzaga.

He designed some pornographic prints that caused so much public outrage that the engraver, Marcantonio ◊Raimondi (c. 1488–1534), was imprisoned. The poet Pietro ◊Aretino, however, was inspired to write sonnets about them. Among Giulio's other works as a painter are *The Martyrdom of St Stephen* (Genoa), *The Holy Family* (Dresden), *Mary and Jesus* (Louvre, Paris), and *Madonna della Gatta* (Naples).

Giunti (Junta) Press

Italian printing house established by Luca-Antonio Giunti (1457–1538) in Venice in the 1480s. The more important branch of the firm was at Florence, where Filippo Giunti (1450–1517) printed from 1497 until his death. The business was carried on by his descendants until the early 17th century. Filippo Giunti printed the first Greek edition of Plutarch's *Lives* in 1517.

The Venetian branch of the family lasted until 1642, and there was a third branch printing at Lyons (1520–92). The Giunti Press came into conflict with their Venetian rival, the printing house of Aldus ◊Manutius, in the first years of the 16th century, probably over the right to monopolize ◊italic type.

Glareanus, Henricus (REAL NAME HEINRICH LORIS) (1488–1563)

Swiss music theorist. He studied the relationship between the Greek and the church modes and wrote

GLASS IN THE RENAISSANCE

DURING THE 14TH CENTURY Venice became a very wealthy trading nation through the importation of porcelain, spices, textiles, and other luxury items from the East. The arts flourished and there was a resurgence in the art of making glass vessels. With the introduction in the mid-15th century of *cristallo,* so-called after its resemblance to rock-crystal, glass became her most important and valuable export, not only to the rest of Europe but also to the Near East.

By the early 13th century Venetian glassworkers had formed themselves into an 'Arti' (guild), a typical association under state control that also doubled as a school. The earliest surviving statute of 1271, the Capitolare de Fiolari, contained 46 articles. These set out the basic rules of a highly organized industry, that aimed at guaranteeing the quality of the finished product. They also enforced an annual rest period, originally for five months, that permitted the furnaces to be repaired, while preserving valuable fuel resources and allowing time for the glass to be sold. In 1291 the glass industry was moved to the island of Murano, allegedly to protect the city from the risk of fire, but it also helped later to prevent its secrets from leaking out, thereby preserving their monopoly.

Like other decorative arts in the 15th century, glassmaking benefited from scientific experiments being carried out in Venice and Padua. Around 1450, Angelo Barovier, the first important member of a very influential glassmaking family, developed a new high-quality glass called 'cristallo'. It was very clear and limpid, obtained from the scrupulous choice of raw materials which were put through a number of purifying processes. It was soon imitated by other Murano glass factories and achieved almost overnight fame. In order to protect this valuable product, the Serenissima imposed new bans on the movement of her glassworkers, punishable by fines, imprisonment, and even bodily harm. However, they did travel, lured by tempting offers from abroad and in this way centres manufacturing glass 'a la façon de Venise', sprang up throughout Europe, from Spain to the Low Countries, and even in England, where Giacomo Verzelini was granted a 21-year monopoly in 1574. In contrast, glassworkers from Altare, an important glassmaking centre outside Genoa, could and indeed were encouraged to leave and spread their knowledge, most travelling to France.

Most late 15th- and 16th-century glass was gilded and enamelled. The glass was either colourless or made in deep rich colours like emerald green, blue, or purple, and occasionally in opaque white 'lattimo' glass imitating expensive Chinese porcelain. The vessels produced included footed goblets, pilgrim flasks, footed salvers, and deep ribbed standing bowls, while the designs on them included simple geometric motifs (intersecting circles or scale patterns), possibly inspired by mosaics. More luxury pieces were decorated with portraits, influenced by contemporary artists like ◊Pietro della Francesca and ◊Vittore Carpaccio, while 'coppe nuziali' had idealized portraits of the bride and groom, sometimes combined with allegorical scenes, like the Fountain of Love. Glasses were commissioned from all over Europe; the earliest to survive celebrates the marriage in 1495 of Michael Behaim of Nuremberg with Katerina Lochnerin, who are unusually represented by depictions of their name saints rather than by portraits.

Coats of arms were also widely used, the flat sides of pilgrim flasks and the central reserves of salvers lending themselves especially to the display of armorials or medallions containing religious scenes or animals. Whole services were similarly decorated like that made, possibly as a diplomatic gift, to celebrate the marriage of ◊Anne of Brittany to ◊Louis XII of France in 1499. A sufficient number of pieces survive, enamelled with the arms of a Medici pope, either ◊Leo X (1513–21) or ◊Clement VII (1523–34), to surmise the existence of a papal service. However, differences in their quality suggest that they were made over a number of years, possibly as replacement pieces. An inventory compiled on the death of ◊Catherine de Medici in 1589 includes blue gilded glass pots and candlesticks of probable Venetian origin and 13 pieces made at the St Germain-en-Laye glasshouse, founded by her husband, ◊Henry II, in June 1551 under the

continued

direction of a Bolognese, Theseo Mutio.

In the early 16th century, motifs derived from classical antiquity, especially grotesques, were increasingly favoured, initially inspired from the recent discoveries of Roman wall-paintings and copied from contemporary engravings. Glassworkers also experimented with ancient Roman glassmaking techniques and by the 1490s they were able to make '*millefiori*' or mosaic glass, mostly miniature objects, intended for princely Kunstkammers rather than for use. They also produced 'calcedonia' glass made in imitation of semi-precious banded stones like jasper and agate, whose invention is also accredited to Angelo Barovier sometime before 1460.

Another important development in the late 1520s, attributed to the Serena brothers, was '*vetro a filigrana*' in which patterns of opaque white canes are imbedded in colourless cristallo. Throughout the century these designs became more complicated, resulting in '*vetro a reticello*' in which bubbles of air were trapped between the white canes. The production of 'ice-glass' with its multi-cracked surface also involved great skill, achieved by repeatedly plunging the hot glass into cold water without breaking it.

All the glasses mentioned above were executed at the glasshouse while the vessel was still hot or had to be re-heated, but they also decorated their glasses when cold, either with diamond-engraving or reverse painting. Delicate engraving with the point of a diamond probably

originated with Vincenzo di Angelo dal Gallo, who, although working from around 1534, was only granted a privilege in 1549. This is quite close in date to a service of armorial plates with grotesques, engraved with the arms of another Medici pope, ◊Pius IV (1559–65). In cold-painting, the decoration was produced by temporarily affixing a print to the inside of the vessel and tracing the outlines to the underside with black paint which were then infilled in colours. As the colours are unfired this type of decoration is unstable and because of the fragility of Renaissance glass in general the small quantity surviving today, mostly preserved in museums, is better known from the inventories, for example, of kings and nobles across Europe.

MARTINE NEWBY

---

treatises, notably *Isagoge in Musicen* (1516) and *Dodecachordon* (1547), containing his new theory of 12 church modes.

He studied music at Berne and Cologne, and taught at Basel from 1515 and again from 1522, after holding a professorship in Paris from 1517 on the recommendation of Erasmus of Rotterdam. In 1529 he settled at Freiburg im Breislau, Germany.

Gloucester, Humfrey, DUKE OF GLOUCESTER (1390–1447)

Youngest son of Henry IV of England. He fought in France with his brother, ◊Henry V, whose policies he attempted to continue after his death. Though he was appointed 'defender' of Henry VI, his power was limited by the minority council. His championing of a vigorous war policy left him increasingly isolated as financial resources and military success became scarce. He was accused of plotting the king's death in February 1447 and died in custody five days later.

From about 1430, Gloucester – 'son, brother, and uncle of kings', as he styled himself – was keen to play

the part of magnificent prince. He commissioned literary works and, from 1436, employed a humanist as his secretary. He amassed a library to rival that of his brother John, Duke of Bedford, and demonstrated his generosity by giving over 400 manuscripts to Oxford University. His career may, in reality, have been lacklustre but this was glossed over by the authors, English and Italian, who sought his patronage.

Gloucester's patronage, c. 1430–47

Gloucester attracted the attention of several humanists but, like so many patrons, his cultural interests were not confined to Italian fashions.

c. 1431	Commissions John ◊Lydgate to write *The Fall of Princes*
1432	Writes to Leonardo ◊Bruni suggesting he translate Aristotle's *Politics*
1433	Carries out building work at his palace of Greenwich
1436	Employs Tito Livio ◊Frulovisi as his secretary, who writes the *Humfrois*, an epic poem in praise of Gloucester
1437	Lapo da ◊Castiglionchio, writing from Italy,

dedicates works to Gloucester

1438 Pietro ◊del Monte dedicates *De Vitiorum Differencia* to Gloucester

c. **1438** Antonio ◊Beccaria, who replaces Frulovisi as Gloucester's secretary, dedicates translations to him

1439 John Capgrave presents Gloucester with biblical commentary

c. **1440** John Whethamstede presents his *Granarium* to Gloucester

c. **1444** English translation of Palladius dedicated to Gloucester

c. **1446** Nicholas Upton dedicates to Gloucester *De Studio Militari*

Goes, Hugo van der (*c.* 1440–1482)

Flemish painter. Chiefly active in Ghent. His works were highly praised by Italian artists, particularly his *Portinari* Altarpiece (*c.* 1475, Uffizi, Florence), typically rich both in symbolism and naturalistic detail.

He began with small panels warmly coloured and detailed in the van ◊Eyck fashion, but from about 1474 he worked on a larger scale, using cool and translucent colour and often expressing great emotional intensity. His best-known work, the *Portinari* Altarpiece, was executed for the agent of the Medici at Bruges, Tommaso Portinari. It made a great impression on the Florentines, being closely studied by Domenico ◊Ghirlandaio, and Goes was favourably mentioned by the historian Giorgio ◊Vasari.

Other works are the *Adoration of the Magi* (Staatliche Museen, Berlin), *Death of the Virgin* (*c.* 1480, Musée Communale des Beaux Arts, Bruges), and *Monk Meditating* (Metropolitan Museum, New York).

Goes became a monk in the Roode-Clooster, Brussels in 1475 but continued to paint, though suffering intermittently in the last years of his life from fits of severe depression.

Góis, Damião de (1502–1574)

Portuguese scholar and chronicler, educated at the court of ◊Manuel I. In 1521 he began his European travels as a diplomat and secretary. The legend that Erasmus died in his arms is probably apocryphal. During his travels he published numerous works in Latin, among these a description of Ethiopia (initially two separate texts, published together in 1544 as *Fides, Religio, Moresque Ethiopum/On the Beliefs,*

Religion and Customs of the Ethiopians) and an account of Portuguese activities in India (*Commentarius Rerum Gestarum in India a Lusitanis,* 1539). Imprisoned in 1542 for resisting the French at Louvain, he finally returned to Lisbon in 1558 and was appointed royal archivist and chronicler. Parts I and II of his chronicle on Manuel I appeared in 1566 while Parts III and IV were published in 1567, the same year as his chronicle on Prince João. He was, however, imprisoned by the Inquisition in 1571 for his philosophical opinions, and died in obscure circumstances shortly afterwards.

Gomar, Francis (FRANZISKUS GOMARUS) (1563–1641)

Flemish Calvinist theologian. Born in Bruges, he was educated in Germany and then England, graduating at Cambridge. He became a professor of theology at Leyden and the leading opponent of Arminius. When the views of Arminius gained support, Gomar left Leyden and finally became professor of theology at Saumur. A postumous work, *Lyra Alcidiana*, appeared in 1645. See Synod of ◊Dort.

Gombert, Nicolas (*c.* 1495–*c.* 1556)

Flemish composer. His music was admired for its sombre colours and close-knit textures.

Gombert was a pupil of Josquin Desprez. He was in service at the Emperor Charles V's chapel in Flanders from 1562 and became maître des enfants (master of the choirboys) in 1529; later he became a canon at Tournai and in 1537 went to Spain with 20 singers and held a post in the imperial chapel in Madrid. He was exiled in 1540 for gross indecency with his choirboys.

Works include:
Ten Masses, 160 motets, psalms; about 80 chansons.

Gomez, Diego (1440–1482)

Portuguese navigator who discovered the coast of Liberia during a voyage sponsored by ◊Henry the Navigator (1458–60).

Gonçalves, Nuno (*c.* 1450–1471)

Portuguese artist. He was court painter to ◊Afonso V. What little of his work survives includes the St Vincent polyptych (*c.* 1465–67, National Museum of

Art, Lisbon). Covering six panels, it depicts Portuguese society in the form of a crowded gallery, with figures ranging from Alfonso and ◊Henry the Navigator to clerics and fishermen. His work owes much to contemporary Flemish painting in its striking realism and bold use of colour.

gonfaloniere

In Medieval and Renaissance Italy, an official responsible for a specific area of a city. In Florence the title was attached to the chief member of the council of magistrates. The word derives from *gonfalone* (military banner), which, by extension, also came to mean a subdivision of a city with its own section of militia.

Góngora y Argote, Luis de (1561–1627)

Irascible Castilian poet and priest. Of a cultured family, he failed his degree at Salamanca due to excessive nightlife and gambling. His father obtained him an ecclesiastical benefice, but in 1589 the bishop accused him of gambling and not singing in the choir – to which Góngora responded that it was impossible to sing as he was between a priest who sang too loud and too long, and another who was deaf and knew not when to stop. Despite this defence, the chapter sent him away on missions around Spain; that same year he achieved fame for twelve ballads published in Pedro de Moncayo's anthology, *Flor de Romances Nuevos/The Flower of New Ballads*. In 1619 he became chaplain to Philip III and spent his final years in his native Córdoba, dying of apoplexy as he prepared his collected works for publication. (They appeared later in 1627, under the grand title of *Obras en verso del Homero español/Poetic works by the Spanish Homer*.)

Despite the mutual, bitter dislike between Góngora and his contemporary ◊Quevedo, they shared a similar literary aesthetic, even if they considered it from different vantage points. Góngora's highly-wrought imagery and Latinate syntax, classified by another as ◊culteranismo and which, in the hands of less-skilled poets, would be pejoratively termed 'gongorismo', had a significant impact on the poetry of his time. Claiming he had transformed Castilian into a language as noble as Latin, Góngora wrote poetry on pastoral, satirical, amorous, and heroic themes (although, perhaps surprisingly, rarely on religious

topics). In 1605 he published a series of songs and sonnets in another anthology, *Flor de poetas ilustres/The Flower of Illustrious Poets*; in 1613 there appeared his *Fábula de Polifemo y Galatea/Tale of Polyphemeus and Galatea*, a free adaptation of Book XII of Ovid's *Metamorphoses*. In his incomplete *Soledades/Solitudes* narrative considerations practically vanish beside Góngora's pursuit of metaphor. The impact of the *Soledades* may be gauged by the fact that Quevedo lampooned them shortly after publication – and in the 17th century a third *Soledad* was added to Góngora's two (of a projected four) by León y Mansilla. Meanwhile, Góngora's two plays made little impact on the Castilian literary scene.

Gonzaga, Federico II (1500–1540)

Marchese of Mantua from the death of his father, Francesco II, in 1519; created Duke of Mantua by Charles V in 1530. Being awarded the title of duke reflected his long (though not completely consistent) service to the emperor.

Federico was both a collector and a commissioner of art. It is said that a formative influence on his art appreciation was his time as a hostage in ◊Julius II's Rome; certainly, later he tried to purchase paintings by ◊Michelangelo for his collection (to no avail) – but his taste was certainly not confined to the latest Roman styles. For example, in 1535 he purchased 120 Flemish landscapes (for Federico, quantity mattered). He commissioned a portrait of himself from ◊Titian and was an important patron of his work, but the artist of whom he made most use was Raphael's heir, ◊Giulio Romano. It was Giulio who designed and decorated Federico's villa, the Palazzo del ◊Té.

Gonzaga, Ludovico (1412–1478)

Marchese of Mantua from the death of his father, Gianfrancesco, in 1444. Married, in 1433, to Barbara of Brandenburg, the granddaughter of Emperor Sigismund, this symbolized the imperial favour of the family. Ludovico's attention was directed towards Italian matters: before he became Marchese, he served as a soldier both for and (briefly) against Milan. As Marchese, his policy saw him closely tied to the new Sforza dynasty of Milan.

Ludovico was concerned to demonstrate the magnificence of his family, as did other dynasties in con-

THE GONZAGA DYNASTY OF MANTUA

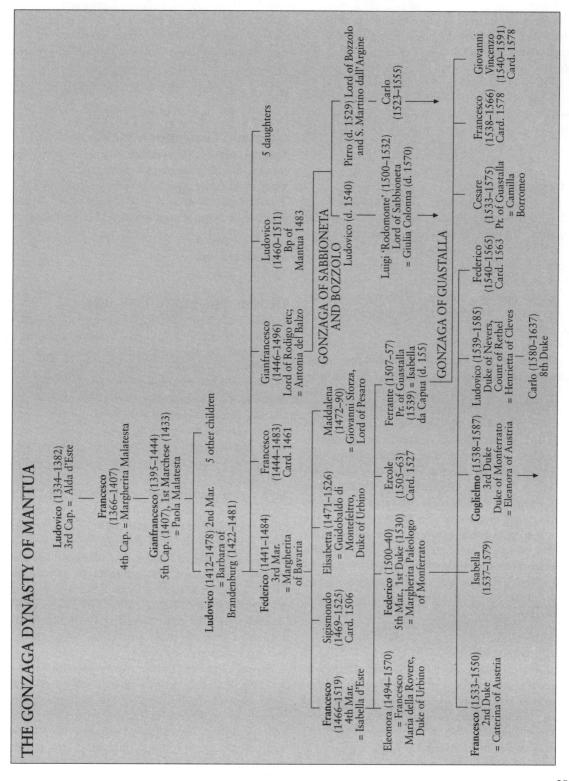

Ludovico (1334–1382)
3rd Cap. = Alda d'Este

Francesco
(1366–1407)
4th Cap. = Margherita Malatesta

Gianfrancesco (1395–1444)
5th Cap. (1407), 1st Marchese (1433)
= Paola Malatesta

Ludovico (1412–1478) 2nd Mar.   5 other children
= Barbara of
Brandenburg (1422–1481)

Federico (1441–1484)
3rd Mar.
= Margherita
of Bavaria

Francesco
(1444–1483)
Card. 1461

Gianfrancesco
(1446–1496)
Lord of Rodigo etc;
= Antonia del Balzo

Ludovico
(1460–1511)
Bp of
Mantua 1483

5 daughters

**GONZAGA OF SABBIONETA
AND BOZZOLO**

Ludovico (d. 1540)

Pirro (d. 1529) Lord of Bozzolo
and S. Martino dall'Argine

Francesco
(1466–1519)
4th Mar.
= Isabella d'Este

Sigismondo
(1469–1525)
Card. 1506

Elisabetta (1471–1526)
= Guidobaldo di
Montefeltro,
Duke of Urbino

Maddalena
(1472–90)
= Giovanni Sforza,
Lord of Pesaro

Luigi 'Rodomonte' (1500–1532)
Lord of Sabbioneta
= Giulia Colonna (d. 1570)

Carlo
(1523–1555)

Eleonora (1494–1570)
= Francesco
Maria della Rovere,
Duke of Urbino

Federico (1500–40)
5th Mar, 1st Duke (1530)
= Margherita Paleologo
of Monferrato

Ercole
(1505–63)
Card. 1527

Ferrante (1507–57)
Pr. of Guastalla
(1539) = Isabella
da Capua (d. 155)

GONZAGA OF GUASTALLA

Isabella
(1537–1579)

Guglielmo (1538–1587)
3rd Duke
Duke of Monferrato
= Eleonora of Austria

Ludovico (1539–1585)
Duke of Nevers,
Count of Rethel
= Henrietta of Cleves

Federico
(1540–1565)
Card. 1563

Cesare
(1533–1575)
Pr. of Guastalla
= Camilla
Borromeo

Francesco
(1538–1566)
Card. 1578

Giovanni
Vincenzo
(1540–1591)
Card. 1578

Francesco (1533–1550)
2nd Duke
= Caterina of Austria

Carlo (1580–1637)
8th Duke

trol of a city. He himself had received an education in *studia humanitatis* from none less than ◊Vittorino da Feltre, whom his father had brought to the city. Ludovico asked for Cosimo de' ◊Medici's financial assistance in his plans for urban development and he also employed Florentine architects, including Luca Fancelli and Leon Battista ◊Alberti. In art, however, Ludovico looked to Padua, from where he brought Andrea ◊Mantegna to paint frescoes for his palace.

Gonzaga dynasty

Ruling family of Mantua. **Luigi Gonzaga** (*c.* 1268–1360) seized power in 1328 and took the title of captain. The title went as part of the inheritance, but in 1433 the Emperor ◊Sigismund bestowed on **Gianfrancesco Gonzaga** (1395–1444) the title of Marchese. Another emperor, ◊Charles V, rounded off this rise in prestige, making Gianfrancesco's great-great-grandson, **Federico II ◊Gonzaga** duke of Mantua in 1530.

The Gonzaga followed the customary policy to consolidate their position: dynastic marriages. **Francesco II Gonzaga** (1466–1519), for example, married Isabella d' ◊Este linking the family with the rulers of Ferrara – and incidentally helping to continue the reputation for cultural patronage fully established by Francesco's grandfather, **Ludovico ◊Gonzaga**, the second marchese. Marriage was also a means of securing the fortunes of younger sons: Ludovico's son **Gianfrancesco Gonzaga** (1446–1496) married Antonia del Balzo, Princess of Altamura, and established the Bozzolo line of the family. An ecclesiastical career was the other career path for younger sons: Gianfrancesco's brother, **Francesco Gonzaga** (1444–1483) became a cardinal (and compiled an expensive collection of artworks – including tapestries and ancient gems – and manuscripts).

Googe, Barnabe (1540–1594)

English poet. He was a friend of George Turberville and imitated his style and the metres of his poems. His best-known work is *Eclogues, Epitaphs and Sonnets* (1563). The eclogues are among the earliest pastorals in English.

Googe was born in Alvingham, Lincolnshire. He studied both at Christ's College, Cambridge, and at New College, Oxford, then travelled on the Continent. On his return he joined his relative, William Cecil, whom he served in Ireland, and became one of the gentlemen pensioners of Queen Elizabeth I.

Gorzanis, Giacomo (*c.* 1525–AFTER 1575)

Italian composer. He published four books of lute music, including numerous dance suites in two or three movements. One of these, consisting of a *passo e mezzo* and *padovana* (1561), provides an early example of 'sonata' used as a title. He was blind.

Gossaert, Jan

Flemish painter, known as ◊Mabuse.

Gosson, Stephen (*c.* 1554–1624)

English playwright, satirist, and clergyman. Moved by a sermon preached in London during an outbreak of the plague, he abandoned the theatre and became one of its severest critics in his prose satire *The School of Abuse* (1579). It is written in euphuistic style (see ◊euphuism) and was dedicated to Philip ◊Sidney, who did not receive it well; it is believed to have evoked his *Apology for Poetry* (1595). Gosson took orders in 1584 and died rector of St Botolph's, London.

Gothic art

Style that succeeded Romanesque as the most popular force in European art and prevailed in most countries, particularly in northern Europe, from the late 12th century to the beginning of the 16th century, when it gave way to Renaissance influence. The term 'Gothic' was coined with reference to architecture, and it is only in architecture that it has a clear meaning, with pointed arches being the most obvious characteristic. The term is used as a convenient label for other visual arts of the period, but its meaning in these contexts is rarely precise.

Several types of sculpture are considered to be typical of the Gothic period, most notably spectacular ensembles of figures around the portals of great cathedrals, particularly in France, where the Gothic style originated. These figures usually echo the long and graceful forms of the architecture. This was also a great age of woodcarving, with elaborate sets of choir stalls, their spiky pierced forms recalling the tracery and pinnacles of Gothic architecture. England and Spain have the richest surviving collections of choir stalls. In smaller-scale sculpture, the spirit of the Gothic period is seen particularly in statuettes of the Virgin and Child. These were often in ivory and typically have a graceful swaying pose following the natural shape of the tusk.

This swaying elegance is considered characteristic of Gothic art and is also found in the manuscript illumination of the time. Illumination and stained glass were the two principal forms of painting in the Gothic period, and individual easel paintings were still something of a rarity. Easel paintings first became common in Italy, where the Gothic style took root much less firmly than in other parts of Europe. Because of its Roman heritage, Italy was more influenced by Classical art than was the rest of Europe, and this restrained the more exuberant features of Gothic art. Climatic factors came into play, too; because it is a sunny country, the windows of medieval churches in Italy tended to be smaller than those in northern Europe, encouraging frescos on the large areas of flat wall space, rather than stained glass in the windows, as the dominant form of large-scale painting.

Goudimel, Claude (*c*. 1514–1572)

French composer. He contributed chansons for several voices to many collections, also four-part settings to a book of odes by the Roman poet Horace and to another of sacred songs (*chansons spirituelles*) by Marc-Antoine de Muret (1526–85) in 1555, and settings of French translations of the psalms, including a complete Protestant psalter.

After studying at Paris University, Goudimel then worked with the publisher Nicolas du Chemin as a proofreader and later as a business partner. He first appeared as a composer in Paris in 1549, when he contributed chansons to a book published by du Chemin. About 1557, having become a Huguenot, he went to live at Metz with the Protestant colony there, and composed his first complete psalter in 1564. About ten years later he left for Besançon, and afterwards for Lyon, where he died in the massacre of the Huguenots in August 1572.

Goudimel wrote Masses, motets, and chansons, but it is for his psalm settings that he is remembered. They range in style from motetlike works to simple harmonizations.

Works include:
Five Masses, three Magnificats, psalms in motet form and other works for the Catholic Church; psalms, including a complete psalter, for the Protestant Church; sacred songs and numerous secular chansons for several voices.

Goujon, Jean (*c*. 1510–*c*. 1565)

French Renaissance sculptor. His style developed under the influence of ◊Primaticcio and ◊Cellini at Fontainebleau, and is exemplified by the slender nymphs in bas relief on his *Fountain of the Innocents* (1549, Louvre, Paris).

Gower, John (*c*. 1330–1408)

English poet. He is remembered for his *Confessio Amantis/Lover's Confession*, written in English (1386–90) and consisting of tales and discussions about love taken from the Roman poet Ovid, the ◊*Gesta Romanorum*, and other sources. He also wrote *Speculum Meditantis/The Mirror of One Meditating* (in French), discovered in Cambridge in 1895, and *Vox Clamantis/Voice of One Crying* (1382–84) (in Latin). He was a friend of Geoffrey ◊Chaucer who dubbed him 'moral Gower'.

The *Speculum Meditantis*, which was lost for centuries, is a discussion of the ethical theme of virtue in rationality. The *Vox Clamantis* gives an account of the Peasants' Revolt of 1381, while attacking the misgovernment and social evils that had led to it. His third major poem, the *Confessio Amantis*, is the earliest large collection of tales in English and its main theme is the relations between, and eventual reconciliation of, the demands of love and rationality.

Gower represented the serious and cultivated man of his time, in which he was reckoned the equal of Geoffrey Chaucer, but as a poet he is given short attention by critics for being prolix.

Gozzoli, Benozzo (*c*. 1421–1497)

Florentine painter. He is known for his fresco *The Procession of the Magi* (1459–61) in the Chapel of the Palazzo Medici-Riccardi, Florence, where the walls are crowded with figures, many of them portraits of the Medici family.

He trained as a goldsmith and worked with ◊Ghiberti and Fra ◊Angelico, but his style reflects the paintings of ◊Gentile da Fabriano.

Graf, Urs (1485–1527/28)

Swiss painter, engraver, and goldsmith. He served as a mercenary and his drawings are obsessed with the life and death of contemporary soldiers, portraying the horrors with stark authenticity.

He was trained and worked in Basel. Like his Swiss contemporary Hans Leu, a painter and engraver of Zürich, also a Swiss mercenary, Graf may have taken part with the imperial forces in the ◊Sack of Rome in 1527.

Grandi, Alessandro (c. 1575–c. 1630)

Italian composer. His church music was in part inspired by the spacious architecture of St Mark's, Venice, and many of his motets are in the concertato style, with singers positioned in different parts of the church to give a 'stereophonic' effect. His later motets employ instrumental accompaniments and anticipate the sacred concertos of Schütz and other north European masters.

Grandi may have studied under Giovanni Gabrieli at Venice. He was maestro di cappella at Santo Spirito, Ferrara, 1610–17, and then at St Mark's, where he sang under Monteverdi's direction and became his deputy in 1620. In 1627 he became choirmaster at the Church of Santa Maria Maggiore at Bergamo. He died of the plague.

Works include:

Five Masses, about 200 motets, psalms; madrigals; cantatas, arias for solo voice.

Granvelle, Antoine Perrenot de (1517–1586)

French diplomat and prelate, adviser to Holy Roman Emperor Charles V and Philip II of Spain. As president of the Netherlands' Council of State (1559–64), he introduced the Inquisition to the Netherlands, where he provoked such hostility that Philip II was obliged to recall him.

He was born in Besançon, eastern France, which was then part of the Holy Roman Empire. He was a diplomat in the service of Charles V, became bishop of Arras in 1543, and imperial chancellor in 1550. In 1554 he helped with the negotiations for the marriage of the future Philip II and Mary I of England. After Charles V's abdication in 1555 he served Philip II of Spain, negotiating a number of important treaties and acting as prime minister to the regent in the Low Countries (1559–64). He was created cardinal in 1561. His career after his recall from the Netherlands was less important. He returned from retirement to be viceroy of Naples (1571–75), then president of the supreme council of Italy (1579–84) and later of Castile.

Gray, William (c. 1414–1478)

English cleric, bishop of Ely from 1454. After studying at Oxford, Gray continued his education on the Continent, first at Cologne, Germany, from 1442, then at Padua, Italy, from 1445, and finally with Battista ◊Guarino da Verona at Ferrara, Italy, from 1446. The lavishness of his entourage deluded his hosts into thinking that he must be of royal blood. He commissioned and bought a large number of manuscripts, some from ◊Vespasiano da Bisticci. He also patronized scholars, including John ◊Free and Niccolò ◊Perotti. On his death, he left his library to his Oxford college, Balliol.

Grazzini, Anton Francesco (1503–1584)

Florentine writer. His realistic *novelle* (tales) about Florence collected in *Le cene* (*The Suppers*), were not published until 1756. To contemporaries he was best known as a poet of burlesque verses and Petrarchan lyrics. He also wrote seven comedies, and was a founder member of the Accademia della Crusca. (See ◊academy).

Grazzini was born in Florence; otherwise little is known of his early life and education. One of the founders of the Accademia degli Umidi in Florence in 1540, which worked to promote the vernacular in literature, he adopted the name 'Il Lasca' (roach, or mullet); he was, however, expelled from the academy in 1547. He edited the poetry of Francesco ◊Berni in 1548 and others.

Among his comedies are: *La Gelosia*, *La Spiritata*, *I Parentadi*, and *La Pinzochera*.

Great Schism

The period 1378–1417, when there were two (from 1409, three) claimants for the papal tiara.

The schism was occasioned by the papal election which followed the death of Gregory XI, who had returned the papacy to Rome from Avignon in 1377. The election of Urban VI, an Italian – and one, at that, who was happy to offend his cardinals – alienated the majority of French cardinals, who objected to being in Rome. They elected Clement VII as ◊antipope, who returned to Avignon in 1379. Contemporary tensions between secular rulers, such as between the kings of England and France, meant that, for the time, different powers were willing to line up behind different papal claimants. However, at the turn of the century the popes both in Rome and Avignon found themselves with decreasing support and menaced by secular forces. This created circumstances favourable for a ◊General Council of the Church to discuss reconciliation, but the attempt at Pisa in 1409 (see ◊Pisa, Council of) only added another pope to the list of claimants. The pressure for an end to the schism finally came from another secular ruler, the Holy Roman Emperor ◊Sigismund, who urged the convening of the Council of ◊Constance (1414–18). The Council secured the resignation or deposition of the remaining claimants, and ◊Martin V was elected pope of the reunified Catholic Church in 1417.

Greco, El (DOMÉNIKOS THEOTOKOPOULOS) (1541–1614)

Spanish painter called 'the Greek' because he was born in Crete. He studied in Italy, worked in Rome from about 1570, and by 1577 had settled in Toledo. He painted elegant portraits and intensely emotional religious scenes with increasingly distorted figures and unearthly light, such as *The Burial of Count Orgaz* (1586, Church of S Tomé, Toledo).

His passionate insistence on rhythm and movement and vehement desire for intensity of expression were conveyed by the elongation and distortion of figures, and unusual and disturbing colour schemes with calculated clashes of crimson, lemon yellow, green, and blue, and livid flesh tones. Perspective and normal effects of lighting were disregarded, and the young El Greco is recorded as having said that the daylight blinded him to the inner light. The characteristic El

Greco can be seen in the *Martyrdom of St Maurice* (1581–84, Madrid, Escorial). The huge *Burial of Count Orgaz* combined austere dignity with rapturous sublimity. Later compositions include *The Agony in the Garden* (National Gallery, London, and other versions) and the soaring vertical ascent of *Pentecost*, *Resurrection*, and *Adoration of the Shepherds* (Prado, Madrid).

training He was trained by Greek monks in his native island of Crete as an icon painter in the Byzantine tradition, and habitually signed his paintings in Greek characters. Crete was then a Venetian possession, and as a young artist he went to Venice. He is stated to have been a pupil of Titian, though his early work seems to owe more to Jacopo Bassano (*c.* 1510–1592) and Tintoretto, and it is possible that he was also influenced by Antonio Correggio.

Rome In 1570, as recorded by his friend the Dalmatian miniature painter Giulio ◊Clovio (1498–1578), who gained him an introduction to Cardinal Alessandro Farnese (1520–1589), he went on to Rome, where he stayed for six years. It is said that he spoke in somewhat contemptuous terms of Michelangelo's *Last Judgement*, though his *Christ Driving the Traders from the Temple* (in several versions) shows him to have borrowed figures and details of composition not only from the Venetians but also from Michelangelo and Raphael.

Toledo El Greco settled in Toledo in 1577, his aim no doubt in going to Spain being to work for Philip II, a lover of Venetian art. Failing to please the king's taste, he did not take up residence in the royal capital, Madrid. Toledo, however, was still much the larger of the two cities, a centre of industry and craft and also the ecclesiastical capital, headquarters of the Jesuits and the Counter-Reformation. A foreigner when he arrived, speaking only Greek and Italian, El Greco stayed in Toledo for the rest of his life, and the religious and spiritual character of his works links him inseparably with the spirit of the time and place. His work was evidently much approved and in demand, though the decay of the city seems to have brought him to poverty in his later years.

work Italian influences remained in his work until about 1580, and in his first commissions at Toledo. These included a now dismembered altarpiece for Santo Domingo el Antiguo, the *Trinity* (Prado) and

Assumption (Chicago), the latter based on the *Assumption* of Titian, and the *Espolio/Disrobing of Christ* for Toledo Cathedral.

The later period of his life produced portraits superbly characterized (and refuting the supposition that El Greco's elongations in other works were due to some defect of eyesight). *Cardinal Niño de Guevara* (New York, Metropolitan Museum) is one of his great portraits, and a remarkable collection is in the Prado. His single pure landscape, *View of Toledo* (Metropolitan Museum), typically selects the intense and abnormal atmosphere of storm. El Greco may have been the first painter to exploit the mysterious and rich effects of shadow produced by artificial light, as in his *Boy Blowing on Coals* (Naples).

influence The many duplicates, revisions, and versions of his paintings suggest a busy studio, though the part played by assistants does not seem clear and he had no follower of note. This is hardly surprising in view of his essential individuality. His complex inheritance as an artist, his background and personal genius, combine to give a unique quality to his achievement. On Spanish painting his influence was small, though Diego Velázquez studied his portraiture and method of design.

Greene, Robert (1558–1592)

English dramatist and pamphleteer. His most popular play was the patriotic comedy *Friar Bacon and Friar Bungay*, printed in 1594. Among his prose romances, *Pandosto* (1588) gave Shakespeare the plot for *A Winter's Tale*. The autobiographical *A Groats-Worth of Wit, Bought with a Million of Repentance* (1592) contains an attack on Shakespeare as 'an upstart crow'.

plays Those of his plays that survive are *Orlando furioso* (1594) and *Alphonsus King of Aragón* (1599), tragedies in the style of Christopher Marlowe; *Friar Bacon and Friar Bungay*; and *The Scottish History of James the Fourth* (1598), a romantic comedy; he has also been credited with *George a Greene, the Pinner of Wakefield* (1599).

romances His prose romances include *Namillia* (1580–83), *Guydonius, the Card of Fancy* (1584), *Perimedes the Blacksmith* (1588), *Menaphon* (1589), later reprinted as *Greene's Arcadia*, and *Tully's Love* (1589). Some of these contain beautiful lyrical pieces.

pamphlets In his pamphlets, Greene turned from idealism to sordid realism. They include *Euphues his Censure of Philautus* (1587), a continuation of John Lyly's work, which provoked the critic Gabriel Harvey to sneer at Greene as 'Euphues' Ape'. Others are *Greene's Mourning Garment* (1590), *Never Too Late* (1590), *Farewell to Folly* (1591), and *A Quip for an Upstart Courtier* (1592). He also wrote interesting accounts of low London life and the swindlers who infested the city.

Gregoriana

Jesuit college founded in Rome as the Collegium Romanum by Ignatius ◊Loyola in 1551. In 1584 it was made into a university by Pope ◊Gregory XIII. It was the earliest modern seminary and the model for later foundations. Many of the college's pupils becoming missionaries and teachers in northern Europe and the Far East.

Gregory XIII (BORN UGO BONCOMPAGNI) (1502–1585)

Pope from 1572. His education and early career was in law at the University of Bologna and it was for his legal skills that Pius IV employed him at the Council of Trent; Pius later made him a cardinal in 1565. As pope, Gregory supported militant attempts to reimpose Catholicism on Christendom: the Massacre of ◊St Bartholomew was celebrated, plots were hatched against Elizabeth I of England.

Gregory is perhaps best remembered for his reform of the calendar published in 1582 and accepted across Catholic Europe (England did not introduce it until the 18th century). Gregory also reconstituted the Roman College as the Gregorian University in 1584.

Grenon, Nicolas (c. 1380–1456)

French composer. He wrote sacred Latin music and chansons.

The earliest mention of Grenon is at Paris in 1399. He later worked at Laon and Cambrai cathedrals and at the Burgundian court chapel under Duke John the Fearless. He was master of the choirboys at the papal chapel (1425–27), and finally returned to Cambrai where he was for many years Guillaume Dufay's neighbour and was probably an influence on the younger composer.

Greville, Fulke (1554–1628)

1st Baron Brooke, English poet and courtier. His biography of his friend Philip ◊Sidney, the *Life of Sir Philip Sidney* (1652), enhanced the posthumous myth surrounding that figure. Greville's other works include *Caelica* (1633), a sequence of poems in different metres; and *The Tragedy of Mustapha* (1609) and *The Tragedy of Alaham* (1633), both modelled on the Roman Seneca. He was knighted in 1603 and was made a baron in 1621.

Greville was born at Beauchamp Court, Warwickshire, and educated at Shrewsbury School, where his lifelong friendship with Sidney began, and Jesus College, Cambridge. He entered the court in 1577, after travelling abroad, and combined a public career with his literary pursuits, being a member of Parliament, treasurer of the navy 1598–1614, and chancellor of the Treasury 1614–21. He was stabbed to death by a servant. The epitaph he composed for himself was: 'Servant to Queen Elizabeth, Councellor to King James, Friend to Sir Philip Sidney. Trophaeum Peccati.'

Grévin, Jacques (1538–1570)

French playwright, poet, and doctor. Like his friend the poet ◊Ronsard, he was an advocate of classical standards in French literature. Among his plays is the tragedy *César* (1560), which has similarities with Marc-Antoine Muret's Latin version of the story of Julius Caesar. Grévin's poetry, published in *Olimpe* (1560), is reminiscent of Ronsard's, but about this time Grévin converted to Protestantism and their friendship ended.

Grévin was born at Clermont-en-Beauvaisis and studied medicine at the university of Paris. *La Trésorière*, based on an earlier lost comedy called *La Maubertine*, was first performed at the college of Beauvais in 1558. He also wrote *Les ébahis* (1562), a comedy about three unlikely suitors.

Grévin became physician to Margaret of Savoy in 1561 and moved to her court at Turin, where he died.

Grimald, Nicholas (1519–1562)

English poet and theologian. He is remembered for his contributions to *Tottel's Songes and Sonettes* (1557). He was also the first poet after the Earl of ◊Surrey to use blank verse. Two Latin tragedies by

Grimald are still extant: *Archipropheta sive Johannes Baptista* (1548) and *Christus Redivivus* (1543). He also translated Cicero's *De Officiis* and Virgil's *Georgics*.

Grimald was born in Huntingdonshire and educated at Cambridge. He became a probationer fellow of Merton College, Oxford in 1541, and chaplain to Bishop ◊Ridley in 1547. His connection with Ridley led to his imprisonment and he is said to have escaped only by recanting.

Grimani, Domenico (1461–1523)

Venetian cleric and patron. The son of Antonio Grimani, Doge of Venice (1434–1523; ruled 1521–23), Domenico's career was at the papal curia, where he was secretary from 1491. His father bought him a cardinal's hat; he became patriarch of Aquileia in 1497, resigning in 1517 (and being succeeded by three of his nephews). The pope employed him in the proceedings leading to the condemnation of Johannes ◊Reuchlin; Venice employed him as an envoy to the pope.

Grimani's education had brought him into contact with the Florentine circle around Lorenzo de' ◊Medici. He himself became a well-known collector of books and works of art. His library, which included the Grimani Breviary (now in the Biblioteca Marciana, Venice), consisted of 15,000 volumes. His art collection comprised both Classical sculpture (removed from ancient sites in Rome) and modern art, ranging from works by ◊Raphael and ◊Titian to northern artists such as Albrecht ◊Dürer, Joachim ◊Patinir and, in particular, Hieronymus ◊Bosch. On his death some of his sculpture and Flemish paintings were left to the Republic of Venice, while over half of his books were to go to a public library that he had founded at the monastery of S Antonio di Castello. The rest remained in the hands of his family, much passing eventually to his nephew Giovanni ◊Grimani.

Grimani, Giovanni (c. 1500–1593)

Venetian cleric and patron. The nephew of Domenico ◊Grimani, he became, like him, the patriarch of Aquileia. He was an architectural patron, presiding over the rebuilding of the Palazzo Grimani and commissioning work for the family chapel in S Francesco della Vigna, which was carried out by Tiziano Aspetti. Like his uncle, he collected ancient sculpture and Flemish art; also like him, he left much of his collection to the Republic of Venice.

Grindal, Edmund (c. 1519–1583)

English cleric and archbishop of Canterbury (1575–77). He served as a chaplain to Edward VI and during the reign of Mary I went into exile in Germany where he was influenced by Calvinist views. When Elizabeth I came to the throne in 1558, he returned to England and became bishop of London in 1559, archbishop of York in 1570, and finally archbishop of Canterbury in 1575. He antagonized the queen and her court with his Puritan ethic and was removed as archbishop of Canterbury in 1577 after a dispute over 'prophesying', meetings of the clergy at which evangelical sermons were preached.

Gringore, Pierre (GRINGOIRE) (c. 1475–c. 1538)

French poet and dramatist. His works contain satires on contemporary politics, and his comedies attacked people of all ranks. His chief works are *La chasse du cerf des cerfs* (1510), *Le jeu du prince des sots* (1512), in which he satirized Pope Julius II, *Le mystère de Saint-Louis* (c. 1524), and *Heures de Nostre-Dame* (1525). In his later years he wrote religious poetry.

Gringore was born in Caen. He first wrote allegorical and moral poems, and then wrote for the stage. He was a member of the *Enfants sans Souci*, a Parisian theatrical company. His later years were spent serving the Duke of Lorraine.

grisaille

Monochrome painting in shades of grey, either used as a ground for an oil painting, or as a work of art in its own right simulating the effect of bas relief. The latter technique was used by Andrea ◊Mantegna.

Grocyn, William (c. 1446–1519)

English humanist and scholar. He studied in Italy and on his return in 1491 he was ordained a priest. He began to teach Greek at Exeter College, Oxford, the first time in England the subject had been taught publicly. His importance lies in his encouragement of *studia humanitatis* in England. Among his pupils were Thomas ◊More, and also ◊Erasmus, who left an account of Grocyn in his letters.

Very little is known about his life before his matriculation at New College, Oxford, in 1465. In 1481 he was appointed reader in divinity at Magdalen College. In 1488 he went to Italy to study Greek at Florence and Rome with Chalcondyles and ◊Politian. Grocyn died at Maidstone, leaving a library of 105 printed books and 17 manuscripts. None of Grocyn's own writings survives.

In Erasmus's letters Grocyn appears as a man who combined traditional scholastic theology with a respect for new learning and a commitment to the highest standards of scholarship.

grotesque

Fanciful mural or sculptural decorations incorporating a profusion of human, animal, and plant forms.

Such decorations were found during excavations of Roman houses at the beginning of the 16th century, notably at the Domus Aurea (Golden House) of Emperor Nero, and the Baths of Emperor Titus. Discovered in underground chambers (grottoes) they became known as *grotteschi*.

The artist ◊Raphael and his followers quickly established grotesque motifs as a facet of their style, particularly in their frescoes. Early examples of grotesque ornament in architecture occur in Pinturicchio's cathedral library ceilings at Siena 1502, and Perugino's ceiling of the Cambio in Perugia c. 1500.

Groto, Luigi (1541–1585)

Blind Italian poet and playwright. He wrote mainly in Italian but also in Latin, Spanish, and Venetian dialect. His works include the extravagant and metrically complex verses of his collection *Rime/Poems* (1577), and plays like the tragedy *Dalida* (1572) (a Senecan horror drama). His other works include *Hadriana* (1578), a dramatization of the Romeo and Juliet story, and the comedies *Emilia* (1579), *Tesoro* (1580), and *Alteria* (1584).

Grünewald, Matthias (MATHIS GOTHARDT-NEITHARDT) (c. 1475–1528)

German painter, architect, and engineer. His altarpiece at Isenheim, southern Alsace, (1515, Unterlinden Museum, Colmar, France), with its grotesquely tortured figure of Jesus and its radiant *Resurrection*, is his most important work.

During 1508–1514 he was painter to the archbishop of Mainz in Aschaffenburg, and after 1514 to the elector of Mainz, Albrecht von Brandenburg (1490–1545). His later years were occupied by a series of paintings ordered by the elector of Mainz for the Cathedral of Halle (where Grünewald also had the function of hydraulic engineer).

To his contemporaries he was 'Matthis of Aschaffenburg'. He was trained in Alsace in the style of Martin Schongauer (though unlike the latter he produced no engravings), and is first mentioned in 1501 in the archives of Seligenstadt, near Aschaffenburg.

On the Isenheim altarpiece there are *Crucifixion* on the closed shutters, *Mourning* on the predella, *Nativity and Concert of Angels*, and *Annunciation* and *Resurrection*. When fully opened, it shows St Anthony and scenes of his temptation and his visit to St Paul in the desert. Although it retained many medieval characteristics, this complex work brought a new emotional range to German art. Apart from the Isenheim altarpiece, Grünewald's remaining work is fragmentary: *Christ Mocked* (Munich); a *Crucifixion* (Basel); parts of altarpieces in Stuppach, Freiburg im Breisgau, Karlsruhe, and Aschaffenburg; a fine late work (part of the Halle commission) is *The Meeting of St Erasmus and St Maurice* (Munich).

Guarini, Giovanni Battista (1538–1612)

Italian poet, author of a blank verse pastoral drama *Il pastor fido/The Faithful Shepherd* (1589). His other works include a comedy, lyric poems, and his *Trattato della politica libertà/Treatise on Political Liberty* (unpublished until the 19th century) which, despite its title, argues for the preferability of tyranny over republicanism.

Guarino, Battista (1434–1503)

Italian humanist scholar and educator. He was the son of ◊Guarino da Verona and he followed his father's footsteps in his native Ferrara, teaching Greek to scholars who came to him from as far afield as Germany and England. Of his pupils, the one who probably had the greatest impact on Renaissance Greek studies was the publisher Aldus ◊Manutius.

In 1459 he wrote the treatise *De Ordine Docendi et Studendi* which embodies his father's ideas on the teaching and studying of Classical languages. His *Poemata* appeared in 1496. He also translated several works.

Guarino da Verona (GUARINO GUARINI) (1374–1460)

Humanist educator and writer from Verona and based for the second half of his career in Ferrara. A pupil of Manuel Chrysoloras, he returned with him to Constantinople and stayed there until 1408. Back in Italy, he taught in Venice, Florence, Padua, and – from 1429, at the invitation of Marchese Niccolò d'Este – at Ferrara. In the city ruled by the ◊Este dynasty, he presided over both a flourishing school and a literary circle which also included Giovanni ◊Aurispa.

His writings comprised mainly of translations from Greek, in particular of Plutarch essays; he also produced a voluminous correspondence and entered into controversies with other humanists like Poggio Bracciolini. In his own time, however, he was best known for his teaching – it is unclear how novel or inspirational his lessons actually were, but they certainly attracted students from across Europe and he surpassed in his celebrity even ◊Vittorino da Feltre and Gasparino ◊Barzizza.

> What can I say of the amazing quantity of Guarino's famous disciples? His house could worthily be called a workshop of eloquence; from his school countless princes emerged, as many as out of the Trojan horse.
>
> ~
>
> LUDOVICO CARBONE (1435–1482), funeral oration on Guarino da Verona, 1460

Guerrero, Francisco (1528–1599)

Spanish composer. He published a large number of works, both religious and secular, and earned himself a reputation in Spain second only to that of Tomás de

Victoria as a composer of church music in the 16th century. His works include Masses, requiems, motets, psalms, and Passions in a flowing polyphonic style; they were much admired for their complex canonic devices and remained in use long after his death, especially in South America.

He studied under his brother Pedro Guerrero and Fernández de Castilleja at Seville Cathedral, where he was a chorister (1542–46); he also had some lessons from Cristobál de Morales as a child. In 1546 he was appointed maestro de capilla at the Cathedral of Jaén, and after the death of Morales to that of Málaga, though he never lived there, but filled posts at Seville Cathedral from 1549 until he succeeded Castilleja as maestro de capilla in March 1574. He visited Lisbon, Rome (twice), Venice, and in 1588 went to the Holy Land. Many of his works were published in France and Italy.

Works include:
Eighteen Masses, about 150 liturgical pieces, including motets, psalms, vespers, Magnificats, Te Deum; sacred and secular songs.

Guevara, Fray Antonio (?1480–1545)

Castilian friar and author with an imaginative approach to scholarship. Raised at the court of ◊Ferdinand and ◊Isabella, he entered the Franciscan Order in 1504 and in 1535 accompanied ◊Charles V in his Tunis expedition. He became Bishop of the modest See of Mondoñedo in 1537.

If his career in the priesthood was less than golden, his fame as author of educational works soon spread. Among his numerous works were his 1528 *Libro aureo de Marco Aurélio/Golden Book of Marcus Aurelius*, which appeared in a pirate edition (it ran to a further 25 before the 17th century was out), and its expanded version, now entitled *Libro llamado relox de príncipes* appeared in an authorized form the following year. Running to 16 Castilian editions, it was also translated into English in 1557 as *Diall of princes* by Sir Thomas ◊North, and it influenced Englishman John ◊Lyly's 1579 *Euphues or Anatomy of Wit*. Guevara's casual invention of references and allusions was attacked by ◊Cervantes in his *Don ◊Quixote*.

Guiccardini, Francesco (1483–1540)

Florentine politician, political commentator, and historian. Born to wealth and position, with which went the duty of political involvement, he served Piero ◊Soderini's Republic as a diplomat, and acted as a highly placed official for the ◊Medici as both rulers of Florence and popes. His *Storia d'Italia/ History of Italy* (1537–40) was printed in 1561 (English translation 1579).

Guiccardini was a member of one of the leading mercantile families in Florence and married into another, the Salviati, in 1508. After an early education in *studia humanitatis*, he learnt law; in 1511 he was employed as a Florentine ambassador to Spain. For Pope Leo X, he was governor of Modena in 1516 and Reggio in 1517; for Clement VII, he was papal president of the Romagna from 1524, papal lieutenant General in 1526 (and at the inauspicious time of the ◊Sack of Rome), and governor of Bologna 1531–34. In Florence, he served both Alessandro de' Medici and Cosimo I.

> Anyone who wants to live totally in accord with God's will must remove himself from the affairs of this world, and it is difficult to live in this world without offending God.
>
> ～
>
> FRANCESCO GUICCARDINI, *Dialogue on the Government of Florence*, book II

His writings were, in part, the habits of a Florentine of his status: there was little that was unusual in his penning *Ricordanze/Memoirs* or *Ricordi/Maxims*, or a family history. His reflections on politics were not confined to these works: as well as his histories (the early *Storia Fiorentine/Florentine History* (1508–09) and his *History of Italy*), he produced a *Discourse on How to Order the Popular Government of Florence* (1512) and a *Dialogo del reggimento di Firenze/Dialogue on the Government of Florence* (1521–24). The cynicism apparent in his writings – his realization that politics and piety make impossible bedfellows – echoes that of his friend and colleague Niccolò ◊Machiavelli. Guiccardini did not always see eye to eye with his colleague, however, as is clear in his *Considerazioni sui discorsi del Machiavelli/Reflections on the Discourses of Machiavelli* (1530). For Guicciardini, the mixed constitution of contemporary Venice was the government most worthy of emulation, not the ancient Roman Republic with its populist elements.

Guiglelmo de Marcillat (1467–1529)

See ◊Marcillat, Guiglelmo de.

Gustavus Vasa (GUSTAVUS I OR GUSTAF I) (1496–1560)

King of Sweden from 1523, when he was elected after leading the Swedish revolt against Danish rule. He united and pacified the country and established Lutheranism as the state religion.

Gutenberg, Johannes (GENSFLEISCH) (c. 1398–1468)

German printer, the inventor of European printing from movable metal type (although Laurens Janszoon ◊Coster has a rival claim).

Gutenberg began work on the process in the 1440s and in 1450 set up a printing business in Mainz. By 1456 he had produced the first printed Bible (known as the Gutenberg Bible). It is not known what other books he printed.

He punched and engraved a steel character (letter shape) into a piece of copper to form a mould which he filled with molten metal. The letters were in Gothic script and of equal height.

Gutenberg was born in Mainz and set up a printing firm in Strasbourg in the late 1430s, where he may have invented movable type. This business folded, as did the subsequent one in Mainz with Johann Fust (c. 1400–1466) as a backer: Fust seized the press for nonpayment of the loan. Gutenberg is believed to have gone on to set up a third press and print the Mazarin and Bamberg Bibles. In 1462 Mainz was involved in a local feud, and in the upheaval Gutenberg was expelled from the city for five years before being reinstated, offered a pension, and given tax exemption.

Habsburg (HAPSBURG)

European royal family, former imperial house of Austria–Hungary. A Habsburg, Rudolf I, became king of Germany in 1273 and began the family's control of Austria and Styria. They acquired a series of lands and titles, including that of Holy Roman Emperor which they held during 1273–91, 1298–1308, 1438–1740, and 1745–1806. The Habsburgs reached the zenith of their power under the emperor Charles V (1519–1556) who divided his lands, creating an Austrian Habsburg line (which ruled until 1918) and a Spanish line (which ruled to 1700).

The name comes from the family castle in Aargau, Switzerland.

Hacomblene (HACOMPLAYNT), Robert (c. 1456–1528)

English composer. He was scholar of Eton, 1469–72, and of King's College, Cambridge from 1472. He was a fellow at Cambridge, 1475–93, and provost from 1509 until his death. A *Salve Regina* by him is in the Eton Choirbook.

Hakluyt, Richard (c. 1552–1616)

English geographer whose chief work is *The Principal Navigations, Voyages and Discoveries of the English Nation* (1598–1600). He was assisted by Sir Walter Raleigh.

He lectured on cartography at Oxford, became geographical adviser to the East India Company, and was an original member of the Virginia Company.

Hall, Edward (c. 1498–1547)

English lawyer and chronicler who wrote *The Union of the Noble and Illustre Families of Lancaster and York*. It chronicles the success of the ◊Tudor dynasty supposedly bringing the War of the Roses to an end. A first edition appeared in 1542, but the second edition, published posthumously in 1548, is considered the standard version. The book was widely used by other historians, notably Raphael ◊Holinshed, and was also used by Shakespeare as a source for his history plays.

Commonly called *Hall's Chronicle* it was continued after his death by Richard Grafton, but because of its Protestant bias, it was prohibited during the reign of Mary I.

Born in London, Hall was educated at Eton and Cambridge. In 1532 he was appointed common serjeant (a position in the legal system) and from 1533–40 was a reader at Grey's Inn in London. In later years he was a judge of the sheriff's court. He became a member of parliament for Bridgnorth in Shropshire in 1542 and was a commissioner to the inquiry into transgressions against the Six Articles (1539).

halo, OR NIMBUS

Radiance encircling the heads of saints and holy persons in art. It is also called an **aureole**, especially when surrounding the whole figure.

Hampton, John (c. 1455–AFTER 1522)

English composer. He was master of the choristers at Worcester Priory (1484–1522). He is represented in the Eton Choirbook.

Hampton Court Conference

A conference of the Anglican Church held at Hampton Court Palace near London in 1604. Presided over by King James I, its aim was to consider the objections ◊Puritans had raised to certain Anglican rites, ceremonies, and prayers. Few concessions were made to Puritan demands for change, but the Conference did lead to a major new translation of the Bible, the Authorized Version of 1611.

The Puritan demands were embodied in the Millenary Petition of 1603 (so called because it had a thousand supporters in clergy). John Rainolds was the leading spokesman for the Puritans, and the archbishop of Canterbury, Richard Bancroft (1544–1610), led the bishops' side.

THE HABSBURG DYNASTY IN THE FIFTEENTH CENTURY

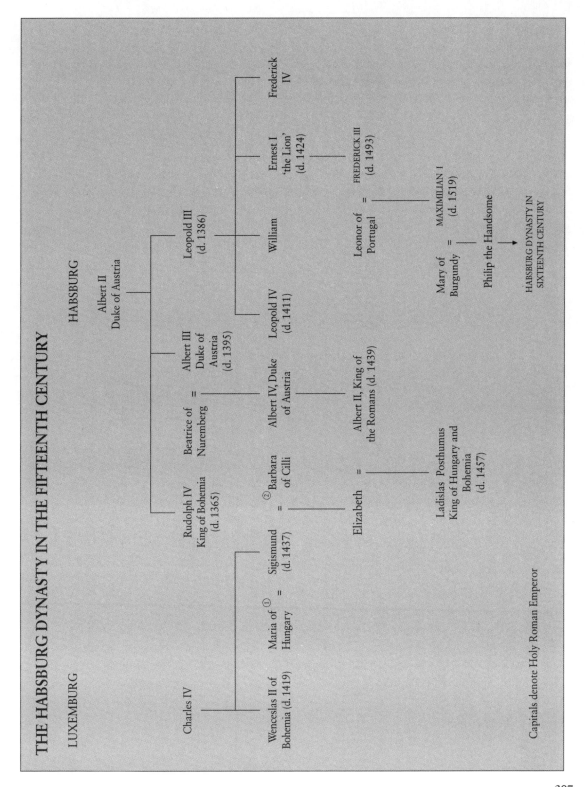

LUXEMBURG

HABSBURG

Albert II
Duke of Austria

Charles IV

Wenceslas II of
Bohemia (d. 1419)

Maria of ① = Sigismund
Hungary   (d. 1437)

Rudolph IV
King of Bohemia
(d. 1365)

Beatrice of = Albert III
Nuremberg   Duke of
                 Austria
                 (d. 1395)

Leopold III
(d. 1386)

② Barbara
= of Cilli

Elizabeth = Albert IV, Duke
              of Austria

Albert IV, Duke
of Austria

Leopold IV
(d. 1411)

Ernest I
'the Lion'
(d. 1424)

William

Frederick
IV

Albert II, King of
the Romans (d. 1439)

Ladislas Posthumus
King of Hungary and
Bohemia
(d. 1457)

Leonor of = FREDERICK III
Portugal   (d. 1493)

Mary of = MAXIMILIAN I
Burgundy   (d. 1519)

Philip the Handsome

→ HABSBURG DYNASTY IN
SIXTEENTH CENTURY

Capitals denote Holy Roman Emperor

THE HABSBURG DYNASTY IN THE SIXTEENTH CENTURY

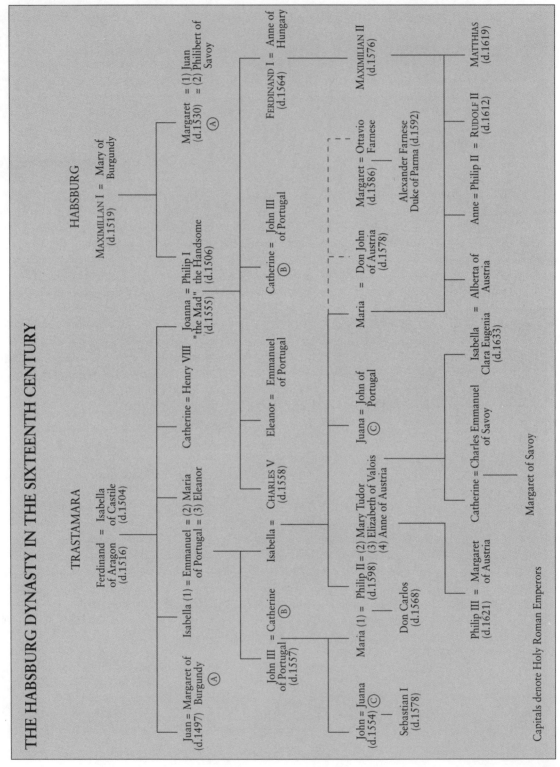

TRASTAMARA

HABSBURG

MAXIMILIAN I = Mary of
(d.1519)   Burgundy

Ferdinand = Isabella
of Aragon   of Castile
(d.1516)   (d.1504)

Margaret = (1) Juan
(d.1530) = (2) Philibert of
Ⓐ   Savoy

Juan = Margaret of
(d.1497) Burgundy
Ⓐ

Isabella (1) = Emmanuel
        = (2) Maria
        = (3) Eleanor

Catherine = Henry VIII

Joanna = Philip I
"the Mad" the Handsome
(d.1555)   (d.1506)

FERDINAND I = Anne of
(d.1564)   Hungary

MAXIMILIAN II
(d.1576)

John III = Catherine
of Portugal Ⓑ
(d.1557)

Isabella =   CHARLES V
             (d.1558)

Eleanor = Emmanuel
          of Portugal

Catherine = John III
Ⓑ   of Portugal

Maria = Don John
        of Austria
        (d.1578)

Margaret = Ottavio
(d.1586)   Farnese

Anne = Philip II = RUDOLF II
                   (d.1612)

MATTHIAS
(d.1619)

John = Juana
(d.1554) Ⓒ

Maria (1) = Philip II = (2) Mary Tudor
(d.1598) (3) Elizabeth of Valois
          (4) Anne of Austria

Juana = John of
Ⓒ   Portugal

Alexander Farnese
Duke of Parma (d.1592)

Isabella = Alberta of
Clara Eugenia Austria
(d.1633)

Sebastian I
(d.1578)

Don Carlos
(d.1568)

Catherine = Charles Emmanuel
            of Savoy

Philip III = Margaret
(d.1621)   of Austria

Margaret of Savoy

Capitals denote Holy Roman Emperors

The bishops rejected the Puritans' demands on theological grounds, and King James decided in favour of the bishops, arguing that the logic of the Puritan position meant 'no bishop, no king'. He did, however, accept Rainolds's suggestion that a new English translation of the Bible should be made, and a strong panel of theologians and scholars was set up to undertake the work.

Handl, Jacob (Jacobus Gallus)(1550–1591)

Slovene composer. He was a prolific composer of church music, and wrote 16 Masses, motets, a Te Deum, and a cycle of music for the liturgical year. He also wrote German songs and other secular works, many of which show the influence of Franco-Flemish composers. Contemporary critics complained about the complexity of his music – his four-volume *Opus Musicum* (1586–91) included two pieces scored for 24 voices.

Handl was born in Ribniča near Ljubljana, and went to Austria in the mid-1560s. He was a singer in the Chapel of Emperor Maximilian II in Vienna (1574–75). He then travelled through Austria, Bohemia, Silesia, and Moravia, and was choirmaster to the Bishop of Olomouc (1579–85). By mid-1586 he was cantor at the Church of St Jan na Brzehu in Prague, where he remained until his death.

Hapsburg

See ◊Habsburg.

Hardyng, John (1378–c. 1465)

English rhyming chronicler. *Hardyng's Chronicle* gives an inaccurate history of England from the earliest times down to his own day, the first edition being Lancastrian in tone, the second Yorkist.

Harington, John (1561–1612)

English writer and translator. He translated Ludovico ◊Ariosto's *Orlando furioso* (1591) and was the author of *The Metamorphosis of Ajax* (1596), a ribald history of the privy ('jakes'). Elizabeth I of England reputedly referred to him as 'that saucy poet, my godson'; she banished him from court on several occasions.

Harington was born at Kelston Park near Bath and educated at Cambridge. He became a courtier of Queen Elizabeth I and in 1599 he served in Ireland under the Earl of Essex, by whom he was knighted on the field. He was appointed tutor to Prince Henry by James I, with whom he had ingratiated himself by his *Tract on the Succession to the Crown* (1602). His collected *Epigrams* were published in 1613.

Harvey, Gabriel (c. 1545–1630)

English poet and critic. His views on literature led him to attack the dramatist Robert Greene in *Four Letters and Certain Sonnets* (1592), and to conduct an acrimonious controversy with dramatist and satirist Thomas Nashe, to which he contributed *Four Letters* (1592) and *Pierce's Supererogation* (1593). He was a lifelong friend of the poet Edmund Spenser.

He was born at Saffron Walden, Essex, and educated at Christ's College, Cambridge.

Harvey, William (1578–1657)

English physician who discovered the circulation of blood. In 1628 he published his book *De Motu Cordis/On the Motion of the Heart and the Blood in Animals*. He also explored the development of chick and deer embryos.

Harvey's discovery marked the beginning of the end of medicine as taught by ◊Galen, which had been accepted for 1,400 years.

Harvey was born in Folkestone, Kent, and studied at Cambridge and at Padua, Italy, under Geronimo ◊Fabricius. He worked at St Bartholomew's Hospital, London, and served as a professor there from 1615–43. From 1618 he was court physician to James I and later to Charles I.

Examining the heart and blood vessels of mammals, Harvey deduced that the blood in the veins must flow only towards the heart. He also calculated the amount of blood that left the heart at each beat, and realized that the same blood must be circulating continuously around the body. He reasoned that it passes from the right side of the heart to the left through the lungs (pulmonary circulation).

Harvey also published *Exercitationes de Generatione Animalium/Anatomical Exercitations Concerning the Generation of Living Creatures* in 1651.

Hassler, Hans Leo (1564–1612)

German organist and composer. He wrote considerable quantities of church music in Latin and German, in addition to many secular songs in German and Italian, and other pieces. He was one of the first Germans to study in Italy, and the polychoral techniques and rich sonorities of his Masses and motets show the influence of the Venetians.

Hassler was born in Nuremberg and was taught by his father, Isaac Hassler (*c.* 1530–1591), who was himself an organist. After an appointment at Nuremberg he was sent to Venice for further study under Andrea Gabrieli. He was organist to Octavian Fugger at Augsburg (1585–1600); he published many works there and established a wide reputation. Having returned to Nuremberg as organist of the Church of Our Lady, he married and went to live at Ulm in 1604, but soon went into the service of the Emperor Rudolf in Prague. In 1608 he became organist to Christian II, the Elector of Saxony at Dresden, but suffered from tuberculosis and died during a visit with the Elector to Frankfurt.

Although Hassler was a Protestant, his early works are all for the Catholic Church. His German church music is somewhat conservative, and though it often uses Lutheran melodies, it shows the influence of Roland de Lassus. He was famous for his Italian madrigals and canzonettes, and German songs were widely known: the tune of his love song, 'Mein G'müt ist mir verwirret' (1601), was used for the Lutheran hymn, 'O Haupt voll Blut und Wunden' which features in Bach's St Matthew Passion.

Works include:

Masses, Magnificats, hymn tunes, motets (including two collections *Sacrae Cantiones* and *Sacri Concentus*), fugal psalms, and Christian songs; Italian canzonets for four voices, Italian and German madrigals, *Lustgarten neuer Teutscher Gesäng* (32 German songs for four to eight voices, 1601); ricercari, toccatas, and other pieces for organ.

hatching

In art, lines parallel or crossed (cross-hatching) by which tone or shadow is created. It is also found in the form of brushwork used in tempera painting and fresco to convey a depth or gradation of tone otherwise difficult to obtain in these media.

Hatton, Sir Christopher (1540–1591)

Lord Chancellor (1587–91) and favourite of Queen Elizabeth I of England. He first came to the queen's attention with his dancing and became an influential and conservative courtier. As a Privy Councillor from 1577, he acted as a government spokesman in the Commons and in Council supported the Earl of Leicester's hardline anti-Spanish foreign policy. He took a conservative line on the religious status quo, playing a leading part in the trials of Catholic conspirators and Mary Queen of Scots in 1586, and as Lord Chancellor, working hard to suppress extreme Puritans and religious separatists.

Haughton, William (*c.* 1575–1605)

English dramatist. He collaborated with Henry ◊Chettle and Thomas ◊Dekker on many plays, but was sole author of the popular comedy *Englishmen for my Money* about 1598, and possibly of *Grim the Collier of Croyden* about 1600. He is also supposed to have written part of *The Pleasant Comodie of Patient Grissill* (1603).

Hawes, Stephen (*c.* 1475–*c.* 1523)

English poet. His principal works are two long moral allegories, *The Example of Virtue* (1504) and *The Pastime of Pleasure* (1509) written in the tradition of John ◊Lydgate.

Hawes was probably born in Suffolk. He was educated at Oxford and travelled in Europe afterwards. He was attached to the court of Henry VII, gaining entry by his knowledge of English poetry and literature.

Hayne van Ghizeghem (*c.* 1445–BETWEEN 1472 AND 1497)

Franco-Flemish composer. His life is documented only for the years 1457–72, which he spent at the court of Burgundy. His entire surviving output is of French chansons, several of which were among the most successful of their age, including 'De tous biens plaine', 'Allez regretz', and 'Amours, amours'.

Hebreo, Leone (EBREO) (?1460–1521)

Lisbon-born Jewish physician and author. The son of Jehuda ◊Abravanel, he led the same peripatetic

PICTURE GALLERY
AND
PLATE SECTION

Detail from the Sistine Chapel ceiling by Michelangelo Buonarroti. *The Bridgeman Art Library*

PICTURE GALLERY

Every art gallery has a partial collection, reflecting the foibles of its original collectors or revealing the rationale of its acquisition policy. The images that follow are similar: they are not intended to provide a whistle-stop tour through all that is 'best' in Renaissance art – the criteria to decide such questions change from generation to generation, if not from individual to individual. Instead, this exhibition is meant to provide some sense of themes that recur in Renaissance art. The attempt is to suggest how art was defined and used by its Renaissance producers, viewers, and collectors.

A Wealth of Belongings [plates I–IV]

The usual focus of discussions of Renaissance art is on the large scale, on paintings, sculpture, and architecture. However, a highly prized element of any collector's belongings involved what might too often be dismissed as 'decorative arts.' These might be part of the decoration of a room – tiles (or azulejos (see feature)), for example, or tapestries – or they might be movable objects, like Oriental carpets or glass products (see feature). Arguably, the increased availability of an increased range of objects, along with the increased desire to have and to hold these things, created one of the most significant developments of the 15th and 16th centuries – that is, an eclectic and conspicuous material culture.

The images presented here are intended to suggest some of the colourful objects which might inhabit a cultured, and rich, household. The vogue for majolica dishes depicting figures or a narrative (*istoriato*) [plate I] was a particular Renaissance phenomenon. Originally having imported glazed earthenware from, for example, Majorca (thus the name majolica), Italian towns came to imitate and to develop this art form. Italian majolica was already being produced in the 14th century but, in the late 15th and early 16th centuries, it became something of an industry centred on previously small towns like Faenza; the earthenware was exported not only across Christendom but outside Europe to, for example, Egypt. The images represented on *istoriato* majolica could reflect the fashions of 'high art' with the pictures imitating recent paintings or engravings (a workshop in Gubbio, for example, produced an image of Hercules strikingly similar to one painted by Antonio Pollaiuolo (now in the Ashmolean Museum, Oxford)), or more generally suggesting classical interests, like the scene from the tale of Jason and the Argonauts painted on the dish presented here. On the other hand, the images on both majolica and enamel dishes were often simpler, with a pattern surrounding a central lunette of a portrait image [plate II].

Tuscan Traditions of Art [plates V–VI]

When, in the first decades of the 15th century, Filippo ◊Brunelleschi and ◊Massacio experimented with perspective and classicising architecture, they found an artistic companion to the literary interests of their fellow Florentines, Niccolò Niccoli and Leonardo Bruni. The activities of this handful of characters could, with exaggeration, be taken as the starting point of the 'Renaissance.' In art, however, as in scholarship, there were local traditions, stretching back over a century, which foreshadowed the events of the early quattrocento.

The position of ◊Giotto in the pantheon of Renaissance artists was assured by Giorgio Vasari's construction of a Florence-centred history of art (see feature). Along with Cimabue, Giotto was depicted in the *Lives of the Artists* as the artist who had first 'revived' the classical skill at painting. There is an irony to the premier position given to Giotto: much of his most celebrated work was undertaken outside his home city, in particular at the ◊Arena Chapel in Padua. The artists who, at about the same time, were working in Florence actually included one from Florence's neighbour and rival, Siena. Vasari did not overlook this painter, Simone ◊Martini, all together in his *Lives,* although he congratulates Martini most of all for his good fortune in being the contemporary and friend of that Florentine scholar, ◊Petrarch.

What is not clear from Vasari, however, is that there was not one but two traditions of painting in Tuscany in the trecento, one centred on Florence, the other on Siena. Sienese art, in particular, had a strong civic element, with ◊Duccio and Ambrogio ◊Lorenzetti – like Simone Martini – being given important commissions for the cathedral and Palazzo Publico. The Florentine tradition, as exemplified by Giotto, was crucially concerned to break away from the rich Byzantine style of art. So, in the fresco of *The Meeting at the Golden Gate* [plate VI], despite the number of figures included, there is a sense of space, even sparseness; at the same time, there is an attempt to create the impression of depth and of the three dimensional. The focus of the painting is on the gesture of the kiss; the men and women are depicted with an unusual attention to the their features and to the curves of their drapery. There is, though, something sculptural in these figures; in contrast, Simone Martini's *Jesus in the Temple* [plate V] shows a greater delicacy. The gold background reflects the continuing influence of Byzantine styles in Sienese art, but, like Giotto, Martini is particularly concerned to express emotions through gestures. The hand gestures of Jesus' parents, who had wondered where their son was, only to find him precociously debating with the Elders in the Temple, suggest their worry and annoyance. And the Christ Child, with his crossed arms, appears the epitome of a petulant teenager.

Retelling the Tale (1): The Annunciation [plates VII–X]

The Annunciation – when the angel Gabriel informs the Virgin Mary that she will miraculously give birth to the Son of God – was one of the most popular of ◊Bible stories depicted in art. Its basic elements were constant: the angel on the left, the virgin reading on the right, with often a lily present to symbolise purity. Ingenuity lay not so much in the choice of subject matter, but in the expression of this well-known story.

One artist could be called upon to produce more than one image of the Annunciation during their career – Fra ◊Angelico, for example, painted at least four for various monasteries of his own Dominican order. In some of these, like that for S. Domenico, Cortona [plate VII], the central image was, as it were, placed in context, not only by the introduction of classicising architecture, but also by the presentation of other narratives. So, in the background at the left, Adam and Eve are shown being ejected from the Garden of Eden – it was their original sin and its consequences from which Mary's son, Jesus, would save mankind; this altarpiece also gives an example of a ◊predella narrating the life of the patron saint. Contrast this busy painting with the pared-down image Fra Angelico painted for one of the cells of the monastery of San Marco in Florence (rebuilt with the money of Cosimo de' ◊Medici): not only is the archi-

tectural backdrop much simpler, but the painting concentrates on the two central figures [plate VIII]. Yet, at the same time, they are not alone: they are observed by a figure who, by his white habit and black cloak is recognizably a Dominican monk, and by the blood running from his head is identifiable as Peter Martyr, a Dominican saint who had been hacked to death.

If these two paintings show how one artist can adopt different styles, the depictions by Lorenzo di ◊Credi and ◊Leonardo suggest how fashions in Florentine art had changed by the late 15th century. Credi's painting [plate IX], in particular, displays a preoccupation with the posture of the characters and the technique of ◊*contrapposto;* the backdrop shows an increased concern to depict classicising architecture and the landscape in harmonious symmetry. Leonardo da Vinci was Lorenzo di Credi's fellow-pupil at ◊Verrocchio's workshop; his subdued image, however, reflects his own idiosyncratic approach to the latest fashions [plate X]. Unusually, the Annunciation is placed *al fresco,* with classicising elements confined to Mary's ornamental bookrest and with symmetry consciously ignored. The intent remains, however, to provide a fresh and affecting image of the central mystery of Christianity.

Jerome: Scholar and Hermit [plates XI–XII]

Christian tradition did not provide only Bible stories to be art subjects. The range of saints provided useful material for religious art. What is more, they could — like the tales of Roman heroes — provide morally uplifting examples. Indeed, of the ancient figures thought worthy of emulation, one of the most popular was the Church Father, St Jerome. He could, however, be imitated in two contrasting ways.

Jerome (c. 342–420) was educated in Rome but spent some years as a hermit in Syria. He eventually settled in Bethlehem where he established a monastic community; there he produced his voluminous writings – letters, polemics, sermons and, of immeasurable importance, the Latin translation of the Bible, the Vulgate. For a later translator of the New Testament, ◊Erasmus, Jerome was a role model: Erasmus wrote a *Life of Jerome* and portraits of the Dutchman even mimic the iconography of the Doctor of the Church. Erasmus' emulation may be extreme but it was only part of a wider vogue. The scholar Jerome was a popular artistic subject, being depicted, for example, by Domenico ◊Ghirlandaio [plate XI].

Ghirlandaio's fresco was commissioned in 1480 alongside another of St Augustine by Sandro ◊Botticelli for the Chiesa degli Ognissanti, Florence. Ghirlandaio depicts in detail the saint's contemporary-looking *studiolo,* with its desk covered by a fashionable oriental carpet and with the lectern flanked by glasses, scissors and inkwells. The strips of paper hanging from the shelves, with their writing in Hebrew and Greek, symbolize Jerome's translating activities; his cardinal's hat also rests, between a leather-bound book and china vases, on the top shelf.

Unusually, however, there is no sign in Ghirlandaio's work of the saint's symbolic animal. Legend told of a lion wandering into Jerome's monastery with a thorn in its paw; his colleagues fled but the saint nursed the lion, removing the thorn and winning the lion's devotion. Paintings of Jerome in his study, like that of ◊Antonello da Messina, often include a lion as his emblem; it also appears in Marco Meloni's (*fl.*1504-37) painting of Jerome in the desert [plate XII]. This was the other popular image of the saint: the hermit contemplating Christ on the cross and beating his chest in penitence. Jerome himself explained that his penitence began after a dream in which he imagined a heavenly tribunal punishing him for his enthusiasm for pagan writings – a tale which might seem to make him a problematic role-model for humanists. But, as Lorenzo ◊Valla and Eramsus explained, the lesson of penitent Jerome was not to reject *studia humanitatis,* merely to avoid excessive interest in such studies to the exclusion of sincere Christian devotion.

Patrons and Collectors [plates XIII–XVI]

Crucial to the cultural activities of the Renaissance was the ability of scholars and artists to convince the rich that their money was well spent on patronage and collecting. These were two related processes: on the one hand, a prince was urged to encourage cultural achievements and, on the other, he was supposed to demonstrate his recognition of their quality. The wealthy and powerful allowed themselves to be convinced of the need to be magnificent for several reasons.

Aeneas Sylvius Piccolomini is hardly a typical case. An accomplished humanist scholar in his own right, when he was elected pope and (with wordplay on Virgil's hero 'pious Aeneas') took the name ◊Pius II, he had the resources to execute a project more lavish than most patrons could afford: rebuilding the village of his birth as a city named after himself, Pienza. Merchants like the Rucellai in Florence could call on Leon Battista ◊Alberti to construct a classical-style palace, architects like ◊Filarete could dream of building an ideal city for the Sforza of Milan, but Pius was able to oversee an attempt to make a vision of a Renaissance city a reality. With other patrons, their claim to be personally involved in a project might be rhetoric created by their clients, but Pius II did discuss in detail with his architect, Bernardo ◊Rossellino, the plans to construct the central piazza, with its cathedral carrying prominently Pius' coat of arms [plate XIII].

Patronage could also glorify one's relatives: after his death, Aneas Sylvius became a source of pride for the Piccolomini family. His nephew, Francesco (who himself was elected – albeit briefly – pope, remembering his uncle by taking the name Pius III) commissioned from ◊Pinturricho a series of frescoes for the Piccolomini library in Siena cathedral which narrated the eventful career of Pius II. One of these, for example, pictures a surprisingly healthy pontiff (considering the scene commemorated occurred just before Pius II's death) at Ancona preparing for a crusade against the Ottomans [plate XIV].

A different type of character and of patron is presented by Philip II, king of Spain a century after Pius II had been pope. Like many patrons, Philip's most ostentatious projects were architectural, designed most often by Juan de ◊Herrera; they included Philip's austere palace, El ◊Escorial near Madrid, and the classical-fronted monastery of São Vicente de Fora in Lisbon, rebuilt as a manifestation of Philip's authority as king of Portugal from 1580.

Philip's court also attracted artists, including El ◊Greco. Philip himself appears (bottom right, in black) in the 1578 *Adoration of the Name of Jesus,* where the Catholic rulers of Europe kneel in (somewhat wishful) harmony before the symbol 'IHS' – the Greek first letters of 'Jesus' [plate XV]. Despite this painting, El Greco, like other artists, found Philip a difficult patron to please – indeed, the king often seemed to prefer dead painters. In particular, the more bizarre works of El Bosco (that is, Hieronymus ◊Bosch) proved to Philip's taste. His collection included *The Garden of Earthly Delights* and three copies of the *Temptations of St. Antony,* although probably not the one presented here [plate XVI]. This copy is testimony to Bosch's Iberian popularity before Philip's reign: it may have been bought by Damião de ◊Go, like other artists, found Philip a d

The Female as Artist and Art-Subject [plates XVII–XX]

Philip II's court was not only home to the works of the likes of Bosch or El Greco; it also provided an audience for the productions of women artists. Philip employed Sofonisba ◊Anguissola, for example, as a lady-in-waiting to his wife; she was also a painter in her own right. She specialized in portraits, like *The Game of Chess,* in which she depicted her sisters [plate XVIII]. The picture may be fanciful but its image of elegantly-dressed girls, pursuing a cultured pastime on a table covered with a fashionable oriental rug, suggests the comfortable lifestyle which Anguissola and her siblings enjoyed. For her, painting was not a profession but, like chess, a courtly accomplishment – and one that few of her male colleagues mastered with such success.

Anguissola was a phenomenon at the Spanish court but other courts could boast of similarly gifted women: in England, for example, Levina ◊Teerlinc was a miniaturist before the days of Nicholas ◊Hilliard; an English girl, Elizabeth ◊Weston, was skilled in a more literary way, impressing the Prague court of ◊Rudolf II with her Latin poems. These women, indeed, made something of a living out of their abilities but not quite to the extent of Lavinia ◊Fontana. Like Teerlinc, Fontana was the daughter of an artist from whom she learnt her trade. In contrast to other female artists, she did

not produce just portraits; instead, she received commissions for religious paintings. Her *Holy Family with Sleeping Christ Child* [plate XVII], for example, was produced for Philip II himself.

Women, then, could act as the producers of art, just as some could – as in the case of Isabella d'◊Este – be its patron. Yet, overwhelmingly, the position of the female was the subject of art, whether it be in portraits, in religious pieces or in more secular images, like those of Lucretia discussed below. The naked female form became a subject of art, though it was surely not given the anatomical attention devoted to the male body. There is something coy in Albrecht ◊Dürer's representation of a small-breasted Eve, with a bunch of leaves covering her pudenda, even before she has had a chance to bite from the apple of knowledge and learn of her nudity [plate XIX]. If, though, we see in this a fascination with fleshy curves of her body which also appears in the art, say, of ◊Giorgione, nudity could be made ugly, as Matthias ◊Grünewald's *Dead Lovers* graphically shows [plate XX]. The emaciated, wrinkled figures are grotesquely gnawed by insects and reptiles to emphasise a lesson as well known in the Renaissance as at any other moment: remember, you shall die.

Retelling the Tale (2): The Rape of Lucretia [plates XXI–XXIII]

Renaissance art was by no means characterized by the victory of the profane over the sacred: the enduring popularity of images of the Annunciation is enough to demonstrate that. At the same time, the reportoire of artists was complemented by a store of classical tales, sometimes employed alongside Christian symbolism (as in Raphael's frescoes for the Vatican Stanze), sometimes used on their own to provide a moral message. The tale of Lucretia was an example of the latter.

Lucretia was hardly a recherché figure, her story available in the ancient historian Livy and often repeated. Lucretia was the wife of a Roman patrician, known for her modest virtue, who lived in the reign of Rome's seventh king, Tarquin the Proud. Tarquin's son, Sextus, was determined to prove that even the most faithful would succumb to his charms: when she did not, he had her by force. On the return of her husband and his friend, Marcus Brutus, Lucretia revealed what had happened and killed herself before their eyes. Sextus' rape became the cause for Brutus to raise a revolt, expelling the kings and establishing the Roman Republic.

Lucretia's tale could teach several lessons: it told women of the virtue of modesty, it warned men of the dangers of tyranny. In literature, it was retold by Coluccio ◊Salutati and by William ◊Shakespeare. In art, it was depicted in various media, from *cassone* panels to bronze reliefs, as well as being chosen as a subject by succeeding generations of artists.

The pictures show how three 16th century artists presented this well-known tale. ◊Parmigian-ino chooses the most typical depiction by portraying Lucretia at the moment of her suicide [plate XXI]. But, despite her open mouth and raised eyes, the emphasis is not on her agony but on her beauty: half-dressed in antique clothes, Parmigianino uses his characteristic techniques, like the elongated neck, to heighten her sensuality. In contrast to the near-serenity of this picture, vigour and violence are the keynotes of ◊Palma il Giovane's depiction of the moment of rape [plate XXII]. The drama is expressed not only by the positioning of the figures, with, at the centre, the taut muscles of Sextus' virile forearm, but by Palma's command of ◊chiaroscuro.

Most unusual, however, is the early 16th century painting of Ambrosius Benson, whose career reflects the international nature of Renaissance art: born in Italy, a naturalized citizen of Bruges, his paintings often found a market in Spain. His modern-dress, even domestic *Lucretia* is a narrative painting, combining the rape (in the background) and the suicide [plate XXIII]. There is not here the same interest in effects of lighting or in anatomy, but, as with Parmigianino, there is a sensuality to the dying Lucretia, achieved by the diaphonous cloth which does not so much cover as reveal her torso. As with the other paintings, little is left to the imagination; but, as with all, the viewer is left to recall the conventional moral.

Church as 'Art Gallery': Santa Maria Novella, Florence [plates XXIV–XXVII]

Individual princes or nobles might be magnificent patrons of art, but the most consistent venues for artistic production were ecclesiastical establishments. The work might not always be paid for by the Church or monastic order – individuals could vie for the honour of embellishing the House of God – but the result was that churches could become like living art galleries. The *locus classicus* of this process of cultural enrichment is Santa Maria Novella in the heart of Florence.

Nowadays, the church announces itself with its marble façade [plate XXIV] the upper part of which was designed by Leon Battista Alberti and paid for by Giovanni ◊Rucellai – the patron is recorded in the inscription running just beneath the sun-lunette at the top of the façade. This, though, was only completed in 1470; the inside of the church had already provided the setting for artistic commissions. Like San Marco, where Fra Angelico was to paint his frescoes (including *The Annunciation* [plate VIII]), Santa Maria Novella was a Dominican convent. In a chapel off the cloisters to the north of the church, Andrea di Bonaiuto produced a set of frescoes in *c*.1365; these celebrate the achievements of the Dominican Order, including the intellectual *Triumph of St. Thomas Aquinas* [plate XXVI].

Aquinas, whose formulations of doctrine and Aristotelian learning were the source of scholastic teachings, was to remain a revered figure to the humanists of the 15th and 16th centuries.

In the church itself, a small-scale commission resulted in a work of immeasurable artistic influence: Masaccio's *The Trinity* [plate XXV], painted between 1425 and his early death in 1428. The fresco depicts God the Father holding the crucified Jesus Christ above whose head hovers a dove, symbolising the Holy Spirit. The Trinity are watched not only by the Virgin and John the Evangelist but also by the donors, an elderly Florentine merchant named Lenzi and his wife. What, however, makes the fresco so striking is both the precociously classical architecture depicted and the unprecedented command of vanishing-point perspective seen in the receding arched ceiling. If any one work presents a programme of artistic reform for early quattrocento Florence, this is it.

Masaccio's fresco stands isolated in the north aisle of the church but, later in the century, there was a spate of redecoration in other parts of Santa Maria Novella. The chapel patronized by Florentine patrician Filippo Strozzi, for example, received garish frescoes by Filippino Lippi; the most prized area, the sanctuary behind the high altar, was painted in the early 1480s by Domenico Ghirlandaio, at the expense of another rich merchant, Giovanni Tornabuoni. These frescoes depict the lives of the Virgin Mary and John the Baptist, including *Herod's Feast* [plate XXVII]. Ghirlandaio's Biblical figures are said to be portraits of his Florentine contemporaries; in the architectural construction of this fresco, there is a clear debt to the tradition of classicising art that was given impetus by Masaccio's short career.

Classical Inspiration [plates XXVIII–XXIX]

Some of the classical tales which artists from the late 15th century chose to represent were not as familiar, or as straightforward, as that of Lucretia. Increasingly, there was an interest in the more intricate and allegorical, sometimes to the point of making modern positive identification of a painting's subject problematic.

One of the more popular of these new tales was that of the Calumny of Apelles. The ancient Greek writer, Lucian, whose short, often ironic, works themselves enjoyed a vogue in the 15th and early 16th centuries, told a story about the pre-eminent Greek artist, ◊Apelles. At one point in his career, Apelles was traduced to Alexander; in response, not only did Apelles prove his innocence but he got his revenge on his accuser by producing a painting which provided an allegory of calumny, including figures like rumour and envy. Lucian gave a detailed description of this painting which became the best-known example of ◊ekphrasis. Several artists gave themselves the task of emulating Apelles and recreating his painting; among these artists was Sandro Botticelli [plate XXVIII]. His work does not simply depict all that Lucian had written; it also places it into a classicizing setting, complete with statues like those which had recently been placed in the alcoves around the Florentine Or Sanmichele (by, for example, ◊Donatello). Moreover, the frieze running round the top and bottom of the walls included imagined classical scenes: most significant is that at the bottom right which is itself a depiction of *The Centaur Family* by the other well-known ancient artist, ◊Zeuxis, based on another ekphrasis by Lucian.

In this case, Botticelli's source and intent is transparent but in other cases, like the over-famous *Primavera*, the image is mysterious enough to engender unending debate. Similarly, the work of ◊Piero di Cosimo has proved difficult to interpret – which is perhaps fitting for a character who appears in Vasari's description as bizarre, if not downright mad. His *Forest Fire*, with its apparently whimisical depiction of animals with human faces [plate XXIX], is one of a series of paintings with a similar theme. It would appear that the source for all of them is the narrative of evolution given in De Rerum Natura by the ancient Roman author, ◊Lucretius – a writer who, despite being incompatible with Christianity, enjoyed some popularity in the Medicean circle of late fifteenth century Florence. Presumably this source was recognisable in Piero di Cosimo's works to those in that rarefied circle, but it is legitimate to wonder how many of even his contemporary viewers fully appreciated the allegory. That is to say, that if one looks at such a picture and is confused or uncertain about its meaning, one might well be recreating a Renaissance way of seeing.

Plate I: Majolica dish (Christie's, London). *e.t. archive*

Plate II: Venetian enamelled dark-amethyst two-handled flask (Christie's, London). *Christie's Images*

Plate III: Reliquary coffer in gold and mother-of-pearl (Diocesan Museum, Mantua). *e.t. archive*

Plate IV: Venetian enamel dish, *c.* 1500 (Christie's, London). *Christie's Images*

Plate V: Simone Martini, *Jesus in the Temple*, 1342 (Walker Art Gallery, Liverpool). *AKG London*

Plate VI: Giotto, *The Meeting at the Golden Gate, c.* 1305 (Cappella degli Scrovegni, Padua). *The Bridgeman Art Library*

Plate VII:
Fra Angelico, *The Annunciation*, *c.* 1432 (Museo Diocesano, Cortona). *e.t. archive*

Plate VIII:
Fra Angelico, *The Annunciation with St. Peter Martyr* (San Marco, Florence). *AKG London/Orsi Battaglini*

Plate IX:
Lorenzo di Credi, *The Annunciation* (Uffizi, Florence). *e.t. archive*

Plate X:
Leonardo da Vinci, *The Annunciation*, (Uffizi, Florence). *AKG London/Erich Lessing*

Plate XII: Anon. (attrib. Marco Meloni), *St Jerome in Penitence* (Galleria e Museo Estense, Modena). *The Bridgeman Art Library*

Plate XI: Domenico Ghirlandaio, *St Jerome in his Study*, 1480 (Chiesa degli Ognissanti, Florence). *The Bridgeman Art Library*

Plate XIII:
Bernardo Rossellino,
Pienza Cathedral,
1459-62. *The Bridgeman
Art Library*

Plate XIV:
Bernardino Pinturicchio,
Pius II at Ancona, 1502-5
(Piccolomini Library,
Siena Cathedral). *AKG
London/Erich Lessing*

Plate XV: El Greco, *Adoration of the Name of Jesus*, 1578 (El Escorial). *The Bridgeman Art Library*

Plate XVI: Hieronymus Bosch, *The Temptation of St Antony* (Museu National de Arte Antiga, Lisbon). *The Bridgeman Art Library*

Plate XVII:
Lavinia Fontana, *The Holy Family* (Gemäldegalerie, Dresden). *AKG London*

Plate XVIII:
Sofonisba Anguissola, *The Game of Chess*, 1555 (Muzeum Narodowe, Poznán, Poland). *AKG London/Erich Lessing*

Plate XX: Matthias Grünewald, *The Dead Lovers*
(Musée de l'Oeuvre de Notre Dame,
Strasbourg). *The Bridgeman Art Library*

Plate XIX: Albrecht Dürer, *Eve*, 1507
(Prado, Madrid). *e.t. archive*

Plate XXI:
Parmigianino,
Lucretia, c. 1540
(Galleria Nazionale
di Capodimonte,
Naples). *AKG London*

Plate XXII:
Palma il Giovane, *The Rape of Lucretia, c.*
1570 (Staatliche
Kunstsammlungen,
Kassel). *AKG London*

Plate XXIII: Ambrosius Benson, *Lucretia* (Phillips Auctioneers, London). *The Bridgeman Art Library*

Plate XXIV: Leon Battista Alberti, façade to Santa Maria Novella, Florence. *AKG London/Erich Lessing*

Plate XXV: Masaccio, *The Trinity*, 1428 (Santa Maria Novella, Florence). *The Bridgeman Art Library*

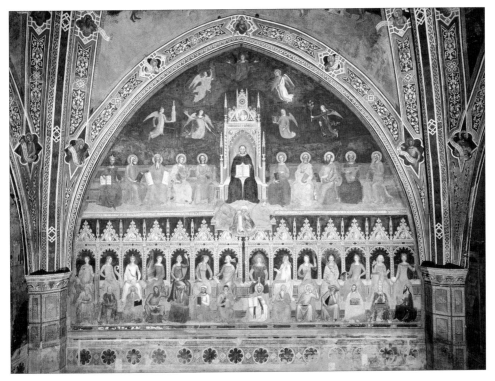

Plate XXVI: Andrea di Bonaiuto, *Triumph of Thomas Aquinas*, *c.* 1380 (Santa Maria Novella, Florence). *AKG London*

Plate XXVII: Domenico Ghirlandaio, *Herod's Feast*, 1478 (Santa Maria Novella, Florence). *AKG London*

Plate XXVIII: Sandro Botticelli, *The Calumny of Apelles, c.* 1495 (Uffizi, Florence). *e.t. archive*

Plate XXIX: Piero di Cosimo, *The Forest Fire* (Ashmolean Museum, Oxford). *The Bridgeman Art Library*

existence as his father, with whom he eventually settled at Venice. His *Dialoghi di amore/Dialogues on Love* (Rome, 1535) argued that love was the source of universal life: an argument which influenced many 16th-century writers including ◊Cervantes (who transcribed passages into his ◊pastoral novel *La Galatea*) and ◊Camões. The *Dialoghi* were first translated into Castilian in 1568 and subsequently retranslated by ◊Garcilaso 'el Inca' (and banned by the Inquisition) in 1590.

Heemskerk, Maerten Jacobsz (MAERTEN VAN VEEN) van (1498–1574)

Dutch painter. Strongly influenced by Italian art of the early 16th century, he painted portraits and religious subjects such as *St Luke Painting the Likeness of the Virgin and Child* (Frans Hals Museum, Haarlem). The drawings of Classical art that he did in Rome (1532–36) are important documents of the state of Roman monuments at the time.

He was born in Heemskerk, north Holland, and studied in Haarlem with Cornelisz., Willemz, and Jan Scorel. He absorbed Italian influence both indirectly through the imitation of Jan ◊Mabuse and later directly by study of Renaissance artists on his visit to Rome. He was particularly impressed by the art of Michelangelo and by ancient Roman statues. When he returned to the Netherlands, the influence of ◊Michelangelo was apparent in his huge pictures with muscle-bound figures in violent movement, although his later style became gentler and more subtle.

His *Self-portrait* (1533, Fitzwilliam Museum, Cambridge) has the Colosseum in Rome as its background. Other works are *Crucifixion* (Ghent), *Judgement of Momus* (Berlin), and *Triumph of Silenus* (Vienna).

Heere, Lucas de (1534–1584)

Flemish painter and designer. Born in Ghent, de Heere was taught by Frans Floris and he, in turn, taught Carel van ◊Mander in the late 1560s. He worked in France and England as well as Ghent. Among his best-known paintings is *Solomon and the Queen of Sheba* (1559) in St Bavo's Cathedral in Ghent.

Also attributed to him is the design of the Valois tapestries in 1582 (Uffizi, Florence), woven in Flanders to celebrate the arrival there of the soon-to-be-discredited Francis, Duke of (Alençon-)Anjou, in his role of 'defender of the liberties of the Netherlands'.

Hegius (VON HEEK), Alexander (c. 1433–1498)

German humanist and educator. He was born at Heek, Westphalia, and was a pupil of both Thomas à Kempis and Rudolphus Agricola. His school in Deventer in the Netherlands, which he opened in 1474, played an important role in the development of humanism in northern Europe, its pupils including ◊Erasmus and the future ◊Adrian VI. In his teaching he stressed the importance of reading original Classical sources rather than medieval commentaries on them.

Hegius produced a number of works that were published posthumously, but his real importance rests more on his teaching methods and his rejection of the formalism of medieval scholastic education. Although he stressed the importance of Greek, his knowledge of the language was considerably inferior to his grasp of Latin.

Heidelberg Catechism

A Protestant confession of faith, drawn up in 1562. It was written by the theologians Kaspar Olevianus and Zacharias Ursinus at the request of the Elector Frederick III. It maintained the doctrines of ◊Calvin and ◊Bullinger, but expressed moderately so as to conciliate the Lutherans. It was accepted by the annual synod of the Palatinate in 1563 and at the Synod of ◊Dort in 1619. It was translated into English in 1572.

Heintz, Joseph (1564–1609)

Swiss painter and draughtsman. He trained in Basle, Switzerland, and finished his artistic education in Italy – in Rome about 1584–87 and Venice 1587–91. He was called to the court of the Holy Roman Emperor Rudolf II in 1591 where he acted as artist and artistic adviser, being sent abroad on several missions. His works include both religious and erotic paintings, for example *Venus and Adonis*, as well as royal portraits.

Helvetic Confessions

Two confessions of faith (1536, 1562), drawn up by the Reformed Church in Switzerland. The First Helvetic Confession was compiled by ◊Bullinger, Myconius, and others. It is sometimes referred to as the second Confession of Basel. The Second Helvetic Confession was written by Bullinger, and a revised version was published in 1566 as the official creed of the Swiss cantons. By 1578 it had been adopted by several reformed churches.

Heminge (HEMMINGS), John (1556–1630)

English actor. He was a member of Richard ◊Burbage's company and later his business manager. He held several shares in the Globe and Blackfriars playhouses. He and his fellow actor John Condell (died 1627) were responsible for printing many of Shakespeare's plays in the first published edition of any of his works, known as the First Folio, 1623.

Hemmel, Sigmund (DIED 1564)

German composer. He composed the first complete polyphonic metrical psalter in Germany (published at Tübingen in 1569). He also wrote German and Latin sacred songs, and a Mass.

Henry IV (HENRY BOLINGBROKE) (1367–1413)

King of England from 1399, the son of John of Gaunt. In 1398 he was banished by Richard II but returned 1399 to head a revolt and be accepted as king by Parliament. He was succeeded by his son Henry V.

He had difficulty in keeping the support of Parliament and the clergy, and had to deal with baronial unrest and Owen Glendower's rising in Wales. In order to win support he had to conciliate the Church by a law for the burning of heretics, and to make many concessions to Parliament.

Henry V (1387–1422)

King of England from 1413, son of Henry IV. His reign was dominated by his determination to reopen the Hundred Years' War. He defeated the French at Agincourt (25 October 1415) and, having occupied much of Normandy, forced Charles VI to agree the Treaty of Troyes (1420). By this, he married Charles's daughter and gained recognition as heir to the French throne. However, he died within two years, leaving his infant son Henry VI with two kingdoms to rule.

Henry advanced his French ambitions by diplomacy as well as war. His military success relied on Burgundian support; his international standing was increased by his alliance with the Holy Roman Emperor ◊Sigismund (incidentally ensuring the end of the ◊Great Schism). Illustrious in life, Henry's lustre only increased after his death. Tito Livio ◊Frulovisi wrote his Latin biography in about 1438, which Pier Candido ◊Decembrio translated into Italian; the English version of 1513 influenced Raphael ◊Holinshed. By the time Shakespeare wrote *Henry V*, Henry had come to epitomize bloodily successful English expansionism.

Henry VI (1421–1471)

King of England and France from 1422, son of Henry V. He was eight months old at his succession, and his minority was dominated by his uncles, John, Duke of Bedford and ◊Humfrey, Duke of Gloucester. Henry, formally at least, assumed royal power in the late 1430s, but he proved incapable of leadership even before his first bout of madness in 1453. His insanity created a struggle of power between the court circle and Richard, Duke of York, whose son ◊Edward IV deposed Henry in 1461, captured him in 1465, and (after an attempted readeption in 1470) had him murdered in 1471. (See Wars of the ◊Roses.)

As Henry reached adulthood, his father's legacy of war in France was proving an impossible burden. These problems were turned into disaster by his vacuous, impotent character. Henry was so politically giftless that he could be accounted saintly: he gained a reputation as a devout king, devoted to educational patronage. Henry Chichele, archbishop of Canterbury, declared him his cofounder of All Souls College, Oxford, and it was in the king's name that the twin foundations of King's College, Cambridge, and ◊Eton College, Windsor, were created – but, even in this project, it is unclear how far he was personally involved.

Henry VII (1457–1509)

King of England from 1485. An exile with a tenuous claim to the throne, Henry was propelled to power by his defeat of ◊Richard III at the Battle of Bosworth. He attempted a symbolic reconciliation with the Yorkists by marrying ◊Edward IV's daughter, Elizabeth of York (1466–1503). Henry's reign was not completely free from sedition but, partly through his careful management of the nobility, he achieved relative peace. He continued several of the policies of ◊Edward IV. He died with a reputation for avarice, leaving a fortune for his son ◊Henry VIII.

Rather disingenuously, Henry presented himself as ending the Wars of the ◊Roses – for this, he called upon the assistance of the arts. A *grex poetarum* (flock of poets) who bleated out royal propaganda passed through his court; it included Pietro ◊Carmeliano and Bernard ◊André. Both André and Polydore ◊Vergil worked on histories amenable to the king. Henry's patronage was not confined to scholarship; he ordered the grand rebuilding of Greenwich Palace, London, to a design of Robert Vertue.

Henry's reign manifested a sharp sense of the symbolic but, ironically, so many symbols were used that they sent out confused messages. The heraldic emblem of the ◊Tudor rose was developed, symbolizing reconciliation; but this was often used alongside the portcullis, the badge of Henry's mother's family, the Beauforts, who had done so much to undermine peace in ◊Henry VI's reign. Again, Henry, with his paternal Welsh lineage, liked to stress his 'British' kingship and so called his eldest son Arthur (1486–1502); but the humanist poets at court celebrated his birth with rather different, classical motifs, like the return of the Golden Age.

Henry VIII (1491–1547)

King of England from 1509 when he succeeded his father, ◊Henry VII. His reign divides into two halves of nearly equal length. For the first half of his reign, Henry attempted to establish himself as a European monarch, reviving the English claim to France so hotly pursued by his ancestor, ◊Henry V, and acting as a significant player on the international diplomatic sign. In this, he was assisted from the mid-1510s by his own cardinal-minister, Thomas ◊Wolsey. And in this period, Henry was married to the Spanish princess, Catherine of Aragon.

Henry's perennial concern for an heir inaugurated the transformations of the second half of his reign. The only offspring of Catherine who survived childhood was a girl, Mary; Henry required a son. He sought a divorce from his now menopausal wife; Wolsey failed to secure papal agreement to this and was duly sacrificed. Henry's choice of a replacement wife, Anne ◊Boleyn, had connections with the evangelical movement on the Continent, as did Henry's new minister, Thomas ◊Cromwell. They provided a resolution to the divorce issue: the Break with Rome. In its wake, there were tentative moves away from Catholic orthodoxy but, in the swirl of factional politics, impermanence was the keynote to religious policy – as it was to Henry's marriages. Anne Boleyn fell, and in the last ten years of his reign Henry had four wives (Jane Seymour, Anne of Cleves, Catherine Howard, and Catherine Parr).

Part of Henry's bid to appear every inch the successful prince was to ape the mélange of styles fashionable in international high culture. Early in his reign, for example, he employed Pietro ◊Torrigiano to design his father's funerary monument. As well as Italian, there were French influences, especially in the 1530s through the circle around Anne Boleyn; the English equivalent, though, to Jean ◊Clouet as court artist was a German, Hans ◊Holbein the Younger. Most of Henry's interest, like that of other princes, was directed to building projects, which included his temporary palace created for the meeting with Francis I in 1520 called the Field of the Cloth of Gold (see ◊chivalry). More permanent (but now destroyed) were his palaces at, for example, Whitehall and Nonsuch.

While Henry aimed at an appearance of cultured suavity, the policies of the second half of his reign hardly assisted learning in his realm. In particular, the ◊Dissolution of the Monasteries involved the dispersal of some ancient libraries which worried even Protestants like John ◊Leland; it also left many monasteries, into which previous generations' artistic patronage had been invested, delapidated or ransacked for stone. Taken as a whole, the balance sheet of Henry's contribution to culture must read (like his dying bank balance): substantially in debt.

Henry II (1519–1559)

King of France from 1547. It is ironic, considering the tensions between him and his father, Francis I, which overshadowed the early 1540s, that Henry's reign in many ways saw, not a reversal, but a continuation of policy. War with Charles V – and later his son, Philip II – continued to be a major concern: Henry's equivalent of ◊Pavia was St Quentin in 1557 where his troops were heavily defeated. It is, however, also ironic that his reign ended just as the peace of Cateau-Cambresis was agreed and there was a chance of change in direction: at the celebratory tournament, Henry was fatally wounded.

In patronage also, Henry continued Francis's projects, for example, carrying through Pierre Lescot's plans for the Louvre, creating the present Cour Carrée. He also continued the patronage of artists decorating the new palace of ◊Fontainebleau. At the same time, he made Philibert de L'Orme superintendent of royal buildings: he had previously been the architect of the Château of Anet for Diane de Poitiers, Henry II's mistress. For Henry he designed, for example, the tomb of Francis I at St Denis.

Henry IV (1553–1610)

King of France from 1589. Son of Antoine de Bourbon and Jeanne, Queen of Navarre, he was brought up as a Protestant and from 1576 led the ◊Huguenots. On his accession he settled the religious question by adopting Catholicism while tolerating Protestantism. He restored peace and strong government to France and brought back prosperity by measures for the promotion of industry and agriculture and the improvement of communications. He was assassinated by a Catholic extremist.

Henryson, Robert (c. 1430–c. 1505)

Scottish poet. His works include versions of Aesop's fables (*The Moral Fables of Esope the Phrygian*), an early pastoral, *Robene and Makyne*, and *The Testament of Cresseid*, a work once attributed to Geoffrey Chaucer, which continues Chaucer's story of *Troilus and Criseyde* by depicting the betrayal and wretched afterlife of Troilus.

A master of arts, possibly of Glasgow University, Henryson was a schoolteacher attached to Dunfermline Abbey, and also practised as a notary.

Henry the Navigator (1394–1460)

Portuguese prince, the fourth son of John I. He is credited with setting up a school for navigators in 1419 and under his patronage Portuguese sailors explored and colonized Madeira, the Cape Verde Islands, and the Azores; they sailed down the African coast almost to Sierra Leone.

Henslowe, Philip (DIED 1616)

English theatre manager. He owned the Fortune, Hope, and Rose Theatres in London. He wrote a diary, in which he kept his accounts of transactions for his theatres, and of loans and payments to actors and dramatists. The diary provides invaluable material evidence for the study of the English theatre in the age of Shakespeare.

herbal

A book describing the medicinal properties of plants, often including illustrations. The earliest herbals are described by Pliny the Elder in the 1st century BC. In the Renaissance, the earliest printed herbal dates from 1477. A whole series followed in the 16th century, including Otto Brunfels' *Herbarum Vivae Eicones* (1530–36), Jerome Bock (1539), and Leonhart Fuchs (1542). (See feature on Botany.)

Heroldt, Johannes (c. 1550–1603)

German composer. His works include a setting of the *St Matthew Passion* for six voices, published at Graz in 1594.

Herrera, Fernando de (1534–1597)

Seville-born poet, esteemed by his contemporaries, who attended the literary gatherings of the Count of Gelves, in part drawn by a (probably unconsummated) love for Gelves's wife. She inspired a number of his poems, such as the ◊pastoral fable *Los amores de Lausino y Corona/The Loves of Lausino and Corona*, but it seems after her death in 1591 he confined himself mostly to prose works, few of which survive. In 1580 he produced a controversial (because somewhat critical) edition of ◊Garcilaso's poetry; his edition of his own appeared in 1582. Another edition, *Versos/Poems*, appeared in 1619.

Herrera, Juan de (c. 1530–1597)

Spanish architect who built El ◊Escorial (beginning in 1572). It was there he developed the plain and austere style for which he is remembered, known as *desnudo* ('bare') or *desornamentado* ('unornamented'). His style found many imitators in Spain and its South American colonies.

Herrera was born in Mobellán and educated at Valladolid, after which he travelled with Philip II to Flanders and Italy (1547–51). During this time Herrera indulged his primary interest in the sciences, but also became familiar with the ideals of contemporary Italian artists. In 1563 he was appointed assistant to Juan Bautista de Toledo (died 1567), the court architect in charge of the building of the Escorial. After Bautista's death Herrera was able to impose his own distinctive style on the plans drawn up by Bautista.

Herrera also designed a palace at Aranjuez in 1569 and the exchange at Seville in 1582, both of which were executed in his characteristic simplified manner. Later, in his role as royal inspector of monuments, he worked on but did not complete the cathedral at Valladolid in 1585. His style was copied by his successors in the post of royal architect and others, and he had many imitators throughout Spain, though there was also a reaction against the severity of his style, a love of rich ornament being a recurrent feature of Spanish architecture.

He also amassed a notable library of mathematical and scientific books, invented navigational instruments, and founded the academy of mathematics at Madrid in 1582.

Hey, Jean

See ◊Master of Moulins.

Heywood, John (c. 1497–c. 1580)

English poet and playwright. He is chiefly remembered as a writer of interludes, which differed from those of his predecessors in that he portrayed social types rather than qualities personified. He also excelled as a writer of epigrams.

Among his works are *The Pardoner and the Frere* (1533), *Johan Johan* (1533), *The Play of the Wether* (1533), *The Four PP* (c. 1545), *Proverbs* (1546), *Two Hundred Epigrams* (1555), and the allegorical poem *The Spider and the Flie* (1566).

Heywood was probably born in London. He seems to have been introduced at court by Thomas More and to have been a favourite in the time of Henry VIII, Edward VI, and Mary, on account of his ready wit and skill in music. When Elizabeth I ascended the throne, however, he retired to Belgium.

Heywood, Thomas (c. 1570–c. 1650)

English actor and dramatist. He wrote or adapted over 220 plays, including the domestic tragedy *A Woman Kilde with Kindnesse* (1602–03). He also wrote an *Apology for Actors* (1612), in answer to attacks on the morality of the theatre.

Hilliard, Nicholas (c. 1547–1619)

English miniaturist and goldsmith. Court artist to Elizabeth I and James I, he painted many leading figures of Tudor and Stuart society, including Francis Drake, Walter Raleigh, and Mary Queen of Scots, as well as several portraits of Elizabeth I herself. Some of his minatures, in particular *An Unknown Young Man Amid Roses* (c. 1590, Victoria and Albert Museum, London), place the sitter in a closely observed natural setting.

Hilliard wrote, but never published, a book on his practice, *The Arte of Limninge*, in 1593. In this, he says he based his style on that of Hans ◊Holbein the Younger, but he also probably learned from contemporary French artists (he visited France in the 1570s); he seems not, on the other hand, to have imitated Levina ◊Teelinc. After 1600 he was gradually superseded by his pupil Isaac Oliver. His son **Lawrence Hilliard** (1582–after 1640) was also a miniaturist.

His works can be seen in the National Portrait Gallery, London, and the Victoria and Albert Museum, London.

Hoby, Sir Thomas (1530–1566)

English diplomat and translator. Born in Leominster, Hoby went to Cambridge before undertaking extensive travels on the Continent. An expert linguist, he was knighted and sent as ambassador to France in 1566, but died in Paris a few months later. During an earlier stay in Paris (1552–53), Hoby translated Baldassare ◊Castiglione's *Il cortegiano/The Courtier*, eventually printed in 1561; it proved popular and was

THE HISTORY OF ART IN THE RENAISSANCE

WRITING ON ART in the Renaissance is dominated by the monumental work of Giorgio ◊Vasari, *Le vite de' pi eccelenti architetti, pittori, et sculteri italiani/The Lives of the Most Excellent Italian Architects, Painters, and Sculptors,* first published in 1550, revised and significantly enlarged in 1568. Commonly held as the father of modern day art history, Vasari was the first person to attempt a comprehensive history of art and artists in Italy. Yet while Vasari was immensely important to the study of art in the Renaissance, he was by no means the only individual to write about art; rather, his work was in large part a codification of previous critics' views on art. Florentine scholars dominated the study of art in the 15th century, although other major cities such as Rome, Milan, and Venice also made significant contributions to the development of a history of art, as became apparent in the 16th century.

Artists and scholars prior to Vasari wrote documentary as well as theoretical works on art. The rise of such literary pursuits occurred in the 15th century, with the Florentine goldsmith and sculptor Lorenzo Ghiberti's *Commentari/Commentaries,* likely written in about 1447, although not published until much later. Divided into three parts, Ghiberti's first book described the artists of ancient Rome, drawing heavily on the *Natural History* of Pliny the Elder. Of greater importance to the development of the history of art were the second and third books which recorded notices of 14th-century artists and detailed his own views and practices as an artist. Despite its small manuscript circulation, the *Commentaries* was the single most important source for information for early Italian artists and provided Vasari, who for a short time was in the workshop of a relative of Ghiberti, with much of his information on early Italian artists.

At roughly the same time as Ghiberti, his compatriot the architect and scholar Leon Battista Alberti published seperate treatises on the three branches of art, *De Re Aedificatoria/On Architecture, De Pictura/On Painting* and *De Statua/On Sculpture* (1436–64). Alberti attempted to codify the artistic precepts necessary to the creation of successful works of art. Although Alberti did not provide histories of specific artists, he was immensely influential as the first theoretician on art. Another practising artist who wrote on the theory of art, with a particular emphasis on architecture, was the eccentric Florentine artist working in Milan known as ◊Filarete. His treatise, divided into 25 books and dated 1467, was another attempt to provide a theoretical framework for a variety of disciplines, including engineering and military planning.

Towards the end of the 15th century, there was a significant increase in the number of scholars and artists writing on art. This interest was divided between theoretical treatises and brief biographies of artists. The modern appreciation of Renaissance art theory has been overwhelmed by the discovery of the notebooks of ◊Leonardo da Vinci. The extensive writings covering subjects ranging from anatomy to atmospheric conditions attempted to provide not only a theoretical framework for the would-be artist, but also investigated forces acting upon nature, an understanding of which was crucial to the effective depiction of figures and forms. Outside Florence, towards the middle of the century, Venetian theoreticians sought to provide an varied interpretation of art that contrasted with the prevalent Tuscan interpretation.

In contrast to Florentine artists and writers who focused on the study of ◊*disegno,* in Venice a greater emphasis was placed upon ◊*colore* and the effects of atmospheric conditions on paintings. This view was articulated in Ludvico Dolce's *Dialgo della pittura intitolato L'Aretino/Dialogue on Painting Entitled The Aretine* (1557). Further studies into the practice and method of painting were extoled in Paolo Pino's *Dialogo della pittura/Dialogue on Painting* (1548) and in Michelangelo Biondo's *De nobilissima pittura/On the Most Nobile Painting* (1549). While touching on individual artists, these publications more generally articulated a theoretical framework on what constituted desirable and successful elements to the art of painting.

In addition to the increase in the number of treatises dealing with theoretical issues in art, there was also a rise in the number of writers collecting notices on the lives of

continued

individuals artists. In Rome, the influential ◊Paolo Govio composed several short biographies of artists including ◊Michelangelo, ◊Raphael, and ◊Leonardo da Vinci in his *De Viris Illustribus/On Illustrious Men* (before 1524). These brief biographies focused on the positive qualities of the artists rather than attempting to catalogue their works of art. In Florence three sources provided detailed information on artists and specific works of art: Giovanni Battista Gelli's *Capricci del bottaio/Caprices of the Cooper,* written towards the middle of the century, and the two anonymous manuscripts, *Il libro di Antonio Billi/The Book of Antonio Billi,* composed between 1481 and 1530, and the *Anonimo Magliabechiano/Anonymous Magliabechian,* (about 1540). While Gelli attempted to include both anecdotal as well as factual information on Florentine artists in a lively, popular, Tuscan style, the two anonymous sources were collections of specific facts about artists rather than proper literary works. Close in spirit to these authors, were the memoirs of ◊Baccio Bandinelli, ◊Benvenuto Cellini, ◊Raffaello da Montelupo, ◊Federico Zuccaro and the biography of Michelangelo composed by his student Asciano Condivi. Collectively, these Roman and Florentine texts indicate that there was a significant interest both prior to and contemporaneous with ◊Vasari in recording the achievements of individual artists.

Vasari's publication of the *Lives of the Artists,* saw the codification of the numerous theoretical and biographical treatises on art of the preceeding two centuries. Born out of the examples of ◊Lorenzo Ghiberti, ◊Paolo Giovio and others, Vasari uniquely composed a coherent and comprehensive collection of historical facts and anecdotal information on the artists of the Italian Renaissance. His tripartite view of the development of art, mirroring the three stages of man, has profoundly influenced subsequent art historical thought. As a highly successful artist in his own right, Vasari's own views on art permeate the *Lives,* making it a benchmark for later commentators on art, such as Raffaele Borghini, in his *Il Riposo/The Ripose* (1584) and the *Schilderboek/Book of Artists* of Karl van Mander (1604).

RICHARD REED

Further Reading
J Schlosser, *Die Kunstliteratur* (Vienna, 1924); P Rubin, *Giorgio Vasari: Art and History* (London, 1995)

---

several times reprinted. Hoby's wife **Elizabeth Hoby** (1528–1609) was also a skilled linguist.

Hoefnagel, Georg (1542–1600)

Flemish draughtsman. The son of an Antwerp diamond dealer, Hoefnagel travelled extensively before entering into the service of the wealthy Fugger family in Germany and eventually of ◊Rudolf II in Prague (from 1591). His travels, often accompanied by his friend, the geographer ◊Ortelius, resulted in his topographical drawings, engravings of which appeared in Georg Braun and Franz Hogenberg's six-volume *Civitates Orbis Terrarum* (1572–1618).

His travels included visits to Spain and France during 1561–67, England in 1569, and Italy in 1577. He specialized in botanical drawings, some which were made for the emperor Rudolf; for him he also illustrated a calligraphy primer by the Hungarian scholar, Georg Bocskay.

Hoefnagel's son **Jakob Hoefnagel** (1575–*c.* 1630) followed him as a miniature painter in the imperial service.

Holbein, Hans, THE ELDER (*c.* 1464–1524)

German painter. Painting mainly religious works, he belonged to the school of Rogier van der ◊Weyden and Hans Memling in his early paintings but showed Italiante influence in such a work as the *Basilica of St Paul* (1502, Staatsgalerie, Augsburg). His principal work is the altarpiece *St Sebastian* (1515–17, Alte Pinakothek, Munich). He was the father of Hans ◊Holbein the Younger.

Financial failure ended his career as artist at Augsburg and ill success then seems to have pursued him at Isenheim and elsewhere. He had a strong sense of character in portrait drawings (as in the sketchbooks preserved in Berlin), which reappears in the works of his son.

Holbein, Hans, THE YOUNGER (1497–1543)

German painter and woodcut artist who spent much of his career as a portrait artist at the court of Henry VIII of England. One of the finest graphic artists of his age, he executed a woodcut series *Dance of Death* about 1525, and designed title pages for Luther's New Testament and Thomas ◊More's *Utopia*.

He was born in Augsburg. In 1515 he went to Basel, where he became friendly with the scholar and humanist Erasmus and illustrated his *Praise of Folly*. He painted three portraits of Erasmus in 1523.

He travelled widely in Europe and while in England as painter to Henry VIII he created a remarkable evocation of the English court in a series of graphic, perceptive portraits. Among his sitters were Henry VIII and Thomas More. During his time at the English court, he also painted miniature portraits, inspiring Nicholas Hilliard. One of his pictures of this period is *The (French) Ambassadors* (1533, National Gallery, London). Pronounced Renaissance influence emerged in the *Meyer Madonna* 1526, a fine altarpiece in Darmstadt.

He was trained by his father, Hans Holbein the Elder, and by Hans Burgkmair, and worked in the family studio as a boy, together with his brother Ambrosius. In 1515 he went to Basel with Ambrosius (a painter of promise who died in 1519) and for some years found constant employment in the prosperous Swiss city, where he became a naturalized Swiss citizen in 1520. Working for the printer-publishers Amerbach and Froben, he showed himself a remarkable designer for books. His illustrations for Erasmus's *Praise of Folly* were as popular as the book itself. Later he designed a title page for More's *Utopia* as well as for Luther's German translation of the New Testament, and the *Dance of Death* series, in the woodcuts made from his designs by Hans Lutzelberger, ranks with Albrecht Dürer's *Apocalypse* as one of the masterpieces of European graphic art. He made numerous designs for goldsmiths' work and stained glass, was much occupied with mural decoration (a *Peasants' Dance* for a house in Basel and paintings for the town hall) and also executed some religious works – *Dead Christ* (1521, Basel) and *Madonna* (1522, Solothurn) – though his mastery of portraiture was already most in evidence. It appears in his portraits of Burgomaster Meyer and his wife in 1516 and Bonifazius Amerbach in 1519 (Basel), and the *Madonna of the Burgomaster Meyer* (Darmstadt) is in effect a magnificent portrait group.

Holbein had a passing contact with Italy in a journey to Milan in 1518, and visited Bourges in France in 1524, where he may have seen works by Jean ◊Clouet (at this time he adopted a method of chalk drawing comparable with that of the French portraitist), but a cardinal event was his introduction to Thomas More in England in 1526, on the recommendation of Erasmus. He stayed until 1528, painting the More family (an informal group of which copies and an original drawing exist); portraits of Warham, the archbishop of Canterbury, and Bishop John ◊Fisher; and making a superb series of portrait drawings (Royal Collection, Windsor). He then returned to Basel to finish his work at the town hall, painting also a portrait of his wife and children.

From 1532 London was his headquarters. He painted the German merchants of the steelyard, for example Jörg Gyze (Berlin), *The Ambassadors*, remarkable in technical skill and use of ◊anamorphosis and became court painter to Henry VIII in 1536. The dynastic group for the Privy Chamber at Whitehall, including Henry VII, Henry VIII, Jane Seymour, and Elizabeth of York, was destroyed by fire in 1698, but in other works Holbein has left an imperishable record of the Tudors. Of his numerous portrayals of Henry VIII, an authentic example is in the Thyssen Collection. He was compelled to paint elaborate details of court dress, but his later work is remarkable for an exquisite refinement of line and essential simplicity of design, as in the portrait he was sent to make at Brussels of the Duchess of Milan in 1537 (National Gallery, London), and that of Anne of Cleves in 1539 (Louvre, Paris). His other work in England included ornamental designs (for example, the drawing for the *Jane Seymour Cup*, Bodleian Library, Oxford) and miniatures, beautiful examples of which are in the Victoria and Albert Museum. Holbein, though he may have inspired the miniaturist Hilliard in some degree, stands alone in the history of the English School and may be called a great internationalist of portraiture.

Holborne, Anthony (1584–1602)

English composer. He was in the service of Queen Elizabeth I. His collection *The Cittharn Schoole* (1597) contains pieces for cittern and bass viol, as well as three-part songs by his brother William. A further collection, *Pavans, Galliards, Almains and Other Short Aeirs*, was published in 1599.

Holinshed, Raphael (HOLLINGSHEAD) (*c.* 1520–*c.* 1580)

English historian. He published two volumes of the *Chronicles of England, Scotland, and Ireland* (1578), which are a mixture of fact and legend. The *Chronicles* were used as a principal source by Elizabethan dramatists for their plots. Nearly all Shakespeare's English history plays, as well as *Macbeth, King Lear*, and *Cymbeline*, are based on Holinshed's work.

Holinshed was probably born in Cheshire. He went to London early in Elizabeth I's reign, and was employed as a translator in Reginald Wolfe's printing office, helping him in the compilation of his *Universal History*. Wolfe died before the work was completed, and it was left to Holinshed to finish in an abridged form. It appeared as the *Chronicles of England, Scotland, and Ireland*. A second enlarged edition was published in 1587. The *Chronicles* like those of ◊Hall basically subscribe to the 'Tudor myth of history', advancing the view that Henry VII was a national saviour, restoring peace and order after the anarchy of the Wars of the Roses.

Holland, Philemon (1552–1637)

English translator. Working both as a doctor and a school teacher, he made his reputation with his translations from Classical writers, including Pliny, Suetonius, Plutarch, and Xenophon. His translations are characterized by immense learning combined with a fine feeling for the emotional tone of the original.

Holland was born in Chelmsford, Essex, the son of a Protestant clergyman who fled to Europe during Mary's reign. Holland took his MA at Cambridge in 1574 and subsequently studied medicine. He then settled in Coventry where he spent the rest of his life teaching, practising medicine, and translating the classics. These included works by Livy (1600), Pliny's *Natural History* (1601), Plutarch's *Moralia* (1603), works by Suetonius (1606), Ammianus Marcellinus (1609), and Xenophon's *Cyropaedia* (1632). In addition he translated Camden's *Britannia* into English in 1610. A few medical translations were issued posthumously.

Holy Roman Emperor

Elected overlord of German-speaking cities and principalities which made up the Holy Roman Empire. From 1356, the electors – seven ecclesiastical and secular princes – were firmly established. When, on the death of the previous emperor, a candidate gained a majority vote from the electors and was then crowned at Aachen, he was officially titled King of the Romans. To become Holy Roman Emperor, the ruler had formally to be crowned in Rome by the pope. There was, however, no real change in power after the second coronation and a ruler elected but not yet crowned was still viewed as emperor.

Though the position was elective and any monarch could present themselves as a candidate, the election tended to be dominated by one family: in the late 14th and early 15th century, it was the House of Luxemburg. After the death of Emperor Sigismund, the title effectively passed to his in-laws, the Habsburg family. Despite contested elections, in particular in 1519 when Francis I of France and Henry VIII of England both were candidates, the title continued in the Habsburg family until the 19th century.

Hooker, Richard (*c.* 1554–1600)

English theologian, author of *The Laws of Ecclesiastical Polity* (1594), a defence of the episcopalian system of the Church of England.

Hooper, John (*c.* 1495–1555)

English Protestant reformer. He adopted the views of the Swiss Protestant Ulrich ◊Zwingli and was appointed bishop of Gloucester in 1550. He was burned to death for heresy.

Hopfer, Daniel (*c.* 1470–1536)

German engraver and designer. He is thought to be the first to have made prints by ◊etching (as opposed to engraving). He produced some of the earliest original etched portraits, a number of religious illustrations (on Reformation lines), scenes of everyday life, such as village festivals, and a large number of repro-

HOMOSEXUALITY AND MALE HOMOEROTICISM

THE CONCEPT OF the homosexual is modern: the medieval term 'sodomy' covered a multitude of sins, including masturbation, incest, sex with nuns, and bestiality – any kind of sexual deviance from the 'norm'. But 'sodomy' began to become a byword for buggery, and homosexual activity generally, in the Renaissance era; most tellingly, in 1527 a Florentine nobleman was fined for crimes explicitly *per buggerone*. By 1600 Francis ◊Bacon's *New Atlantis* forwarded 'masculine love' as a distinct erotic category (indeed, his mother wrote to him complaining of his 'foul sins' with various male servants). The anachronistic search for the origins of gay 'identity politics' or for a homosexual subculture has been over-normative in the context of European Renaissance culture. Nevertheless, explicitly homophile activity was one of many potentially subversive pursuits which flourished more grandly in the 15th and 16th centuries than at any other time since antiquity.

It is perverse that as the 'unmentionable vice' was discussed with ever-growing gusto from 1300, religious persecution *and* secular prosecution, especially in Italian civic culture, increased to keep pace. One unpublished 16th-century source translates:

'The mighty impose penalties on those who [commit sodomy] for no other reason than this: since it is their own profession, they don't want common people to use it ….'

But extensive legal evidence of homosexual sex among the *petite gens* tends to give the lie to this popular notion. Same-sex bonding ('homosociality') right across society, and particularly in military and clerical orders, led to homosexual activity. As a result of economic instability and population shifts after 1300 the age of majority and marriage for men was considerably higher than that of women: this was particularly true, despite heavy policing, in the Italian city-states, with predictable results.

The prevalence of the notion is nonetheless understandable: homoerotic language and imagery pervaded the spectrum of Renaissance high culture; less elite expressions have not survived. The most powerful (and obvious) factor in the burgeoning of homoerotic imagery was the fashion for the literature, art, and history of classical antiquity – with its explicit statues and paintings, and its stories of Achilles and Patroclus, Alexander and Hephaistion, and Marcus Aurelius and Antinus. A fashion developed for images of the gorgeous young Ganymede seized by the lusting Jove in the form of an eagle – in literature too, from ◊Dante to Robert ◊Barnfield. But while the classical tradition was grandiose, it was also open to satire: the libation Beccadelli's 'epitaph' suggests on spilling on a homosexual's grave was certainly *not* wine. Similarly, the Christian 'moralization' of certain literary classics in medieval culture (Ovid being the most notable victim of this semantic bowdlerization) was turned on its head in a case from Brescia in 1530: a 22-year-old man accused of buggery invoked the example of Christ 'and His catamite', the 'beloved disciple' John: why should he not follow the Master in taking as his altar 'a lovely bum'?

A deeply problematic aspect of the homophile classical heritage was faced by the philosophers who strove to resurrect the ideas and ideals of ◊Plato. Marsilio ◊Ficino and his peers attempted to distinguish the mystical, transcendental Platonic homoeroticism – *amor Socraticus* – from the unchaste sodomite lusts of which Socrates and Alcibiades were, nonetheless, suspected. In 1455 ◊George of Trebizond accused the new ◊Academy of this *Platonica venus*; ◊Bessarion countered by pointing out Plato's disgust for the carnal, a line adopted by most 'Academicians'. Yet the correspondence between Giovanni ◊Pico della Mirandola and the younger Girolamo Benivieni reveals a passionate attachment; the language of Ficino's dedication of his Plato commentary of 1469 to the young Giovanni Cavalcanti reverberates with the love that dare not speak its name.

Indeed, homosexual love was rarely celebrated overtly, even among its most evident practitioners: ◊Michaelangelo's sonnets reveal a deep ambivalence about his love for boys – but *la donna é dissimil troppo* ('women are just too different'). The gender pronouns of his sonnets were switched to female before their (posthumous) publication. Benvenuto ◊Cellini, convicted for 'sodomy'– meaning almost exclusively, by now,

continued

seducing boys – in 1557, while privately unrepentant, was nonetheless furious at his public 'outing' by an enemy. Burlesque literary forms permitted more overt, though often negative, images of 'inverted' behaviour: hence Beccadelli's *Hermaphroditus*, ◊Chaucer 's *Pardoner*, ◊Boccaccio's cuckolded husband who beds both his wife and her lover; the anonymous 16th-century Italian treatise *La Cazzaria* ('Prick-ery'), and the 'one-liner' circulating in England in about 1600: *habuimus regem Elizabetham, habemus reginam Jacobem* ('we had a *King* in Elizabeth: now we have a *Queen*, James'). The diarist Stefano Infessura cattily implied that ◊Sixtus IV made his barber a cardinal not for his tonsorial skills but for quite different services to Sixtus' son.

However, the temptation gleefully to 'reclaim' or 'out' Renaissance figures as gay obscures the essential point of how far male homosexual imagery and actions were a part of mainstream high culture *and* popular street life (until the repressive measures of the 'reformed' later 16th century arguably pushed homosexuality 'underground'). Few *exclusively* gay figures, even among Italian artists, existed – ◊'il Sodoma', Giulio ◊Romano, ◊Correggio, ◊Parmigianino; but plenty of men imitated the culture of ancient Greece in loving boys and women (not equally). ◊Molière may have enjoyed both sexes: his forerunner Jodell

certainly did. ◊Shakespeare's much-debated dedication of sonnet 20 to 'the master-mistress of [his] passion' is one of many intriguing fragments of 'evidence'; Kit ◊Marlowe's writings

were less coy again. On the whole, Renaissance homosexual love followed the ancient Greek model of *erastos – eromenos* – not two adult males who could switch roles, but a bearded 'giver' and an adolescent 'reciever'. As in the ancient Greek custom, Renaissance men who desired younger youths still reserved their scorn for two adult males together; of course, there was no place for lesbians in any of this; this was not 'modern', but, rather, a revived classical homosexuality entirely appropriate to Renaissance aesthetics. Beccadelli, for example, gleefully advocates boys' bottoms as a source of infinite delight; but concerning the submissive tendencies of a mature acquaintance his explicit words drip with venom.

To paraphrase: If just one virile part of each man to whom Mamuriano has been a passive partner is placed on his back and if he carried that weight any distance then 'Mamuriano, you would be stronger than an ox.'

AMANDA COLLINS

Further Reading

M Goodich, *The Unmentionable Vice* (Santa Barbara, 1979); A M Rocke, *Forbidden Friendships* (Oxford, 1996)

Classical literature provided an embarrassment of riches when it came to stories of homosexual lust. One was that of Jupiter's rape of the boy Ganymede, whom he abducted by taking on the disguise of an eagle — a moment recorded in Benvenuto Cellini's bronze statuette (Bargello, Florence) ◊Cellini *e.t. archive*

ductions of Italian art, which made him a significant popularizer of the Italian style in Germany.

Hopfer was born at Kaufbeuren, but from 1493 he was a citizen of Augsburg. He was also a designer of decorations, publishing 50 plates of ornamental motifs, which included Gothic foliage and Renaissance ◊grotesques. Like other graphic artists of the time, he etched decoration on ceremonial parade armour, which formed a major part of his work.

Horace (FULL NAME QUINTUS HORATIUS FLACCUS) (65–8 BC)

Roman lyric poet and satirist. He became a leading poet under the patronage of Emperor Augustus. His works include *Satires* (35–30 BC); the four books of *Odes* (*c.* 25–24 BC); *Epistles*, a series of verse letters; and an influential critical work, *Ars poetica*.

Horace's works were well known before the 15th century: there was no need for them to be 'rediscovered' in the Renaissance. Some humanists considered editorial work necessary: in 1482, Cristoforo ◊Landino produced an edition which was prefixed by a praise of Horace by ◊Politian, suitably written in a form imitating Horace's poetry. However, while interest ranged across his oeuvre, especial attention was increasingly paid to the *Ars poetica*, his theoretical discussion of poetry. It is significant that in the second half of the 16th century, this work was the most frequently translated into vernaculars. At the same time, Horace was being used as a model, for example by the French ◊*Pléiade* poets, for their own attempts at the creation of a national poetry. Similarly, in early 17th-century England, while Ben ◊Jonson's dramatic works owed much to Tacitus, poems like 'To Penshurst' (the former home of Sir Philip ◊Sidney), had Horatian inspiration.

Horwood, William (DIED 1484)

English composer. He became master of the choristers at Lincoln Cathedral in 1477. His music, consisting of Latin antiphons and a Magnificat, is included in the Eton Choirbook; a fragmentary *Kyrie* has also survived.

Hours, Book of

In medieval Europe, a collection of liturgical prayers for the use of the faithful.

Books of Hours appeared in England in the 13th century, and contained short prayers and illustrations, with each prayer suitable for a different hour of the day, in honour of the Virgin Mary. The enormous demand for Books of Hours was a stimulus for the development of Gothic illumination. A notable example is the *Très Riches Heures du Duc de Berry*, illustrated in the early 15th century by the ◊Limbourg brothers.

Huber, Wolf (1490–1533)

German painter and graphic artist. Mainly noted for his woodcuts, with their depictions of landscapes, he worked at Ratisbon and Passau where he was court painter to the prince bishops.

Hudson, Henry (*c.* 1565–1611)

English explorer. Under the auspices of the Muscovy Company (1607–08), he made two unsuccessful attempts to find the Northeast Passage to China. In September 1609, commissioned by the Dutch East India Company, he reached New York Bay and sailed 240 km/150 mi up the river that now bears his name, establishing Dutch claims to the area. In 1610 he sailed from London in the *Discovery* and entered what is now the Hudson Strait. After an icebound winter, he was turned adrift by a mutinous crew in what is now Hudson Bay.

Huguenot

French Protestant in the 16th century; the term referred mainly to Calvinists. Persecuted under Francis I and Henry II, the Huguenots survived both an attempt to exterminate them (the Massacre of ◊St Bartholomew on 24 August 1572) and the religious wars of the next 30 years. In 1598 ◊Henry IV (himself formerly a Huguenot) granted them toleration under the Edict of ◊Nantes. Louis XIV revoked the edict in 1685, attempting their forcible conversion, and 400,000 emigrated.

Huguet, Jaume (1420–1490)

Catalan painter. He was a leading artist of the Catalan Gothic School and a painter of altarpieces. Among his works are the retables of *St Abdon* and *St Sennen* (1460, Church of San Miguel de Terrasa) and that of *The Corporation of St Stephen* (1462, part of the predella, Museum of Barcelona).

The wealthy city guilds kept him busily employed on these offerings to the church and his altarpieces were also exported to Sardinia, then under Spanish dominion. Huguet's richly patterned altarpieces are distinct in tranquil, poetic feeling. Other examples include those of St Augustine (six large panels, Barcelona) and of the Constable de Porting (Santa Agueda, Barcelona).

humanism

Term coined in the early 19th century to describe an education centred on Classical literature. In later generations, 'humanism' came to mean something much grander, being defined as nothing short of 'the intellectual movement of the Renaissance'. The 15th and 16th centuries, however, saw no such single movement or philosophy which united all humanists; taken in this broad sense, the term is not only redundant but misleading. If, however, there was a common thread connecting Renaissance scholars together, it was their interest in what they called *studia humanitatis* (*see feature*).

humours, theory of

Theory that the human body was composed of four kinds of fluid: phlegm, blood, choler or yellow bile, and melancholy or black bile. Physical and mental characteristics were explained by different proportions of humours in individuals.

An excess of phlegm produced a 'phlegmatic', or calm, temperament; of blood a 'sanguine', or passionate, one; of yellow bile a 'choleric', or irascible, temperament; and of black bile a 'melancholy', or depressive, one. The Greek physician Galen connected the theory to that of the four elements: the phlegmatic was associated with water, the sanguine with air, the choleric with fire, and the melancholic with earth. An imbalance of the humours could supposedly be treated by diet.

Hunyadi, János Corvinus (*c.* 1387–1456)

Hungarian politician and general. Born in Transylvania, reputedly the son of the emperor ◊Sigismund, he won battles against the Turks from the 1440s. In 1456 he defeated them at Belgrade, but died shortly afterwards of the plague. His son, ◊Matthias Corvinus, however, was made king of Hungary.

Hurtado de Mendoza, Diego (1503–1575)

Spanish soldier, diplomat, author, and bibliophile, he counted ◊Santillana among his ancestors and studied Greek, Latin, Hebrew, and Arabic at Granada and Salamanca. He fought at Pavia (1525) and Tunis (1535). In England 1537–38, his diplomatic skills failed to marry ◊Henry VIII with Charles V's niece; he was ambassador in Venice 1539–47 where he enthusiastically collected Greek manuscripts, corresponded with ◊Boscà, patronized the ◊Aldine Press and probably wrote the anonymous 1547 *Diálogo entre Caronte y el ánima de Pedro Luis Farnesio, hijo del Papa Paulo III/Dialogue between Caron and the Soul of Pedro Luis Farnesio, Son of Pope Paul III*. Recalled to Spain in 1554 and banished by Philip II in 1568, his experiences quelling the morisco rising 1568–71 appeared in his book *La Guerra de Granada*. Partially published in 1610 and 1627, the first, error-strewn complete version appeared in 1730. He bequeathed his magnificent library to ◊Philip II's royal library at El Escorial.

Huss, John (CZECH JAN HUS) (*c.* 1373–1415)

Bohemian Christian church reformer, rector of Prague University from 1402, who was excommunicated for attacks on ecclesiastical abuses. He was summoned before the Council of Constance in 1414, defended the English reformer John Wyclif, rejected the pope's authority, and was burned at the stake. His followers were called Hussites.

Hutten, Ulrich von (1488–1523)

German humanist and knight. His early writings divided between his outspoken attacks on Duke Ulrich of Württemberg and his outspoken support for the cause of humanist *bonae litterae*/good letters. In particular, he was instrumental in the satirical *Epistolae Obscurorum Vvirorum/Letters of Obscure Men* (1515) attacking Johann ◊Reuchlin's opponents. However, he took Erasmian criticisms of the church further and, when the Luther affair began, became a vigorous supporter of Martin ◊Luther.

He was born in the Castle of Steckelberg, near Fulda, Hesse. He went to the monastery at Fulda but left in 1505, going to the universities at Cologne, Erfurt, and Frankfurt-an-der-Oder, where he took his masters degree and published his first poems. From there he went to Wittenberg and Leipzig, and then travelled to Italy, where he served in the emperor's army.

In 1517 Hutten was made poet laureate by Emperor Maximilian. In the same year he entered the service of the archbishop of Mainz and the following year published an edition of Valla's *Donation of Constantine* with a sarcastic dedication to the pope. In 1520 his enthusiastic support of Martin Luther (expressed in several Latin and German tracts) resulted in his dismissal from the archbishop's service, and Hutten resumed his wanderings.

He urged the knights of the empire to take up arms against the Catholic Church but did not take part in Franz von Sickingen's abortive 'Knights' War'. He died of syphilis in Zürich while under the protection of the reformer Ulrich ◊Zwingli.

Hypnerotomachia Polifili (Dream of Polyphilius)

An Italian prose romance published in 1499.

Written in both Latin and Italian by the Dominican monk Francesco ◊Colonna (1433–1527), it describes a lover's search for his mistress. Printed by Aldus ◊Manutius, it was celebrated for the beauty of its woodcut illustrations and typography.

The anonymous woodcut illustrations reflect the influence of both Andrea ◊Mantegna and Giovanni Bellini; several of them record contemporary Italian garden designs, and others are remarkable as architectural fantasies.

The text was translated into French by Jean Martin and Jacques Ghorry in 1546 and published, with extra pictures, in a format almost as beautiful as the original. An incomplete English version appeared as *The Strife of Love in a Dreame* (1592).

India, Sigismondo d' (*c.* 1582–1629)

Italian composer. His highly chromatic madrigals have been valued as second only to those of ◊Monteverdi.

He left his native Sicily to work as director of music at the Turin court of the Duke of Savoy (1611–23). His madrigal collections were published in eight books (1606–24) at Milan and Venice. In 1625 his sacred drama *Sant' Eustachio* was produced in Cardinal Maurizio's palace at Rome. The following year he moved to Modena. Other important influences on his style came from Luca Marenzio and the chromaticism of Gesualdo.

Innocent VIII (BORN GIOVANNI BATTISTA CIBÒ) (1432–1492)

Pope from 1484. Elected with the support of the future Julius II, the latter played a leading role in his pontificate. These years saw a decline in papal hold over Rome with the two noble families, the Colonna and the Orsini, taking control into their own warring hands. Meanwhile, Innocent concentrated on trying to undermine the power of ◊Ferrante of Naples, inciting a revolt against him – which failed.

As a patron, Innocent's largest project was the building of the Villa Belvedere on the Vatican Hill, the interior of which imitated ancient art, with the vaults echoing those in the recently refound Golden House of Nero. The frescoes, by Pinturicchio, also imitated Classical decoration. For this project, Innocent also attracted Andrea ◊Mantegna to Rome; Mantegna painted the altarpiece of the Baptism (destroyed) for Belvedere's chapel.

Of symbolic importance for Innocent was the arrival in Rome in 1492 of the Holy Lance, which was claimed to have pierced Christ on the Cross. It was presented to him by the Sultan Bayezid II, and to house it, Innocent had a tabernacle built with a fresco by Pinturrichio. It was for this relic's arrival that Innocent wished to be remembered: his tomb, by Antonio ◊Pollaiuolo, depicts him holding the lance.

Innocenzo da Imola (*c.* 1490–*c.* 1545)

Italian painter. Based in Bologna from 1517, he produced a series of religious frescoes and altarpieces, strongly influenced by the style of ◊Raphael. He also trained other artists, including Francesco ◊Primaticcio and Prospero Fontana.

Inquisition

Tribunal of the Roman Catholic Church established in 1233 to suppress heresy originally by excommunication. The Inquisition operated in France, Italy, Spain, and the Holy Roman Empire, and was especially active after the Reformation; it was later extended to the Americas. Its trials were conducted in secret, under torture, and penalties ranged from fines, through flogging and imprisonment, to death by burning.

During the course of the Spanish Inquisition, until its abolition in 1834, some 60,000 cases were tried. The Roman Inquisition was established in 1542 to combat the growth of Protestantism. Despite bare statistics, however, it is unclear how thorough or effective the Inquisition ever was.

Institutes

The familiar name for *Christianae Religionis Institutio/Institutes of the Christian Religion* (1536), the principal text of Calvinism. Written by the French religious reformer John ◊Calvin, it is the clearest and ablest systematic exposition of the ideals that inspired the second generation of Protestant reformers and their followers.

The first edition, published in Basel, Switzerland, was a brief manual of six chapters based on the framework of the catechism and intended as a short textbook of reformed orthodoxy. Its success prompted Calvin to expand it considerably, so that by the time of the definitive edition of 1559 it was five times its original length.

Its 80 chapters and four books now comprised a complete handbook of the reformed religion: a systematic theology based on the Bible, a manual of ethics, a guidebook to the Protestant creed, and a comprehensive survey of Reformation theological controversy.

It was soon translated into the languages of those countries influenced by Calvinism, including French in 1541 (by Calvin himself), Dutch in 1560, and English in 1561.

interlude (SOMETIMES TUDOR INTERLUDE)

In 16th-century England, a short dramatic work, often comical, performed in the intervals of a banquet or court pageant, or between the parts of mystery plays. The characters were usually traditional personifications, such as Mercy, Youth, or Gluttony. Interludes appeared in the transitional period (*c.* 1500–*c.* 1575) between the medieval religious drama (mystery, morality, and miracle plays) and Elizabethan drama.

John ◊Heywood was the first English playwright to treat the interlude as an independent dramatic form and to use characters who were social types (for example, friars or pedlars) rather than moral qualities. An example is his farcical interlude *The Pardoner and the Friar* (1533).

intermedii (OR INTERMEZZI)

In 15th- and 16th-century Italy, musical or dramatic interludes played between the acts of a play or during the intervals of a banquet. The musical *intermedii* consisted of instrumental pieces played out of sight of the audience. The dramatic *intermedii* were stage spectacles performed by singers, dancers, and actors in costume. These were broadly similar to the English ◊interlude.

In its combination of music and drama, *intermedii* can be regarded as an important forerunner of opera.

Intermedii were first performed during the intervals of Renaissance plays – the court of 15th-century Ferrara was particularly important in their development. Sometimes the subject matter of the *intermedii* was connected with that of the play, though more often unrelated pastoral scenes with allegorical figures were presented. The Medici court in Florence was the scene of many lavish entertainments, the most spectacular being that performed in 1589 at the wedding of Christine of Lorraine and Ferdinando de' Medici, for which the music was provided by leading composers, including Marenzio and ◊Caccini.

Isaac, Henricus (HEINRICH) (c. 1450–1517)

Flemish composer. He was a prolific composer of songs and instrumental music, and wrote a *Choralis Constantinus* consisting of 58 offices for the whole year; but he is popularly remembered for the song 'Innsbruck ich muss dich lassen', later harmonized by J S Bach. His wide travel is reflected in the various national influences in his music. He was a major contemporary of Josquin Desprez, Jacob Obrecht, and Pierre de La Rue.

Isaac was born at Brabant. In about 1484, when he seems to have been at Innsbruck and in touch with Paul Hofhaimer there, he went via Ferrara to Florence as musician to the Medici family. He sang in the choir at the Chapel of San Giovanni at Florence, and was regularly employed at the cathedral from 1485. He visited Rome in 1489, and married Bartolomea Bello, the daughter of a wealthy butcher.

Lorenzo de' Medici died in 1492 and subsequently Isaac accepted an invitation from the Emperor Maximilian, who visited Pisa in 1496, to join the Imperial court, just then about to be transferred from Augsburg to Vienna. He seems to have visited Innsbruck again to be formally appointed and was possibly appointed in Augsburg too. His duties were not arduous, so that he was able to live by turns in Vienna, Innsbruck, Constance (all connected with the court), and Italy. He also spent much time at the court of Ercole d'Este, Duke of Ferrara, and during his last years he remained at Florence.

Works include:

Many Masses, about 50 motets, sequences, Lamentation *Oratio Jeremiae*, 58 four-part settings of the offices under the title *Choralis Constantinus*, the first polyphonic cycle of liturgical works for the ecclesiastical year: four-part Monodia on the death of Lorenzo de' Medici (words by Poliziano); many German, Italian, French, and Latin songs (including 'Innsbruck, ich muss dich lassen', which may not be his own tune), 58 instrumental pieces in three–five parts, 29 domestic pieces in two–five parts.

Isabella (I), THE CATHOLIC (1451–1504)

Queen of Castile from 1474, after the death of her brother Henry IV. By her marriage with ◊Ferdinand of Aragon in 1469, the crowns of two of the Christian states in the Spanish peninsula cemented their dynastic link. Her youngest daughter was Catherine of Aragon, first wife of Henry VIII of England.

Under Isabella and her husband (the Catholic King), the reconquista was finally fulfilled with the taking of the Moorish city of Granada in 1492. She introduced the ◊Inquisition into Castile, expelled the Jews, and gave financial encouragement to ◊Columbus.

Isenheim Altar

Altarpiece by the German painter Matthias ◊Grünewald (1510–15), executed for the convent of the order of St Anthony at Isenheim, Alsace.

It is a polyptych showing in its original complete form a collaboration between the painter and the woodcarver Backoffen. Backoffen's work is a centre-piece of St Anthony enthroned, with St Augustine and St Jerome, and carvings in the predella of Christ and the 12 apostles. The painted scenes by Grünewald, presented by the opening or closing of the several panels, are: St Anthony assisting the hermit Paul; the temptation of St Anthony; the Annunciation; the Virgin among angelic musicians; the Virgin and Child; the Resurrection; and the Crucifixion. On the predella, when closed, there is a ◊pietà. In two wings flanking the closed centrepiece (Crucifixion) are St Anthony and St Sebastian, the latter the supposed portrait of the artist.

italic script

A script developed by early humanists alongside ◊*littera antiqua*. Its invention is credited to Niccolò ◊Niccoli. In essence, a sloped, joined-up version of *littera antiqua*, which would have been quicker to write than the other script, it became itself a book-hand, being perfected by scribes like Bartolomeo Sanvito (1435–1511). In print, it was the favoured typeface of Aldus ◊Manutius.

Ivan (III), THE GREAT (1440–1505)

Grand Duke of Muscovy from 1462. He revolted against Tatar overlordship by refusing tribute to Grand Khan Ahmed in 1480. He claimed the title of tsar (Caesar), and used the double-headed eagle as the Russian state emblem.

Ivan (IV), THE TERRIBLE (1530–1584)

Grand Duke of Muscovy from 1533. He assumed power in 1544 and was crowned as first tsar of Russia in 1547. He conquered Kazan in 1552, Astrakhan in 1556, and Siberia in 1581. He reformed the legal code and local administration in 1555 and established trade relations with England. In his last years he alternated between debauchery and religious austerities, executing thousands and, in rage, his own son.

Ivan attempted to centralize his rule in Muscovy. He campaigned against the Tatars of Kazan, Astrakhan, and elsewhere, but his policy of forming Russia into an empire led to the fruitless 24-year Livonian war. His regime was marked by brutality, evidenced by the destruction (sacking) of Novgorod.

Jachet (JAQUET) da Mantova (DIED 1559)

Flemish singer and composer. He was attached to San Pietro Cathedral at Mantua (1527–58), and wrote Masses, Magnificats, motets, psalms, hymns, and other pieces.

Jacobean

Style in the arts, particularly in architecture and furniture, during the reign of James I (1603–25) in England. Following the general lines of Elizabethan design, but using Classical features with greater complexity and with more profuse ornamentation, it adopted many motifs from contemporary Italian design.

A sudden change to full-blown Palladin architecture occurred early in the 17th century, when Inigo ◊Jones appeared upon the scene and designed the Queen's House at Greenwich (1617–35), and the Banqueting House in Whitehall (1619–22).

Jacobello del Fiore (c. 1370–1439)

Italian painter. The son of Francesco del Fiore, Jacobello was a pupil of Gentile da Fabriano and adopted a similar style when he began painting in 1394. His earliest surviving work is the *Madonna della Misericordia* (1407). Other works include the *Lion of St Mark* (1415) (Palazzo Ducale, Venice) and the *Coronation of the Virgin* (1438), a copy of the well-known painting by Gauriento. He was president of the guild of painters in Venice (1415–36).

James IV (1473–1513)

King of Scotland from 1488. He came to the throne after his followers murdered his father, James III, at Sauchieburn. His reign was internally peaceful, but he allied himself with France against England, invaded in 1513, and was defeated and killed at the Battle of Flodden. James IV was a patron of poets and architects as well as a military leader.

In 1503 he married Margaret Tudor (1489–1541, daughter of Henry VII), which eventually led to his descendants succeeding to the English crown. He was succeeded by his son James V.

James V (1512–1542)

King of Scotland from 1513, who assumed power in 1528. During the long period of his minority, he was caught in a struggle between pro-French and pro-English factions. When he assumed power, he allied himself with France and upheld Catholicism against the Protestants. Following an attack on Scottish territory by Henry VIII's forces, he was defeated near the border at Solway Moss in 1542.

Son of James IV and Margaret Tudor, he succeeded his father at the age of one year. His first wife, Madeline, daughter of King Francis I of France, died in 1537; the following year he married Mary of Guise. Their daughter, Mary Queen of Scots, succeeded him.

James I (1566–1625)

King of England from 1603 and Scotland (as **James VI**) from 1567. The son of Mary Queen of Scots and her second husband, Lord Darnley, he succeeded to the Scottish throne on the enforced abdication of his mother and assumed power in 1583. He established a strong centralized authority, and in 1589 married Anne of Denmark (1574–1619).

As successor to Elizabeth I in England, he alienated the Puritans by his High Church views and Parliament by his assertion of divine right, and was generally unpopular because of his favourites, such as Buckingham, and his schemes for an alliance with Spain. He was succeeded by his son Charles I.

As king of Scotland, he curbed the power of the nobility, although his attempts to limit the authority of the Kirk (Church of Scotland) were less successful.

Upon his accession to the English throne on the death of Elizabeth I, James acted mainly upon the advice of Robert Cecil, Earl of Salisbury, but on the latter's death all restraint vanished.

His religious policy consisted of asserting the supreme authority of the crown and suppressing both Puritans and Catholics who objected. The preparation of the Authorized Version of the Bible in English, published in 1611, was ordered by James.

He thwarted Guy Fawkes's plot to blow up Parliament during its opening in 1605. The gunpowder plot, with its anti-Catholic reaction, gave James a temporary popularity which soon dissipated. His foreign policy, aimed primarily at achieving closer relations with Spain, was also disliked.

James's childhood and adolescence were unhappy, abnormal, and precarious; he had various guardians, whose treatment of him differed widely. His education, although thorough, was weighted with Presbyterian and Calvinist political doctrine, and his character – highly intelligent and sensitive, but also fundamentally shallow, vain, and exhibitionist – reacted violently to this.

His political philosophy turned to the theory of the divine right of kings, in striking contrast to the practical experiences of his childhood. He also sought solace with extravagant and unsavoury male favourites who, in later years, were to have a damaging effect on his prestige and state affairs. His economic opportunism, with its disastrous effects on commerce, alienated city interests. Puritan influence and political awareness were increasing fast among the rural landowners, whose influence James never appreciated. His willingness to compromise politically, even while continuing to talk in terms of absolutism, largely accounts for the superficial stability of his reign. However, the effects of many of his actions were long term, becoming fully obvious only after his death. The marriage of James's daughter Elizabeth to Frederic V, Elector Palatine and King of Bohemia, was to result in the eventual Hanoverian succession to the British throne.

Janequin, Clément (c. 1472–c. 1560)

French composer of chansons and psalms. He was choirmaster of Angers Cathedral (1534–37) and then based in Paris from 1549.

His songs of the 1520s–30s are witty and richly textured in imitative effects, for example 'Le Chant des oiseaux'/'Birdsong', 'La Chasse'/'The Hunt', and 'Les Cris de Paris'/'Street Cries of Paris'.

'La Bataille de Marignan'/'The Battle of Marignan' (1515) incorporates the sounds of warriors fighting.

Janyns, Henry (LIVED 15TH CENTURY)

English stonemason. He was in charge of the building of St George's Chapel, Windsor Castle, in the 1470s. He followed his father, Robert, in his career; he worked on the chapel of ◊Eton College and was appointed by Edward IV master mason of the work at Windsor.

Jenson, Nicolas (1420–1480)

French printer, active in Venice from about 1470. He experimented with a roman typeface (first used in Strasbourg and Rome by 1467) following a ◊littera antiqua script. In the following decade he issued about 70 books, mostly Latin or Greek classics including, for example, an edition of Pliny's *Historia naturalis/Natural History* (1472).

Jenson was born at Sommevoie, near Troyes, and moved to Venice after learning to print in Germany, perhaps at Mainz. Though Jenson was noted for his use of roman type, he certainly did not use this exclusively. Indeed, after 1473, he appears to have decreased the number of editions printed with this typography, using instead a Gothic typeface. At the same time, he was one of the first printers to have a Greek font, which may have been influenced by the interest of Francesco ◊Filelfo. The attempt with his various fonts was to make his printed books look as much like a manuscript as possible.

Many of his books were illuminated and decorated by hand, as though they were manuscripts, and special copies of some were printed on vellum. However, they had potential disadvantages to manuscripts. Though hand-written copies were naturally liable to individual errors, printed copies were in danger of replicating mistakes on a larger scale. In particular, Jenson's books sometimes relied on earlier printings and perpetuated the errors already made.

Jodelle, Etienne (1532–1573)

Parisian poet and playwright. He was a member of the ◊Pléiades and followed the group's classicizing agenda in his *Cléopatre captive* (1553), the first tragedy in French to imitate Seneca. He also wrote another tragedy about a female suicide, *Didon* (based on Virgil), and a comedy, *Eugène*. These were printed with his poems, *Euvres et meslanges poetiques* (1574).

John XXIII (BORN BALDASSARE COSSA) (c. 1370–1419)

Anti-pope 1410–15. Born of Neapolitan noble stock, Baldassare Cossa (or Coscia) became cardinal-legate of Bologna and, in his attempt to defend the city against the *condottieri* of Milan and Naples, he supported the Council of ◊Pisa. When the Pisan pope Alexander V died, Cossa was elected his successor but found he had to rely on one of those same threatening *condottieri*, Ladislas of Naples. After Ladislas's death, the Emperor Sigismund persuaded John XXIII to attend the Council of Constance, where, faced with a heavy list of charges, he was deposed and imprisoned. But, in the year of his death, this supposed murderous, incestous sodomite was reappointed cardinal-bishop; and when he died, the Florentines, whose ally he had been, treated him with honour: he was buried in the baptistery, in a tomb designed by ◊Donatello and ◊Michelozzo.

John I (1357–1433)

King of Portugal from 1385. An illegitimate son of Pedro I, he was elected by the Cortes (parliament). His claim was supported by an English army against the rival king of Castile, thus establishing the Anglo-Portuguese Alliance in 1386.

He married Philippa of Lancaster, daughter of John of Gaunt.

John of Austria, Don (1547–1578)

Spanish soldier, the illegitimate son of the Holy Roman Emperor Charles V. He defeated the Turks at the Battle of Lepanto in 1571.

John captured Tunis in 1573 but quickly lost it. He was appointed governor general of the Netherlands in 1576 but discovered that real power lay in the hands of William of Orange. John withdrew in 1577 and then attacked and defeated the patriot army at Gemblours on 31 January 1578 with the support of reinforcements from Philip II of Spain. Lack of money stopped him from going any farther. He died of fever.

John of the Cross, St (1542–1591)

Spanish Carmelite friar from 1564, who was imprisoned several times for attempting to impose the reforms laid down by St ◊Teresa of Avila. His verse describes spiritual ecstasy.

He was persecuted and sent to the monastery of Ubeda until his death. He was beatified in 1674 and canonized in 1726. Feast day is 24 November.

Johnson, John (c. 1540–1595)

English lutenist and composer. He was attached to Queen Elizabeth's court and possibly also to the household of Sir Thomas Kitson at Hengrave Hall, Suffolk, and in London (1572–74). He took part in Leicester's entertainments at Kenilworth Castle in 1575. He wrote lute solos and duets.

Johnson, Robert (c. 1500–1554)

Scottish priest and composer. He fled to England as a heretic and settled at Windsor, where he may have been chaplain to Anne ◊Boleyn. He wrote Latin motets, English services and prayers, In Nomines for instruments, and songs.

Johnson, Robert (c. 1583–1633)

English lutenist and composer, presumed to be a son of John ◊Johnson. He was taught music at the expense of Sir George Carey, husband of Sir Thomas Kitson's granddaughter, in whose household he was brought up, and was appointed lutenist to James I in 1604. He taught Prince Henry and remained in his post under Charles I.

Works include:
Songs for several voices; songs to the lute; catches; pieces for viols; also songs in Shakespeare's *Tempest*, in Fletcher's *Valentinian*, and *The Mad Lover*.

Jonas, Justus (JODOCUS KOCH) (1493–1555)

German Lutheran jurist and theologian. A firm friend and admirer of Martin ◊Luther, Jonas took a prominent part in the Protestant cause. He attended both the Colloquy of Marburg in 1529 and the Diet of ◊Augsburg in 1530, and translated a number of Luther's Latin works into German along with the *Loci communes* of ◊Melanchthon.

Jonas was born at Nordhausen and proved to be an able scholar whose precocious talents attracted the notice of ◊Erasmus. He became professor of law at Erfurt in 1518, and in 1521 professor of theology at Wittenberg. In 1541 Jonas left Wittenberg to take up a post in Halle where, as superintendent of the area's churches, he supervised the organization of the local reform. Forced to leave Halle by the Schmalkaldic war (Schmalkaldic League) he eventually settled in Eisleben, where he remained until his death.

Jones, Inigo (1573–1652)

English Classical architect. He introduced the Palladian style to England. He was employed by James I to design scenery for Ben Jonson's masques and was appointed Surveyor of the King's Works 1615–42. He designed the Queen's House, Greenwich, 1616–35, and the Banqueting House in Whitehall, London, 1619–22.

Little is known of his life, beyond the fact that he was born in London, and appears to have travelled a great deal, particularly in Italy. It is possible that he was sent to Italy to study by William Herbert, 3rd Earl of Pembroke. At any rate he was in Venice around 1603 when he was sent for by the King of Denmark. A quite unfounded legend suggests that he designed the palaces of Rosenborg and Frederiksborg. He accompanied Anne of Denmark to the English court in 1604, where (through his designs for masques) he introduced the new Italian perspective scenery into England and also the proscenium arch. In 1615, after another visit to Italy, Jones became surveyor-general of the royal buildings. He held the same offices under Charles I.

The Civil War interrupted his activities (his loyalty to the Stuarts caused him to be fined twice) and other examples of his work are not numerous. Besides the Queen's House and the Whitehall Banqueting House, his only buildings still surviving are the chapel of Marlborough House, London (1623–27), and part of Wilton House, Wiltshire, including the 'Double Cube Room' (1649–52); but a good example of his work is to be found in St Paul's, Covent Garden, burnt down in 1795, but re-erected in the same style; this was part of his design of Covent Garden Piazza, on which the market was afterwards built; an early example of an architecturally conceived civic space. He may have designed Lindsey House in Lincoln's Inn Fields, around 1640.

Jones, Robert (c. 1485–c. 1536)

English composer. He was a Gentleman of the Chapel Royal from 1513. He composed a song,

'Who shall have my fair lady', a Mass, *Spes Nostra*, and a Magnificat.

Jones, Robert (c. 1570–c. 1617)

English lutenist and composer. He worked for several patrons and took a degree in music at Oxford University in 1597. In 1610, with Philip Rosseter and others, he obtained a patent to train children for the Queen's revels, and in 1615 they were allowed to erect a theatre in Blackfriars, but its opening was subsequently prohibited.

Works include:

Madrigals, five books of *Songs and Ayres* to the lute, anthems.

Jonghelinck, Jakob (1530–1606)

Dutch sculptor and medallist. After studying in Milan with Leone ◊Leoni, Jonghelinck, who was born in Antwerp, returned to the Netherlands in 1555. Among his best-known works, sculpted from 1558–1566, is the Gothic-style tomb of Duke Charles the Bold of Burgundy (who had died nearly a century earlier), for the Church of Our Lady in Bruges.

As this tomb was situated beside the late 15th-century tomb of Charles's daughter, Mary of Burgundy, Jonghelinck imitated the style of the earlier artist, an example of antiquarianism rare in 16th-century art. Although Jonghelinck's life-size bronze of the infamous Duke of ◊Alva in the Antwerp citadel was destroyed during the revolt of 1577, its appearance is reflected in a bust of the same sitter now in New York.

Jonghelinck's bronzes are technically very accomplished and his portraits have considerable characterization.

Jonson, Ben(jamin) (1572–1637)

English dramatist, poet, and critic. *Every Man in his Humour* (1598) established the English 'comedy of humours', in which each character embodies a 'humour', or vice, such as greed, lust, or avarice. This was followed by *Cynthia's Revels* (1600) and *The Poetaster* (1601). His first extant tragedy is *Sejanus* (1603), with Burbage and Shakespeare as members of the original cast. His great comedies are *Volpone, or The Fox* (1606), *The Alchemist* (1610), and

◊*Bartholomew Fair* (1614). He wrote extensively for court entertainment in the form of ◊masques produced with scenic designer Inigo ◊Jones.

He was born in Westminster, London, and entered the theatre as an actor and dramatist in 1597. In 1598 he narrowly escaped the gallows for killing a fellow player in a duel; his goods were confiscated and he was imprisoned. In prison he became a Catholic, but 12 years later reverted to Protestantism. His first comedy, *Every Man in his Humour*, was performed by the Lord Chamberlain's Servants at the Globe Theatre, London. The play was successful, and Jonson was at once enrolled on the list of the leading dramatists. His next plays were *Every Man out of his Humour* (1599), *Cynthia's Revels*, *The Poetaster*, and *Sejanus*. These were followed by *Volpone, Epicoene, or The Silent Woman* (1609), *The Alchemist*, and *Bartholomew Fair*. These are regarded as Jonson's greatest plays, in which he most brilliantly and profoundly exposes the nature of folly, and subtly but pervasively offers a standard of moral sanity by which to judge all excess. They were followed by *The Devil is an Ass* (1616) and, after a long absence from the stage, *The Staple of News* (1626), *The New Inn* (1629), *The Magnetic Lady* (1632), and *The Sad Shepherd* (1635).

Jonson collaborated with Marston and Chapman in *Eastward Ho!* (1605), and shared their imprisonment when official exception was taken to the satirization of James I's Scottish policy. He also wrote numerous poems ('Drink to me only with thine eyes'), and some works in prose. In 1619 he received the laureateship and a small pension from the king, but he died in poverty. He was buried in Westminster Abbey.

Josquin Desprez (DES PRÉS) (1440–1521)

Franco-Flemish composer. His synthesis of Flemish structural counterpoint and Italian harmonic expression, acquired in the service of the Rome papal chapel (1484–1503), marks a peak in Renaissance vocal music. In addition to masses on secular as well as sacred themes, including the *Missa 'L'Homme armé'/ Mass on 'The Armed Man'* (1504), he also wrote secular chansons such as 'El Grillo'/'The Cricket' employing imitative vocal effects.

Juan de Flandes (DIED 1519)

Flemish painter, active in Spain from 1496. He was appointed court painter to Queen Isabella that year and after her death spent the last years of his life in Palencia. A characteristic work is the *Raising of Lazarus* (Prado, Madrid), one of a series of six panels originally in the Church of St Lazarus in Palencia.

Judgement of Sisamnes

Pair of paintings by the Flemish artist Gerard ◊David (1498, Musée Communal, Bruges, Belgium). The subjects were taken from the Greek historian Herodotus, according to whom Sisamnes, one of King Cambyses' judges, was convicted of corruption and ordered to be flayed alive.

The first panel shows the arrest of the corrupt judge, the second the punishment being carried out. The paintings were originally executed for the Hall of Justice in Bruges.

Julius II (BORN GIULIANO DELLA ROVERE) (c. 1445–1513)

Pope from 1503. Born near Savona, he owed his early elevation to the cardinalate to his uncle, ◊Sixtus IV. His own pontificate was dominated by war: he built up the papacy's territorial power by crushing Cesare Borgia, removing the Baglioni from Perugia, and expelling Giovanni Bentivoglio from Bologna in 1506; Julius personally took charge of these campaigns. He also took on the might of the French; Louis XII, as he could not defeat him decisively with arms, tried to undermine his power by invoking the mantra of ◊'conciliarism': however, his creation, the 'schismatic' council of Pisa, did not receive wide support. Julius's response was to call his own Lateran Council, which continued under Leo X.

In his uncle's pontificate, the della Rovere cardinal was employed as military commander and diplomat. On Sixtus's death, rumours suggested he was instrumental in securing the election of Innocent VIII; rumours also claimed that this had made della Rovere 'more than pope'. Whatever his influence over Innocent, he had no such power in the next pontificate. Hostility between him and Rodrigo Borgia had

Julius II Michelangelo, *Moses, c.* 1520 (San Pietro in Vincoli, Rome). The grandiose plans for Michelangelo's tomb for Pope Julius II were repeatedly revised and reduced. The figure of Moses, tugging his beard as a sign of awe of God, was one of the few statues in the original designs which was finally used. *e.t. archive*

for St Peter's (in the inscriptions and heraldry of his commissions, Julius repeatedly emphasized his relationship to the first della Rovere pope). At the same time, he continued his uncle's patronage of the cathedral in their home town, Savona, where he commissioned, for example, an altarpiece by Vincenzo ◊Foppa; he also had a Palazzo della Rovere built in Savona in 1495, to a design of Giuliano da Sangallo.

As pope, his commissions were often grand – sometimes too grand to be finished; but if they remain incomplete, they were at least by the hands of some of the leading artists in Rome in the first decade of the 16th century. Julius's own tomb was extravagantly designed by Michelangelo (a much reduced version finally completed in 1547), the Belvedere courtyard and the façade of St Peter's by Bramante. The façade of St Peter's was part of the restoration work that Julius continued following the example of Nicholas V and Sixtus IV; in Julius's lifetime, Bramante's plans only really got as far as demolishing large parts of the ancient basilica. More successful were two artistic commissions: one was the frescoes for Julius's Vatican apartments, the Stanze della Segnatura, painted by ◊Raphael in 1508–11 (the cycle includes *The School of Athens*). The other was the ceiling of the chapel which bears his uncle's name and was painted by a reluctant Michelangelo 1508–12.

flared up beside Innocent's deathbed, but he could not stop Borgia's election as ◊Alexander VI; his reaction was to go into exile from Rome. After Alexander's death (and the brief pontificate of Pius III), he negotiated with the other cardinals so successfully that his election was a foregone conclusion even before the conclave began.

Julius II acted, both when he was pope and in his earlier days as a cardinal, as a lavish artistic patron. When a cardinal, he had two palaces built and redesigned a third – this, at Santi Apostoli, incorporated rooms from the palace of Cardinal Bessarion; it was decorated with frescoes by ◊Perugino and Bernardino ◊Pinturrichio; in its garden, was displayed the cardinal's collection of antique sculpture, including the ◊*Apollo Belvedere* (moved to Belvedere when he became pope). He also commissioned from Antonio ◊Pollaiuolo the tomb of his uncle, Sixtus IV

> Certainly worthy of great glory, if he had been a secular prince.
>
> ◇
>
> FRANCESCO GUICCIARDINI, summing up Julius II's achievements

Julius III (BORN GIOVANNI MARIA CIOCCHI DEL MONTE) (1487–1555)

Pope from 1550. He succeeded his uncle as archbishop of Siponto in 1511 and, after serving several popes as diplomat and administrator, was made a cardinal by ◊Paul III in 1536 and, with Cardinal Reginald ◊Pole, became copresident of the Council of Trent. There was imperial opposition to his election (he had shown himself to be no supporter of Charles V) but in subsequent years the intricacies of international politics meant that he had to turn to Charles as an ally.

As a patron, he continued the employment of Michelangelo on St Peter's (despite opposition) and also had him design his own residence, the Villa Giulia, which was built by Bartolommeo ◊Ammannati and Giorgio ◊Vasari in 1555. He also appointed Giovanni Pierluigi da ◊Palestrina as the Vatican's choirmaster, and Marcello Cervini as the librarian. He attracted dedications from, among others, Paolo ◊Giovo and Ascanio ◊Condivi.

Juni, Juan de (c. 1507–1577)

French-born Spanish sculptor. His early works include architectural portrait medallions (1536) for the façade of the Church of San Marcos, León. He is best known for the polychromed wood carving *The Entombment of Christ* (1539–44, Valladolid Museum), an expression of his great technical skill and also the emotionalism popular in Spanish art at this time.

Probably born in Burgundy, Juni moved to León in 1533, and settled in Valladolid in 1540.

Justus of Ghent (GIUSTO DA GUANTO) (LIVED 15TH CENTURY)

Flemish painter, active in Urbino, Italy, in the 1460s–1480s. He was, according to ◊Vesapasiano da Bisticci, called to Italy by ◊Federigo da Montefeltro of Urbino, but before he reached the court, he probably went to Rome and then produced an altarpiece of the *Communion of the Apostles* for an Urbino confraternity (1473–74, Palazzo Ducale, Urbino). A large-nosed figure in that painting is recognizable as Federigo and it was for him that Justus painted, among other things, 28 portraits of *Famous Men* (for the duke's *studiolo*) and a painting depicting the duke's learned interests, *Frederigo da Montefeltro, His Son Guidobaldo and Others Listening to a Discourse* (Royal Collection, Hampton Court).

If, as is commonly assumed, Justus of Ghent is identifiable with Joos van Wassenhove, he had an early career in the Netherlands and was a friend of Hugo van der Goes.

Juvenal (c. AD 60–140)

Ancient Roman satirical poet, of whose life very little is known.

Despite Sicco Polenton's claim that Juvenal's poetry fell into slumber for a millennium, humanists merely continued earlier scholars' interest in the *Satires*. ◊Guarino, his son Battista ◊Guarini, and Cristoforo ◊Landino were among those who lectured on Juvenal; Domizio ◊Calderini in 1474, Giorgio ◊Merula in 1478 and, outside Italy, Josse ◊Bade in 1498 produced early printed commentaries. The *Satires* was also one of the first publications from Fichet's Sorbonne Press. Pier Candido ◊Decembrio wrote a life of Juvenal, and Filelfo's own *Satires* was influenced by him.

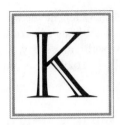

Keating, Geoffrey (SEATHRÚN CÉITINN) (c. 1580–c. 1645)

Irish Gaelic poet and historian. He wrote his *Forus Feasa ar Eirinn/A Basis for Knowledge about Ireland* about 1630. In it he refutes other commentators on Ireland, particularly the Elizabethan chroniclers of the preceding generation, and produces the first attempt at a complete compendium of history and legendary material. He also wrote poetry, in densely wrought assonantal metres.

He was born in Burges, County Tipperary. Educated at Bordeaux and Salamanca, he returned to Ireland as a Catholic priest in 1610.

Kemp, Will (DIED 1603)

English clown. A member of several Elizabethan theatre companies, he joined the Chamberlain's Men in 1594, acting in the roles of Dogberry in Shakespeare's *Much Ado About Nothing* and Peter in *Romeo and Juliet*. He published *Kempe's Nine Days' Wonder* (1600), an account of his nine-day dance to Norwich from London.

Kepler, Johannes (1571–1630)

German mathematician and astronomer. He formulated what are now called **Kepler's laws** of planetary motion: (1) the orbit of each planet is an ellipse with the Sun at one of the foci; (2) the radius vector of each planet sweeps out equal areas in equal times; (3) the squares of the periods of the planets are proportional to the cubes of their mean distances from the Sun. Kepler's laws are the basis of our understanding of the Solar System, and such scientists as Isaac Newton built on his ideas.

Kepler was one of the first advocates of Sun-centred cosmology, as put forward by ◊Copernicus. Unlike Copernicus and ◊Galileo, Kepler rejected the Greek and medieval belief that orbits must be circular in order to maintain the fabric of the cosmos in a state of perfection.

early work Kepler also produced a calendar of predictions for the year 1595 which proved uncanny in its accuracy. In 1596, he published his *Prodromus Dissertationum Cosmographicarum seu Mysterium Cosmographicum* in which he demonstrated that the five Platonic solids (the only five regular polyhedrons) could be fitted alternately inside a series of spheres to form a 'nest'. The nest described quite accurately (within 5%) the distances of the planets from the Sun. Kepler regarded this discovery as a divine inspiration that revealed the secret of the Universe. Written in accordance with Copernican theories, it brought Kepler to the attention of all European astronomers.

In 1601 Kepler was bequeathed all of Tycho ◊Brahe's data on planetary motion. He had already made a bet that, given Tycho's unfinished tables, he could find an accurate planetary orbit within a week. It was five years before Kepler obtained his first planetary orbit, that of Mars. His analysis of these data led to the discovery of his three laws. In 1604 his attention was diverted from the planets by his observation of the appearance of a new star, 'Kepler's nova'. Kepler had observed the first supernova visible since the one discovered by Brahe in 1572.

Kepler's laws Kepler's first two laws of planetary motion were published in *Astronomia Nova* (1609). The first law stated that planets travel in elliptical rather than circular, or epicyclic, orbits and that the Sun occupies one of the two foci of the ellipses. The second law established the Sun as the main force governing the orbits of the planets. It stated that the line joining the Sun and a planet traverses equal areas of space in equal periods of time, so that the planets move more quickly when they are nearer the Sun. He also suggested that the Sun itself rotates, a theory that was confirmed using Galileo's observations of sunspots, and he postulated that this established some sort of 'magnetic' interaction between the planets and the Sun, driving them in orbit. This idea, although incorrect, was an important precursor of Newton's gravitational theory.

Kepler's third law was published in *De Harmonices Mundi*. It described in precise mathematical language the link between the distances of the planets from the

Sun and their velocities – specifically, that the orbital velocity of a planet is inversely proportional to its distance from the Sun.

Rudolphine Tables and other work Kepler finally completed and published the *Rudolphine Tables* (1627) based on Brahe's observations. These were the first modern astronomical tables, enabling astronomers to calculate the positions of the planets at any time in the past, present, or future. The publication also included other vital information, such as a map of the world, a catalogue of stars, and the latest aid to computation, logarithms.

other works Kepler's second book on optics, the *Dioptrice*, was published in 1611. The *Epitome*, intended as an introduction to Copernican astronomy, was an effective summary of Kepler's life's work in theoretical astronomy. It was a long treatise of seven books, published over a period of four years, and it had more impact than any other astronomical text of the mid-17th century. Kepler wrote the first science-fiction story, *Somnium*, describing a man who travelled to the Moon. It was published in 1631, a year after his death. He had published 33 works and left 22 volumes of manuscript and much correspondence.

life Kepler was born in Weil der Stadt in Baden-Württemberg, and studied at Tübingen. He originally intended to prepare for the ministry of the Lutheran Church, but instead became lecturer in astronomy at the University of Graz in about 1594. As a Lutheran Protestant, he was expelled twice from Graz; then from Prague in 1612; then from Linz, Austria, from where he moved to Ulm. His *Prodromus Dissertationum Cosmographicarum seu Mysterium Cosmographicum* won him the friendship of Brahe and Galileo.

Kepler became assistant to Brahe in 1600, and succeeded him in 1601 as mathematician to Holy Roman Emperor Rudolf II. Rudolf was more interested in astrology than in astronomy, and Kepler was of great value to him and to his successor, Matthias, because of his knowledge of the casting of nativities. Kepler himself believed in the subject, and one of the publications that brought him fame during his lifetime was an astrological one, *De Fundamentis Astrologiae* (1602).

After Rudolf's death, Kepler remained in favour and continued his astronomical research. He was invited to England after he dedicated *Harmonices Mundi* to James I. Although in constant poverty at a court that rarely paid him a salary, Kepler refused the invitation. In about 1629, he became astrologer to Wallenstein.

Kerle, Jacob van (*c.* 1531–1591)

Flemish composer. He spent some time in Italy, partly in Rome in the service of Otto von Truchsess, cardinal-archbishop of Augsburg, in whose service he was (1562–75). He was with the cardinal at Augsburg at times, and may have attended the Council of Trent with him (1562–63). Later he became canon of Cambrai, but was often in Vienna and Prague attending on the Emperor Rudolf.

Works include:
Preces, commissioned by the cardinal of Augsburg in 1562, Masses, motets, Te Deums, Magnificats, hymns, *Sacrae Cantiones*.

Khair ed-Din, KNOWN AS BARBAROSSA (ITALIAN 'REDBEARD') (*c.* 1465–1546)

Turkish corsair and admiral of the Ottoman fleet. He harassed European shipping and settlements in the Mediterranean, capturing Algiers from the Spanish in 1519, and gradually took control of all the North African states. He later won several victories against the fleet of Emperor ◊Charles V. His campaigns severely weakened Spain's influence in the Mediterranean.

Of Armenian stock, he was raised on the Greek island of Lesbos, and later moved to Djerba. He began his career with his brother **Horuk** (Aruj) (*c.* 1474–1518). They took Algiers in 1515 but the Arab inhabitants combined with Spanish forces and defeated the brothers in 1518, Horuk being killed near Oran. Barbarossa retook Algiers in 1519 and was proclaimed its ruler by the Turkish sultan Selim I. In 1533 he became admiral of the Turkish fleet.

His success in the Mediterranean finally brought about a response from Emperor Charles V. The Emperor's fleet, under the Italian admiral Andrea ◊Doria, won early engagements, driving Barbarossa out of Tunis in 1535, but lost to Barbarossa in sea battles in the Gulf of Arta in 1538, off Crete in 1540, and off Algiers in 1541. It was in response to these attacks that Barbarossa began plundering coastal towns in Italy, Greece, and Spain. In 1543 Barbarossa helped the French king Francis I – the unlikely ally of Sultan Suleiman – to capture Nice, then a part of Savoy.

King of the Romans
See ◊Holy Roman Emperor.

Kirbye, George (c. 1565–1634)
English composer. He first appeared as the most copious contributor, except John Farmer, to Thomas East's psalter *The Whole Book of Psalmes* (1592). In 1598 he married Anne Saxye, and he seems to have lived at that time at Rushbrooke near Bury St Edmunds, Suffolk, as domestic musician at the residence of Sir Robert Jermyn. In 1597 he dedicated his book of 24 madrigals to Jermyn's daughters. In 1601 he contributed a madrigal to *The Triumphes of Oriana*.

Works include:
Motets, a hymn; madrigals; pavane for viols.

Knox, John (c. 1505–1572)
Scottish Protestant reformer, founder of the Church of Scotland. He spent several years in exile for his beliefs, including a period in Geneva where he met John ◊Calvin. He returned to Scotland in 1559 to promote Presbyterianism. His books include *First Blast of the Trumpet Against the Monstrous Regiment of Women* (1558).

Originally a Roman Catholic priest, Knox is thought to have been converted by the reformer George Wishart. When Wishart was burned for heresy, Knox went into hiding, but later preached the reformed doctrines.

Captured by French troops in Scotland in 1547, he was imprisoned in France, sentenced to the galleys, and released only by the intercession of the British government in 1549. In England he assisted in compiling the Prayer Book, as a royal chaplain from 1551. On Mary's accession in 1553 he fled the country and in 1557 was, in his absence, condemned to be burned. In 1559 he returned to Scotland. He was tried for treason but acquitted in 1563. He wrote a *History of the Reformation in Scotland* (1586).

Kochanowski, Jan (JOHANNES COCHANOVIUS) (1530–1584)
Polish poet whose work comprises mainly lyrics and elegies, both in Latin and Polish. Influenced by contemporary French classicism, his works include *Treny* (1580), a cycle of elegies on the death of his infant daughter, Urszula, who died in 1579.

A native of Sycyn, Kochanowski was educated at Kraków and Königsberg and visited Italy and then Paris, where he met the poet Pierre ◊Ronsard. He returned to Poland in 1559 with an extensive knowledge of Classical and Italian literature. His *Foricoena*, not published until 1584, dates from this period, as do his Latin lyrics and elegies.

He briefly attached himself to the court, attaining the position of royal secretary in 1567. In this period, Kochanowski began to write in Polish as well as Latin. His *Szachy/Chess* (1566) is based on the mock-heroic *Scacchia Ludus* by the Italian poet Marco Vida. In 1570 he retired from the court to settle on an estate at Czarnolas.

His later works include *Fraszki/Trifles* (1584), a collection of sparkling epigrams, and *Pieśni/Songs* (1586), verse much influenced by the odes of ◊Horace, as are his lyrical renderings of the psalms. He also wrote one verse play, *Odprawa posłów greckich/The Dismissal of the Greek Envoys* (1578), based on an incident in the third book of Homer's *Iliad* and modelled on the lines of Classical Greek tragedy.

Kraft, Adam (c. 1460–c. 1508)
German sculptor. He worked in an elaborate late Gothic style, as seen in his tabernacle in the Church of St Lawrence in Nuremberg (1493–96), for which he made not only the sculptures but also the whole highly imaginative architectural edifice – a tiered spire about 19 metres (62 feet) high.

Kraft's work was all produced in his native Nuremberg, where he was given the most prestigious commissions. Among his finest works are his seven reliefs of the Stations of the Cross near the entrance to St John's Church (1505–08). His outstanding work, however, is the tabernacle in the Church of St Lawrence, where there are, among the many figures of humans and animals, portraits of Kraft himself and two apprentices, kneeling and supporting the base of the structure.

Kulmbach, Hans Suess (Süss) von
(c. 1475–1522)

German painter. As a young man, he collaborated with Albrecht ◊Dürer in designing woodcuts, and after 1508 he designed numerous stained-glass windows. When Dürer gave up the execution of altarpieces in 1510, Kulmbach emerged as a major painter of triptychs in Germany.

About 1500 he left his native Kulmbach for Nuremberg, where he studied in Dürer's workshop and was also influenced by the visiting Venetian artist Jacopo de' Barbari. Next to ◊Baldung Grien, Kulmbach was Dürer's most important pupil, with a personal style quite distinct from that of his master.

In 1511 Kulmbach obtained citizenship of his adopted town and became an independent artist. He visited Poland in 1514 and later three of his dozen or so altarpieces were exported to Kraków in Poland. He also painted a number of portraits of considerable ability.

Kyd, Thomas (c. 1557–1595)

English dramatist. He was the author of a bloody revenge tragedy, *The Spanish Tragedy* (printed about 1590), which anticipated elements present in Shakespeare's *Hamlet*.

His *Pompey the Great* (1594) was translated from the French of Robert ◊Garnier. He probably wrote *Solyman and Perseda* (1592), and perhaps had a part in *Arden of Feversham* (1592), the first of many domestic tragedies.

Kyd was born in London, the son of a scrivener. He was a schoolfellow of Edmund Spenser at Merchant Taylors', but little is known of his life. He became one of the bohemian literary set of his day, was a close associate of Christopher Marlowe in his last years and, like him, was charged with atheism; after being imprisoned for this he spent his last years in poverty.

Labé, Louise (PEN NAME OF LOUISE CHARLY) (c. 1524–c. 1566)

French poet. She was a member of the poets, led by Maurice ◊Scève, who flourished in her native Lyons in the 16th century. Her poetic works, published in 1555, consist of three elegies and 24 love sonnets, inspired by Petrarch, that combine realism and intense feeling.

Born in Lyons, she became the wife of a wealthy rope maker (cordier), acquiring the nickname 'La Belle Cordière'. She was an accomplished horsewoman and fencer, and as a young woman she is thought to have fought in the army, disguised as a man, and taking the name Captain Loys.

Among her works is the prose discourse on love, Débat de Folie et d'Amour/Dispute on Folly and Love.

La Boétie, Etienne de (1530–1563)

French writer. He was born at Sarlat, Dordogne, and was well known through his friendship with ◊Montaigne. His Discours de la servitude volontaire, or Contr'un (about 1549), denouncing tyrants and passionately advocating liberty, was used polemically by Huguenots after its publication in 1574.

Ladislas (1380–1414)

King of Naples from 1386. The heir of the ◊Anjou dynasty, he became king when he was six, but his reign was harried by the French claimants to his throne. Despite this, Ladislas led an aggressive policy, twice taking Rome and threatening the northern cities. As with Giangaleazzo ◊Visconti, the menace was ended not by military defeat but by fatal illness.

Lafreri, Antonio (ANTOINE LAFRÉRY) (c.1512–1577)

French-born Italian engraver and publisher. Lafreri is best known for devising 'Lafreri atlases' – atlases in which sheet maps by various cartographers are bound into a single (unique) volume according to each customer's requirements.

Born in Orgelet in France, Lafreri settled in Rome as an engraver in 1544, but by 1553 had moved into publishing. A particularly sumptuous production was his Speculum Romanae Magnificentiae/The Mirror of Roman Magnificence (1575), but he was also known for his output of prints by Marcantonio ◊Raimondi. Lafreri's own imprint occurs on a number of atlases issued between 1556 and 1572, the later ones under the title of Tavole moderne di geografia.

La Grotte, Nicolas de (c. 1530–c. 1600)

French composer and keyboard player. He published settings of poems by ◊Ronsard in 1569 and examples of musique mesurée à l'antique. In 1583 he published with Claude Le Jeune pieces for the Ballet comique de la Royne.

La Hèle (HELLE), Georges de (1547–1586)

Flemish composer. He wrote Masses, motets, and chansons; some of his works were destroyed in a fire at Madrid in 1734.

He was a chorister at the royal chapel in Madrid in his youth. In 1578 he was choirmaster at Tournai Cathedral, but was probably back in Spain by 1580. He won two prizes at the Puy de Musique at Evreux in 1576.

Laib, Konrad (LIVED MID-15TH CENTURY)

Austrian painter. He was active in Salzburg. His work shows both Italian and German traits; an example is his crowded and ornamental Crucifixion (Kunsthistorisches Museum, Vienna).

Lambe, Walter (c. 1452–c. 1500)

English composer. His known music was all included in the Eton Choirbook: it consists of a Magnificat and five votive antiphons (a sixth can be completed from another manuscript; another is partially lost, and four more completely so).

He was King's Scholar at Eton in 1467 (aged 15), and clerk at St George's, Windsor, from 1479 to 1499, acting as master of the choristers (1480–84) (at first jointly with William Edmunds).

Lambert, Francis (1486–1530)

French-born religious reformer. A Franciscan famous as a preacher, he abandoned his order and travelled to Zürich to meet ◊Zwingli and then to Wittenberg in 1523 to meet Martin ◊Luther. He was appointed professor of Bible studies at Marburg University in 1527. In 1529, on the debate over the Eucharist, he openly advocated the position of ◊Zwingli, denying the real presence, alienating his Lutheran supporters.

The son of a papal official at Avignon, he joined the Franciscan Order there in 1507 and became famous as a preacher. After 1517 he travelled through France, Italy, and Switzerland, his study of the Bible and the religious reformers causing him to abandon Catholicism.

In 1526 he was summoned to Hesse by the landgrave, Philip, who entrusted Lambert with the setting up of a Reformed Church in his domains and appointed him to a professorship at the new university of Marburg, the first Protestant university. He died of the plague, leaving a number of works that include a polemic against Erasmus (1525), and commentaries on the Song of Songs (1524) and on the Book of Revelation (1528).

Landi, Stefano (c. 1586–1639)

Italian singer and composer. He was maestro di cappella at Padua about 1620 and in Rome from 1624, and sang alto in the papal chapel from 1630. His sacred opera *Il Sant' Alessio* has been successfully revived at Rome and Innsbruck in 1981 and at Los Angeles in 1988.

Works include:
The operas *La morte d'Orfeo* (1619) and *Il Sant' Alessio* (1631); Masses and psalms; madrigals and cantatas; arias for one voice.

Landini, Francesco (c. 1325–1397)

Italian organist, lutenist, composer, and poet. He was one of the chief exponents of the Italian ◊ars nova. Although blind from early childhood, he became a skilled player of various instruments, in particular the portative organ, and was organist at the Church of San Lorenzo, Florence (1369–96).

He was born in Florence and spent most of his life there, but also visited Venice, where he was highly acclaimed. As a composer he is remarkable for his madrigals and *caccie*, both forms that later underwent considerable development.

Works include:
Madrigals, *ballate*, and other pieces.

Landino, Christoforo (1424–1498)

Italian humanist and professor of poetry at the Florentine Studio. A central figure of Florentine university life, Landino composed the first Platonic dialogue of the Italian Renaissance, the *Disputationes Camaldulenses*, a treatise on the relative merits of the active and contemplative lives. A member of the informal Platonic Academy of Florence (see feature), Landino's Christian Platonic interpretation of the great poets culminated in influential studies of Horace, Virgil, Dante, and Petrarch. He also translated Pliny into Italian.

Landino constitutes an important link between the earlier era of Florentine humanism and the later Platonic Academy of Florence. His work seeks to vindicate the early humanist enthusiasm for ancient poetry and philosophy, expressed by Petrarch, Boccaccio, Salutati, and Traversari, whom he praises in the preface to his influential commentary on the *Divine Comedy*. Landino found in the Tuscan verse of Dante, Petrarch, and Boccaccio the thought of Plato and his successors. In his interpretation of ancient poetry, Landino seeks to attain a spiritual reading harmonizing pagan and Christian thought. In 1453 Landino encouraged Ficino to compose his first work, the *Institutiones ad Platonicam Disciplinam*, which Landino recommended to Cosimo.

Languet, Hubert (1518–1581)

French writer and diplomat. He travelled widely in Europe before entering the service of Augustus I, Elector of Saxony, in 1559, whom he represented at the French court from 1561–72. He narrowly escaped the Massacre of ◊St Bartholomew in 1572, and later served Augustus at the imperial court from 1573–77. His extensive correspondence is a valuable source for 16th-century history.

The anonymous treatise *Vindicia Contra Tyrannos/ Against Tyranny* (1579), which expounds the doctrine of resistance to tyranny by constitutional means, is sometimes attributed to him (others suggest Philippe du ◊Plessis-Mornay as the author, some think it may have been a combined effort). He retired to the Netherlands and may also have helped ◊William the Silent draft his *Apologia* against the king of Spain, published in 1581. He accompanied on his tour round Europe Philip ◊Sidney, whom he considered his protégé and with whom he may have been in love.

Born at Vitteaux in Burgundy, he was educated by Jean Perrelle, a distinguished Greek scholar, and then studied at Poitiers 1536–39, Bologna, and Padua. In 1549, after meeting ◊Melanchthon at Wittenberg, he became a Protestant.

La Noue, François de (1531–1591)

French soldier and writer. He was widely known as 'Bras-de-Fer' ('Iron Arm') because an arm lost in battle was replaced by an iron one. He fought on the ◊Huguenot side in the French Wars of Religion. While in prison he wrote *Discours politiques et militaires/Political and Military Discourses* (1587), a graphic account of the period that combines his memoirs as a soldier with a plea for religious toleration.

La Noue was born in Nantes and converted to Protestantism in 1558. Following the Massacre of St Bartholomew in 1572 he was in charge of the defence of La Rochelle from 1574–78. In 1580 he was captured while fighting against the Spanish in the Netherlands and spent five years in prison. On his return to France he entered the service of Henry IV and fought at the Battle of Ivry in March 1590. He died a year later of wounds received in battle.

Laocoon

Ancient sculpture, refound in Rome in 1506. It became part of the papal collection of ancient statuary, like the ◊*Apollo Belvedere*. It was prized for its intricate entwining of a series of figures and was frequently studied by artists like Giuliano da Sangallo and Michelangelo who believed it to be a sculpture described in Pliny the Elder's *Natural History*. ◊Vasari tells of an occasion when ◊Bramante set four young sculptors, including Alonso ◊Berruguete and Jacopo ◊Sansovino, to copy in competition the *Laocoon*; their efforts were judged by Raphael who declared Jacopo Sansovino's the best – this version was subsequently cast in bronze for Cardinal Domenico ◊Grimani.

La Rue, Pierre de (c. 1460–1518)

Flemish composer. He was a pupil of Ockeghem, and was in the service by turns of the court of Burgundy, Charles V, and Margaret of Austria. He was appointed prebendary of Courtrai and later of Namur.

Works include:
Thirty-one Masses, seven Magnificats, Requiem, 38 motets; chansons.

Las Casas, Bartolomé de (1474–1566)

Spanish missionary, historian, and colonial reformer, known as **the Apostle of the Indies.** He was one of the first Europeans to call for the abolition of Indian slavery in Latin America. He took part in the conquest of Cuba in 1513, but subsequently worked for Native American freedom in the Spanish colonies. *Apologetica historia de las Indias* (first published 1875–76) is his account of Indian traditions and his witnessing of Spanish oppression of the Indians.

Las Casas sailed to Hispaniola in the West Indies in 1502 and was ordained priest there in 1512. From Cuba he returned to Spain in 1515 to plead for the Indian cause, winning the support of the Holy Roman Emperor Charles V. In what is now Venezuela he unsuccessfully attempted to found a settlement of free Indians. In 1530, shortly before the conquest of Peru, he persuaded the Spanish government to forbid slavery there. In 1542 he became bishop of Chiapas in southern Mexico. He returned finally to Spain in 1547.

Lassus, Roland de (ALSO KNOWN AS ORLANDO DI LASSO) (c. 1532–1594)

Franco-Flemish composer. His works include polyphonic sacred music, songs, and madrigals, including settings of poems by his friend ◊Ronsard, such as 'Bonjour mon coeur'/'Good day my heart' (1564).

La Taille, Jean de (1540–1608)

French dramatist. Among his works are the biblical tragedies *Saul le furieux* (1572) (to which he prefaced the essay 'Art de la tragédie') and *La Famine, ou les Gabéonites* (1573), and the comedies *Le Négromant* and *Les Corrivaux* (both 1573).

Latimer, Hugh (*c.* 1485–1555)
English bishop. After his conversion to Protestantism in 1524 he was imprisoned several times but was protected by Cardinal ◊Wolsey and ◊Henry VIII. After the accession of the Catholic Mary, he was burned for heresy.

Latimer was appointed bishop of Worcester in 1535, but resigned in 1539. Under Edward VI his sermons denouncing social injustice won him great influence, but he was arrested in 1553, once Mary was on the throne, and two years later he was burned at the stake in Oxford.

Laurana, Francesco (*c.* 1430–*c.* 1502)
Dalmatian sculptor and medallist who worked in Naples, Provence, and Sicily. His work includes a series of portrait busts of women connected with the royal house of Naples, including those of Battista Sforza (Bargello, Florence) and Beatrice of Aragon (Kunsthistorisches Museum, Vienna). He sometimes worked in collaboration with Luciano ◊Laurana.

Laurana probably trained in Ragusa (near Dubrovnik) under Pietro di Martino da Milano. The first definite record of him is as one of the sculptors working on the triumphal arch of ◊Alfonso V at Castelnuovo in Naples 1453, after which he moved in 1461 to Marseille and to the court of ◊René of Anjou, for whom he executed several medals in the style of ◊Pisanello. Besides these, he also produced a number of reliefs and worked on the Mastrantonio chapel at the Church of San Francesco in Palermo, Sicily (1468).

Laurana, Luciano (*c.* 1422–1479)
Dalmatian architect. A relative of the sculptor Francesco ◊Laurana, he worked in Italy, in particular designing part of the ducal palace of Urbino for ◊Federigo da Montefeltro. It was later completed by the Sienese architect Francesco di Giorgio and is known to have inspired ◊Bramante.

Luciano was born at Lo Vrana, near Zara (Zadar in Croatia), and is first recorded as working in Urbino in 1467. The next year he was appointed the principal

architect on the construction of the ducal palace. His main contribution was the courtyard of the palace and the façade, which resembled the triumphal arch of Alfonso V at Castelnuovo in Naples, upon which his relative Francesco worked in the 1450s.

Laurenziana, Bibliotheca
Library in Florence, opened in 1571. It was built to house the valuable collection of books and manuscripts founded by Cosimo de' Medici and enlarged by other members of the Medici family in the 15th and 16th centuries.

The library building was designed by ◊Michelangelo for Pope Clement VII (Giulio de' Medici) in 1523 in the cloisters of the church of San Lorenzo and includes such features as a carved ceiling, mosaic floor, and carved benches all made to Michelangelo's designs. The library's staircase was completed by Bartolommeo ◊Ammanati and Giorgio ◊Vasari in 1559.

In 1808 the Medici library at the convent of San Marco was combined with the Laurenziana to form the present Bibliotheca Medicea Laurenziana.

Layolle, François de (Francesco dell' Aiolle) (1492–*c.* 1540)
French organist and composer. He was Benvenuto ◊Cellini's music teacher; worked at the church of SS Annunziate, Florence, until 1518. His son Aleman Layolle afterwards taught Cellini's daughter and became organist at Lyon by 1521.

Works include:
Masses, motets; canzoni, madrigals.

Lazarillo de Tormes
Eponymous narrator of the Spanish novel *La vida de Lazarillo de Tormes y de sus fortunas y adversidades/ The Life of Lazarillo de Tormes and His Fortunes and Misfortunes*. Although the anonymous author does not describe the narrator Lazarillo as a *pícaro* ('rogue'), some have considered this the first ◊picaresque novel. Published in 1554 at Burgos, Antwerp, and Alcalá de Henares, the Alcalá edition contains probably spurious interpolations, the last of which suggests a sequel that in fact appeared at Antwerp in 1555. Accurately dating the composition of the work and identifying the author have proved impossible, but the work's sophis-

tication suggests an educated person.

The plot is episodic: Lazarillo serves a series of different, disreputable masters, and learns that social advancement is possible only by deception. The tale closes with Lazarillo as a town crier, believing himself a social success, but cuckolded by his employer and oblivious to the social opprobrium attached to his employment. Although not the first Spanish work to involve low-life characters (La ◊Celestina, for example, is earlier), Lazarillo was original in that its narrative purports to be an autobiography. Its popularity is attested by several translations, among these an English one of 1586.

Lechner, Leonhard (c. 1553–1606)

Austrian composer. He was music director (1584–85) to Count Eitel Friedrich of Hohenzollern at Hechingen and in 1595 was appointed to a similar post at the court of Württemberg at Stuttgart.

After studying with ◊Lassus in the court chapel at Munich, he became a schoolmaster at Nuremberg in 1570. In 1579 he began to publish a revised edition of Lassus's works.

Works include:

Masses, motets, Magnificat, psalms, introits, wedding motet for the Elector Johann Georg I of Saxony; sacred and 160 secular German songs for two–five voices in seven published books; St John Passion (1594).

L'Ecluse, Charles de (CLUSIUS) (1525–1609)

French botanist who published one of the earliest known books on Spanish flora. He translated botanical works, and wrote *Rariorum Aliquot Stirpium per Hispanias Observatarum Historia* in 1576, a description of his observations of rare flora in Spain during an expedition (1564–65).

L'Ecluse was born in Arras, France to a wealthy family in which it was the tradition to study law. This he dutifully did and obtained his licence to practice law in 1548 from the University of Louvain. However, from childhood onwards he had expressed a great interest in plant life and, in 1551, persuaded his father to let him go to Provence in southern France to collect botanical specimens for a local dignitary, Guillaume Roudelet. This led to him translating botanical works, and also completing his own original works.

He was appointed professor of botany at the University of Leiden in 1593. He was delighted to hold this post because the University was rapidly becoming known as a centre for science and medicine as well as theology and the classics. He continued to work in Leiden until his death at the age of 84.

Lefèvre d'Etaples, Jacques (FABER STAPULENSIS) (c. 1453–1536)

French humanist and theologian. He studied Greek in Italy and translated several works by Aristotle. He also published studies of the Scriptures (which influenced Martin ◊Luther) and made the first translation of the Bible into French.

Born at Etaples, Lefèvre became a priest and a teacher of philosophy in Paris. He went to Italy in the 1480s and studied there for several years, his main influence being the scholar Ermolao ◊Barbaro. Lefèvre's main interest was Aristotle, though he was also aware of contemporary neo-Platonism and read the works of medieval mystics.

Around 1505 he was teaching Greek in Paris. In 1507 he won the support of a former pupil, Guillaume Briçonnet, then bishop of Lodèeve, who made him the librarian of the abbey of St Germain-des-Prés. Lefèvre later moved to Meaux, where Briçonnet was now bishop.

During these years Lefèvre turned his attention from Greek classics to the scriptures, publishing his *Commentaires sur les épîtres de Saint Paul/ Commentary on the Epistles of St Paul* in 1512, a work that helped to form Luther's views on grace and faith. This was followed in 1522 by a commentary on the Gospels and in 1523 by the first French translation of the New Testament (from the Vulgate). This was followed in 1528 by his translation of the Old Testament.

Lefèvre's works aroused the antagonism of the scholars of the Sorbonne in Paris and in 1525 he had to take refuge in Strasbourg, where he became tutor to the children of the French king Francis I. He soon retired to Nérac, where he enjoyed the protection of ◊Marguerite of Navarre for the last five years of his life.

Le Franc, Guillaume (DIED 1570)

French composer. A Protestant, he fled to Switzerland, and settled at Geneva in 1541. He established a school of music there, becoming master of the children and singer at the cathedral the following year, and edited Calvin's Genevan Psalter, in which Bourgeois and Marot also had a hand. In 1545 he left for the cathedral of Lausanne, and in 1565 issued a new Psalter there with some tunes of his own.

Leicester, Robert Dudley, Earl of Leicester (c. 1532–1588)

English courtier. Son of the Duke of Northumberland, he was created Earl of Leicester in 1564. He led the disastrous military expedition (1585–87) sent to help the Netherlands against Spain. Despite this failure, he retained the favour of Queen Elizabeth I, who gave him command of the army prepared to resist the threat of Spanish invasion in 1588.

His father was executed in 1553 for supporting Lady Jane Grey's claim to the throne, and Leicester was himself briefly imprisoned in the Tower of London. His good looks attracted Queen Elizabeth, who made him Master of the Horse in 1558 and a privy councillor in 1559. He was a supporter of the Protestant cause.

Elizabeth might have married him if he had not been already married to Amy Robsart. When his wife died in 1560 after a fall downstairs, Leicester was suspected of murdering her. In 1578 he secretly married the widow of the Earl of Essex.

Le Jeune, Claude (CLAUDIN) (c. 1530–1600)

Franco-Flemish composer. He worked for most of his life in Paris. Having become a Huguenot, he tried to escape from Paris during the siege of 1588, and his manuscripts were saved from seizure by the Catholic soldiers by his colleague Jacques Mauduit, himself a Catholic. Later Le Jeune became chamber musician to the king. Like Jean-Antoine de Baïf (1532–1589) and Mauduit, he was an exponent of *musique mesurée*.

Works include:

Motets, psalms set to rhymed versions in measured music and also to tunes in the Genevan Psalter set for three voices; chansons, madrigals; instrumental fantasies, and other pieces.

Leland, John (c. 1506–1552)

English poet and antiquary. Educated at St Paul's (by William ◊Lily), Cambridge, Oxford, and Paris, Leland came to the attention of the court with his Latin poetry. Having gained royal favour, he was appointed to be 'king's antiquary' and in that capacity toured England in 1534–43 making notes on the ancient sites that existed. Though a Protestant, he was dismayed by the destruction of libraries which was a consequence of the dissolution of the monasteries; he urged Henry VIII to take the contents of the libraries into his ownership, but only a few collections were saved that way.

Little that Leland wrote was printed in his lifetime, though manuscripts of his works were known to other scholars, like John Bale. In his last years, he went mad (a result, it is sometimes said, of excessive antiquarianism).

Leo X (BORN GIOVANNI DE' MEDICI) (1475–1521)

Pope from 1513. Second son of Lorenzo de' Medici 'the Magnificent', his birth ensured him privileged access to promotion. He was made a cardinal (in secret) in 1489 when he was 13; when his family were ejected from Florence, his position in Rome was a rallying point for them. He enjoyed Julius II's favour and, on his death, was elected pope. His pontificate was dominated by relations with France, from the time of the young Francis I's victory at Marignano (leading to the Concordat of ◊Bologna) to the alliance with Charles V in 1521 which saw the French pushed out of Lombardy.

At the same time, the church faced internal divisions. In response to the 'schismatic' Council of Pisa, Julius II had convened the Fifth Lateran Council and this continued under Leo until 1517. Leo himself faced a plot on his life, in which three cardinals were implicated –and, as a result, cardinal Alfonso Petrucci was executed. In his last years, another threat arose: the Luther affair. It was Leo that pronounced the condemnation of Luther in the bull *Exsurge Domine* (1520).

Fat and ugly, according to one Venetian, Leo had been educated by, among others, ◊Politian. ◊Erasmus, at least, hoped on his election for a new age of peace and scholarship (but then he was contrasting Leo with his own *bête-noire*, Julius II). Peace there certainly was not, but scholarship fared better. As in previous pontificates, the curia was a humanist-

the ◊Inquisition in 1572 for preferring the Hebrew Biblical text to the Vulgate and for translating the 'Song of Songs' from Hebrew to Castilian, he was declared innocent in 1576 and returned to Salamanca, obtaining the chair of Holy Scripture in 1579. His works published during this period include the intellectually bold *De los nombres de Cristo/On the Names of Christ* (1583). He was appointed Provincial of his Order in Castile days before he died.

Although León's translation of, and commentary on the 'Song of Songs' and his *Exposición del Libro del Job/Commentary on the Book of Job* were never published, he achieved literary and scholarly fame both during and after his lifetime. His poetry, influenced stylistically and thematically by ◊Horace, was first published in 1631 by Francisco de ◊Quevedo. Demonstrating the expressive possibilities of Castilian by his translations from Classical Latin and Biblical Hebrew, León regretted the Church's recent ban on vernacular translations of the Bible in *De los nombres de Cristo*.

hive including, for example, Pietro ◊Bembo. Leo also founded in Rome in 1513 a college of Greek with Janus Lascaris (1445–1534) as its first director.

The tradition of artistic patronage also continued. Julius and Bramante had planned the renovation of St Peter's; Leo appointed a group of architects, first led by Bramante, and including Antonio da Sangallo, to execute the immense task. Raphael was also employed on that enterprise, as well as the continuing decoration of the papal chambers in the Vatican.

León, Luis de (1527 OR 1528–1591)

Castilian friar, scholar, and poet. Of an influential family, he became an Augustinian friar in 1544. He read theology at Salamanca, obtaining the chair of theology there in 1561. Arrested and imprisoned by

Leonardo da Vinci (1452–1519)

Florentine painter, sculptor, architect, engineer, and scientist. He was active in Florence, Milan, and, from 1516, in France. His pictures and drawings were hugely influential for their innovative compositional design and mastery of light. His notebooks and sketches show an immensely inventive and enquiring mind, studying aspects of the natural and scientific world from anatomy and botany to aerodynamics and hydraulics.

Leonardo was the illegitimate son of a Florentine lawyer. He displayed unusual gifts from his earliest years in music and drawing. He was apprenticed in the workshop of Andrea del ◊Verrocchio, where he studied as a pupil with Botticelli, Perugino, and Lorenzo di Credi. Leonardo likely painted the kneeling angel in his master's *Baptism* (Uffizi, Florence) which, the contemporary art historian Giorgio Vasari notes, was recognized by Verrocchio as superior to his own figures. He later developed the use of both ◊*chiaroscuro* and ◊*sfumato*. Both techniques helped explore the emotional depth and complexity of his subjects, as can be seen in unfinished Uffizi *Adoration of the Magi*.

Before his departure for Milan in 1482, Leonardo began to devote himself to projects and studies in architecture, hydraulics, mechanics, engineering, astronomy, geology, and anatomy. As military and naval engineer and secondly as sculptor and painter to the city's ruler Lodovico Sforza, he was employed in a wide range of projects, including the unfinished bronze equestrian monument to Francesco Sforza. During this period he also painted the portrait of Cecilia Gallerani (Kraków) and, in partnership with Ambrogio da Predis, the *Virgin of the Rocks* (National Gallery, London). It was during this period that he painted the fresco of the *Last Supper* in the refectory of Sta Maria delle Grazie, which was tremendously influential despite the ruinous experimental fresco technique employed by him; an engraving of it was made by Marcantonio ◊Raimondi.

In 1500 Leonardo travelled to Venice, where he may have met the painter ◊Giorgione, who was greatly impressed by his treatment of light and shade. He was in Rome in the employ of Cesare Borgia in 1502, mapping out the country and planning canals, harbours, and other works, and in 1503 was commissioned to produce a battle scene on the walls of the Council Hall of Florence. Michelangelo was at the same time commissioned for a similar work, and the cartoons of both aroused great admiration, Leonardo's cartoon of *The Battle of ◊Anghiari* being finished in two years and exhibited with that of Michelangelo. Although neither work was completed, the cartoons were avidly studied by contemporary artists who created numerous copies, among them the young Raphael.

Leonardo later travelled to France, where he enjoyed the patronage of Francis I for the last years of his life. His last painting was *St John the Baptist* (*c.* 1514–15, Louvre, Paris). His many drawings explore both scientific and artistic themes. His superb skill at drawing was highly prized in the 15th and 16th centuries for his expressive use of *chiaroscuro* to define his compositions, as can be seen in the *Virgin and St Anne* (National Gallery, London).

His voluminous notebooks and diagrammatic drawings show a profound research into general scientific laws demonstrable by observation and experiment, although much of his studies were drawn from previous engineers. His inventions ranged from complex cranes to pulley systems, lathes, drilling machines, a paddle-wheel boat, flying machines, and an underwater breathing apparatus. The notes for an unfinished treatise on painting and his remarks on the observation of accidental effects in nature were of considerable importance to later artists.

Leone Ebreo

See ◊Hebreo, Leone.

Leoni, Leone (*c.* 1509–1590)

Tuscan sculptor, engraver, and medallist. He is best known for his bronze portraits and medals of patrons, rulers, and artists such as ◊Charles V and ◊Michelangelo, and in particular for his statues for el ◊Escorial in Spain, sculpted for Philip II. His sculptural style was one of strong and elegant naturalism.

Leoni was born at Arezzo and trained as a goldsmith, but none of his work in that medium has survived. Leoni first worked in Venice and then in Rome, where he was coin engraver at the papal mint 1537–40. He held the same post at the mint in Milan from 1542. As court sculptor and medallist to Emperor Charles V (from 1546) Leoni travelled to Germany and Brussels, besides attending the emperor on his visits to Italy. Later he executed portraits of Philip II of Spain, Empress Isabella, and Maria of Portugal, and collaborated with his son Pompeo ◊Leoni on a range of statuary for el Escorial. He spent the last years of his life in Milan, where the tomb of Gian Giacomo de' Medici in the cathedral (1560–62) is an important example of his work.

Leoni, Pompeo (*c.* 1531–1608)

Italian sculptor, goldsmith, and medallist, son of Leone ◊Leoni. He spent much of his life in Spain, working mostly for Philip II. The chapel of the Escorial contains his most famous sculptures, the larger-than-life bronze statues flanking the main altar.

Leoniceno, Niccolò (1428–1524)

Italian humanist teacher and Greek scholar. Educated at Padua, he taught at Ferrara (where Pietro ◊Bembo and Thomas Linacre were among his pupils). He translated works by the anatomist Galen and discussed that author's scientific method in 1508. His medical knowledge led to his being called upon to provide an opinion of the new disease of the 1490s: ◊syphilis.

Leopolita, Martinus (Marcin Lwowczyk) (c. 1540–1589)

Polish composer who might have studied under Sebastian Z Felsztyna and Jan Jeleń of Tuchola. He was a member of the College of Roratists (*Cappella Rorantistarum*), established at the Royal Chapel at the Wawel royal residence in Kraków in 1543, and court composer there from 1560.

Works include:
Masses, including *Missa Paschalis*, motets; secular songs for several voices, and other pieces.

Lescot, Pierre (1515–1578)

French architect. His most famous work is at the Louvre in Paris, where he designed a square court known as the Cour Carrée (1546–51). On this and other projects he worked closely with the sculptor Jean ◊Goujon. His designs, which played an important role in the development of French architecture, show the influence of the architecture of both the Italian Renaissance and ancient Rome.

Born into a wealthy family of lawyers, Lescot first studied painting. He probably never visited Italy but became acquainted with Classical ideals through books and the study of Roman ruins in France.

His design for the Cour Carrée combined Classical and traditional French features. Jean Goujon provided it with a wealth of sculptures, most in low-relief, and the court was completed under Claude Perrault in the 17th century.

Other major works included the Fontaine des Innocents (1547–49) in Paris and the Hôtel de Ligneris (now the Musée Carnavalet) (1545). Several other influential works have been destroyed.

Leto, Pomponio Giulio (Julius Pomponius Laetus) (1428–1498)

Italian humanist and teacher. A dedicated scholar of Latin, who even adopted an ancient Roman lifestyle, he played the leading role in the founding of the ◊Roman Academy in the late 1450s, which developed in imitation of the Platonic Academy in Florence (see feature).

Born in Calabria, an illegitimate member of the Sanseverini family, he was educated by the scholar Lorenzo ◊Valla. He was a totally dedicated Latinist, refusing even to learn Greek, and he modelled his life on that of Cato the Elder (Marcus Porcius Cato).

L'Héritier, Jean (c. 1480–after 1552)

French composer. He wrote Masses, motets, and other pieces.

He was a pupil of Josquin Desprez. In the 1520s he was in Rome, and was music director to the Cardinal de Vermont at Avignon 1540–41.

L'Hôpital, Michel de (1507–1573)

French lawyer and political figure. As chancellor (1560–68) he sought to reach a compromise in the conflict between Catholics and Protestants in France. With the resumption of the Wars of Religion in 1567, however, ◊Catherine de' Medici lost confidence in him and his policy of religious toleration, and he retired to his estates.

L'Hôpital had a distinguished career in French political life. He became councillor of the *parlement* of Paris in 1537, and in 1547 was Henry II's envoy to the Council of ◊Trent. In 1553 he became Master of Requests (responsible for petitions to the king), and in 1555 president of the finance ministry, the *chambre des comptes*. As chancellor (1560–68) he worked for judicial reform and joined the moderate Catholics (the *politiques*) in their search for a compromise to end religious conflict. His most important work on this issue was the Edict of Orléans (1566).

His *Epistolarum seu sermonum libri VI* appeared posthumously in 1585.

Libavius, Andreas (c. 1560–1616)

German chemist. A prolific writer and controversialist, he is best known for his *Alchemia* (1597), considered the first textbook of modern chemistry. With over 200 illustrations, is a prime source of information on the practical aspects of 16th-century chemistry.

Libavius played an important role in ridding chemistry of its links with alchemy and giving chemistry a scientific basis. He developed a rudimentary system of chemical analysis and discovered stannic chloride, $SnCl_4$. Born at Halle, the son of a weaver, Libavius studied at Jena university, then worked initially as a doctor. From 1588, however, he was a teacher of history and literature, first at Jena, and then at Rothenburg (1591–1607) and Coburg (1607–16).

Ligorio, Pirro (c. 1500–1583)

Italian architect, born in Naples. He designed the Villa d'Este at Tivoli near Rome (1550–69) for his patron Cardinal Ippolito d'Este. Incorporating both landscape features and a terraced garden, Ligorio's plan shows the influence of both ◊Bramante and ◊Raphael. He also worked on the Vatican.

Ligorio also built the Casino in the Vatican gardens for Pope Pius IV (1558–62), but in 1565 was dismissed as Michelangelo's successor at St Peter's after altering Michelangelo's designs. He was also known as a painter and an antiquarian, although he was suspected of forging certain Roman antiquities (see feature on forgery). Several of Ligorio's buildings were also adorned with stucco decorations by him, including the Casino in the Vatican.

Ligozzi, Jacopo (c. 1547–1626)

Italian painter. Born in Verona, he moved to Florence, where in 1575 he became a court painter to the Medici. In this role he painted scenes from Florentine history for the Palazzo Vecchio, Florence. His paintings in the monastery of Ognissanti, Florence, show his characteristic use of warm colour. He was also a fine draughtsman, noted for his detailed pen drawings.

Lily, William (c. 1468–1522)

English teacher and humanist. Returning from a pilgrimage to Jerusalem he learned Greek in Rhodes, where he was taught by refuges from Constantinople, and then spent several years studying Greek and Latin in Rome and Venice. He became the first teacher of Greek in London, and in 1512 was appointed headmaster of John ◊Colet's foundation St Paul's School in London.

Born at Odiham, Hampshire, Lily was the godson of the scholar William ◊Grocyn. He studied at Magdalen College, Oxford, graduating in 1486 and setting off on his pilgrimage soon after.

He was a friend of Thomas ◊More, with whom he collaborated in the translation of Greek epigrams into Latin elegiacs (*Progymnasmata*, 1518), and John ◊Colet, for whom he produced his Latin syntax with rules in English, *Grammatices Rudimenta/Simple Grammar*, which was published with Colet's *Aeditio* in 1527. He also published a book of Latin verses attacking a rival schoolmaster.

Limbourg brothers

Franco-Flemish painters, **Paul** (Pol), **Herman**, and Jan (Hennequin, Janneken), active in the late 14th and early 15th centuries, first in Paris, then at the ducal court of Burgundy. They produced richly detailed manuscript illuminations, including two Books of ◊Hours.

Patronized by Jean de Berry, Duke of Burgundy, from about 1404, they illustrated two Books of Hours that are masterpieces of the International Gothic style, the *Belles Heures* about 1408 (Metropolitan Museum of Art, New York), and *Les Très Riches Heures du Duc de Berry* about 1413–15 (Musée Condé, Chantilly). Their miniature paintings include a series of scenes representing the months, presenting an almost fairytale world of pinnacled castles with lords and ladies, full of detail and brilliant decorative effects. All three brothers were dead by 1416.

Linacre, Thomas (c. 1460–1524)

English humanist, physician to Henry VIII, from whom he obtained a charter in 1518 to found the Royal College of Physicians, of which he was first president.

Lindsay (LYNDSAY), David (1490–1555)

Scottish poet. He was attached to the Scottish court in 1508, and until 1522 was 'usher' to James V of Scotland. His works include the allegorical poem *The Dreme* (*c.* 1528); *The Testament and Complaynt of our Soverane Lordis Papyngo* (*parrot*), a satire on the court, prelates, and nobles; *Answer to the Kingis Flyting*, a reprimand of the king's licentiousness; and the morality play *Ane Satyre of the Thrie Estatis* (1540), denouncing the clergy.

His longest poem, *The Monarchie*, giving an account of the rise and fall of Syria, Persia, Greece, and Rome, also ends in an attack on the Church of Rome. Others include *The Complaynt of Bagsche*; *The Testament of Squire Meldrum* (1550), a kind of romance; *Kitteis Confessioun*, an attack on the church; and *Ane Descriptioun of Pedder Coffeis* (*Pedlars*), a study in low life.

Lippershey, Hans (*c.* 1570–*c.* 1619)

Dutch lensmaker, credited with inventing the telescope in 1608.

Lippi, Filippino (*c.* 1457–1504)

Florentine painter. He was trained by his father Filippo ◊Lippi and ◊Botticelli. His most important works are frescoes in the Strozzi Chapel of Sta Maria Novella in Florence, painted in a graceful but also dramatic and at times bizarre style.

He painted many altarpieces and frescoes, most of which show the grace and delicacy he derived from Botticelli, especially in the depiction of figures and the treatment of light, fluttering draperies. His earlier works include the *Vision of St Bernard*, an altarpiece in the chapel of the Badia, Florence; the *Madonna and Child with Sts Victor, John the Baptist, Bernard, and Zenobius*, (1485, Uffizi, Florence); and the *Virgin and Child with Sts Jerome and Dominic*, (1485, National Gallery, London).

In 1484 he completed the frescoes left unfinished by Masaccio in Sta Maria del Carmine. He was in Rome for some years from 1488 and painted frescoes of scenes from the life of St Thomas Aquinas for a chapel in Sta Maria sopra Minerva. Frescoes for the Strozzi Chapel in Sta Maria Novella, Florence (1500–02) were his last important undertaking. A notable altarpiece of the later Florentine period is *The Adoration of the Magi*, (1496, Uffizi, Florence).

Lippi, Fra Filippo (*c.* 1406–1469)

Florentine painter. His most important works include frescoes depicting the lives of St Stephen and St John the Baptist (1452–66) (Prato Cathedral), which in their use of perspective and grouping of figures show the influence of ◊Masaccio. He also painted many altarpieces featuring the Madonna.

Lippi was born in Florence and patronized by the Medici family. The painter and biographer Giorgio ◊Vasari gave a colourful account of his life including how, as a monk, he was tried in the 1450s for abducting a nun (the mother of his son Filippino ◊Lippi).

A Carmelite monk in early life, he is first mentioned as a painter 1431 and in his early work formed his style on that of Masaccio. He lost two church offices after being convicted of forgery. Pardoned and made chaplain of the convent of Sta Margherita in Prato, he then eloped with a nun, Lucrezia Buti, by whom he had two children, one of them the painter Filippino Lippi. A dispensation arranged by the Medici sanctioned their marriage.

Of his frescoes in Prato Cathedral, depicting events in the lives of St John the Baptist and St Stephen, the most important is the *Death of St Stephen*, in the background of which he introduced a portrait of himself, and that of Salome dancing.

His last years were spent in Spoleto, where with his pupil, Fra Diamante, he worked on frescoes of the life of the Virgin for the cathedral. He also painted many panel pictures and created that wistful type of beauty in his Madonnas (owing something to Fra ◊Angelico) which was to be an ideal pursued by many Florentine masters of the 15th century.

Lipsius, Justus (JOEST LIPS) (1547–1606)

Dutch scholar and teacher. One of the leading Latin scholars of his age, Lipsius is noted for important editions of the Classical authors Tacitus and Seneca. These works popularized a terse prose style that can be seen, for example, in the works of Francis ◊Bacon. His own writings developed a neo-stoicism combining Christianity with ancient stoic philosophy.

He was educated at the Catholic university of

Louvain, he then went to Italy as secretary to Cardinal ◊Granvelle. Returning via Vienna he then taught at the Lutheran university of Jena, where he became a Lutheran. He married a Catholic and returned to lecture at Louvain. In 1579 he accepted an invitation to the Calvinist university of Leyden where he was professor of Roman history for 12 years. He then reverted to Catholicism and spent the last 14 years of his life teaching at Louvain, where he died.

His major editions of Tacitus (1574) (second edition 1600) and Seneca (1605) combine critical insight with wide knowledge of Roman social and political history. He published his much admired and translated book on stoicism, *De Constantia*, in 1584.

littera antiqua (ALSO KNOWN AS LETTERA ANTICA)

Script which, in its printed version, is known as Roman type. Invented probably by ◊Poggio Bracciolini in the very first years of the quattrocento, it was an attempt (as the name suggests) to return to ancient handwriting. What they imitated, however, was not Classical script but what was found in Carolingian manuscripts. Its introduction was, in part, the result of an old man's complaints: Coluccio Salutati found the writing in recent manuscripts too small for his tired eyes and Poggio provided for him something easier to read.

Alongside the ◊italic script, this humanist bookhand became a symbol of their revolution. Classical texts came to be copied in *littera antiqua*, and decorated with the appropriate ◊*bianchi girari* initials, presenting novel-looking, attractive manuscripts. When print was introduced to Italy, some printers experimented with creating a *littera antiqua* type, in particular Nicholas ◊Jenson. Testimony to the enduring success of these experiments is the typeface of this book.

littera antiqua Title page of a mid-15th century manuscript of Petrarch's *Trionfi*, written in *littera antiqua* and illuminated with *bianchi girari* border (Biblioteca Nazionale Centrale, Florence). ◊Petrarch. *Bridgeman Art Library*

Lloyd (FLOYD), John (*c.* 1475–1523)

English composer. He sang at the funeral of ◊Henry VIII's infant son Prince Henry in 1511 and was present at the Field of the Cloth of Gold in 1520.

Lobo, Alonso (*c.* 1555–1617)

Spanish composer. He was a choirboy at Seville Cathedral and assistant to the maestro de capilla from 1591; in 1604 he became maestro de capilla there himself. He was influenced by Palestrina, Victoria, and Guerrero.

Works include:

Liber Primus Missarum (1602), containing six Masses and seven motets; Credo romano, three passions, Lamentations, psalms, hymns.

Lobo, Duarte (ALSO CALLED LOPEZ OR LUPUS) (1565–1646)

Portuguese composer. He was widely known as a composer of polyphonic church music, which he published in six books.

He studied under Manuel Mendes (1547–1605) at Evora and later became choirmaster there. Afterwards he went to Lisbon with an appointment to the Royal Hospital and became maestro di cappella at the cathedral about 1590.

Works include:
Masses, offices for the dead, canticles, motets, and much other church music.

Lochner, Stephan (c. 1400–1451)
German painter. Active in Cologne from 1442, where most of his work still remains, notably the *Virgin in the Rose Garden* (c. 1440, Wallraf-Richartz Museum) and *Adoration of the Magi*, (1448, Cologne Cathedral). His work combines the indigenous German style with the naturalism of Flemish painting.

Lodge, Thomas (c. 1558–1625)
English author. His romance *Rosalynde* (1590) was the basis of Shakespeare's play *As You Like It*. He excelled as a lyric poet, and *Glaucus and Scilla* appeared in 1589; his main volume of verse, *Phillis*, a collection of amorous sonnets, was published in 1593, and *A Fig for Momus* in 1598.

He also wrote two dramas, *The Wounds of Civile War* and, in collaboration with Robert Greene (1558–1592), *A Looking-Glass for London and England*, both 1594, and he translated the works of Seneca and Josephus.

Lodge was born in West Ham and educated at Merchant Taylors' and Trinity College, Oxford. He entered Lincoln's Inn in 1578, but for variety and adventure he took part in two sea expeditions against the Spaniards near the Azores and Canary Islands 1589–91. He studied medicine in Avignon, France, about 1595 and practised as a doctor during the latter part of his life.

Lohet, Simon (c. 1550–1611)
German organist and composer. He was appointed organist to the court of Württemberg at Stuttgart in 1571.

Works include:
Pieces in fugal style, canzoni, and hymn-tune fantasies for organ.

Lomazzo, Giovanni Paolo (1538–1600)
Italian painter and art theoretician. He worked as a painter until the age of 33, when he went blind and turned to writing on the theory of art producing, for example, his popular *Trattato dell'arte de la pittura/Treatise on the Art of Painting* in 1584.

Born in Milan, Lomazzo trained as a painter under Gaudenzio ◊Ferrari and worked at the court of Duke Cosimo of Florence. His influential *Trattato dell'arte de la pittura* is a work in seven parts, dealing with proportion, movement, colour, light, perspective, technique, and art history. It was translated into English as *A Tracte Containing the Artes of Curious Paintinge, Carvinge, and Building* in 1598.

In 1587 he published a volume of verse, *Rime*, and in 1590 his art treatise *Idea del tempio della pittura*.

Lombard, Lambert (1505–1566)
Flemish painter, engraver, architect, and poet. He visited Italy during 1537–38 and became known as a Romanist, introducing his many Flemish pupils to Italian art. He was more important as a theorist than as an artist.

Lombardo
Family of Venetian sculptors and architects. **Pietro Lombardo** (1435–1515) was an architect who designed the Palazzo Vendramin in Venice (1500–1509), and produced many tombs for Venetian churches, often assisted by his son **Tullio Lombardo** (c. 1455–1532), notably the Mocenigo tomb in SS Giovanni e Paolo in 1481. Tullio also sculpted portrait reliefs. His brother Antonio (c. 1458–1516) worked for a time in Ferrara, where he produced mythological pieces for Alfonso I d'Este. All three worked in a classicising style.

Lope de Rueda (c. 1505–1565)
Sevillian gold-beater, strolling player, and playwright, whose rather turgid prose plays were published posthumously by his friend, the scholar, editor, and publisher Joan Timoneda (two collections in 1567, and in an anthology of other playwrights in 1570). Lope de Rueda's 'pasos' – short, farcical interludes, many of which are interpolated into his comedies – constitute his major contribution to Spanish drama.

Almost plotless and written in prose, their humour consisted in the attention to dialogue and local detail. One such is his 1548 *Las aceitunas/The Olives*, in which a peasant couple argue over the olives' selling price before the trees have even been planted.

Lopes, Fernão (?C. 1380–AFTER 1459)

Portuguese chronicler of the Avis dynasty. A 1418 document refers to him as keeper of the royal archive (at St George's Castle, Lisbon); a 1422 document reveals he was also confidential secretary to one of João I's younger sons, Fernando (who died imprisoned in Tangiers in 1443). In 1428 he was described as public notary to João I. João's successor, ◊Duarte, appointed him royal secretary, also instructing him in 1434 to chronicle the lives of all Portuguese kings to the death of João I.

Lopes's chronicles of the reigns of Duarte's three immediate predecessors (Pedro I, Fernando I, and João I) are all that has survived and even the last of these is incomplete. Although Lopes's immediate successor to the post of royal chronicler, ◊Zurara, did not plagarize and destroy his writings as Rui de Pina was to do, he rejected Lopes's use of archival documents in favour of rhetorically embellished eye-witness accounts. Yet if Lopes is often taken at his word as a historian striving for objectivity through use of documents and collation of chronicle sources, his observation (in his chronicle on João I) that he considers worthless any chronicles at variance with his own suggests he too had a penchant for destroying competing accounts. Numerous 16th- and 17th-century manuscripts of Lopes's three chronicles survive, but none of them was printed until 1644.

López, Iñigo López de Mendoza

Another name of the Spanish poet ◊Santillana.

López de Ayala, Pero (1332–1407)

Chancellor of Castile, historian, and poet, he began his career at the court of Pedro I 'the Cruel' (becoming admiral of the fleet in the war against Aragon), but changed allegiance when Enrique was proclaimed king over Pedro in 1366. His court career continued under Juan I, whom he accompanied in his unsuccessful campaign to claim the Portuguese throne, despite having advised against it. Ayala was captured at the decisive Battle of Aljubarrota (1385); during his two-year Portuguese imprisonment he began his *Rimado del Palacio/Palace verses* (its contents included personal reminiscences, criticism of contemporary society, and prayers) and completed a derivative treatise on falconry. He remained at court after Juan's death in 1390, but when the young Enrique became king, he returned to his native Alava (in the Basque country) to complete his *Rimado* and to begin the first Castilian chronicles on events within living memory. Enrique named him chancellor in 1399.

Ayala chronicled the reigns of the four kings he served: Pedro I and Enrique II (both chronicles completed before 1483), and Juan I and Enrique III (completed 1393–1407). The *Crónica del Rey Don Pedro/Chronicle of King Pedro* was first published in 1495; in 1526 it was republished together with the chronicles of Enrique II and Juan. Ayala's reliance on eyewitness accounts over documentary sources aroused the hostility of ◊Fernão Lopes, in any case ill-disposed towards Castile. Ayala also translated Livy (Books I, II, and IV), published 1497, and rendered the first eight books of Boccaccio's *De Casibus Virorum Illustrium/On the Fall of Illustrious Men* into Castilian as *Cayda de principes/The Fall of Princes* (published 1495).

Lorenzetti, Ambrogio (?1290s–1348)

Sienese fresco- and panel-painter who deliberately took over the mantle of ◊Duccio and Simone ◊Martini. Ambrogio's commission (1338–39) to decorate the Sienese council chamber resulted in unprecedented panoramic evocations of life in the ideal type and antitype of city and *contado* (the city's economically dependent hinterland), and groupings of allegorical, superhuman (both sacred and diabolic) figures to govern those cities. Ambrogio's work demonstrated explicitly how, in the ideology of the trecento urban republic, civic and secular were far from synonymous.

Details of Ambrogio's life are unknown. The secular landscapes, architectonic distribution, and *all'antica* near-nude females of his civic works powerfully recall Classical fresco, though the allegories are late-medieval. The stylistic influence of Duccio and

Lorenzetti Ambrogio Lorenzetti's fresco cycle celebrating the virtues of republican government was commissioned for the Palazzo Publico of Siena. *e.t. archive*

- *Presentation in the Temple* (1342)
- *Annunciation* (1344)

Undated:
- *Mary Magdalene and Dorothy* (c. 1320s)
- *Madonna del Latte*
- *Madonna and Child in Swaddling Bands*

Disputed works:
- Talamone city-scape and Trasimeno lake-side landscape
- *Allegory of Redemption*

Lorenzetti, Pietro, (c. 1280–c. 1348)

Sienese fresco- and panel-painter long confused with and overshadowed by his younger brother ◊Ambrogio, partly owing to a mistake by ◊Vasari. The trademark gestures of his sacred figures – the tender facial expressions, the indicative jerk of the thumb, and the streaming processions which anticipate International ◊Gothic – were almost unprecedented. In his *Birth of the Virgin* (1342) Pietro also developed an *ad hoc* linear perspective for the representation of internal architectural space which pushed forward ◊Giotto's volumetric solutions to anticipate the Classical barrel-vault of the 15th century.

Simone affected Ambrogio's play of light and colour and the sinuosity of his fabrics, though there are Giottesque tones in his idiosyncratic, unmathematical perspective. The inventive solutions to the depiction of interior space pioneered by his elder brother ◊Piero influenced Ambrogio's temple in his *Presentation in the Temple* (1342).

Pietro, whose life and career is almost undocumented, also executed a sequence of frescoes in the lower church at Assisi illustrating the life and passion of Christ. This included innovations such as the horrifyingly realistic image of the hanged Judas, the depiction of the passing of time in the rising and setting of the moon, and the panicky hustling of spectators, possibly influenced by the crowd scenes of sculptor Giovanni Pisano (Pietro was also a friend of the sculptor Tino di Camaino).

Surviving attributed works:
- *Madonna of Vico L'Abate* (c. 1319)
- *Madonna and Child with SS Nicolaus and Proclus* (c. 1332)
- *Stories from the Life of St Nicolaus* (c. 1332)
- Massa Marittima *Maestà* (c. 1335)
- Sant'Agostino *Maestà* (c. 1335-8)
- San Galgano *Maestà* (c. 1335-8)
- *The Martyrdom of the Seven Franciscans* (1336–37)
- *Allegories of Good and Bad Government* (1338–39)
- *The 'Little' Maestà* (c. 1340)

Surviving works:
- Arezzo polyptych (1320)
- Passion frescoes, *Stigmatization of St Francis, Madonna and Child with SS Francis and John the Evangelist*, Assisi (c. 1320s)

- The Carmine altarpiece (1327–28)
- Frescoes at San Francesco, Siena (c. 1336–37)
- The Uffizi *Madonna and Child* (1340)
- The Cortona *Madonna and Child* (c. 1340)
- *The Birth of the Virgin* (after 1336–42)

Lorenzo Monaco (ADOPTED NAME OF PIERO DI GIOVANNI) (1370–1422)

Italian painter. He produced illuminated manuscripts, altarpieces, and frescoes. Among his paintings are *Coronation of the Virgin*, (1413) and *Adoration of the Magi*, (1420–22, both Uffizi, Florence).

He was born in Siena and settled in Florence as a Camaldolese monk. He introduced a Gothic element into Florentine art, to be seen in his elongated figures and decorative colour – his *Annunciation* (Accademia, Florence) is already close in feeling to the work of his successor, Fra ◊Angelico. His own development, however, also shows the gradual assimilation of elements of Florentine styles such as that of Agnolo ◊Gaddi, a follower of Giotto.

lost-wax technique

Method of making sculptures; see ◊*cire perdue*.

Lotto, Lorenzo (c. 1480–1556)

Venetian painter active in Bergamo, Treviso, Venice, Ancona, and Rome. His early works were influenced by Giovanni ◊Bellini. He painted religious works but is best known for his portraits, which often convey a sense of unease or an air of melancholy.

He evolved a rich and imaginative style, as in the *Prothonotary Apostolic, Giuliano* (National Gallery). *A Lady as Lucretia* (also National Gallery) well represents a type of his work which inspired the young Caravaggio. His most celebrated altarpieces are in the churches of the Carmine and SS Giovanni e Paolo, Venice, the cathedral at Asola and at Monte San Giusto near Ancona, where the church contains a *Crucifixion* with 23 life-size figures. The last two years of his life were spent in monastic retreat in the Santa Casa monastery at Loreto.

Louis XI (1423–1483)

King of France from 1461. He broke the power of the nobility (headed by ◊Charles the Bold) by intrigue and military power.

Louis XII (1462–1515)

King of France from 1498. He was Duke of Orléans until he succeeded his cousin Charles VIII to the throne. His reign was devoted to Italian wars.

Lovati, Lovato (1241–1309)

Italian notary, judge, and author, born in Padua. Perhaps Lovati himself would judge his greatest moment to be his discovery in 1283–84 of a tomb which he identified as that of Antenor, the mythical founder of his city. He was, as it happens, wide of the mark, but the incident suggests how civic pride could be entwined with classicizing interests. Those interests were also reflected in his reading of little-known ancient authors and in his writing of a short treatise unravelling the mysteries of the metre of Seneca's *Tragedies*. (See ◊prehumanists.)

Loyola, St Ignatius (BORN IÑIGO LÓPEZ DE RECALDE) (1491–1556)

Spanish noble who founded the Jesuit order in 1534, also called the Society of Jesus.

His deep interest in the religious life began in 1521, when reading the life of Jesus while recuperating from a war wound.

He visited the Holy Land in 1523, studied in Spain and Paris, where he took vows with St Francis Xavier, and was ordained in 1537. He then moved to Rome and with the approval of Pope Paul III began the Society of Jesus, sending missionaries to Brazil, India, and Japan, and founding Jesuit schools. Canonized in 1622. Feast day is 31 July.

Lucas van Leyden (1494–1533)

Dutch painter and engraver. Active in Leiden and Antwerp, he was a pioneer of Netherlandish genre scenes, for example *The Chess Players* (c. 1510, Staatliche Museen, Berlin). His woodcuts and engravings, often more highly regarded than his paintings, were inspired by Albrecht ◊Dürer.

Lucas was a pupil of Cornelisz. Engelbrechts. He settled at Antwerp, where he met Dürer in 1521. Though the engravings and woodcuts by which he won early fame show Dürer's influence, they possess a distinctive charm and inventiveness of their own which is characteristic in all his work. His paintings show an Italian influence, his unusual colour and pictorial imagination being exemplified in *Lot and his Daughters* (Louvre, Paris).

Lucas earned a high reputation in his own day, even being praised by the Italian artist and art historian ◊Vasari.

Lucretius (TITUS LUCRETIUS CARUS)
(*c.* 99–55 BC)

Ancient Roman poet and Epicurean philosopher whose *De rerum natura/On the Nature of Things* envisaged the whole universe as a combination of atoms.

Although a few medieval scholars knew *De rerum natura* – including, perhaps, the Paduan ◊prehumanists – the work circulated widely only after ◊Poggio found a copy in 1417. Humanists equally praised the poem for its poetry and condemned it for its un-Christian tenets (although ◊Ficino, always keen to Christianize writers, suggested that Lucretius could be reconciled to true religion). Although *De rerum natura* rarely entered the classroom (indeed, in Florence, it was banned), it was printed (28 times between the *editio princeps* in 1473 and 1400), commented upon (Gian Battista Pio, 1511; Denys Lambin, 1563), read (by, for example, ◊Montaigne and Francis ◊Bacon), imitated (by ◊Marullus and Bartolomeo ◊Scala), and used as an artistic source (by ◊Piero di Cosimo).

Ludford, Nicholas (*c.* 1485–*c.* 1557)

English composer. He wrote seven festal Masses, motets, a Magnificat, and a unique set of seven Masses for the daily Mass of Our Lady. He was long active at the Royal Chapel of St Stephen, Westminster.

Luini, Bernardino (*c.* 1460–?*c.* 1530)

Italian painter. He worked primarily in Milan where he came under the influence of ◊Leonardo da Vinci who had a tremendous impact on his art. Considered to be among Leonardo's most faithful followers, his paintings are characterized by the skilful use of ◊*sfumato* which he employed in numerous religious paintings.

Luis de León, Fray (*c.* 1527–1591)

Spanish poet, writer, and translator. An Augustinian friar, he spent most of his life as a teacher at Salamanca University. In his lifetime he was recognized as one of the greatest Spanish prose writers of his age, his most important work being *De los nombres de Cristo* (1583), a meditation on the names applied to Christ. The same originality can be seen in his few poems (not published until 1631).

Born the eldest son of a judge in Belmonte, La Mancha, Luis de León entered the university of Salamanca about 1541, and then joined the Augustinian order, taking vows in 1544. He was elected to the chair of St Thomas Aquinas in 1561.

After the decrees of the Council of ◊Trent were promulgated in Spain in 1564, there was pressure to impose orthodoxy on university teachers. For various reasons he fell foul of the Inquisition (he was secretly denounced by rival professors) and was imprisoned during 1572–76. The possible reasons include his translation of the biblical *Song of Songs* made privately for a cousin who was a nun, a work that was thought licentious; his public criticism of the Vulgate; and perhaps even the fact that a great-grandmother was a *conversa* (a convert from Judaism). Finally acquitted, he returned to Salamanca, holding the chairs of moral philosophy from 1578 and biblical studies from 1579. He became provincial of the Augustinian order in Castile shortly before his death.

His 29 poems were influenced by Virgil, Horace, and neo-Platonic philosophy and are, like those of St John of the Cross, highly personal expressions of intense religious feeling. They include odes that are among the best examples of the *lira* stanza introduced into Spanish by Garcilaso de la Vega.

His *De los nombres de Cristo*, written while he was in prison, is a dialogue on the scriptural names of Christ ('the Way', the 'Shepherd', the 'Bridegroom' and so on). He also wrote *La perfecta casada* (1583), a commentary on chapter 31 of the Book of Proverbs expounding the duties of a married woman. He was as fluent a writer in Latin as in Spanish, and also translated works by Pindar, Seneca, Tibullus, Bembo, and della Casa.

Luna, Álvaro de (*c.* 1390–1453)

Spanish statesman and poet. The tutor of King John II of Castile, he became very powerful, and as constable from 1423 was the virtual ruler of Castile. The hostility of the king's second wife, Isabella of Portugal, brought about his downfall, and he was executed at Valladolid after a mock trial for witchcraft. His poems appeared in *Cancionero de Baena* in 1445.

An illegitimate member of a family of wealthy *conversos* (converts to Catholicism from Judaism), de Luna became the tutor of John II about 1410 and began his climb to power when the young John II of Castile came of age in 1419. Despite the hostility of the king's Trastámara cousins and their supporters among the old aristocracy, the king came to rely heavily on de Luna. Although driven from court by his opponents in 1427 and again in 1439, he returned on both occasions and consolidated his power. He fought and defeated the Moors in Granada in 1441, and after the Castilian defeat of the Aragonese at Olmedo in 1445 he was elected grand master of the Order of Santiago.

Among his writings was a treatise in defence of women, *Libro de las virtuosas e claras mugeres* (1446).

Lupo, Thomas

English composer and player of stringed instruments. His father Joseph (died 1616), his uncle Ambrose (died 1591), and his son Theophilus (fl. 1628–42) are also known as composers, but Thomas is distinguished by his pavanes and fantasies for viol consort, particularly in five and six voices.

Lusiads, The Os Lusíadas

Epic poem in ten *cantos* by Luis de ◊Camões. Dedicated to King Sebastião of Portugal, it celebrates Vasco da ◊Gama's discovery of the sea-route to India, as well as Camões's own poetic self. Interspersing his narrative of contemporary events with scenes involving pagan gods – gods which, moreover, intervened in the events of the voyage – was both innovatory and open to criticisms of heresy. However, the Portuguese censor of the first, 1572, edition excused the presence of such pagan characters on the grounds that they were no more than decorative ornaments for a fictitious poem. Not so the 1584 editors, who erased all reference to gods and goddesses.

Os Lusíadas was an instant – and huge – success, both in Portugal and Spain. By 1600, there had been four Portuguese editions (1572, 1584, 1591, and 1597) and three different Castilian translations (two in 1580, another in 1591). Even so, Manuel de Faria e Sousa felt compelled to publish a monumental edition and commentary (written in Castilian) in 1639, to ensure Camões's consecration as the greatest poet ever, and *Os Lusíadas* as a work second only to the Bible. Although Sousa's commentary apparently inspired ◊Lope de Vega to appreciate the epic (having hitherto preferred Camões's lyrics), Lope continued to hold Camões second to ◊Garcilaso de la Vega. Meanwhile, despite the Portuguese Tomé de Faria's Latin translation in 1622, the work's fame did not spread beyond the Iberian peninsula until the mid-17th century, when English (1655) and Italian (1658) translations appeared.

Lusitano, Vicente (DIED AFTER 1553)

Portuguese music theorist and composer. He was known as Vicente de Olivença in Portugal, but was called Lusitano ('the Portuguese') in Rome, where he settled about 1550. In 1551 he had a dispute with Nicola Vicentino, which was settled in his favour, with Ghiselin Danckerts and Bartolomeo Escobedo as judges. He published a treatise on cantus firmus in 1553.

Works include:
Motets *Epigrammata*, and other pieces.

Luther, Martin (1483–1546)

German monk whom circumstances turned into the pre-eminent leader of Protestant reform. In his early years, Luther taught at the new University of Wittenberg, where his ideas were formed by reading both humanist works and Augustine. He gained attention, however, for his criticism of the selling of indulgences (which the papacy claimed could assist the soul through purgatory to heaven); his 95 theses of 1517, intended to cause debate, aroused more than that – they brought on him the Dominicans' accusations of heresy. Luther had to admit that his position had similarities to that of Jan Huss but he refused to recant. Instead, he developed his theology in opposition to the Catholic Church; a combination of political support and the unprecedented spread of his ideas by print made Lutheranism impossible to repress.

Luther's theology developed in response to events around him. Before the events of 1517, he already had thought out his crucial doctrine of 'justification by grace through faith alone' which came to be a denial of Catholic belief that good works could assist in one's salvation. In the period between 1517 and the Diet of Worms of 1521 (where he was outlawed by Charles V), he produced a set of tracts expounding and developing his thoughts further. Through his career, he was an indefatigable popularizer of his views, translating the Bible into German as well as producing hymns and pamphlets. In the process, however, it was easy for internal contradictions in his ideas to appear.

At first, Luther's position seemed acceptable to reformers within the Catholic Church like ◊Erasmus. His plight seemed akin to that of Johannes ◊Reuchlin, who had also been attacked by the Dominicans; and Luther gained support from some German humanists, like Ulrich von ◊Hutten (who had already expressed – anonymously – a strident position on the Reuchlin affair). However, his increasing vehemence and his clear break from the Catholic Church alienated many reforming figures, including Erasmus and Reuchlin. Erasmus eventually entered controversy with Luther on the issue of free will, which Luther denied.

Lutheranism

The faith which emerged from the various writings of Martin Luther and Philip ◊Melanchthon. Given some sort of formulaic statement by the Confession of Augsburg (1530), it was the religion adopted by several German princes as well as by the kings of Denmark (under Christian III) and Sweden (first under Gustav Vasa but only permanently in 1593). There were also Lutherans in France, tolerated until the Day of Placards in 1534, and in England, where under Henry VIII hesitant and incomplete moves were made towards evangelical religion. From the middle of the 16th century, Lutheranism was challenged by the success of Jean Calvin's Reformed Protestantism.

Luyton, Karel (c. 1556–1620)

Flemish organist and composer. He was in the service of the Emperor Maximilian II at Prague in 1576, and when Maximilian died, was appointed to the Emperor Rudolf II in the same capacity. He succeeded Philippe de Monte as court composer from 1603.

Works include:

Masses, motets, Lamentations, *Sacrae Cantiones*, Italian madrigals; *Fuga Suavissima* and *Ricercare* for organ.

Luzzaschi, Luzzasco (c. 1545–1607)

Italian organist and composer. He wrote some sacred works, but his madrigals are his best-known compositions. His skilfully composed five-part madrigals were his most popular works; the later ones show an increased use of homophony.

Luzzaschi was a pupil of Cipriano de Rore at Ferrara and in 1561 became a singer at the Este court there. In 1564 he became court organist, and was also active as a composer and teacher; Frescobaldi was one of his organ pupils. By 1570 he was directing the duke's chamber music, and by 1576 was his organist and maestro di cappella. He was also organist at Ferrara Cathedral and the Accademia della Morte. Here he composed madrigals for the celebrated 'singing ladies' of Ferrara, a group of virtuoso singers who performed for private audiences. His *Madrigali per cantare, et sonare a 1–3 soprani* (1601) contains some of these pieces with their fully notated keyboard accompaniments, which were long kept secret. From 1597 Luzzaschi served cardinal Pietro Aldobrandini, who controlled Ferrara when the city passed to the papacy.

Works include:

Motets, *Sacrae Cantiones*, madrigals; organ music, and other pieces. His *Madrigali per cantare et sonare* (1601) are for three voices and have keyboard accompaniments.

Lydgate, John (c. 1370–1449)

English Benedictine monk and poet. His numerous works range from fables and satires to lives of saints and religious lyrics; his large-scale poems include *The Troy Book* (1412–21) (commissioned by Henry V), *The Siege of Thebes* (1420–22), and *The Fall of Princes* (1431–38) (commissioned by Humfrey, Duke of ◊Gloucester).

Lydgate was educated at the monastery of Bury St Edmunds, Suffolk, and spent much of his life there (in the 15th and 16th centuries – when his works proved popular – he was often called 'the Monk of Bury'). Although his career was not as cosmopolitan as that of Geoffrey ◊Chaucer (whom he regarded as his poetic 'master'), he did spend several years in Lancastrian France about 1426–29, where he was patronized by Richard Beauchamp, Earl of Warwick, and his works reflect knowledge of trends in French and Latin literature. In particular, *The Fall of Princes* is an adaptation of Laurent de Premierfait's French version of Boccaccio's *De Casibus Virorum Illustrium* and also includes a section indebted to a declamation by Coluccio ◊Salutati.

Lyly, John (*c.* 1553–1606)

English dramatist and author. His romance *Euphues, or the Anatomy of Wit* (1578), with its elaborate stylistic devices, gave rise to the word ◊euphuism for a mannered rhetorical style. It was followed by a second part, *Euphues and his England* (1580).

The story line of *Euphues* is little more than a basis for the characters to engage in debate on the manners and values of the age. The prose style is chiefly characterized by a continuous straining after antithesis and epigram.

Lyly was born in Kent. He studied at Magdalen College, Oxford, graduating with an MA degree in 1575, and also at Cambridge, graduating with an MA in 1579. The publication of *Euphues, or the Anatomy of Wit* brought him instant fame; the second part brought him to the notice of Lord Burghley, who gave him some employment. After this he wrote sophisticated plays to be performed at court by the children's acting companies, among which were *Campaspe* (1584), *Sapho and Phao* (1584), *Endymion* (1591), and *Midas* (1592). In 1589 he championed the cause of the bishops in the ◊Marprelate controversy and published a tract entitled *Pappe with an Hatchet*. In 1589 he entered Parliament for Hinton, being subsequently elected for Aylesbury in 1593, for Appleby in 1597, and again for Aylesbury in 1601.

Mabuse, Jan (ADOPTED NAME OF JAN GOSSAERT) (c. 1478–c. 1533)

Flemish painter. His visit to Italy in 1508 started a new vogue in Flanders for Italianate ornament and Classical detail in painting, including sculptural nude figures, as in his *Neptune and Amphitrite* (*c.* 1516, Staatliche Museen, Berlin).

His early works, in a purely Flemish style, include the *Adoration of the Magi* (National Gallery, London), and *The Upright Judges* (Musée Royal des Beaux-Arts, Antwerp). His triptych of *Adam and Eve*, (1516, Berlin), on the other hand, clearly shows the influence of his visit to Italy.

Machaut, Guillaume de (1300–1377)

French poet and composer. Born in Champagne, he was in the service of John of Bohemia for 30 years and, later, of King John the Good of France. He gave the ballade and rondo forms a new individuality and ensured their lasting popularity. His *Messe de Nostre Dame* about 1360, written for Reims Cathedral, is an early masterpiece of *ars nova*, 'new (musical) art', exploiting unusual rhythmic complexities.

Machiavelli, Niccolò (1469–1527)

Florentine diplomat and author. He rose to prominence after the fall of Girolamo ◊Savonarola, serving the Republic as chancellor (from 1498), military administrator, and diplomat. With the return of the Medici in 1512, he was removed from office; the following year, he was implicated in an anti-Medicean plot and tortured. Though he had earlier written a verse chronicle, it was in the following years that he really took to writing, producing his own idiosyncratic versions of a mirror-for-princes work (*Il Principe/The Prince, c.* 1513), a commentary on a Classical text (*Discorsi sopra la Prima Deca di Tito Livio/◊Discourses on the First Ten Books of Livy, c.* 1515–19) and a city history (*Istorie Fiorentine/Florentine Histories,* 1525), as well as comedies (*Andria,* based on Terence, 1517; *Mandragola* 1518; *Clizia,* based on Plautus, 1525), biography (*The Life of Castruccio Castracani,* 1520) and a discussion of military matters (*Arte della Guerra/The Art of War,* 1520 – the only work of his to be printed, in 1521, in his lifetime).

Machiavelli's writings were, for the most part, written for the delectation of a few, sometimes with the expectation of patronage: his short treatise, *The Prince,* was originally intended for Giuliano de' Medici and then dedicated to Lorenzo de' Medici (died 1519); similarly, the *Florentine Histories* were commissioned by the Medici family and dedicated to Clement VII. This desire for Medicean patronage was somewhat ironic considering Machiavelli's own career and the circumstances of his major work, the *Discourses.* One of the dedicatees of these was Cosimo Rucellai who owned the ◊Orti Oricellari, where a group of people met and discussed politics – often with an anti-Medicean bias. The apparent contradictions between his works (not to mention his diabolical treatment at the hands of subsequent generations) have made it difficult to discern his political and ethical outlook.

The one work in which Machiavelli could be said to have a professional interest was *The Art of War,* written as a reflection on the patent inadequacies of Florentine arms in the face of the French invasions. Machiavelli's solution was hardly original: his preference for a citizen militia was a commonplace in the writings of Florentine humanists stretching back to Leonardo ◊Bruni. This combination of formative influences – Florence's present woes and its past intellectual glories – moulded his other works. Florentines' gullible acceptance of Savonarola's 'prophecies'; their inability to create a secure republican government under Piero ◊Soderini; the success, meanwhile, of worldly, warrior popes – such circumstances informed Machiavelli's attitudes. And in formulating his response, Machiavelli worked within the local humanist tradition but also (like any ambitious humanist) used his rhetoric to subvert elements of it. His studied worldweariness and his rejection of the belief (inherited from Bruni) in the importance of civic harmony were surely intended to be a salutary shock to the few who read his works; the publication of his major writings after his death meant that they could shock many more than he had intended.

Shock they certainly did, making, by the late 16th century, Machiavelli's name a byword for immorality. The venom, in the writings of, for example, Giovanni ◊Botero, was most often directed against *The Prince* – arguably not a good indicator of Machiavelli's attitudes. Indeed, in the 17th century, a lesser tradition in praise of Machiavelli concentrated instead on his *Discourses*. However, by that point, another author with a cynical, quasi-republican outlook was enjoying a European vogue: ◊Tacitus.

Madonna of the Rocks

Title of two paintings, both of which have been attributed to ◊Leonardo da Vinci, one in the Louvre, Paris, the other in the National Gallery, London. Arguments about who exactly painted them – Leonardo or assistants under his direction – are still unresolved, though it is generally believed that the National Gallery version is by Leonardo himself.

On 25 April 1483 Leonardo, in partnership with Ambrogio da Predis (*c.* 1455–after 1508) and the latter's half-brother Evangelista (died after 1490), contracted to paint a work for the confraternity of the Immaculate Conception in Milan, for the chapel adjoining their Church of S Francesco. The centre-piece was to be painted by 'the Florentine' (Leonardo), the side panels by da Predis. Between 1490 and 1494 the artists claimed more pay. Argument dragged on for years and the picture was reclaimed.

In 1506 the confraternity agreed to pay an extra sum but the work finally delivered seems to have been a different version from that originally painted. The first version is generally considered to be the painting now in the Louvre. A question on which there have been different opinions is whether the National Gallery picture, which was definitely that finally accepted and hung in the confraternity's chapel, was by Leonardo or his assistant. Comparison with the wings of the altarpiece by da Predis, also in the National Gallery, shows so different a level of skill as to lead to the conclusion that the London *Madonna* is indeed a mature work by Leonardo himself.

madrigal

Form of secular song in four or five parts, usually sung without instrumental accompaniment. It originated in 14th-century Italy. Madrigal composers include Andrea Gabrieli, Monteverdi, Thomas Morley, and Orlando Gibbons.

maestà (ITALIAN 'IN MAJESTY')

In Christian art, a depiction of the enthroned Madonna and Child surrounded by angels and saints. Examples include Duccio's *Maestà Altarpiece*, (1309–11, Cathedral Museum, Siena) and Giotto's *Madonna Enthroned* (*c.* 1310, Uffizi, Florence).

Maestlin, Michael (1550–1631)

German astronomer and mathematician. Like many Renaissance astronomers, he was caught between the old and the modern view of the universe: in private he supported the Copernican system, but in public and in his treatise *Epitome Astronomiae* (1582), he continued to expound the Ptolemaic system. Nevertheless, it was as a pupil of Maestlin at Tübingen university that ◊Kepler first studied Copernican astronomy.

His support for the Copernican system came from direct observation of two phenomena that challenged the traditional view that the stars and planets were unchanging: the 'new star' of 1572 and the comets of 1577 and 1580.

Educated at Tübingen university, Maestlin became, in 1576, a Lutheran pastor. He also served as mathematics professor at the universities of Heidelberg and Tübingen. Maestlin also edited Kepler's Copernican treatise, *Mysterium Cosmographicum* (1596).

Magellan, Ferdinand (*c.* 1480–1521)

Portuguese navigator. In 1519 he set sail in the *Victoria* from Seville with the intention of reaching the East Indies by a westerly route. He sailed through the **Strait of Magellan** at the tip of South America, crossed an ocean he named the Pacific, and in 1521 reached the Philippines, where he was killed in a battle with the islanders. His companions returned to Seville in 1522, completing the voyage under del ◊Cano.

Magellan was brought up at court and entered the royal service, but later transferred his services to Spain. He and his Malay slave, Enrique de Malacca, are considered the first circumnavigators of the globe, since they had once sailed from the Philippines to Europe.

Maggior Consiglio (ITALIAN 'GREAT COUNCIL')

The ruling body of Venice during the Middle Ages and the Renaissance. All adult males of the aristocracy had a lifelong hereditary right to sit on the council. Throughout the Renaissance the Maggior Consiglio functioned mainly as a pool from which members could be drawn for other councils and committees of state, such as the senate (with about 200 members) and the ◊Council of Ten, all under the chairmanship of the doge.

The closure (*serrata*) of the membership to all except aristocratic families took place in 1297, and from 1325 their names were recorded in the *Libro d'oro/Golden Book*.

The Venetian council was copied in Florence on the fall of the Medici in 1494 and became the basis of the republican constitution there until 1512.

Mainardi, Sebastiano (DIED 1513)

Italian painter. Active from 1493 in Florence, he is said to have collaborated with Domenico ◊Ghirlandaio in a fresco of *The Assumption of the Virgin* (Sta Croce, Florence), and a series of frescoes in San Gimignano, Tuscany, has been attributed to him.

He was a pupil and assistant of Ghirlandaio, whose sister he married. Many of the works ascribed to him should more accurately be described as from the studio of or by a follower of Ghirlandaio.

Maitland, Richard, OF LETHINGTON (1496–1586)

Scottish poet, lawyer, and historian. All his verses were written after his 60th year, and consist mostly of laments for the state of Scotland, the feuds of the nobles, and the discontent of the common people. Maitland's principal historical work is the *Historie and Cronicle of the Hous and Surename of Seytoun*. He also made a collection of early Scottish poetry in two

manuscript volumes (Pepysian Library, Magdalene College, Cambridge). Knighted in 1551–52.

He studied at St Andrews University and in France, and on his return to Scotland was successively employed by James V, the Regent Arran, and Mary of Lorraine. He became a lord of the court of session in 1561, and Lord Privy Seal in 1562.

majolica (OR MAIOLICA)

Tin-glazed earthenware and the richly decorated enamel pottery produced in Italy from the 15th century. The name derives from the Italian form of Mallorca, the island from where Moorish lustreware made in Spain was shipped to Italy.

Malherbe, François de (1555–1628)

French poet and grammarian. He became court poet about 1605 under Henry IV, received a pension from his widow Marie de' Medici, and was patronized by Louis XIII. He advocated reform of language and versification, criticizing the innovations of the ◊Pléiade poets, and established the 12-syllable alexandrine as the standard form of French verse.

Malherbe was born in Caen. He accompanied Henry of Angoulême, son of Henry II, when he went to Provence as governor in 1579 and remained attached to his household until the prince's death in 1585, after which he was patronized by Henry IV.

Malory, Thomas (c. 1410–1471)

English author. He is known for the prose romance *Le Morte D'Arthur* (c. 1470), printed in 1485, which relates the exploits of King Arthur's knights of the Round Table and the quest for the Holy Grail. Knight of the shire from 1445.

Malory is thought to have been the Warwickshire landowner of that name who was member of Parliament for Warwick in 1445 and was subsequently charged with rape, theft, and attempted murder. If that is so, he must have compiled *Le Morte D'Arthur* during his 20 years in and out of prison. Based on an unidentified 'French book', with imaginative additions from other sources, it is the fullest version of the legends of King Arthur, and a notable contribution to English prose.

Malouel (MAELWAEL), Jean (DIED 1415)

Netherlandish painter. He worked in Paris for Isabeau of Bavaria, wife of Charles VI of France, and then in Dijon, where he was appointed in 1397 court painter to the Duke of Burgundy, ◊Philip the Bold. He continued in Burgundian employ under Philip's son and successor, John the Fearless, until his own death. The only work that has been confidently ascribed to him is a circular *Pietà* (Louvre, Paris), painted for Philip the Bold.

He had some part in the decoration of the Chartreuse of Champmol built under the auspices of Philip the Bold. It is possible that he began *The Crucifixion and Martyrdom of St Denis* (Louvre) which is mainly the work of Henri ◊Bellechose, his successor as Burgundian court painter. Lost works by Malouel include a portrait of John the Fearless, made as a gift to João I of Portugal.

Mander, Karel van (1584–1606)

Dutch art historian and painter. His biographical work on artists, *Het schilderboeck/The Book of Painters* (1604), is a valuable source of information on Dutch and Flemish art. It was modelled on Giorgio ◊Vasari's *Lives of the Artists*.

Mander studied art in Ghent and Rome, his own work being a blend of Flemish and Italian Mannerist styles. After a wide variety of experience he settled in Haarlem, where he founded an Academy of Painting.

Manetti, Giannozzo (1396–1459)

Florentine biblical scholar. A member of the scholarly avant-garde in Florence, Manetti learnt his Greek from Ambrogio ◊Traversari. His career took him to ◊Nicholas V's Rome and to ◊Alfonso the Magnanimous' Naples. It was in the latter city that Manetti used the Greek and Hebrew that he had learnt to undertake the task of retranslating the Bible: he completed the New Testament and the Psalms.

mannerism

Modern critical term to describe a style of 16th century art. Its origins are supposed to be an admiration for the work of ◊Michelangelo demonstrated, in part, by exaggerating the expressive distortion of his figures. The term, which is ill-defined and over-used, originates from another ill-defined, but contemporary, term: ◊*maniera*.

Manrique, Jorge (c. 1440–1479)

Castilian poet and soldier whose biography is obscure. Manrique came from a powerful noble family: his father was Master of the Order of Santiago (1474), his uncle was the poet Gómez ◊Manrique. His father's death from cancer in 1476 inspired his most enduringly famous poem, 'Coplas que fizo por la muerte de su padre'/'Verses Composed on the Death of His Father', a meditation on the transience of life, inevitability of death, and unfailing consolation of salvation through Christ. Jorge Manrique himself died in a skirmish against supporters of the royal pretender, Juana 'la Beltraneja'.

Only 49 poems are attributed with any certainty to Manrique. Although famed as a poet when alive, his *Coplas*, was first published in about 1490 in the *Cancionero de Ramón Llavia*. A selection of his other poetry appeared in four successive editions of the *Cancionero General* (first edition 1511), the *Coplas* being added in Juan Cromberger's 1535 edition. Juan de Valdés praised the form and content of the *Coplas*, which was set to music in 1557 and became the subject of numerous glosses, the first of these being Alonso de Cervantes's *Glosa famosísima/Most Famous Gloss* (1501).

Mantegna, Andrea (c. 1431–1506)

Italian painter and engrave. He painted religious and mythological subjects, his works noted for their ◊*all'antica* style taking elements from Roman antique architecture and sculpture, and for their innovative use of perspective.

Mantegna was born in Vicenza. He was brought up and trained by Francesco ◊Squarcione at Padua, his master entering him in the guild of painters before he was eleven. Like Squarcione, and indeed most north Italian artists, he was influenced by the scuptures of ◊Donatello at Padua, and he was later impressed by the paintings of the Florentines, ◊Uccello and Filippo ◊Lippi. As well as Florentine styles, Mantegna was influenced by Venetian fashion, in particular the style of Jacopo Bellini, whose daughter Lodovisia he married 1453.

MANIERA

HE TERM *MANIERA* WAS repeatedly used by Giorgio ◊Vasari and other 16th-century writers to describe the manner in which an artist executed a sculpture, painting, or building. A word which proved problematic to define even in the Renaissance, *maniera* has been overtaken in the critical literature by a preference for the term 'mannerism'. This modern coinage has evoked fierce debate over its exact meaning but can be characterized as the type of 16th century Italian art that favoured attenuated and improperly proportioned forms to create unbalanced works of art, most notably in painting. An examination of Vasari's attempt at defining *maniera* both reveals the difficulties in applying the term to art and suggests the anachronisms involved in talking about 'mannerism'.

Vasari employed the term *maniera* throughout the *Lives of the Artists,* yet was not able to provide an exact definition of the word. Rather, he noted that good *maniera* was attained by an artist who frequently practised portraying the most beautiful forms available from nature and employing them in a work of art. Vasari's inability to provide a concise meaning suggests the difficulty that artists and theoreticians alike shared in employing a term which was universally used but not precisely defined. Although Vasari included *maniera* as one of the five most desirable qualities that a truly great artist must possess, he was not consistent with the term and often used it to simply express the way in which a particular artist worked, either as a positive, neutral, or even negative judgement. This inconsistency in usage suggests a further danger in relying upon *maniera* as a viable term to express artistic skill of a high calibre.

The modern term 'mannerism' presents many of the same difficulties in definition and usage. Originally used as a critical term to describe Italian art from about 1520 onward as bizarre and unconventional based on the elongation of forms and the use of jarring colour contrasts, it later was viewed in a more positive light as a stylish style.

Though the usage was inconsistent, what did not change was the desire to create a distinct and separate term to describe a particular period of Italian art. Placed in opposition to the classically inspired and balanced art of ◊Michelangelo, ◊Raphael, and ◊Leonardo da Vinci, the term 'mannerism' provided a convenient means of isolating the art of the so-called 'High Renaissance' from the art produced after and often directly inspired by these same masters.

In contrast to 'mannerism', the term *maniera* was employed in the Renaissance by writers such as ◊Vasari equally to artists from the 14th and 16th centuries. The division of Italian art into multiple periods implied by 'mannerism' would not have been understood during the Renaissance, where old and new styles of art were considered as individual stages in the advancement of art as a whole. Artists active in the so-called mannerist period did not view their own work in opposition to the past, but rather saw a continuous progression owing to their frequent study and borrowing of motifs from earlier artists. ◊Vasari, who employed the term *maniera* more comprehensively than any other writer, was aware of the difficulty of applying a single definition to the term, and ultimately abandoned his attempt to use it consistently as a descriptive term.

RICHARD REED

Further Reading
J Shearman, *Mannerism* (London, 1990); E Cropper's introduction to C H Smyth, *Mannerism and Maniera* (Vienna, 1992)

Becoming the Gonzaga family's court painter in 1460, he painted the frescoes of the Camera degli Sposi (Bridal Chamber) in the Castello, which portrayed the Gonzaga family on the walls, and the first Renaissance illusionistic ceiling painting above. His Vatican frescoes of 1488 were later destroyed, but the series of tempera paintings of the *Triumph of Caesar* (1490) for the Gonzagas survives at Hampton Court, London.

Early paintings that won him fame were his frescoes in the Eremitani church at Padua, 1449–54. These were mainly destroyed in World War II,

though two sections moved to Venice remain. Also from this period is *The Agony in the Garden*, (*c.* 1455, National Gallery, London). The background was probably taken in essentials from a drawing by Jacopo Bellini, but the sculptural quality, the effects of perspective and foreshortening, and the austerity of form, were Mantegna's own.

He went to Verona in 1459 and painted an altar-piece for the Church of St Zeno, then moved to Mantua in 1460 at the invitation of Lodovico Gonzaga, remaining in the service of the Gonzagas for the rest of his life. Among the frescoes he undertook for them was the Camera degli Sposi of the Castello di Corte, the painted cupola of the ceiling representing figures foreshortened round a balcony with open sky beyond, a feat of an illusionism later imitated by Correggio and Baroque painters.

Mantegna Andrea Mantegna, *The Agony in the Garden* (National Gallery, London). Mantegna's painting of Jesus just before his arrest demonstrates the artist's fascination both with the skill of foreshortening and with architecture, classical and contemporary. *e.t. archive*

Cartoons for the decoration of a theatre in this palace (not carried out) constitute the famous *Triumph of Caesar*, in nine large sections, painted in tempera, 1482–92, bought with other treasures of the Gonzagas by Charles I of England. While this work was in progess Mantegna visited Rome to paint frescoes in the Chapel of the Belvedere (since destroyed). The cartoons again show his fascination with Classical antiquity and suggest an attempt to rival Roman narrative relief sculpture in painting.

Later pictures include the *Lamentation* (Brera, Milan), with its dramatic foreshortening of the body of the dead Christ, the *Madonna della Vittoria* (Louvre, Paris), celebrating a Mantuan victory over the French, and two paintings intended for the boudoir of Isabella ◊d'Este at Mantua, the *Parnassus* and *Virtue Triumphant over Vice* (Louvre, Paris), in which Mantegna shows a graceful fancy strikingly different from his usual austerity. As an engraver he was highly original in the style and straight-line shading of his religious and mythological copperplates.

Manuel I (1469–1521)

Portuguese king from 1495. That his reign coincided with Portugal's successful expansion in Africa and India, with attendant profits, led to his sobriquet 'the Fortunate'. He commemorated Portugal's new-found wealth and conquests by adopting a navigational instrument, the armillary sphere, as a royal symbol, and by initiating a series of building projects, including the construction of the Hieronymite monastery at Belém (Lisbon), begun by a French architect in 1502. The penchant for twisted columns and figurative decorations carved around doors and windows which these royal buildings displayed, led them to be classified as ◊Manueline by 19th-century historians.

Manuel Deutsch, Nicolaus (1484–1530)

Swiss painter, poet, and reformer. His works included a *Dance of Death* (of which only copies exist) for a monastery in Bern and the *Beheading of John the Baptist* (Basel) in an ornate and fanciful style with much curious detail. He studied painting in Colmar and in Venice under Titian. In later years he was active in diplomacy and public affairs and as an advocate of the Reformation.

Manueline style (PORTUGUESE 'ARTE MANUELINA')

A style in Portuguese architecture associated with the reign of King ◊Manuel I (1495–1521), under whom numerous monasteries and churches were built. A richly ornate style, it is characterized by a profusion of organic forms – such as coral, tree branches, artichokes – and carved stone rope, thickly knotted and twisted round windows, doorways and pinnacles.

The monasteries at Tomar, Batalha, Belém, and Alcobaça are examples of Manueline style, which was also exported to Portuguese possessions overseas.

It was contemporaneous with and partly influenced by the early ◊plateresque style in Spain and, like plateresque, incorporates mudéjar elements as well as echoes of contemporary Italian architectural fashion.

Manutius, Aldus (LATINIZED NAME OF ALDO MANUZIO) (*c.* 1452–1515)

Italian teacher and printer. Roman by birth, his first career seems to have been as a teacher active in Ferrara and Carpi (where he taught Giovanni Pico della Mirandola's nephews). Around 1490, however, he moved to Venice and changed careers. He promoted the idea of producing editions of Classical authors in the original Greek and in 1495 became a junior partner to the publisher, Andrea Torresani (1451–1528), whose daughter he later married. What became known as the Aldine Press produced a series of small-format editions in Greek and Latin, both of Classical and humanist authors.

Aldus's publishing venture was a good deed in a bad world: it seems that in 1505 his company was in financial difficulty. It recovered, however, and the tradition of publishing continued under his sons, in particular **Paolo Manuzio** (1512–74).

The Aldine publications included celebrated editions of Classical authors, both Latin (for example ◊Pliny the Younger) and Greek. Illustrated printed books were rare, but the ◊*Hypermachia Polifili* did appear from the press. This was also an example of modern authors being represented; other living authors whose works appeared with the distinctive anchor and dolphin imprint included Erasmus, who spent three years in Venice. The work practices of Aldus's printing house, like those of other printers (for example, Badius Ascensius) involved a group of people working on the textual editing; in other words, there was the aura of a scholarly enterprise. Indeed, some of Aldus's books stated they were produced in the Aldine Academy. Aldus certainly dreamt of founding a society of Greek speakers – the so-called ◊Neakademia – but this came to nothing; Aldus's ◊academy was more like the printing house equivalent to earlier informal gatherings of like-minded scholars.

Marburg, Colloquy of

A conference held in 1529 in Marburg, Germany, in an attempt to reconcile the Zwinglian and Lutheran evangelical movements. Summoned by Philip, Landgrave of Hesse, it was attended by ◊Luther and ◊Melanchthon on the German side, and by ◊Zwingli, Oecolampadius, and ◊Bucer on the Swiss. Though there was agreement on most of the articles, the striking point was the issue of the real presence in the Eucharist: Zwingli denied that the bread became the body of Christ or even (as Luther suggests – consubstantiation) was both bread and body.

March, Ausiàs (c. 1395–1460)

Catalan poet. His *Cants d'amor* and *Cants de mort*, show the influence of the troubadours, ◊Dante, and ◊Petrarch.

Marciana, Bibliotheca (FLORENCE)

The library of the Dominican convent of San Marco in Florence. The basis of the collection was the library of some 800 volumes accumulated by the scholar Niccolò ◊Niccoli. On his death the collection passed into the stewardship of a group of Florentines, including ◊Cosimo de' Medici, who was patron of San Marco. The building commissioned to hold the collection was designed by ◊Michelozzo in 1441.

Many of the texts were dispersed or destroyed by the religious reformer ◊Savonarola and his followers. In 1508 the collection was bought by Pope Leo X and returned to Florence in 1532 by Clement VII. In 1808 the collection was amalgamated with that of the ◊Laurenziana.

Marciana, Bibliotheca (VENICE)

The library housed in the Libreria Sansoviniana (Sansovino Library) in Piazzetta San Marco, Venice. The foundation of the collection was the gift of manuscripts made by Cardinal ◊Bessarion to the Venetian senate in 1468. This was augmented by the bequest of Domenico ◊Grimani. The building, begun in 1536, was designed by Jacopo ◊Sansovino; it was completed by Scamozzi in the 1580s. The interior is decorated with paintings by ◊Titian, ◊Tintoretto, ◊Veronese, and Andrea ◊Schiavone.

Marcillat, Guiglelmo de (1467–1529)

French glass painter active in Italy. Born in La Châtre, he transferred to Italy in *c.* 1506, where he became a Dominican friar and spent most of his life working in and around Arezzo. He gained renown for his painted windows in the Vatican commissioned by ◊Leo X and ◊Julius II.

Marcillat advanced the art of glass painting by perfecting a viable method for shading glass with both iron and copper based colours. Following his work in Rome, he settled in Arezzo where he executed an ambitious project to provide painted windows and also to fresco the vaults of the cathedral (*c.* 1516–26). The latter project was unprecedented in that it was the first attempt in Tuscany to quote ◊Michelangelo's Sistine Ceiling. Highly prolific in his career as a glass painter, he employed an extensive workshop based in Arezzo that continued following his death.

Marenzio, Luca (c. 1553–1599)

Italian singer and composer. He is the most important of the Italian madrigalists, having written over 400. His madrigals were introduced into England through music editor Nicholas Yonge's (died 1619) *Musica Transalpina* in 1588 and he was in correspondence with Dowland in 1595.

Born at Coccaglio, near Brescia, Marenzio studied with Giovanni Contino (1513–1574), organist at Brescia Cathedral, and published his first work in 1581. Soon afterwards he went to Rome, where he served cardinal Cristoforo Madruzzo from around 1574 until 1578, when he became maestro di cappella to Cardinal d'Este until 1586. During this time he published many madrigals, and began to gain an international reputation as a composer. In 1588 he entered the service of Ferdinando de' Medici and in 1589 contributed two *intermeddi* for wedding festivities in Florence. Later that year he returned to Rome, where he was employed by Virginio Orsini, Duke of Bracciano, until 1593. His next patron, cardinal Cinzio Aldobrandini, recommended Marenzio as music director to the king of Poland. He was in Warsaw during 1596–98, at the court of Sigismondo (Zygmunt) III of Poland. About 1599, however, he returned to Rome and became organist at the papal chapel.

Marenzio published 18 books of madrigals for

4–10 voices (1580–99), as well as five books of villanelles and two books of motets. Many of the madrigals he wrote before 1587 are settings of pastoral texts whose authors include the poet Petrarch; these were widely imitated in Europe, and in England by Thomas Morley. As he grew older, Marenzio's madrigals became increasingly serious in tone, with melancholy texts and more dissonance and chromaticism in the music.

Works include:
Mass, motets, *Sacri concenti*; over 400 madrigals, *Villanelle ed arie alla napolitana* (five volumes).

Margaret of Austria (1480–1530)

The regent and governor of the Netherlands for ◊Charles V from 1507–15 and from 1519–30. She was the daughter of ◊Maximilian I and Mary of Burgundy. She extended Habsburg domination in the Netherlands and pursued a foreign policy favourable to England and hostile to France. She negotiated the Peace of Cambrai in 1529 with Louise of Savoy (who represented Francis I of France), known as the *Paix des Dames* ('Ladies' Peace').

She was also a noted patron of the arts. She employed the sculptor Konrad ◊Meit of Worms and the painter Bernard van ◊Orley and encouraged writers and scholars. The palace built for her at Malines (1507–26) combined Renaissance decoration with a basically Gothic structure.

Marguerite of Navarre (ALSO KNOWN AS MARGARET D'ANGOULÊME) (1492–1549)

Queen of Navarre from 1527, French poet, and author of the 'Heptaméron' (1558), a collection of stories in imitation of Boccaccio's 'Decameron'. The sister of Francis I of France, she was born in Angoulême. Her second husband (1527) was Henri d'Albret, King of Navarre.

Mariana, Juan de (c. 1535–1624)

Spanish historian. A Jesuit priest, he taught in Rome, Sicily, Paris, Flanders, and Spain, his most important work being his *Historiae de Rebus Hispaniae/History of Spain* (1592). This drew together every source available and included a wealth of legendary and anecdotal material from the earliest times to the death of Ferdinand in 1516. His works reflect an enlightened and liberal point of view in Spanish scholarship.

He also wrote a number of essays on political theory and other subjects, including the controversial study of kingship *De Rege et Regis Institutione* (1599), which contained arguments in favour of violent opposition to tyrannical kings. This tract was thought to have inspired the Gunpowder Plot.

The illegitimate son of the dean of the collegiate church of Talavera de la Reina, Mariana entered the Jesuit novitiate in 1554, studied at Alcalá, and was ordained in 1561.

The first edition of *Historiae de rebus Hispaniae* appeared in 20 volumes, and was enlarged to 30 volumes in the 1605 edition, the expanded text now covering the reigns of Charles V and Philip II. The book was noted in particular for its impeccable style, modelled on that of the Roman historian Livy.

Marini (MARINO), Giambattista (1569–1625)

Neapolitan poet. His first published works were lyrics (*Rime* 1602) and poetical ◊ekphrasis (*La Galeria* 1614). His most successful epic was *Adone* (1623), a retelling of the classical story of Adonis, dedicated to Louis XIII. He aimed to surprise by the use of startling metaphors, hyperboles, antitheses, and other literary devices. His ornate and self-conscious style, termed 'Marinism', influenced early 17th-century poetry in Italy, France, and England.

Intended for the law, Marini left his profession and led a wandering, dissolute life, often in debt. When he was imprisoned for immorality in 1611, his release was secured through admirers of his poetry. In 1615 he left Italy for Paris, where he lived under the patronage of Marie de' Medici. He returned to Italy 1623.

Markham, Gervase (JERVIS) (1568–1637)

English poet, translator, and writer. Among his works are a continuation of Philip ◊Sidney's *Arcadia*, a poem on the death in a naval battle of Richard Granville, *The Discourse of Horsemanshippe* (1593), *Cavelarice, or the English Horseman* (1607), *Country Contentments* (1615), *A Way to Get Wealth* (1623), various books on agriculture, and some plays.

Markham was born in Cottam, Nottinghamshire. He served as a soldier in the Low Countries and

Ireland, but retired into civil life about 1593. He was a prolific translator, compiler, and original writer. It has been suggested that he is the 'rival poet' of Shakespeare's sonnets.

Marlowe, Christopher (1564–1593)

English dramatist and poet. He was one of the early, and most popular, playwrights for the London stage. Seven tragedies by him survive: *Tamburlaine the Great* parts I and II, *Dr Faustus*, *Edward II*, *The Jew of Malta*, *The Massacre at Paris*, and *Dido, Queen of Carthage*. He also wrote translations of the Roman poets Ovid and Lucan, as well as *Hero and Leander*, a poem retelling the ancient tale of a pair of doomed lovers, which was published with a continuation by George Chapman after Marlowe's death.

Marlowe was born in Canterbury, Kent, where his father was a shoemaker. He went to Corpus Christi College, Cambridge, and while there he seems, like many others, to have been recruited by Francis Walsingham as an information gatherer or intelligence agent. He graduated in 1587, about the time that *Tamburlaine* was first performed in London. In the course of a short and violent life, Marlowe was in trouble with the law several times, for a range of crimes from forgery to involvement in a street fight that left one man dead. Shortly before his death, he was under investigation suspected of the crime of atheism, an accusation based in part on cross-examinatin of his friend and former roommate Thomas ◊Kyd. He was stabbed to death in Deptford, south London, supposedly in an argument over a bill but possibly for more political reasons.

The chronology of his plays is uncertain, with the early printings offering few clues: *Dr Faustus*, for instance, exists in two markedly different posthumous editions, suggesting the work of collaborators, and *Dido*, on its first appearance in 1594, was published under the joint names of Marlowe and Thomas ◊Nashe. The playwright Ben Jonson praised Marlowe's 'mighty line' – the splendour of the poetry in the plays. The tragedies are also remarkable for the magnetic charisma of their protagonists, who resist easy moral categorization: as in the case of Dr Faustus, who gains magic powers by selling his soul to the Devil, or Tamburlaine, who sets about conquering the world nation by nation, or Barabas in *The Jew of Malta*, who,

despite murdering several people, is in many ways the most sympathetic character of the play.

Marmion, Simon (*c.* 1422–1489)

French painter and miniaturist of the Franco-Flemish School. Active in Amiens, Valenciennes, and Tournai, he illuminated manuscripts for Philip the Good, Duke of Burgundy.

He painted panels illustrating the *Life of St Bertin* (1459) for the abbey of St-Omer, southeast of Calais (St Bertin was a missionary in the region in the 7th century). Several panels are lost but there are parts in the Staatliche Museum, Berlin, and in the National Gallery, London, showing a notable delicacy of style.

Marnix, Philipp van (Heer van Sainte Aldegonde) (1538–1598)

Dutch Calvinist theologian and statesman. An adviser of William of Orange, he played a prominent part in drafting the Pacification of Ghent in 1576. He wrote a number of influential polemical works, including *De biênkorf der heilige roomsche kerche/The Beehive of the Holy Roman Church* (1569), a satirical attack on the Catholic Church (in the style of ◊Rabelais), which was translated into English as early as 1579.

Born a member of the lesser Netherlands nobility in Brussels, Marnix studied in Geneva as a young man and became a personal disciple of the reformers ◊Calvin and ◊Beza. He took part in the insurrection against Spain in 1566 and was consequently forced to go into exile in Germany, where he helped organize the Synod of Emden in 1571. Returning to Holland in 1572 he became a close political and religious advisor to William of Orange. As mayor of Antwerp (1583–85) he defended the city against Alexander, Duke of Parma.

He published his *De biênkorf der heilige roomsche kerche* (sometimes known as *De Roomsche Byenkorf*) under the pen name Isaac Rabbotenus. He also made a translation of the Psalms into Dutch.

Marot, Clément (1496–1544)

French poet. He is known for his translation of the Psalms (1539–43). His best verse is found in his rondeaux, epigrams, and epistles. He restored naturalness and simplicity to French poetry, replacing artificial excess of ornament and allegory by native grace, and his achievement became a model for later writers of light verse. Among others, La Fontaine imitated the *style marotique*.

His other works include translations and allegories, such as his translation of the first and second books of Ovid's *Metamorphoses*, his *Temple de Cupido* (1515), and his allegorical satire *L'Enfer*. His paraphrases of the Psalms reveal his metrical originality, and he also helped introduce the sonnet to France.

Marot was born in Cahors. In 1518 he entered the service of Marguerite of Navarre. Later he was in the service of Francis I whom he accompanied to Italy in 1524. In 1534, suspected of sympathies with Lutheranism, he had to flee to the court of Queen Margaret and later to that of the Duchess of Ferrara. He returned to France in 1536 on condition of a formal recantation, but once more was forced to leave, his translation of the Psalms having been condemned by the Sorbonne. He went to Geneva but the austerity demanded of the true Calvinist was beyond him and he continued on to Turin, where he died.

Marprelate controversy

Pamphleteering attack on the clergy of the Church of England in 1588 and 1589 made by a Puritan writer or writers, who took the pseudonym of **Martin Marprelate.** The pamphlets were printed by John Penry, a Welsh Puritan. His press was seized, and he was charged with inciting rebellion and hanged in 1593.

marrano (SPANISH *MARRANO* 'PIG')

Spanish or Portuguese Jew who, during the 14th and 15th centuries, converted to Christianity continued to adhere secretly to Judaism and carry out Jewish rites. During the Spanish ◊Inquisition thousands were burned at the stake as 'heretics'.

Marston, John (1576–1634)

English satirist and dramatist. His early plays, the revenge tragedies *Antonio and Mellida* and *Antonio's Revenge* (1599), were followed by a number of satirical comedies including *What You Will* (1601), *The Malcontent* (1604), and *The Dutch Courtesan* (1605).

Marston also collaborated with dramatists George ◊Chapman and Ben ◊Jonson in *Eastward Ho* (1605),

which satirized the Scottish followers of James I, and for which the authors were imprisoned. His own satires include *The Metamorphosis of Pygmalion's Image* (1598) and *The Scourge of Villanie* (1598).

He was probably born in Coventry. Educated at Brasenose College, Oxford, he studied law at the Middle Temple. As early as 1601 he was satirized under the name of Demetrius in Jonson's *The Poetaster*. However, in 1604, Marston dedicated *The Malcontent* to Jonson, with expressions of affection and esteem, and a year later he was collaborating with Jonson.

Martial (MARCUS VALERIUS MARTIALIS) (*c*. AD 41–*c*. 104)

Latin poet and epigrammatist. His poetry, often obscene, is keenly observant of all classes in contemporary Rome. His most extensive work were his 12 books of *Epigrams* (AD 86–102); other writings included *Liber Spectaculorum* (written to commemorate the opening of the Colosseum in AD 80), parts of which were rediscovered in the 14th century, perhaps by ◊Boccaccio.

Before the end of the 14th century, Martial's epigrams were studied by only a few scholars, including Lovato ◊Lovati and Albertino ◊Mussato. For the humanists of the early 15th century, however, Martial was a popular author, often read (by, for example, Gasparino ◊Barzizza and Francesco ◊Barbaro), quoted (by, say, Lorenzo ◊Valla in his *Elegentiae*), and imitated (by, for instance, ◊Panormita in his *Hermaphroditus*). Later in the century, Pomponio ◊Leto worked on glossing the *Epigrams*; his colleague, Niccolò ◊Perotti, was – alongside Domizio ◊Calderini and Giorgio ◊Merula – an early commentator on Martial.

Outside Italy, selected epigrams were imitated in French by Clément ◊Marot in 1544 and translated into English by T Kendall in 1577.

Martin V (BORN **ODDONE COLONNA**) (1368–1431)

Pope from 1417, elected at the Council of ◊Constance. A member of the powerful Roman family of the Colonna, Martin's pontificate was dedicated to reinvigorating papal power in Rome, Italy, and across Europe (in the process enriching his own family). His reign opened inauspiciously with the pope having to haggle his way to Rome, which he reached in 1420. He soon proved himself, however, to be no-one's puppet and the secular rulers who made his election possible found they could expect few favours. His political astuteness was demonstrated in his dealing with the issue of ◊conciliarism: he convened, as required, a council in Pavia but, absenting himself from it, was able to ensure it achieved absolutely nothing. He was, though, probably fortunate to die when he did: he had given way to pressure to call another council but it had yet to meet in ◊Basel.

Martin's curia was a very Italian bureaucracy, providing job opportunities to a series of scholars with interest in *studia humanitatis*. ◊Poggio Bracciolini, for example, Andrea ◊Fiocchi, or Cencio de' ◊Rustici. The Pope, like any great prince, also had works dedicated to him, like Leonardo ◊Bruni's translation of Aristotle's *Ethics*. Martin was also an artistic patron, commissioning the building of a palace for his own residence (Palazzo Colonna, Rome) and perhaps patronizing ◊Masolino and ◊Michelozzo. His policies, in other words, set a precedent for support of Renaissance fashions which was developed by his successors.

Martini, Simone (*c.* 1284–1344)

Italian artist working mainly in Siena in the 1320s, but also employed in Angevin Naples, at Assisi, and in Papal Avignon. His exquisite works, recalling that of the greatest Gothic sculptors (the Pisani family), but in the two-dimensional media of panel and fresco, are the meeting point of ◊Giotto's calm, monumental compositional style and his (assumed) master Duccio's passionate, sinuous use of line and colour. His spectacular yet subtle use of incised and enamelled metals and cut glass enhanced already beautiful artistry and left a lasting legacy.

Martini was commissioned in 1315 to provide a Maestà in the secular heart of Siena, mirroring Duccio's version in the Cathedral. This suggests he was already a well-known public artist (and contextualises the much-contested attribution of the Guidoricchio da Foligno fresco.) His reputation took him to the Neapolitan and Papal courts; his connec-

tion with Petrarch in Avignon is well-evidenced by two Petrarchan *canzoni*. Martini's response to the new 'cult of antiquity' infuses the iconography of the Martin chapel, and his cover design for Petrarch's copy of Virgil's *Georgics*.

Surviving works:
- *Maestà* (1315, restored by Simone in 1321)
- San Martino Chapel frescoes (before 1317; or late 1330s)
- St Louis d'Anjou altarpiece (1317)
- Santa Caterina polyptych (1319)
- Beato Agostino Novello altarpiece (before 1324)
- *Annunciazione/Annunciation* (with Lippo Memmi) (1333)
- Frontispiece, Ambrosian Virgil (*c.* 1330s)
- Polyptych of the Passion of Christ (*c.* 1340s)
- Orsini polyptych (*c.* 1340s)
- Notre-Dame-des-Doms frescoes (*c.* 1336–40s)
- *Holy Family* (1342)

Marullus, Michael (*c.* 1453–1500)

Italian soldier and humanist poet. He was born in Ancona but claimed to be of Byzantine descent. In the 1470s, he spent his time fighting the Turks; in late 1494, he was in the French army invading Italy, but in 1500 he fought against Cesare ◊Borgia and his French troops. Between these bouts of bloody activity, Marullus wrote *Epigrammata* and *Hymni Naturales*, which imitated the Roman poets Horace, Catullus, and Lucretius (to the extent that he sounded, Erasmus complained, 'just like a pagan').

Mary Queen of Scots (1542–1587)

Queen of Scotland (1542–67). Also known as **Mary Stuart**, she was the daughter of James V. Mary's connection with the English royal line from Henry VII made her a threat to Elizabeth I's hold on the English throne, especially as she represented a champion of the Catholic cause. She was married three times. After her forced abdication she was imprisoned but escaped in 1568 to England. Elizabeth I held her prisoner, while the Roman Catholics, who regarded Mary as rightful queen of England, formed many conspiracies to place her on the throne, and for complicity in one of these she was executed.

Mary's mother was the French Mary of Guise. Born in Linlithgow (now in Lothian region, Scotland), Mary was sent to France, where she married the dauphin, later Francis II. After his death she returned to Scotland in 1561, which, during her absence, had become Protestant. She married her cousin, the Earl of Darnley in 1565, but they soon quarrelled, and Darnley took part in the murder of Mary's secretary, Rizzio. In 1567 Darnley was assassinated as the result of a conspiracy formed by the Earl of Bothwell, possibly with Mary's connivance, and shortly after Bothwell married her. A rebellion followed; defeated at Carberry Hill, Mary abdicated and was imprisoned. She escaped in 1568, raised an army, and after its defeat at Langside fled to England, only to be imprisoned again. A plot against Elizabeth I devised by Anthony Babington led to her trial and execution at Fotheringay Castle in 1587.

Mary, Duchess of Burgundy (1457–1482)

Daughter of Charles the Bold, Duke of Burgundy. She married Maximilian of Austria in 1477, thus bringing the Low Countries into the possession of the Habsburgs and, ultimately, of Spain.

Mary of Hungary (1505–1558)

Queen Consort of Hungary (1522–26). The younger sister of Emperor ◊Charles V, she was known as **Mary of Austria** before her marriage to King Louis II of Hungary and Bohemia in 1522. She was appointed regent of the Netherlands in 1531, a post that she held until 1556, the year of Charles's abdication: she retired with him to Spain. Though discontent with the Spanish rule was growing in the Netherlands, she ruled with a moderation that successfully avoided provocation.

With the death of her husband at the battle of ◊Mohács in 1526, Mary remained childless and Louis' realms passed to her family, the Habsburgs. It was Mary who persuaded an assembly of Hungarian nobles at Pressburg to elect her brother Ferdinand (later Emperor Ferdinand I) as their king, and she later mediated between Ferdinand and Charles in their quarrel over the succession to the empire.

She was a keen patron of the arts, employing Jacques ◊Dubroeucq as architect at her castles of Binche and Mariemont and furnishing them with pictures by the great Flemish masters and by ◊Titian. She also received dedications from ◊Erasmus (*Vidua Christiana/Christian Widow* 1528) and – more wor-

ringly to her staunch Catholic family – from Luther (*Vier trüstliche Psalmen* 1526).

Mary Tudor (1516–1558)

Queen of England from 1553. The elder daughter of Henry VIII by Catherine of Aragon, Mary was committed to Roman Catholicism. On the death of her younger brother, Edward VI, the Duke of Northumberland tried to continue his rule by having his daughter-in-law, Lady Jane Grey, declared queen. Support rallied, however, to Mary, setting the tone for her reign: its keynote was widespread obedience.

Aided by Cardinal Reginald ◊Pole, Mary reintroduced Catholic ceremonies and papal authority, reversing both the Reformation of Edward's reign and the Break with Rome of Henry VIII's reign. Despite the lurid reports of the burning of Protestants which were later given classic expression by John ◊Foxe's *Book of Martyrs*, the return to the traditional church met with little opposition and, in some quarters, relieved support. Mary's return to earlier Tudor policy and a Spanish alliance, involving her marriage to Philip II, was less welcome but, apart from the ineffectual Wyatt's rebellion in 1554, accepted. She did, however, fail to impose the reversal of the ◊Dissolution of the Monasteries. Her final failure was a personal one: her premature death, childless, leaving the throne to her younger, and Protestant, half-sister, Elizabeth.

Masaccio, Tommaso di Giovanni di Simone Guidi (1401–*c.* 1428)

Italian painter. Although he died at an early age, Masaccio had an immense impact on the direction of 15th-century painting owing to his application of a coherent three-dimensional space and linear perspective to his compositions.

Eulogized by the art historian Giorgio Vasari as furthering the advances made by Giotto to achieve a greater sense of space and volume (see feature on History of Art), Masaccio was the first Florentine artist to apply these qualities systematically to his paintings. His fresco cycle depicting scenes from the life of St Peter in the Brancacci chapel in Florence, executed in collaboration with ◊Masolino da Panicale, was considered a milestone in the development of painting during the 15th and 16th centuries for its coherent narrative structure, and was studied assiduously by later artists.

He executed numerous altarpieces and private devotional compositions in which he attempted to explore the same problems of linear perspective and substantial, sculptural figures in traditional subjects, such as the *Virgin and Child Enthroned* (1426, National Gallery, London).

Masip, Juan Vicente de (1475–1550)

Spanish painter. His religious paintings show the influence of ◊Raphael Sanzio, though they are individual in colour and detail. His *Martyrdom of St Agnes* and *The Visitation* (both Prado, Madrid) are examples.

His son **Juan Vicente de Masip the Younger** (1523–1579), also known as Juan de Juanes, whose reputation long overshadowed that of his father, developed a dramatic but artificial style, as in his *Last Supper* (Prado, Madrid)). He was capable of vigorous portraiture, as in *Don Luis de Castellà de Vilanova* (Prado).

Maso di Banco (LIVED LATE 14TH CENTURY)

Italian painter. He was one of the principal followers of Giotto, mainly known by his frescoes of *The Life of St Sylvester* in the Bardi Chapel of Sta Croce, Florence.

Masolino (TOMMASO DA PANICALE) (c. 1383– c. 1447)

Italian painter. He worked with ◊Masaccio on the fresco cycle in the Brancacci Chapel of Santa Maria del Carmine, Florence, 1425–28. Though he shared Masaccio's enthusiasm for the newly discovered technique of perspective, he reverted, after the younger man's death, to his own preferred decorative style, moving away from the Renaissance novelty.

A goldsmith in his youth, he is believed to have worked under Lorenzo ◊Ghiberti on the baptistery doors at Florence (1403–07), before turning to painting. Other works besides the Brancacci Chapel include a Madonna, dated 1423 (Bremen), frescoes at Castiglione d'Olona (c. 1435), and an altarpiece, parts of which are in the galleries of Naples, Philadelphia, and London.

masque

Spectacular court entertainment with a fantastic or mythological theme in which music, dance, and extravagant costumes and scenic design figured larger than plot. Originating in Italy, where members of the court actively participated in the performances, the masque reached its height of popularity at the English court between 1600 and 1640, with the collaboration of Ben ◊Jonson as writer and Inigo ◊Jones as stage designer. John Milton also wrote masque verses. Composers included Thomas ◊Campion, John Coperario, Henry Lawes, William ◊Byrd, and Henry Purcell.

The masque had great influence on the development of ballet and opera, and the elaborate frame in which it was performed developed into the proscenium arch.

Master of Avignon

Anonymous French painter of the School of Avignon who painted the *Avignon Pietà* about 1450 (Louvre, Paris). In its emotional feeling and simplicity and breadth of treatment, it is a great work for its time.

Master of 1499 (LIVED LATE 15TH CENTURY)

Anonymous Flemish painter who worked in Bruges. There are four works attributed to him in the Musée des Beaux-Arts, Antwerp, the reverse side of a panel of the *Madonna* bearing the date 1499.

Master of Moulins (MAÎTRE DE MOULINS, ALSO KNOWN AS THE MASTER OF THE BOURBONS) (LIVED LATE 15TH–EARLY 16TH CENTURY)

Anonymous painter, probably Dutch, working at the Bourbon court in Moulins (now in Allier *département*). His *Triptych of the Virgin in Glory* (c. 1498–1500, Moulins Cathedral) shows both Flemish and Italian influences.

The central panel of the triptych shows the Virgin and Child surrounded by angels. The donor, Pierre II, Duke of Bourbon (died 1503), appears with his wife and daughter in the wings. The influence of the Flemish artist Hugo van der ◊Goes appears most clearly in *The Nativity* (Musée Rodin, Autun) and *St Victor with a Donor* (Art Gallery, Glasgow).

The Master of Moulins, once identified with Jean de ◊Perréal, is now thought to have been called Jean Hey, who painted *Ecce Homo* (Brussels) in a similar style to the Moulins altarpiece.

Master of Spes Nostra (LIVED LATE 15TH CENTURY)

Anonymous Netherlandish painter. The most important work attributed to the Master of Spes Nostra is the allegorical painting *The Vanity of Human Life* (Rijksmuseum, Amsterdam).

Master of St Giles (LIVED EARLY 16TH CENTURY)

Anonymous painter of Netherlandish training, active in Paris in 1500. The artist is named after two pictures in the National Gallery, London: *St Giles and the Hind* and *The Mass of St Giles*. The style is that of the School of Bruges.

Master of the Death of the Virgin (LIVED EARLY 16TH CENTURY)

Anonymous Netherlandish painter. Thought to be responsible for a large group of works, he derived his name from two altarpieces of *The Death of the Virgin* – one in Cologne and one in Munich. He is known to have been active 1507–37, and is sometimes identified with Joos van ◊Cleve.

Master of the Female Half-Lengths (LIVED EARLY 16TH CENTURY)

Anonymous Netherlandish painter. He painted a large group of works featuring young women, distinctive by their oval features and almond-shaped eyes, playing musical instruments or reading.

He is part of the Antwerp School, though related in style to the Bruges masters Ambrosius Benson and Adriaen Isenbrant.

Master of the Housebook (LIVED LATE 15TH CENTURY)

Anonymous German painter and engraver. He is called after the drawings in the *Hausbuch* of Castle Wolfegg in the Rhineland. His engravings show scenes of everyday life. One of his paintings is *The Lovers of Gotha* (Castle Museum, Gotha).

Master of the Legend of St Lucy (LIVED LATE 15TH CENTURY)

Anonymous Netherlandish painter. He is named after the altarpiece *Scenes from the Life of St Lucy* in the church of St Jacques, Bruges. He worked in Bruges in a style influenced by Hans Memling and Gerard David.

Master of the Legend of St Ursula (LIVED LATE 15TH CENTURY)

Anonymous Netherlandish painter. He was named after the diptych *Four Scenes from the Legend of St Ursula* in the Convent of Les Söurs Noires, Bruges. He was active in Bruges, and his work shows the influence of Hans ◊Memling.

Master of the Life of Mary (LIVED SECOND HALF OF THE 15TH CENTURY)

Anonymous German painter and stained-glass designer. He is named after the panels of *The Life of the Virgin* from the church of St Ursula, Cologne. Their style suggests a Netherlandish training. He was active in Cologne.

Master of the Virgo inter Virgines (LIVED SECOND HALF OF THE 15TH CENTURY)

Anonymous Netherlandish painter. He probably worked in Delft, and is named after the painting *The Virgin and Child with Four Female Saints* (Rijksmuseum, Amsterdam).

Master of Třebon, OR OF WITTINGAU (LIVED MID–LATE 14TH CENTURY)

Anonymous Bohemian Gothic painter. He created the paintings that form part of an altarpiece in the Augustinian church at Třebon, now in the National Gallery, Prague. The outstanding panel is *The Resurrection* about 1380.

The panels combine the Gothic tradition of art in Bohemia with influences coming from Italy and France. *The Resurrection* in particular shows its creator to have been an innovator in the use of light and shade and a designer of great originality and power.

Mästlin, Michael (1550–1631)

German astronomer and mathematician who was one of the first scholars to accept and teach Polish astronomer ◊Copernicus's observation that the Earth orbits the Sun. One of Mästlin's pupils was German mathematician Johannes ◊Kepler.

Mästlin was born in Göppingen, Baden-Württemberg, and studied at Tübingen. In 1580 he became professor of mathematics at Heidelberg and in 1584 at Tübingen, where he taught for 47 years.

In 1573, Mästlin published an essay concerning the nova that had appeared the previous year. Its location in relation to known stars convinced him that the nova was a new star – which implied, contrary to traditional belief, that things could come into being in the spheres beyond the Moon.

Observation of the comets of 1577 and 1580 convinced Mästlin that they were also located beyond the Moon. Together with other observations, this led him explicitly to argue against the traditional cosmology of Aristotle.

However, Mästlin's *Epitome of Astronomy* (1582), a popular introduction to the subject, propounded a traditional cosmology because this was easier to teach.

Matsys (MASSYS OR METSYS), Quentin(*c.* 1465–1530)

Flemish painter. Active in Antwerp, he marked the transition from early Flemish art to that influenced by Italian styles. He painted religious subjects, and portraits set against landscapes or realistic interiors. One of his best-known works is *The Money Changer and his Wife* (1514, Louvre, Paris).

Massys Quentin Massys, *Ecce Homo,* 1518–20 (Prado, Madrid). Like Gerard David's treatment of the same subject, this picture reflects the popularity in Dutch art of the subject of Christ's Passion. *e.t. archive*

He is noted in particular for the refinement and delicacy of his female figures, in which he seems to show acquaintance with the work of Leonardo, and for landscape backgrounds related in character to those of his contemporary at Antwerp, Joachim ◊Patinir.

His sons **Cornelis** (*c.* 1508–*c.* 80) and **Jan** (*c.* 1509–75) were also painters.

He was the son of a metalworker and clockmaker at Louvain and trained there and perhaps in the studio of Dirck ◊Bouts. His art represents two phases of transition: not only from early Netherlandish art, represented by Memling and Gerard David, to that of Italian influence, but also from the declining city of Bruges to the newly flourishing city of Antwerp, where he became a member of the Painters' Guild in 1491.

Other works include the *St Anne Altarpiece,* (1509, Musées Royaux, Brussels), the *Lamentation over Christ,* (1511, Musées Royaux, Antwerp), and a portrait of *Erasmus,* (1517, Museo Nazionale, Rome).

Matteo di Giovanni (1435–1495)

Italian painter. He was active in Siena and his work has the traditional delicacy and charm of the early Sienese School. An example is *The Assumption of the Virgin* (National Gallery, London).

He painted parts of a triptych for the Cathedral of Sansepolcro, southeast Tuscany (now in the museum in Sansepolcro), of which the centre panel, by ◊Piero della Francesca, is *The Baptism of Christ* (National Gallery).

Matthias Corvinus (*c.* 1440–1490)

King of Hungary from 1458. The son of János Hunyadi, Matthias Corvinus was declared king on the death without heirs of King Ladislas. Though his reign opened with a minority, he soon took control and begun campaigns against the Ottomans. His reign also saw conflict with the emperor, Frederick III, and with the 'heretical' King George of Bohemia, against whom Matthias Corvinus launched a crusade.

Matthias attracted the notice of humanists and the pope alike. His position on the frontier with the Ottomans made him, as Marsilio ◊Ficino put it, a potential saviour of Christendom. Matthias equally wished to be seen as a prince in the Italian mould; he married in 1476 Beatrice, the daughter of Ferrante of Naples, and adopted Italian fashions – perhaps influenced by members of his court like János Vitez (*c.* 1408–72). Like other Renaissance patrons (for example, Frederigo da Montefeltro) Matthias was most concerned with buildings: he had Buda palace modified in the Florentine style; the work on this was headed by a Florentine, Chimenti di Leonardo Camicia, who employed Italian and Hungarian craftsmen. Matthias also had the palace at Visegrád altered, and built a villa at Nyék. Nor was Matthias dismissive of humanist interests. He collected manuscripts, creating the Corviniana library (whose librarian was Taddeo Ugoleto).

Mattioli, Pierandrea (1501–1577)

Sienese physician and botanist. His encyclopedic study of plants *Commentarii a Dioscodie/ Commentaries on Dioscorides* (1544) brings together Classical, Medieval, and Renaissance knowledge of plants and th,eir uses in medicine. He moved to Bohemia in 1554 and became physician to the Emperor ◊Ferdinand I

He studied in Padua, and travelled widely in Italy to collect plants. His *Commentarii a Dioscodie*, intended as a practical guide for doctors, was first published in Venice and went into many editions and translations: it appeared first in Latin, and then in Italian (three versions) in 1554. It also appeared in German, French, and Czech. It goes beyond the plants described by the Greek doctor Dioscorides (1st century AD) and includes Mattioli's own discoveries and reports from his correspondents.

The two series of illustrations, one first published in the Venice edition of 1554, the larger ones appearing in a Prague version of 1562, and both copied repeatedly, are unusual in representing massed foliage, fruit, and flowers instead of single twigs or plants.

Mauduit, Jacques (1557–1627)

French lutenist and composer. He was, like his father before him, registrar to the courts of justice in Paris, but became famous as a musician. In 1588 he saved the manuscripts of his Huguenot friend Claude Le Jeune from destruction by Catholic soldiers, though he was himself a Catholic.

In 1581 he won first prize at the annual Puy de Musique at Evreux, and he was associated with Jean-Antoine de Baïf (1532–1589) in his experiments with *musique mesurée*, though after Baïf's death he relaxed the rigid subordination of music to verbal rhythm in his settings of verse.

Works include:
Requiem on the death of the poet Ronsard (1585), motets, chansons, chansonnettes mesurées for four voices, and other pieces.

Maximilian I (1459–1519)

Holy Roman Emperor from 1493, the son of Emperor Frederick III. Through a combination of dynastic marriages and diplomacy (backed up by military threats), Maximilian was able to build up the Habsburg inheritance. He himself married Mary of Burgundy, and after her death in 1582, held onto Burgundian lands; his son, ◊Philip the Handsome, was married to Joanna, the daughter of ◊Ferdinand

Maximilian II (1527–1576)

Holy Roman Emperor 1564–76.
Maximilian was the eldest son of Emperor
Ferdinand I and Anna of Hungary. He married his cousin Maria, daughter of ◊Charles
V, in 1548. Like his father he was mainly
engaged in defending the empire's eastern
border against the Turks and trying to
ensure peaceful coexistence between
Catholics and Protestants in Habsburg
lands – like his father, he adopted a tolerant
policy in religious matters. He was succeeded by his son Rudolf II.

Born in Vienna, but educated mainly in
Spain, he shared his father's taste for the
arts and sciences. He tried unsuccessfully to
lure the composer ◊Palestrina and the sculptor ◊Giambologna to his court in Vienna.
The artists who did work for him include
◊Arcimboldo and ◊Spranger, and the architect and sculptor Hans Mont of Ghent.

His tolerance in religious issues led some
to believe that he was secretly a Lutheran, a
belief given some weight by his deathbed
refusal to receive the Catholic sacrament.

and ◊Isabella. The eventual legatee of these arrangements was Maximilian's grandson, Charles V.

Maximilian was keen to promote his glory and did
so in part in his own writings. His entourage also
provided patronage for Germans with humanist interests, like Willibald ◊Pirckheimer and Konrad
Peutinger (1465–1547); he also attracted dedications
from other scholars like Ulrich von ◊Hutten. It was
probably through Pirckheimer that Albrecht ◊Dürer
was provided with imperial artistic commissions,
including a portrait (one among many) of
Maximilian.

Maynard, John (1577–AFTER 1614)

English lutenist and composer. He was connected
with the school of St Julian in Hertfordshire, and at
some time in the service of Lady Joan Thynne at
Cause Castle in Shropshire.

Works include:

Pavanes and galliards for the lute; an organ piece; lessons
for lute and bass viol and for lyra-viol; 12 songs *The XII
Wonders of the World*, describing various characters, for
voice, lute, and viola da gamba.

Mayone, Ascanio (c. 1565–1627)

Italian composer. He studied with Jean de Macque in Naples, was appointed organist at the Annunziata, Naples, in 1593 and maestro di cappella there from 1621.

Works include:

Madrigals, and solo and chamber instrumental music. His two volumes of keyboard music, *Capricci per sonar* (1603, 1609) contain canzonas and toccatas in an advanced idiom.

Mazzoni, Guido (PAGANINO) (c. 1450–1518)

Italian sculptor. Born at Modena, Mazzoni worked there and at Ferrara, Venice, Naples, and France, specializing in dramatic and realistic Nativity and Lamentation scenes. In 1495 he travelled with Charles VIII from Naples to France and helped to popularize recent Italian styles there. Much of the realism in these works was achieved through the use of masks taken from the living and the dead.

In 1498 he worked on a monument to Charles VIII in the abbey of St Denis (destroyed in 1793) and later executed an equestrian statue of Louis XII at Blois. Subsequently he was approached by Henry VIII of England to design a monument for Henry VII in Westminster Abbey, a project which was later undertaken by Pietro ◊Torrigiano.

Meckenen (ALSO MEKENEN, MECHELN), Israel von (c. 1445–1503)

German engraver and goldsmith. He is usually identified with the painter Meister Israel, 18 of whose works hang in the Pinakothek of Munich. They are religious in subject, and are clearly influenced by Jan van ◊Eyck.

Medici, Cosimo de' (KNOWN AS 'PATER PATRIAE') (1389–1464)

Florentine banker and politician, founder of Medicean political power. On his father's death in 1429, Cosimo became leader of the Medici family and inherited not only a fortune and a thriving business but also a policy of protecting the family interests by increasing involvement in politics. This involved Cosimo in clashes with other leading families, most notably the ◊Albizzi; accusing him of attempting to undermine the regime, they had him arrested in 1433 and exiled. Some, like Francesco ◊Filelfo, welcomed this move, but the Medici still had friends in Florence and, securing a majority of office-holders, were able to have the expulsion quashed. Cosimo returned and had the Albizzi themselves exiled.

1434 did not, however, create a Medici tyranny; Florence continued to be ruled by an oligarchy of families. Indeed, one of the reasons for Cosimo's success was his ability to act self-effacingly as a private citizen. It was only when he was dead that the city's government was willing to accord him the title of 'Pater Patriae' ('father of the fatherland'). At the same time, Cosimo's advice was a persuasive factor in decisions. So, for example, it can be credited to him that Florence jettisoned its traditional animosity to Milan and forged an alliance with the city.

Meanwhile, Cosimo also built up the family business, opening up more branches so that by the time of his death it not only had outlets in most of the major Italian cities but as far afield as Geneva and London.

Self-effacing he may have been but it did not follow that he was understated in his patronage. For sure, many of the commissions with which he was involved were communal or guild decisions: for example, he was on the committee that selected Ghiberti to sculpt statues for Orsanmichele. At the same time, he made sure that the Medici's position was apparent by commissioning the family palace from ◊Michelozzo da Bartolommeo. The Palazzo Medici stands diagonally opposite the church the Medici adopted, S Lorenzo, whose rebuilding designed by ◊Brunelleschi had begun under the patronage of Cosimo's father and which he continued. Cosimo, however, also had a project for another church, that of S Marco which came to house Fra ◊Angelico frescoes and Niccolò ◊Niccoli's book collection.

Niccoli, indeed, was one of several scholars with whom Cosimo was acquainted. Though himself no devotee of *studia humanitatis*, Cosimo did support those who promoted those studies. Some of the Florentine humanist coterie, like Leonardo ◊Bruni, may have had an ambivalent view towards the man

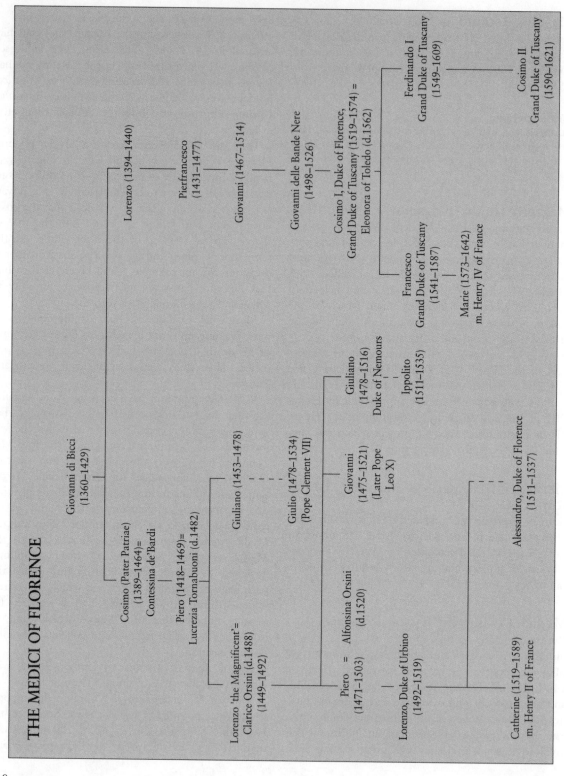

THE MEDICI OF FLORENCE

Giovanni di Bicci
(1360–1429)

Cosimo (Pater Patriae)
(1389–1464)=
Contessina de'Bardi

Lorenzo (1394–1440)

Piero (1418–1469)=
Lucrezia Tornabuoni (d.1482)

Pierfrancesco
(1431–1477)

Lorenzo 'the Magnificent'=
Clarice Orsini (d.1488)
(1449–1492)

Giuliano (1453–1478)

Giovanni (1467–1514)

Giovanni delle Bande Nere
(1498–1526)

Piero = Alfonsina Orsini
(1471–1503)   (d.1520)

Giovanni
(1475–1521)
(Later Pope
Leo X)

Giulio (1478–1534)
(Pope Clement VII)

Giuliano
(1478–1516)
Duke of Nemours

Ippolito
(1511–1535)

Cosimo I, Duke of Florence,
Grand Duke of Tuscany (1519–1574) =
Eleonora of Toledo (d.1562)

Lorenzo, Duke of Urbino
(1492–1519)

Alessandro, Duke of Florence
(1511–1537)

Catherine (1519–1589)
m. Henry II of France

Francesco
Grand Duke of Tuscany
(1541–1587)

Ferdinando I
Grand Duke of Tuscany
(1549–1609)

Marie (1573–1642)
m. Henry IV of France

Cosimo II
Grand Duke of Tuscany
(1590–1621)

who broke Albizzi power but replaced it with his own. He provided them, however, with financial assistance and with an influential supporter; like most Florentines, they could not afford to alienate him.

Medici, Cosimo (I) de', GRAND DUKE OF TUSCANY (1519–1574)

Florentine ruler from 1537, Grand Duke of Tuscany from 1569. Cosimo was descended in the male line not from his namesake but from the cadet branch of the family: he owed his insertion as Florence's ruler at the age of 18 to one relative's murder of another, Alessandro. He owed his elevation to Charles V who wanted to secure the status quo; he owed his survival to Alessandro Vitelli's defeat of anti-Medicean exiles at Montemurlo in 1539. Cosimo slowly extricated himself from subservience to Charles V and expanded his territory, taking Siena in 1554–56.

In the 1560s he took an ever-smaller part in government, making his son **Francesco de' Medici** (1541–87) his regent. But it was Cosimo himself who took the grandiloquent title he eventually prised out of Pius V.

Cosimo was keen to emphasize a continuity of Medicean control in Florence, stretching from the first Cosimo. His patronage, therefore, both continued family traditions (he commissioned works from ◊Pontormo and ◊Bronzino for S Lorenzo, for example) and back-projected his own rule onto his forefathers: Giorgio ◊Vasari's decorations of the Palazzo Vecchio celebrated the Medici as a princely dynasty. It was also Vasari that designed the new Medicean palace between the Palazzo Vecchio and the Arno: Gli Uffizi (The Offices). For other 'public' works, Cosimo employed Bartolommeo ◊Ammanati, adding, for example, the Fountain of Neptune to the Piazza della Signoria. With such patronage, Florence was converted from a republican to a princely city.

Medici family

Florentine banking family which came to dominate the city from 1434 until their expulsion in 1494, only to return after the failure of Piero ◊Soderini's republic in 1512 and eventually to become the titled rulers of Florence as the Grand Dukes of Tuscany. Along the way, they produced two popes, ◊Leo X and ◊Clement VII, as well as wives to various European princes, including ◊Catherine de' Medici.

With the collapse of the ◊Acciaiuoli and ◊Bardi family banks in the mid-14th century, there were opportunities for other families to take over their role. By the beginning of the 15th century, **Giovanni di Bicci de' Medici** (1360–1429) had filled the position. After his death, his son, ◊Cosimo, suffered some political difficulties but, from 1434, was able increasingly to influence the direction of Florentine politics. On his death, however, he left his son **Piero de' Medici** (1418–69) with financial problems and the potential resentment of fellow Florentines. Piero weathered this storm only to die in 1469. The hope of the family then became Piero's own son, ◊Lorenzo de' Medici at the time barely out of his teens; but in the next decades he was able to convert influence into a stranglehold and to turn his grandfather's cultural interests into grand patronage.

Throughout the 15th century, though, Medici control of Florence depended on the person of the family's leading member and the support of the city's other leading families. None of the Medici could be sure of this cooperation, as Lorenzo learnt in 1478 when the ◊Pazzi conspiracy occurred – and as his son, **Piero de' Medici** (1471–1503) discovered when, faced with the danger of French invasion, the other families deserted and ousted him in 1494. The less aristocratic republics of the hell-fire preacher ◊Savonarola and of Piero Soderini also foundered, ultimately because of the continuing French menace: the Medici were restored in 1512, with **Giovanni** (elected pope as Leo X the next year) and **Lorenzo de' Medici** (1492–1519) the leading members in the first instance.

Yet, even now, Medicean authority was not securely established. Another foreign invasion, this time by imperial forces of ◊Charles V, signalled another expulsion of the family, in the wake of the ◊Sack of Rome in 1527 which left the second Medici pope, Clement VII, diplomatically stranded. However, an alliance between pope and emperor saw the Medici reimposed on Florence in 1530 with **Alessandro de' Medici** (1511–1537) heading the government and taking the title in 1532 of 'Duke of the Florentine Republic'. He suffered the weakness of a tyrant – a perpetual sense of insecurity – a concern ironically vindicated by his assassination at the hands

of a member of his own family in 1537. In the aftermath of this, the clan moved quickly to insert another Medici into power: a second ◊Cosimo de' Medici took control and increasingly proved himself an independent politician. In 1569, he achieved for the family an hereditary title: Grand Duke of Tuscany.

Medici, Lorenzo de' (KNOWN AS 'THE MAGNIFICENT') (1449–1492)

Florentine politician and author. The head of the Medici family from his father's death in 1469, he built upon the powerbase created by his grandfather, Cosimo, a quasi-princely position in the republic. Though the sobriquet 'il Magnifico' ('the Magnificent') was merely a sign of respect to a man of standing, he was certainly regarded by other rulers – and, increasingly, by fellow Florentines – as the boss of the city. This was not to everybody's liking: internal and external opposition was crystallized in the ◊Pazzi conspiracy in 1478. Such open confrontation was rare, however, and counterproductive: Lorenzo tied more closely around him the strings of the constitution, as well as the bonds of loyalty of other leading families.

By the second half of the 15th century, the skills for which Florentines were renowned were not just financial but also artistic. It was commonsense for Lorenzo to take on, with all his other roles, that of a broker for cultural exports. A symbol of the new entente with ◊Sixtus IV after the Pazzi war was the sending to Rome of a group of Florentine artists to assist with the decorating of the ◊Sistine Chapel. He also offered to Ferrante of Naples the services of Giuliano da Sangallo, whom he himself employed on a series of projects, like his villa at Poggio a Caiano. It was other members of the Medici clan who commissioned works of art like Sandro ◊Botticelli's *Primavera* but the complex mythological allegory of such paintings owes something to the circle around Lorenzo. There was no formal ◊Platonic Academy for Lorenzo to patronize but he did share an interest in the writings of Plato and the neo-Platonists with, for example, Marsilio ◊Ficino, ◊Pico della Mirandola, and Cristoforo Landino. Lorenzo was himself a poet and certainly assisted the careers of other writers; ◊Politian found employment at the Medici 'court' – and may have advised artists like Botticelli (for the *Primavera*) and Michelangelo (for his *Battle of Lapiths and Centaurs*) on their Classical subjects. Michelangelo, furthermore, was one of the sculptors who visited the Medici garden where Bertoldo di Giovanni presided over Lorenzo's collection of ancient sculpture. However far Lorenzo was engaged in these activities, it was as the enlightened patron that he was remembered, or mythologized, in the 16th century.

It would have been impossible to find a better tyrant or a more likeable one.

~

FRANCESCO GUICCIARDINI's verdict on Lorenzo de' Medici in his *History of Florence*

Meistergesang

Form of sung poetry that developed in Germany during the 14th and 15th centuries and flourished in the 16th. It was performed solo by members of guilds of *Meistersinger* (mastersingers), according to strict rules of versification and music.

At first religious but later also secular, *Meistergesang* developed out of the medieval courtly love song (*Minnesang*) as poetry and music became forms of relaxation for members of the urban trade guilds.

Meit, Konrad (*c.* 1480–1551)

German sculptor. Working mainly in boxwood, alabaster, and metal, he made many small portrait busts and statuettes in a Classical style, fusing together Italian and northern elements, in works like his alabaster nude *Judith* (*c.* 1510–15).

Meit was born at Worms. From 1506 to 1510 he worked at the court of Frederick, Elector of Saxony, in Wittenberg. The rest of his life was spent in the Netherlands, where he was court sculptor to the regent, ◊Margaret of Austria.

He also produced several monumental sculptures for the tombs of Margaret, her husband and her mother-in-law (1526–32) at Brou, Bourg-en-Bresse. Little work remains from Meit's period in Antwerp after Margaret's death in 1530.

Mel, Rinaldo del (*c.* 1554–*c.* 1598)

Flemish composer. After serving at the Portuguese court, he went to Rome in 1580, where he entered the service of Cardinal Gabriele Paleotti (1522–97) and may have studied under Palestrina. He was at Liège (1587–91), in the household of Ernst, Duke of Bavaria, but he rejoined Paleotti at Bologna, who appointed him maestro di cappella at Magliano Cathedral.

Works include:
Motets, *Sacrae Cantiones*, a Litany; 12 volumes of *madrigaletti* and spiritual madrigals.

Melanchthon, Philip (ASSUMED NAME OF PHILIP SCHWARZERD) (1497–1560)

German humanist and Lutheran theologian. Melanchthon's early employment was as a teacher at his university, Tübingen, and as an editor of printed works, including the *Clarorum Virorum Epistolae/ Letters of Famous Men* written in support of his uncle, Johann ◊Reuchlin. He was appointed professor of Greek at Wittenberg in 1518 and there became an ally of Martin ◊Luther. It was Melanchthon who produced the Confession of ◊Augsburg in 1530.

While still a boy, his scholarship impressed his uncle, Reuchlin, who gave him the pseudonym Melanchthon as a Greek translation for his family name (meaning 'black earth'). His early work on printed editions also earned him the praise of Erasmus, but Melanchthon was willing to forgo the support of these scholars in his defence of Luther's theology. While the latter was in the Wartburg, Melanchthon produced his own *Loci Communes Rerum Theologicarum/Commonplaces of Theology* (1521) which later formed the basis of the Augsburg Confession, and which was translated into German in 1555. Melanchthon became effectively the leading diplomat of the Lutheran cause, both assisting like-minded communities across Germany and also attempting to find grounds for reconciliation with the Catholic Church. After Luther's death, his moderate (Philippist) position had its supporters but was rejected by more radical Lutherans.

Melozzo da Forlì, Francesco (1438–1494)

Italian painter. A disciple of ◊Piero della Francesca, he was active in Urbino and Rome. A fresco in the Church of SS Apostoli, Rome, is an example of his work which includes characteristic figures of angelic musicians. For Sixtus IV, he painted a fresco celebrating the pope's patronage of the Vatican library.

In Urbino he probably collaborated with the Flemish painter ◊Justus of Ghent (active *c.* 1460–80) on the portraits of famous men and personifications of the liberal arts for ◊Federigo da Montefeltro's *studiolo*.

He is said to have been the inventor of a form of

foreshortening – ◊*sotto in sù* – which caused figures on a painted ceiling or interior dome to look as if they were floating overhead in space.

Melville, Andrew (1545–1622)

Scottish reformer and humanist. He studied in Paris and taught in Geneva, and from 1574 held academic posts in Scotland. Several times moderator of the General Assembly of the Presbyterian Church in Scotland, he was largely responsible for its constitution. At the ◊Hampton Court Conference in 1606 he criticized the royal supremacy and was briefly imprisoned in the Tower of London until 1611.

He was born at Baldovie, near Forfar, and learnt Greek at Montrose grammar school from Pierre de Marsiliers. He studied at St Andrews University in Scotland before studying oriental languages, law, and mathematics at Paris (1564–66), where he was influenced by the new methods of Petrus ◊Ramus. He became regent of St Marceon College at Poitiers in 1566 but soon left for Switzerland, where he occupied the chair of Latin at the Geneva Academy (1568–73).

On his return to Scotland he became principal of Glasgow University (1574–80) and then St Mary's College, St Andrews University (1580–97). A staunch defender of Presbyterianism, he helped to bring about the fall of episcopacy in Scotland and to draft the *Second Book of Discipline* about 1581. His extreme views made him many enemies and he was forced to flee to England in 1584. He soon returned and in 1570 was made rector of St Andrews, a position he held until 1597.

After his release from the Tower of London in 1611 he went to France and spent the rest of his life as professor of biblical theology at Sedan.

Melzi, Francesco de' (c. 1491–1568)

Italian painter. He was a friend and pupil of Leonardo da Vinci and is responsible for the preservation of Leonardo's writings, which, with other belongings, were bequeathed to him. The *Vertumnus and Pomona* (Staatliche Museen, Berlin) may be by him.

Memling (MEMLINC), Hans (c. 1430–1494)

Flemish painter. He was probably a pupil of van der ◊Weyden, but his style is calmer and softer. He painted religious subjects and also portraits, including *Tommaso Portinari and His Wife* about 1480 (Metropolitan Museum of Art, New York).

His works, which were highly regarded in Renaissance Italy, where they influenced ◊Perugino and others, include: *The Mystic Marriage of St Catherine* (Hospital of St John, Bruges); the Donne Triptych (National Gallery, London), which includes both a self-portrait and a portrait of the English donor, Sir John Donne; *Bathsheba* (Staatsgalerie, Stuttgart), a life-sized nude; and such fine portraits as that of Guillaume Moreel and his wife (Musée des Beaux-Arts, Brussels).

Memling was born in Seligenstadt near Frankfurt-am-Main, Germany, but settled in Bruges about 1466, and was town painter there (1475–87). He had a prosperous career, producing religious paintings of great beauty and portraits of dignified reticence, anticipating those of Hans Holbein the Younger. His landscape backgrounds have a charm and delicacy that was particularly appreciated by Italian artists of his day. Though he adopted elements of style from van Eyck, Dirck Bouts, and above all van der Weyden, he showed little development in his work, except in his later years when he introduced some Italian decorative motives.

Memmi, Lippo, DI FILIPPUCCIO (DIED 1356)

Italian painter. He was active in Siena and Avignon, and often worked with ◊Simone Martini. The fresco over the door of the convent of the Servites in Siena is one of his principal works.

He was the son and pupil of the painter **Memmo di Filippuccio.**

Mena, Juan de (1411–1456)

Cordoban poet and author, whose features, apparently, were 'pale and worn from study'. He was patronized by Juan II and his powerful favourite, Alvaro de Luna (to whose book on *Virtuous Women* he contributed a prefatory poem). In 1442 he translated *The Iliad* into Castilian verse (it was published in 1519); unfortunately his Latin source was taken from a defective copy. Juan appointed him royal chronicler, but Mena is better known for his poetry. This, although couched in traditional (that is, not Italianate) Castilian metres, eschewed the rhythms and language of popular speech, being characterized by complex syntax, the use of Castilian words in their original, Latin, sense, and a fondness for allegorical and mythological subjects. In 1444 he produced the densely written *Laberinto de la fortuna/Fortune's Labyrinth*, a three-hundred-stanza didactic poetic allegory in which the Castilian past and present are revealed to Everyman by Providence, a heavenly vision ended before the revelation of the future by a eulogy of his patron Luna. Admired and imitated by contemporaries, it was published in the 1480s and was the subject of an obscene 16th-century parody, the *Caragicomedia/ The Penis-Comedy*. Luna's execution in 1453 and Juan's death in 1454 robbed Mena suddenly of his patrons. Forced to seek a wider audience, it seems he attempted to simplify his style: the result was the *Coplas de los siete pecados mortales/ Verses on the Seven Deadly Sins* (1500).

Mendoza, Antonio de (c. 1490–1552)

First Spanish viceroy of New Spain (Mexico) (1535–51). He attempted to develop agriculture and mining and supported the church in its attempts to convert the Indians. The system he established lasted until the 19th century. He was subsequently viceroy of Peru (1551–52).

Menéndez de Avilés, Pedro (1519–1574)

Spanish colonial administrator in America. Philip II of Spain granted him the right to establish a colony in Florida to counter French presence there. In 1565 he founded St Augustine and destroyed the French outpost at Fort Caroline.

Born in Avilés, Spain, he saw service in the navy of Charles V and was named to the vital post of captain general of the Indies fleet in 1554. His later attempts to establish colonies in the Chesapeake region were unsuccessful but Menéndez maintained a firm Spanish claim on the Florida peninsula.

Merbecke, John (MARBECK) (c. 1505–c. 1585)

English composer and writer. He compiled *The Booke of Common Praier Noted* (1550), the first musical setting of an Anglican prayer book. He was lay clerk and organist at St George's Chapel, Windsor from 1531. In 1543 he was arrested and in 1544 tried and con-demned for heresy as a Calvinist, but he was pardoned and allowed to retain his office.

His concordance of the English Bible, the first complete edition, was published in 1550. After Edward VI's accession, Merbecke compiled *The Booke of Common Praier Noted*. It was the first book of its kind, and used adaptations of plainsong in addition to music written by Merbecke himself. Merbecke's other surviving works are a large-scale Mass, two motets, and an anthem.

Works include:

Mass and two motets (probably early); carol 'A Virgine and Mother'; *The Booke of Common Praier Noted* [set to notes] (1550, first version authorized by Edward VI).

Mercator, Gerardus (LATINIZED FORM OF GERHARD KREMER) (1512–1594)

Flemish mapmaker who devised **Mercator's projection** in which the parallels and meridians on maps are drawn uniformly at 90°. The projection continues to be used, in particular for navigational charts, because compass courses can be drawn as straight lines, but the true area of countries is increasingly distorted the further north or south they are from the Equator.

Mersenne, Marin (1588–1648)

French monk, mathematician, philosopher, and music theorist. His treatises include the two-volume *Harmonie universelle*, published at Paris in 1636–37, with a section on instruments, 'Questions harmoniques de la nature des sons'.

Educated at Le Mans and La Flèche, he became a Minorite friar, and was ordained in 1612. He taught philosophy at Nevers and then studied mathematics and music in Paris, where his colleagues included Descartes and the elder Pascal. He corresponded with scholars in England, Holland, and Italy, the last of which he visited three times.

Merula, Giorgio (1430/31–1494)

Humanist teacher, editor, and commentator on Classical texts, born in Alessandria (Piedmont), Italy. A fractious character (but perhaps most humanists were), Merula had a career which was dogged by academic disputes with the likes of ◊Politian and Cornelio ◊Vitelli. These controversies were sparked off by his commentaries and editions on authors like Martial, Cicero, and Plautus. When he was not arguing, Merula taught, first in Venice from 1465–82, then, at the invitation of Lodovico Sforza, in Milan from 1482–94, where his pupils included ◊Baldassare Castiglione. For the Sforzas, Merula also wrote a history of Milanese rulers.

Merulo, Claudio (ADOPTED NAME OF CLAUDIO MERLOTTI) (1533–1604)

Italian organist, teacher, and composer. Famous in his lifetime for his organ playing, he is best known today for his keyboard music.

He was appointed organist at Brescia in 1556 and second organist at St Mark's, Venice, in 1557, advancing to first organist in 1564. In 1584 he left Venice, visited the court of Mantua, and became organist to the ducal chapel at Parma.

Works include:
Intermezzi for Dolce's *Le Troiane* (1566) and Cornelio Frangipani's *La tragedia* (1574); Masses, motets, *Sacrae Cantiones*, Litanies; madrigals; toccatas and ricercari for organ.

metaphysical poets

Group of early 17th-century English poets whose work is characterized by ingenious, highly intricate wordplay and unlikely or paradoxical imagery. They used rhetorical and literary devices, such as paradox, hyperbole, and elaborately developed conceits, in such a way as to engage the reader by their humour, strangeness, or sheer outrageousness. Among the exponents of this genre are John ◊Donne, George Herbert, Andrew Marvell, Richard Crashaw, and Henry Vaughan.

Michelangelo (PROPERLY MICHELANGELO DI LODOVICO BUONARROTI) (1475–1564)

Florentine sculptor, painter, architect, and poet. Active in Florence and Rome, he was heralded as the leading artist of the 16th century, celebrated in two biographies – those of Giorgio ◊Vasari and Ascanio ◊Condivi – while he still lived. In Vasari's view of art history (see feature on History of Art), he was the ultimate genius of the revival of art: the aura which surrounded the man meant that his art – sculpture, painting, and architecture – had a profound influence on the generations immediately following him.

Born in Caprese outside of Florence, he was apprenticed at the age of 13 to the painter Domenico ◊Ghirlandaio, before attracting the patronage of Lorenzo de' ◊Medici, in whose sculpture garden he studied antique works under the guidance of the custodian Bertoldo. *The Battle of Centaurs and Lapiths* (Casa Buonarotti, Florence) was amongst his earliest sculptures in relief and shows the influence of antique sarcophagi on his art. Central to his practice as an artist was his emphasis on the primacy of ◊*disegno*, and his interest in the portrayal of monumental human figures and elaborate poses.

He travelled to Rome in 1496, where he studied antique buildings and sculpture, in addition to sculpt-

Michelangelo Daniele da Volterra, bust of the bearded Michelangelo, giving some sense of his squashed nose (broken in his youth by Pietro Torrigiano) (Bargello, Florence). *AKG London/Erich Lessing*

ing the monumental *Pietà* (St Peters, Rome). On his return to Florence he received the commission to sculpt a figure for the Cathedral of Florence from a massive piece of discarded Carrara marble. On the completion of the *David* (Accademia, Florence), he received critical acclaim for the sophistication of the larger than life sculpture. With his *Holy Family* (Uffizi, Florence), painted in 1503, he confirmed his status as an artist capable in painting as well as sculpture. He received the commission to paint a large fresco in the Council Hall of Florence of the Battle of Cascina, alongside ◊Leonardo da Vinci. Both artists left their work unfinished, though Michelangelo may have learned from the latter's cartoon a new energy of movement and intensity of expression.

Called to Rome by ◊Julius II to execute the pope's tomb, he was allotted the commission to decorate the ceiling of the ◊Sistine Chapel. Michelangelo completed the ceiling in an astonishingly short space of time, working largely without assistants; the work confirmed his status as one of the leading artists of his day. He remained principally occupied with sculptural and architectural projects for the remainder of his career; of the few paintings he executed, the most controversial was the *Last Judgement* of the Sistine Chapel where he demonstrated his life-long interest in the portrayal of the human figure (and his weak grasp on theological orthodoxy). Among his most prominent projects was his design for the sepulchral chapel of the Medici family in the church of San Lorenzo, Florence, which involved both architectural as well as sculptural decorations. A synthesis of his interests in antique sculpture and architecture, the chapel was used as a training ground for artists of the 16th century. The architectural designs of his later years in Rome, which included the dome of St Peters, had an immense influence of the emergence of the Baroque.

Michelozzo The courtyard of the Palazzo Medici (now Palazzo Medici-Riccardi) in Florence, designed by Michele Michelozzo. *AKG London/Jochen Remmer*

In addition to his works of art, he was a prolific poet whose sonnets were revered by his contemporaries (see Vitturia Colonna). On his death in Rome in 1564, his body was transported to Florence where he was buried in the church of Santa Croce in an elaborate ceremony organised by the Accademia del Disegno.

Michelozzo di Bartolomeo (1396–1472)

Italian sculptor and architect. He worked with ◊Ghiberti and ◊Donatello. Although overshadowed by such contemporaries as ◊Brunelleschi and ◊Alberti, he was the chosen architect of Cosimo de' Medici and was commissioned by him to design the Palazzo de' ◊Medici (now Palazzo Medici-Riccardi, Florence), begun in the 1440s, and the library of the monastery of San Marco, about 1436.

Middleton, Thomas (1580–1627)

English dramatist. He produced numerous romantic plays, tragedies, and realistic comedies, both alone and in collaboration, including *A Fair Quarrel* (1617), *The Changeling* (1622), and *The Spanish Gypsy* (1623) with William Rowley; *The Roaring Girl* (1611) with Thomas ◊Dekker; and (alone) *Women Beware Women* (1621). He also composed many pageants and masques.

Other plays include *A Trick to Catch the Old One* (c. 1604–07), *Your Five Gallants* (1604–07), *The Familie of Love* (1608), *A Mad World, My Masters* (1609), *A Chaste Maid in Cheapside* (c. 1611), *No Wit, No Help Like a Woman's* (c. 1613), *More Dissemblers Besides Women* (c. 1615), and *The Witch* (c. 1615).

Middleton's work is wide-ranging and varied in quality. His work shows a particular sympathy with and insight into female psychology.

Middleton was born in London and educated at Queen's College, Oxford. He started his writing career in 1597 with a poem, 'The Wisdom of Solomon Paraphrased'. Soon be became a professional writer for the theatre, collaborating with Thomas Dekker, John Webster, William Rowley, and others. He also wrote verse satires and satirical prose pamphlets such as *The Black Book* (1604). Middleton was employed writing masques and entertainments for civic occasions in London, finally being appointed

city chronologer in 1620. In 1624, his satirical anti-Spanish comedy *A Game at Chess*, which represented prominent politicians as chess pieces, played for nine days to packed crowds before being banned by the Privy Council.

Milán, Luis (c. 1500–AFTER 1561)

Spanish vihuelist and composer. His works were all published in *El Maestro* (1536), the earliest surviving vihuela collection. They include fantasies and pavans for vihuela, Spanish and Portuguese *villancicos*, Spanish ballads, and Italian sonnets for voice and vihuela. He was one of the first composers to write tempo indications.

He was the son of a nobleman, Don Luis de Milán. He visited Italy and Portugal.

Milton, John (c. 1563–1647)

English composer, father of John Milton the poet. He is said to have received a gold medal from a Polish prince for an In Nomine in 40 parts.

He was educated at Christ Church, Oxford. After being cast out by his father as a Protestant, he went to London, and in 1600 became a member of the Scriveners' Company, marrying Sarah Jeffrey about that time. Having made a fair fortune as a scribe, he retired to Horton in Buckinghamshire in 1632, but after his wife's death moved to Reading about 1640. In 1643 he returned to London, where he lived with his son John.

Works include:

Various sacred pieces for several voices; madrigal contribution to *The Triumphes of Oriana*, four vocal pieces contributed to Leighton's *Teares or Lamentacions*; two tunes for Ravenscroft's Psalter; five fancies for viols.

Mirror for Magistrates

English book published in 1559 consisting of 19 tragic stories written in verse written by various authors. The stories are told by figures from English history – such as Richard III and Edward VI – who describe their rise to power and subsequent downfall. The book became very popular (enlarged editions appeared in 1563, 1578, and 1610) and influenced Shake-speare's history plays.

Written by William Baldwin, George Ferrers, and

others, the stories were a continuation of John ◊Lydgate's long poem *Fall of Princes*, which was itself a version of a book by ◊Boccaccio.

Mocetto, Girolamo (*c.* 1470–1531)

Italian artist of the Venetian School. His works reflect the influence of Andrea Mantegna and Giovanni ◊Bellini. He worked in a series of media: engravings (like his *Calumny of Apelles* about 1500, after Mantegna), oil paintings (for example, *The Massacre of the Innocents* about 1500, National Gallery, London), and – in a medium closer to that of his family background of glass painting – stained glass (for SS Giovanni e Paolo, Venice, about 1515).

Mohács, Battle of

Turkish victory over a Hungarian army on 29 August 1526; the battle marked the end of the medieval kingdom of Hungary. King Louis II of Hungary's 25,000-strong army was attacked by a Turkish army of about 100,000 troops under Suleiman the Magnificent and totally destroyed; 24,000 Hungarians were killed, including Louis. This left the road to Buda open, and the Turks sacked the city on 12 September 1526.

Molza, Francesco Maria (1489–1544)

Italian poet. His *Ninfa Tiberina* (1538) has a place in the history of pastoral poetry.

Momper, Joos (Jodocus) de, THE YOUNGER (1564–1635)

Flemish landscape painter. Like his immediate predecessor Pieter ◊Brueghel the Elder, he often gave his landscapes a high viewpoint, his panoramas inspired by his journeys through Switzerland and Italy. Typical of his winter scenes is *The Flight from Egypt* (Ashmolean Museum, Oxford).

Momper was born in Antwerp, the principal member of a family of artists and son-in-law of the painter Joos de Momper (1500–1559). He worked in a landscape style that was a link between Pieter Brueghel and Adam ◊Elsheimer, and often employed other Antwerp painters, such as Jan 'Velvet' Brueghel, to paint in incidental figures.

Monet, Jan (*c.* 1480–*c.* 1550)

Flemish sculptor. Monet's chief works were alabaster altarpieces, such as those at Halle (1533) and Brussels (1538–41). These works were the first Renaissance sculptural altarpieces in the Netherlands, their architectural and stylistic repertory consisting of Classical or Italianate motifs. He worked in Spain for many years.

By 1497 he was working in Barcelona, and in 1512–13 in Aix-en-Provence. He was in Barcelona again in 1516 and the following year worked beside Bartolomé Ordóñez on the decoration of the choir of the cathedral there, after which he may have visited Naples. In 1521 he met Albrecht Dürer at Antwerp and the following year Emperor Charles V appointed him a court artist. From about 1524/25 until his death he was resident at Malines.

Montagna, Bartolommeo (BARTOLOMMEO CINCANI) (1450–1523)

Italian painter. His religious works, their simplicity of design and sobriety of colour strongly influenced by Andrea ◊Mantegna, made him the leading artist of Vicenza. His chief work is the altarpiece (1499) of S Michele in Vicenza (later removed to Milan).

Montagna was born in Orzinuovi, near Brescia, and probably trained in Venice under Mantegna. Other Venetian influences are those of Alvise Vivarini, Gentile Bellini, and Vittore Carpaccio.

Montaigne, Michel Eyquem de (1533–1592)

French writer. He is regarded as the creator of the essay form. In 1580 he published the first two volumes of his *Essais*; the third volume appeared in 1588, and the definitive edition was issued posthumously in 1595. In his writings Montaigne considers all aspects of life from an urbanely sceptical viewpoint. He is critical of human pride and suspicious of philosophy and religion, seeking his own independent path to self-knowledge. Francis ◊Bacon was among the thinkers who have been challenged and stimulated by his work, and through the translation by John Florio in 1603, he influenced Shakespeare and other English writers.

He was born at the Château de Montaigne near Bordeaux, studied law, and in 1554 became a counsellor of the Bordeaux *parlement*. Little is known of his earlier life, except that he regularly visited Paris and the court of Francis II. In 1569 he published his translation of the *Theologia Naturalis* of Raymond Sebond (a 15th-century professor of Toulouse), and in the same year edited the works of his friend Etienne de ◊La Boétie. In 1571 he retired to his estates, relinquishing his magistracy, and began to write his *Essais* 1572. The ironical *Apologie de Raymond Sebond* about 1576 reveals the full extent of his sceptical philosophy, refusing to trust the reasoning and rationality of other philosophies. He toured Germany, Switzerland, and Italy (1580–81), returning upon his election as mayor of Bordeaux, a post he held until 1585.

Monte, Philippe de (1521–1603)

Flemish composer. He was a prolific polyphonist; about 40 of his Masses, 300 motets, 45 chansons, and over 1,100 madrigals survive. Among his friends were the composers Roland de ◊Lassus and William ◊Byrd. Monte's secular music enjoyed widespread popularity, as the distribution of his publications and manuscripts testifies.

Monte was born in Malines, and went to Italy while still young. He served the Pinelli family in Naples (1542–51) as singer, teacher, and composer. In 1554 he left Naples and went to the Netherlands. He was in England (1554–55) as a member of the choir of Philip II of Spain, when he met William Byrd and his family; by 1558 he had returned to Italy. In 1568 he went to Vienna as Kapellmeister to the Emperor Maximilian II, after whose death in 1576 he followed the next emperor, ◊Rudolf II, to Prague. He served the emperor for the rest of his life, and was made a canon of Cambrai Cathedral, but did not reside there.

Many of his Masses are based on motets by contemporary composers. His madrigal settings follow the text closely (most of the texts are by contemporary pastoral poets such as ◊Guarini); his later madrigals are simpler in form and increasingly homophonous.

Works include:

Around 40 Masses, motets; over 30 books of madrigals, including 1,073 secular and 144 spiritual works. His

motet *Super Flumina Babylonis* was sent to Byrd in 1583, to which the latter responded with *Quomodo Cantabimus* in 1584.

Montemayor, Jorge de (1519–1561)

Portuguese poet and musician, born at Montemor-o-Velho (hence his surname) near Coimbra. He travelled to England in ◊Philip II's entourage in 1554; the same year he published a collection of his poetry. This was re-printed in 1558, with a second collection added, and promptly banned by the Inquisition in 1559. They did not, however, censor his most famous work, written in Castilian despite his Portuguese nationality, which also appeared in 1558–59: *La* ◊*Diana*. Despite his promises, Montemayor never produced a sequel to this ◊pastoral best seller. In 1560 he translated Ausias March's Catalan poetry to Castilian, and the following year was murdered in obscure circumstances in Piedmont.

Monteverdi, Claudio Giovanni Antonio (1567–1643)

Italian composer. He contributed to the development of the opera with *La favola d'Orfeo/The Legend of Orpheus* (1607 and *L'incoronazione di Poppea/The Coronation of Poppea* (1642). He also wrote madrigals, motets, and sacred music, notably the *Vespers* (1610).

Born in Cremona, he was in the service of the Duke of Mantua about 1591–1612, and was director of music at St Mark's, Venice, from 1613. He was first to use an orchestra and to reveal the dramatic possibilities of the operatic form. His first opera *Orfeo* was produced for the carnival at Mantua in 1607.

Monteverdi was the son of a doctor. He was a chorister at Cremona Cathedral and a pupil of Ingegneri, he then became an organist and viol player and in 1583, aged 16, published sacred madrigals. About 1591 he entered the service of the Duke of Mantua, Vincenzo Gonzaga, as a viol player and singer, and there married the harpist Claudia Cataneo. He was in Gonzaga's retinue in the war against the Turks on the Danube and again in Flanders in 1599. He probably heard Peri's *Euridice* at Florence in 1600, and in 1602 was made music master to the court of Mantua. His wife died in 1607 after a long illness, and in the same year Monteverdi finished his first opera, *La favola d'Orfeo*; this remains the earliest opera to be regularly performed today. His next opera, *Arianna*, now lost except for the famous 'Lament', made him widely famous. Meanwhile Monteverdi had written his first five books of madrigals, which are scarcely less important in the development of their species. In 1610 he dedicated his collection of church music, the *Vespers*, to Pope Paul V; from the opening chorus, based on the Toccata of *Orfeo*, and through to the concluding Magnificat, it is evident that the art of music is moving away for the first time from private use and into the public domain.

When Francesco Gonzaga succeeded his brother to the dukedom in 1612, he quarrelled with Monteverdi, who left for Cremona to wait for a new appointment. This came from Venice in 1613, where he was was appointed maestro to St Mark's, the most coveted church appointment in north Italy. He remained there until his death, adding church music of great splendour to his previous output. He had by this time written much church music and numerous madrigals. His church music makes supremely effective use of the particular architecture of St Mark's, deploying separate groups of instruments and singers in order to exploit antiphonal effects. The nine books of madrigals develop from the small-scale pieces of 1587 to the hugely extended forms in Book 8 of 1638. In 1630 he took holy orders after escaping the plague at Venice. In 1639 the second public opera theatre in Venice, the Teatro dei SS Giovanni e Paolo, was opened with Monteverdi's *Adone*, and *Arianna* was revived the same year when the Teatro di San Moisè was inaugurated. Two further operas survive from this period: *Il ritorno d'Ulisse in patria* (1641), and his last opera *L'Incoronazione di Poppea*, widely performed today in an increasing variety of editions.

Works include:

Operas *Orfeo* (1607), *Arianna* (lost except the 'Lament', 1608), *Il combattimento di Tancredi e Clorinda* (after Tasso, 1624), *Il ritorno d'Ulisse in patria* (1640), *L'incoronazione di Poppea* (1642), and about a dozen lost stage works; ballets *Ballo delle ingrate* (1608) and *Tirsi e Clori* (1619); Masses, Magnificats, and psalms; *Vespers* (1610), *Sancta Maria* for voice and eight instruments; 40 sacred madrigals; 21 *canzonette* for three voices; nine books of secular madrigals containing 250, including book VIII, *Madrigali guerrieri e amorosi/Madrigals of love and war*; 26 madrigals published in various collections; 25 *Scherzi musicali* for one to three voices (1607).

Montezuma II (1466–1520)

Aztec emperor of Mexico. He succeeded his uncle in 1502. Although he was a great warrior and legislator, heavy centralized taxation provoked resentment in outlying areas. When the Spanish conquistador Hernán ◊Cortés landed at Veracruz in 1519 and attempted to march on Tenochtitlán, he was well received by the inhabitants and made Montezuma his prisoner. The emperor was restored to his throne as a vassal of Spain, but dissident groups among his subjects rebelled and killed him.

Montgomerie, Alexander (*c.* 1556–*c.* 1610)

Scottish poet. His chief poem is *The Cherrie and the Slae* (1597), written in a 14-line stanza, of which Montgomerie may have been the inventor. Montgomerie also introduced the sonnet to Scotland. Other works are *The Flyting betwixt Montgomery and Polwart* (1621) and *The Mindes Melodie* (1605), a version of 15 of the Psalms, with other pieces.

Montgomerie was born in Ayrshire. He held office in the Scottish court in 1577 and became one of James VI's 'Castalian Band' of court poets.

Montluc, Blaise de Lasseran-Massencôme, Seigneur de (*c.* 1500–1577)

French soldier. His military career began in 1521 and culminated in his appointment as Marshal of France in 1574. A supporter of the Guise in the early years of the Wars of Religion, he was remembered for his severe repression of the ◊Huguenots. His autobiographical *Commentaires* (1592) gives a detailed account 16th-century warfare.

Montluc was born at St-Puy and spent his early years at court, as page and archer to the Duke of Lorraine. During his career he took part in five pitched battles and more than 200 skirmishes. As governor of Siena (1554–55) he distinguished himself in the heroic defence of that city against imperial and Florentine forces.

Montmorency, Anne de (1493–1567)

French soldier. Became Marshal of France in 1522, and Constable in 1538. He distinguished himself in the wars between Francis I and Emperor ◊Charles V, and after the French defeat at the battle of Pavia in 1525 negotiated Francis I's release. He later played a leading role in fighting the Huguenots in the early stages of the French Wars of Religion (1562–98).

Named after his godmother, Anne of Brittany, he was a boyhood friend of Francis I. He played a central role in the king's military campaigns. His first successes were during the Italian Wars, when he distinguished himself at Marignano in 1515, and at Mézières in 1521.

He exercised great influence at court, becoming Constable of France after his successes against Charles V's imperial forces in Provence and Savoy. Power struggles within the court led to his banishment in 1541. He was restored to the court and to power by Henry II, who made him a duke in 1551. He fought against Spain until his capture at St-Quentin in 1557, being released when the Treaty of Chateau-Cambréesis was signed in 1559.

The Guise family, now in power, drove him from Francis II's court, though during the minority of Charles IX he joined the Duke of Guise and Marshal St André in the triumvirate that sought to resist the influence of Catherine de' Medici. He fought on the Catholic side in the Wars of Religion, winning the first battle of the war at Dreux. Later taken prisoner he was released in 1563, and was killed at the siege of Paris.

Mor, Anthonis (ANTHONIS MOR VAN DASHORST/ANTONIO MORO) (c. 1517–1577)

Dutch portraitist. He became court painter to the Spanish rulers in the Netherlands in 1549 and was widely patronized at the courts of Europe. Suitably formal and austere, his portraits of contemporary European royalty greatly influenced development of the genre.

Born in Utrecht, he trained under Scorel. Subsequently he travelled extensively and rarely settled for long in one place. He developed a type of formal portrait derived in pose from ◊Titian and ◊Moroni (whom he studied in Italy), but with Flemish precision of detail in delineating features and costume which made him very popular.

He visited Italy, Spain, Portugal, and England, where he painted a portrait of Mary I in 1554 (Prado, Madrid) at the time of her marriage to Philip II of Spain. He was an important influence on portrait painting in the Netherlands and Spain, but less so in England, where he made a brief visit, because of the strong ◊Holbein tradition. Knighted c. 1553.

Morales, Ambrosio de (1513–1591)

Spanish historian and antiquarian, he continued Florián De Ocampo's 1543 *General Chronicle of Spain* using the same cautious, investigative methods as ◊Zurita. His two-volume *Corónica General de España/General Chronicle of Spain* appeared in 1574–77. In 1575, at the request of ◊Philip II, he compiled an inventory of all manuscripts, inscriptions and holy relics in León, Galicia, and Asturias, while later in his career he was called upon to defend ◊Zurita's work. Morales's defence, entitled *Apologia/Apology* was published in 1610.

Morales, Cristóbal (c. 1500–1553)

Spanish composer. He wrote many masses and motets which rank him among the finest contrapuntists of his time. Palestrina based a mass on his motet *O Sacrum Convivium*.

He studied at Seville under the cathedral maestro de capilla Fernández de Castilleja. He was maestro de capilla at Avila (1526–30), and some time later went to Rome, where he was ordained a priest and became cantor in the Pontifical Chapel in 1535. In 1545 he was given leave to visit Spain, but did not return, remaining as maestro de capilla at Toledo and Málaga, and serving in the household of the Duke of Arcos at Marchena.

Works include:

Twenty-one Masses, 16 Magnificats, 91 motets, Lamentations and other church music; cantatas for the peace conference at Nice (1538) and for Ippolito d'Este; madrigals.

Morales, Luis de (1509–1586)

Spanish painter. He worked in isolation, developing a style that brought both Flemish and Italian elements to a strong Spanish tradition. A typical work, often repeated with slight variations, is *The Virgin and Child* (Prado, Madrid).

Morales was born in Extremadura. Little is known of his career, though it is thought possible that he worked in Valencia and Seville as well as Badajoz, where he died. In style he seems to have acquired some Italian mannerisms through the Italianate Flemish painters of the time, such as Quentin ◊Matsys.

morality play

Didactic medieval European verse drama, in part a development of the ◊mystery play (or miracle play), in which human characters are replaced by personified virtues and vices, the limited humorous elements being provided by the Devil. In England, morality plays, such as *Everyman*, flourished in the 15th century. They exerted an influence on the development of Elizabethan drama and comedy.

More, (St) Thomas (1478–1535)

London lawyer and author. In his career he moved from being an Erasmian humorist who supported church reform to a fervent anti-Lutheran polemicist to, finally, a man seeking martyrdom. In this varied life, the high point came in the late 1510s, when his ◊*Utopia* was published and when he entered the service of ◊Henry VIII (eventually becoming Lord Chancellor in 1529).

Though his professional training was in the common law, More also learned Greek. It was as an exercise at testing their skills in the ancient language that More and Erasmus first collaborated on a set of Latin translations from Lucian in 1505. On his second visit to England in 1509, Erasmus stayed with More (and conceived the idea of his ◊*Praise of Folly*); it was also Erasmus who later assisted in the publication of both the *Utopia* and More's Latin poems (some of which he had written alongside William ◊Lily). What irrevocably altered for More this career of increasing literary and professional success was the Luther affair. While Erasmus reacted with tempered distaste, for More the only fitting response to this threat to Christendom was uncompromising opposition.

Alongside, then, his official duties, More produced a series of anti-evangelical works and entered into long-winded written debate with William ◊Tyndale (for example, in the *Confutation* 1532–33). At the same time, however, More found the established order under attack from a different direction: by his own king's radical attempt to achieve a divorce.

Elevated to the chancellorship left vacant by the fall of Thomas Wolsey (who had failed to secure the divorce), More resigned the position of chancellor in 1532 when the Break with Rome became royal policy. Not only that, but he avoided taking the new oath of allegiance that Henry, and Thomas Cromwell, introduced and which stated that the king was the rightful head of the church. This opposition eventually led to More's arrest. Confined in the Tower of London, More produced his final writings – spiritual works which include *Dialogue of Comfort against Tribulation* (1534). Faced with a show trial that condemned him for treason, More wrote these works with the certainty of imminent death. He was executed in 1535.

Erasmus described More as 'having a special loathing of tyranny'. This preoccupation explains his interest in Richard III, though his *History of Richard III*, which he wrote in the early 1510s, was left unfinished and unpublished. It was not merely a historical interest; like Erasmus, More was concerned about the direction in which kings like Henry VIII were going. Yet again, however, the focus of his concerns turned in the 1520s: for More, the Lutherans, denying free will, made God into a tyrant. It was not the case that such men could be treated in a civilized fashion; in his eyes, they were the enemies of civilization.

Moretto, Alessandro Bonvicino (1498–1554)

Italian painter. He worked in Brescia, painting primarily portraits, his style based on that of his teacher Giovanni ◊Bellini and his fellow pupil ◊Titian. He also produced church frescoes and a number of altarpieces. A fine example of his portraiture is the *Count Martinengo Cesaresco* (National Gallery, London).

He was also sensitive to northern European influences, his *Portrait of a Gentleman* (1526, National Gallery) – one of the first full-length and life-size portraits in Italian art – being indebted to Lucas ◊Cranach the elder.

Morisco

A Spanish Moor or his descendants who accepted Christian baptism. They were all expelled from Spain in 1609.

Morley, Thomas (*c.* 1557–*c.* 1602)

English composer. He wrote consort music, madrigals, and airs including the lute song 'It was a lover and his lass' for Shakespeare's play *As You Like It* (1599). He edited a collection of Italian madrigals *The Triumphs of Oriana* (1601), and published an influential keyboard tutor *A Plaine and Easie Introduction to Practicall Musicke* (1597). He was also organist at St Paul's Cathedral, London.

Moroni, Giambattista (1510–1578)

Italian painter. His portraits won the praise of ◊Titian; he also painted many religious works. His quiet and straightforwardly realistic style, without formality of pose or deep analysis of character, enabled him to portray a type perfectly, as in *The Tailor*, (*c.* 1570, National Gallery, London).

Moroni was born in Albino, Bergamo. He was a pupil of Alessandro ◊Moretto, from whom he inherited the practice of painting full-size, often full-length, portraits.

Morton, Robert (*c.* 1430–*c.* 1476)

English singer and composer. He composed French chansons, of which two were among the most popular of their day. He was employed at the court of Burgundy (1457–76), under Philip the Good and Charles the Bold.

Moser, Lucan (1430–1450)

German painter. He worked in Ulm. His altarpiece of *St Mary Magdalene* (1431), in the church in Tiefenbrunn, is an advanced work for its time and place. Its realistic detail suggests some acquaintance with painting in France and the southern Netherlands.

Mostaert, Jan (1475–1556)

Dutch painter. As court painter to ◊Margaret of Austria, he produced portraits of richly dressed sitters with elaborate backgrounds; he also painted religious subjects. He was one of the first to introduce a Renaissance element into Netherlandish painting.

He was born in Haarlem and probably trained with ◊Geertgen tot Sint Jans – his style is clearly indebted to Geertgen's. Besides his portraits, he also painted pictures of the New World – one of the first artists to do so – though he in fact never visited it.

Mouton, Jean (*c.* 1459–1522)

French composer. He was in the service of Louis XII and François I, and became canon of Thérouanne, which he left probably on its being taken by the English in 1513, and afterwards of the collegiate church of Saint-Quentin.

He was a pupil of Josquin Desprez.

Works include:

Fourteen Masses, 110 motets, psalms, *Alleluia* and *In illo tempore* for Easter, *Noe, Noe, Psallite* for Christmas, and other pieces.

Mostaert Jan Mostaert, *Christ Crowned with Thorns*, *c.* 1510 (National Gallery, London). *e.t. archive*

Mühlberg, Battle of

Battle fought near the German town of Mühlberg, on the bank of the River Elbe, in 1547. It was a victory for the forces under the personal command of Emperor ◊Charles V over a Lutheran alliance led by John Frederick, Elector of Saxony. By this triumph Charles hoped he was in a position to achieve religious harmony in his German realms and at the Interim of ◊Augsburg the following year he attempted to draw up the necessary settlement.

A portrait of Charles on horseback (now in the Prado, Madrid) was painted by ◊Titian to celebrate the victory.

Multscher, Hans (1400–1467)

German painter and sculptor. He worked in Ulm producing carved and painted altarpieces. His principal work is the *Wurzach Altarpiece*, 1437 (Berlin), the *Nativity* which shows a dramatic use of a realism – derived from Netherlandish art – in the strongly individualized figures.

Munday (MUNDY), Anthony (1553–1633)

English dramatist and miscellaneous writer. In 1605 he was appointed chief pageant writer for the City of London, and is best remembered for these entertainments. There are 18 plays ascribed to Munday, among them *The Downfall of Robert Earl of Huntingdon* (1601), followed by *The Death of Robert of Huntingdon*, in which he collaborated with Henry Chettle, and *John a Kent and John a Cumber*, performed about 1594.

He also wrote anti-Catholic pamphlets, translated romances, contributed several lyrics, some under the name of 'Shepherd Tony', to the collection of Elizabethan poetry *England's Helicon* (1600), and published an enlarged edition of Stow's *Survey of London* (1618).

He was born in London and went to Rome in 1578, probably as a spy to report on the English Jesuit College there. On his return to England in 1579 he became an actor, and later a member of the Earl of Oxford's company.

Mundy, John (c. 1555–1630)

English organist and composer. He studied under his father, William Mundy, became a Gentleman of the Chapel Royal in London, and succeeded Marbeck as one of the organists of St George's Chapel, Windsor, about 1585.

Works include:

Anthems, *Songs and Psalmes* for three to five voices; madrigals (one in *The Triumphes of Oriana*); virginal pieces including the 'Weather' fantasia.

Münster, Sebastian (1489–1552)

German theologian and geographer. He wrote *Cosmographia Universalis/Universal Cosmography* printed in 1544, complete with woodcuts and maps (very detailed for Germany and Western Europe, less so for the New World and Asia).

Münster was born at Ingelheim and educated at the universities of Tübingen and Heidelberg. He became a Franciscan monk in 1505, but after becoming an evangelical in 1529 he moved to Switzerland and was appointed to the chair of mathematics at Basel university in 1536. A formidable linguist, he produced Hebrew and Chaldean grammars as well as an edition of the Hebrew Bible (1534–35). He published *Horologiographia* (1531), on the use of sundials, and an edition of Ptolemy's *Geography* (1540). He died of the plague.

Murner, Thomas (1475–1537)

German satirist. A Franciscan friar, he developed a reputation for biting satire, with works like his *Die Narrenbeschweerung/Fools' Exorcism* (1512). Though he was critical of corruption within the Catholic Church, he was passionately opposed to the Lutheran Reformation and attacked it in several vitriolic satires.

Born in Oberehnheim in Alsace, Murner grew up in Strasbourg and took orders as a Franciscan friar there in 1491. He then studied theology and taught at Fribourg, Cologne, Paris, Rostock, and Kraków, and later studied law at Basel. In both his preaching and his writing, he combined popular sayings and imagery with a love of the grotesque and scurrilous. More biting than Sebastian ◊Brant's gentle satire, Murner's was directed first at folly in general, as in his *Die Narrenbeschweerung*, modelled on Brant's *Narrenschyff*. His later works, like *Von dem grossen Lutherischen Narren, wie in doctor Murner beschworen hat Of the Great Lutheran Fool, as Doctor Murner has*

Exorcised Him (1522) were preoccupied with attacking Luther and his followers. His other works include anti-Lutheran pamphlets, theological works in Latin, and a translation of Virgil's *Aeneid* into German verse.

Mussato, Albertino (1261–1329)

Italian scholar and lawyer, born in Padua. Mussato's writings consciously imitated Classical authors: his history *De Gestis Henrici VII Caesaris/On the Deeds of Emperor Henry VII* was modelled on the Roman historians Livy and Sallust; his tragedy *Ecerinis* reflected an interest, which he shared with his teacher Lovato ◊Lovati, in Seneca's plays. For the latter work, the purpose of which was 'to inveigh against tyranny' – at the very time that Padua was being menaced by Cangrande della Scala – Mussato was crowned ◊poet laureate in his home town in 1315.

Mussato's example was remembered by Petrarch, and Salutati called him 'the first cultivator of eloquence'. On the basis of such claims, historians have described him as the leading ◊prehumanist.

Myconius, Oswald (OSWALD GEISSHÄUSLER) (1488–1552)

Swiss religious reformer. He was a close friend of Ulrich ◊Zwingli and a collaborator in his reforming work. His writings included a number of biblical commentaries and the first biography of Zwingli, published in 1536.

Myconius was born at Lucerne and studied in Rottweil and Basel before coming to Zürich to teach in the cathedral school there. He played an influential role in securing the appointment of his friend Ulrich ◊Zwingli as minister. In 1531 Myconius was called to Basel, where he succeeded Oecolampadius as chief minister, and he remained there for the rest of his life. He supervised the publication of the Basel Confession of 1534 and helped draft the first Helvetic Confession of 1536.

mystery play (MIRACLE PLAY)

Medieval religious drama based on stories from the Bible. Mystery plays were performed around the time of church festivals, reaching their height in Europe during the 15th and 16th centuries. A whole cycle running from the Creation to the Last Judgement was performed in separate scenes on mobile wagons by various town guilds, usually on the festival of Corpus Christi in midsummer.

Four English cycles survive: Coventry, Wakefield (or Townley), Chester, and York. Versions are still performed, such as the York cycle in York.

Naich, Hubert (*c.* 1513–AFTER 1546)

Flemish composer. He lived at Rome, where he was a member of the Accademia degli Amici. He published a book of madrigals there about 1540.

Naldini, Giovan Battista (*c.* 1537–1591)

Florentine painter. He was adopted by ◊Pontormo with whom he studied ◊*disegno*, before working with Giorgio ◊Vasari on the decoration of the Palazzo Vecchio, Florence. His drawings were highly esteemed in his day for the bold use of contour line and were avidly collected. Although best known for his altarpieces in major Florentine churches such as Santa Maria del Carmine and Santa Maria Novella, he also visited Rome twice where he executed altarpieces and frescoes in the churches of Trinità dei Monti and San Giovanni Decollato.

Nanni di Banco (*c.* 1384–1421)

Florentine sculptor. He worked on several of the great civic commissions of 15th-century Florence. He remained independent of ◊Donatello's sculptural innovations, using conservative techniques to create Classical imagery. His major work, commissioned for a niche at Orsanmichele, is *Quattro Santi Coronati* about 1413, a group of four Roman sculptors who were also Christian martyrs.

His relief *Assumption* (1414–21) over the Porta della Mandorla of Florence Cathedral prefigures Baroque style. But for an early death, his career might have rivalled Donatello's.

Nantes, Edict of

Decree by which Henry IV of France granted religious freedom to the ◊Huguenots in 1598. It was revoked in 1685 by Louis XIV.

Naogeorgus, Thomas (THOMAS KIRCHMAIER) (1511–1563)

German polemical dramatist. A Protestant pastor, he used Latin drama as a vehicle for his Reformation polemic against the pope and the Catholic Church. His *Pammachius* (1538), representing the pope as Antichrist, is one of the best examples of this drama. It was acted in Cambridge in 1545.

Mercator (1540) is an Everyman play. The many plays that followed were less successful. Naogeorgus also translated the tragedies of the Greek dramatist Sophocles into Latin.

Napier, John (1550–1617)

8th Laird of Merchiston, Scottish mathematician who invented logarithms in 1614 and 'Napier's bones', an early mechanical calculating device for multiplication and division.

It was Napier who first used and then popularized the decimal point to separate the whole number part from the fractional part of a number.

Napier was born in Merchiston Castle, near Edinburgh, and studied at St Andrews. He never occupied any professional post.

English mathematician Henry Briggs went to Edinburgh in 1616 and later to discuss the logarithmic tables with Napier. Together they worked out improvements, such as the idea of using the base ten.

Napier also made advances in scientific farming, especially by the use of salt as a fertilizer. In 1597 he patented a hydraulic screw by means of which water could be removed from flooded coal pits.

Napier published a denunciation of the Roman Catholic Church, *A Plaine Discovery of the Whole Revelation of St John* (1593), as well as *Mirifici Logarithmorum Canonis Descriptio/Description of the Marvellous Canon of Logarithms* (1614) and *Mirifici Logarithmorum Canonis Constructio* (1619). In *Rabdologiae* ('numeration by little rods') (1617) he explained his mechanical calculating system and showed how square roots could be extracted by the manipulation of counters on a chessboard.

Nardi, Jacopo (1476–1563)

Florentine political figure and historian. A committed republican, he held various offices after the exiling of the Medici from Florence in 1494, and played an active role in their second expulsion in 1527. On their return in 1530 Nardi himself was exiled. His most important work is a history of Florence published posthumously in 1582.

Nardi was born in Florence and belonged to the intellectual circle of the ◊Orti Oricellari. His earliest works were two comedies based on tales in ◊Boccaccio: *L'Amicizia* (written 1502–12) and *I due felici rivali* (performed in 1513). His history of Florence, *Istorie della città di Firenze* (1582), which covers the period 1498–1537, is mainly valuable for the period 1512–30, when Nardi was deeply involved in the political events on the anti-Medici side.

Following his exile from Florence in 1530 he lived in Venice.

Narváez, Pánfilo de (*c.* 1480–1525)

Spanish conquistador and explorer. Narváez was largely responsible for bringing Cuba under Spanish control in 1511. The governor of Cuba sent him to Mexico in 1520 to reassert authority over Hernán ◊Cortés. Defeated, he was held captive for two years. He drowned during an expedition to Florida after a fruitless detour for gold split his party.

Nashe, Thomas (1567–1601)

English poet, satirist, and anti-Puritan pamphleteer. He was drawn into the Martin ◊Marprelate controversy and wrote at least three attacks on the Martinists. Among his later works are the satirical *Pierce Pennilesse, his Supplication to the Divell* (1592) and the religious *Christes Teares over Jerusalem* (1593); *The Unfortunate Traveller* (1594) is a picaresque narrative mingling literary parody and mock-historical fantasy.

He was born in Lowestoft, Suffolk, graduated from Cambridge University in 1586, and settled in London about 1588. His first publication was an acrid review of recent literature prefixed to Robert Greene's *Menaphon*, a topic which he discussed at greater length in *The Anatomie of Absurditie* (1589). After this he was engaged in the Marprelate controversy for a time. He published *Pierce Pennilesse* as a reply to Richard Harvey, who had criticized his preface to Greene's work, and followed this with *Strange News, of the Intercepting certaine Letters* (1592), in response to Gabriel Harvey's attack on Greene. *Christes Teares over Jerusalem*, like Greene's pamphlets, is a picture of loose life in London, denouncing immorality; *The Terrors of the Night* (1594) deals with ghosts and superstitions. In 1596 Nashe published *Have with You to Saffron Walden* (1596), a pamphlet of brilliant, devastatingly inventive abuse aimed at Harvey. The following year he collaborated with Ben ◊Jonson on a (now lost) comedy, *The Isle of Dogs*. On the run from the authorities, who found the scurrilous satire contained within the play less than amusing, Nashe went into hiding in Yarmouth, Norfolk, and began *Lenten Stuffe* (1599), a surreal, rambling pamphlet in praise of smoked herring. He died in London, perhaps from plague. Two works not printed in his lifetime were *Summer's Last Will and Testament*, a play written for Archbishop Whitgift in his country retreat in Croydon, and 'The Choice of Valentines', a long comic poem on the subject of the dildo, which attained considerable notoriety.

Naumburg Convention

A meeting of German princes and Protestant theologians in 1561 designed to achieve doctrinal unity in accordance with the Confession of ◊Augsburg. It failed because the Lutherans insisted on the original articles of 1530 (*invariata*) and the Calvinists preferred those of 1540 (*variata*). A papal invitation to send delegates to the Council of ◊Trent was declined.

Navagiero, Andrea (1483–1529)

Venetian scholar, poet, and diplomat. He edited Latin texts for the Aldine Press and worked as librarian for what was to become the Biblioteca ◊Marciana. He was the Venetian ambassador to France and also Spain, where he met the poet Joan ◊Boscà.

Navagiero was born into an eminent Venetian family. He studied in Padua, where he learned Greek and particularly interested himself in the odes of the Greek poet Pindar. The first Greek edition of Pindar 1513 was dedicated to Navagiero by Aldus ◊Manutius, for whose press Navagiero edited Latin authors, most notably Cicero. In 1506 Navagiero was appointed to succeed Sabellico as librarian of St Mark's Basilica. Navagiero's own writings included

Ludus/Game (1530), a set of Latin poems that influenced, in particular, the French *Pléiade* poets, Joachim ◊du Bellay, and ◊Ronsard. Among his many friends was ◊Fracastoro, who made Navagiero the mouthpiece for his views on poetry in the dialogue *Naugerius* (1555) – the garden setting for this dialogue recalls Navagiero's renowned garden at Murano. He was also friendly with Pietro ◊Bembo, with whom he visited Rome, and with ◊Raphael, who painted his portrait. In 1526, as Venetian ambassador, he went to Spain, where he met Boscá and introduced him to Italian poetic metres, which Boscá was the first to naturalize in Spanish. Navagiero brought back with him from Spain to Italy the then newly discovered potato and other exotics, including possibly a banana. He was next sent on an embassy to Francis I of France, but died while at Blois. His *Orationes Duae Carminaque Nonnulla/Two Speeches and Several Poems* were published posthumously in Venice in 1530.

Navarro, Juan (*c.* 1530–1580)

Spanish composer. He was highly regarded as a polyphonist, and his church music was popular in Spain, Portugal, and Mexico for some time.

After the death of Cristóbal Morales in 1553 he competed unsuccessfully for the post of maestro de capilla at Málaga Cathedral, but he later obtained a similar post in Salamanca. He visited Rome in 1590, where his nephew Fernando Navarro Salazar arranged for the publication of some of his church music.

Works include:

Psalms, hymns, Magnificats and other church music, madrigals, and other pieces.

Neakademia (TRANSLITERATED GREEK 'NEW ACADEMY')

An aspiration of Aldus ◊Manutius and his friends. Manutius and his friends talked, half-jokingly, half-seriously, of forming an ◊academy like that of Plato's where the only language spoken would be Greek (with fines for those who broke this rule). It is unlikely that this playful plan came to anything, but Manutius was for some time wedded to the concept of an academy. He considered his printing house worthy of the appellation and hoped (vainly) to arrange

the founding of a Greek college, probably in Germany. Despite its lack of substance, the *Neakademia* remained a potent symbol of a humanist desire to bring together a coterie of Greek-speaking scholars.

He is where he can at last found his imagined Academy,

Since there was for Aldus no place in this world.

'Foolish age' he said, 'and unworthy earth, farewell'

And transferred his work to the Elysian Fields.

~

WILLIBALD PIRCKHEIMER on the death of Aldus Manutius and his *Neakademia*

Neapolitan Academy

Name given to the tradition of humanist coteries at Naples. An example of an informal ◊academy, its first manifestation in the 1440s centred on the scholars at the court of ◊Alfonso V the Magnanimous, in particular Antonio ◊Beccadelli. A little later it became known as the Accademia Pontaniana after its new leading member, ◊Pontano.

Nebrija, Elio Antonio Martinez de Cala, de (1442–1522)

Spanish Classical scholar and grammarian, he studied at Salamanca until 1461, when he was granted a scholarship to study at the Collegio di San Clemente in Bologna. He remained there until 1470, diligently learning Classical philology. In 1475 he began a 38-year career as professor of grammar and rhetoric at Salamanca university, only interrupted by periods of literary activity 1486–1505 and 1508–09 (when he was appointed royal chronicler). His arrogance denied him the chair of Greek at Salamanca (which fell vacant in 1513); piqued, he left for Seville and then Alcalá, where ◊Ximénes de Cisneros held him in such high esteem that he informed the university's rector that Nebrija could work as he pleased.

Nebrija's classical and philological erudition enabled him to provide his countrymen for the first time with reliable works on Latin and Castilian grammar. In 1481 he published his *Introductiones Latin/Introductions to Latin* which in 1486, at the request of ◊Isabella 'the Catholic', was translated into Castilian. 1492 witnessed not only the appearance of his Latin-Castilian dictionary, but also Nebrija's publication of the first grammar to describe a modern European language: the *Gramatica sobre la lengua española/Grammar of the Spanish Language*. Dedicated to the crusading Isabella, its preface promised its value as a tool to instruct the conquered of the New World. Around 1495 he published a Castilian-Latin dictionary (expanded and reprinted in 1516), while between 1514 and 1517 he played a significant role in the production of the ◊Complutensian Bible. In 1517 he also produced a work aimed at standardizing Castilian spelling: the *Reglas de orthographia en la lengua castellana*. Despite all this grammatical labour, however, Nebrija did marry – and had six children (who perhaps inspired his, unpublished, *De Liberis Educandis/On the Education of Children* of 1509).

Nenna, Pomponio (*c.* 1550–BEFORE 1613)

Italian composer. He lived mainly at Naples and taught Gesualdo, Prince of Venosa (1594–99). He moved to Rome about 1608.

Works include:

Two books of responsories and nine books of madrigals.

Neri, Filippo (SAINT) (1515–1595)

Florentine cleric who organized the Congregation of the Oratory. He built the oratory over the Church of St Jerome, Rome, where prayer meetings were held and scenes from the Bible performed with music, originating the musical form ◊oratorio. Feast day 26 May.

Neroccio di Bartolommeo Landi (1447–1500)

Sienese sculptor and painter who worked in the tradition of Simone ◊Martini. He was the brother-in-law of the painter Francesco di Giorgio Martini (1439–1502), with whom he conducted a workshop.

Niccoli, Niccolò (1364–1437)

Quintessential *arbiter elegantiarum* of the early Florentine humanist circle. Although he wrote little, he was an influential figure in the Florentine circle that first gathered around Coluccio ◊Salutati. In Leonardo ◊Bruni's *Dialogi ad Petrum Paulum*

Histrum, Niccoli is the pivotal character, declaring his admiration of everything antique, to the dispraise of recent literature. Niccoli was an avid collector of manuscripts of Classical texts (urging ◊Poggio Bracciolini to search for them), and was fascinated with the minutiae of the Latin language. While his most loyal friend Poggio developed the ◊*littera antiqua* script, Niccoli is credited with making the first attempts at an ◊italic script.

His detractors, who included Francesco ◊Filelfo and, at one point, Leonardo Bruni, provide in their invectives most of our information about this enigmatic figure. They mocked not only his private life; his fascination with details like the issue of Latin ◊diphthongs was also ridiculed. On his death, he had his large book collection put into the hands of a group of Florentine citizens (including Poggio, Bruni, Ambrogio Traversari, and Cosimo de' ◊Medici) to be disposed of as they would. It eventually became the core of the Florentine Biblioteca ◊Marciana.

Niccolò di Liberatore (NICCOLÒ DA FOLIGNO) (1456–1502)

Italian painter of the Umbrian School. Although provincial in style, he was able to give the tenseness of emotion to his religious compositions which distinguishes such works as his *Christ on the Cross*, (1487, National Gallery, London).

His early work is related to that of Benozzo di Lese, though afterwards he appears to have been influenced by such Venetians as Antonio Vivarini and Carlo Crivelli.

Nicholas V (BORN TOMASSO PARENTUCELLI) (1397–1455)

Humanist book collector, pope from 1447. Born near La Spezia, Parentucelli was educated in Bologna. He became secretary to Niccolò Albergati, bishop of Bologna, in 1421 and with him travelled across Europe and attended the Councils of Basel and Florence. ◊Eugenius IV made Parentucelli bishop of Bologna in succession to Albergati in 1444. In succession to Eugenius himself, he was elected pope. As Nicholas V, he envisaged both the rebuilding of Rome and the building up of the papal library.

Parentucelli was himself a Classical scholar, who, in his travels with Albergati, discovered some little-known ancient texts. Perhaps influenced by Ambrogio ◊Traversari, he showed a special interest in patristic literature. As pope, he gathered at the curia a series of scholars to translate Greek texts, including Niccolò ◊Perotti. He was not only concerned to make the Vatican into a storehouse of ancient knowledge; he was also the first pope seriously to consider the rebuilding of Rome and of St Peter's, calling upon the services of, for example, Leon Battista ◊Alberti.

For all these plans, however, Nicholas's pontificate was overshadowed by the *annus horribilis* of 1453. In that year, the pope was faced with a conspiracy, led by Stefano Porcari, aiming (like Cola di ◊Rienzo a century earlier) to restore Roman 'liberty'. More importantly than an ineffectual plot with a leader who was quickly hanged was the event in the East: the fall of Constantinople. It is ironic that a pope keen to increase the West's knowledge of Greek learning should witness the final collapse of the Greek-speaking Byzantine Empire before the advance of the Ottomans.

Nicholas of Cusa (1401–1464)

Theologian from Kues in the German-speaking lands. He attended the Council of ◊Basel and wrote in support of the conciliarist position: his *De Concordantia Catholica* (1433) introduced into the debate a neoplatonic concept of the harmony of the universe. However, he abandoned his ◊conciliarism in the mid-1430s and received instead papal employment and, in 1446, a cardinal's hat. He was employed as a diplomat both to Constantinople and in his homeland. In the wake of the Ottoman capture of Constantinople in 1453, Nicholas produced *De Pace Fidei/On the Peace of the Faith* promoting the cause of crusade; ◊Pius II called on his services when promoting his own plans for crusade.

Nicholas was educated at Heidelberg and Padua and was, in his early life, a protégé of cardinal Giordano Orsini. Well acquainted with the humanist circles in Italy, he became what might be called a corresponding member of these coteries. He built up a notable library of Classical, humanist, and theological works; and he involved himself in the recov-

ery of ancient literature. It has been suggested that it was at Nicholas's instigation that Conrad ◊Sweynheym and Arnold ◊Pannartz ventured to introduce the printing press to Italy; at least his secretary, Giovanni Andrea Bussi, was very much involved in that enterprise.

Nicholson, Richard (DIED 1639)

English organist and composer. In 1595 he became choirmaster and organist at Magdalen College, Oxford, took a degree in music in 1596, and became the first professor of music there in 1627.

Works include:

Anthems, madrigals (one in *The Triumphes of Oriana*), music for viols, 'dialogue' (or song cycle) for three voices 'Joane, quoth John'.

Nielsen, Hans (c. 1580–c. 1626)

Danish lutenist and composer. After learning music as a choirboy in the royal chapel at Copenhagen, he studied with Giovanni Gabrieli at Venice (1599–1606), and with the English lutenist Richard Howett at Wolfenbüttel (1606–08). After that he was lutenist at the Danish court until 1611, when he was dismissed and went to Heidelberg University. In 1623 he was appointed vice director of the royal chapel in succession to Mogens Pedersøn.

Norfolk, Thomas Howard, 3rd duke (1473–1554)

Brother-in-law of Henry VII and a leading Catholic politician under Henry VIII and Mary Tudor. He was appointed Lord High Admiral in 1531 and served at the Battle of Flodden. He led various campaigns against the French in the 1520s and returned to England to oppose Wolsey. He subsequently saw two nieces, Anne Boleyn and Catherine Howard, marry Henry VIII. His willingness to preside over his nieces' trials and executions proved his loyalty to the king, even though he remained conservative in religion and opposed Thomas Cromwell's reforms. He was arrested in 1546 when his son and heir, Henry Howard, Earl of Surrey, claimed during Henry's last illness that his father should be protector for the young Edward VI. Though his son was beheaded, the duke was saved by Henry's own death, and he was released from the Tower by Queen Mary I.

North, Sir Thomas (*c.* 1535–*c.* 1601)

English translator. His translations include Plutarch's *Lives*, which appeared in 1579 as *Lives of the Noble Grecians and Romans.* ◊Shakespeare drew heavily on this translation for his Roman plays (*Julius Caesar*, *Antony and Cleopatra*, and *Coriolanus*).

North's first translation was of the Spanish adaptation of Marcus Aurelius: *Reloy de principes* by Antonio de ◊Guevara. North's version, *The Diall of Princes* (1557), is partially based on a French translation.

North's translation of Plutarch was not taken directly from the Greek, but from a 1559 version by the French translator Jacques ◊Amyot. North's version is neither scholarly nor accurate: both Amyot and North embellished Plutarch's rather dry prose style. Nevertheless it was very popular; a second edition (1603) augmented the text with translations of other Classical biographies.

He was the second son of the 1st Lord North. After possibly studying at Cambridge, he entered Lincoln's Field Inn in 1557, though he seems to have devoted himself to literature rather than law. In 1574 he accompanied his brother on an embassy to France. He was knighted in 1591.

North also published *The Morall Philosophy of Doni* (1570), a translation of a collection of Oriental fables by the Italian writer Anton Francesco Doni (1513–74).

Northumberland, John Dudley, Duke of (*c.* 1502–1553)

English politician. He was chief minister from 1551 until Edward VI's death in 1553. He tried to place his daughter-in-law Lady Jane Grey on the throne, and was executed on Mary I's accession.

Son of the privy councillor Edmund Dudley (beheaded 1510), he overthrew Edward Seymour, Duke of Somerset, as protector to the young Edward VI and, having married one of his sons to Lady Jane Grey (fifth in line to the throne), persuaded the king to sign a document excluding his half-sisters from the succession, thereby hoping to retain his authority

after Edward's death. Knighted in 1523, made Earl in 1547.

Another of his sons, Robert, Earl of Leicester, became one of Elizabeth I's favourites.

Norton, Thomas (1532–1584)

English dramatist. He collaborated with Thomas ◊Sackville in the composition of the tragedy *Gorboduc* (1561).

Norton was born in London. He became a lawyer and entered Parliament in 1558. In 1571 he was appointed to the office of Remembrancer of the City of London (a kind of envoy to Parliament).

Nostradamus (LATINIZED NAME OF MICHEL DE NÔTREDAME) (1503–1566)

Medic and self-professed orthodox Christian of Provençal Jewish family origins, who lost his family in the plagues of the 1530s and wandered the roads of Europe developing a reputation as a mystic, alchemist, and prophet. Summoned to Paris by ◊Catherine de' Medici in 1556, the trip financially crippled him but by the time of his death a decade later he had amassed a fortune of nearly 3,500 crowns, possibly because of the near-accuracy of his prediction that all Catherine's sons would be kings.

Nostradamus's *Centuries* were mainly complete by 1557; each 'century', composed in fashionable vernacular quatrains and using perversely obscure language, predicted more than a hundred years of events to come and were as popular in the later 16th century as in any time since.

Núñez de Balboa, Vasco (*c.* 1475–1517)

Castilian adventurer who discovered the Pacific Ocean. Leaving Spain in 1501, he eventually arrived in Darien (Panama) after stowing away in a barrel to escape debtors. Founding a settlement there, he left on 1 September 1513 to discover the 'South Sea' (the Pacific), sighted on 26 September. He was beheaded on spurious charges of treason at Acla in January 1517.

Núñez de Toledo y Guzmán, Hernán (1475–1553)

Classical scholar born at Valladolid, he was also

NUMEROLOGY

THE ANCIENT SCIENCE of numerology, divining symbolic meaning in the 'pure' abstract language of number, remained of widespread interest in the Renaissance period as a means of proving that order stands behind the flux of human experience. A common argument ran from Plato to Augustine and on to Galileo that ignorance of the language of number and mathematics excluded one from comprehending the great universal design.

The attitude of Renaissance scholars such as Pico della Mirandola, Ficino, Agrippa, or Bongo towards the multiple strands and conflicting theories of number symbolism is significant. They inherited the accreted deliberations of generations, a tangle of idiosyncratic systems and discrete interpretations, where Mesopotamian astrological lore and the classical Greek philosophy of the Pythagorean and Platonic traditions had long been appropriated and modified by the medieval enthusiasm for exhaustive exploration of the allegorical number symbolism of the Bible. However, able to access classical texts directly as well as through the filter of later exegesis, and demonstrating in addition a lively interest in Orphic, Gnostic, Cabalist, and Hermetic writing, the Renaissance approach is audaciously broad. Rather than medieval quiddity, we find a new desire for syncretic wisdom.

The Greeks conceived of number as spatial form. Using pebbles as markers, it is easy to see how the numbers from 1 to 4 can be said to express the basic geometric principles of universal order • is a point, •–• is a line, △ a surface, and △ a pyramid. Having arrived at a three-dimensional solid body, the extension of number in spatial terms is complete: the universe can be seen to be composed of these numbers alone. Moreover, the sum of these numbers will set the limit of the physical universe and of course 1+2+3+4 = 10, the *decad*. This limit leaves nothing to be added and therefore the number ten is equivalent to perfection. Based on these mathematical proposals, each of the numbers from one to ten acquires a complex set of symbolic significances but most rewarding for the Renaissance imagination remained the Pythagorean idea of proportional correspondences or ratio established by the core series 1–4, (for example, the ratios 1:4, 2:3, 3:4). The best known of these ratios is the *diapason,* the ratio 1:2, which functions as the interval of an octave and as the concord through all the notes of the scale. Pythagoras had been the first to show how such mathematical ratios determined musical concord, a movable bridge controlling vibration on a single stretched string meant that musical notes could be considered as mathematical intervals upon a line, but such basic ratios of proportion and order were thought to be on open display throughout the universe, determining the order of the heavens (for example, the distances between the spheres in the Ptolemaic cosmology) as well as of the Earth.

Plato elaborated upon this system of universal harmony. The *Timaeus* proposes a mathematical process of creation where the actions of the creator provide us with an ascending series of seven numbers defining an ideal musical scale. The series consists of the *monad* (1), then the first even and odd numbers (2, 3), their squares (4, 9) and their cubes (8, 27), and is commonly arranged in the shape of the Greek letter *lambda*, λ.

A number of influential attributions can be read off from this diagram, most significantly the division of even numbers representing matter from odd numbers representing soul.

Acceptance of the ahistorical premise (traceable to the work of Philo) that Plato was somehow influenced by Moses meant that classical philosophy could be conflated with the mysteries of Christian salvation. Plato's *Timaeus* could therefore be read as a commentary on *Genesis,* just as the four-cornered chariot in *Ezekiel* could be linked to the Pythagorean system's preoccupation with fours, or explanation of the paradoxical doctrine of the Trinity could rely on classical arguments where the *monad* (1) contains the potential for all numbers and therefore contains within itself the creative principle while the *triad* (3) is the first prime number, indivisible in itself. However, it was the abstract patternings of truth revealed by such correspondences that was of

continued

conceptual significance to the Renaissance Neoplatonists, over and above the literal connection of individual units with specific symbolic values. Exploring such correspondences led some into esoteric mysticism but equally it offered many a new liberation of thought. Johannes Kepler, for example, took the principle of proportional order in the movement of the planets from Plato and continued to maintain that principle even when he came to formulate his radical laws of planetary motion based on elliptical orbits rather than circular ones.

The employment of complex proportional schemes across a wide range of creative disciplines is the most rewarding aspect of the Renaissance interest in numerology. In music, architecture, and literature, composition based on numerical principles had the additional value of imitating universal structures, so that the activity of the artist could be thought both to embody and to further the divine creational order. Recognizing such inherent compositional harmonics can be particularly difficult in the field of poetry: Tasso's *Gerusalemme liberata,* for example, is said to favour an eight-line stanza form because of the association of 8 with the diapason and the symbolic weight of the number as the cube of two. English Renaissance poetry is less rigid in its approach but it is often equally preoccupied with number games. Spenser often employs sophisticated patternings (see Hieatt's reading of the *Epithalamion*), but such formal thinking is equally characteristic of the work of Philip Sidney, John Donne, and John Milton, amongst others. Although certain systems may prove too specialized to be of general interest, it remains beneficial to keep alert for obvious structural markers: the relevance of five, the number representing justice, in the Fifth Sestiad of Chapman's *Hero and Leander* and the fifth book of Spenser's *The Faerie Queene,* for example, or the significance of the lines marking the midpoint of Milton's *Paradise Lost.* The concept of universal order that stands behind such numerological harmonies was embraced by English poets up to John Dryden but, thereafter, verbal and structural patterning is employed for its aesthetic rather than symbolic value.

MARGARET KEAN

Further Reading
Christopher Butler, *Number Symbolism* (London, 1970); A Kent Hieatt, *Short Time's Endless Monument* (New York, 1960)

known as *Pinciano,* after the Latin name for his birthplace, and "El comendador griego"/"The Greek leader", a reference to his erudition. Between 1490 and 1498 he studied with the aid of a rare Castilian scholarship at the Collegio di San Clemente in Bologna. He also produced a confused commentary on the works of Juan de ◊Mena (1490, reprinted 1505). On his return he became tutor to the Mendoza family in Granada until ◊Ximénes de Cisneros sought his expertise for the ◊Complutensian Bible, in preparation at Alcalá de Henares, where Guzmán was appointed professor of rhetoric. In 1513 he succeeded ◊Nebrija to the chair of Greek at Salamanca. His works of Classical scholarship include critical editions of the works of Seneca (1529), Pomponius Mela (1542), and Pliny (1544), as well as a Castilian translation of Aneas Sylvius Piccolomini's Latin history of Bohemia. In 1555 he produced a compendium of Castilian proverbs or sayings, the *Refranes o proverbios en romance.*

Obrecht, Jacob (c. 1450–1505)

Flemish composer. His mostly polyphonic sacred music (which in style predates that of Josquin Desprez) centred on the Mass. He was innovative, developing borrowed material, and using a secular fixed ◊cantus firmus in his *Missa super Maria zart*. He also wrote motets and secular works. He worked as a Kapellmeister in Utrecht, Antwerp, and Bruges. He died of the plague.

He was born at Bergen-op-Zoom and studied at Louvain University. He directed the singers at Utrecht (1476–78), Bergen-op-Zoom (1479–84), then at Cambrai, at Bruges in 1486 and 1490, and elsewhere in the Low Countries. He was obliged to resign in 1500, and after a spell at Antwerp (1501–02) went to Italy for his health. He had already spent six months at the ducal court of Ferrara in 1487–88 and returned there in 1504 as head of Ercole d'Este's choir, only to die of plague the following year.

Works include:
Twenty-seven Masses, including *Fortuna Desperata*, *Maria zart*, and *Sub Tuum Praesidium*; motets, chansons.

oil painting

Painting technique using ground pigments mixed with oil, usually linseed. The technique is generally held to originate in the Netherlands, possibly in the workshop of Jan van ◊Eyck. Although ◊Antonello da Messina is generally credited with importing it into Italy, it was already known to Cennino ◊Cennini.

The advantage of oil painting over tempera or fresco is that it dries slowly, giving the artist greater flexibility in executing a composition. It is also possible to make corrections once oil paint has dried by adding additional layers of paint.

technique The process of grinding pigments to which oil was added was a time-consuming process generally given to junior members in an artist's workshop to carry out. Oil paint is then applied to a prepared panel, canvas, paper, or mural surface. The artist may paint multiple layers of oils to create greater luminosity than can be achieved with ◊tempera or ◊fresco. The finished oil painting was generally covered with a thin layer of varnish to protect the colours from damage.

Okeghem (OR OCKENHEIM, OCKEGHEM, HOQUEGAN), Johannes (Jean d') (c. 1421–c. 1497)

Flemish composer of church music. His works include the antiphon *Alma Redemptoris Mater* and the richly contrapuntal *Missa Prolationum/Prolation Mass*, employing complex canonic imitation in multiple parts at different levels. He was court composer to Charles VII, Louis XI, and Charles VIII of France.

He was a chorister at Antwerp Cathedral until 1444, was in the service of Charles, Duke of Bourbon at Moulins (1446–48), and in the service of the French court from about 1452, where he became the first maître de chapelle. Louis XI appointed him treasurer of Saint-Martin at Tours, where he lived during the latter part of his life, though he visited Spain in 1469.

Works include:
Ten Masses, including *Ecce Ancilla Domini*, *L'homme armé*, and *Mi-mi*; motets; French chansons.

Oldenbarneveldt, Johan van (1547–1619)

Dutch politician, a leading figure in the Netherlands' struggle for independence from Spain. He helped William the Silent negotiate the Union of Utrecht in 1579.

As leader of the Republican party he opposed the war policy of stadholder (magistrate) Maurice of Orange and negotiated a 12-year truce with Spain in 1609. His support of the Remonstrants (Arminians) in the religious strife against Maurice and the Gomarists (Calvinists) effected his downfall and he was arrested and executed.

Oliver, Isaac (c. 1565–1617)

English miniaturist. A Huguenot refugee, he studied under Nicholas ◊Hilliard but a formative influence was also a visit to Venice in the 1590s. He became a court artist in the reign of James I. He produced, as well as portrait minatures (for example of the poet John ◊Donne), minatures on religious subjects, following the example of Giulio ◊Clovio.

Born in Rouen, he went to England in 1568. In contrast to Hilliard who had avoided shadow, Oliver made use of light and shade in his minatures. Because of his more Continental style, he proved popular at the court of James I, and was Hilliard's main rival from about 1600. His son **Peter Oliver** (1594–1648) was also 'limner' (painter of miniatures) to the Stuart Court, working in his father's style.

oratorio

Dramatic, nonscenic musical setting of religious texts, scored for orchestra, chorus, and solo voices. Its origins lie in the *Laude spirituali* performed by St Philip ◊Neri's Oratory in Rome in the 16th century, followed by the first definitive oratorio in the 17th century by Cavalieri.

Orcagna, Andrea (ANDREA DI CIONE) (1308–1368)

Florentine painter, sculptor, and architect. He was to some extent a follower of Giotto, though his style marks a rejection of Giotto's monumental simplicity and a return to the rich and decorative qualities of Gothic painting. His chief work is the altarpiece *Christ Enthroned* (1357) in the Strozzi Chapel of Sta Maria Novella, Florence.

His other great work, as both architect and sculptor, is the church and tabernacle of Orsanmichele, Florence. His relief sculpture on the tabernacle, *The Death and Assumption of the Virgin* (1355–59), shows the clear influence of the sculptor Andrea Pisano.

Orcagna's brothers **Jacopo di Cione** (also known as Robiccia) and **Nardo di Cione** were also painters, and are said to have completed works left unfinished by Andrea.

Orcagna's return to a more conventional manner in religious subjects has been associated with a change in religious feeling, or a desire for the security of tradition, after the bubonic plague that beset Florence and Siena in 1348.

Orellana, Francisco de (*c.* 1500–*c.* 1549)

Spanish explorer who travelled with Francesco ◊Pizarro from Guayaquil, on the Pacific coast of South America, to Quito in the Andes. He was the first person known to have navigated the full length of the Amazon from the Napo River to the Atlantic Ocean (1541–43).

Orlando Furioso

Poem written in 1516 by Ludovico ◊Ariosto, first published in 1516 (revised 1522, 1532) as a sequel to Matteo Maria ◊Boiardo's *Orlando innamorato* (1487). The poem describes the unrequited love of Orlando for Angelica, set against the war between Saracens (Arabs) and Christians during the reign of the first Holy Roman Emperor, Charlemagne. The work was a success in Ariosto's own lifetime; it was later translated into French, Spanish, English (by Sir John ◊Harington), and Polish.

Orley, Bernard van (1490–1541)

Flemish painter and tapestry designer. Although he probably never visited Italy, Orley, like his rival Jan ◊Gossaert, helped to introduce High Renaissance motifs and styles to Flemish art. His paintings, mainly on religious and mythological subjects, include the altarpiece *The Patience of Job* (1521, Musée Royaux des Beaux-Arts, Brussels), which reflects the influence of Andrea ◊Mantegna and Raphael.

He made a number of designs for tapestries, such as *The Life of Abraham* (Hampton Court, London) and *Maximilian's Hunts* (Louvre, Paris); the latter in particular demonstrates his move from a traditional two-dimensional style of tapestry to one that, imitating Raphael, attempts to create a sense of depth and perspective. He also designed stained-glass windows for the Cathedral of St Gudule, Brussels.

He was born in Brussels and studied with his father, the painter Valentijn Orley. He was appointed court painter to Margaret of Austria in 1518.

Orta, Garcia da (*c.* 1500–1568)

Portuguese physician and scholar who not only studied at Lisbon, but in Alcalá and Salamanca as well (the influence of these Spanish universities on his scholarship is difficult to gauge). He went to India as chief physician in 1534, where he practiced successfully and carried out meticulous research on local medicine based on his own observations. The results of these practical investigations were published in his *Coloquios dos simples e drogas [...] da India/Conversations on Indian Medicines and their Constituent Drugs* (Goa, 1563), which he had apparently translated from his original Latin only at his friends' insistence. Orta's work surfaced in Flanders and was translated into Latin by Carolus Clusius (1567). Clusius's Latin version enjoyed considerable success, and its wide circulation meant it tended to be used for subsequent translations into the vernacular. Meanwhile, Orta's use of empirical methods alerted the suspicions of the Inquisition – his *Coloquios* were placed on the prohibited index (all but removing the work from circulation) and he was tried and condemned posthumously by the Inquisition at Goa.

Ortelius (OERTEL), Abraham (1527–1598)

Dutch mapmaker and printer. He published what has been called the first modern atlas, his *Theatrum Orbis Terrarum* (1570). It consisted of engravings by various cartographers, including Georg ◊Hoefnagel and himself; it was the first atlas to cover all areas of the globe. He also produced a heart-shaped map of the world printed in 1564. From 1573 he was geographer to Philip II of Spain.

Ortelius was born in Antwerp and trained as an engraver before establishing himself as a dealer in maps and antiquities. He travelled widely to collect and sell maps, many of which he illustrated or coloured before sale.

He made many contacts – for example, Hoefnagel, who travelled with him to Italy in 1578 – but it was his friendship with the mapmaker ◊Mercator that prompted his active involvement in cartography. In 1577 he visited England and helped the antiquarian William ◊Camden with his topographical work *Britannia*.

The *Theatrum Orbis Terrarum* proved immensely popular, running to seven editions by the end of the century; translated and abridged versions also appeared. He was appointed geographer to Philip II

despite suspicions that he might have Protestant inclinations.

Orti Oricellari

Gardens of the Rucellai family, situated off Via della Scala, Florence. Under both Bernardo di Giovanni ◊Rucellai and his grandson Cosimo, the gardens were the meeting place for a group of intellectuals which included in the 1510s the political theorist Niccolò ◊Machiavelli.

The gardens were laid out by Bernardo, who imported rare plants so that the Orti could reflect the range of flora mentioned in Classical literature. The discussions held there often had a political dimension: from 1502 to 1506 they reflected Bernardo's aristocratic discontent with Piero ◊Soderini's Republic. Discontent was still the keynote in the 1510s and 1520s but it was now directed against Bernardo's in-laws, the ◊Medici family.

Ortiz, Diego (*c.* 1510–*c.* 1570)

Spanish composer. He went to Naples in 1555 to become maestro de capilla to the viceroy, the Duke of Alva. While there, he worked with many other Spanish musicians, including Francisco de Salinas. He wrote an important treatise on ornamentation in viol music, the *Trattado de Glosas*, published in two editions (Spanish and Italian) at Rome in 1553.

Works include:
Motets; variations for bass viol.

Orto, Marbrianus de (ADOPTED NAME OF MARBRIANUS DUJARDIN) (*c.* 1460–1529)

Flemish singer and composer. He changed his name when he went to Rome, where he was a singer in the papal chapel (1484–94), with Josquin Desprez. Early in the 16th century he became chaplain and singer at the court of Philip the Fair of Burgundy.

Works include:
Masses, motets, and other church music; chansons.

Othello

Tragedy by William ◊Shakespeare, first performed in 1604–05. Othello, a Moorish commander in the

Venetian army, is persuaded by Iago that his wife Desdemona is having an affair with his friend Cassio. Othello murders Desdemona; on discovering her innocence, he kills himself.

Ouwater, Albert (AELBERT) van (LIVED 15TH CENTURY)

Netherlandish painter. Only one work has definitely been attributed to him, *The Raising of Lazarus* (Staatliche Museen, Berlin). He was a follower of Jan van Eyck and Dirk Bouts, and is traditionally regarded as the master of ◊Geertgen tot Sint Jans.

He was presumably born in Ouwater, though he was closely associated with Haarlem. Another work that is probably by him is a *Madonna* in the Metropolitan Museum, New York.

Owen, John (c. 1560–1622)

Welsh epigrammatist. His Latin epigrams, which have a high degree of sense and wit, gained him much praise, and were translated into English, French, German, and Spanish.

He was born in Plas Du, Caernarvonshire (Gwynedd). Educated at Winchester and Oxford, he became headmaster of King Henry VIII's School at Warwick.

Oxford, Edward de Vere, 17th Earl of Oxford (1550–1604)

English courtier and poet, credited with around 15 surviving lyric poems. He went to Cambridge University at the age of eight and succeeded to the earldom and hereditary office of Lord Great Chamberlain at the age of 12.

He was tutored by his uncle Arthur Golding, the translator of Ovid. Of unruly temperament, he quarrelled with many people, including – famously – a quarrel with Sir Philip ◊Sidney in 1579 that started on a tennis court and threatened to become murderous. Though he was certainly a literary patron and received dedications of works by various writers, there is no factual basis for the conspiracy claims made by T J Looney and others that he was the secret author of the works attributed to William Shakespeare.

Pacher, Michael (1430–1498)

Austrian painter and wood sculptor. He was one of the principal late-Gothic masters of the carved and painted altarpiece, such as that in the Church of St Wolfgang on the Abersee, Upper Austria, produced 1471–81.

He had some contact with Venice, Padua, and Mantua, where Andrea ◊Mantegna was his contemporary, though Italian influence appears mainly in the concentration of perspective on a focal point and in some details of ornament. Pacher executed altarpieces in Gries, Neustift, Salzburg, and other places in his native region. His *Coronation of the Virgin* (1471–81) is in the Pinakothek, Munich.

Pagani, Gregorio (1558–1605)

Florentine painter. A fine colourist, he helped to renew Florentine art during the last years of the 16th century. *The Family of Tobit* and frescoes in the Church of Santa Maria Novella, which are his best-known works, are all in Florence.

Painter, William (c. 1525–1590)

English translator. He is remembered for his two-volume *Palace of Pleasure* (1566–67), an anthology of more than 100 stories taken from a wide range of writers, including Livy, Plutarch, Giraldi (Cinthio), Boccaccio, Bandello, and Marguerite of Navarre. The stories were adapted by many English writers and dramatists, notably Shakespeare, who uses material from this book in *Romeo and Juliet*, *Timon of Athens*, *All's Well That Ends Well*, and *The Rape of Lucrece*.

Probably born in London, he was educated at Cambridge and became a schoolmaster in Kent.

Paix, Jakob (1556–AFTER 1623)

German composer. He wrote German songs and Latin church music, but his chief work was his collection of keyboard music, published in 1583, which included original compositions as well as highly ornamented arrangements of songs and motets.

He was organist at Lauingen, Swabia (1576–1601), and court organist at Neuburg an der Donau (1601–17).

Palestrina, Giovanni Pierluigi da (c. 1525–1594)

Italian composer. He wrote secular and sacred choral music, and is regarded as the outstanding exponent of Renaissance ◊counterpoint. Apart from motets and madrigals, he also wrote 105 masses, including *Missa Papae Marcelli*.

Palissy, Bernard (1510–1589)

French potter. He made richly coloured rustic pieces, such as dishes with realistic modelled fish and reptiles. He was favoured by the queen, Catherine de' Medici, but was imprisoned in the Bastille as a ◊Huguenot in 1588 and died there.

Palladio, Andrea (1508–1580)

Italian architect who created harmonious and balanced classical structures. He designed numerous palaces and country houses in and around Vicenza, making use of Roman Classical forms, symmetry, and proportion. The Villa Malcontenta and the Villa Rotonda are examples of houses designed from 1540 for patrician families of the Venetian Republic. He also designed churches in Venice and published his studies of Classical form in several illustrated books.

His ideas were imitated in England in the early 17th century by Inigo ◊Jones.

Palladio was born at Padua, and studied in Vicenza and Rome. His style was an attempt to revive the severity and dignity of Roman architecture, and was derived from Vitruvius and from a study of the Roman monuments that remained. He greatly influenced the architecture of his day by his work, *I quattro libri dell'Architettura/The Four Books of Architecture*

(1570), which was immediately translated into most European languages. His buildings included the Palazzo della Ragione, Vicenza (commissioned 1545); and the churches of S Giorgio Maggiore (begun 1566) and Il Redentore (begun 1576) at Venice.

S Giorgio Maggiore is a Benedictine monastery whose design is an interpretation of the Basilica of Maxentius and a development from Palladio's own rebuilding of Sta Giustina in Padua, a Benedictine sister house.

Pallavicino, Benedetto (1551–1601)

Italian composer. He was in the service of the Duke of Mantua from 1582, and succeeded Giaches de Wert as maestro di cappella there in 1596, but retired to the monastery of Camaldoli in Tuscany in 1601.

Works include:

Masses, psalms, and other church music; ten volumes of madrigals.

Palma il Giovane, Jacopo Palma, THE YOUNGER (1544–1628)

Italian painter. Active mostly in Venice, he blended elements of mid-sixteenth century Roman and Venetian styles. He painted mainly religious and historical subjects.

He studied in Rome (1567–75), but was also strongly influenced by three of the major figures of Venetian art: ◊Titian, ◊Tintoretto, and Paolo ◊Veronese. Many of his commissions were executed for Venice, such as his frescoes for the Doge's Palace, but a number of his works were ordered from other Italian cities. When Tintoretto died in 1594, Palma Giovane became the leading artist in Venice.

He was the grand-nephew of ◊Palma Vecchio.

Palma Vecchio, Jacopo (Giacomo) d'Antonio de Negreti, THE ELDER (1480–1528)

Italian painter. Active in Venice, he was strongly influenced by his contemporaries ◊Giorgione and ◊Titian. He painted mostly religious subjects and portraits, including *The Holy Family with Saints* (completed by Titian; Accademia, Venice) and *Portrait of a Poet* (probably Ariosto; National Gallery, London), a work formerly attributed to Titian.

Among Palma's most important works are the *St*

Barbara Altarpiece in the Church of Sta Maria Formosa, Venice; *Portrait of a Lady* (Museo Poldi Pezzoli, Milan); and *The Three Sisters* (Gemäldegalerie Alte Meister, Dresden).

He was born in Serinalta, near Bergamo, and probably studied under Giovanni ◊Bellini. He adopted the name Palma and was later called Vecchio to distinguish him from his grand-nephew ◊Palma Giovane.

Paminger, Leonhard (1495–1567)

Austrian composer. He became a Lutheran and published religious pamphlets and a series of motets for the Lutheran year.

He was educated at the monastery of St Nicholas at Passau, then studied in Vienna, but returned to Passau in 1513 to become a teacher and later secretary at the monastery.

Works include:

Latin motets, German hymns, psalms, and other pieces.

Pannartz, Arnold (DIED c. 1476)

German cleric who was the business partner of Conrad ◊Sweynheym in the enterprise of introducing the printing press into Italy.

Pannemaker family

Family of 16th-century Flemish tapestry weavers, based in Brussels. The most famous tapestry weavers of their age, they worked for several European leaders and popes, but their main patrons were members of the Habsburg dynasty. One of their most important commissions, for Pope Leo X, was to weave a set of tapestries of New Testament subjects from cartoons by ◊Raphael. (See Renaissance ◊tapestry.)

Pieter I Pannemaker (active from 1510) was a follower of the artist Pieter van Aelst. Pieter was the first of his family to gain imperial patronage, with a commission from Maximilian I, and in 1523 he also worked for Margaret of Austria. Pieter II and Willem continued to work for the Habsburgs.

Among their prolific output was the series of 12 tapestries (completed in 1535) depicting Charles V's campaign to capture Tunis, after designs by the artist Vermeyen. At the end of the 1570s the pre-eminence of the Pannemakers was overtaken by the Geubels family.

Panormita
See Antonio Beccadelli.

Pantoja de la Cruz, Juan (1551–1608)
Spanish painter. He was the pupil of Sánchez ◊Coello, whom he succeeded as court painter to Philip II. Like his master, he was influenced by Titian and Anthonis Mor, and painted in Coello's formal style a number of stately portraits with much highly finished detail of costume.

papalism
Theory of government of the Christian church, based on the belief that the pope had received from Christ the duty and right to rule the church as a monarch. This was worked out in the 15th century on behalf of Pope ◊Eugenius IV in response to the challenge of ◊conciliarism, which originated at the Council of Basel and advocated the supremacy of general councils.

Papalism, constructed with reference not only to canon law but also to Aristotelianism, was presented in treatises and in diplomatic encounters by papal servants like Antonio de' Roselli, Juan de Torquemada, and Pietro ◊Del Monte.

Parabosco, Girolamo (1520 OR 1524–1557)
Italian composer and organist. He was well known for improvisations on the organ. He published two pieces in the miscellaneous collection of instrumental music *Musica Nova* (1540).

He studied with Adrian Willaert in Venice. In 1551 he succeeded Jachet Buus as first organist at St Mark's, Venice, a post which he held until his death.

Paracelsus (ADOPTED NAME OF THEOPHRASTUS BOMBASTUS VON HOHENHEIM) (1493–1541)
Swiss physician, alchemist, and scientist who developed the idea that minerals and chemicals might have medical uses (iatrochemistry). He introduced the use of laudanum (which he named) for pain-killing purposes.

Overturning the contemporary view of illness as an imbalance of the four humours (see ◊humours, theory of), Paracelsus sought an external agency as the source of disease. This encouraged new modes of treatment, supplanting, for example, bloodletting, and opened the way for new ideas on the source of infection.

Paracelsus was extremely successful as a doctor. His descriptions of miners' diseases first identified silicosis and tuberculosis as occupational hazards. He recognized goitre as endemic and related to minerals in drinking water, and originated a medical account of chorea, rather than believing this nervous disease to be caused by possession by spirits. Paracelsus was the first to distinguish the congenital from the infectious form of ◊syphilis, and showed that it could be treated with carefully controlled doses of a mercury compound.

Paracelsus was born in Einsiedeln, Schwyz canton. Like many of his contemporaries, he became a wandering scholar, studying at Vienna, Basel, and several universities in Italy. He was a military surgeon in Venice and the Netherlands and is said to have visited England, Scotland, Russia, Egypt, and Constantinople. Having practised as a physician in Austria, he became professor of medicine at Basel in 1527, but scandalized other academics by lecturing in German rather than Latin and by his savage attacks on the Classical medical texts – he burned the works of ◊Galen and Avicenna in public – and was forced to leave Basel in 1528. In 1541 he was appointed physician to Duke Ernst of Bavaria.

Paracelsus was the disseminator in Europe of the medieval Islamic alchemists' theory that matter is composed of only three elements: salt, sulphur, and mercury. His study of alchemy helped to develop it into chemistry and produced new, nontoxic compounds for medicinal use; he discovered new substances arising from the reaction of metals and described various organic compounds, including ether. He was the first to devise such advanced laboratory techniques as the concentration of alcohol by freezing. Paracelsus also devised a specific nomenclature for substances already known but not precisely defined, and his attempt to construct a system of grouping chemicals according to their susceptibility to similar processes was the first of its kind.

Paré, Ambroise (c. 1509–1590)
French surgeon who introduced modern principles to the treatment of wounds. As a military surgeon, Paré developed new ways of treating wounds and

amputations, which greatly reduced the death rate among the wounded. He abandoned the practice of cauterization (sealing with heat), using balms and soothing lotions instead, and used ligatures to tie off blood vessels.

Paré eventually became chief surgeon to Charles IX. He also made important contributions to dentistry and childbirth, and invented an artificial hand.

Paré was born in Mayenne *département* and trained in Paris. His book *La Méthode de traicter les playes faites par les arquebuses et aultres bastons à feu/ Method of Treating Wounds Inflicted by Arquebuses and Other Guns* (1545) became a standard work in European armies, and was followed by a number of works on anatomy.

Parker, Matthew (1504–1575)

English cleric. He was converted to Protestantism at Cambridge University. He received high preferment under Henry VIII and Edward VI, and as archbishop of Canterbury from 1559 was largely responsible for the Elizabethan religious settlement (the formal establishment of the Church of England).

Parmigianino, (Girolamo) Francesco (Maria Mazzola) (1503–1540)

Italian painter and etcher. One of the leading Parman artists of the 16th century, he painted religious subjects and portraits in a sensual style; his slender, elongated figures demonstrate his highly elegant and personal interpretation of form. He was one of the first Italian artists to make original etchings.

A member of a family of artists who initially instructed him in painting, he later became a follower of ◊Correggio, and was inspired by the art of ◊Raphael and ◊Michelangelo after a trip to Rome in 1523. Following the ◊Sack of Rome in 1527, Parmigianino returned to his native Parma. He was influenced by the study of both northern and central Italian art, combining strong draughtsmanship and monumental, graceful figures with a subtle use of diffused light, as can be seen in the Bologna *Virgin and Child with St Margaret* (*c.* 1528). The immense sophistication of his paintings, characterized by a highly keyed colour palette and attention to decora-

tive details, were influential to later 16th-century artists who admired his eclectic style.

He authorized or undertook numerous etchings of his own compositions, which were widely circulated throughout Europe. His drawings were avidly collected during the 17th and 18th centuries.

Parsons, John (*c.* 1575–1623)

English composer. He wrote a Burial Service, which Purcell used in 1685 for the funeral of Charles II.

He became parish clerk and organist at St Margaret's Church, Westminster, in 1616, and in 1621 organist and choirmaster of Westminster Abbey.

pastoral novel

The term 'pastoral' can broadly be used to describe works in both prose and poetry which take as their theme the praise of country life over a city existence, and which narrate the love affairs of shepherds and shepherdesses (or aristocratic characters disguised as such). It is a setting which derives from Classical poetry, and it was taken up by ◊Petrarch, Jacopo Sannazaro, and ◊Tasso. The Castilian *novela pastoril* ('pastoral novel') shared this ideal, country setting, and alternated prose and verse to narrate the various happy or unhappy loves of shepherds and shepherdesses (both genuine and disguised), who co-exist and consult with a host of gods, nymphs, and enchantresses. The treatment of the different aspects of the shepherds' love was mostly inspired by Leone ◊Hebreo's philosophy in his *Dialoghi/Dialogues*.

The pastoral novel was extremely popular in 16th-century Spain; the most successful, and perhaps archetypal work of the genre was ◊Montemayor's *La ◊Diana*.

Patay, Battle of

Battle fought on 18 June 1429 at the village of Patay, 21 km/13 mi northwest of Orléans, France, during the Hundred Years' War, in which the French under the Duke of Alençon and Joan of Arc surprised the English, captured John Talbot, and inflicted heavy casualties.

In the wake of their failure to take Orléans, Lord Talbot and John Fastolf mustered 3,500 men in a good defensive position at Patay. They were surprised by the French, who charged into the vanguard of archers unprotected by stakes. Talbot was wounded and captured, with the loss of 2,000 men; Fastolf escaped with the remnant.

Patinir (ALSO PATENIER OR PATINIER), Joachim (c. 1485–1524)

Flemish painter. He produced religious scenes like *Landscape with St Jerome* (*c.* 1520, National Gallery, London) in which the landscape dominates and the small figures are dwarfed by their setting.

Born at Dinant or Bouvignes, he may have been a pupil of Quentin ◊Matsys with whom he collaborated, or he may have worked in the workshop of Gerard ◊David. After a brief period in Bruges, he spent his working life in Antwerp. In 1521 he met Dürer, who mentions him as a landscape painter. He is known to have painted landscape backgrounds for other artists' works. He had a large following, many anonymous paintings being of his 'school', and his works strongly influenced Herri met de ◊Bles and Pieter ◊Brueghel the Elder.

Paul II (BORN PIETRO BARBO) (1417–1471)

Pope from 1464. Born into an affluent Venetian patrician family, the future Paul II was made a cardinal in 1440 at the age of 23 by the Venetian pope, ◊Eugenius IV. He served as an administrator to successive popes; in his own pontificate, he continued Pius II's plans for a crusade against the Ottomans and strengthened papal control in central Italy.

As a cardinal and pope, Paul II displayed a taste for the expensive and the grand, building his Roman palace (now Palazzo Venezia) and collecting there tapestries, gems, and manuscripts (he took over a large part, for example, of the collection of Pietro del Monte). In the eyes of scholars, his reputation has been done no favours by his treatment of Pomponio ◊Leto and his 'Roman Academy': with rumours of sodomy and, more importantly, astrological predictions of the pope's imminent death, Paul II arrested members of the coterie in 1468 and had some of them tortured. This treatment gained him a damning biography by one of his victims, ◊Platina.

Paul III (BORN ALESSANDRO FARNESE) (1468–1549)

Pope from 1534. Born into the noble Farnese family, high church office may have been his expectation but he was assisted by his own abilities and by other factors. He was created a cardinal in 1493 by ◊Alexander VI, whose mistresses included Farnese's sister. Under Alexander and his successors, he collected ecclesiastical and administrative positions which were lucrative and influential. Elected in succession to Clement VII, he combined a nepotistic desire to forward his family with a determination to reform the church, the culmination of which was the convening of the Council of Trent.

The future Paul III had been educated in Rome (by Pomponio ◊Leto) and in Florence (by ◊Politian), where a fellow pupil was the future ◊Leo X. He considered that humanist learning was essential to reform and to its purpose of dispelling the Protestant threat. Accordingly, while his first appointments to the cardinalate had included his own grandsons, he made moves in 1535 to elect Erasmus a cardinal. This came to nothing but his promotions did include Reginald ◊Pole, Gasparo Contarini, and Gian Pietro Carafa (the future ◊Paul IV), all of whom were appointed to a committee to report on reform (the *Consilium de Emendenda Ecclesia*, 1538). Paul similarly supported the new monastic orders, recognising the Jesuits in 1540 and the Ursulines in 1544.

At the same time, Paul III considered magnificence a crucial element of the papacy's image, especially as a means of erasing the memory of the ◊Sack of Rome: symbolically, he had a sculpted angel placed on top of the Castel Sant' Angelo in 1544 to replace the one destroyed in the Sack. He fostered Clement VII's plan for the altarwall of the ◊Sistine Chapel, commissioning ◊Michelangelo to paint the *Last Judgement* (but worrying about the level of nudity in it). Michelangelo had been appointed 1535 papal painter, architect and sculptor; after he completed the work in the Sistine Chapel, Paul III directed him, despite his growing ill health, to fresco his private chapel, the Capella Paolina, with images of the Conversion of Saul and the Martyrdom of St Peter 1542–50 – frescoes which provide a striking contrast to the brightly coloured *Last Judgement*. On the death of Antonio da ◊Sangallo, Michelangelo was also appointed the architect of the new St Peter's. Beyond the walls of the Vatican, Paul III completed the Palazzo Farnese, which he had begun in 1514–15

PATRONAGE OF ART

THE DEMAND FOR works of art during the Renaissance is dominated by commissions from wealthy religious institutions and individuals who wished tangibly to demonstrate their piety. During the 14th and part of the 15th century, artistic patronage was confined largely to the production of devotional images, which also took the form of civic monuments commissioned by the leading citizens or the administration of a city. Towards the mid-15th century and increasingly into the 16th, demand arose for secular imagery. In a similar fashion, the status and role of the patron evolved significantly, with the rise of independent patronage by prominent individuals who wished to commemorate family achievements with works of art.

Artistic patronage in the 14th century was confined almost exclusively to religious or civic institutions which commissioned images that exemplified the values or practices of the given group. Churches and lay religious confraternities were a principal source of patronage, often wishing to commemorate an important event with a painting, sculpture, or even a building, as was the case with the church of Orsanmichele in Florence which was transformed from a grain loft following a miraculous occurence. In many cases, prominent families provided the financial backing for large enterprises of this nature

which were beyond the means of the general populace.

In the 15th century, patronage began to slowly break from the rigid hierarchy characteristic of the past century. Although institutions continued to dominate the market for religious images, increasingly, leading families vied with each other to commission works of art to decorate private chapels and palaces, such as the Carafa Chapel painted by ◊Filippino Lippi in the church of Santa Maria Sopra Minerva in Rome. With the rise of independent patrons, came an increase in the demand for secular subjects, including portraits and mythogical or historical subjects. Although once confined to princely or immensely wealthy families, the desire for portraiture and other secular imagery became attainable by the merchant class. Mythological and

historical events became increasingly popular with erudite families such as the Medici, whose interest in antiquity spawned such works as *The Calumny of Apelles* by Sandro ◊Botticelli (Uffizi, Florence).

By the 16th century, patronage was no longer confined to institutions or powerful families, but came increasingly within the range of the general populace. A growing demand for works of art encouraged the establishment of large workshops under the direction of a single master, such as that of ◊Andrea del Sarto, which in addition to large-scale decorative commissions and altarpieces, also produced multiple copies of traditional subjects including the Virgin and Child with saints. Although prevalent in the previous century, large workshops producing multiple copies or variations of stock

continued

Filippino Lippi, *Virgin and Child with Tanai de' Nerli and his wife*, 1494. The Florentine Nerli commissioned this painting for their chapel in the recently completed church of Santo Spirito (designed by Brunelleschi). They appear prominently in the alterpiece. ◊Lippi, Filippino e.t. archive

images became increasingly prevalent with the rise in affluence of merchants and tradesmen. The broadening of the market for works of art also carried over into less traditional vocations, with painters, sculptors, and architects including ◊Agnolo Bronzino and ◊Antonio da Sangallo designing theatrical sets for dramatic representations.

With the increase in status and wealth of powerful families, a flourishing industry grew up around the decoration and embellishment of private palaces. Once the exclusive territory of popes and princes, prominent families sought to confirm their status through elaborate commissions to decorate both the interior and exterior of their palaces. This liberal form of patronage required artists to mobilize highly

skilled workshops which specialized in working in multiple media, including sculpture, stucco, fresco, and oil paintings. These decorations generally took the form of allegorical themes or subjects from antiquity which represented or personified the deeds of a given family, such as in ◊Raphael's decorations for the Villa Farnesina, Rome.

The 16th century commensurately saw the rise in the dynastic ambitions of the papacy and princely families of Italy, such as the Gonzaga in Mantua and the Medici in Florence. Artistic patronage benefited from these expansionist tendencies, as immensely wealthy patrons sought to eulogize their families through elaborate commissions, which included the renovation and decoration of palaces

as was the case with the Palazzo Vecchio in Florence, and the creation of elaborate and often impossibly lavish monuments such as the ill-fated tomb project of Pope Julius II which ◊Michelangelo laboured on unsuccessfully for a number of decades. Vast sums of money were devoted to projects which were well beyond the means of lesser patrons in a bid to employ leading artists to produce paintings, sculptures, and palaces of unprecedented grandeur and opulence.

RICHARD REED

Further Reading
M Hollingsworth, *Patronage in Renaissance Italy: from 1400 to the early sixteenth century* (London, 1994)

---

while a cardinal and which was designed by Antonio da Sangallo. Once again, when Sangallo died, Michelangelo was assigned yet another task to adapt the design of the palace.

Paul IV (BORN GIAN PIETRO CARAFA) (1476–1559)

Pope from 1555. Noted for his commitment to church reform, he had been made a cardinal by Paul III in 1535 and appointed to a comission to investigate reform. By the time he became pope, he was 79; by then, all possibility of reconciliation with the Protestants had passed and repression concerned him more than reform. Politically, he was virulently anti-Spanish, going as far as excommunicating Philip II.

His pontificate was not noted for its artistic patronage though this may reflect as much the brevity of his reign as his austere tendencies. For sure, he asked Michelangelo to make his Sistine Chapel fresco, the *Last Judgement*, more modest, but he did not baulk when the reply was a straight

'no'. His building work involved destroying frescoes by Taddeo Zuccaro and Raphael but this was hardly unprecedented. And, above all, he was concerned that the work on St Peter's should continue, though he himself did not live to see much advance.

Paumann, Conrad (c. 1410–1473)

German composer and organist. He travelled widely through France, Italy, Germany, and Austria as an organist and is believed to have invented a form of lute tablature. His treatise, *Fundamentum Organisandi* (1452), gives examples of the ornamentation of chant, with keyboard arrangements of chants and secular melodies.

Paumann was born in Nuremberg. Blind from birth, he was educated by the Grundherr family of Nuremberg, learnt the organ and composition, and was organist at St Sebald's Church in the 1440s. In 1450 he was appointed organist to Duke Albrecht III of Bavaria at Munich, and retained the post for the rest of his life. Few of his compositions survive, probably because he could not write them down.

Works include:
Fundamentum Organisandi/Principles of Composition,
(1452), laid out in keyboard tablature, which exists in several versions; organ arrangement of monophonic and polyphonic pieces; and a German song, 'Wiplich figur'.

Pavia, Battle of

Battle fought in 1525 between France and the Holy Roman Empire. The Habsburg emperor Charles V defeated and captured Francis I of France; the battle marked the beginning of Habsburg dominance in Italy. Francis was held in Spain for a year. To obtain his release he signed away any claims he had to Italy (the Treaty of Madrid) but, on his return to France, disowned the treaty and organized a league against Charles V.

Pazzi conspiracy

Attempt to assassinate the leading ◊Medici on 26 April 1478. The Pazzi family were one of the patrician clans of Florence. Like the Medici, they made their money in banking and demonstrated their position by acts of architectural patronage: they commissioned the austere Pazzi chapel at S Croce from Filippo ◊Brunelleschi in the 1420s. In the third quarter of the quattrocento, however, they felt themselves to be increasingly sidelined by Lorenzo de' ◊Medici's regime. Supported by Sixtus IV, Francesco de' Pazzi persuaded the head of the family, Jacopo, that they had to rid Florence of Medici tyranny.

The plan was to kill both Lorenzo and his younger brother Giuliano de' Medici while they attended mass in the cathedral. When the time came, Francesco de' Pazzi successfully stabbed Giuliano to death, although he wounded himself in the process and his fellow conspirators inflicted only a wound to Lorenzo's throat. Lorenzo escaped, the conspirators failed to raise popular support, were captured and themselves killed. In the aftermath, the pope and Ferrante of Naples declared war on Florence; the city was saved from invasion, in part, by Lorenzo's personal embassy to Ferrante in December 1479. Peace was agreed in the following year.

A failed rebellion is worse than not rebelling. Lorenzo's survival became part of the Medici myth, with, for example, ◊Politian quickly producing an unsympathetic account of the conspiracy. In its wake, Lorenzo took the opportunity to tighten his control of Florentine affairs; the Pazzi war did see the Medici bank suffer and close some its branches, but in their home city, the family's standing was increased, not cut down.

Jacopo de' Pazzi's body was dragged naked through the city by the noose with which he had been hanged; then he was thrown into the Arno river, the waters of which were at their highest. Truly a great example of fortune, to see a man of such wealth fall into such unprosperity with such ruin and such contempt!

NICCOLÒ MACHIAVELLI, *Florentine Histories,* finding a conventional moral message in the killing of the Pazzi

---

Pedro, CONSTABLE OF PORTUGAL (1429–1466)

Portuguese noble, constable of Portugal from 1443. His father Pedro, Duke of Coimbra, acting as regent for Afonso V, furthered his own political interests by appointing his son constable (*condestável*) in 1443 and Master of the Order of Avis in 1444. His father's death and Afonso V's victory in 1449 caused Pedro to flee to Castile, returning to Portugal and collaboration with Afonso in 1456. His final years were spent fighting in Morocco and stirring up trouble in Catalonia.

Aside from his request to Iñigo ◊Santillana for an anthology of his poems, Pedro himself was author of several works, and set a much-followed precedent for Portuguese writers by composing in both Portuguese and Castilian. In 1453 he translated his *Satire on Happy and Unhappy Life*, written earlier in Portuguese, into Castilian; shortly after he composed the Castilian poem 'Coplas del menesprecio de las cosas fermosas del mundo'/'Lines on Scorning the Beautiful Things of the World', which he dedicated to Afonso V.

Pedro, PRINCE AND DUKE OF COIMBRA (1392–1449)

Regent of Portugal during ◊Afonso V's minority, soldier, and author. The peripatetic fourth son of João I, he took part in the 1415 conquest of Ceuta and between 1425 and 1428 travelled Europe where, *inter alia*, he established commercial contacts for the Portuguese and fought with the Hungarian army against the Turks. In Venice, in 1428, he may have acquired (and later partly translated to Portuguese) an account of Marco Polo's travels (*The Book of Marco Polo*), which, appended to the original text, was published in 1502. He also wrote to Don ◊Duarte from Bruges, suggesting Oxford or Paris as models for Portuguese universities. Becoming regent on Duarte's untimely death (1438), he summoned the Italian scholar Matteo Pisano to act as Afonso's tutor. He died fighting his former ward at the battle of Alfarrobeira.

As well as commissioning a translation of Cicero's *De Officiis*, the *Livro dos ofcios/Book of Duties* (1433–33), Pedro dedicated his paraphrase of Seneca's *De beneficiis/Livro da Virtuosa Bemfeitoria/ The Book of Virtuous Good Deeds* (*c.* 1433) to his bookish brother Duarte. The earliest poem in Resende's ◊*cancioneiro, Geral,* is Pedro's panegyric (*c.* 1440–48) of his friend Juan de ◊Mena. Rui de Pina also attributes translations of Giles of Rome's *De regimine principum* and Vegetius' *De re militari* to his pen, although these, like the manual for confession which he also lists, appear to be lost.

Pedro was the subject of Gómez de Santo Estebán's curious work entitled *Libro del Infante Don Pedro de Portugal/Book of Prince Pedro of Portugal.* Published at Burgos in 1563, it recounts a fictitious journey made by Pedro to the Holy Land. Translated into Portuguese in 1602, it enjoyed considerable success in both languages.

Peele, George (*c.* 1558–*c.* 1596)

English dramatist and poet. His surviving plays are a pastoral, *The Arraignment of Paris* (1584), *Edward I* (1593), *The Battle of Alcazar* (1594), a fantastic comedy, *The Old Wives' Tale* (1595), and the tragedy, *David and Bethsabe* (1599). He wrote many miscellaneous verses, the best perhaps being the 'gratulatory poem' *The Honour of the Garter* (1593).

Peele was born in London. From Christ's Hospital he went to Oxford, where he had a reputation as a poet and wrote his *Tale of Troy* (1589). It is generally assumed that he became an actor, but nothing is known of his performances.

Peffenhauser, Anton (PFEFFENHAUSER) (*c.* 1525–1603)

German armourer from Augsburg. He specialized in plate armour that was for ceremonial parade rather than combat, producing magnificently decorated suits of armour that were extremely elaborate. His clients included German princes, members of the court of Philip II of Spain, and King Sebastian of Portugal.

Peletier, Jacques (KNOWN AS PELETIER DU MANS) (1517–1582)

French poet. He was a member of the ◊*Pléiade* group of poets. His literary works include a translation of ◊Horace's *Ars poetica* (1545), an *Art poétique* of his own (1555), and poems, *Euvres poétiques* (1547). He was also well known as a mathematician.

Pembroke, Mary, Countess of Pembroke (1561–1621)

English poet. The sister of Philip ◊Sidney, she married Henry Herbert, Earl of Pembroke in 1577. It was at her suggestion that Sidney wrote his *Arcadia*, and she completed his translation of the Psalms after his death. She was the patron of Samuel ◊Daniel, Ben ◊Jonson, and other poets, and herself wrote several works. She also translated Philippe de Mornay's *A Discourse of Life and Death* (1592).

Penni, Giovan Francesco (KNOWN AS IL FATTORE) (*c.* 1488–*c.* 1528)

Italian painter. Trained together with ◊Giulio Romano in the workshop of ◊Raphael in Rome, where he excelled at the study of ◊*disegno*. He collaborated on the Vatican Logge and the tapestry cartoons for the Sistine Chapel with Raphael, and upon his death aided in the completion of the private rooms of ◊Julius II, known as the *Stanze*. He painted altarpieces in Tuscany and Rome before travelling to Naples where he died. His accomplishments as a draughtsman and his fidelity to the style of his master – seen, for example, in the *Madonna of the veil*, in the Capodimonte in Naples – earned him widespread recognition in his day.

Pérez de Guzmán, Fernán (*c*. 1378–*c*. 1460)

Castilian poet and chronicler. Among his works are *Crónica del rey Juan II*; *Generaciones y semblanzas*, a terse account of the illustrious men of his time; and *Loores de los claros varones de España*, a rhymed chronicle. His poetical works consist mainly of hymns and moral pieces. He was the nephew of Pedro ◊López de Ayala.

Peri, Jacopo (1561–1633)

Roman composer who lived in Florence in the service of the Medici. His experimental melodic opera *Euridice* (1600) established the opera form and influenced Monteverdi. His first opera, *Dafne* (1597) believed to be the earliest opera, is now lost.

Peri was a pupil of Cristoforo Malvezzi, then became a canon at the church of San Lorenzo at Florence. He was attached to the Medici court from about 1588, and was later appointed their maestro di cappella and chamberlain. He became a member of the progressive artists grouped round Count Giovanni Bardi, with the composers Giulio Caccini, Jacopo Corsi, and Vincenzo Galilei, and the poet Ottavio Rinuccini. In their endeavour to revive Greek drama with the kind of music they imagined to be genuinely Greek, they stumbled on the invention of opera. They discarded counterpoint in favour of melody and expressive harmony. Peri, with Caccini , experimented in musical declamation to a suitable accompaniment, and they thus became the earliest composers of recitative. They may also be considered the world's first operatic composers.

Works include:

Operas *Dafne* (1598), *Euridice* (1600), *Tetide* (1608), *Adone* (1611), tournament with music *La precedenza delle dame* (1625); parts of operas (with others) *La guerra d'amore* and *Flora* (with Gagliano); several ballets; *Lamento d'Iole* for soprano and instruments, madrigals, sonnets, and arias in *Songbook* of 1609.

Perino del Vaga (1501–1547)

Florentine painter. A pupil and assistant of ◊Raphael

Sanzio in Rome, he carried out decorations in the Logge of the Vatican from Raphael's designs. What might be called his trademark were his frescoes painted so as to simulate bronze reliefs. Late in his career (after a decade spent mainly in Genoa working for Andrea ◊Doria), he produced a group of these to supplement Raphael's frescoes in the Vatican Stanze della Segnatura; from this commission followed his last major work, the decoration of ◊Paul III's suite in the Castel Sant' Angelo.

Perotti, Niccolò (1429–1480)

Italian cleric and humanist writer, born in Fano. After an education at the feet of ◊Vittorino da Feltre and ◊Guarino da Verona, Perotti entered the household of, first, William ◊Gray, and then Cardinal ◊Bessarion (whose life he described in 1472). He acted as one of Pope ◊Nicholas V's translators, rendering, for example, the first books of the Greek historian Polybius into Latin (1452–54). Papal secretary from 1455, he was made archbishop of Siponto in 1458. Although his later career was as a papal governor, he continued his scholarly pursuits, editing the works of the Roman writers Pliny and Martial.

Like most humanists, Perotti was not averse to scholarly controversy: he openly criticized Domizio ◊Calderini for his work on Martial. Perotti's own Martial commentary was presented in the *Cornucopia*, which was printed only after his death. His posthumous fame perhaps rested not only on this work but equally – maybe even more so – on his grammatical writings, which gained Europe-wide popularity: in 1480s Oxford, for example, it was a source for John ◊Anwykyll's textbook.

Perréal, Jean (JEHAN DE PARIS) (*c*. 1457–1530)

French painter, illustrator, and poet. Active from 1485, he was court painter to successive French kings – Charles VIII, Louis XII, and Francis I – and was also employed by Margaret of Austria. He gained a high reputation for his portraits; those which survive – for example, of Charles VIII and Anne of Brittany (Paris, Bibliothèque Nationale, MS. lat. 1190) – are manuscript minatures.

He worked in Lyon but was often sent elsewhere on various commissions, visiting Italy, where Franco Gonzaga, Marchese of Mantua, commissioned a portrait from him, and England. As well as his artistic achievements, Perréal was known in literary circles; one of his sitters, Pierre Sala, dedicated to him a treatise on friendship.

He was once identified with the ◊Master of Moulins, but this is now rejected on stylistic grounds.

Perugino, Pietro (PIETRO DI CRISTOFORO VANNUCCI) (c. 1450–1523)

Painter from Perugia. Early in his career, he was employed by ◊Sixtus IV, most notably on the frescoes for the ◊Sistine Chapel. Later he was based in his hometown where ◊Raphael was his pupil. But, with his skills continually in demand, he also ran a studio in Florence and accepted commissions from Orvieto, Mantua, Siena, and Naples.

Perugino may have been a pupil of ◊Piero della Francesca and was probably an assistant to Verrocchio, his style being formed at Florence. Frescoes in the Palazzo Communale at Perugia in 1475 were one of his undertakings. Sixtus IV commissioned him in c. 1469 to produce a fresco in the old basilica of St Peter's; subsequently, the pope employed him as one of the painters for the Sistine Chapel; he may have been in overall charge of the enterprise. One of his frescoes for the chapel, *The Delivery of the Keys to St Peter*, reflects his interest in creating a sense of space in his art.

His later works included frescoes for the Collegio del Cambio, Perugia (c. 1496), the *Crucifixion with Saints* (1496, Florence, Santa Maria Maddalena de' Pazzi), and the altarpiece *Virgin and Child with St Michael and St Raphael* (1498, National Gallery, London), in which, it has been speculatively suggested, there is a trace of the young Raphael's handiwork. Perugino's contemporary standing is reflected in the desire of Isabella d' ◊Este to commission a painting from him; however, in this case, Isabella (or her advisor) insisted on providing unusually detailed instructions about the content and style of the painting that they left little room for invention on the part of the artist. The resulting painting is the *Battle between Love and Chastity* (1503–05, Louvre, Paris).

Peruzzi, Baldassare Tommaso (1481–1536)

Sienese architect and painter. Apart from five years (1527–32), he worked mainly in Rome. His first significant work was a villa for Agostino Chigi (now the Villa Farnesina), 1509–11, where the decoration was by Raphael and assistants, including Peruzzi himself. He succeeded ◊Raphael as architect to St Peter's in 1520, but returned to Siena in 1527, after the ◊Sack of Rome, where he worked with Antonio da ◊Sangallo the Younger on the Villa Caprarola in 1530. His final work, the Palazzo Massimo alle Colonne, Rome, 1532–36, was sited at a difficult location (it is at a sharp curve in the road) and consequently has several unorthodox features.

Pesellino (FRANCESCO DI STEFANO) (1422–1457)

Florentine painter. He was probably a pupil of Fra Filippo ◊Lippi, whose style is echoed in Posellino's *Annunciation* (Courtauld Institute, London). The *Trinity with Saints* altarpiece, (1460, National Gallery, London) which was left incomplete at Pesellino's death was finished by assistants in Lippi's workshop. Pesellino was one of the painters who specialized in the decoration of *cassoni* (bridal chests).

Petit, Jean (LIVED 16TH CENTURY)

Parisian bookseller and publisher who published over his career more than 1000 volumes. A rich and influential figure, he had, as well as his shop in Paris, branches in Lyon and Rouen. He assisted Josse ◊Bade in setting up his printing house and they later acted as partners in several publishing ventures.

Petrarch (PETRARCA), Francesco (1304–1374)

Italian poet and early humanist scholar, born in Arezzo to Florentine exiles who moved to Avignon in 1311. Petrarch wrote vernacular sonnets and Latin verse in emulation of Classical literature, focussing first upon an idealized beloved, the unobtainable 'Laura', and later upon more abstract notions of moral perfection, connected to Classical Roman *virtus*. Petrarch's discovery (at Verona in 1345) and his lifelong imitation of Cicero's letters helped nurture a humanist, essentially epistolary, scholarly culture.

Petrarch's 50-year career incorporated the discovery and edition of ancient texts, and creative composition in classicizing metre; each element made a distinctive contribution to the subsequent course of scholarship and literature. His collected Italian poetry (the *Rerum Fragmentum Vulgarium/Vernacular Pieces* or *Canzioniere/Sonnets*) offered a synthesis of Italian stylistic achievement to date (it became a literary genre). Meanwhile, though he had no Greek, Petrarch's *Latinitas* was more refined than that of any contemporary scholar (or many afterwards, according to Pietro ◊Bembo).

Petrarch's writings, much more self-consciously (and querulously) autobiographical (hence *Posteritati/Letter to Posterity*, late 1350s) than those of his peers and predecessors, reveal many of the ideological currents – and conflicts – of the early Renaissance period. Over and over Petrarch exposed the ridiculous demonization of the antique in medieval Christian culture and defended classical literary interests against detractors (in the *Invectiva*

Petrarch Justus of Ghent, portrait of Petrarch, one of the series of paintings of illustrious scholars for the studiolo of Federigo da Montefeltro at his palace in Urbino. *AKG London*

Contra Medicum 1352–53, for example). Nonetheless Petrarch was obliged to assert his own Christian orthodoxy over and over, for example in the Augustinian-inspired apologia *Secretum/Secret* (*c.* ?1343–53) or *De Ignorantia/On Ignorance* (1367), which reclaims Cicero as a proto-Christian. Indeed, certain of Petrarch's visionary sonnets (no XX, 'Spirto Gentil/Noble Spirit') reveal a mystical tendency reminiscent of Dante's sacro-political Christian imperial dream. Petrarch's contribution to the revival of the study of Classical literature, in terms of the re-edition, or the discovery and edition of lost texts, and the development of a literary style to match these, was extensive. The Livian-inspired histories provided in *De Viris Illustris/On Famous Men* (*c.* 1338–74) and *Rerum Memorandum Libri/Of Memorable Things* (134?), with both the ideal republicanism and the new finesse of his Latin epic on Scipio, the *Africa* (*c.* 1339–44), with the antique imagery evoked in the vernacular *Trionfi/Triumphs* (*c.* 1373), and with the enormous epistolary collections (*Familiares/Letters to Friends, Seniles/Letters in Old Age, Sine Nomine/ 'Anonymous' Letters*), spanning decades, Petrarch laid down a range of Latin writings – a set of humanist 'core' texts. Petrarch attempted to introduce a new 'age of enlightenment' celebrating ancient Roman high culture, and deliberately insulated subsequent generations from what he saw as medieval obscurantism. His self-conscious 'break' with the past was elaborated by successive humanist scholars to such a persuasive extent that the exhilarating notion of *rinascimento* was often then, and frequently since, claimed to have begun with his work.

The young Petrarch was sent to learn law at Montpellier and Bologna but abandoned this life ◊Bruni reports that Petrarch thought it 'tedious and gross') in favour of a literary career on the edge of the Provençal Papal court. Patronage was an ongoing problem, since Petrarch's temperament was not suited to political intrigue; he usually avoided and even more frequently castigated the sordid realities of political or diplomatic missions, though obliged to temporize. In the latter half of his life he managed to escape Avignon, either in seclusion on his Vaucluse property or by travelling between the courts of Italian civic rulers. Works such as *De Vita Solitaria/On the Solitary Life* (1346) and *De Otio*

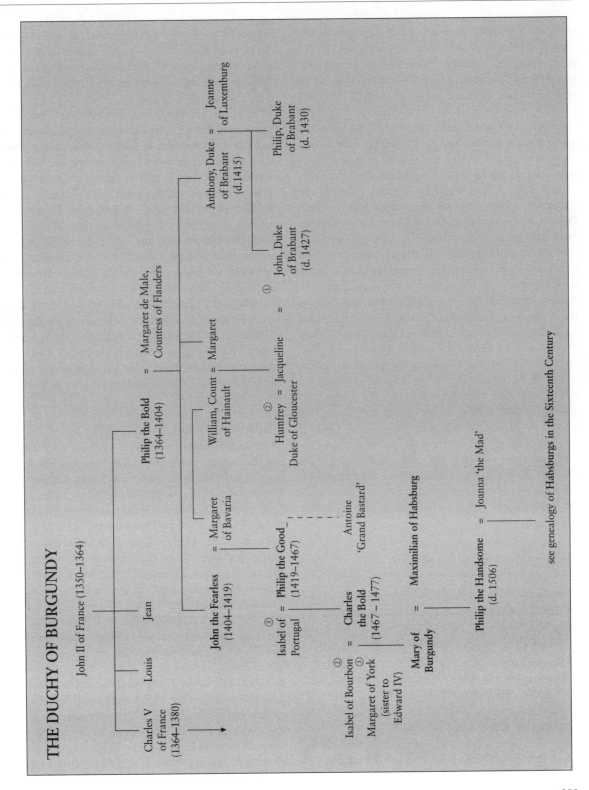

THE DUCHY OF BURGUNDY

John II of France (1350–1364)

Charles V of France (1364–1380)

Louis

Jean

Philip the Bold (1364–1404) = Margaret de Male, Countess of Flanders

John the Fearless (1404–1419)

Margaret = William, Count of Hainault = Margaret of Bavaria

Anthony, Duke of Brabant (d.1415) = Jeanne of Luxemburg

Humfrey = Jacqueline = John, Duke of Brabant (d. 1427)
Duke of Gloucester

Philip, Duke of Brabant (d. 1430)

Isabel of Portugal = Philip the Good (1419–1467)

Antoine 'Grand Bastard'

Isabel of Bourbon =
Margaret of York (sister to Edward IV) = Charles the Bold (1467–1477)

Mary of Burgundy = Maximilian of Habsburg

Philip the Handsome (d. 1506) = Joanna 'the Mad'

see genealogy of Habsburgs in the Sixteenth Century

Religioso/On Holy Retreat (1347) effectively reframed the debate over the relative virtues of the active (political, military, 'Dantean') life versus religious retreat, presenting Cicero's compromise, *otium cum dignitate* ('leisure spent properly'). Petrarch loathed Avignon and its hypocrisy, as his more polemical verse made clear. Despite this, he secured a living for his middle age by embracing holy orders (he also provided for his old age, despite his clerical vows, by fathering two illegitimate children who helped support him when he became elderly). His allegiance to antique political concepts was considerably more constant than his loyalty to any contemporary individual power-broker (emperor, lord, or cardinal): republican-minded friends were less than impressed by his acceptance of support from princes. Several impractical attempts at active participation in governmental reform – his participation from afar in the revolution of Cola di ◊Rienzo, for example – led to disillusionment and retreat to the purely literary evocation of an idealized antiquity. Once the euphoria of the heady years following his spectacular coronation as Poet Laureate on the Capitol in Rome (*c.* 1341) had faded, Petrarch had to face the perspectual divorce of the notion of the revival of Roman (as lauded by Dante, Marsilius of Padua, and Cola di Rienzo) from the intellectual revival of Roman culture: written late in life, *De Remediis Utrius Fortunis/Remedies against Good and Ill Fortune* (*c.* 1364) is considerably more sanguine on, *inter alia*, the unlikelihood of the restoration of Roman world dominion.

Pevernage, André (1543–1591)

Flemish composer. After holding an appointment at Courtrai 1565–85, he moved to Antwerp about 1587 and became choirmaster at the cathedral, holding the post until his death. Apart from cultivating church music, he held weekly concerts at his house.

Works include:

Cantiones sacrae and other church music; madrigals and five volumes of chansons; ode to St Cecilia.

Philip the Bold (1342–1404)

Youngest son of John II of France (1350–64), who invested him and his heirs with the duchy of Burgundy in 1363. By his marriage in 1369 to Margaret of Male, heiress to the county of Flanders, he was able to increase his lands, inheriting the title in 1384. With this acquisition began the pretensions of the House of Burgundy.

Philip, in emulation of his brother Charles of France, was keen to appear the cultured prince. He built up a manuscript collection, although it could not compare in number or illumination with the French royal library and it lacked, except service books, any works in the language of culture: Latin. He also patronized scholars like Jean Gerson and received dedications from others like Christine de Pisan. His architectural and artistic commissions centred on the Carthusian monastery of Champinol; this Charterhouse was designed by the Parisian Drouet de Dammartin, decorated with sculptures by Jehan de Marville and ◊Claus Sluter, and provided with altarpieces by Jean ◊Malouel and Melchior ◊Broederlam.

Philip's son and successor, John the Fearless, continued Philip's policy of cultural patronage. But it was Philip's grandson, Philip the Good, who developed the policy so that Burgundy became seen as a cultural leader of Europe.

Philip the Good (1396–1467)

Duke of Burgundy from 1419. He succeeded following the murder of his father, John the Fearless, by his cousin, the French dauphin (the future Charles VII). In the wake of that, he pursued an alliance with Henry V of England against the French crown. That alliance, however, was eventually abandoned at the Congress of Arras in 1435. Philip's shifting loyalties had consistently one aim: the further increase of Burgundian power. This was an intent which he achieved with remarkable success, annexing, for example, the lands of Hainault to his duchy (1433). With his aggrandizing statecraft went a policy of quasi-regal magnificence: his court became renowned as a cultural centre, with Jan van Eyck his court painter and the composer Gilles Binchois his chaplain.

Philip the Good's patronage contrasted with his grandfather's in that Philip the Bold had lavished money on building projects. The younger Philip was less concerned about this aspect; it was left to town councils to provide the main architectural commissions of the mid-century. Nor was sculpture a major concern of Philip's although he did belatedly commission a tomb for his father in 1443; the craftsman for this; the Aragonese Juan de la Huerta, left Burgundy without finishing it and the work was completed by Antoine le Moiturier in 1470 – after Philip's own death.

Philip the Good's patronage was directed more to movable art-works like tapestries, paintings, and illuminated manuscripts. Philip's collection of manuscripts was built up over the second part of his reign, perhaps following the example of some of his own subjects. Ducal patronage nurtured the local traditions in illumination and script, so that the layout of a Burgundian manuscript became an internationally recognised style to rival that of humanist *littera antiqua* manuscripts. Some of Philip's manuscripts contained texts dedicated to him, often translated into French or Latin text, like Jean Wauguelin's *Chroniques de Hainaut* or a version of Boccaccio's *Decameron* (which also inspired the *Cent nouvelles nouvelles/Hundreds new stories* written at Philip's court late in the reign).

Above all, through, there was a concern for ◊chivalry and spectacle. Philip founded the chivalric order of the Golden Fleece in 1431, which like the English Order of the Garter, met once a year and eventually included foreign princes (the first elected was ◊Alfonso V of Aragon). Philip also promoted the cause of crusade in the 1450s when this was a live-issue across Christendom: it provided him with an opportunity to hold a legendarily extravagant banquet, the Feast of the Pheasant in 1454. Such events were not just an excuse for excess: they could also play an important political role, emphasising the magnificence of Philip's court and assisting Burgundian diplomacy.

Philip (I) the Handsome (1478–1506)

Duke of Burgundy from 1482, King of Castile from 1504. The son of the Holy Roman Emperor, Maximilian, he succeeded to the duchy of Burgundy on the death of his mother. Marrying in 1496 Joanna, the daughter of Ferdinand and Isabella, he became the king of Castile on his mother-in-law's death, but, as Ferdinand pressed to hold the regency, he and his wife had to travel to Spain to assert their right. Philip's death there left his wife so distraught that she earned the sobriquet 'the Mad'.

Following an earlier trip to Spain in 1503, Philip's return to the Low Countries was celebrated by ◊Erasmus in his *Panegyricus/Panegyric*.

Philip II (1527–1598)

King of Spain from 1556. He was born at Valladolid, the son of the Habsburg emperor Charles V, and in 1554 married Queen Mary of England. On his father's abdication 1556 he inherited Spain, the Netherlands, and the Spanish possessions in Italy and the Americas, and in 1580 he annexed Portugal. His intolerance and lack of understanding of the Netherlanders drove them into revolt. Political and religious differences combined to involve him in war with England (sending the unsuccessful ◊Spanish Armada against them) and, after 1589, with France. (See also Picture Gallery).

Philips, Peter (1561–1628)

English organist and composer. He was famous as an organist throughout the Netherlands, and was probably the best-known English composer in northern Europe. His collections of madrigals and motets are Roman in style, with Italianate word painting and polyphony; they were reprinted many times in Antwerp.

Philips sang in the choir of St Paul's Cathedral as a boy. He left England in 1582, probably because he was a Roman Catholic; he was received there at the English College, where he became organist. He travelled in Italy and Spain, settled at Antwerp in 1590, and became a canon at the collegiate church of Soignies. In 1585 he entered the service of Lord Thomas Paget, and spent five years travelling through Italy, Spain, and France. He settled in Brussels in 1589, and on Paget's death in 1590, moved to Antwerp. In 1593, returning from a visit to hear Jan Sweelinck play in Amsterdam, he was arrested on suspicion of being involved in a plot to assassinate Queen Elizabeth; he was released. In 1597 he entered the household of the Archduke Albert in Brussels; he was appointed organist at the royal chapel there in 1611, and remained there until the Archduke's death in 1621. He was then appointed chaplain of the church of Saint-Germain at Tirlemont and in about 1623 became canon of Béthune, but may not have resided at either place.

Some of Philips' large output of keyboard music is preserved in the Fitzwilliam Virginal Book. It belongs to the English tradition, with the most inventive pieces being based on madrigals

Works include:

Masses, 106 motets published in *Paradisus Sacris Cantionibus* (Antwerp, 1628), hymns, *Sacrae Cantiones*, madrigals; fantasies, pavanes, and galliards for various instruments; organ and virginal pieces.

Phinot (FINOT), Dominique (*c.* 1510–*c.* 1555)

French composer. He was associated with the courts of Urbino and Pesaro in Italy and wrote many motets and chansons.

picaresque

Literary term which became current in the 19th century, derived from the mid-16th-century Castilian insult 'pícaro' ('person mocked for being poor'). It refers to prose work of episodic plot and variable length, narrated in the first or third person. These fictional narratives concern unscrupulous, often unpleasant characters whose actions (and the actions of those around them) provide both comedy and a critique of contemporary society. The picaresque novel originated in Spain, enjoying popularity there between the mid-15th and the mid-17th centuries. The 1554 work ◊*Lazarillo de Tormes* is accepted by some as the first example of this slippery genre; other scholars prefer Mateo ◊Alemán's *Guzmán de Alfarache* (Part I, 1599), arguing that *Lazarillo* is merely its precursor.

Piccolomini, Aeneas Sylvius

See ◊Pius II.

Pico della Mirandola, Giovanni (1463–1494)

Italian minor noble and philosopher. Pico's short career was mainly spent in Florence in the circle around Lorenzo de' ◊Medici 'the Magnificent'. Though he was friends with Marsilio ◊Ficino and was involved in the discussions described as 'the Platonic academy', Pico's first interest was in the Arab commentator on Aristotle, Averroes. This interest and his fascination with the *cabbala* raised questions about his orthodoxy from Innocent VIII; it was only by the intervention of Lorenzo de' Medici that he escaped long imprisonment.

Giovanni Pico's nephew, **Gianfrancesco Pico della Mirandola** (1469–1533) collected together his uncle's

works and published them, with a biography imagining him as a paragon of virtue (1496). The *Life* and some of Pico's writings were subsequently translated into English by Thomas ◊More and printed in 1510.

Pienza

A Renaissance new town. Originally a small settlement called Corsignano, its most famous son, ◊Pius II, raised it to a city named after him. The pope planned, on designs worked out with Bernardo Rosellino, to create a symmetrical set of buildings and roads, centred on a small piazza with a palace, cathedral and town hall. Pius also expected his cardinals to build their own palaces in this remote location – some like the Frenchman, Jean Jouffroy, did. The city, however, remained incomplete at Pius's death.

Many churches in the cities of Italy are equal in size or even larger and not a few have more famous marble-work or paintings, but it will be difficult for anyone to think of a church as pleasingly proportioned as the Cathedral of St Matthew in Pienza.

FLAVIO BIONDO in conversation with Bernardo Rosellino about Pius II's city

---

Piero della Francesca (*c.* 1420–1492)

Painter from Borgon San Sepolcro in Umbria. Active in Arezzo and Urbino, he was one of the major artists of the 15th century. His work has a solemn stillness and unusually solid figures, luminous colour, and carefully calculated compositional harmonies. It includes several important fresco series, and panel paintings such as the *Flagellation of Christ* (*c.* 1455, Ducal Palace, Urbino), which is remarkable for its use of perspective.

Formal and austere, all his works, of whatever size or medium, show in their use of colour, perspective, and composition a fascination with mathematical order. His largest scale work is the fresco series *The Legend of the True Cross* (the Church of San Francesco, Arezzo) 1452–60; other works include the fresco *The Resurrection of Christ* (Pinacoteca, Borgo San Sepulcro); and the panel altarpiece *Madonna with the*

Duke of Urbino as Donor (Brera, Milan). The two famous panel paintings in the National Gallery, London, the *Baptism of Christ* and the *Nativity*, though closely related in style, are considered to be an early and late work respectively.

His portraits include *Federigo da Montefeltro* (*c.* 1470) and *Battista Sforza* (*c.* 1470, both Uffizi, Florence).

The oil method of these portraits suggests some acquaintance with Netherlandish painting, but in general the art of Piero is strongly individual in its poetry and contemplative spirit, and the feeling of intellectual force conveyed by its abstract treatment of space and form.

He was probably the pupil of Domenico Veneziano, and is first mentioned in 1439 when he was an assistant of Domenico, then painting frescoes in Sant' Egidio in Florence. He returned to his native town, no doubt with a valuable store of Florentine science, including that of perspective, and was employed there on panel paintings and frescoes. He also worked at Urbino, where he had the patronage of the Federigo da Montefeltro and his wife, of whom he painted famous portraits (Uffizi, Florence).

He visited Rome, where he painted frescoes in the Vatican for ◊Nicholas V. These were immense works in the Vatican library, in poor condition as early as the 16th century, when Raphael was commissioned to replace them. He also worked in Ferrara, Rimini, and Arezzo, where he painted his masterpieces of fresco 1452–60. He returned regularly to Borgo San Sepulcro, to which he seems to have been very attached. He gave up painting when about 60, as his sight was failing, and devoted himself to mathematical and philosophical studies. Two written treatises remain on the laws of perspective and mathematics.

Piero di Cosimo (*c.* 1462–*c.* 1521)

Florentine, idiosyncratic (if not mentally unstable) painter. As well as religious paintings, he produced inventive pictures of mythological subjects, often featuring fauns and centaurs, like the *Forest Fire* (Ashmolean Museum, Oxford).

The son of Lorenzo di Piero, he was the pupil of Cosimo ◊Rosselli, whose Christian name he adopted. Though influenced by Signorelli and Leonardo, he had a personal and whimsical imagination, which

gives a vivid life to his representations of the satyrs and centaurs of classical fable, and also shows itself in the various animals he introduced into his pictures.

His *Perseus and Andromeda* (Uffizi, Florence) presents a typically fantastic dragon, and his mythological scene, formerly known as *The Death of Procris* (National Gallery, London), like the work of his contemporary Botticelli in its delicate pathos, introduces a strange-looking faun.

Besides the paintings that survive, however, Piero produced, like many of his contemporaries, transient artwork lost to posterity. Giorgio ◊Vasari talks in his colourful life of Piero di Cosimo of his terrifying inventions made for the Carnival. He assisted Cosimo Rosselli in his frescoes in the ◊Sistine Chapel 1481–82. He was also the author of some strongly characterized portraits that have an element of Leonardesque caricature. He was the master of Andrea del Sarto.

> He kept himself constantly shut up and would not let himself be seen at work, leading the life of a man who was less a man than a beast. He would never have his rooms swept, he would only eat when hunger came to him, and he would not let his garden be worked or his fruit-trees pruned; for it pleased him to see everything wild, like his own nature, and he declared that Nature's own things should be left to her to look after, without lifting a hand to them.
>
> ~
>
> GIORGIO VASARI, *Lives*, on Piero di Cosimo

pietà (ITALIAN 'PITY')

A depiction of the Virgin Mary mourning over the body of Christ. See also ◊Biblical stories in art feature.

Pinturicchio (PINTORICCHIO, PSEUDONYM OF BERNARDINO DI BETTO) (*c.* 1454–1513)

Painter from Perugia. He produced fresco series for both the Borgia Apartments in the Vatican, painted in the 1490s, and in the Piccolomini Library of Siena Cathedral, 1503–08, illustrating the history of ◊Pius II.

He went to Rome 1481 as one of ◊Perugino's

assistants in the decorating of the ◊Sistine Chapel. He became very successful, his skill in large-scale narrative – pageants rich in detail and incident – proving popular with both church and nobility. An example of his work on a smaller scale is *The Return of Odysseus* (National Gallery, London).

Pirckheimer, Willibald (1470–1530)

German book-collector and humanist. His own writings included translations from Greek into Latin, and from both Classical languages into German. He also wrote *Bellum Helveticum/The Swiss War* (not published until 1610), a vivid account of his experiences in a military campaign in 1499. A renowned figure in German humanist circles, he was a correspondent of ◊Erasmus (they did not, however, meet) and also knew Philip ◊Melanchthon: in the early 1520s, he tended towards support of the Lutherans but later, like Erasmus, wrote against them (*De Vera Christi Carne/On Christ's True Body*, 1527).

Pirckheimer was born at Eichstätt into a wealthy Nuremberg commercial family with scholarly interests. He was sent to Padua and Pavia to study law, but showed more interest in Greek, philosophy, and the sciences. From his return in 1495 until 1523 he was a Nuremberg city councillor, and he led a contingent from Nuremberg in the Swiss war of 1499.

At the request of Emperor Maximilian I, he translated the *Hieroglyphica* of the Egyptian Horapollo from Greek into Latin, which provided inspiration for the two monumental woodcut celebrations of the Emperor (*Ehrenpforte/Triumphal Arch*, 1517; *Triumphzug/ Triumph*, 1526) for which some of the illustrations were provided by Pirckheimer's friend Albrecht ◊Dürer. It was probably through Pirckheimer that Dürer was introduced to the Emperor. Pirckheimer himself, in recognition of this and other imperial commissions, was an imperial councillor from 1514. His wealth enabled him to build up one of the largest private libraries in Germany, to collect ancient coins, and to hold open house for other scholars.

Pisa, Council of

◊General Council of the Church held in Pisa, Italy, in 1409 in an attempt to end the ◊Great Schism. It failed, managing instead to add another line of claimants to the dispute.

The Great Schism meant there was a pope in Rome and a rival pope in Avignon. The council was called by cardinals formerly of both factions. Deposing both existing popes (neither of whom recognized the council), they elected instead the cardinal archbishop of Milan, the learned Greek Peter Philargis, as Alexander V. The council quickly ended, leaving Alexander reliant on Baldassare Cossa, cardinal legate of Bologna (who in the following year was to succeed him as Pope John XXIII).

Pisanello (NICKNAME OF ANTONIO PISANO) (c. 1395–c. 1455)

Italian painter and medallist. He painted religious works and portraits in a style untouched by recent Florentine innovations, as in *Madonna and Child with St George and St Anthony Abbot* (c. 1445, National Gallery, London). He was also an outstanding portrait medallist. His frescoes in the Palazzo Ducale in Mantua were rediscovered after World War II.

life His early life was spent at Verona, where he was trained and worked with Gentile da Fabriano, completing frescoes (now destroyed) by Gentile, in Venice and Rome. As a painter and producer of portrait medallions moved from one Italian court to another, working for the Gonzagas in Mantua, the Visconti in Pavia, Sigismondo Malatesta in Rimini, Leonello d'Este in Ferrara, and, from 1448, for ◊Alfonso of Aragon in Naples.

work Of the few examples of his frescoes that remain, the *Annunciation* in the church of S Fermo, Verona, 1423–24, and the *St George* at Sta Anastasia, Verona, 1437–38, show his ornate manner, and on a small scale *The Legend of St Eustace* and *Madonna and Child with St George and St Anthony Abbot* (both National Gallery) are leading examples. He excelled in relief portraiture, and his drawings from nature, especially his beautiful animal studies, show an observation surpassing the conventions of the belated Gothic style.

The most important collection of his drawings is that of the *Codex Vallardi* of the Louvre, Paris, and the Victoria and Albert Museum in London has a notable collection of the medals.

Pisano, Andrea (c. 1290–c. 1348)

Italian sculptor. He made the earliest bronze doors for the Baptistery of Florence Cathedral, completed

Pisano, Andrea Grammar master and schoolchildren. *e.t. archive*

in 1336. He completed the campanile for the cathedral, designed by Giotto.

Pius II (BORN AENEAS SYLVIUS PICCOLOMINI) (1405–1464)

Pope from 1458. As celebrated before his election for his humanist writings as he was as pope for his attempts to organise a crusade. There was, however, a fissure between his two characters: the humanist had also been a supporter of ◊conciliarism; when Piccolomini was elected pope, he publicly declared his rejection of his previous writings advising others to abandon Aeneas and follow Pius.

Born near Siena, where he went to university, Piccolomini's early employment was as secretary to a string of ecclesiastics, including cardinal Niccolò

Albergati. In his entourage, he arrived at the Council of ◊Basel, where he was to remain for a decade (apart from a diplomatic mission to Scotland 1435–36, a place where he found the men unwelcoming and the women all too friendly). At Basel, he wrote a history of its deeds, *De Gestis Basiliensis Concilii* (1440) and became its spokesman in 1442. However, with the Council being increasingly ineffectual, in the same year, he entered the service of the emperor, Frederick III. Frederick often employed him as an emissary to Rome, where Piccolomini also received ecclesiastical preferment: bishop from 1449, cardinal from 1456.

Alongside his professional duties, Piccolomini produced a series of writings, of which two works of 1444 were the most popular: a novella, *De Duo Amantibus/Tale of Two Lovers* and an anticourt satire *De Curialium Miseriis/On the Miseries of Courtiers*. Other writings included biographies (*De Viris Aetate sua Claris/On Famous Men of his Age*, finished in 1450; *Historia Friderici Imperatoris/History of Frederick III*, completed before 1458) and tracts recanting his previous conciliarism.

As pope, he wrote increasingly less, although he did produce his autobiography, the *Commentaries*, both justifying his life and admitting his sins (which had included fathering a child by a married woman). However, in his pontificate his cultural interests were turned instead to patronage, in particular to converting his hometown, Corsignano, into ◊Pienza. Such interests, though, did not become preoccupations: the overriding concern of the pope was to organise a crusade to recapture Constantinople. He arranged a meeting of the rulers of Europe to discuss the plan – the Congress of Mantua 1459–60. While, like earlier general councils, this afforded scholars the chance to meet and to buy books (Vespasiano da ◊Bisticci visited it), it did not provide the Europe-wide support of which Pius had dreamt. He persisted, however, and arranged for a navy to meet at Ancona. He died there waiting for it to arrive.

Pius's life was remembered not only by his *Commentaries*; it was later remembered in frescoes in the Piccolomini library of the cathedral in Siena, commissioned from ◊Pinturicchio by Pius II's nephew, Francesco Piccolomini, who himself became pope taking the name Pius III but dying two months after his election in 1503.

Pius IV (born Giovanni Angelo de' Medici) (1499–1565)

Pope from 1559. Blessed with the Medici name, but not with their blood, he was born in Milan to a minor noble family. He achieved papal favour under Paul III and was made cardinal 1549. He was a continual advocate of a pro-Spanish policy which caused him difficulties in the pontificate of Paul IV; on Paul's death, however, he was elected (after three months of debate in conclave) his successor. During his pontificate, he relied on the assistance of his nephew, Cardinal Borromeo, and reconvened the Council of Trent which had been dormant for ten years.

The future Pius's own training had been in canon law and it was as a lawyer, as well as a diplomat, that he was employed by Paul III. As pope, he showed a wider interest in learning, revitalising the Roman university and patronizing the printing press of Paolo Manuzio (Aldus ◊Manutius's son). At the same time, Pius IV imitated the Medici popes, whose coat of arms duke Cosimo de' Medici allowed him to adopt, in his grandiose building projects, which included the building of S Maria degli Angeli in the ancient Baths of Diocletian to a design by Michelangelo, as well as laying out the Borgo Pio between the Vatican and the Castel Sant' Angelo.

Pius V (born Antonio Ghislieri) (1504–1572)

Pope from 1566. His early career was in the Inquisition, a role which brought him the support of Paul IV who made him a cardinal in 1558. From the beginning of his own pontification, he stressed his determination to carry out the reforms of the Council of Trent. He also excommunicated Elizabeth I of England, and organized the expedition against the Turks that won the victory of Lepanto.

Pizarro, Francisco (1475–1541)

Castilian adventurer, unofficial governor of Peru from 1535. There is a (false) legend that Pizarro was suckled by a Trujillo sow as a baby. He was practically illiterate. In 1509 he sailed for Santo Domingo. He accompanied Núñez de Balboa ◊Vasco on his 1513 expedition to find the Pacific Ocean, which alerted him to the existence of Peru. Arriving there in 1532, he seized control by murdering ◊Atahualpa in 1533. He fixed his capital at coastal Lima in 1535, but his hold was precarious, as his former friend Diego de Almagro claimed Andean Cuzco. Almagro's murder by Pizarro's brother in 1538 increased the tension, and Pizarro was murdered at his Lima palace by Almagro's supporters.

Placards, Day of

On 18 October 1534 Parisians woke up to find a set of broadsheets proclaiming the Zwinglian view of the Mass posted across their city. This outburst of fly-posting proved self-defeating. ◊Francis I, who had previously been fairly tolerant of evangelical views (at least in court circles), set about cracking down on heresy: burnings followed. The spate of repression, however, decreased after the edict of Coucy in 1535 which (optimistically) declared that heresy did not need to be persecuted as it had already been eradicated.

The author of the anonymous broadsheets remained a mystery in the 16th century; it seems to have been a French exile in Switzerland, Antoine Marcourt. Francis's ire is said to have been aroused by finding one of the placards outside his bedchamber. In the wake of the event, members of the court with Protestant leanings were especially in danger: Clément ◊Marot, for example, fled to the court of Marguerite of Navarre.

plateresque (Spanish 'plateresco')

Style of Spanish architecture in vogue during the first two thirds of the 16th century. The word was coined by a 17th-century historian to describe Seville Cathedral Royal Chapel and subsequently came to refer to a highly decorative, hybrid style which incorporated elements of Arabic, Gothic, and Renaissance Italian designs in its execution. Characteristic features include an abundance of medallions, niches, and columns decorated with bas-relief garlands.

Two outstanding examples of the plateresque style are the façades of the universities of Alcalá de Henares (by Rodrigo Gil de Hontañón, begun in 1542, completed in 1552) and of Salamanca (by Juan de Alava, about 1525).

THE PLATONIC ACADEMY OF FLORENCE

IN HIS PREFACE to his 1492 edition of Plotinus, the enigmatic, lyre-playing philosopher priest, Marsilio Ficino, described the foundation of a new Platonic Academy in the West. This Academy had been first conceived at the Council of Florence (1439) by the great Cosimo de' Medici, who heard Gemistos Plethon 'disputing like another Plato on the Platonic mysteries'. From this time Cosimo had 'conceived deep in his mind a kind of Academy, to give birth to at the first opportune moment'. Thus Cosimo destined Ficino, 'while still a boy, to the labour, educating me from that day forth to this very thing'. The direct fruits of these labours were Ficino's translations of Hermes Trismegistus, Plato, Plotinus, a number of Middle Platonists, and finally Dionysius the Areopagite. Ficino and his fellow Platonists believed that they had received and revived an ancient philosophical revelation handed down from the ancient Egyptians via Moses and Hermes thrice-blessed, transmitted through Orpheus and Pythagoras and consummated in Plato. The Academy sought to reveal the compatibility and utility of this religious philosophy to the Christian Faith.

Like many early Church fathers, Ficino and his fellow Platonists found much that was good, true, and beautiful in the world of antiquity. The great thinkers of all ages were witness to one truth, as Ficino wrote in the *De Amore*: 'Above the soul of man there must be some single wisdom which is not divided among various concepts, but is a single wisdom from whose single truth the manifold truth of men derives'. The numerous classically inspired works carried out by Ficino's philosophical companions (Pico's *Heptaplus* and *Conclusiones,* Poliziano's *Epictetus,* Landino's commentaries on Virgil and Dante, Giovanni Nesi's Pythagorean interpretations) bear witness to this enthusiasm.

The exact nature of the Platonic Academy has always intrigued scholars of the Renaissance period. Some have envisaged an institution which met regularly, celebrated Plato's feast day with symposia (as in the *De Amore)*, and comprised 'members' – including Giovanni Pico della Mirandola, Lorenzo the Magnificent, Poliziano, and Cristoforo Landino – who cooperated throughout their lives in re-establishing Platonic wisdom in the West. Recent scholarship has questioned the existence of any institutional association of Platonists around Ficino. Ficino himself, who often employed metaphorical or allegorical expressions, used the term 'Academy' at different times to denote different things. Yet Ficino's revived 'Academy' did indeed give rise to a group of philosophical friends, united by a shared enthusiasm for Plato. These friends met for philosophical discussion and religious contemplation at Careggi or the Camaldolese house of S Maria degli Angeli, where the exposition of Christian Platonism accompanied the recitation of the *Psalms.* For this circle, the ancient theology consisted of a spiritual experience which closely resembled, in both form and content, the Christian monastic life. In a letter to two friends cured by his spiritual medicines Ficino wrote how 'you paid your respects to the Academy, as if it were your own doctor. You then asked for and heard the sound of the lyre and the singing of hymns'. Attendents of these meetings included Lorenzo de' Medici's three sons, Piero, Giovanni, and Giuliano, Girolamo Benivieni, and Giovanni Pico della Mirandola. Accompanying this religious devotion was an aesthetic vision of love and beauty which linked the earthly with the divine. To Ficino and his companions, earthly desire was solely a rung on the ladder leading to the divine: 'He who uses love properly certainly praises the beauty of the body, but through that contemplates the higher beauty of the soul, the Mind and God, and admires and loves that more strongly'. The Academy believed that the soul, through Divine Love, 'kindled by the flames of virtue, and growing stronger from celestial rays, seeks to return to the sublime heights of heaven'.

After Ficino's death in 1499, the teachings of the Academy were perpetuated by his Florentine disciple Francesco da Diacetto, whose *De Pulchro* and *De Amore* further developed the philosophy of earthly and celestial love. In Venice the Aldine Academy – with links to the Florentine circles around Diacetto became another centre of

continued

Platonic enthusiasm. The Aldine editor of Dante, Pietro Bembo, praised Platonic philosophy through the mouth of a hermit in his *Asolani* of the early 1500s. Ficino's follower Baldassare da Castiglione popularized these themes of the Platonic Academy in his book of the *Courtier* (1507–08), where he affirms: 'Beauty is goodness, and so true love of beauty is good and holy'. The *Courtier* consists of a series of discussions set at Urbino, and attended by several loyal Ficinians, including Diacetto and Giuliano de' Medici. Here Pietro Bembo ends his masterpiece with a eulogy of love worthy of the Platonic Academy of Florence:

'O most sacred Love...with the rays of your light cleanse our eyes of their misty ignorance, so that they may no longer prize mortal beauty but know that the things which they first thought to see are not, and that those they did not see truly are. Accept the sacrifice of our souls; and burn them in the living flame that consumes all earthly dross, so that wholly freed from the body we may unite with divine beauty in a sweet and perpetual bond and that we, liberated from our own selves, like true lovers can be transformed into the object of our love'.

DENNIS LACKNER

Further Reading
Raymond Marcel, *Marsile Ficin (1433–1499)* (Paris); James Hankins; 'Cosimo de' Medici and the 'Platonic Academy''; *Journal of the Warburg and Courtauld Institutes*, 53 (1990), 144–62 and idem 'The Myth of the Platonic Academy of Florence', *Renaissance Quarterly* (1991), 429–75

Platina (PEN NAME OF BARTOLOMMEO DEI SACCHI) (1421–1481)

Italian humanist author. His varied career began with a spell as a mercenary soldier but he seems to have decided he preferred letters to arms. He entered the service of Federico I Gonzaga, marchese of Mantua, as a tutor to his children; to his employer, he dedicated his mirror-for-princes tract, *De Principe*. Later, Platina settled in Rome as secretary to one his former pupils, now cardinal Francesco Gonzaga. In the pontificate of ◊Paul II, his involvement in the circle around Pomponio ◊Leto led to his arrest in 1468, an indignity he did not forget when he came to write that pope's biography. His fortunes, however, reached their height in the next pontificate, when Sixtus IV appointed him librarian of the Vatican Library.

His writings included a life of ◊Vittorino da Feltre, a panegyric of cardinal ◊Bessarion, a history of Mantua written in 1466–69 and his influential (but hastily written) *Liber de Vita Christi ac Omnium Pontificum* (1471–74). He also

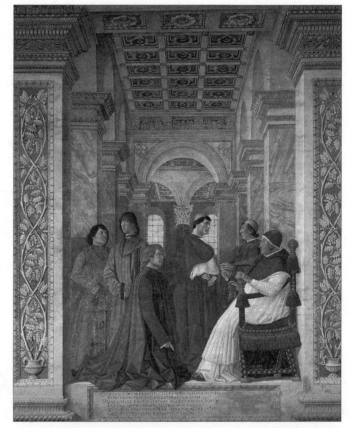

Platina Melozzo da Forli, fresco *c.* 1476 (transferred onto canvas) of Sixtus IV appointing Platina as librarian of the Vatican library (Pinacoteca Vaticana). Platina kneels before the pope, while around Sixtus crowd his nephews, including (second left) the future Julius II. *AKG London/Erich Lessing*

produced editions of Classical texts, including one of Josephus's *Jewish War* which was printed by Pannartz in 1475.

Plautus, Titus Maccius (*c.* 250–*c.* 184 BC)

Roman comic dramatist. Born in Umbria, he settled in Rome and began writing plays in about 224 BC. Twenty-one comedies survive in his name; 35 other titles are known.

Eight Plautus plays were known before the 15th century and 12 more were added by a discovery of ◊Nicholas of Cusa. Plautus was repeatedly imitated by humanist playwrights like Tito Livio ◊Frulovisi, ◊Machiavelli, and ◊Ariosto; the first printed edition of his works was made by Giorgio ◊Merula in 1472. In the 16th century, some of Plautus' plays were also translated into most European vernaculars.

Pléiade, La

group of seven poets in 16th-century France, led by Pierre ◊Ronsard, who aimed to break away from the medieval poetic tradition by seeking inspiration in Classical Greek and Latin works, and to make the French language a suitable medium for all literary purposes. The other poets, according to Ronsard, were Joaquim ◊du Bellay, Jean Antoine de ◊Baïf, Rémi ◊Belleau, Etienne ◊Jodelle, Pontus de Tyard (1521–1605), and Jacques ◊Peletier, but the name of the humanist scholar Jean ◊Dorat is sometimes substituted for that of Peletier. The views of the group were first set out in du Bellay's *Défense et illustration de la langue française* (1549), and the name is derived from the seven stars of the Pleiades group.

Plethon (ADOPTED NAME OF GEORGIUS GEMISTUS) (*c.* 1360–1452)

Byzantine teacher, whose pupils included ◊Bessarion. Late in life, Plethon was a member of the Orthodox delegation to the Council of ◊Florence. At this time, he produced (in Greek) the discussion *De Differentiis Platonis et Aristotelis/On the Differences Between Plato and Aristotle* (1439); this not only praised Plato but criticized Aristotle, whose philosophy, Plethon claimed, was irreconcilable with Christianity. Plethon's reading of Plato, however, influenced as it was by ◊Plotinus, did not provide an interpretation

that accorded with Christianity as understood by his Catholic humanist audience. Indeed, some of his contemporaries – most vociferously ◊George of Trebizond – considered that his Platonism had led him into paganism.

Pleydenwurff, Hans (*c.* 1420–1472)

German painter. He was active in Nuremberg after 1450. In his *Crucifixion* altarpiece about 1460 (Alte Pinakothek, Munich), the influence of Netherlandish art appears in the rich detail and elaborate landscape background.

Pliny (GAIUS PLINIUS SECUNDUS), THE ELDER (*c.* AD 23–79)

Ancient Roman scientific encyclopedist and historian. Many of his works have been lost, but in *Historia naturalis/ Natural History*, probably completed in AD 77, Pliny surveys all the known sciences of his day, notably astronomy, meteorology, geography, mineralogy, zoology, and botany.

The *Natural History* was well known before the 15th century, although it and its author suffered some tribulations. The medieval Pliny was, for several centuries, a composite character, rolling into one the encyclopedist and his letter-writing nephew. An attempt to dispel this confusion was made by one of the ◊prehumanists, Giovanni Mansionario (active 1305–20). There had also arisen – as was inevitable in a culture of manuscripts – defects in the text of the *Natural History*; an attempt to remove these was first made by ◊Guarino da Verona's 'critical edition' of the text, and this was also a concern of later commentators.

The *Natural History*, indeed, gained a certain vogue in the second half of the 15th century. Not only was it one of the earliest books printed in Italy (Venice, 1469) and not only was it translated into Italian by Cristoforo ◊Landino (a version which was printed three times in the 15th century); it also attracted the interest of a series of humanists, including Niccolò ◊Perotti (whose work was enlarged by Cornelio ◊Vitelli), ◊Politian, and Ermolao Barbaro the Younger. In part, this interest was inspired by Pliny's unusual vocabulary; in part, because his work provided an entrée into a world of learning which, to a large extent, had otherwise been lost. This world

LONDON'S OPEN-AIR PLAYHOUSES

WITH THE PLAYS of Shakespeare, Marlowe, and Jonson now firmly established in the literary canon, it can be hard to appreciate fully the contemporary struggle involved in the establishment of professional theatre in Elizabethan and Jacobean London. The position of the acting company in early Elizabethan England was precarious to say the least. The social status of the actor lay on a par with beggars and vagabonds and the law required that troupes of players find an aristocratic patron who would accept nominal responsibility for them. Even with a powerful sponsor, the authorities of the City of London disapproved of acting as a morally corrupting influence, considering mass audiences a threat to political stability and public health. (Under both Elizabeth and James, outbreaks of plague in London would result in the temporary closure of all playhouses.) The obstacles to establishing professional acting companies within the capital were all too real but the potential returns from an urban audience eager for entertainment proved sufficient incentive for some hardy entrepreneurs.

The first attempt to provide a purpose-built theatrical venue, the Red Lion in Stepney, dates from the mid-1560s but, then as now, location dictates business success and it is with the opening in 1576 of the aptly named Theatre in Shoreditch that the story of the London playhouses really accelerates. Built to the north of the city walls on the site of the dissolved Holywell Priory, the Theatre lay outside the jurisdiction of the City authorities but was easily accessible by its target audience. The man of vision behind the project was James Burbage (c. 1530–97), carpenter, actor, and theatre manager. His success with the Theatre would be emulated by others as playhouses mushroomed on the skirts of the city – the Curtain, the Rose, the Swan, the Globe, and the Fortune were all extant by 1600.

By the 1590s, there were two dominant acting companies competing for business in London, the Lord Admiral's Men and the Lord Chamberlain's Men. The Lord Admiral's Men had the star actor Edward Alleyn (1566–1622) and the company was financed by the businessman Philip Henslowe (c. 1550–1616), who built the Rose, the first playhouse on the south bank of the Thames, in 1587. Henslowe's *Diary,* a detailed account of economic transactions in the theatre business, recording house takings, loans made to actors, payments made to dramatists, and so on, provides crucial primary evidence for the historian. That it should be available to us at all is indirect proof of his business acumen. By 1592 Edward Alleyn had married Henslowe's stepdaughter and the two men remained close business partners thereafter. Growing financial security for Alleyn led to his founding of Dulwich College in 1613 and it is Alleyn who left Henslowe's papers to the library there.

Formed in 1594, the Lord Chamberlain's Men (later the King's Men under James I) arranged their affairs somewhat differently. Rather than relying on an external financier, members of the company shared both profits and costs. First among equals in the company was James Burbage's son, Richard (c. 1569–1619). He played the lead in the major tragedies written specifically for the company by their resident playwright, Shakespeare, but just as much a crowd-puller for the company as Burbage was the clown, William Kempe (?–c.1603). Associated with the Lord Chamberlain's Men until 1599, Kempe was renowned for his visual style of humour. He danced the jigs that closed each comic performance and, undoubtedly, his fame in this regard was a great asset in attracting audiences to the company's productions.

The Lord Chamberlain's Men were commonly housed at the Theatre but the lease on the land expired in 1597, and negotiations between James Burbage's sons and the landlord were abortive. The doubtful legality of what happened next has become a celebrated story, clear evidence of the high stakes required for theatrical success. In December of 1598 the Burbage brothers had the Theatre dismantled and, the following month, the timbers crossed the Thames to become building materials in the construction of the new playhouse, the Globe. The Lord Chamberlain's Men's midnight flit south of the river also offers us a clear picture of how shareholdings worked within the company. It cost £700 to build the

continued

Globe. Richard Burbage and his brother Cuthbert put up half the capital and five other 'sharers' including Kempe and Shakespeare raised the remainder. The actor-shareholders had become in effect their own landlords at the Globe.

Elizabethan theatre design developed from the temporary staging used in inn yards and animal-baiting arenas. The 'wooden O' was a polygonal building where a raised apron stage extended out into the spectators' courtyard, encircled on three sides by tiered galleries. Playgoers chose either to stand in the uncovered yard or to pay more money for a seat in a gallery. The stage itself would have been almost entirely bare, using virtually no representational scenery and employing only simple mechanical illusions. Costumes, however, would have been luxurious: a major part of a company's assets lay in their stock of velvet robes and embroidered gowns. The public season ran from autumn to summer and performances took place in the afternoons to make use of natural light. The turnover of plays in a season could be staggering: the Lord Admiral's Men in 1594–95 presented 38 plays, 21 of them new. Certain plays might well call for more roles than there were actors in a company and so the doubling of parts was standard practice, as was the employment of 'hired men', actors paid by the week to take on minor roles. Moreover, as no women acted on the English public stage before the Restoration, the women's parts were played by boys. Individual playhouses certainly attracted different audiences and the variant states of extant playtexts suggests that plays could also be easily adapted to suit requirements but it seems undeniable that the growth of this form of popular culture in London affected a wide cross-section of society: merchants and their wives, lawyers, whores, visitors, apprentices, young aristocrats, pickpockets, and servants all visited the London theatres until their closure in 1642 at the start of the English Civil War.

MARGARET KEAN

Further Reading
Andrew Gurr, *The Shakespearian Playing Companies* (Oxford: Clarendon Press, 1996)

---

included that of ancient art: Pliny, for example, provided an ◊ekphrasis of a statue which was identified with the rediscovered ◊*Laocoon*. For this reason – and because of his discussion of the high standing of ancient artists – Pliny's work became of interest to artists as well as to scholars.

While so many books have not been as much disguarded as shipwrecked, while they have not as much been lost as annihilated, we are not completely hated by the gods when Pliny survives; he, however mutilated, incomplete and mangled he is, can sustain us.

∼

ERMOLAO BARBARO on the survival of Pliny the Elder's *Natural History*

Pliny (GAIUS PLINIUS CAECILIUS SECUNDUS), THE YOUNGER (*c.* AD 61–113)

Ancient Roman administrator, nephew of ◊Pliny the Elder. His literary remains consist mainly of his correspondence; among his surviving letters are those describing the eruption of Vesuvius, his uncle's death, and his correspondence with the emperor Trajan. To the emperor, he also addressed a *Panegyric*.

Pliny's *Letters*, though well known, did not circulate in their complete form until the 16th century. The only complete manuscript, dating from the 5th century, survived in Paris, where it was 'discovered' by Giovanni ◊Giocondo some time around the turn of the century. Combining the most recent printed editions and his own transcription of the relevant sections of this manuscript, Guillaume ◊Budé was the first person to have a complete 'edition' of the *Letters*, but this was only for his private study. Around the same time, Aldus ◊Manutius heard of the Paris manuscript and managed to get it transported to Venice; his complete edition was printed in 1508.

Pliny's *Panegyric*, meanwhile, was a 15th-century rediscovery: a manuscript of it was found in Mainz by Giovanni ◊Aurispa in 1433. It soon gained a Europe-wide circulation (Pier Candido ◊Decembrio sent a copy to ◊Humfrey, Duke of Gloucester) and was translated into several vernacular languages. In print, it often appeared with Pliny's letters, as in the Aldine edition.

Plotinus (AD 204/05–270)

Platonist philosopher. Egyptian by birth, he taught in Rome, where his pupils included Porphyry, who later edited Plotinus' philosophical discussions, the *Enneads*. He had a plan to build a city governed by Plato's political ideas; perhaps fortunately for human happiness, the scheme came to nothing.

Early 15th-century humanists including Giovanni ◊Aurispa and Francesco ◊Filelfo had copies of Plotinus, but interest in his work seems to have come later in the century. When Argyropoulos lectured in Florence in 1457, he made use of the *Enneads*, which was eventually translated by Marsilio ◊Ficino in 1484–92, complete with a commentary. This edition was widely read and influenced men as diverse as Robert ◊Gaguin, John ◊Colet, and Giordano ◊Bruno.

Plummer, John (c. 1410–c. 1484)

English composer. His surviving works consist of four antiphons for two and four voices, a Mass, *Omnipotens Pater*, and a Mass fragment.

He was a clerk of the Chapel Royal by 1441 and in 1444 became the first official master of its children. In about 1458 he became verger at St George's Chapel, Windsor, while continuing as a member of the Chapel Royal; he held the Windsor post until 1484.

poet laureate

Poet celebrated for their work by being crowned with a laurel wreath. An ancient Roman custom, it was revived in 14th-century Italy. Albertino ◊Mussato was crowned in 1315 by his fellow Paduans; and in emulation, ◊Petrarch orchestrated his own crowning on the Capitoline Hill, Rome, in 1341. These examples set precedents which were much repeated across Europe: for example, in England in the early 16th century, John ◊Skelton boasted of having been crowned three times over.

The concept of an English poet laureate as an official royal verse writer dates only from the 17th century.

Poggio Bracciolini (1380–1459)

Versatile Florentine humanist of Niccolò ◊Niccoli's circle. He created the humanist script, ◊*littera antiqua*; he discovered – or, as he put it, 'liberated' – manuscripts of hitherto little-known Classical texts held in northern European monasteries; he developed the humanist dialogue form; and, in his last years, he was chancellor of Florence (1453–59). He had a keen eye for the humorous (and for pretty women), but he also had a devout sense of Christian morality.

Poggio was a humanist in his leisure time; his day job, from 1403, was as a papal secretary. In this capacity, he attended the Council of ◊Constance, but spent his time searching monastic libraries for rare Classical works. Poggio's literary activity began relatively late in life; beginning with his time in England (1419–22), he wrote letters to Niccoli which he later published. His first dialogue, *Contra Avaritiam*, appeared in 1428; others, including *De Infelicitate Principum* (1440) and *De Varietate Fortunae* (1448) followed. In later life, he wrote in a series of genres: a *Historia Florentina* (1457), a Latin translation of ◊Xenophon's *Cyropedia* (1446), a series of invectives (he fell into bitter dispute with, at one point, Lorenzo ◊Valla, at another, Francesco ◊Filelfo) and a scurrilous – and popular – set of ◊*Facetiae*.

Pole, Reginald (1500–1558)

English cleric. A cousin of ◊Henry VIII, he alienated himself from the king by his opposition to his divorce. Pole left England in 1532 and, in 1536, wrote a tract attacking Henry; in the same year, he was made a cardinal. He settled in Rome, where he moved in literary and church-reforming circles, which included Vittoria ◊Colonna. On the accession of Mary, however, he returned to his homeland to assist with the rebuilding of Catholic England, becoming archbishop of Canterbury in 1536. His efforts were overshadowed, ironically by his former colleague, now Paul IV's, accusations of heresy against him. He died on the same day as Mary.

Politian, Angelo Poliziano (PEN NAME OF ANGELO AMBROGINI) (1454–1494)

Italian humanist poet and Classical scholar. Educated in Florence by, among others, John ◊Argyropoulos, Cristoforo ◊Landino, and Marsilio Ficino, Politian came to the attention of Lorenzo de' ◊Medici when he dedicated to him his translation of part of Homer's *Iliad* in 1470. Poems in Greek, Latin, and the *volgare* followed, including his *Stanze per la giostra di Giuliano de' Medici/Verses on the Joust of Giuliano de' Medici* begun in 1475, but left unfinished probably because of Giuliano's murder by the Pazzi in 1478 – an incident that provoked Politian's *Sallustianum De Pactiana Coniuratione Comment-arium*. He was appointed tutor to Lorenzo's son, Piero de' Medici, in 1475, and professor of Greek and Latin at the Florentine *studio* in 1480. Much of his philological work, for example on Pliny's *Natural History*, was collected together in his *Miscellaneorum Centuria* (1489).

Pollaiuolo, Antonio del (*c.* 1432–1498) AND Piero del (*c.* 1441–*c.* 1496)

Florentine brothers who ran an artistic workshop in their home town and later in Rome. Antonio, considered by contemporaries the better artist (Lorenzo de' ◊Medici called him 'the leading artist of this city, perhaps of all time'), specialized in sculpture and was known for his detailed study of the male ◊anatomy; Piero concentrated on painting. Together they produced works like the altarpiece, *The Martyrdom of St Sebastian* (1475, National Gallery, London). Their largest commissions were the tombs of ◊Innocent VIII (commissioned by himself) and of ◊Sixtus IV (paid for by the future ◊Julius II).

Piero's individual work included a fresco cycle of *Virtues* (1469, Uffizi, Florence) and an *Annunciation* (*c.* 1470, Gemäldegalerie, Berlin). Antonio's work in different media – his bronze statuette of *Hercules and Antaeus*, *c.* 1475–80 for example, or his engraving, *The Battle of the Nude Gods* (*c.* 1470–5) – were noted for their fascinations with anatomy. Giorgio ◊Vasari praised *The Martyrdom of St Sebastian* because it carefully depicted the tense muscles of archers straining to reload their crossbows.

Ponce de León, Juan (*c.* 1460–1521)

Spanish soldier and explorer. He is believed to have sailed with Columbus in 1493, and served 1502–04 in Hispaniola. He conquered Puerto Rico in 1508, and was made governor in 1509. In 1513 he was the first European to reach Florida.

He returned to Spain 1514 to report his 'discovery' of Florida (which he thought was an island), and was given permission by King Ferdinand to colonize it. He died in Cuba from an arrow wound.

Pontan, Jirí (ALSO KNOWN AS PONTANUS) (*c.* 1550–1614)

Hungarian writer and Jesuit priest. He combined the religious fervour of his order with a cosmopolitan intellectual outlook, which was characteristic of the court circle of ◊Rudolf II, of which he was a member. He wrote poetry, orations, and scientific works, and amassed a large library.

Pontano, Giovanni (1429–1503)

Italian humanist and poet. His Latin poetry includes *Amorum Libri Duo* and *De Amore Coniugali*. He also wrote *De Bello Napoletano* describing his master ◊Alfonso V's fight to secure the kingdom of Naples.

He was born in Cerreto, Umbria. At the age of 18 he entered the service of Alfonso V, under whom, and his successor, Ferrante I, he occupied high office. Pontano became a key figure in what is called to ◊Neapolitan Academy.

Pontormo, Jacopo da (KNOWN AS JACOPO CARUCCI) (1494–1557)

Italian painter. He produced a wide variety of compositions in Florence throughout his career, and was praised by contemporaries for his virtuosity as a draughtsman and strong compositional design. His bold, expressive figures and striking colour contrasts were hugely influential to later artists, including ◊Bronzino.

Born in a small town outside of Florence, Pontormo was briefly employed in the workshop of ◊Andrea del Sarto, although his status may have been as a collaborator rather than an apprentice. He developed a highly individual style characterized by detailed figure studies from life, combined with the dramatic manipulation of light and shadow to define forms crisply, as can be seen in the *Virgin and Child with Saints* (*c.* 1530), in San Michele in Visdomini, Florence.

During the 1520s his work underwent a change of style under the influence of ◊Michelangelo, which placed renewed emphasis on the human form, as can be seen in the frescos for the Medici villa at Poggio a Caiano. He was also inspired by the engravings of ◊Dürer, whose compositions strongly influenced his frescoes at the Certosa of Florence. He was occupied on the ambitious project to fresco the choir of the Medici church of San Lorenzo, Florence, in the last decade of his life, which he left unfinished on his death and the work he had done was later destroyed.

A fragment of his personal diary from his later years survives, and provides a direct testimony to his introverted and lonely character.

Poppi, Francesco (KNOWN AS FRANCESCO MORANDINI) (c. 1544–1597)

Italian painter. Follower of Giorgio ◊Vasari who collaborated on the painted decorations of the Palazzo Vecchio in Florence, he was a prolific artist who produced altarpieces for a wide range of patrons throughout Tuscany. Revered in his day for his sophisticated use of vivid colours and graceful, elegant forms which were inspired by his mastery of ◊*disegno*, characterisic examples of his work are his paintings for the *studiolo* of Francesco de' Medici, Florence.

Pordenone, Giovanni Antonio Sacchi (1483–1539)

Painter from Friuli, Italy. He painted religious frescoes and altarpieces in various cities of northern Italy. Pordenone is associated with the Venetian School and his work shows the fashionable 16th-century tendency (sometimes described as Mannerism) towards exaggeration.

It is assumed that he visited Rome, from the traces of the influence of ◊Raphael Sanzio and ◊Michelangelo that have been detected in his style.

Porta, Costanzo (c. 1529–1601)

Italian monk and composer. He was a pupil of Adrian Willaert at Venice. He took holy orders and became choirmaster at Osimo near Ancona 1552–64, then went to Padua to take up a similar post at the Cappella Antoniana, the church of the Minorite order to which he belonged. He left for a time to work at Ravenna 1567–74, then at Loreto 1574–80. He returned to Ravenna and lived there 1580–89.

Works include:

Fifteen masses, 200 motets, psalms, hymns, introits, and other church music, five books of madrigals 1555–86.

Porta, Giambattista della (c. 1541–1615)

Italian physicist. He helped found the Accademia dei Oziosi and the Academia Secretorum Naturae, where groups of students could discuss scientific ideas. He wrote *Magia Naturalis/Natural Magic* (1558) which considers magic as techniques for controlling nature, and various works on optics, gardening, and physiognomy.

The Academia Secretorum Naturae was closed by Pope Paul V in 1610 at the instigation of the Inquisition.

Portinaro, Francesco (c. 1520–AFTER 1578)

Italian composer. He was associated with the *Accademia degli Elevati* at Padua in 1557, and later with the d'Este family at Ferrara and Tivoli. His three books of motets and six of madrigals were published at Venice.

Postel, Guillaume (1510–1581)

French scholar, philologist, philosopher, cabalist, traveller, and novelist. Postel had an extraordinary career in France and Italy and produced over 60 works: an agitator for liberal reform at the Council of Trent, his flirtation with doctrinal heresy also included his self-identification in a messianic role and his condemnation by Rome in 1555. Postel's mystical, prophetic writings are even more obscure, certainly more scholarly and possibly more fascinating to contemporaries than those of ◊Nostradamus.

Power, Leonel (c. 1375–1445)

English composer and theorist. He wrote a treatise on the singing of descant and composed Masses, including *Alma Redemptoris*, motets, and other church music.

Praise of Folly, The (LATIN 'ENCOMIUM MORIAE')

A prose satire written in Latin by ◊Erasmus and published in 1511. In a fashion of which Lucian would have been proud, Erasmus damns by praising many forms of human folly, not even sparing contemporary theologians. This last point made his work controversial, with Martin Dorp the first to attack it in 1515, exciting responses from both Erasmus and his English friend, Thomas ◊More. The work was an extraordinary bestseller: 42 Latin editions appeared in Erasmus's lifetime and it was soon translated into French (1520), German (1520), and English (1549).

It was written in its earliest form at the London home of Thomas More, and its Latin title – *Encomium Moriae* – is a pun on More's name, *moros* being 'fool' in Greek.

predella

Base of an altarpiece, often painted with a series of incidents connected with the subjects of the main panels; for example, scenes from a saint's life.

THE POWER OF PROPHECY, 1200–1600: APOLLO REDIVIVUS

THE RENAISSANCE PERIOD witnessed a particularly intense outpouring of mysterious insight and inspired visionary activity; an outpouring that flooded and sometimes threatened to drown rulers and ruled alike. The term 'prophecy' has two meanings; the first, 'speaking forth', *praedicatio* (hence 'prediction'), describes preaching an interpretation of Scripture. Such exegeses, packaged as injunctions for the present, could veer dangerously close to heresy, offering a threat to eschatological doctrine and to social stability. The rise of the mendicant orders after 1200, often itinerant preachers whose sermons roused audiences to hysteria, brought skilled prophesying into the Renaissance marketplace. These *praedicatores* often slid into the second mode of 'prophecy' – prognostication – operating outside the control of local political or ecclesiastical entities, and/or using non-canonical texts: local office-holders were often powerless to control what they saw, from their perspective accurately, as dangerous, heretical rabble-rousers.

This was not, however, a merely popular phenomenon: the power of prophecy to disturb and obsess its audiences was felt in the courts of Renaissance lords and popes alike. The mysterious writings of Joachim of Fiore (d.1202), partly heretical, had a profound influence on understandings of the history of the Church and the world throughout the later Renaissance period. As well as

symbolically dividing time itself, his works included two particularly influential prophecies: the first, that an order of holy men, *viri spirituales*, would purify the world – an inheritance seized by the 'spiritual' Franciscans. Second, he anticipated a *pastor angelicus*, a future 'holy leader' of humanity. Throughout the Renaissance, a temporal but sacred ruler, usually a past emperor reborn, was sought with increasing fervour: in Emperor Henry VII by ◊Dante, in Charles IV in the 1350s by ◊Cola di Rienzo and ◊Petrarch, and in ◊Charles V in the 1520s; in ◊Charles VII of France, by ◊Joan of Arc, in the 1420s, and in his descendent ◊Charles VIII, invader of Italy in the 1490s.

Disastrous political and economic events from 1300 belied and undermined the literary promise of a new Golden Age; the resulting foreboding was as much a part of Renaissance culture as optimism and anticipation. During the ◊Avignon exile, one seer after another pressured the papacy to return to Rome, his 'spouse', the New Jerusalem prophesied in the Book of Revelation. The return to Rome after 1378 brought only temporary relief; prophets swiftly claimed one or other ◊Schismatic pope as the Antichrist foretold in Revelation. The malaise at the vulnerable centre of Christendom, Rome, was still evident a century later; the Sack by 'Holy Roman' troops in 1527 acquired a profoundly symbolic meaning as a foreboding of holocaust. It was even more obvious on the margins of Christendom; the

incursions of the ◊Ottoman Turks, following the definitive collapse of Constantinople in 1454, heralded the arrival of the forces of Antichrist in the predictions of cardinals and village wise-women alike. And the prophetic writing was not merely on the wall: the new printing presses of the Renaissance era permitted the distribution of broadsheets, with images of prodigies and portents, across the whole of society. *Fin de siècle* tensions accelerated the process: the discovery in 1492 of the New World was frequently interpreted as a positive sign of Christ's imminent return to earth – the Second Coming – when all peoples would be converted.

The danger of prognostication as a threat to ecclesiastical as well as civic authority approached a zenith around 1500. The challenge to papal executive authority offered by ◊conciliarism marched side by side with cries, often couched in apocalyptic language, for the reform of a corrupt institution, beginning at the top – the pope. These cries came not least from within the curia itself, which around 1500 housed a number of cardinals and other senior prelates who preached prophetically while operating politically (most notably ◊Egidio of Viterbo). When ◊Leo X was elected in 1511 he attempted, through the Fifth Lateran ◊Council, to curb prophetic activity – partly a personal grudge against the memory of the hell-fire preacher ◊Savonarola,

continued

whose cries of damnation helped exile his ◊Medici forebears from Florence in 1494. But the presence of so many 'pro-prophecy' churchmen pulled the punch of Leo's Bull of 1516, *Supernae majestatis praesidio*.

It was already too late to stem the tide towards reform. The ◊German Reformation was fuelled by apocalyptic images of pope as Antichrist, or the Beast (Romanist opponents asserted the same of ◊Luther, of course), circulating in print. It took the decrees the ◊Council of Trent to stem the flow of Catholic predictions. The subsequent crackdown on unorthodox preaching, discrediting the authenticity of prophetic (even of scholarly) inspiration, was typified in 1600 by the trial and burning of Giordano ◊Bruno.

Meanwhile, non-biblical prophesying in the north could attract the attention of the witch hunters. And well before *Supernae* drew a firmer line between biblical interpretation and other arcane forms of divination, the practice of consulting astrologers (such as ◊Pierre d'Ailly and ◊Annio of Viterbo) at courts across Europe had taken hold. Astrology, in fact, was a Renaissance 'science', like alchemy, which enjoyed a measure of respectability. This form of foretelling the future had powerful ancient antecedents, of course. New scientific modes of discerning the future are a distinct, generally overlooked aspect of the celebrated classical heritage of Rome and Greece 'renewed' by Renaissance intellectuals.

Sacrifice, smoke, blood, and visions of the future took less elevated, if equally 'classical' forms, too. The practitioners of such arts occupied a precarious position – sometimes uncomfortably close to the pyre – within the patronage of the elite. The relationship of John Dee and his scrying stone with ◊Elizabeth I, the mixed reaction to Michel de Nôtredame (◊'Nostradamus') at the French royal court, and the reception of Guillaume ◊Postel by the Medici dukes of Florence, all testify to the simultaneous suspicion and fascination in which such charismatic figures were held in the later 16th century.

Every feature, then, of Renaissance culture and history had its prophetic *alter ego*: the revival of classical ideas and ideals, the sharpening of textual scholarship, the geographical discoveries, the printing press, and communication between rulers and ruled; the witch hunts and the Inquisition, Protestant and Catholic Reformations, the incursions of the Turks in the east and the new, grandiose monarchical styles of the west. Renaissance 'divines' enjoyed ecstatic or troubled visions of the future rather than 'enlightenment': indeed, the self-conscious identification of a new age, involving rebirth and regeneration, owed a considerable debt to the prevalence of prophetic modes of thought across European society.

AMANDA COLLINS

Further Reading

O Niccoli, *Prophecy and People in Renaissance Italy* (Princeton, 1990); M E Reeves, *The Influence of Prophecy in the Later Middle Ages* (Oxford, 1969)

pre-humanists

The term 'pre-humanists' (or 'proto-humanists') was invented in the mid-20th century to describe a handful of late 13th- and early 14th-century Italian scholars. Their interests have struck historians as having notable similarities with the activities of the likes of Petrarch or Poggio; they are, in other words, thought to anticipate the humanists.

In some cases, their reputation as precursors originates with humanists themselves: for Albertino Mussato (and for the less well-documented Geri d'Arezzo), a place among the revivers of learning was set aside by Coluccio Salutati; similarly, the learning of Mussato's teacher, Lovato Lovati, was praised by Petrarch. For all their rhetoric of achieving a rebirth, early humanists were aware that they were not the first scholars in medieval history.

It is also easy to draw parallels with later scholarly interests: in Lovati's delight in referring to rare Roman writers, like Catullus; in Benzo d'Alessandria's touring of libraries in search of Classical manuscripts; in Giovanni Mansionario's desire to unravel the confusion over the identity of Pliny. These pre-humanists also shared with the devotees of *studia humanitatis* a sense of their civic identity. Yet, to call these – and other – earlier writers 'pre-humanists' is to use the perspective of hindsight. Their interests may have been echoed by the generations following Petrarch but, equally, they were not unprecedented in medieval Europe. They could plausibly be seen as examples of the fitful, localized fascination in the Classical world which repeatedly appears in the so-called Middle Ages.

Previtali, Andrea (ANDREA CORDELIAGHI) (c. 1470–1528)

Painter from near Bergamo. He worked in Venice and (from 1511) Bergamo, and painted religious subjects and portraits. He was a pupil of Giovanni Bellini, and his later work was influenced by Lorenzo ◊Lotto.

Primaticcio, Francesco (c. 1504–1570)

Bolognese painter, sculptor, architect, and decorator. Sent to France in 1532 to assist with the decoration of the palace at ◊Fontainebleau, he worked alongside Rosso ◊Fiorentino, and developed an innovatory combination of painting and stucco work.

Primaticcio first worked under ◊Giulio Romano in the Palazzo del Tè at Mantua. When Giulio Romano was invited to France by Francis I, he refused but recommended instead his young assistant. At first, Primaticcio was Rosso's subordinate, but he took charge of the Fontainebleau decorations on the latter's death in 1540. In Henry II's reign, Primaticcio was assisted by Niccolò dell' Abbate, to whom he delegated much of the execution of his own designs. The little of his work that has survived there includes his stucco and fresco work in the *Chambre de la Duchesse d'Étampes* (c. 1541). In 1559 he was employed by Catherine de' Medici and had his workshop in Paris.

print

The invention and success of printing by movable type, first used by Johann Gutenberg in Mainz in the 1450s, was arguably the most significant cultural event of the 15th century; it was also a development that originally owed nothing to those fashions now described as 'Renaissance'. A German invention, using a gothic (or black-letter) typeface, the first printed books were Bibles and devotional works. Indeed, these – along with school texts – long remained the most popular publications.

At the same time, however, men with humanist interests began to consider the potential of print for their own studies. Aeneas Sylvius Piccolomini (later Pius II) wrote an enthusiastic report of Gutenberg's Bible; ◊Nicholas of Cusa encouraged a couple of printers, Arnold ◊Pannartz and Conrad ◊Sweynheym, to set up the first press in Italy at the monastery of Subiaco in 1465. These two Germans were advised by Nicholas of Cusa's former secretary, Giovanni Andrea Bussi, ensuring that, from the introduction of print into Italy, the new technology showed an interest in Classical and humanist works. Others, such as the bookseller ◊Vespasiano da Bisticci, might have doubted the quality of printed books and could have pointed to several early and inaccurate editions to confirm their fears. But these well-founded concerns did not stop printers like Nicholas ◊Jenson and Aldus ◊Manutius establishing their own printing houses and producing humanist texts in appropriate humanist typefaces. Such ventures sometimes ran into financial difficulties but they survived and ensured the dissemination of Greek works and rare Latin classics, as well as the latest humanist outpourings, at a rate unthinkable in a manuscript culture.

Printers in other countries did not follow far behind these Italians in founding presses that produced as part of their output Renaissance texts: Badius Ascensius in Paris, for example, followed in that city by the Estienne family, or the Froben press in Basel, which proved popular with ◊Erasmus. The art of printing spread with relative speed across Europe, ensuring that a whole range of texts – conservative or subversive, learned or popular – were produced. Print may have ensured that early Renaissance fashions did not die but it also assisted other developments: Martin Luther considered print 'God's greatest act of grace' to the Protestant Reformations; printers' need to promote accessible (that is, sellable) products assisted the rise of vernaculars in the 16th century. In other words, print assisted transformations to Latin Christendom that neither its German inventors nor its humanist promoters could have envisaged, let alone endorsed.

Procaccini, Ercole (1520–1591)

Milanese painter. He was the head of a family of considerable influence in the development of painting in Milan, where he founded a teaching academy. His three sons, **Camillo Procaccini** (1546–1629), **Giulio Cesare Procaccini** (1548–1626), and **Carlo Antonio Procaccini** (1555–1605), were painters who also trained numerous Milanese artists.

prostitution

See ◊*cortigiana onesta*

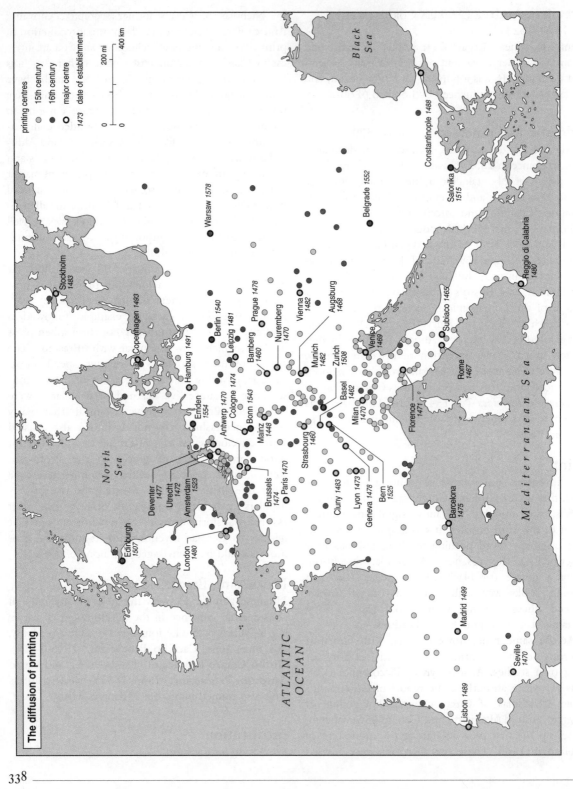

The diffusion of printing

printing centres

15th century
16th century
major centre
1473 date of establishment

400 km
200 mi

Black Sea

Constantinople *1488*

Salonika *1515*

Reggio di Calabria *1480*

Belgrade *1552*

Warsaw *1578*

Stockholm *1483*

Copenhagen *1493*

Hamburg *1491*

Berlin *1540*

Leipzig *1481*

Prague *1478*

Vienna *1482*

Augsburg *1468*

Nuremberg *1470*

Bamberg *1460*

Munich *1482*

Zurich *1508*

Venice *1469*

Subiaco *1465*

Emden *1554*

Antwerp *1470*

Cologne *1474*

Bonn *1543*

Mainz *1448*

Basel *1462*

Milan *1470*

Rome *1467*

Florence *1471*

Mediterranean Sea

Deventer *1477*

Utrecht *1472*

Amsterdam *1523*

Brussels *1474*

Paris *1470*

Strasbourg *1460*

Cluny *1483*

Lyon *1473*

Geneva *1478*

Bern *1525*

Barcelona *1475*

North Sea

Edinburgh *1507*

London *1480*

Madrid *1499*

Seville *1470*

ATLANTIC OCEAN

Lisbon *1489*

Provost (PREVOST), Jan (1465–1529)

Flemish painter. His work marks the transition from 15th-century to 16th-century Flemish painting. He followed Gerard ◊David in his early work, though with a somewhat coarse effort towards realism in facial expression. After 1521 he modelled his style on that of the German artist Albrecht Dürer, who stayed with him in Bruges.

He studied in Valenciennes (now in France) with Simon ◊Marmion, whose widow he married. Having worked in Antwerp, he settled in Bruges 1494, where he enjoyed a successful career.

Pullois, Jean (c. 1420–1478)

Flemish composer. His output consists mainly of songs but also includes some sacred music. He is important as one of the few named composers active during Dufay's middle years.

He was a singer in the Burgundian court chapel until 1463, then was choirmaster at Antwerp 1444–47. He sang at the papal chapel in Rome 1447–68. His single Mass cycle may really be the work of an English composer.

Puritan

From 1564, a member of the Church of England who wished to eliminate Roman Catholic survivals in church ritual, or substitute a presbyterian for an episcopal form of church government. The term also covers the separatists who withdrew from the church altogether. The Puritans were increasingly identified with the parliamentary opposition under James I and Charles I.

Puschmann, Adam Zacharias (1532–1600)

German master singer. He was a pupil of Hans Sachs at Nuremberg 1566–60. He wrote about 200 Meisterlider (master-songs), and in 1574 published a treatise on master-singing, containing songs of his own as well as by Sachs, Behaim, and others.

Pygott, Richard (c. 1485–1552)

English composer. He was in Wolsey's private chapel in 1517 as master of the children and in 1533 became a Gentleman of the Chapel Royal. Later he was given a living allowance at Coggeshall monastery in Essex and a canonry at Tamworth, but lost some of the benefits at the dissolution of the monasteries; Henry VIII, however, and after him Edward VI, retained his services.

Works include:

Masses, motets, *Salve Regina*; carols and other pieces.

Quagliati, Paolo (c. 1555–1628)

Italian composer. He was organist at the church of Santa Maria Maggiore in Rome from 1601. For the wedding of Carlo Gesualdo's daughter, Isabella, in 1623 he wrote a collection of instrumental pieces, entitled *La sfera armoniosa*.

Works include:

The dramatic cantata *Carro di fedeltà d'amore* (1806); motets; spiritual and secular madrigals and canzonets; organ and harpsichord works.

quattrocento (ITALIAN 'FOUR HUNDRED')

Denotes the 1400s and used in relation to Italian culture of the 15th century.

Quercia, Jacopo della (c. 1374–1438)

Sienese sculptor. He was a contemporary of ◊Donatello and ◊Ghiberti. His major works were a fountain for his hometown of Siena, the Fonte Gaia 1414–19 (Palazzo Pubblico, Siena), and the main portal at San Petronio, Bologna, 1425–38.

His turbulent style and powerful figures influenced ◊Michelangelo, whose painting *The Creation of Adam* (1511, Sistine Chapel, Vatican) was inspired by Jacopo's relief panel of the same subject at San Petronio.

questione della lingua (ITALIAN 'THE LANGUAGE QUESTION')

Debate over which dialect of the Italian peninsula was best suited for literary expression. It was an issue discussed in the early 16th century with different solutions advanced by the likes of Pietro ◊Bembo, Baldassare ◊Castiglione, and Niccolò ◊Machiavelli.

Discussion of the *volgare* had its origins in the early 14th century, with ◊Dante's *De vulgari eloquentia/On Vernacular Eloquence* (1304–06).

Dante discussed the suitability of various dialects for poetic composition, finding all excellent in part but none perfect. While the *tre corone* (three crowns) – Dante, Boccaccio, and Petrarch – wrote in the vernacular as well as Latin, the enterprise of *studia humanitatis* (see feature) was, naturally, focused on composition in the ancient tongue.

In the late 15th century, however, there was increased interest in the *volgare* as a mode of expression, which necessarily raised the question of which dialect was most appropriate. Pietro Bembo, in *Prose della volgar lingua/Writings in the Vernacular Tongue* (1525), argued that just as Virgil and Cicero had become the exemplars of Latin style, so Petrarch and Boccaccio were the models for Italian composition. This promotion of an archaic Tuscan style was supported by Leonardo Salviati and the Accademia della Crusca; though it was the most favoured response to the *questione*, other writers suggested different solutions. Castiglione, for example, promoted a *lingua cortigiana* (courtly language), reflecting actual usage in the Italian courts. Machiavelli, on the other hand, in his *Discorso o Dialogo intorno a la nostra lingua/Discourse or Dialogue on Our Language* (1525), rejected Bembo's old-fashioned Tuscan for contemporary Florentine usage.

Quixote, Don

Eponymous principal character of ◊Cervantes's two-part novel (Part I: 1605, Part II: 1615). The work concerns the (mis)adventures of Alonso Quijano, a nobleman of extremely modest means, whose obsessive readings of chivalric romances eventually convince him to ride out as a knight himself. He changes his name to Don Quixote, acquires an old nag as a steed (calling it Rocinante), and chooses as his lady a local girl, Aldonza Lorenzo, renaming her Dulcinea del Toboso in accordance with his chivalric fantasies. Thus prepared, he rides forth, always interpreting unextraordinary encounters and situations in terms of the extraordinary and literary. Hence a group of windmills become giants to be challenged, and a flock of sheep become an army to be fought. Quixote's actions are naturally misunderstood by his fellow human beings; as a result he is frequently subjected to vicious beatings. Undeterred, Quixote resumes his wanderings, now accompanied by Sancho Panza, a local man who agrees to act as his 'squire' in return for lordship of the first country they should conquer. By the end of Part I, the pair have returned to their anonymous La Mancha village, Sancho none the richer and Don Quixote none the less obsessed by chivalry. Although 'the author' observes that Don Quixote sallied forth a third time (to Zaragoza), he claims he could find no reliable information on his new adventures. No second part, therefore, is announced, and perhaps it would not have appeared had not the shadowy Fernández de Avellaneda published a spurious second part in 1614. Cervantes' Part Two appeared the following year – Don Quixote and Sancho's adventures are deliberately not set in Zaragoza, to emphasize the falseness of Avellaneda's continuation. The work closes with Don Quixote's death: after losing a joust in Barcelona, his victorious opponent bars him from taking up arms for a year. A broken man, Don Quixote returns to his village, falls ill and, shortly before he dies, realizes the folly of his literary obsession and returns to his senses.

The comic and complex texts which are Parts I and II of the *Quixote*, rich in intertextual references and literary games, enjoyed great popularity. Aside from the three 1605 editions, there were a further three (the last was 1610) before Part II appeared. Meanwhile, Part II was reprinted twice in 1616, but it was not until 1637 that both parts were published together. The first translation was Shelton's extremely free English version of 1612, closely followed by Oudin's French translation of 1614. Testament to the *Quixote*'s English popularity was a second edition of Part I in 1617; the translation of Part II appeared in 1620.

Rabelais, François (c. 1495–1553)

French satirist, monk, and physician. His name has become synonymous with bawdy humour. He was educated in the humanist tradition and was the author of satirical allegories, including a cycle known as ◊Gargantua and Pantagruel which included *La Vie estimable du grand Gargantua, père de Pantagruel/ The Inestimable Life of the Great Gargantua, Father of Pantagruel*, the first to be written, but published in 1534, two years after *Les Horribles et Épouvantables Faits et prouesses du très renommé Pantagruel/The Horrible and Dreadful Deeds and Prowess of the Very Renowned Pantagruel* (1532).

Raffaellino del Garbo (RAFFAELLE CAPPONI) (1470–1526)

Italian painter. He was active in Florence, and probably the pupil of Filippino ◊Lippi, whom he is said to have assisted in the frescoes of Sta Maria sopra Minerva, Rome.

Raimondi, Marcantonio (1480–1534)

Bolognese engraver, active in Rome. He engraved many works by ◊Raphael Sanzio and his pupils, becoming the first and perhaps the most eminent of reproductive engravers. His works were important in spreading Raphael's style throughout Europe, and in disseminating copies of Albrecht ◊Dürer's work throughout Italy.

He trained and worked in Bologna as a goldsmith and engraver under Francesco ◊Francia. He moved to Rome in 1510 where he worked for Raphael. He remained in Rome until the Sack in 1527. As well as copies of Raphael's works, his engravings included ones of ◊Giulio Romano's art, of ◊Leonardo da Vinci's *Last Supper*, and of Classical statues.

Raleigh (RALEGH), Walter (c. 1552–1618)

English adventurer, writer, and courtier to Queen Elizabeth I. He organized expeditions to colonize North America 1584–87, all unsuccessful, and made exploratory voyages to South America 1595 and 1616. His aggressive actions against Spanish interests, including attacks on Spanish ports, brought him into conflict with the pacific James I. He was imprisoned for treason 1603–16 and executed on his return from an unsuccessful final expedition to South America. He is traditionally credited with introducing the potato to Europe and popularizing the use of tobacco.

Born in Devon, England, Raleigh became a confidant of Queen Elizabeth I and was knighted in 1584. He led a gold-seeking expedition to the Orinoco River in South America 1595 (described in his *Discoverie of Guiana* 1596).

After James I's accession to the English throne 1603, Raleigh was condemned to death on a charge of conspiracy, but was reprieved and imprisoned in the Tower of London, where he wrote his unfinished *History of the World*. Released in 1616 to lead a second expedition to the Orinoco, which failed disastrously, he was beheaded on his return under the charges of his former sentence.

Ramis de Pareja, Bartolome (c. 1440–AFTER 1491)

Spanish theorist and composer. He wrote a theoretical work in which he devised a way of tuning the monochord and wrote church music.

After lecturing at Salamanca he went to Italy, living at Bologna 1480–82 and later in Rome.

Ramus, Petrus (LATINIZED NAME OF PIERRE DE LA RAMÉE) (1515–1572)

French philosopher and logician. He sought to improve the syllogistic logic of Greek philosopher Aristotle with the rhetoric of Roman orator Cicero. In the 17th century, Ramism was a serious rival to Aristotelian logic in Britain, New England, and Germany.

Aristotelian logic had already been criticized by Lorenzo ◊Valla. Francis I suppressed Ramus's works 1544, but Henry II lifted the ban 1547. From 1551,

Ramus was professor of philosophy and eloquence at the Collège de France. Around 1561 he became a Protestant. He was murdered by hired assassins. His works include *Dialectique/Dialectic* 1555.

Raphael (RAFFAELLO) Sanzio (1483–1520)

Painter and architect born in Urbino and eventually settled in Rome. He painted portraits and mythological and religious works, noted for their harmony of colour and composition. He was active in Perugia, Florence, and (from 1508) Rome, where he painted frescoes in the Vatican. Among his best-known works are *The Marriage of the Virgin* (1504) (Brera, Milan) and the fresco *The School of Athens* (1509–11) (Vatican, Rome).

Raphael was the son of Giovanni Santi (died 1494), a painter at the court of Urbino. In 1499 he went to Perugia, where he worked with ◊Perugino, whose graceful style is reflected in Raphael's *Marriage of the Virgin*. This work also shows his early concern for harmonious disposition of figures in the pictorial space.

In Florence 1504–08 he studied the works of Leonardo da Vinci, Michelangelo, Masaccio, and Fra Bartolommeo. His paintings of this period include the *Ansidei Madonna*. Pope Julius II commissioned him to decorate the papal apartments (the Stanze della Segnatura) in the Vatican. Raphael's first fresco series there, *The School of Athens*, is a complex but Classically composed grouping of Greek philosophers and mathematicians, centred on the figures of Plato and Aristotle. A second series of frescoes 1511–14 includes the dramatic and richly coloured *Mass of Bolsena*.

Raphael received many commissions and within the next few years he produced mythological frescoes in the Villa Farnesina in Rome 1511–12; cartoons for tapestries for the Sistine Chapel in the Vatican; the *Sistine Madonna* about 1512; and portraits, for example of Baldassare Castiglione about 1515.

When he was eight years old Raphael's mother died, and two years later his father. He may have begun his apprenticeship as a painter with his father, and later possibly continued with Timoteo Viti in Urbino, and subsequently Perugino in Perugia, where he also came under the influence of Pintoricchio. Perugino's art influenced Raphael at an early age as the early Crucifixion in the National Gallery, London, demonstrates. Raphael's *Vision of a Knight* (National Gallery, London), *St Michael and St George* (Louvre, Paris), and *The Three Graces* (Chantilly) were all painted during his early days in Urbino.

During his years in Florence he was influenced not only by Michelangelo and Leonardo da Vinci, but also by Fra Bartolommeo. With an extraordinary power of assimilation, he profited from the individ-

Raphael Raphael, *The Madonna of the Chair* c. 1516 (Uffizi, Florence). *e.t. achive*

ual attributes of many masters, though never becoming an imitator of any one. He combined a mastery of workmanship with a personal conception of design and form. Some of the chief paintings of this period are *La Madonna del Granduca* (Pitti, Florence), *Madonna del Giardino, Holy Family with the Lamb*, the *Ansidei Madonna, The Entombment of Christ*, and *St Catherine* (all National Gallery, London).

About 1508 Raphael went to Rome and by 1509 was working for Pope Julius II on the decoration of apartments in the Vatican, the whole of the fresco work soon being entrusted to him. His work in the Stanza della Segnatura included *The Dispute of the Sacrament* and the *School of Athens;* those in the Stanza di Eliodoro, the *Deliverance of St Peter from Prison* and *The Miracle of the Mass of Bolsena*. The frescoes also reflect the influence of Michelangelo's Sistine Chapel ceiling (unveiled 1512).

During the last six years of his life in Rome he produced many celebrated works, including *St Cecilia*, the *Madonna di S Sisto*, and *The Transfiguration* (unfinished at his death).

The large number of commissions Raphael received resulted in the organization of a large workshop, in the charge of ◊Giulio Romano. His versatility and powers of assimilation are further proved by the impressive development of his portraiture, from the early Leonardesque *Doni* portraits, to the Roman style of *La Donna Velata* (Pitti, Florence) and *Beazzano and Navagero* (Doria Gallery, Rome).

In 1514 he succeeded Bramante as the chief architect of St Peter's, and produced an entirely new plan, which was never carried out. Among other buildings he designed in Rome were the Palazzo Bronconio del Aquila, S Eligio degli Orefici, the Chigi Chapel in Sta Maria del Popolo, the Villa Madama, and Palazzo Vidoni.

Raselius (BORN RASEL), Andreas (*c.* 1563–1602)

German clergyman, theorist, and composer. He wrote a treatise on the hexachord, set hymn and psalm tunes in five parts, and composed German motets.

He studied at the Lutheran University of Heidelberg, became cantor at Regensburg 1584–

1600, and was then music director to the Elector Palatine at Heidelberg.

Ravenscroft, Thomas (*c.* 1582–*c.* 1633)

English composer. He was a chorister at St Paul's Cathedral under Edward Pearce, took a degree in music at Cambridge University in 1607, and was music master at Christ's Hospital 1618–22.

Works include:

Anthems, 55 of the 105 hymn-tune settings contained in his Psalter; madrigals, some of the four-part songs *The Pleasures of Five Usuall Recreations* in his treatise on notation *A Briefe Discourse* (1614) are by himself; some of the rounds and catches in the collections *Pammelia* (1609), *Deuteromelia* (1609), and *Melismata* (1611) are probably of his own composing.

reform and Reformation

The 15th and 16th centuries saw a Catholic Church which was both vibrant and resilient, criticized and ultimately weakened. Only in retrospect are the dividing lines between internal attempts at reform and external, 'heretical' attacks clearcut. Those who wanted to improve their church often used strident, even exaggerated criticisms to emphasis the necessity of what they were doing; those whose theology became defined as heresy often began with wishing radically to reform the Catholic Church from within. Indeed, there were few rules by which to decide whether new writings were orthodox or heretical.

15th century heresies The end of the 14th and the beginning of the 15th century saw two heresies in Europe: in England, that of John ◊Wyclif and the Lollards; in the Czech lands, that of Jan ◊Huss. The two were related – Huss's works being influenced by Wyclif's – and similarities: geographically isolated, they survived at all because of secular support. In the case of Wycliffites, however, this was a brief phase, soon replaced by determined and successful repression. In the case of Hussites, however, the support of the dypsomaniac king Wenceslas provided more enduring protection. Though Huss himself was burnt at the Council of ◊Constance, his movement took on national proportions and left another Council, that of ◊Basel, with the necessity of coming to a compromise with the heretics rather than crushing them.

reform and the humanist contribution From the view of the popes, reinstalled in Rome, heresies on the margins of Europe were only one difficulty, less immediate than, say, ◊conciliarism or the particularist tendencies of certain monarchs, exemplified by Charles VII of France's Pragmatic Sanction of ◊Bourges. At the same time, the pope was also a secular ruler whether he liked it or not (and some certainly did seem to put their heart into it): the lands of the Italian papal state (supposedly donated to the popes by the first Christian emperor, Constantine) were eyed by other rulers in the peninsula with suspicion or greed. So, for example, Alfonso V was in continual conflict with the pope, and was willing to use the weapons of scholarship on his side: this was the genesis of Lorenzo ◊Valla's attack on the Donation of Constantine. This is one instance where humanist philology was turned against the papacy, but some popes – like Nicholas V and Pius II – were willing to turn humanist skills to their own advantage. *Studia humanitatis* did not strictly include theology but, from the earliest stages, there was humanist interest not only in Classical but also in patristic texts with Ambrogio ◊Traversari in particular translating a series of works by the Church Fathers. And for the Catholic Church this bore fruit at the Council of ◊Florence. In the following decades, some scholars, like Marsilio ◊Ficino, engaged in a different exercise, trying to draw connections between Christianity and Platonism; this, though, was confined to a few esoteric circles. The interest in patristic and biblical scholarship had a wider vogue: in the early 16th century, scholarship on the Bible was reflected, in particular, in the Complutensian *Polyglot* and Erasmus's *Novum Instrumentum*.

dividing between criticism and heresy Erasmian scholars in the first two decades of the 16th century, like John ◊Colet in England, were outspoken critics of the standards of the clergy. Others, like Thomas ◊More, mocked what he saw as the superstitious elements in the cults of pilgrimage. These criticisms were not so much a sign of the absolute failure of the church but of the attempts of a few to improve their church in the way they wished. Their outspokenness, however, left them open to charges of heresy themselves – Erasmus's religion was certainly considered by some suspect – and there was one *cause célèbre* in

the 1510s: the claim that Johann ◊Reuchlin's reading of Hebrew works was in itself heretical.

The affair of Martin ◊Luther seemed, at first, like others which had gone before. Increasingly, however, as the divide between Luther and Catholic tradition increased, Erasmus, More, and Reuchlin turned against a movement they saw as undermining their own efforts at internal reform.

the evangelical reformers – Luther and Zwingli In the German-speaking lands of the 1520s, there were several movements against the Catholic Church, which gradually became defined against each other. Radical Anabaptist groups appeared, preaching social as well as religious revolution; the connection between heresy and sedition was a long-established one and other reformers were concerned to distance themselves from these elements. The two most influential movements were those led by Martin Luther and Philip ◊Melanchthon from Wittenberg and that by Ulrich ◊Zwingli in Zürich. Preachers, as much as the printed word, spread their ideas to the autonomous cities of the Empire and the Swiss Confederation, many of which took up one of these faiths. At the same time, Luther and Zwingli attempted to negotiate a position uniting the ideas they were both developing, only to disagree implacably at the Colloquy of Marburg in 1529 over the issue of the Mass. While cities provided pockets of support, political influence was provided by the few princes in Germany and Scandinavia who converted to Lutheranism, attracted in part by the teaching that allowed them to take over church lands and thus enrich themselves.

attempts at ending the schism While there were points of disagreement between different reformers within and outside the Catholic Church, there was at this stage no firm boundaries of faith. Indeed, while some like Charles V were concerned to suppress heresy, some Catholic clerics believed that a reconciliation of the 'Protestants' (as they were generically called from 1529) with the church was still possible. Cardinal Contarini met Philip Melanchthon in 1541 at Regensburg to discuss their differences and came close to accord. Contarini, indeed, reflected a vein of Catholic thought (represented by both clerics, like Reginald ◊Pole, and lay-people, including Vittoria ◊Colonna) which was both humanist and open to evangelical ideas of reform; this tradition was doomed when its declared enemy, Gian Pietro Carafa, was elected Pope ◊Paul IV, the archetype of so-called Counter-Reformation zeal.

the second generation – Jean Calvin's Reformed Church By 1555, Lutheranism had secured institutional recognition by the Peace of Augsburg but by this stage, a more coherent and organized movement had appeared in Geneva, where Jean Calvin, assisted by Guillaume Farel, had established his idea of a reformed city-state. In the second half of the 16th century, it was this brand of Protestantism which enjoyed international success: it spread to France (where they were called Huguenots), to Scotland (under the leadership of John Knox), to the Netherlands, and to England (where those who supported it completely, against the mixed theology of the church established under Edward VI and Elizabeth, were dubbed Puritans). It provided a potent, and increasingly radical religious element to political conflicts like the Wars of Religion in France, the Revolt of the Netherlands and, in the 17th century, the Thirty Years' War.

Regiomontanus (ADOPTED NAME OF JOHANNES MÜLLER) (1436–1476)

German astronomer. He compiled astronomical tables, translated Ptolemy's *Almagest* from Greek into Latin, and assisted in the reform of the Julian calendar.

Johannes Müller adopted the name Regiomontanus as a Latinized form of his birthplace Königsberg while studying in Vienna. At the age of 15, he was appointed to the Faculty of Astronomy in Vienna. He lived in Italy 1461–68, spent the next three years at the court of the king of Hungary, and settled in Nuremberg 1471. He installed a printing press in his house and so became one of the first publishers of astronomical and scientific literature. He went to Rome 1475, invited by the pope to assist in amending the notoriously incorrect ecclesiastical calendar.

In 1467, Regiomontanus started compiling trigonometric and astronomical tables, but these too were not published until after his death. Regiomontanus's *Ephemerides* (1474) was the first publication of its kind to be printed (by himself); it gave the positions of the heavenly bodies for every day 1475–1506. He published his *Tabulae Directionum* (1475).

After Regiomontanus's death, the statement 'the motion of the stars must vary a tiny bit on account of the motion of the Earth' was found in his handwriting. This has led some people to believe that Regiomontanus gave ◊Copernicus the idea that the Earth moves round the Sun.

Regis, Jean (*c.* 1430–*c.* 1495)

Flemish composer. He wrote two Masses, including one on *L'Homme armé*, songs in parts, eight motets, and other pieces.

He was choirmaster at Antwerp Cathedral and was Dufay's secretary at Cambrai in the 1440s. He went about 1451 to Soignies, and remained there.

Régnier, Mathurin (1573–1613)

French poet. His works 1608–12, chiefly satires, attempt (as the ◊Pléiade poets had done with other genres) to raise this type of work to Classical perfection. The satires are characterized by the combination of comic realism and social criticism.

He was born in Chartres and became a canon of the cathedral there; he enjoyed the patronage of Henry IV.

Rej, Mikołaj (1505–1569)

Polish writer. His work is transitional between the medieval tradition and the Reformation; for example, a verse debate (1543) 'between the squire, the bailiff, and the parson'. Rej was self-educated and was an eager moralist. His poetry collection *Zwierciadło/The Looking Glass* (1568) is both a personal reflection and a mirror of the age, and includes his best-known work, 'Zi.ywot człowieka poczciwego/The Life of an Honest Man'.

Religion, Wars of

Series of civil wars 1562–89 in France between Catholics and (Protestant) Huguenots. Each side was led by noble families which competed for influence over a weakened monarchy. The most infamous event was the Massacre of ◊St Bartholomew 1572, carried out on the orders of the Catholic faction led by

◊Catherine de' Medici and the Duke of Guise. After 1584, the heir apparent to the French throne was the Huguenot Henry of Navarre. This prompted further hostilities, but after his accession as Henry IV in 1589, he was able to maintain his hold on power, partly through military victory and partly by converting to Catholicism in 1593.

He introduced the Edict of Nantes 1598, guaranteeing freedom of worship throughout his kingdom.

René the Good (DUKE OF ANJOU) (1409–1480)

French claimant to the lands of the ◊Anjou dynasty. Continuing the conflict against Alfonso V, he failed to secure the kingdom of Naples. Dynastic promotion was better achieved through marriage alliances than war: his daughter became the bride to ◊Henry VI of England (although this achievement also did not prove durable).

Exaggerated claims for nobles' cultural activities are often made (in the case, say, of John ◊Tiptoft) and René of Anjou has dubiously been claimed to have illuminated his own manuscripts. Although that should probably be discounted, he was one of the aristocratic authors of the 15th century: he produced chivalric, devotional, and allegorical works.

René was also a patron of Italian art; he owned works by Luca della Robbia and medals by Francesco Laurana and Pietro di Martino da Milano, both of whom made trips to Provence. The duke's major commission, however, of his tomb (now destroyed), which apparently represented him as a skeleton enthroned, went to a French sculptor, Jacques Morel.

1448	Founds the chivalric *Ordre du Croissan*/Order of the Crescent
1452	Composes *Le Livre des Tournois,* dedicated to Charles of Anjou
c. **1455**	Dedicates to the lawyer and academic Jean Bernard his mystical work *Le Mortifiement de vaine plaisance*
1457	Writes the allegorical romance *Le Livre du coeur d'amour épris*
1472	Commissions his tomb for Angers Cathedral (destroyed 1769)

Reuchlin, Johannes (1454/55–1522)

German scholar of Greek, Hebrew, and the kabbala.

Educated at Freiburg, Paris, and Basel, Reuchlin began and ended his career with teaching; in the years around the turn of the century, he was in the service of Count Eberhard (the Bearded) of Württemberg and with him travelled across Europe. Reuchlin's works were wide-ranging but controversy attached to one aspect of his output: his interest in Hebrew.

Reuchlin, who produced a Hebrew grammar 1506, became embroiled in debate when Johann Pfefferkorn began campaigning for the suppression of all Hebrew books. Reuchlin opposed this and brought upon himself the enmity of the Dominican order, who charged him before the pope. Reuchlin was not slow to show that he had international scholarly opinion on his side: he had printed *Clarorum in Virorum Epistolae/Letters of Famous Men* 1514 (enlarged 1519), collecting together letters written in support of him. In the following years (1515–17) similar collections entitled *Epistolae Obscurorum Virorum/Letters of Obscure Men* appeared anonymously, satirizing Reuchlin's opponents (Ulrich von ◊Hutten was one of their main authors). Reuchlin was eventually convicted but was not imprisoned: in his last years, he was teaching Greek and Hebrew at Tübingen.

Many people say, in their simplicity, that it is not possible that Pfefferkorn wrote that Latin defence against the *Epistolae Clarorum Virorum* because he has never learnt a word of Latin. But I reply that that objection does not hold because Johannes Pfefferkorn could have written down what he had heard in sermons or in meetings or when students and friars visited him or when he himself went to the bath.

～

'BROTHER SIMON WORST' on the Reuchlin affair – a joke-letter from *Epistolae Obscurorum Virorum*

Reuchlin's other works included a Latin dictionary 1478, two comedies in Latin 1498 and 1504, and a couple of kabbalistic dialogues; he also worked on ◊Erasmus' edition of Jerome. Erasmus supported him in the controversy with Pfefferkorn, although this became increasingly hazardous: when the Luther affair broke, some of Luther's supporters drew parallels with Reuchlin's case, allowing Erasmus' critics to make a link between him and heresy. Erasmus' response was to stress the differences between the two cases and to point out that Reuchlin himself did not support Luther. Indeed, Reuchlin was willing to alienate former allies, like Hutten and his own grand-nephew Philip ◊Melanchthon, in his desire to stand by Catholic orthodoxy.

revenge tragedy

Form of Elizabethan and Jacobean drama in which revenge provides the mainspring of the action. It is usually characterized by bloody deeds, intrigue, and high melodrama. It was pioneered by Thomas Kyd with *The Spanish Tragedy* (*c.* 1588), Shakespeare's *Titus Andronicus* (c. 1593), and Cyril Tourneur's *The Revenger's Tragedy* (1607). Its influence is apparent in tragedies such as Shakespeare's *Hamlet* and *Macbeth*.

Riccio, (Antonio) Teodoro (*c.* 1540–AFTER 1599)

Italian composer. After holding the post of choirmaster at a church at Brescia, he was appointed music director by the Margrave of Brandenburg-Ansbach. He settled there and followed the margrave to Königsberg in 1579, having become a Lutheran, and returned to Ansbach with his patron in 1586. Johann Eccard served under him there from 1581 and succeeded him at his death.

Works include:

Motets and other church music; madrigals, *Canzoni alla napoletana*; some of his canzonas are based on themes by Gabrieli.

Rich, Barnabe (1542–1617)

English writer. His romances include *Rich, his Farewell to the Military Profession* (1581) (which provided the plot for Shakespeare's *Twelfth Night*), *The Strange and Wonderful Adventures of Don Simonides* (1581–84), and *Faults, Faults, and Nothing Else but Faults* (1606). He also wrote pamphlets on military subjects and memoirs.

Richard III (1452–1485)

King of England from 1483. Youngest brother of Edward IV, he supported him loyally through his reign. However, on Edward's death, he did not extend such loyalty to his nephews: Richard deposed Edward's teenage son, had him and his brother imprisoned in the Tower of London, and declared himself king. His actions could not but cause suspicion and from suspicion unrest grew. What proved fatal was the small-scale invasion of Henry Tudor (Henry VII) who defeated and killed Richard at the Battle of Bosworth, 22 August 1485.

Many kings died with a reputation for tyranny but Richard was an exceptional case. Even before his death, there were rumours that he had killed his nephews; in the years after 1485, some considered him an Antichrist. For Thomas ◊More, he was a suitable candidate to represent archetypal evil kingship. This two-dimensional image became the standard interpretation of Richard, reflected, for example, in the mid-century chronicles and in Shakespeare's play.

Ridley, Nicholas (*c.* 1500–1555)

English Protestant bishop. He became chaplain to Henry VIII 1541, and bishop of London in 1550. He took an active part in the Reformation and supported Lady Jane Grey's claim to the throne. After Mary's accession he was arrested and burned as a heretic.

Riemenschneider, Tilman (*c.* 1460–1531)

German sculptor. He was the head of a large and successful workshop in Würzburg from 1483 and an active participant in the political and religious struggles of his time. He is best known for his limewood sculptures, such as *St Matthew* (1495–1505, Berlin-Dahlem, Staatliche Museum).

Rienzo, Cola di (*c.* 1313–1354)

Plebeian Roman lawyer with visionary tendencies who, in his 1347 revolution, restored a short-lived 'Roman Republic'. Cola's idea of ancient Rome meeting an apocalyptic New Jerusalem, within a unified Italy, under a Classical-style Tribune, owed its inspiration to a remarkable range of sources, incorporating the monarchical dreams and civic metaphysics of ◊Dante, the nascent literary humanism of ◊Petrarch (Cola's supporter and would-be advisor) the legal governmental theories of his near-contemporaries Bartolus and Baldus, and the prophetic language of radical Franciscan prophets.

Chased quickly from Rome both for heresy and for over-taxing a pressured populace, Cola soon faced imprisonment in Prague by the Roman Emperor, Charles IV, and then in Avignon by the Roman Pope, Clement VI. His rhetorical skills persuaded Clement's successor, Innocent VI, to send Cola back to Rome in 1353–54 at the head of a task force; but within a few weeks of his glorious march into Rome – staged as both Christ's entry to Jerusalem and a Classical Imperial triumph – he was brutally assassinated.

Robbia, della

Italian family of sculptors and architects. They were active in Florence. **Luca della Robbia** (1400–1482) created a number of major works in Florence, notably the marble *cantoria* (singing gallery) in the cathedral 1431–38 (Museo del Duomo), with lively groups of choristers. Luca also developed a characteristic style of glazed terracotta work.

Andrea della Robbia (1435–1525), Luca's nephew and pupil, and Andrea's sons continued the family business, inheriting the formula for the vitreous terracotta glaze. The blue-and-white medallions of foundling children 1463–66 on the Ospedale degli Innocenti, Florence, are typical. Many later works are more elaborate and highly coloured, such as the frieze 1522 on the façade of the Ospedale del Ceppo, Pistoia.

Giovanni della Robbia (1469–1529), Andrea's son, and **Girolamo della Robbia** (1488–1566) produced terracottas for Fontainebleau in France.

Roberti, Ercole d'Antonio de (1450–1496)

Italian painter. He was active in Ferrara, and worked for the Este court. Principal works include a *Pietà* (Walker Gallery, Liverpool), two scenes from the Passion (Gemäldegalerie Alter Meister, Dresden), and *The Israelites Gathering Manna* (National Gallery, London).

He was probably a pupil of Francesco Cossa, with whom he may have worked in Bologna, and he was influenced by Cosimo ◊Tura and also by Jacopo Bellini. Another remarkable work is an altarpiece of 1480 (Brera, Milan).

Rodio, Rocco (*c.* 1535–SHORTLY AFTER 1615)

Italian composer. He wrote church music (including ten Masses), madrigals, and instrumental music, and a treatise, *Regole di Musica*, which was published at Naples in 1600, though it is now known only from its second and third editions (1609 and 1626), edited by his pupil Giovanni Battista Olifante.

Roelas, Juan de las (*c.* 1558–1625)

Castilian painter. He worked in Seville, using a style strongly influenced by Venetian art. Among his principal religious paintings are *Death of St Isidore* and *Martyrdom of St Andrew* (1609, Seville Museum). Francisco de Zurbarán was his pupil.

It is not clear whether Roelas visited Venice, but the Venetian influence, particularly that of Paolo ◊Veronese, is the most distinctive feature of his style.

Roelas became a priest about 1600 and painted huge, dramatic altarpieces for churches in Seville which are among the greatest work produced in Spain at the time, but he has remained comparatively unknown because almost none of his work is to be found outside his native city.

Rojas, Fernando de (*c.* 1473/76–1541)

Castilian lawyer and author, of *converso* (Jewish converts to Christianity) parentage. He read law at Salamanca university, and seems to have graduated around the time when his continuation of an earlier, anonymous prose fiction was published, probably in 1499, as the *Comedia de Calisto y Melibea/Comedy of Calisto and Melibea*. He then produced an expanded and retitled version, the *Tragicomedia de Calisto y Melibea/Tragicomedy of Calisto and Melibea* (*c.* 1502). Both works were enormously popular; the *Tragicomedia*, which superseded the *Comedia*, became known as *La ◊Celestina*. Despite this acclaim it seems Rojas never wrote anything else, dedicating the rest of his life to a successful legal career.

Roman Academy

Name given to a successive groups of humanists in Rome from the second half of the 15th century up to the ◊Sack of Rome. Like many ◊academies, these were informal gatherings. They began with the coterie of scholars around Pomponio ◊Leto (including ◊Platina) who enjoyed the dubious honour of

349

arousing the suspicion of ◊Paul II. Though Paul dispersed the group, Leto was not deterred. Later incarnations of the 'academy' received the patronage of Paul's successors, ◊Julius II and ◊Leo X.

Romanino, Girolamo (1485–1566)

Italian painter. A fine colourist, influenced by ◊Giorgione and ◊Titian, he is best known for four frescoes in the cathedral of Cremona (1519–20). Among his other works are *The Madonna* (Doria Gallery, Rome) and *Nativity* (National Gallery, London).

He painted chiefly in his native city, Brescia, but travelled very extensively.

Romero, Mateo (KNOWN AS MAESTRO CAPITÁN) (c. 1575–1647)

Spanish singer, composer, and priest. He joined the Flemish section of the royal chapel at Madrid in 1594; he was a pupil of Philippe Rogier, whom he succeeded as maestro de capilla in 1598. He was ordained priest in 1609 and retired with a pension in 1633, but was sent on a musical mission to Portugal in 1638.

Works include:

Motets and other church music; secular songs for three and four voices, including settings of poems by Lope de Vega.

Ronsard, Pierre de (1524–1585)

French poet. He was the leader of the ◊Pléiade group of poets. Under the patronage of Charles IX, he published original verse in a lightly sensitive style, including odes and love sonnets, such as *Odes* (1550), *Les Amours/Lovers* (1552–53), and the 'Marie' cycle, *Continuation des amours/Lovers Continued* (1555–56). He also produced a theoretical treatise *Art poétique* (1565).

Rore, Cipriano de (c. 1516–1565)

Flemish composer. He spent much of his life in Italy, where he was a prolific composer of madrigals and sacred music. He wrote 125 madrigals, most of which are contained in the ten books he published 1542–46. His works made a strong impression on Monteverdi.

He studied under Adrian Willaert at Venice, where he was a singer at St Mark's, and began to publish madrigals in 1542. He left Venice about 1550 to enter the service of Duke Ercole II d'Este at Ferrara. In 1558 he visited his parents at Antwerp and the court of Margaret of Parma, governor of the Netherlands, at Brussels, into the service of whose husband, Ottavio Farnese, Duke of Parma, he passed in 1561. In 1563 he succeeded Willaert as maestro di cappella of St Mark's, Venice, but returned to Parma the following year.

Rore's parody Masses and motets follow the style of the previous generation, but it is for his madrigals that he is chiefly remembered. He set many of Petrarch's texts in his earlier madrigals; in the later ones he became more aware of sensitive treatment of the text.

Works include:

Five Masses, 65 motets, one Passion and other church music; 125 madrigals; instrumental fantasies and ricercari, and other pieces.

Roses, Wars of the

Intermittent civil strife in England from the 1450s to 1487. Failure in the Hundred Years' War and incompetent government at home created vociferous opposition to the court circle around Henry VI. The opposition was led by Richard, Duke of York, who eventually claimed the throne for himself. Although he was killed in battle in 1460, his son won the crown as Edward IV. Fighting recurred in 1470–71, when the Lancastrians invaded, and in 1483–87, when first ◊Richard III and then Henry VII usurped the throne.

The name Wars of the Roses is a misleading 19th-century invention. Certainly, using a red (Lancaster) and a white (York) rose as symbols of the conflict began early – it is the basis, for example, of Henry VII's symbol, the ◊Tudor rose. However, the idea that the late 15th century was a period of unremitting conflict only brought to an end by Henry VII was a myth successfully propagated by Tudor writers like Polydore ◊Vergil.

Rosselli, Cosimo (1439–1507)

Florentine painter. He was one of the team of painters commissioned by Pope Sixtus IV to paint frescoes in the ◊Sistine Chapel, contributing four works including the *Last Supper*.

Giorgio Vasari tells a story that Rosselli's works were mocked by his colleagues working in the Sistine Chapel – until Sixtus IV, awed by the amount of gold Rosselli used, declared them the best. On his return to Florence, Rosselli produced the fresco *Procession of the Miraculous Chalice* (1485) for the church of Sant' Ambrogio, as well as altarpieces. More importantly, he established an influential workshop where the likes of Piero di Cosimo and Fra Bartolommeo trained.

Cosimo's brother, **Francesco Rosselli** (1448–1513) was also a painter, as well as an illuminator, who worked briefly for ◊Matthias Corvinas of Hungary.

Rossellino, Bernardo (1409–1464) AND Antonio (1427–1479)

Florentine sculptor brothers. They worked together on the tomb in the Chapel of the Cardinal of Portugal in S Miniato al Monte, Florence. Bernardo was responsible for the tomb of Leonardo ◊Bruni in S Croce, Florence, and was the architect for ◊Pius II's pet project of ◊Pienza.

Rosseter, Philip (1567 OR 1568–1623)

English lutenist and composer. He worked in London and was associated with Robert Jones, Philip Kingham, and Reeve in the theatre life of the capital. From 1609 he worked with Robert Keysar, managing a company of boy actors, known as the Children of Whitefriars (from 1610 the Children of the Queen's Revels). From 1615 the company performed at the Blackfriars theatre. Rosseter published a book of songs to the lute with Thomas Campion; some if not all of the words by Campion and about half of the music by Rosseter.

Works include:

A Booke of Ayres with lute, orpheoreon, and bass viol; *Lessons for the Consort* for six instruments by various composers.

Rosso, Giovanni Battista di Jacopo
(CALLED **ROSSO FIORENTINO**) (1494–1540)

Florentine painter. He was active in Florence, Rome, Venice and, from 1530, France, where he was in charge of the decoration of ◊Fontainebleau palace. A nomadic lifestyle was not unusual for an artist, but in Rosso's case it seems to have been necessitated by his sharp and injudicious tongue. Giorgio ◊Vasari claims that, in the end, an overhasty allegation against one of his assistants caused recriminations and Rosso's suicide.

Born in Florence, Rosso studied under ◊Andrea del Sarto and worked in Florence from 1513–23. In 1524 he went to Rome hoping to work in the Vatican. Instead, through Antonio da Sangallo (whom he soon antagonized), he decorated the Cesi Chapel in Sta Maria della Pace. He left Rome when it was sacked in 1527, travelled to Venice and, from there, was invited by ◊Francis I to his court. From the time of his arrival in France, his work was taken up with decorating Fontainebleau, where he was joined in 1532 by Francesco ◊Primaticcio. His *Moses Defending the Daughters of Jethro*, (1523, Uffizi, Florence) and his *Dead Christ*, (1526, Museum of Fine Art, Boston) demonstrate how strongly he was influenced by Michelangelo's Sistine Chapel ceiling.

Rottenhammer, Johann (1564–1623)

German painter. He travelled to Venice 1589 and spent many years there and in Rome. He painted small pictures on copper of mythological scenes in an Italianate style. Settling in Augsburg in 1606, he worked for the Count von Schaunburg at Bückeburg, executing wall and ceiling decorations.

Rout of San Romano, The

Series of three paintings executed in the 1450s by the Italian artist Paolo ◊Uccello (Uffizi, Florence; Louvre, Paris; and the National Gallery, London). They depict a battle or skirmish fought between the Florentines and Sienese 1432 at San Romano (between Florence and Pisa), a minor incident of the long-continuing rivalry between Florence and Siena.

The pictures were framed together in the palace of the Medici in Florence. It is probable that the National Gallery picture hung on the left, the Uffizi in the centre, and the Louvre on the right. The Florentine commander Niccolò da Tolentino has been identified in the National Gallery version by his device of knotted cords ('Solomon's knot') appearing on the standard.

Rucellai, Bernardo di Giovanni
(1448–1514)

Florentine patrician and diplomat, the son of Giovanni di Paolo Rucellai. While his father, related to the Strozzi family, had been effectively ostracized from Florentine politics under the Medici for several decades, Bernardo was allowed to marry in 1466 into the ruling family. He became a friend and adviser to Lorenzo de' ◊Medici 'the Magnificent', serving regularly as an ambassador. He was among those leading figures of Florence who turned against Piero de' Medici. Rucellai's dissatisfication continued after 1494, when he felt the constitution became too populist. He withdrew from politics in 1502 and went into voluntary exile in 1506.

Rucellai was, in his early days, a disciple of Marsilio ◊Ficino and he was himself something of a writer, producing, among other works, *De Bello Italico/On the Italian War*, a history of the French invasion of 1494, and an antiquarian work, *De Urbe Romana/On the City of Rome* (*c.* 1500). He also laid out the gardens that became known as the ◊Orti Oricellari and began the intellectual discussions there.

If you read his history, you would say he was another Sallust

or, at least, that his writings were from Sallust's times.

∽

ERASMUS' double-edged praise of Bernardo Rucellai's *De Bello Italico*

Rucellai, Cosimo (LIVED EARLY 16TH CENTURY)

Florentine patrician, grandson of Bernardo di Giovanni ◊Rucellai. If his Christian name, Cosimo, signified his family's closeness to the Medici regime, it proved ironic. During Piero ◊Soderini's Florentine republic (1502–12) and after, he presided over discussions at the ◊Orti Oricellari, which were anti-Medicean in character. Among the frequenters of the

gardens was Niccolò Machiavelli, who dedicated his *Discorsi/ Discourses* (1531) to Cosimo Rucellai and also included his host as a interlocutor in his *L'Arte della guerra/The Art of War* (1520).

Rucellai, Giovanni (1475–1525)

Florentine poet of a patrician Florentine family. He wrote two tragedies in the style of the Greek dramatist Euripides, *Rosamunda* (1515) and *Oreste* (1525), and also a didactic poem on bees, *Le Api* (1539) (edited by his brother Palla), based on the fourth book of the Roman poet Virgil's *Georgics*.

He was a grandson of Bernardo di Giovanni ◊Rucellai. A cleric, he was frequently employed as a diplomat by the Medici popes.

Rucellai, Giovanni di Paolo (1403–1481)

Florentine patrician and architectural patron in Florence. The Rucellai family's money came from their cloth-trading activities; Giovanni used this wealth for cultural patronage, in particular two ostentatious building works, both designed by Leon Battista ◊Alberti: his

Rucellai The façade of Palazzo Rucellai, Florence, designed by Leon Battista Alberti. This was one of the two of Rucellai's major commissions, the other being the façade of Santa Maria Novella (see picture gallery). *AKG London*

family palace, begun in 1446, and the upper façade of the church of Santa Maria Novella (1456–70), replete with Rucellai's heraldic symbol, the wind-filled sail (a device he borrowed from the d'Este dynasty). These works, he recorded, were to the glory of God, the city, and (last and least) himself.

Ruckers, Hans (*c.* 1530–1598)

Flemish harpsichord and virginal maker. He founded a business at Antwerp in 1584, producing instruments which provided contrast in register and tone. He was succeeded by his sons Joannes (1578–1642) and Andries (1579– *c.* 1645). About 100 instruments made by members of the Ruckers family survive, in both single and two-manual versions.

Rudolf II (1552–1612)

Holy Roman Emperor from 1576, when he succeeded his father, Maximilian II. During his reign, the continuing Catholic attempts to reverse the concessions to Protestants made in the Peace of Augsburg led to a gradual paralysis of the imperial bureaucracy. Rudolf's later years were also marked by conflict with his brother and heir presumptive, Matthias.

Rudolf moved his capital from Vienna to Prague in 1583; there he consciously cultivated his court as an artistic and intellectual centre. The artists around him, like Hans von ◊Aachen, Joseph ◊Heintz, and Bartholomeus ◊Spranger (who sometimes worked closely together, for example collaborating on an altarpiece in 1598), have collectively been called 'Prague Mannerists' for whom (reflecting Rudolf's tastes) strained virtuosity, unabashed eroticism, and intricate allegory were key stylistic components. The circle also included Giuseppe ◊Arcimboldo, whose work defies any simple categorization.

Rudolf not only commissioned art; he also collected it – in particular, he liked paintings by Albrecht ◊Dürer and Pieter ◊Brueghel. He was not, however, interested only in art: he patronized music (his chief musician was Philippe de ◊Monte), collected clocks, and gathered a menagerie at his palace (he took the death of his pet lion as an omen of his own demise – rightly, as it turned out). He also gained a reputation for an unhealthy fascination with the occult; certainly, interest in alchemy

and magic were fashionable at his court and both John ◊Dee in 1584 and Giordano ◊Bruno in 1588 passed through it. But a simple division can not be drawn between 'superstitious' and 'scientific' interests: the astronomers Tycho ◊Brahe and Johannes ◊Kepler both accepted Rudolf's invitation to work in Prague.

Whoever so desires nowadays has only to go to Prague to the greatest art patron in the world at present, the Roman Emperor Rudolf II; there he may see ... a remarkable number of outstanding and precious, curious, unusual and priceless works.

KAREL VAN MANDER, 1604

Rueda, Lope de (*c.* 1510–1565)

Spanish dramatist. His comedies are modelled largely on those of Italian authors of the early 16th century. His short sketches, or *pasos*, include such witty interludes as *El convidado* (1546) and *Las aceitunas* (1548).

He organized a strolling company of players, whose performances laid the foundations of the popular theatre in Madrid and Seville.

Ruffo, Vincenzo (*c.* 1510–1587)

Italian male soprano and composer. His sacred music shows the influence of Tridentine reforms, which insisted on verbal clarity.

He held the post of maestro di cappella at Verona Cathedral from 1554 and at Milan 1563–72. He occupied a similar post at Pistoia 1574–79, then returned to Milan.

Works include:
Masses, motets, Magnificat, psalms, and other church music; madrigals.

Rustici, Cencio de' (*c.* 1390–*c.* 1445) (ALSO KNOWN AS CINCIUS ROMANUS)

Roman cleric and humanist translator. He was born in Rome of a wealthy family, and learned Greek from ◊Chrysoloras in 1410–15; from 1411 his career was spent in the papal curia. He attended the Council of

◊Constance and in 1416 accompanied Poggio and Bartolomeo da Montepulciano on their trip to St Gall, where they found Quintilian. His literary works include a set of epistles and translations of Plato's *De Virtute* and the *Axiochus*, a meditation on death also thought to be by Plato; the latter (dedicated to cardinal Orsini) proved popular across Europe. (See also feature on rediscovery of classical literature).

Sack of Rome

Looting of the city of Rome by imperial troops in 1527. In the aftermath of Charles V's capture of Francis I at the Battle of Pavia in 1525, the various powers of Italy attempted to create an alliance to push his forces out of Italy. ◊Clement VII, however, preferred to secure a truce with the emperor but this proved short-lived. In March 1527, Charles's army, under the control of the Duke of Bourbon, entered the papal states and advanced on Rome. They attacked on 6 May and, though Bourbon was killed in the assault, broke into the city. The troops – unruly and unpaid – went on the rampage.

During the Sack, several monuments were destroyed and palaces ransacked; much of Angelo ◊Colocci's collection of ancient inscriptions, for example, was lost. The stories of what occurred in those days may be exaggerated – one soldier claimed that 12,000 people had been killed – but the shock of events was real. For some, including (incongruously) Pietro ◊Aretino, it was a judgement of God for the sins of the papacy. Apart from the loss of art and of libraries, the Sack had a wider cultural effect: some of the artists then in Rome were captured and ransomed, others fled (like ◊Parmigianino or Giulio ◊Clovio). Overall, the result was a dispersal, albeit short-lived, of the artistic community which had been so active in the previous years under the Medici popes.

Sackville, Thomas, LORD BUCKHURST, 1ST EARL OF DORSET (1536–1608)

English poet and politician. He collaborated with Thomas Norton on *Ferrex and Porrex* (1561), afterwards called *Gorboduc*. Written in blank verse, this was one of the earliest English tragedies. He also contributed to the influential ◊*Mirror for Magistrates*, intended as a continuation of John ◊Lydgate's *Fall of Princes*. An influential figure in Elizabeth's last years, he held offices of Privy Councillor, Lord Steward, and Lord Treasurer.

He was born in Buckhurst, Sussex, educated at Oxford and Cambridge, and studied law in London. He was made Baron Buckhurst in 1567 and Earl in 1604.

Sacred and Profane Love

Painting of about 1516 by ◊Titian (Borghese Gallery, Rome). An early work, painted when he was still strongly influenced by Giorgione, it is richly sensuous and poetic in feeling.

The title by which it was known in Titian's lifetime, when it was in the collection of cardinal Scipio Borghese, was *Beauty Clothed and Unclothed* – the symbolism lends itself to various interpretations.

Sá de Miranda, Francisco (c. 1481–1558)

Portuguese poet who studied at Lisbon. His poems first appeared in Resende's ◊*Cancioneiro Geral* (1516), suggesting early court connections. Between 1521 and 1527 he was in Italy. His reasons for going are as obscure as his activities there, but the subsequent impact upon the structure and imagery of his poetry is clear enough. The reasons for his move to rural northern Portugal in 1530 are also obscure, but he remained in touch with court life, preparing a manuscript of his complete works in the early 1550s in response to Prince João's request. His life ended sadly: his eldest son was killed in Africa in 1553; his wife died in 1555, while Prince João had died in 1554.

Over half of Sá de Miranda's poetry was written in Castilian, which he tended to use when composing in the Italian style in imitation of ◊Boscà and ◊Garcilaso. On his return from Italy, he introduced Portuguese poets to the Italian hendecasyllabic (11-syllable) line, and to certain Italian poetic forms, in particular the sonnet and the eclogue (a short pastoral poem). He also breathed new life into traditional Portuguese metres by introducing new themes and imagery (as in his five Portuguese *Sátiras/Satires*). Mourned by contemporary poets on his death, all his works were first printed posthumously. The first of these was his *Comedia dos estrangeiros/The Comedy of the Foreigners* (1559). Probably composed on his return from Italy, its originality lay in its Classical plot structure of complex intrigue and resolution, its dialogues in prose, not verse, and its refusal to mock the foreigners' non-Portuguese languages. His other play *Vilhalpandos/ The Boastful Soldiers* was published the following year. Sá de Miranda's collected poems, *As Obras/Collected Works*, was published in 1595 and reprinted five times throughout the 17th century.

St Bartholomew, Massacre of

Slaughter of ◊Huguenots (Protestants) in Paris, 24 August–17 September 1572, and until 3 October in the provinces. About 25,000 people are believed to have been killed. When ◊Catherine de' Medici's plot to have Admiral ◊Coligny assassinated failed, she resolved to have all the Huguenot leaders killed, persuading her son Charles IX it was in the interest of public safety.

Catherine received congratulations from all the Catholic powers, and the pope ordered a medal to be struck.

Saint-Gelais, Mellin de (1491–1558)

French poet. Together with Clément ◊Marot, he introduced the Italian sonnet into French literature, but was soon eclipsed by Pierre Ronsard and the ◊*Pléiade* poets. His tragedy *Sophonisbe* was performed in 1559.

St Peter's Cathedral

Cathedral church of the papacy in the Vatican, Rome, built 1506–1626. Begun by ◊Julius II, successive popes called upon the services of leading italian architects including Donato ◊Bramante and ◊Michelangelo.

The present basilica stands on the site once occupied by a chapel built over the tomb of St Peter by Pope Anacletus at the beginning of the 2nd century. In the place of this chapel Constantine the Great erected a basilica in 330, and it was here that Charlemagne was crowned Emperor of the West on Christmas Eve, 800. Pope ◊Nicholas V first planned in 1452 to reconstruct the basilica, and work began in 1506 through the commission of Pope Julius II.

Julius II commissioned Bramante, who planned a church in the form of a Greek cross with a central dome. On the death of Bramante, Raphael was placed in charge of the work by Pope Leo X. ◊Raphael produced a design in the form of a Latin cross, but when he died, ◊Peruzzi, who succeeded him, returned to the idea of a Greek cross. In 1536 Antonio da ◊Sangallo, the younger, produced a new plan for the completion of the structure, but this plan was later abandoned when Michelangelo became the responsible architect. Michelangelo reverted to the basic design of Bramante, and his work was continued after his death by Vignola, Pirro Ligorio, and Giacomo della Porta. Pope Paul V, however, again reverted to a Latin cross, and the nave was accordingly extended by Carlo Maderno (1556–1629), who also built the façade 1606–12.

The cathedral has an internal length of 180 m/600 ft and a width at the transepts of 135 m/450 ft. The dome has an internal diameter of 42 m/137 ft and rises externally 138 m/452 ft to the crowning cross of the lantern.

St Quentin, Battle of

In the war between Henry II of France and Philip II of Spain, a Spanish victory over the French 10 August 1557 at St Quentin, a French town 150 km/95 mi northwest of Paris.

A Spanish force, estimated at 5,000 cavalry and 3,000 foot under Duke Philibert of Savoy was threatening St Quentin and the Constable of France, the Duc de Montmorency, set out to relieve it with a 20,000-strong army of mainly French troops, but including some German mercenaries. Their route lay through a narrow valley, at which the Spanish set up an ambush. This proved so effective that Montmorency lost some 15,000 troops and all but two of his guns were captured. The Spanish lost only 50 troops and were able to deal with St Quentin at their leisure.

saint's play

Medieval religious drama, popular throughout Western Europe. The plays dramatized incidents from the lives and deaths of the saints, with the purpose of instructing the audience in the basic Christian doctrines and to show the possibility of defeating worldly temptation and enjoying eternal salvation.

Only three English saints' plays survived the political suppression of Catholic drama at the time of the Protestant Reformation: *The Conversion of St Paul* (*c.* 1500), *Mary Magdalene* (*c.* 1500), and the Cornish play *St Meriasek* (1504).

Salinas, Francisco de (1513–1590)

Spanish organist, theorist, and folk-song investigator. In his treatise *De Musica Libri Septem* (1579) he quotes the tunes of many Spanish folk songs.

He was the son of an official in the treasury of Charles V and became blind at the age of ten, whereupon his parents decided to let him study music. He was taken to Rome in 1538, where he met the lutenist Francesco da Milano and became a great admirer of Lassus. In 1558 he became organist to the Duke of Alba, viceroy of Naples, under Diego Ortiz. In 1561 he returned to Spain, became organist at León in 1563 and professor of music at Salamanca University, 1567. There he got to know the poet Luis de León, who wrote a poem on his organ playing.

Salutati, Coluccio (1331–1406)

Florentine humanist scholar and chancellor of that city. The self-appointed heir to Petrarch, Salutati can be credited with creating the first coterie of scholars devoted to *studia humanitatis*. His job as chancellor was to produce speeches and letters on behalf of the city, which he did with a new attention to Classical rhetoric. At the same time, he produced works on a range of topics from the efficacy of monastic life to Julius Caesar's right to be remembered as emperor. He gathered young scholars around him, such as Leonardo ◊Bruni, and arranged for Manuel ◊Chrysoloras to teach Greek in Florence.

His work proved controversial in his lifetime, with some critics claiming that his interest in what he called *studia humanitatis* was at the expense of proper reading of Christian literature. This was an accusation he and his protégés vehemently denied: it was the spur to one of Bruni's first works, his translation of St ◊Basil's tract on education. It was also the issue that lay behind Salutati's (unfinished) chief work, his *On the Labours of Hercules*, in which he tried to provide an allegorical reading of Classical myths to demonstrate their use to Christians.

In many ways, Salutati's scholarship was left behind by the next generation which he had helped to nurture. Although he himself knew no Greek, his protégés learned it and could read ancient texts beyond his grasp. The most indefatigable of those translators was Leonardo Bruni, whose early dialogue, the *Dialogi ad Petrum Paulum Histrum*, can be read as a rejection of Salutati's belief in a tradition of letters going back to Petrarch and beyond. Later, Poggio Bracciolini's first dialogue, *De Avaritia*, includes a satire on the tradition of allegorical interpretation of Classical works – a tradition into which *On the Labours of Hercules* obviously fits.

Salutati's major works

c. **1381**	*De Seculo et Religione/On the Secular and the Religious Life*
c. **1398**	*De Fato et Fortuna/On Fate and Fortune*
1390	*De Verecundia/On Shame*
1399	*De Nobilitate Legum et Medicine/On the Relative Nobility of Law and Medicine*
1400	*De Tyranno/About the Tyrant*
1403–04	*Invectiva contra Antonium Luscum/Invective against Antonio Loschi*
1390–1406	*De Laboribus Herculis/On the Labours of Hercules* (a first version written 1378–82; second version left unfinished at Salutati's death)

Salviati, Francesco (ADOPTED NAME OF FRANCESCO DEI ROSSI) (1510–1563)

Italian painter. He painted religious and Classical subjects in fresco (including the *Story of Psyche* in the Palazzo Grimani, Venice), as well as portraits. A fine example of his portraiture is *Portrait of a Boy* (National Gallery, London).

Salviati studied under several painters in his youth, among them Andrea del Sarto. He worked in Florence, Venice, and Rome with an interval in Paris 1554–56. His works include *The Triumph of Camillus* (Bargello, Florence) and *The Descent from the Cross* (Louvre, Paris).

Sambucus, Johannes (LATINIZED NAME OF JÁNOS ZSAMBOKY) (1531–1584)

Hungarian historian and Classical scholar. Sambucus was educated in Germany (by Philip ◊Melanchthon), France, and Italy (graduating in medicine from Padua). He lived for some time in the Netherlands, where he became friends with Christopher Plantin, who published his popular *Emblemata* (1564). In the same year, he was called to Vienna as imperial historiographer to Maximilian II and, later, Rudolf II. His publications also include patristic commentaries and editions of the work of an early Hungarian humanist, Janus Pannonius.

Sanctorius, Sanctorius (1561–1636)

Italian physiologist who pioneered the study of metabolism and invented the clinical thermometer and a device for measuring pulse rate.

Sanctorius introduced quantitative methods into medicine. For 30 years he weighed both himself and his food, drink, and waste products. He determined that over half of normal weight loss is due to 'insensible perspiration'.

Sandrin, Pierre Regnault (fl. 1540s–1560s)

French composer. He composed only chansons, of which the majority were published by Attaingnant. Lassus based a Mass on the chanson 'Doulce memoire'.

He was a member of the royal chapel 1543–60, during which time he also travelled to Italy.

Sangallo, Antonio Giamberti dal, THE YOUNGER (c. 1483–1546)

Florentine High Renaissance architect. He worked under ◊Bramante and ◊Peruzzi in Rome. His masterpiece is the monumental Palazzo Farnese, Rome (begun 1513, completed by Michelangelo). Sangallo took over as chief architect of St Peter's in 1539 and expanded on Bramante's original plan, but it was left to Michelangelo, his successor, to make of the building a convincing whole.

Sangallo, Giuliano Giamberti da (c. 1445–1516)

Italian architect and woodworker, born in Florence. He may have designed Bartolomeo ◊Scala's palazzo in the 1470s and he certainly became the favoured architect of Lorenzo de' ◊Medici, for whom he designed the Villa Medici at Poggio a Caiano (c. 1486–1519) and the church of Sta Maria delle

Carceri, Prato. After Lorenzo's death in 1492, Sangallo's fortunes declined. Although he was appointed one of the architects of St Peter's Basilica, Rome, in 1514 by the Medici Pope Leo X, his health was failing and he was overshadowed by Raphael.

Sangallo's earliest work was on choir stalls in Florence and Pisa, and throughout his life he continued to produce woodwork with his brother Antonio. But, as the art historian Giorgio ◊Vasari observed, 'woodworkers become architects', and so did Sangallo. He may have designed Bartolomeo Scala's palazzo in the 1470s. His classicizing style owed something to Brunelleschi and something to his own study of ancient buildings and writings (in particular, those of Vitruvius). As well as the commissions for Lorenzo, Sangallo designed the Florentine palazzo of Giuliano Gondi in 1490.

After the exile of the Medici, Sangallo entered the service of Cardinal Giuliano della Rovere, designing his palace in Savona and travelling with him to France. When this patron was elected Pope ◊Julius II, Sangallo travelled to Rome but failed to gain major commissions. He returned to republican Florence and turned his talents to military architecture, until he was called back to Rome by Leo X.

Sannazaro, Jacopo (1456–1530)

Italian poet and humanist. He wrote verse and prose in both Latin and Italian. His *Arcadia* (1504) was the first ◊pastoral romance in Italian; it established the form that was later to become very popular throughout Europe.

Sano di Pietro (1406–1481)

Sienese painter. He was a pupil of Stefano di ◊Sassetta, whom he followed in style. Many of his works are preserved in Siena, one of the most highly considered being *St Bernard Preaching*.

Sansovino (ORIGINALLY TATTI), Jacopo (1486–1570)

Florentine architect and sculptor. He was a pupil of Andrea Sansovino (died 1529), whose name he assumed when he accompanied him to Rome in 1505. He studied and began his career in Rome but fled after the sack of the city in 1527 to Venice, where

Santillana, Iñigo López de Mendoza, Marques de (1398–1458)

Castilian noble, poet, and bibliophile. He became friends with Enrique de ◊Villena while serving at the Aragonese court from 1412–18. He was rewarded for bravery at the 1455 battle of Olmedo with the marquisate of Santillana, and celebrated the execution of Juan II's favourite, Alvaro de Luna, with a satirical poem set out as the dead Luna's confession of his sins ('Doctrinal de Privados', 1456). Although he knew no Greek and his Latin was uncertain, he was an avid collector of books, especially translations from the classics and fine manuscripts, some of which were bought from ◊Vespasiano da Bisticci.

In 1449 he responded to a request by Pedro, Constable of Portugal, for a selection of his works, by sending him the *Prohemio e carta/Prologue and Letter*. This was an anthology of his poems prefaced by his considerations on poetry. His authorship of the 1447 *Refranes que dicen las viejas tras el fuego/Old Wives' Fireside Sayings* is unproven; he did, however, commemorate ◊Alfonso V's 1435 victory at Ponza with an Italian-style allegorical play, the *Comedieta de Ponça* (1436).

On his death, he was (with an exaggeration customarily allowed to mourners) remembered both by Italians, like Pier Candido ◊Decembrio, and his compatriots as the man who had introduced Classical learning into Spain.

Sassetta, Stefano di Giovanni (c. 1392–1450)

Italian painter. His work remained true to the International Gothic style of the 14th-century Sienese school, while reflecting contemporary discoveries in spatial representation by Florentine artists. His major work is the altarpiece of St Francis for S Francesco in Borgo San Sepolcro (1437–44, distributed between Villa i Tatti, Florence; the National Gallery, London; and the Louvre, Paris).

most of his major works are found. His principal works include the Loggetta in St Mark's Square (1537–40); the richly decorated Library and Mint (1535–45) opposite the Doge's Palace; and in Rome, the church of S Marcello and the Palazzo Gaddi. The library was greatly admired by Andrea ◊Palladio.

Sansovino is best known for the ◊Biblioteca Marciana (begun 1536), the first fully Classical building in Venice in which the orders were correctly used.

Santi, Giovanni (1450–1494)

Italian painter of the Umbrian School. He is principally of note as the father of ◊Raphael Sanzio. He shows a true sensitivity of feeling in such works as *The Madonna and Child* (National Gallery, London), though the work of his son was evidently inspired by other sources.

Savery, Roelandt (1576–1639)

Flemish painter and etcher. He worked for ◊Henry IV in France and for the Holy Roman Emperor ◊Rudolf II in Prague, becoming personal painter to the emperor Mathias after the death of Rudolf in 1612. He painted landscapes with mythological incident and minutely detailed flowers and animals.

Savile, Henry (1549–1622)

English scholar. His chief works were a collection of early English chronicles, *Rerum Anglicarum Scriptores* (1581), and an edition of St John Chrysostom (1610–13). He also worked on the King James Authorized Version of the Bible.

Savile was born in Bradley, near Halifax, West Yorkshire, and studied at Oxford, where he became warden of Merton College in 1585. He became provost of Eton school in 1596. In 1619 he founded the Savilian professorships of astronomy and geometry at Oxford.

Savoldo, Giovanni Girolamo (1480–1550)

Painter from Brescia, active in Florence, Venice, and Treviso. He foreshadows the realism of Caravaggio in such works as *Mary Magdalene Approaching the Sepulchre* (version in National Gallery, London), and the landscape backgrounds of his religious subjects are remarkable in their effects of light.

He may have trained in Venice, his style being modelled on that of the Venetian Renaissance masters.

Savonarola, Girolamo (1452–1498)

Ferrarese preacher and theologian. Savonarola joined a Dominican monastery in Bologna in 1475, aged 33, but swiftly made up for this late start, acquiring an impressive reputation as a fiery preacher. ◊Lorenzo de' Medici invited him to Florence in 1490; he thundered from his pulpit against worldly power and moral lassitude until the exile of the Medici in 1494. The eventual backlash against his fervent, gloomy, powerful prophetic preaching in 1498 led to his torture and burning.

Savonarola's apocalyptic language both flattered and castigated the Florentine populace as God's chosen, but currently sinful emissaries, who would ultimately purify the world. This 'negative' eschatological aspect of self-important Renaissance civic ideology, with Florence as the archetype and Savonarola as its prophet, was as much a part of Christian urban culture in *c.* 1500 as a renewed interest in, for example, Roman civic architecture: Medicean and Savonarolan Florence were, essentially, the same place.

Scala, Bartolomeo (1430–1497)

Florentine humanist and secretary who became chancellor of the city from 1465. His career was made by his links with the ◊Medici family, which began with his acting as secretary to Pierfranceso de' Medici. His connections, however, also gained him the animosity of another Medicean acolyte, Politian. Scala's writings included a *History of Florence* (written in a tradition begun by Leonardo ◊Bruni, and left unfinished at his death), a dialogue *De Legibus et Iudiciis/On Laws and Judgements*, dedicated to Lorenzo de' ◊Medici, and *De Consolatione/On Consolation*, written on the death of Giovanni de' Medici in 1463.

Scaliger, Joseph Justus (1540–1609)

French scholar. He revolutionized the study of ancient chronology in his editions of Manilius (1579) and *Opus De Emendatione Temporum* (1583), and reconstructed the lost *Chronicle of Eusebius* (1606).

Scaliger was born in Agen, southwest France, son of the scholar and soldier **Julius Caesar Scaliger** (1484–1558) who had been a Ciceronian critic of Erasmus. Under his father's tuition, he became a master of Latin and of textual and historical criticism. He was a professor at Geneva 1572–74 and Leiden from 1593, and edited many Classical texts. He also fought for the Huguenots during the French Wars of Religion.

Scandello, Antonio (1517–1580)

Italian composer. He became a Protestant and was music director (Kapellmeister) at the Elector of Saxony's court chapel at Dresden. Both his church music and secular songs combine Italian and German styles for the first time.

He is first heard of as a cornettist in Bergamo 1541 and was a member of the Saxon court chapel at Dresden in 1553, but he often returned to Brescia for visits, as in 1567, when he and his family took refuge there during the plague at Dresden. Among the court musicians was his brother Angelo Scandello, and also employed at the court was the Italian painter Benedetto Tola, whose daughter Agnese became Scandello's second wife in 1568. In the same year he was appointed Kapellmeister in place of Matthieu Le Maistre, whose assistant he had been for two years. He became involved in quarrels with the German court musicians and the Flemish singers because the Italians received higher pay.

Works include:
Masses, motets, setting for voices of the Passion and Resurrection narrative according to St John (1561), hymn tunes for several voices and other church music; madrigals, epithalamia, *canzoni napoletane* for four voices, sacred and secular German songs for several voices and instruments; lute music.

Scève, Maurice (*c.* 1501–*c.* 1564)

French poet. His works include *Délie, objet de plus haute vertu* (1544), poems on the subject of love; *La Saulsaye* (1547), a shorter pastoral poem; and *Microcosme* (1562), a philosophical poem tracing the history of humans on Earth.

He was the leader of the so-called *poètes lyonnais*, whose verse marks the transition from Clément ◊Marot to Pierre ◊Ronsard. *Délie* is written in more than 400 *dizains*, ten-line stanzas of ten-syllable verse.

Schiavone, Andrea (REAL NAME ANDREA MELDOLLA), CALLED 'THE SLAVONIAN' (1515–1563)

Italian painter of Dalmatian origin. He settled in Venice and painted both religious and mythological subjects. He may have been the pupil of Francesco ◊Parmigianino, but he was influenced by ◊Titian and developed a Venetian richness of colour.

Schlick, Arnolt (BEFORE 1460–AFTER 1521)

German organist, composer, and theorist. In 1511 he published his *Spiegel der Orgelmacher und Organisten*, a treatise on organ building and playing. The *Tabulaturen etlicher Lobgesang und Lidlein*, published at Mainz in 1512, followed; it was the first printed book of keyboard music to appear in Germany, and contained liturgical organ music, lute pieces, and songs with lute.

His early life was spent in Heidelberg, but he subsequently travelled widely: to Frankfurt in 1486, where he played the organ during the festivities for the coronation of Maximilian I; to Holland in 1490; to Strasbourg (many times); to Worms in 1495, where he met Sebastian Virdung; and subsequently to Speyer, Hagenau, and elsewhere. During these journeys he gained an enormous reputation for testing new organs. He also wrote music for the coronation of Charles V in Aachen, 1520. He was blind, probably from infancy.

Schmid(t), Bernhard, THE ELDER (1535–1592)

Composer and poet from Strasbourg. He published a collection of music arranged for organ in two parts: the first contained motets, the second secular songs and dances, published at Strasbourg in 1577.

His son, **Bernhard Schmid(t) the Younger** (1567–1625) was also a composer of organ music.

Schongauer, Martin (*c.* 1450–1491)

German painter and engraver. He worked in the ornate, late Gothic style, his best-known painting being *The Madonna of the Rose-Arbour* (1473) (St Martin's Church, Colmar). He was one of the most important early engravers and helped to transform engraving from a craft to an art.

Deeply influenced by Rogier van ◊Weyden, he in turn influenced many of his contemporaries. The young ◊Dürer, who admired and copied his work, sought him out and, though Schongauer died before they could meet, worked in his studio in Colmar.

Schongauer was the son of the goldsmith, Kaspar Schongauer, and became a freeman of Colmar 1455. From about 1473 he worked in Colmar, where the monastery church has his one entirely authenticated painting, *The Madonna of the Rose-Arbour*. In 1488 he became a citizen of Breisach.

School of Athens, The

Fresco painted 1509 by the Italian Renaissance artist ◊Raphael Sanzio in the Stanza della Segnatura of the Vatican, Rome. It is a companion painting to the *Disputà*. As the latter represents the triumph of Christianity, so *The School of Athens* represents the advance of philosophy and learning.

It shows the colonnade of a stately Temple of Knowledge adorned with statues of Apollo and Minerva. The central figures of the Greek philosophers Plato and Aristotle are surrounded by others symbolic of various forms of science and education.

Not all the characters are identifiable but, as in the *Disputà*, some of the philosophers are actually contemporary portraits – Raphael himself appears, as does a brooding ◊Michelangelo in the foreground and the architect Donato ◊Bramante, as a geometer with compasses.

Schuyt, Cornelis (1557–1616)

Flemish composer. He held a succession of organ appointments in the Netherlands. He published several books of madrigals and a book of instrumental pieces.

He travelled to Italy to study music, returning to the Netherlands in 1581.

Scorel, Jan van (1495–1562)

Dutch painter. Deeply influenced by Italian art, he introduced Renaissance motifs to the northern part of the Low Countries.

Scorel trained in Alkmaar and Utrecht, where he settled. He travelled widely, visiting Germany, Italy, and Palestine (there are portraits by him of Dutch pilgrims to Jerusalem in Utrecht Museum). Appointed keeper of the Belvedere in the Vatican by ◊Adrian (Hadrian) VI (a native of Utrecht), he acquired a deep admiration for the art of ◊Raphael Sanzio and ◊Michelangelo. He returned to Utrecht in 1524 and spent the rest of his life there.

He was highly influential in Holland, his students including Maerten Heemskerk and Anthonis Mor.

Scott, Alexander (c. 1515–1583)

Scottish poet. His work includes a verse homily to ◊Mary Queen of Scots, some comic pieces, and one or two versified psalms. The rest are passionate or cynical love poems.

Sebastiani, Claudius (DIED 1565)

German music theorist. He held organist's posts at Fribourg and Metz, but is famous particularly for his treatise *Bellum Musicale/The Musical War*, published at Strasbourg in 1563.

Sebastiano del Piombo (LUCIANI) (c. 1485–1547)

Venetian painter, he was a pupil of ◊Giorgione and developed a similar style. In 1511 he moved to Rome, where his friendship with Michelangelo (and rivalry with Raphael) inspired his finest works, such as *The Raising of Lazarus* 1517–19 (National Gallery, London).

Michelangelo encouraged him and provided designs for his work, including *The Flagellation* (S Pietro in Montorio, Rome), and the *Pietà* in Viterbo. His portraits include *Clement VII* (Naples Museum) and *Andrea Doria* (Doria Gallery, Rome).

From 1531 Sebastiano was keeper of the papal leaden seal, hence his sobriquet.

Secundus, Johannes (PSEUDONYM OF JAN NICOLAI EVERAERTS, OR EVERTS) (1511–1536)

Dutch humanist poet. Amongst the range of Latin poetry that he wrote in his career, the most influential were his love lyrics *Basia/Kisses* which worked off the Classical poets Horace and Catullus.

He was private secretary to the archbishop of Toledo in Spain, and he accompanied the Holy Roman Emperor Charles V to Tunis 1534.

Segni, Giulio (GIULIO DA MODENA) (1498–1561)

Italian composer. He composed three *ricercari à 4* (published in *Musica Nova* in 1540) and other instrumental works.

After a short period as organist of St Mark's, Venice, 1530–33, he entered the service of Pope Clement VII.

Sellaio, Jacopo del (1441–1493)

Florentine painter. He painted religious and mythological subjects, modelling his style on that of Sandro Botticelli. A *Pietà* 1483 (Staatliche Museen, Berlin) is one of his principal authentic works.

Sellaio was a pupil of Fra Filippo Lippi. A number of Botticellian imitations have been tentatively attributed to him.

Sempill, Robert (c. 1530–1595)

Scottish satirical poet. He wrote *The Sege of the Castel of Edinburgh* in 1573 (first printed 1724), in which he probably took part, and coarsely satirical poems on the life of his times, such as *The Regentis Tragedie* (1570).

Senfl, Ludwig (c. 1486–c. 1542)

Swiss composer. He made imaginative arrangements of traditional German melodies, ranging from chordal harmonization to canons, and is regarded as the most important German-speaking composer of motets and songs during the Reformation.

He studied under Henricus ◊Isaac in Vienna and sang 1496–1513 in the *Hofkapelle* of ◊Maximilian I in Vienna, Augsburg, and Constance. He worked with Isaac in copying a large amount of music which was later published as part of Isaac's *Choralis constantinus* (1550–55), a task Senfl completed around 1520. In 1513 he succeeded Isaac as Kapellmeister to Emperor Maximilian I, holding the post until the emperor's death in 1519. In 1520 he went to Augsburg and in 1523 to Munich, where he settled as first musician at the ducal court of Wilhelm of Bavaria. In 1530 he was in correspondence with Martin ◊Luther.

Works include:

Seven masses, Magnificats, motets and other church music; odes by Horace for voices; about 250 German songs.

Serlio, Sebastiano (1475–1554)

Bolognese architect and painter. He was the author of *Regale generali di architettura/General Rules of Architecture* (published in six parts 1537–51, with a posthumous seventh part 1575),.which set down practical rules for the use of the Classical orders and was used by architects of the Neo-Classical style throughout Europe.

He was born at Bologna, and trained by his father as a painter. He went to Rome in 1514, and became assistant to ◊Peruzzi, whom he accompanied to Venice in 1527 after the ◊sack of Rome. Here he began writing his book. In 1541 he was invited to Paris by Francis I, by whom he was employed at the palace of Fontainebleau for some years. The course of French architecture was to be greatly influenced by his limited number of executed buildings, and even more so by *L'Architettura/Architecture*.

Sermisy, Claudin de (USUALLY KNOWN AS CLAUDIN) (c. 1490–1562)

French composer. He was master of the choristers at the French royal chapel, and wrote about 110 sacred works, including motets, Masses, and a Passion. His reputation, however, both during his lifetime and since, has rested on his chansons, of which about 175 survive. They have attractive melodies and are simpler and more homophonic and syllabic in style than those of his contemporaries. Many of them were arranged by other composers for a variety of vocal and instrumental forces.

He was attached to the Sainte-Chapelle in Paris 1508–14, in 1515 became a singer in the royal chapel just before Louis XII's death, and in the same year his choir competed with the Papal choir before Leo X; he later succeeded Antoine de Longueval as master of the choristers. In 1520, with François I, he met the English king Henry VIII at the Field of the Cloth of Gold. A similar meeting followed in 1532 at Boulogne; and on both occasions the French and English choirs sang together. In 1533 he was made a canon of the Sainte-Chapelle, with a living and a substantial salary attached to it; but his duties there were light and he remained in the royal chapel, with which, under François I, he visited Bologna.

Works include:

Eleven masses, motets; about 175 chansons for several voices.

Servetus, Michael (MIGUEL SERVETO) (1511–1553)

Spanish Anabaptist theologian and physician. He was a pioneer in the study of the circulation of the blood and found that it circulates to the lungs from the right chamber of the heart. He was, however, as noted for his death as for his life: passing through Calvin's Geneva, he was arrested for his unorthodox views on the Trinity (expressed in his treatise *On the Errors of the Trinity*, 1531). After Servetus had been found guilty of heresy, Calvin had him burnt.

Sforza, Ludovico, IL MORO (1451–1508)

Effective ruler of Milan from 1480, duke from 1494. The younger brother of Galeazzo Maria Sforza, he increasingly came to dominate government after the latter's assassination in 1476. Galeazzo Maria's heir, Giangaleazzo was a mere boy; Ludovico took control by taking the titles of governor and lieutenant. In 1494, Giangaleazzo died (there was talk of poison administered at Ludovico's behest) and Ludovico became duke. He did not, however, have long to enjoy full power. Louis XII invaded in 1499 and ousted Ludovico, capturing the former duke the following year. The rest of Ludovico's life was spent in captivity.

It is unclear how Ludovico gained his nickname *il Moro* – presumably he was swarthy in complexion. However tenuous Ludovico's grasp of morality, he suffered from human weakness; though he was by no means faithful to his wife, Beatrice d' Este, her death in 1497 seems to have left him a brooding figure. At the same time, his court enjoyed a reputation for being a cultural centre: it was, after all, the place of employment for ◊Leonardo da Vinci, ◊Bramante and Baldassare ◊Castiglione in these years. Ludovico could be celebrated in panegyrics, for example by Filippo Beroaldo the Elder, as a patron of letters. This was brought to an abrupt end by the events of 1499.

Sforza family

Italian family that ruled the duchy of Milan 1450–99, 1512–15, 1521–24, and 1529–35. Its court was a centre of Renaissance culture and its rulers prominent patrons of the arts.

The family descended from Giacomuzzo, or Muzio, Attendolo (1369–1424), a peasant *condottiere* who adopted the name of Sforza. **Francesco Sforza** (1401–66) succeeded his father in command of the *condottiere*. He served Filippo Maria Visconti, Duke of Milan, and in 1441 married his only daughter, Bianca. On Filippo's death in 1447, Francesco defeated the Venetians, hereditary enemies of Milan, and was acknowledged duke of Milan in 1450. **Galeazzo Maria Sforza** (1444–76) succeeded as duke of Milan in 1466. When he was assassinated, he left a young son, **Giangaleazzo** Sforza (1468–94), who took the title of duke, with his mother as regent. Ludovico ◊Sforza, Giangaleazzo's uncle, supplanted

the regent and took power, eventually becoming duke on his nephew's death in 1494. Though he himself lost the dukedom when the French invaded in 1499, the volatile situation in the following decades meant that both his sons were, briefly, installed in Milan: **Massimiliano** (1490–1530, named after the Holy Roman Emperor) was duke from 1512 until the Francis I's successful invasion of 1515; **Francesco Maria** (1492–1535) held power twice, in 1521–24 and from 1529 until his death in 1535, which left Charles V in control of Milan.

sfumato

Use of shading to blend areas of light and dark together in oil painting to provide a transition between objects such as a figure and the sky. An influential and successful example of this practice is ◊Leonardo da Vinci's *Virgin of the Rocks* (Louvre, Paris, and National Gallery, London).

Shakespeare, William (1564–1616)

English dramatist and poet. Thirty-seven plays attributed to him survive, including the tragedies *Hamlet*, *Macbeth*, *King Lear*, *Romeo and Juliet*, *Othello*, *Antony and Cleopatra*, and others; comedies, such as *As You Like It*, *A Midsummer Night's Dream*, *Twelfth Night*, and *The Taming of the Shrew*; history plays, including *Henry V* and *Richard III*; and romances, including *Cymbeline* and *The Tempest*. Poems include *Venus and Adonis*, *The Rape of Lucrece*, and *Shakespeare's Sonnets*.

life William Shakespeare was born in Stratford-on-Avon. The exact date of his birth is not known, but it is close to April 23, the day on which he also died. His father, John Shakespeare, was a wool dealer and probably a Roman Catholic. Shakespeare was educated at the grammar school but did not go to university, and in 1582 married Anne Hathaway. They had a daughter, Susanna, in 1583, and in 1585 twins, Hamnet (died 1596) and Judith. Shakespeare's movements in these years are unknown, but by the early 1590s he had moved to London and was establishing a reputation as an actor and a writer in the theatre. In 1598 Shakespeare's company, the Lord Chamberlain's Men, were in dispute over the tenancy of their base, the Theatre, and tore it down before using the timbers again to erect a new theatre, the

MILAN: VISCONTI, SFORZA, AND VALOIS

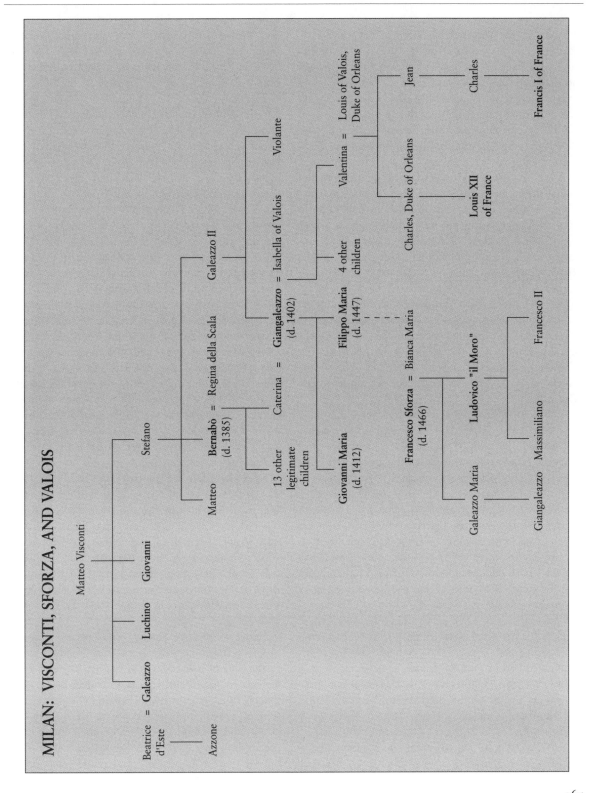

Globe, in the disreputable suburb of Southwark. Shakespeare was a 'sharer' in the company, entitling him to a share of the profits. In 1603 the company attracted the sponsorship of the new monarch James I and became the King's Men. By now Shakespeare was the leading playwright of the company. He continued to maintain links with Stratford, though, and died there on 23 April 1616 and is buried in Holy Trinity Church.

works In the absence of copyright laws, professional dramatists were by and large unwilling to let their plays be printed, as it diminished their value to the theatrical company for which they worked. Nonetheless, several Shakespeare plays were published in his lifetime, sometimes anonymously. But in 1623, seven years after his death, two former colleagues – John Heminges and Henry Condell – organized an edition of Shakespeare's works (the 'First Folio') which included most of Shakespeare's surviving output and cemented his reputation as one of the leading dramatists of the age along with Ben Jonson, Francis Beaumont, and John ◊Fletcher. Within the plays, it is possible to construct an approximate chronology.

before 1598 Shakespeare's earliest surviving plays probably date from the late 1580s and include *Henry VI* parts I, II, and III, *Richard III*, and the gory tragedy *Titus Andronicus*. It can be guessed that he also worked in collaboration with other dramatists at this time; for instance, on the play *Sir Thomas More*. During the plague of 1593–94, and the 18-month closure of the theatres that it caused, Shakespeare wrote two long narrative poems on erotic themes, *Venus and Adonis* (1593) and *The Rape of Lucrece* (1594), both dedicated to the Earl of Southampton. In the mid-1590s, Shakespeare produced a string of comedies, including *The Comedy of Errors*, *A Midsummer Night's Dream*, and *Loves Labours Lost*, as well as further plays about English history, including *Richard II* and *Henry IV* parts I and II. In 1598, Francis Meres, in *Palladis Tamia*, a survey of English poets and playwrights, praised Shakespeare for these works, as well as for 'sugared sonnets' in circulation in manuscript and a mysterious lost play, *Loves Labours Won*.

1598–c. 1608 Shakespeare wrote his major tragedies in these years: *Hamlet*, *Othello*, *King Lear*, *Macbeth*,

and *Antony and Cleopatra*. He also wrote comedies, including *Troilus and Cressida*, *All's Well That Ends Well*, and *Measure for Measure*, so strange and dark in tone that they are often referred to as 'problem plays'.

c. 1608–1616 The publication of Shakespeare's *Sonnets* in 1609 may not reflect the date of their composition, as Meres says that some sonnets by Shakespeare, at least, were in circulation nine years earlier. Shakespeare's late plays, including *Pericles*, *Cymbeline*, *The Winter's Tale*, and *The Tempest*, are often grouped together by critics as 'the romances', since they share common concerns with families parted and reunited, with the redemptive power of art, and with the motif of the sea, although all these ideas occur elsewhere in the Shakespeare canon too. Shakespeare's last plays included *Two Noble Kinsmen* and *Henry VIII*, a collaboration with John Fletcher which was playing at the Globe in 1613 when a misfiring special effect burned the theatre to the ground.

controversies Debate continues about the extent to which Shakespeare worked with collaborators both on canonical plays like *Macbeth* and *Pericles*, and on plays like *Edward III* which is not generally admitted to the Shakespeare canon. Poems whose authorship remains disputed include 'A Funeral Elegy' by WS 1612. Furthermore, with many plays (notably *King Lear*) problems remain over which early version of the play is preferable.

Secondly, there are controversies of interpretation. The argument advanced by 19th-century critics that the plays provide an unproblematic access for the reader into the soul of the historical Shakespeare have now largely been discarded. None the less, controversy continues over the biographical implications of aspects of Shakespeare's work, notably the sonnets, since part of the sequence appears to depict a homosexual relationship between the speaker and a younger man.

Efforts to co-opt Shakespeare's plays for political purposes started as early as 1601, when the followers of the Earl of Essex arranged to have *Richard II* performed as a prelude to his intended coup against Queen Elizabeth, in the belief that the play's depiction of a weak monarch deposed for the country's good would gain sympathy for their cause. Since then, his works have been claimed as celebrating – but in other readings as condemning – nationalism (for instance, *Henry V*), imperialism (for instance, *The Tempest*), and racial discrimination (for instance, *The Merchant of Venice*), to name just three topics. Indeed, Shakespeare's continuing fascination rests to a large extent on the continuing ability of his plays to provoke controversy and debate.

Finally, it is sometimes argued that all the works attributed to Shakespeare were in fact written by someone else acting in a secret conspiracy. Favoured alternative candidates include Edward de Vere, Earl of ◊Oxford (on the grounds that only an aristocrat could have written these plays), Francis ◊Bacon (on the grounds that only a highly educated man could have written these plays), and Christopher ◊Marlowe (on the grounds that Shakespeare's life story was insufficiently romantic for him to have had the inspiration for these plays). All three of these theories are equally plausible; that is, not at all.

Sheppard, John (*c.* 1515–*c.* 1563)

English composer. In 1542 he became organist and choirmaster at Magdalen College, Oxford, and later was in Queen Mary's Chapel Royal.

He learnt music as a choirboy at St Paul's Cathedral in London under Thomas Mulliner.

Works include:

Masses *The Western Wynde*, *The French Masse*, *Be not afraide*, and *Playn Song Mass for a Mene*, 21 Office responds, 18 hymns, motets, two Te Deums, two Magnificats, anthems, and other choral pieces.

Sidney, Philip (1554–1586)

English poet and incompetent soldier. He wrote the sonnet sequence *Astrophel and Stella* (1591), *Arcadia* (1590), a prose romance, and *Apologie for Poetrie* (1595). Politically, Sidney became a charismatic, but hardly powerful, figure supporting a 'forward' foreign policy that would help the Protestant Netherlands against the Spanish.

Sidney was born in Penshurst, Kent. Educated at Christ Church, Oxford, he rounded off his education by a tour around Europe in the company of Hubert ◊Languet. He entered Parliament in 1581, and was knighted in 1583. In 1585 he was made governor of Vlissingen in the Netherlands, and died at Zutphen, fulfilling his desire of fighting the Spanish.

Sidney's reputation, which was high among a few writers and politicians (like Edmund ◊Spenser) in his life, increased immeasurably after his death. He provided the nearest thing the English Calvinists had to a martyr for their cause, whose life was mythologized by Fulke ◊Greville.

Sigismund (1368–1437)

King of Hungary from 1387, Holy Roman Emperor from 1410 (crowned king of the Romans 1414; crowned emperor 1433), and king of Bohemia from 1419, though he actually ruled it only for the last year of his life. Sigismund's reign was overshadowed by two religious issues: the ◊Great Schism and the agitation of the reformer John ◊Huss. Sigismund demonstrated his ability as a European leader in working to end the schism by arranging the Council of ◊Constance 1414–18; his weakness was manifest in his continual failure to suppress the Hussites.

The younger son of the house of Luxemburg, Sigismund owed his conglomeration of lands to his father's foresight and his brother's incompetence. Married to the daughter of Lewis of Hungary, Sigismund inherited that kingdom on his father-in-law's death, though in the following years he faced repeated revolts. Meanwhile, his elder brother Wenceslas (1361–1419) had failed to impress as Holy Roman Emperor or king of Bohemia, being given to heavy drinking rather than high politics. Wenceslas was deposed as emperor in 1400 and was eventually succeeded by Sigismund. On Wenceslas's death in 1419, Sigismund also inherited Bohemia – a poisoned chalice, as Wenceslas had failed to deal with the Hussites. At the Council of Constance Sigismund had promised protection to Huss, but imprisoned him after his condemnation for heresy and acquiesced in his burning in 1415. After unsuccesful crusades against his subjects, Sigismund found the door opened to his second kingdom by the actions of another council of the church, that at ◊Basel.

Sigismund's career was marked by military failures (like the crusade against the Ottomans defeated, at Nicopolis in 1396) and diplomatic successes. His influence at the Council of Constance attracted the attention of humanists and one, Pier Paolo ◊Vergerio, joined his court as his historian. Others, like

Francesco ◊Filelfo and Ambrogio ◊Traversari, visited his court at Buda. Contacts with Italy were fostered by Sigismund's coronation expedition to Italy 1431–33 (his imperial coronation was characteristically recorded in a letter by ◊Poggio Bracciolini). And if Sigismund was not a patron of the new style of Italian art, others in his employ were: the administrator and soldier Pippo Spano (Filippo Scolari) brought the Florentine painter ◊Masolino briefly to Hungary. In other words, there was an acquaintance with the new Italian styles decades before the reign of Sigismund's eventual successor, ◊Matthias Corvinus.

signore

The Italian name for a man who takes control of a city into his own hands. Various *signori*, gaining power in the 13th or 14th century in their particular city, did so by overturning a republican constitution and establishing their own rule without any claim to legitimacy. Signorial control often became hereditary, but was open to challenge for other would-be *signori*.

Examples of signorial regimes are the ◊Visconti in Milan, the d' ◊Este in Ferrara and the ◊Gonzaga in Mantua. A *signore* could rarely act as a tyrant: he often worked through the institutions which existed and with the assistance of the patrician families.

Signorelli, Luca (*c.* 1450–1523)

Painter from Cortona (in Tuscany). Probably trained by ◊Piero della Francesca, his patrons included ◊Sixtus IV and Lorenzo de' ◊Medici. His frescoes of *The End of the World* (1499–1503) in the Cappella di S Brizio, Orvieto Cathedral, according to Michelangelo, inspired elements in his own *Last Judgement*.

One of Signorelli's earliest jobs was as one of the artists of the ◊Sistine Chapel; late on in the work, he contributed two frescoes, one painted over in 1571, the other surviving: *The Testament of Moses*. After his time in Rome, Signorelli produced work for Loreto's Santa Casa (influenced by Verrochio), for Perugia Cathedral (*Virgin and Child with Saints, c.* 1484) and for Lorenzo de' Medici in Florence – his *Court of Pan* involves a complicated and obscure allegory. Later commissions came from a range of towns, including his own hometown where he painted *The*

Lamentation over the Dead Christ (1502). His works, like those of Antonio Pollaiuolo, display a fascination with the male form.

signoria

A word meaning both the rule of a ◊signore and the council ruling a republic like Florence. In Florence, the *signoria* was elected to serve for two months; its members lived in the Palazzo Vecchio for their period of office.

silverpoint

Drawing instrument consisting of silver wire encased in a holder, used on paper prepared with opaque white. An example of silverpoint is Dürer's *Self-portrait* (1484, Albertina, Vienna).

The ground was composed of powdered bones and gumwater, giving an ivory finish, though in Italy, and especially in Florence, tinted grounds were favoured. Being indelible and not liable to smudge, the silverpoint was convenient for the sketchbook, as in that which Dürer took with him on his visit to the Netherlands. Lead, copper, and gold metalpoints were also used, but silver was most popular in the 15th and 16th centuries.

Sinan (1489–1588)

Ottoman architect. He was chief architect to Suleiman the Magnificent from 1538. Among the hundreds of buildings he designed are the Suleimaniye mosque complex in Istanbul 1551–58 and the Selimiye mosque in Adrinople (now Edirne) 1569–74.

Sistine Chapel

Chapel in the papal palace complex of the Vatican, Rome. It was built in about 1477–80 on the site of an earlier large chapel (*capella magna*) by Giovanni del Dolci (died before 1486) at the order of Sixtus IV. The chapel was designed to the proportions of Solomon's temple (its height a half and its width a third of its length).

The first decoration of the Sistine Chapel took place in the early 1480s when, with a new entente between Sixtus and the Florentine Medici rulers, a group of mainly Tuscan artists were sent to Rome to paint its frescoes. This group, probably supervised by Pietro ◊Perugino, comprised Sandro ◊Botticelli, Domenico ◊Ghirlandaio, Cosimo ◊Rosselli, Piero di ◊Cosimo, Luca ◊Signorelli, and Bernardino ◊Pinturicchio. On the altar wall, Perugino painted *The Annunciation of the Virgin Mary* (to which the chapel was dedicated); on the north wall, there was a cycle recording the life of Jesus, and on the south, a cycle of the life of Moses, both being completed on the west wall.

Later popes were not satisfied, however, to leave the chapel as it was. In part, this was because of structural difficulties in the building: the ceiling cracked in 1504 and had to be rebuilt. ◊Julius II commissioned ◊Michelangelo to paint the new ceiling 1508–12. His cycle of frescoes depicted a range of stories from Genesis (for example, *The Creation of Adam*) as well as including images of sybils and seven prophets. Stories of Michelangelo's reluctance to paint this cycle, as well as his often ill-tempered discussions with the pope about it, were recorded by both ◊Vasari and Ascanio ◊Condivi, Michelangelo's first biographers; whether they are true or not, what is not in doubt is the high opinion contemporaries had of this cycle.

Twenty years later, first ◊Clement VII, then Paul III

Sistine Chapel Perugino, Christ giving the keys to Peter, one of the frescoes painted for Sixtus IV's chapel in the Vatican. The subject stressed the power God gave to Peter and his successors, the popes. *AKG London*

Although the work is of such beauty as Your Lordship may imagine, there are those who do not like it; some say that the nudes are not fitting in such a place, showing their parts, even though Michelangelo has exercised considerable tact in this and there are scarcely ten in the whole multitude where you can see their sexual organs. Others complain that the Christ has no beard and is too young...

Nino Sernini to Cardinal Ercole Gonzaga on the controversy of Michelangelo's *Last Judgement*, 1541

talked about replacing the altar fresco with one by Michelangelo: this was the genesis of *The Last Judgement*, completed 1541. This fresco, however, proved more controversial than the ceiling decoration; there were accusations of immodesty and heresy. The plans to destroy it in 1564 were headed off by the project to paint over any appearance of genitalia, a task first undertaken by ◊Daniele da Volterra. His emendations were not enough to calm the palpitations of the more shockable clerics and plans for destruction re-emerged later in the century, only to be dropped once again in favour of further 'tidying up'.

Sixtus IV (born Francesco della Rovere) (1414–1484)

Pope 1471–84. Born near Savona to a family of little note, he rose to become general of the Franciscan order in 1464 and, in 1467, a cardinal. An outside candidate at the conclave of 1471, few could have anticipated that this scholarly monk would turn to power politics and extravagant patronage.

Soon after his election, he broke the promise he had made in the conclave not to create new cardinals and had two nephews – one of them the future ◊Julius II – presented with red hats. His attempts to increase the papacy's political power in Italy brought him into conflict first with the Medici and then with his erstwhile ally, Ferrante of Naples. These intrigues, however, gained him little political advantage.

Sixtus was concerned not just to increase the papacy's political hold; he also wished to enhance its aura of magnificence. Building on Nicholas V's plans,

he ordered a series of improvements to the Vatican and the area around it, for example, having the ancient Pons Agrippae rebuilt (and renamed Ponte Sisto) in 1473. In the Vatican itself, he rebuilt the main chapel as the ◊Sistine Chapel. On the other side of the Tiber, he also had a new church constructed at S Maria del Popolo in 1472–80, and commissioned S Maria della Pace in 1478–83. His artistic patronage extended to his home town, Savona, where he paid for alterations to the cathedral; in this, as in much else, his work was continued by his nephew, the future Julius II.

It was again in the footsteps of Nicholas V that Sixtus treaded when he announced the establishment (or rather embellishment) of the Vatican Library in 1475. This event, and his appointment of ◊Platina as its librarian was recorded in a fresco painted by ◊Melozzo da Forlì. The reading rooms were completed and a room each given to Latin and Greek literature (the Vatican's holdings of Greek texts could only be rivalled by the Medicean collection in Florence and the Biblioteca ◊Marciana in Venice).

Sixtus V (born Felice Peretti) (1521–1590)

Pope from 1585. He supported the Spanish Armada against Britain and the Catholic League against Henry IV of France.

Skelton, John (c. 1460–1529)

English poet. He was tutor to the future Henry VIII, under whom he became ◊poet laureate in effect, if not in name. His satirical poetry includes political attacks on Cardinal ◊Wolsey, such as *Collyn Cloute* (1522). He also wrote *Magnyfycence* (1516), the first secular morality play in English.

Skelton was born in Norfolk and studied at both Oxford and Cambridge universities. He became a priest in 1498 and was given the living of Diss in Norfolk.

His first recorded verses were composed on the death of Edward IV (1483). *Phyllyp Sparowe* (written before 1509) is a parody of the liturgical office for the dead, delivered upon a young lady's pet; *A Ballade of the Scottysshe Kynge* is an attack on Henry VIII's enemies, written after the Battle of Flodden (1513); the rumbustious *The Tunnyng of Elynour Rummynge* (1516) describes the drunks in an alehouse; 'Speke Parrot' (1521), *Collyn Cloute*, and *Why come ye nat to Court* 1522 all combine attacks on the growing influence of Wolsey with criticism of humanist learning.

Sluter, Claus (*c.* 1380–1406)
Netherlandish sculptor, in the service of ◊Philip the Bold of Burgundy. He was active in Dijon (France) and at the Charterhouse in nearby Champinol. For the latter, he worked on the *Well of Moses* about 1395–1403 (now in the grounds of a hospital in Dijon) and the kneeling mourners, or *pleurants*, for the tomb of his patron (Dijon Museum and Cleveland Museum, Ohio), commissioned by Philip the Bold himself but completed under John the Fearless. His style, with its attention to human featues, was continued at the Burgundian court by his nephew, Claus de Werve.

Smythson, Robert (*c.* 1535–1614)
English architect. He built Elizabethan country houses, including Longleat (1568–75), Wollaton Hall (1580–88), and Hardwick Hall (1590–97). Their castlelike silhouettes, symmetry, and large gridded windows are a uniquely romantic English version of Classicism.

Soderini, Piero (1452–1522)
Florentine political leader. With the Medici expelled from Florence in 1494 and with Girolamo ◊Savonarola eventually put to death in 1498, the Florentines attempted to create a durable constitution on the model of Venice's. They decided to elect a *gonfaloniere* for life in 1502: the choice fell to Soderini. His regime, however, faced tensions from the outset: some wanting the Medici back, others wanting a more narrowly patrician government. What eventually did it for Soderini was a united offensive of other Italian powers (including the pope, whose representative was cardinal Giovanni de' Medici) against his ally, the French, in 1512: the Medici were restored.

Soderini's regime, in which Niccolò ◊Machiavelli served, attempted to recreate a culture of Florentine republicanism: in part, this was a matter of policy, with Soderini introducing a citizen militia, a panacea

(or rather placebo) for all military difficulties, prescribed by humanists like Machiavelli. In part, though, it was a case of harnessing the city's recent reputation for outstanding art to the republican cause. Michelangelo, for example, was commissioned to sculpt the *David* which was to symbolize the victory of plucky little Florence over its gargantuan enemies. And both Michelangelo and Leonardo da Vinci were commissioned to paint battle scenes for the Palazzo Vecchio (see ◊Anghiari, Battle of). But if this was to be a republic of arms and letters, its pen proved mightier than its sword.

Sodoma, Il, Giovanni Antonio Bazzi (1477–1549)
Italian painter. Strongly influenced by Leonardo da Vinci, he developed an ornate and graceful style. Much of his best work consists of frescoes on religious and mythological subjects in Siena and Rome, among the finest being *The Life of St Catherine* (1526) (Church of S Domenico, Siena).

Il Sodoma was born in the duchy of Savoy. He went first to Milan and then settled in Siena in 1501, where he completed a series of frescoes depicting the life of St Benedict begun by Luca ◊Signorelli in the Benedictine monastery of Monte Oliveto (1505–08).

In 1508 he visited Rome, where he painted in the Camera della Segnatura of the Vatican, though Pope Julius II was dissatisfied with his work and replaced him with Raphael Sanzio. Also in Rome, Il Sodoma painted the *Marriage of Alexander and Roxana* (1512) in the Villa Farnesina. He did some work in Mantua, Volterra, Florence, and Pisa.

Soest, Konrad von (*c.* 1378–*c.* 1415)
German painter, active in Dortmund from about 1394. His principal works are the altarpiece *Crucifixion* (1404) in Niederwildungen and *Madonna* (1420) in Dortmund.

Solari, Andrea da (1460–1520)
Italian painter. He travelled widely, his style as a consequence combining the influences of Leonardo da Vinci and Venetian and Flemish painting. His *Giovanni Cristoforo Longoni* (1505, National Gallery, London) shows a masterly ability in portraiture.

He was probably born in Milan. His style was formed on Alvise Vivarini and ◊Antonello da Messina during a stay in Venice 1490–93, and on Leonardo da Vinci in Milan. He went to France 1507 and may have visited Flanders, which would account for Flemish influence discernible in his work, but he was back in Italy by 1515.

Somerset, Edward Seymour, 1st Duke of Somerset (*c.* 1506–1552)

English politician. Created Earl of Hertford after Henry VIII's marriage to his sister Jane, he became Duke of Somerset and protector (regent) for Edward VI in 1547. His attempt to check enclosure (the transfer of land from common to private ownership) offended landowners and his moderation in religion upset the Protestants; eventually he was beheaded on a treason charge in 1552. Knighted in1523, Viscount in 1536, Earl in 1537.

Soriano, Francesco (*c.* 1549–1621)

Italian composer. After a first appointment he went to the court of Mantua 1583–86, and then became maestro di cappella in Rome, by turns at Santa Maria Maggiore, St John Lateran, St Peter's in 1603, and the Cappella Giulia 1603–20.

He was a choirboy at the Church of St John Lateran in Rome and studied with various masters including G B Nanini and Palestrina.

Works include:

Masses, an arrangement of Palestrina's *Missa Papae Marcelli* for eight voices, motets, psalms, Magnificat, a Passion, and other church music; madrigals.

sotto in sù (ITALIAN FROM BELOW UPWARDS)

In art, extreme foreshortening, usually in a ceiling painting. It is meant to give a convincing illusion of figures and objects in space when seen from below. It became a familiar feature of Baroque painting.

It may have been invented in the 15th century by Francesco ◊Melozzo da Forlì.

Southampton, Henry Wriothesley, 3rd Earl of Southampton (1573–1624)

English courtier, patron of Shakespeare. Shakespeare dedicated *Venus and Adonis* and *The Rape of Lucrece* to him and may have addressed him in the sonnets.

Spanish Armada

Fleet sent by Philip II of Spain against England in 1588. Consisting of 130 ships, it sailed from Lisbon and carried on a running fight up the Channel with the English fleet of 197 small ships under Howard of Effingham and Francis ◊Drake. The Armada anchored off Calais but fire ships forced it to put to sea, and a general action followed off Gravelines. What remained of the Armada escaped around the north of Scotland and west of Ireland, suffering many losses by storm and shipwreck on the way. Only about half the original fleet returned to Spain.

Spataro, Giovanni (*c.* 1458–1541)

Italian composer and theorist. He was involved in a protracted controversy with the theorist Franchino Gafori, against whom two of his printed treatises are directed. He composed a number of sacred works; six motets and one *laude* are extant.

He was a pupil of Ramos de Pareia and corresponded with Pietro Aron; he was maestro di cappella at San Petronio, Bologna from 1512.

Spenser, Edmund (*c.* 1552–1599)

English poet. His major work is the allegorical epic *The ◊Faerie Queene*, of which six books survive (three published in 1590 and three in 1596). Other books include *The Shepheard's Calendar* (1579), *Astrophel* (1586), the love sonnets *Amoretti*, and the marriage poem *Epithalamion* (1595).

Born in London and educated at Cambridge University, in 1580 he became secretary to the Lord Deputy in Ireland and at Kilcolman Castle completed the first three books of *The Faerie Queene*. In 1598 the castle was burned down by rebels, and Spenser and his family narrowly escaped. He died in London, and was buried in Westminster Abbey.

His attitude towards the Irish problem, expressed in both book five of the *Faerie Queene* and his *View of the Present State of Ireland* was that merciless oppression was the only solution.

Spinello, Aretino (DIED *c.* 1410)

An early Florentine artist, working in the tradition of ◊Giotto, who executed several fresco series in Tuscany. These include those illustrating the life of St Nicholas in the church of S Niccolò, Arezzo, and

THE SONNET

A VOGUE FOR SONNETEERING swept western Europe during the 16th century. In France, Spain, and England, mastery of the sonnet opened up new avenues of self-expression germane to the exploration of emotional anxieties and the detailed contemplation of one's own spiritual and mental state of being. The versatility of the sonnet form – short, witty, and evocative – was greatly attractive but equally the close internal regulation of the structure ordered ideas and gave shape to subjective discourse.

We can use the formal structure of the Petrarchan sonnet as a general exemplar by which to define the sonnet form. It is a 14-line poem, tightly regulated by means of internal syntax and interwoven end rhymes. The poem splits into two sections: an opening *octave* (eight lines) followed by the *sestet* (six lines). The moment of transition, known as the *volta* or turn, will be marked by a change of rhyme and most probably by a thematic shift in the poem's line of thought, so that the description of a scene, say, will give way to a more abstract evaluation. A further subdivision of both rhyme and argument into two *quatrains* (four lines) followed by two *tercets* (three lines) is standard. Petrarch favoured the rhyme scheme ABBA ABBA for the octave, although more complicated variations were available, and a sestet scheme of either CDECDE or CDCDCD. (In the later English modifications of the form, we find an inclination towards closure on a final couplet and the extension to seven of the number of rhymes employed.)

The legacy of Petrarch remains key to comprehending the subject range and status accorded to the sonnet form. The lyric achievement of his *Rime Sparse,* a collection of over three hundred sonnets alongside longer poetic forms, underpinned the artistic endeavour of future generations, endorsing self-expression within the vernacular and consigning a viable language of love to all. The Petrarchan idiom imitated throughout the 16th century was at once uniquely sympathetic to the expression of both erotic and spiritual desire and yet an artificial composite of rhetorical tropes. 'Rime' 134 is an ideal index of Petrarch's sophisticated employment of antithesis to mirror the emotional frustration of the speaker, (he fears and hopes, burns, yet is of ice), but the vast number of mediocre clone sonnets across the 16th century expose a wider set of accessible 'Petrarchan' commonplaces. The lady has eyes like the sun that burns and hair like gold that dazzles; passion buffets the lover like a ship caught in a storm; he besieges an unobtainable fortress; suffers harsh treatment; indulges in erotic dreams; and claims an ultimate victory for his art over the ravages made on mortal beauty by time.

Thomas Wyatt began imitating Petrarch's poems after a visit to Italy in 1527, seeking a public voice, simultaneously anguished yet opaque, that would be suited to the tense realities of court life under Henry VIII. Sonnets by both Wyatt and Surrey are published in the first English anthology, *Tottel's Miscellany* (1557) but, despite this promising start, there is something of a lull in creative interest in the form in England until the 1580s. Meanwhile, in France, Pierre de Ronsard and the group known as *La Pléiade* were active, with Joachim du Bellay encouraging his fellow Frenchmen to write Petrarchan sonnets as a means of cultural regeneration. The English revival of interest in the sonnet is greatly influenced by such contemporary continental practice. The young Spenser turns to du Bellay and the Protestant Clément Marot as his literary models for the sonnets he contributes to the emblem book, *A Theatre for Worldlings* (1569), and later both Philip Sidney and John Milton prove equally conscious of the specifically political application of the poetic form in the cause of continental Protestantism.

The literary self-awareness of the Petrarchan sonnet, where the desire for Laura is also the ambition to gain the *lauro,* the crown of laurel awarded for poetic merit, can only be furthered by the developing sense of a European tradition. The discontinuity between emotional immediacy and its polished expression is actively exploited by sonneteers. The 'penning' of such frustration is presumed to be a male preserve and the moral iniquity of indulging such sinful desires is clear to many of the Elizabethans, strongly influenced by the new doctrines of Calvinism.

continued

Philip Sidney's sequence *Astrophel and Stella,* written in the early 1580s, exploits just this division, ironically exposing the self-delusion of the Petrarchan lover, while Spenser in his 'Amoretti' (1594) aims to transcend moral dubiety by producing a sequence that will admit future consummation through marriage. One intriguing response to the moral issues comes with 'Pamphilia to Amphilanthus', written by Lady Mary Wroth (Philip Sidney's niece) in the 1610s. Wroth's attempts to give voice to a female lover lead to their own frustrations: cultural conventions require Pamphilia to be actively passive, a constant heart betrayed by the infidelity of the male object of desire. One might compare this reversal with the male addressee of Shakespeare's sonnets (published in 1609 but written in the 1590s).

The posthumous publication of Sidney's *Astrophel and Stella* in 1591 sparked a huge outpouring in sonneteering among wits at the Inns of Court, such as John Donne, and beyond: it became a commonplace of the 1590s that any educated young man should be capable of composing a sonnet. Numerous cycles were published by the close of the century, including those by Daniel, Constable, Barnes, Drayton, Lodge, Percy, William Smith, and Tofte. As well as amorous themes, spiritual and metaphysical concerns are uppermost in these writers' collections but one poet capable of utilizing the full range of the sonnet's potential is John Milton. From the 1630s to the 1650s, he turns to the sonnet for a variety of purposes: as an occasional form, to display youthful ability, to deal with political topics, to address friends, to consider his literary ambitions, and to express personal anguish, for example at the death of his wife. Sonneteering was not fashionable in the Augustan age but the sonnet form returned afresh with the Romantics and its lyric potential has continued to be employed by writers up to the present day.

MARGARET KEAN

Further Reading
Michael R G Spiller, *The Development of the Sonnet: an Introduction* (London, 1992)

---

scenes from the life of Pope Alexander III in the Palazzo Pubblico, Siena.

Spinello was born in Arezzo, and worked in Arezzo, Florence, Pisa, and Siena successively. Other frescoes include those in the principal chapel of Sta Maria Maggiore, Florence; in the monasteries of S Miniato (near Florence), S Bernardo (Arezzo), and Monte Oliveto (near Florence); and in the Campo Santo (cemetery), Pisa, illustrating the life of St Raniero.

Sponde, Jean de (1557–1595)
French poet and humanist. His poetry includes 'Les Amours', 'Stances', and 'Sonnets de la mort'. He also wrote the prose *Méditations sur les Psaumes* (1588).

Spranger, Bartholomeus (1546–1611)
Flemish painter, sculptor, and engraver. He trained in Antwerp and then worked (briefly) in Paris before travelling to Italy. He visited Milan and Parma (where he was influenced by the works of ◊Correggio and ◊Parmigianino) and settled in Rome in 1566, where he was patronized by cardinal Alessandro Farnese.

◊Giambologna introduced Spranger to the court of Maximilian II in 1575; he remained at the imperial court for the rest of his life, being one of the court painters to Maximilian's successor, ◊Rudolf II from 1581.

For Rudolf, Spranger produced a series of mythological (for example, *Hercules, Deianeira and Nessus, c.* 1581–2) and allegorical (for instance, *The Triumph of Wisdom, c.* 1591) paintings; his works reflect Flemish and Italian influences, in particular that of Giambologna.

Squarcione, Francesco (1394–1474)
Paduan painter. He is more important as the master of a large workshop and collector of Greek and Roman antiquities than as an artist. His collection, which he used in his teaching, strongly influenced his many pupils, the most important of whom were Andrea ◊Mantegna, Carlo ◊Crivelli, and Cosimo ◊Tura.

Squarcione was a merchant in early life who travelled extensively, especially in Greece, from where he brought back a collection of antiques. He took to painting, his fame as a teacher earning him the title of the 'father of painting'. His influence on the development of the Venetian School was enormous.

A signed work by Squarcione is the polyptych *Madonna and Saints* (1449–52, Museo Civico, Padua).

Stanyhurst, Richard (1547–1618)
Irish scholar, historian, and poet. His translation of the first four books of Virgil's *Aeneid* was published in 1582.

His other writings include *Description of Ireland*, published in Raphael Holinshed's *Chronicles* (1577), and *De Vita S Patricii Hyberniae Apostoli* (1587).

Stappen, Crispinus van (c. 1470–1532)
Flemish composer. He wrote sacred and secular works, including a *strambotto* in praise of the town of Padua.

He became a singer at the Sainte-Chapelle, Paris, in 1492, and shortly afterwards, until 1507, at the Papal Chapel in Rome. In 1524–25 he was maestro di cappella at the Casa Santa, Loreto. He held a canonry at Cambrai from 1504.

Stevinus, Simon (c. 1548–1620)
Flemish scientist who, in physics, developed statics and hydrodynamics; he also introduced decimal notation into Western mathematics.

Stevinus was born in Bruges (now in Belgium). He began work in Antwerp as a clerk and then entered Dutch government service, using his engineering skills to become quartermaster-general to the army. He designed sluices that could be used to flood parts of Holland to defend it from attack.

In statics Stevinus made use of the parallelogram of forces and in dynamics he made a scientific study of pulley systems. In hydrostatics he noted that the pressure exerted by a liquid depends only on its height and is independent of the shape of the vessel containing it. He is supposed to have carried out an experiment (later attributed to Italian physicist Galileo) in which he dropped two unequal weights from a tall building to demonstrate that they fell at the same rate.

Stevinus wrote in the vernacular (a principle he advocated for all scientists). His book on mechanics is *De Beghinselen der Weeghcoust* (1586).

Stobaeus, Johann (1580–1646)
German composer and bass. While attending the university at Königsberg, he studied music with Johann Eccard, and after holding various minor appointments there became Kapellmeister to the Elector of Brandenburg in 1626.

Works include:
Cantiones Sacrae for five to ten voices (published 1624), Magnificats for five to six voices, five-part settings of hymn tunes; Prussian Festival Songs for five to eight voices (with Eccard; two volumes, published 1624 and 1644); sacred and secular occasional compositions.

Stokem (STOKHEM), Johannes (c. 1440–c. 1500)
Flemish composer. A few sacred and secular works by him survive, including four chansons printed in Ottaviano Petrucci's *Odhecaton A* (1501).

He was probably born and spent his early life near Liège. He was in the service of Beatrice of Hungary in the early 1480s and a singer in the papal choir 1487–89. He was a friend of Johannes Tinctoris, who sent him portions of his 12th treatise (all that survives) with a letter.

Stoss, Veit (ALSO KNOWN AS WIT STWOSZ) (c. 1450–1533)
German sculptor and painter. He was active in Nuremberg and Poland. He carved a wooden altarpiece with high relief panels in St Mary's, Kraków, a complicated design with numerous figures that centres on the *Death of the Virgin* (1477–89).

Stoss was born in Nuremberg and returned there from Poland. The figure of *St Roch* about 1510 in Sta Annunziata, Florence, shows his characteristic Flemish realism and bold drapery. Most of his sculptures were brightly painted.

Strada, Jacopo (1515–1588)
Italian antiquary, born in Rome. He was appointed court antiquary by the Holy Roman Emperor Ferdinand I and continued in imperial service all his life. His position and that of his son **Octavio Strada** (1550–1607) was done no harm by his daughter's status as Rudolf II's mistress.

A collector of coins and books, Strada produced for

his patrons *Epitome Thesauri Antiquitatum/ Summary of the Riches of the Ancients*, relating the history of the emperors from Julius Caesar to the present day, with illustrations of coins. His son Octavio also worked on imperial history, posthumously published as *De Vita Imperatorum et Caesarum Romanorum/On the Life of the Roman Emperors* (1615).

Strigel, Bernhard (1460–1528)

German painter. He worked in Memmingen, Bavaria, as portrait painter to the Viennese Habsburg court and, late in life, as court painter to the Holy Roman Emperor Maximilian I. *Sybilla von Freyberg* (Alte Pinakothek, Munich) is an example of his portraits.

Strigel studied in Ulm and later worked in Augsburg with Hans ◊Burgkmair. He imitated the Milanese artist Ambrogio da Predis (*c.* 1455–after 1508) in his profile portraits.

Striggio, Alessandro (*c.* 1535–1592)

Italian composer. He was a nobleman from Mantua, and travelled abroad in a diplomatic capacity, visiting England in 1567. He was celebrated as a composer of madrigals and as a virtuoso player of the lira da gamba and viol. His son, Alessandro ◊Striggio, was a friend of Monteverdi.

Striggio was in the service of Cosimo de' Medici at Florence 1560–74, collaborating with other composers on contributions to the local *intermedi* for great festivities. His music was admired in Italy and abroad, and in 1568 his 40-part motet, *Ecce Beatam Lucem*, was performed at the marriage of Duke Albrecht IV of Bavaria. He subsequently visited several European courts, including that of Ferrara in 1584. He returned to Mantua later that year, to the court of Duke Guglielmo Gonzaga. He published seven books of madrigals (1558–97).

Works include:
Masses, motet in 40 parts for voices and instruments; madrigal comedy *Il cicalamento delle donne al bucato* (1567); intermezzi for performance between the acts of plays; madrigals; various works for voices and instruments in many parts.

studiolo (ITALIAN FOR 'LITTLE STUDY')

Either a cabinet in a study (*studio*) or the room itself. Possessing a well-designed and well-arranged study became a mark of culture for those who could afford it, as much as it was a necessity for scholars. ◊Federigo da Montefeltro's *studiolo*, with its paintings of learned men (whose intellect, it presumably was hoped, would rub off on the room's owner) is an unusually lavish example, but other rulers such as Isabella d'◊Este also paid close attention to their *studioli*. The accoutrements of a study were also a matter of artistic interest, paid special attention in the paintings of St Jerome. (See Picture Gallery).

Sturgeon, Nicholas (*c.* 1390–1454)

English composer. He contributed to the Old Hall Manuscript during the second phase of its existence, when it was in use at the Chapel Royal. Five known works by him survive.

He was a scholar of Winchester College as a child. In 1442, after serving as a clerk of the Chapel Royal, he became a canon of Windsor and precentor of St Paul's Cathedral.

Suetonius (GAIUS SUETONIUS TRANQUILLUS) (*c.* AD 69–*c.* 140)

Ancient Roman historian. His *De Vita Caesarum/ Lives of the Caesars* provided, alongside ◊Tacitus, an essential (and salacious) source for the history of imperial Rome.

Suetonius' histories were widely circulated before the 14th century; if anything, however, there is less sign of interest in Italy than further north. ◊Petrarch, though, owned several manuscripts of Suetonius and, from the last quarter of the 14th century, there was an explosion of interest in his works: *Lives of the Caesars* became one of the must-haves for any self-respecting humanist's library. Commentaries came, as in the case of many other Classical texts, in the second half of the 15th century, with the work of Domizio ◊Calderini and Filippo ◊Beroaldo the Elder, who also wrote a life of Suetonius.

Suleiman (SOLYMAN) (*c.* 1494–1566)

Ottoman sultan from 1520, known as **the Magnificent** and **the Lawgiver**. Under his rule, the Ottoman Empire reached its largest extent. He made conquests in the Balkans, the Mediterranean, Persia, and North Africa, but was defeated at Vienna in 1529

STUDIA HUMANITATIS

THE UNTRANSLATABLE TERM, *studia humanitatis*, was derived from a speech by the man who was, for generations of scholars, the quintessential Roman orator, politician, and philosopher, ◊Cicero. The short-cut translation would be 'humanism' but that way confusion lies: over-used and under-understood, the '-ism' suggests a shared outlook, a wholeness which is not just simplistic – it also fails to express the human diversity of the humanists. So, if we were to be instead literal-minded, we would say *studia humanitatis* meant 'studies of humanity' (thus the modern 'humanities'); straining after a more expressive rendering, we might say that it suggests 'studies of what it is to be human' – but this still does not convey the aura that the phrase held for early humanists, nor the specificity with which later teachers burdened it.

To start in the middle: *studia humanitatis* came to mean a particular educational curriculum, one which involved grammar, rhetoric, poetry, history, and moral philosophy. It was in this sense that, in the late 15th century, it could act as the derivation for the new coinage, *humanista* meaning a man who made his living by teaching the round of subjects just mentioned. And it was in that sense that the term entered the vernaculars – Italian: *umanista*; English: humanist, for example – during the 16th century. It was only in the early 19th century that the concept of 'humanism' was created (first in Germany), defining an education in the classics.

In this sense, then, *studia humanitatis* comes nowhere near to expressing the gamut of intellectual experiences which are usually huddled together under the umbrella-terms 'Renaissance' and 'humanism'. Moreover, while moral philosophy was part of the curriculum a humanist taught, a training in *studia humanitatis* did not commit a student to a particular philosophy. There were certainly implications to the humanist curriculum: a belief in the importance of classical literature (or of particular classical texts which were selected for school use), a recognition that persuasion, not rationality alone, helped win debates – important concepts but not ones which added up to a complete world-view, just as *studia humanitatis* were not a complete education. Many of its students would go on to study law or medicine or theology at university.

Yet, this history of *studia humanitatis* does not take into account its earliest Renaissance uses. The phrase was reintroduced into Latin by ◊Petrarch's discovery of Cicero's speech *Pro Archia* in which the words *studia humanitatis ac litterarum* appeared. Petrarch himself noted the passage but did not use the phrase; the credit for first applying it goes to Coluccio ◊Salutati, who used it in 1369 and repeatedly thereafter. He was followed by his protégé, Leonardo ◊Bruni, and by others outside Florence – in particular, by Gasparino ◊Barzizza. However, when they used the phrase, there was little of the curricular specificity or clarity that it came to have later in the century. Certainly, the term was often used in contrast to other types of learning – Salutati distinguishes it from both *studia secretorum nature* ('studies of the secrets of nature') and *studia divinitatis* (which is something like 'studies of what it is to be divine'); but it was at the same time employed with a certain vagueness. Indeed, in Pier Paolo ◊Vergerio's tract, *De Ingenuis Moribus,* which defines the cycle of subjects that were later called *studia humanitatis,* the phrase does not occur: instead he uses terms like *artes liberales*. Indeed, in this early period, *studia humanitatis* was simply one among several phrases used to describe the interests of these coteries of scholars.

In other words, in its earliest uses, *studia humanitatis* was more like a slogan than a set of beliefs or lessons. It was a shorthand phrase with which to describe the interests of the small bands of writers and teachers who self-importantly declared that they were reviving classical learning. Ironically, it may have been the very vagueness of this term that meant it gained popularity at the expense of similar phrases and thus came to take on its narrow, curricular definition. And as that term became stale, the scholarly avant-garde naturally turned to other slogans or symbols by which to define their novelty: so, for example, different groups of scholars across Italy in the late 15th century each claimed that they constituted a new ◊Academy. Just as those

continued

Centres of learning founded before 1400

university founded
◇ before 1300
◆ 1301–1400

1289 date of foundation
(1263) date of suppression
• important monastic
  or cathedral school

North Sea

York
Peterborough
Cambridge 1209
Oxford c.1190
Canterbury

ATLANTIC OCEAN

Magdeburg
Paderborn
Hildesheim
Utrecht
Corvey
Cologne 1388
Hersfeld
Erfurt 1392
Prague 1348
Cracow 1364, 1397
Tournai
Liège
Fulda
Mainz
Rouen
Laon
Regensburg
Bec
Beauvais
Reims
Metz
Heidelberg 1386
Vienna 1365
Chartres
Paris c.1150
Clairvaux
Buda 1389, (1526)
Orléans 1235
Fleury
Langres
St Gall
Angers 1337
Tours
Citeaux
Cluny
Milan
Lodi
Pavia 1361, 1412
Vicenza 1204
Grenoble 1339, (1475)
Vercelli 1228
Treviso 1318 (1407)
Ferrara 1391, 1442
La Chaise Dieu
Piacenza 1248
Padua 1222
Bologna 1200
Cahors 1332
Reggio 1188
Ravenna
Orange 1364
Florence 1349, 1472
Montpellier 1289
Avignon 1303
Pisa 1343, 1472
Arezzo 1215
Toulouse 1229
Siena 1246
Perugia 1308
Perpignan 1329
Rome 1303, 1431
Palencia 1208–09, (1263)
Huesca 1354
Lérida 1300
Monte Cassino
Salamanca 1227–28, 1243
Valladolid 1346
Naples 1224
Salerno 1173
Coimbra 1308, 1355, 1537
Toledo
Lisbon 1290, 1338, 1377
(Lisbon and Coimbra were sites for one university)
Messina
Seville 1254, (1265), 1377
Monreale

Mediterranean Sea

0 ──── 200 mi
0 ──── 400 km

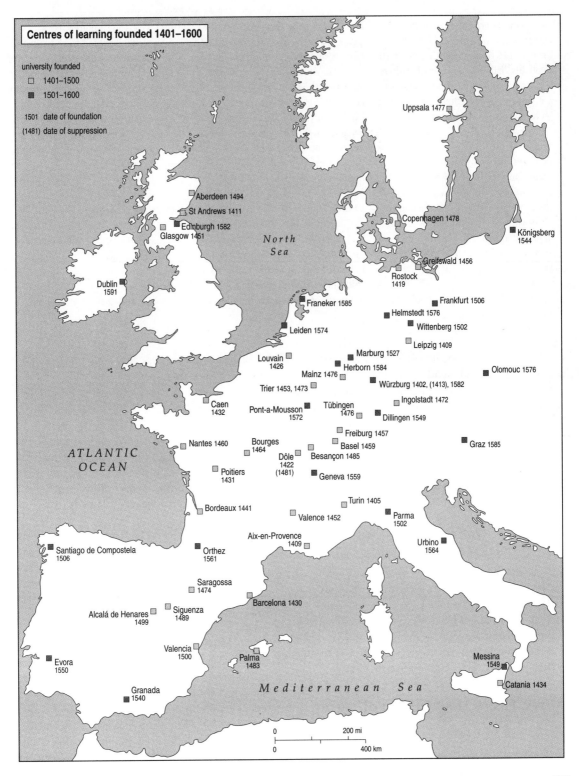

Centres of learning founded 1401–1600

university founded
- ☐ 1401–1500
- ■ 1501–1600

1501 date of foundation
(1481) date of suppression

Uppsala 1477

Aberdeen 1494
St Andrews 1411
Edinburgh 1582
Glasgow 1451

Copenhagen 1478
Königsberg 1544
Greifswald 1456
Rostock 1419

North Sea

Dublin 1591

Franeker 1585
Frankfurt 1506
Helmstedt 1576
Wittenberg 1502
Leiden 1574
Leipzig 1409
Marburg 1527
Louvain 1426
Herborn 1584
Olomouc 1576
Mainz 1476
Würzburg 1402, (1413), 1582
Trier 1453, 1473
Ingolstadt 1472
Caen 1432
Pont-a-Mousson 1572
Tübingen 1476
Dillingen 1549
Freiburg 1457
Nantes 1460
Bourges 1464
Basel 1459
Graz 1585
Dôle 1422 (1481)
Besançon 1485
Poitiers 1431
Geneva 1559

ATLANTIC OCEAN

Turin 1405
Bordeaux 1441
Valence 1452
Parma 1502
Aix-en-Provence 1409
Urbino 1564

Santiago de Compostela 1506
Orthez 1561

Saragossa 1474
Alcalá de Henares 1499
Siguenza 1489
Barcelona 1430

Evora 1550
Valencia 1500
Palma 1483
Messina 1549
Granada 1540
Catania 1434

Mediterranean Sea

0   200 mi
0   400 km

379

'academies' were rarely definite institutions, so before *studia humanitatis* became specific, the term probably had resonances rather than a clear definition. And if we wish to gain a sense of what those resonances were, we can do no better than to study what those who preached it practised. So, for example, these early devotees involved themselves in recovering texts of classical writings; they imitated the eloquent Latin of those ancient authors (in particular, Cicero); they also imitated what they assumed was classical script. They tried to master Greek as well and to translate classical Greek texts into their Ciceronian Latin.

There are, though, two final caveats. First, if men like Leonardo Bruni or ◊Poggio Bracciolini considered that they were assisting *studia humanitatis* when they undertook any of these activities, the term certainly did not cover all their scholarly pursuits. Most importantly, early humanists were often interested in patristic as well as pagan writings but these (on Salutati's usage) were not part of *studia humanitatis*. So, when Ambrogio ◊Traversari translated the Greek Church Fathers into an approximation at Ciceronian Latin, he was using a 'humanist' technique but was engaged in *studia divinitatis*. Second, no one practitioner of *studia humanitatis* could have been expected to follow all the pursuits the term could imply. If

that were the case, then Poggio would have to be excluded from the list of humanists (for failing to learn Greek until late in life) – and so would Bruni (for not involving himself in the hunt for classical texts). In that sense, *studia humanitatis* was an enterprise, not for lonely scholars, but for coteries. It was, in the end, a way of communicating a shared enthusiasm.

DAVID RUNDLE

Further Reading
P O Kristeller, *Renaissance Thought* (New York, 1961); B Kohl, 'The changing concept of the *studia humanitatis* in the early Renaissance', *Renaissance Studies*, vi (1992), 185–209

---

and Valletta (on Malta) in 1565. He was a patron of the arts, a poet, and an administrator.

Suleiman captured Belgrade in 1521, the Mediterranean island of Rhodes in 1522, defeated the Hungarians at Mohács in 1526, and was halted in his advance into Europe only by his failure to take Vienna, capital of the Austro-Hungarian Empire, after a siege from September to October 1529. In 1534 he turned more successfully against Persia, and then in campaigns against the Arab world took almost all of North Africa and the Red Sea port of Aden. Only the Knights of Malta inflicted severe defeat on both his army and fleet when he tried to take Valletta in 1565.

Sully, Maximilien de Béthune, duc de Sully (1560–1641)

French politician, who served with the Protestant ◊Huguenots in the Wars of Religion, and, as Henry IV's superintendent of finances 1598–1611, aided French recovery. He became duke in 1616.

Surrey, Henry Howard, Earl of Surrey (c. 1517–1547)

English courtier and poet. With Thomas ◊Wyatt, he introduced the sonnet to England and was a pioneer

of blank verse. He was executed on a poorly based charge of high treason.

Susato, Tielman (c. 1500– BETWEEN 1561 AND 1564)

Flemish composer, publisher, and editor. He was the outstanding Dutch music publisher of his time. His 11 *Musyck Boexken*, 'little music books', of 1551 contained Dutch songs, dance music, and the *Souter Liedekens* of the composers Clemens non Papa and Gerhard Mes.

He worked in Antwerp from 1529, established his business in 1543, and in 1547 built his own premises 'At the Sign of the Crumhorn'. He also published volumes of Masses, motets, and chansons by the leading composers of his day; many of these include works by himself.

Süss, Hans (VON KULMBACH) (1480–1522)

German painter. Combining German and Italian styles, he acquired a Venetian richness of colour and pursued Albrecht Dürer's linear style with effect in portraits, as seen, for example, in his *Margrave Casimir von Brandenburg* (1511, Alte Pinakothek, Munich).

He was first influenced by the Venetian Jacopo de' ◊Barbari (who worked in Germany under the name of

Jacob Walch), and was later the pupil and friend of Dürer.

Sweelinck, Jan Pieterszoon (1562–1621)

Dutch composer, organist, harpsichordist, and teacher. He was the first composer to write an independent part for the pedal keyboard (pedalboard) in organ works, a technique which reached its peak in J S Bach's organ compositions. He taught many of the next generation's organists of the German school.

He studied under his father, **Pieter Sweelinck**, who became organist at the Old Church at Amsterdam in 1566. His father died in 1573 and he succeeded to his post between 1577 and 1580, holding it to his death. His music was influenced by the English virginalists and the Venetian organists. The poet Joost van den Vondel (1587–1679) wrote an epitaph on his death.

Works include:

Four books of psalms for four to eight voices, including three books of *Psalms of David* (1604–14), *Cantiones sacrae* for several voices; organ fantasias, toccatas, and chorale variations; harpsichord pieces; chansons for five voices, *Rimes françoises et italiennes*.

Sweynheym, Conrad (DIED 1477)

German cleric, who with Arnold ◊Pannartz introduced the printing press into Italy. They set up their press in the Benedictine monastery at Subiaco, near Rome, in 1464, and moved their operations to Rome three years later. Their output had a specifically humanist slant and editors of their printings of Classical authors included ◊Nicholas of Cusa's former secretary, Giovanni Andrea Bussi, and Niccolò ◊Perotti.

syphilis

Venereal disease, probably introduced into Europe in 1494 from the New World. The 'French disease' to most of Europe, to the French it was the 'Neapolitan disease'. It was first apparent among French troops in Naples and soon spread northwards across Europe.

Its name was coined in 1530 by Girolamo ◊Fracastoro who tells the touching tale of Sifilo, a shepherd touched by the *morbus gallicus* (French disease) but eventually cured (with mercury). A few decades earlier, in the wake of the disease's first appearance, a group of physicians met in Ferrara to discuss the matter; among them was Niccolò Leoniceno who insisted that the disease must have existed in the Classical world and found passages in Hippocrates to support his view. It may be that syphilis occurred in Europe before the 1490s, but it was then that it became widespread and claimed some notable victims (like Julius II): the disease seems to have come from the Americas, an import soon reciprocated with the European export of the common cold virus which, being uncommon in the New World, decimated the native Indians in the following decades.

Szamotulczyk, Wacław (WACŁAW Z SZAMOTUŁ) (c. 1524–1560)

Polish composer. He wrote much *a cappella* church music, some of which was published by printers Johann Berg 'Montanus' (died 1563) and his partner Ulrich Neuber (died 1571) of Nuremberg.

He studied at Poznań and at Kraków University, and in 1547 became composer to the king. From 1555 he was Kapellmeister to Prince Michał Radziwiłł.

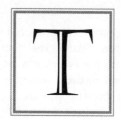

Tacitus, Publius Cornelius (c. AD 56–c. 120)

Ancient roman historian. A public orator in Rome, he was consul under Nerva in 97–98 and proconsul of Asia in 112–113. He wrote histories of the Roman empire, *Annales* and *Historiae*, covering the years AD 14–68 and 69–97 respectively. He also wrote a *Life of Agricola* in 97 (he married Agricola's daughter in 77) and a description of the Germanic tribes, *Germania*, in 98.

The works of Tacitus were all but lost from view for several centuries. A manuscript at Monte Cassino of the *Histories* and part of the *Annals* was noticed and removed in the mid-14th century by either Zenobi da Strada or ◊Boccaccio. It somehow passed into the hands of Niccolò ◊Niccoli who showed it to ◊Poggio Bracciolini. Poggio himself in 1425 found a manuscript of the *Germania* and *Agricola*, in (appropriately) a German monastery, but he was (for once) not brazen enough to remove it; the codex only reached Italy (by the agency of ◊Enoch of Ascoli) in the 1450s. The first books of the *Annals*, however, did not circulate until the early 16th century when Filippo ◊Beroaldo the Younger produced the *editio princeps* in 1515.

Use of Tacitus was made from Leonardo ◊Bruni onwards. For Bruni (and for Poggio Bracciolini), Tacitus provided evidence for the decline of letters under the Roman Empire – which gave one of their supporting arguments for the superiority of republican government. Tacitus was used for less political reason by both Flavio ◊Biondo (in *Roma Instaurata*) and Leon Battista ◊Alberti (in *De Re Aedificatoria*). In the early 16th century, Tacitus received more interest: Francesco Guicciardini may not have been convinced of his use, but Niccolò ◊Machiavelli certainly made use of Tacitus in his republican *Discourses*. Indeed, later in the century, Machiavelli and Tacitus were considered to provide similar

insights into politics, with the latter being read while the former was censured.

The vogue for Tacitus was a phenomenon created in northern Europe. From the 15th century, there was a tradition of understandable local interest in the *Germania* (but seemingly less so, curiously, in the *Agricola*): Aeneas Sylvius Piccolomini, when at the imperial court, quoted the *Germania*, Conrad ◊Celtis lectured on it at Vienna, commentators on it included Philip ◊Melanchthon. One Briton who did show interest in the *Agricola* was the Scotsman William ◊Barclay who produced a commentary printed in Justus ◊Lipsius's 1599 edition of Tacitus. It was, indeed, Justus Lipsius who turned Tacitus into a fashionable author, both for his terse, acerbic comments and his political outlook. Both were imitated, for example, by Ben ◊Jonson whose play *Sejanus* is based on the *Annals*.

Cornelius Tacitus teaches very well the man who lives under a tyrant how to live and conduct himself wisely and just as well teaches the tyrant how to secure his tyranny.

~

FRANCESCO GUICCARDINI'S view on Tacitus

Tagliacozzi, Gaspare (1546–1599)

Italian surgeon who pioneered plastic surgery. He was the first to repair noses lost in duels or through ◊syphilis. He also repaired ears. His method involved taking flaps of skin from the arm and grafting them into place.

Tallis, Thomas (c. 1505–1585)

English composer. He was a master of ◊counterpoint. His works include *Tallis's Canon* ('Glory to thee my God this night') (1567), the antiphonal *Spem in alium non habui* (c. 1573) for 40 voices in various groupings, and a collection of 34 motets, *Cantiones sacrae* (1575), of which 16 are by Tallis and 18 by Byrd.

Tallis was organist at the Benedictine Priory, Dover, in 1532, and held a post at Waltham Abbey before its dissolution in 1540. He became a Gentleman of the Chapel Royal about 1543. He was one of the earliest composers to write for the Anglican liturgy (1547–53) but some of his most ornate music, including the Mass *Puer Natus Est Nobis* dates from the brief Catholic reign of Mary Tudor (1553–58). In 1557 Queen Mary granted him, jointly with Richard Bowyer, Master of the Children in the Chapel Royal, a lease of the manor of Minster, Thanet, and at her death he passed into the service of Elizabeth I, who in 1575 granted him, jointly with Byrd, a patent for the sole right to print music and music paper in English; but two years later, not finding this immediately profitable, they petitioned for an annual grant, which was sanctioned. The two masters were then joint organists at the Chapel Royal. A tune written for Archbishop Parker's Psalter of 1567 was used by Vaughan Williams in his celebrated *Fantasia*. Tallis has become best known for the elaborate and ingenious 40-part motet *Spem in Alium non Habui*. In his last years he and his wife Joan, whom he had married about 1552, lived at their own house at Greenwich.

Works include:

Three Masses, including *Puer Natus Est Nobis* (1554), two Latin Magnificats, two sets of Lamentations for voices, about 40 Latin motets, and other pieces, including *Spem in Alium* in 40 parts; services, psalms, Litanies, about 30 anthems and other English church music; secular vocal pieces; two In Nomines for strings; organ and virginal pieces.

Tannenberg, Battle of

Victory of a combined Polish and Lithuanian army over the Knights of the Teutonic Order in 1410, at Tannenberg, a village in northern Poland (now Grunwald). The battle broke the Knights' hold over Old Prussia (approximately modern Poland); their defeat led to the Treaty of Thorn and to an independent Polish state.

The rule of the Knights in Poland was oppressive and in 1410 the population, led by King Władysław Jagiełło, Grand Duke of Lithuania and king of Poland, rose against them. Władysław led an army of 20,000 to meet some 15,000 Knights near Tannenberg and completely defeated them, slaughtering several thousand Knights.

Tansillio, Luigi (1510–1568)

Italian courtier, soldier, and poet, born in Venosa in southern Italy. He served in administrative and mil-

itary posts under the Spanish viceroys of Naples, taking an active part in many campaigns. As a poet he wrote in a wide range of forms, from sonnets and eclogues in the style of ◊Petrarch, to didactic verse and religious epics. One of his early works, *Il vendemmiatore/The Grape Harvester* (1532), was put on the Index Librorum Prohibitorum for obscenity.

His other works include numerous lyrics, which achieved wide circulation; the religious epic *Le lagrime de S Pietro/The Tears of St Peter* (1585); and *La balia/The Nurse*, written to encourage mothers to nurse their own babies.

Tapissier, Johannes (ADOPTED NAME OF JEAN DE NOYERS) (*c.* 1370–1410)

French composer. Two Mass movements and an isorhythmic motet by him survive, though records indicate that he was a prominent and prolific composer.

Though at the Burgundian court from 1391 to the end of his life, he seems to have been active mainly in Paris.

Tarleton, Richard (DIED 1588)

Elizabethan theatrical clown. He was the most celebrated clown of his time. A member of the Queen's Men theatre company from 1583, he was renowned for the jig, a doggerel song-and-dance routine, and for his extempore humour, which influenced some of the characters in Shakespeare's plays.

Tartaglia (ADOPTED NAME OF NICCOLÒ FONTANA) (*c.* 1499–1557)

Italian mathematician and physicist who specialized in military problems, topography, and mechanical physics.

Tartaglia was born in Brescia, Lombardy. He was called Tartaglia ('stammerer') because of a speech defect resulting from a wound caused by French soldiers sacking the town when he was 12. Although self-educated, he taught at a school in Verona 1516–33. He then moved to Venice, where he eventually became professor of mathematics.

Tartaglia solved the problems of calculating the volume of a tetrahedron from the length of its sides, and of inscribing within a triangle three circles tangent to one another.

He delighted in planning the disposition of artillery, surveying the topography in relation to the best means of defence, and in designing fortifications. He also attempted a study of the motion of projectiles, and formulated **Tartaglia's theorem**: the trajectory of a projectile is a curved line everywhere, and the maximum range at any speed of its projection is obtained with a firing elevation of 45°.

When Tartaglia translated Euclid's *Elements* into Italian 1543, it was the first translation of Euclid into a contemporary European language.

Tasso, Bernardo (1493–1569)

Poet from Bergamo (northern Italy). His career was spent in the service of various Italian princes: his oeuvre included Petrarchan lyrics, Horatian odes, a discourse on poetry (*Ragionamento della poesia*, 1562), and an epic *Amadigi di Gaula*, (1560), based on a Spanish work by Ordoñez de Montalvo.

His son, Torquato ◊Tasso, was also an epic poet.

Tasso, Torquato (1544–1595)

Italian poet. He was the author of the romantic epic poem of the First Crusade *Gerusalemme liberata/ Jerusalem Delivered* completed by 1575 and first published in 1581, which he revised as *Gerusalemme conquistata/Jerusalem Conquered*, published in 1593.

Tasso was born at Sorrento in southern Italy. As a boy accompanied he his father, the poet Bernardo ◊Tasso, into political exile, spending a short time at the court of Urbino and studying at the universities of Padua and Bologna. In these early years he produced *Rinaldo* (1562), a chivalric romance. In 1565 he joined the retinue of Cardinal Luigi d'Este, who took him to Paris, where he was influenced by the works of the ◊Pléiade group of poets. In 1572 Duke Alfonso II d'Este appointed him court poet at Ferrara, where his play *Aminta* was performed in the summer of 1573. By 1575 he had completed the first of his many versions of his epic *Gerusalemme libertata*.

Soon afterwards he betrayed signs of the mental instability that remained with him for the rest of his life. In 1577, after a violent outburst in the presence of Lucrezia d'Este, he was briefly confined: two years later after abusing Duke Alfonso in public, he was confined in the hospital of Sant'Anna from 1579–86. After his release (authorized by Alfonso), he continued his wanderings, though now with the protection of prominent men and women and welcomed by various academies and religious orders. He finally settled at the monastery of Sant'Onofrio in Rome, dying before his coronation as poet laureate, which Pope Clement VIII had intended for him, could take place.

His other works include almost 2000 letters; 28 dialogues on a wide range of subjects; *Discorsi del poema eroico/Treatise on Epic Poetry* (1594), a critical study that throws light on his own poetry; the play *Torrismondo* (1587), based on the tragedy *Oedipus Rex* by the ancient Greek poet Sophocles; *Rime*, consisting of over 1000 of his shorter poems; and the long poem in blank verse *Le sette giornate del mondo creato/The Seven Days of the Creation*.

Tausen, Hans (1495–1561)

Danish religious reformer. Playing a leading role in the Reformation in Denmark, he became known as the 'Danish Luther'. He established the first Lutheran congregation in Denmark, at Viborg, in the mid-1520s, and was appointed Lutheran chaplain to Frederick I in 1526, his preaching at Copenhagen quickly winning him the support of the National Assembly. He drew up confession of faith for the Danish church, but this was considered too conciliatory to the Catholic Church and so rejected in favour of the Confession of ◊Augsburg.

Tausen was born into a peasant family in Birkende on the Island of Fyn. He became a Catholic monk and studied at the universities of Rostock, Copenhagen, and Louvain before going to Wittenberg in Germany to study with Martin ◊Luther in 1523. On his return to Denmark in 1525 he was imprisoned briefly for spreading heretical beliefs, but soon established himself as the leading figure in religious reform. A firm believer in the use of the vernacular, he wrote many hymns and sermons in Danish, and translated part of the New Testament. In late 1530 he taught Hebrew at Copenhagen university, and in 1542 was appointed Lutheran bishop of Ribe.

Taverner, John (c. 1495–1545)

English organist and composer. He wrote masses and motets in polyphonic style, showing great contrapuntal skill, but as a Protestant renounced his art. He was imprisoned in 1528 for heresy, and, as an agent of Thomas Cromwell, assisted in the dissolution of the monasteries.

Teerlinc, Levina (c. 1515–1576)

Netherlandish miniaturist. Her career was spent in England, where she was court painter from 1546. No signed work by her exists but several miniatures have been attributed to her; she may also have produced manuscript illuminations. If she did so, it would support the hypothesis that miniature painting was the continuation of the pre-print and pre-Reformation art of illuminating manuscripts. She was the daughter of the illuminator Simon Benninck (or Bening).

tempera

Painting medium in which powdered pigments are mixed with a water-soluble binding agent such as egg yolk. Tempera is noted for its strong, translucent colours. A form of tempera was used in ancient Egypt, and egg tempera was the foremost medium for panel painting in late Medieval and early Renaissance Europe. It was gradually superseded by oils from the late 15th century onwards.

pure egg tempera In pure egg tempera well-ground inorganic pigments are mixed with egg yolk and water and painted onto a slightly absorbent gesso panel. (The yellow of egg yolk bleaches out, whereas white of egg may turn brown.)

In early Italian painting, the initial lay-in of a design was often done with terra-verde. Colours were then applied to the design in a mixture with flake or zinc white, gradually being strengthened and modelled with glazes or hatches of pure transparent colour.

tempera emulsion Tempera emulsion uses for its medium a well-fused mixture of egg yolk and stand oil, which permits dilution with water. It dries hard sooner and, being more flexible, can be used on canvas prepared with a water ground, that is, with size and gesso. The early Italian procedure is described by a pupil of Giotto, Cennino ◊Cennini.

casein Casein is a variant of egg tempera in which the medium is fresh white curd and a little slaked lime, diluted with water.

After the grandeur of the Roman empire began to decline, architecture grew gradually worse. But (all human things being in perpetual motion) architecture in the times of our fathers and grandfathers, breaking out of the darkness in which it had been for a long time buried, began to show itself once more to the world. Therefore, Bramante, a most excellent man, and an observer of ancient edifices, made most beautiful constructions in Rome.

PALLADIO, *The Four Books of Architecture*, introducing his discussion of the Tempietto

---

Tempietto

The Church of S Pietro in Montorio, Rome, built by Donato ◊Bramante. Its site on the Janiculum was reputedly the place of St Peter's crucifixion. The design, completed in 1502, was based on the writings of ◊Vitruvius: a circular domed building surrounded by Doric columns. It was the one work of contemporary architecture celebrated by Andrea ◊Palladio.

Tè, Palazzo del

A palace near the city of Mantua in northern Italy, built 1525–35. It was designed and decorated by the Italian artist and architect ◊Giulio Romano for Federico II Gonzaga, marchese and (later) duke of Mantua. Its design marked a rejection of the order and restrain of Classical quattrocento architecture in favour of dramatic effects. The most daring of its decorative features is the Sala dei Giganti (Room of Giant), which Romano painted from floor to ceiling with frescoes of the *Fall of the Titans*, a spectacular work showing over-lifesized giants being crushed by falling columns and masonry.

Teresa, of Avila, St (1515–1582)

Castilian mystic who founded an order of nuns in 1562. She was subject to fainting fits, during which she saw visions. She wrote *The Way to Perfection*

385

(1583) and an autobiography, *Life of the Mother Teresa of Jesus* (1611). Her spiritualism was inspired by St ◊John of the Cross. In 1622 she was canonized.

terza rima

Poetical metre used in Dante's *Divine Comedy*, consisting of three-line stanzas in which the second line rhymes with the first and third of the following stanza. Poets who used *terza rima* include ◊Petrarch, ◊Boccaccio, and in English, ◊Chaucer and ◊Wyatt.

Thiard, Pontus de (OR THYARD OR TYARD) (1521–1605)

French poet. He was a member of the ◊*Pléiade* group. His works include three volumes of sonnets, *Erreurs amoureuses* (1549–55), and various essays published as *Discours philosophiques* (1552–58). He became bishop of Chalon in 1578.

Thirty-Nine Articles

Set of articles of faith defining the doctrine of the Church of England, first proposed by a church Convocation in 1563 and given legal status in 1571. The Articles follow the Forty-Two Articles of Archbishop Cranmer (1553); they explicitly condemn Catholic doctrine and are explicitly Calvinist in their theology.

Thomas à Kempis (ADOPTED NAME OF THOMAS HÄMMERKEN) (c. 1380–1471)

German Augustinian monk, author of *De Imitatio Christi/Imitation of Christ* (1441), a devotional handbook of the ◊*devotio moderna*. The work proved quickly popular, being translated into Dutch and French.

Thomas à Kempis lived at the monastery of Zwolle in the Netherlands. He took his name from his birthplace Kempen, near Cologne. He also wrote hymns, sermons, and biographies.

Thorne, John (DIED 1573)

English organist, composer, and poet. He was appointed organist of York Minster in 1542, and worked there in various capacities until two years before his death.

A motet, *Stella Coeli*, was copied by John Baldwin, and another, *Exsultabant Sancti*, survives in organ score. A four-part In Nomine also survives, and there are three poems by him in the same manuscript as Redford's 'Play of Wit and Science' in the British Library and in the 'Paradyse of Daintie Devices' (1576).

Tinctoris, Johannes (c. 1435–c. 1511)

Franco-Flemish music theorist and composer. He wrote a number of important theoretical works and composed Masses, motets, and chansons. His dictionary of musical terms, *Terminorum Musicae Diffinitorium* (1495), was the first of its kind and defines 299 musical terms.

He was born at Nivelles, and studied both law and theology. He was ordained, and became a canon of Poperinghe. He may have been a singer at Cambrai in 1460, under Guillaume Dufay, and in 1463 was choirmaster at Orléans Cathedral. He went to Italy and from about 1472 was in the service of Ferdinand of Aragon, King of Naples, maintaining connections with the court there for at least the next 15 years. He founded a school of music and was in the papal chapel at Rome 1484–1500.

Tinctoris is remembered as one of the most important music theorists of his day; he wrote 12 treatises, two of which were printed. His other writings deal with composition, improvisation, the aesthetics of music, and its role in education and religion.

Tintoretto (ADOPTED NAME OF JACOPO ROBUSTI) (1518–1594)

Venetian painter who produced portraits and religious works of great intensity. Outstanding among his many works is a series of religious works in the Scuola di S Rocco in Venice 1564–88, the dramatic figures lit by a flickering, unearthly light, the space around them distorted into long perspectives. Among his best-known works is *St George and the Dragon* (c. 1570, National Gallery, London).

He was born in Venice, the son of a dyer, hence the name Tintoretto ('little dyer'). He studied under ◊Titian, and was strongly influenced by ◊Michelangelo: it is commonly claimed that his motto was 'Michelangelo's drawing, and Titian's colour'. His works are characterized by broad and dramatic composition, fine draughtsmanship, and a superb use of colour, the scenes spectacularly lit and full of movement.

His works include the *Miracle of St Mark Rescuing a Slave* (1548, Accademia, Venice); his lives of Christ and the Virgin for the Scuola di S Rocco (including the vast *Christ before Pilate* and *The Last Supper*); his *Paradise* (1588), for the Doge's Palace; his *St George and the Dragon*, which demonstrates his characteristic originality in depicting figures in rushing movement; and *The Origin of the Milky Way* (after 1570, National Gallery, London), one of the finest of his allegories.

He also painted a large number of portraits, such as the *Doge Mocenigo* (Accademia, Venice), *Self-Portrait* (Louvre, Paris), and *Vincenzo Morosini* (National Gallery, London). Other works, apart from his religious works on a decorative scale, include *Susanna and the Elders* (Accademia, Vienna).

The characteristic qualities of his works – a wonderfully dramatic sense of movement, space, and lighting – were in part aided by his use of small wax models which he grouped inside a box to create a stagelike setting, changing the figures, lighting, and setting to explore different effects.

Tintoretto spent almost all his career in Venice, where he maintained a busy workshop producing a vast output of religious paintings, portraits, and a number of allegorical and mythological subjects. His son **Domenico** (*c.* 1560–1635) was his assistant in his later works and carried on his workshop, in which another son, **Marco** (1561–1637), and his daughter, **Marietta** (*c.* 1556–1590), were also trained.

Tiptoft, John, 1st Earl of Worcester
(*c.* 1427–1470)
English statesman, created Earl of Worcester in 1449, Constable of England 1462–67. During the civil strife of the 1450s, Tiptoft was absent from England: he went on pilgrimage to Jerusalem and then travelled round Italy. Recalled in 1461 by Edward IV, he was made constable with the task of meting out justice to traitors. His success at this gained him the sobriquet 'the butcher of England'; he displayed similar severity when appointed deputy lieutenant in Ireland in 1467. During the readeption of Henry VI, Tiptoft was captured and executed.

Tiptoft was not only a man of ruthless action; he also contemplated scholarly matters. He studied at Padua University (from where his critics claimed he learned his summary justice) as well as visiting ◊Guarino at Ferrara. Humanists including John ◊Free and Francesco Griffolini presented works to him; he amassed a large library, buying manuscripts from ◊Vespasiano, but of this little survives (although what does suggests that, unusually, he was a conscientious reader of his books).

Tiptoft was not, however, an author. William Caxton printed English translations of Cicero's *De amicitia* and Buonaccorso's *De Nobilitate* claiming they were by Tiptoft but it seems unlikely that he actually wrote them.

Titian (ANGLICIZED FORM OF **Tiziano Vecellio**) (*c.* 1487–1576)
Italian painter. He was the leading painter in Venice during his day where he was considered to be without rival. During his long career he was court painter to ◊Charles V and to his son, Philip II of Spain. He produced a vast number of portraits, religious paintings, and mythological scenes with the aid of a large workshop, including the Venus and Adonis (*c.* 1554, Prado).

He was born in Pieve di Cadore and at nine years old he was apprenticed to mosaicists in Venice, afterwards becoming the pupil of Giovanni ◊Bellini together with ◊Giorgione. It is assumed that they collaborated in 1507–08 on the decoration of the *Fondaco de' Tedeschi* (now destroyed). Titian appears to have been responsible for completing pictures left incomplete at Giorgione's death in 1510, for example the *Concert* (Florence).

Based on the success of several large-scale religious works such as the *Assumption of the Virgin* in the Church of the Friari and the *Entombment* (now in the Louvre, Paris), his reputation increased dramatically. He painted a portrait of Charles V in 1533 which led to a lucrative series of commissions, establishing his fame internationally and making his paintings, and in particular his portraits, greatly demanded. He worked throughout Italy at the invitation of various rulers and popes, and in Augsburg, where he painted Philip of Spain in 1548. From this time onwards he painted mainly in Venice, produc-

Titian Titian, *Mary Magdalen* (Uffizi, Florence). e.t. archive

ing works profound in feeling and notable for remarkable developments in technique.

From the art of Giorgione, he learned and developed a highly personal style notable for its emphasis on ◊*colore* as a means of defining his compositions. His mastery of the effects of light on colour profoundly influenced later Venetian art. His method was complex and deliberate. He laid cooler tones over a solid foundation of red earth colour, and applied films or glazes of transparent colour at intervals, sometimes softening the effect with a finger rather than the brush and adding crisp touches of definition. In this way he achieved his inimitable depth of colour and feeling of rich texture.

Tordesillas, Treaty of

Agreement reached in 1494 when Castile and Portugal divided the uncharted world between themselves. An imaginary line was drawn 370 leagues west of the Azores and the Cape Verde Islands, with Castile receiving all lands discovered to the west, and Portugal those to the east.

The treaty was negotiated because Portugal was unhappy with Spanish pope Alexander VI's four papal bulls of 1493 about a monopoly of navigation and conquest, which were more favourable to Spain.

Torrigiano, Pietro (1472–1528)

Florentine sculptor, employed by ◊Henry VIII of England. He learnt his craft in the Medici gardens from ◊Bertoldo di Giovanni. For a while, he changed career becoming a soldier in Cesare ◊Borgia's army. However, hoping for better reward (it is said) he returned to sculpting and travelled to England, some time between 1506 and 1511. He made several tombs and terracotta busts and worked on Henry VII's grandiose tomb. This, though, was not completed; Torrigiano left in about 1522 and travelled to Seville, Spain.

Torrigiano, like ◊Mazzoni, is an example of the Italian artisan who found lucrative foreign employment and consequently exported a particular Renaissance fashion to cities outside the peninsula. His most substantial work was the bronze and marble tomb of Henry VII and Elizabeth of York (1512–18) in Westminster Abbey, London. In later sculptures, like *St Jerome* (now in the Museo de Bellas Artes, Seville), he worked in polychrome.

Torrigiano has the distinction of being the man who broke the artist Michelangelo's nose. This was not the only time (as Giorgio ◊Vasari describes it) that his hot temper got the better of him: a violent disagreement with a Spanish patron led to his being accused of heresy and dying in custody.

Tourneur, Cyril (1575–1626)

English dramatist. Little is known about his life, and his reputation depends on *The Atheist's Tragedy* (1611), a startling and bitter example of the ◊revenge tragedy. *The Revenger's Tragedy* (1607), once considered to be Tourneur's work, is now thought to be by Thomas ◊Middleton.

Tradescant, John (1570–*c.* 1638)

English gardener and botanist who travelled widely in Europe and is thought to have introduced the cos lettuce to England from the Greek island of that name. He was appointed gardener to Charles I and was succeeded by his son, **John Tradescant the Younger** (1608–1662). The younger Tradescant undertook three plant-collecting trips to Virginia in North America.

The Tradescants introduced many new plants to Britain, including the acacia, lilac, and occidental plane. Tradescant senior is generally considered the earliest collector of plants and other natural history objects.

In 1604 the elder Tradescant became gardener to the Earl of Salisbury, who in 1610 for the first time sent him abroad to collect plants. In 1620 he accompanied an official expedition against the North African Barbary pirates and brought back to England gutta-percha and various fruits and seeds. Later, when he became gardener to Charles I, Tradescant set up his own garden and museum in London. In 1624 he published a catalogue of 750 plants grown in his garden.

The Tradescants' collection of specimens formed the nucleus of the Ashmolean Museum in Oxford. Swedish botanist Carolus Linnaeus named the genus *Tradescantia* (the spiderworts) after the younger Tradescant.

Traversari, Ambrogio (1386–1439)

Florentine scholar; General of the Camaldolese Order from 1430, he translated numerous Greek Fathers into Latin, including Athanasius, John Chrysostom, Basil the Great, and Gregory Nazianzen. He carried out the first ever complete translations of Dionysius the Areopagite and Diogenes Laertius' *Lives of the Philosophers*. Traversari composed, together with ◊Bessarion, the Decree of Union between the Roman Catholic and Orthodox churches at the Council of Florence.

An authority on Classical and Byzantine Greek, Traversari was consulted by humanists such as Lorenzo Valla, Poggio Bracciolini, Leonardo ◊Bruni, and Ermolao ◊Barbaro on literary, stylistic, and linguistic questions. He was a close associate of Niccolò ◊Niccoli and Cosimo de' Medici, and interceded on Cosimo's behalf in 1433 when he was imprisoned. Traversari instituted at S Maria degli Angeli an intellectual circle which included, in addition to the above, Cyriac of Ancona, Leonardo Dati, Mateo Palmieri, and Gianozzo Mannetti. Under his administration at the Angeli, the monastery commissioned (with Medici support) ◊Brunelleschi's Rotunda, the first concentric church of the Renaissance (1430s), and ◊Ghiberti's bronze reliquary with winged victories for saints Protus, Hyacinth, and Nemesius (1426–27), both redolent of the palaeo-Christian world Traversari sought to revive. Traversari's legacy persisted both within the Camaldolese Order and in the secular world. Traversari also oversaw at the monastery a thriving scriptorium which became a centre of ◊*littera antiqua* script.

The early patristic concept of man's divinization through divine love, so prevalent in the Eastern Church Fathers which Traversari translated, came to occupy a central place in the Renaissance *topos* of the dignity of man – expressed by humanists like Gianozzo Manetti and Giovanni ◊Pico della Mirandola. With the support of Cosimo de' Medici and ◊Eugenius IV, Traversari sought to revive this palaeo-Christian spirituality amongst his contemporaries and successors. Exemplified by authors such as Basil the Great and Gregory Nazianzen, Aeneas of Gaza and Dionysius the Areopagite, together with the great patriarch of Constantinople, St John Chrysostom, the subjects of the general's translations contained strong elements of the mystical Platonism of late antiquity. Traversari's patristic scholarship thus proved of central importance to the development of the philosophical Renaissance.

trecento (ITALIAN 'THREE HUNDRED')

Denotes the 1300s and used in relation to Italian culture of the 14th century.

Trent, Council of

Conference held 1545–63 by the Roman Catholic Church at Trento, northern Italy, initiating the so-called ◊Counter-Reformation.

TRANSLATIONS OF THE BIBLE

ON 28TH MAY 1528, John Tybal, from Steeple Bumpstead, a well-known centre of heresy in Essex, was examined by the Bishop of London, Cuthbert Tunstall. Tybal confessed to possession of 'certain books of the four Evangelists in English, of one holy John, & certain Epistles of Peter & Paule', as well as to a number of heterodox beliefs associated with the afterlife of the medieval English heresy of ◊Lollardy. He also revealed the complicity of the curate of his parish, Richard Fox, in his beliefs, and the existence of a network of heretical safe houses in the southeast of England. Having travelled to London in the company of Thomas Hilles, Tybal met with the renegade Augustinian friar, Robert Barnes, at Michaelmas in 1526. Proudly displaying their books to Barnes, Tybal and Hilles were surprised when he showed them little regard and 'made a twit of it, & said, A point for them, for they be not to be regarded toward the new printed Testament in English. For it is of more cleaner English.' Convinced by Barnes of its worth, the two country Lollards parted with three shillings and two pence for a copy of William ◊Tyndale's translation of the New Testament, which had been printed at Worms earlier in the year. Barnes urged them to keep the book secret, and promised that it would make the Latin New Testament seem 'a Cymbal tinkkling, & Brass sounding'.

The books which Tybal had valued so highly before his encounter with Barnes were manuscript copies of a translation of the New Testament into English out of the Latin Vulgate. This was a part of the larger translation of the Bible undertaken in the final quarter of the 14th century by followers of the Oxford heretic, John ◊Wyclif. Over two hundred and fifty manuscripts of the Wycliffite translation survive, the largest number for any English medieval text, indicating its popularity despite the prohibition from 1409 of unauthorized ownership of the Bible in English. The translation preferred by the English Lutheran, Barnes, was that which had been made from the original Greek by William Tyndale, an English exile, which was modelled on Martin ◊Luther's German New Testament of 1522 and whose language echoed both that of Luther and Erasmus. After an abortive attempt at printing his work at Cologne in 1525, Tyndale had finally seen the text through the press in Worms in 1526. Copies were smuggled into England, helping to reignite the hunt for native heresy. At St Paul's in November 1526, Bishop Tunstall preached at a ceremony in which captured copies of Tyndale's New Testament were consigned to the flames.

The writings of Luther had established the importance of vernacular readership of Scripture by the laity for the reformers. Widely publicized in Germany, Luther's ideas touched a chord both with the learned aspirations of contemporary humanists and the devotion of pious lay people. Luther's own mammoth endeavours soon supplemented his New Testament with a German Old Testament, translated from the original Hebrew and published in 1523–24. A complete edition of the German Bible was published for the first time in 1534. By then, Tyndale was well advanced with his own translations out of the original languages of the Bible, having published an edition of the Pentateuch (the first five books of the Old Testament) in 1530. Despite Tyndale's execution for heresy in 1536, a complete edition of the English Bible appeared in 1537, based on his work and supplemented by that of Miles Coverdale (whose own translation of the Bible, based on other contemporary versions in German, Latin, and English, had been published with royal approval in 1535). Through this edition, Tyndale's translation came to influence the subsequent, official revisions of the English Bible, published initially in 1539 and 1568, as well as the extremely popular Geneva Bible, translated by exiles from the Marian persecution, who included Coverdale. All of these versions in turn influenced the committees of translators appointed by the Hampton Court Conference whose work was published in 1611, dedicated to King James I. This, the Authorized Version, won increasing acceptance over the course of the 17th century, and, like Luther's translation in Germany, shaped the language, lives, and minds of generations, being used regularly in

continued

the worship of the Church until the 20th century.

The pattern of development exemplified by the English Bible, from late medieval vernacular versions of the Vulgate, to humanist translations, to authorized editions produced by committees of scholars working for the national church, was repeated elsewhere in Europe, notably in the Netherlands. Here, there was no equivalent to the prohibition against reading the Bible in the vernacular which operated in England because of Wycliffite heresy, and translations of passages of Scripture played a role in the devotion and piety of groups such as the ◊Brethren of the Common Life. The Old Testament was printed in Dutch as early as 1477; a Dutch New Testament was published in 1522, and went through 25 editions by 1530. Numerous versions circulated in the later 16th century, including translations of the Vulgate for a Catholic readership, and one of the tasks of the Synod of Dort

(1618–19) was to establish a committee to oversee an official translation of the Bible for the Calvinist national church, which was eventually published in 1637.

The anxiety of the Catholic Church about unsupervised lay reading of the Bible, and the reaffirmation of the status of the Vulgate by the ◊Council of Trent, helped to limit the spread of vernacular translation during the early modern period. Despite the condemnation of Jan ◊Huss, versions of the Bible in Czech continued to circulate in Bohemia, extending a vernacular tradition which some dated back to St Jerome himself. Persecution of Protestants drove vernacular Bible readership underground here, as it did in many Catholic countries, such as France, Italy, and Spain, where the interests of humanist scholars had originally encouraged the process of translation. Although prepared to sanction translations of the Vulgate for a lay audience under certain circumstances,

the Catholic Church largely abandoned the project of scholarly translation to Protestant authors. In so doing, it terminated one of the most vibrant strands of late medieval piety, and, especially in Italy, associated lay readership even of selected passages of the Bible with suspicions of heresy. Access to the Bible in the vernacular, which had so excited people like Barnes or Tybal, thus became a major point of controversy between Protestants and Catholics throughout Europe, and served to highlight broader differences about the roles of tradition and authority in their respective Churches.

SCOTT MANDELBROTE

Further Reading
Jaroslav Pelikan, Valerie R Hotchkiss, and David Price, *The Reformation of the Bible/The Bible of the Reformation* (New Haven, 1996); Anne Hudson, *The Premature Reformation* (Oxford, 1988); Gigliola Fragnito, *La Bibbia al rogo* (Bologna, 1997)

Très riches Heures du Duc de Berri, Les

Illuminated manuscript painted by the three ◊Limbourg brothers, Paul, Herman, and Jan, about 1413–15 (Musée Condé, Chantilly). It is a Book of Hours (see ◊Hours, Book of) executed for Jean, Duke of Berry, (died 1416), though it was not finished until about 70 years after his death, by the painter Jean Colombe.

The manuscript contains a number of biblical scenes and 12 illustrations depicting the occupations and background of nobles and peasantry for each month of the year. The various châteaux of the duke are minutely depicted, and figures and landscape are combined in such images as the February snow scene, the cavalcade of nobles in spring, and the autumn boar hunt. A map of Rome and a medical-astrological illustration are also included.

triptych

Painting consisting of three panels, usually hinged together with the central panel being twice the width of the wings, which may fold inwards. The triptych developed from the ◊diptych and was used both as a portable altar and, on a larger scale, as an ◊altarpiece.

Trissino, Gian Giorgio (1478–1550)

Venetian dramatist, scholar, and poet. He was interested in linguistic problems, translating ◊Dante's *De Vulgari Eloquentia* into the *volgare* and writing his own treatise *Il Castellano*. He also turned his hand to tragedy, in his *Sofonisba* (written in 1514–15, but not staged until 1562) imitating ancient Greek models. He also produced an epic, *La Italia liberata dai Goti/Italy liberated from the Goths* (1547–48).

Tritonius, Petrus (LATINIZED NAME OF PETER TREYBENREIF) (*c.* 1465–*c.* 1525)

Austrian composer and scholar. He wrote music for Horatian odes for four voices, and in 1524 published a hymn book containing the text of about 130 hymns and blank staves for the music to be written on.

He studied at Vienna and Ingolstadt universities and later became a teacher of Latin and music at the cathedral school of Brixen. He later studied at Padua University, and while in Italy he met the Viennese professor Conrad ◊Celtis, who invited him to settle at Vienna. Once there, he joined Celtis's circle and wrote a setting of Horatian odes, which were published in 1507. Ludwig Senfl later took the tenor parts of these as canti firmi for his own settings, and Paul Hofhaimer imitated Tritonius's settings. On the death of Celtis in 1508 Tritonius returned to the Tyrol and became director of the Latin school at Bozen; in 1513 he was in Halle, and in 1521 he retired to Schwaz am Inn.

Works include:
Hymns in four parts; odes by Horace and other Latin poems set in four parts, and other pieces.

Trombetti, Ascanio (1544–1590)

Italian composer. He wrote four books of madrigals 1573–87. From the 1560s he was in the service of the Signoria of Bologna, where he played the cornett. From 1583 he was maestro di cappella at the Church of S Giovanni at Monte.

Works include:
Motets in 5 to 12 parts for voices and instruments; madrigals for four to five voices, *napolitane* for three voices.

Tromboncino, Bartolomeo (*c.* 1470–AFTER 1534)

Italian composer. He was famous as a composer of *frottole* – songs for several singers or for one singer and instruments – he wrote over 170. He enjoyed brief fame for having murdered his adulterous wife in 1499 and was in the service of another adulteress, Lucrezia Borgia, at Ferrara 1502–08.

He was at the ducal court of Mantua 1487–95, then at Venice, Vicenza, Casale, at Mantua again 1501–13, and then at Ferrara.

Works include:
Lamentations, one motet and 17 *laude*; over 170 *frottole* for four voices.

Tudor dynasty

Dynasty that ruled England from ◊Henry VII's victory at Bosworth in 1485 until Elizabeth I's death in 1603. The dynasty was succeeded by the Scottish royal dynasty, the Stuarts, in the person of James VI.

Originally a Welsh gentry family, the Tudors married into royalty three times in the 15th century. First, Owen Tudor married Katharine of Valois, daughter of Charles VI of France and widow of ◊Henry V. Owen's son, Edmund, took as his wife Margaret ◊Beaufort whose royal blood came from Edward III's son, John of Gaunt; though the Beauforts were Gaunt's illegitimate offspring, they were later legitimized and it was through them that ◊Henry VII made his claim to the throne. Henry secured his hold on the throne by marrying ◊Edward IV's daughter, Elizabeth – although he stressed that he was king in his own right.

Tudor rose

Heraldic emblem adopted by Henry VII and his successors. It comprises a rose with the central petals white and the outer petals red; in other words, it combines a badge of the house of York with one of the house of Lancaster. It symbolized that Henry, by marrying Elizabeth of York, had united the two houses and had (supposedly) brought the Wars of the ◊Roses to an end.

Tura, Cosimo (1430–1495)

Italian painter. A painter of religious and allegorical scenes, he developed a highly individual style of rich and fanciful ornamentation, his forms sharp, spiky, and metallic. His fondness for dolphins as a motif can be seen in *An Allegorical Figure* (*c.* 1455, National Gallery, London).

Tura was the first outstanding representative of the School of Ferrara. He seems to have studied in the Squarcione workshop in Padua and to have been influenced by the sculpturesque style of the young Andrea ◊Mantegna, though not with the same antiquarian or Classical tendency. He worked mainly for the Este court in Ferrara.

THE TUDOR DYNASTY

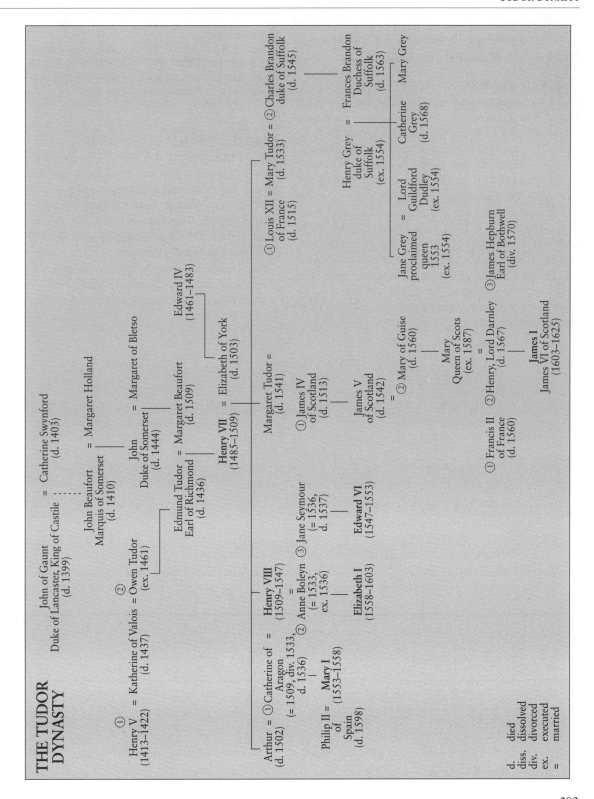

THE TUDOR DYNASTY

John of Gaunt = Catherine Swynford
Duke of Lancaster, King of Castile   (d. 1403)
(d. 1399)

John Beaufort = Margaret Holland
Marquis of Somerset
(d. 1410)

John = Margaret of Bletso
Duke of Somerset
(d. 1444)

Edward IV
(1461–1483)

Edmund Tudor = Margaret Beaufort
Earl of Richmond   (d. 1509)
(d. 1436)

Henry VII = Elizabeth of York
(1485–1509)   (d. 1503)

①
Henry V = Katherine of Valois = Owen Tudor
(1413–1422)   (d. 1437)   (ex. 1461)
②

① Louis XII = Mary Tudor = ② Charles Brandon
of France   (d. 1533)   duke of Suffolk
(d. 1515)   (d. 1545)

Margaret Tudor =
(d. 1541)

① James IV
of Scotland
(d. 1513)

James V
of Scotland
(d. 1542)
=

② Mary of Guise
(d. 1560)

Frances Brandon   Mary Grey
Duchess of
Suffolk
(d. 1563)

=

Henry Grey
duke of
Suffolk
(ex. 1554)

Jane Grey   =   Lord   Catherine
proclaimed   Guildford   Grey
queen   Dudley   (d. 1568)
1553   (ex. 1554)
(ex. 1554)

Mary
Queen of Scots
(ex. 1587)
=

① Francis II   ② Henry, Lord Darnley   ③ James Hepburn
of France   (d. 1567)   Earl of Bothwell
(d. 1560)   (div. 1570)

James I
James VI of Scotland
(1603–1625)

Arthur = ① Catherine of = Henry VIII
(d. 1502)   Aragon   (1509–1547)
(= 1509, div. 1533,   =
d. 1536)   ② Anne Boleyn   ③ Jane Seymour
(= 1533,   (= 1536,
ex. 1536)   d. 1537)

Philip II =   Mary I   Elizabeth I   Edward VI
of   (1553–1558)   (1558–1603)   (1547–1553)
Spain
(d. 1598)

d.   died
diss.   dissolved
div.   divorced
ex.   executed
=   married

Artists whose work is related to his are Francesco Cossa, Ercole de Roberti, and Marco Zoppo.

Tye, Christopher (*c.* 1505–*c.* 1572)

English composer and poet. His music shows considerable acquaintance with contemporary continental composers, for example, the Mass for six voices *Euge Bone*. He wrote a good deal of verse in his later years.

He became a lay clerk at King's College, Cambridge in 1537. In 1543 he was appointed choirmaster at Ely Cathedral; he received a doctorate in music from Cambridge University in 1545, and from Oxford in 1548. In 1561 he resigned his post at Ely and was succeeded by Robert White. Having been ordained, he accepted the living at Doddington-cum-Marche in the Isle of Ely, and for some time later held two other livings in the neighbourhood; but he had to resign them because of carelessness in the matter of payments due.

Works include:
Masses (including *Euge Bone* and *Western Wind*), motets, services, anthems, *The Actes of the Apostles* in English (1533, metrical versions set for four voices dedicated to Edward VI); In Nomines for instruments.

Tyndale, William (*c.* 1492–1536)

English translator of the Bible. The printing of his New Testament was begun in Cologne in 1525 and, after he had been forced to flee, completed in Worms. Tyndale introduced some of the most familiar phrases to the English language, such as 'filthy lucre', and 'God forbid'. He was strangled and burned as a heretic at Vilvorde in Belgium.

His translation heavily influenced that of Miles ♭Coverdale and, later, James I's Authorized Version of the Bible. (See feature on Translations of the Bible).

U

Uccello, Paolo (ADOPTED NAME OF PAOLO DI DONO) (1397–1475)

Florentine painter. He was one of the first to experiment with perspective, though his love of detail, decorative colour, and graceful line remains traditional. His works include *St George and the Dragon* (*c.* 1460, National Gallery, London) and *A Hunt* (*c.* 1460, Ashmolean Museum, Oxford).

Uccello used perspective, though he used it imaginatively rather than with scientific accuracy or consistency. His works in fresco include his painting (in imitation of an equestrian statue) of the English ◊*condottiere* Sir John Hawkwood (1436), in Florence Cathedral, and a series in the Chiostro Verde (Green Cloister) of Santa Maria Novella, Florence, the principal composition being the *Deluge* of about 1445. He is, however, more celebrated for his panel pictures, notably the *Battle of San Romano* (*c.* 1455), three pictures of the battle between the Florentines and the Sienese in 1432 painted for the Medici (Uffizi, Florence; Louvre, Paris; and National Gallery, London). They were intended to be framed together, but each gives an effect of completeness and is wonderfully rich in design.

Trained as a goldsmith, Uccello was apprenticed to ◊Ghiberti about 1407–12, when the latter was working on the doors of the Florentine Baptistry. In 1415 he entered the Physicians' Guild in Florence as a painter. He worked mainly in Florence, with an interlude from 1425 in Venice, where he is said to have produced a mosaic for the façade of St Mark's. He bought a house in Florence in 1442 and evidently prospered for a time, though his old age was reputedly spent in poverty and isolation.

Udall, Nicholas (*c.* 1505–1556)

English schoolmaster and dramatist. He was the author of *Ralph Roister Doister* dated by various scholars around 1540/53, printed 1566–67. It is the first known English comedy and is based on the plays of the Roman comic dramatists Plautus and Terence.

Ugolino di Nerio (DIED 1327)

Italian painter, active in Siena. A signed work by him is the high altarpiece of Sta Croce, Florence, a polyptych, his only authenticated painting (fragments are in the National Gallery, London; in Berlin; and in private collections). A follower of Duccio, he worked in the highly cultivated Byzantine style.

Ugolino of Orvieto (*c.* 1380–1457)

Italian composer and theorist. His *Declaratio Musicae Discipline* (1435) is mainly a practical handbook for the performing musician of his day.

Urfé, Honore d' (1567–1625)

French writer. His main work was a vast and influential pastoral romance, *L'Astrée/Astrea*, the first part of which was published in 1607 and the fifth posthumously in 1627. The final section was completed by his secretary, Balthazar Baro, on the basis of Urfe's notes. This tale of shepherds and shepherdesses in love was inspired by earlier Spanish and Italian works; for example, Torquato ◊Tasso's Arcadian drama *L'Aminta* (1581).

Usper, Francesco (ADOPTED NAME OF FRANCESCO SPONGA) (BEFORE 1570–1641)

Italian priest, organist, and composer. In 1614 he became organist at the Church of San Salvatore at Venice, in 1621 he deputized for Giovanni Battista Grillo (died 1622) as organist at St Mark's, and in 1627 he became principal of the school of St John the Evangelist.

Works include:

Masses, motets, psalms for voices with instruments, vesper psalms for four to eight voices and bass, some for double choir; *La battaglia* for voices and instruments, madrigals; *ricercari* and *arie francesi* in four parts.

Utopia

Political fiction, part dialogue, part description of an imaginary country (Utopia, Greek 'no place'), by Thomas ◊More. Written in Latin probably in 1515, it was published the following year with the assistance of More's friend ◊Erasmus. Erasmus arranged for a series of letters by well-known humanists, like Guillaume ◊Budé, to appear as introduction to the work; both these and the etching of the island of Utopia by Ambrosius Holbein, brother of Hans ◊Holbein the Younger, sustained the pretence that the book recorded a real conversation. The work was a publishing sensation in humanist circles and made More's international reputation.

The work records a conversation between an explorer called Raphael Hythlodaeus (the surname means 'nonsense pedlar'), More's alter ego (Morus), and his friend Peter Giles. Hythlodaeus has just returned from the new-found island of Utopia, which he declares a much wiser and happier state than any in Christendom. Hearing his tale, Morus suggests that he should help improve Europe by advising a king; the debate between Morus and Hythlodaeus about whether his counsel would be heard is the subject of the first book of *Utopia*. The second consists of a description of the island of Utopia and the customs of its inhabitants: for example, they hold property in common, considering gold worthy only to be used for chamber pots. The tale of their habits, so different from those of Europe, ends with Morus's comment that many of these customs would be beneficial (though few could be introduced) – with the exception of the moneyless economy which would be, in the popular opinion, unacceptable.

The humour of *Utopia* lies in the continually shifting nature of the work. In the first book, the debate plays off reality, since More himself was at this time about to join royal service. In the second book, the physical description of Utopia sounds uncannily like that of England, its capital like London; their customs, meanwhile, at times contrast utterly with More's Europe, at others, satirically parallel those of contemporary society. So, for example, the Utopians never make a treaty – unlike European kings, who often make treaties, and as often break them; but if it comes to war, the Utopians do not fight themselves but send in mercenaries, who are highly paid – or would be, if they survived. The use of mercenaries was, of course, established European practice. At other points, the humour is self-deprecating: More the lawyer comments that the Utopians ban lawyers from their country as 'a class of men whose trade is to manipulate cases and multiply quibbles'. The different layers of this humour make it impossible to identify *Utopia* (as many readers have done) as a blueprint of an ideal society. More's purpose is not to construct an alternative, but to deconstruct the absurdities not just of European societies but of human nature.

Utopia was repeatedly reprinted, and often translated into English, German, Italian, and other vernacular, in the decades after its first publication. It also began a literary *topos* – the discovery of an ideal commonwealth – to which several writers contributed in the late 16th and early 17th centuries (although none replicated the ironic ambivalence of More's text). Examples of later utopian works include *Città del Sole/City of the Sun* by the Italian Tommaso ◊Campanella (1568–1639) and Francis ◊Bacon's *New Atlantis* (1626).

VII's curia and then moved to Naples where he headed a group of scholars discussing theology and church reform. His conversations with his disciple Giulia de Gonzaga resulted in his *Alfabeto Cristiano* (1535).

His *Diálogo de la Lengua* (1533–35), a study of the Castilian language by way of its proverbs, circulated only in manuscript until 1737.

Vaet, Jacobus (1529–1567)

Flemish composer. He was choirmaster to Maximilian, King of Bohemia, in the 1560s and succeeded Jachet Buus as chief music director in Vienna in 1564, when his patron became the Emperor Maximilian II.

Works include:
Masses, motets, Magnificats, Te Deum for eight voices and other church music; chansons.

Valdés, Alfonso de (1490–1532)

Castilian scholar, Latin secretary to Charles V from 1529. The older brother of Juan de ◊Valdés, Alfonso was, like his regular correspondent ◊Erasmus, critical of church corruption but also an opponent of Lutheranism.

His works included commentaries on St Paul's Epistles to the Romans and the Corinthians and a Castilian translation of St Matthew's Gospel; however, only two of his writings – *Diálogo de las cosas ocurridas en Roma* and *Diálogo de Mercurio y Carón* – were printed in his lifetime (both in 1530). The first *Dialogue* was a harsh attack on corruption in the Catholic Church, couched as a defence of the 1527 ◊Sack of Rome (it was translated into English in 1590 as *The Sacke of Roome*). *The Dialogue of Mercury and Charon*, meanwhile, condemned evil men by providing examples of good ones. Both dialogues were denounced as heretical but by 1547 had run to four editions.

Valdés, Juan de (c. 1498–1541)

Castilian religious reformer and educator, the younger brother of Alfonso de ◊Valdés. He studied at Alcalá, where in 1529 he published his *Diálogo de Doctrina Cristiana*, which was denounced as heretical. Juan briefly resided in the early 1530s at Clement

Valdivia, Pedro de (c. 1497–1554)

Spanish explorer who travelled to Venezuela about 1530 and accompanied Francisco ◊Pizarro on his second expedition to Peru. He then went south into Chile, where he founded the cities of in Santiago 1541 and Valdivia in 1544. In 1552 he crossed the Andes to explore the Negro River. He was killed by Araucanian Indians.

Valla, Lorenzo (1407–1457)

Italian humanist, born and raised in Rome. He seems to have been self-taught (a condition which brought on him the ridicule of ◊Poggio Bracciolini); Beccadelli invited him to teach in Pavia in 1431. He only remained there for a couple of years, leaving with his friendship with Beccadelli ended. He went first to Milan and then, in 1435, to the court of ◊Alfonso V where he remained for a decade. Though his works had caused him to be tried before the Inquisition in 1444, he was able to find employment in the papal curia under ◊Nicholas V, from 1448, and (that enemy of humanists) ◊Calixtus III.

1428	*De Comparatione Ciceronis Quintilianique*
c. **1431**	*De Voluptate/On Pleasure*
1433	Polemic on the barbarism of Bartolus
c. **1433**	*De Vero Falsoque Bono/On the True and False Good,* a revised version of *On Pleasure* (revised again 1440s)
1435–36	*Adnotationes in Novum Testamentum/Annotations on the New Testament* (revised 1443, 1453)
1435–43	*De Libero Arbitrio/On Free Will*
1438–39	*Dialecticae Disputationes/Dialectical Disputations* (revised 1444, 1453–57)
1440	*De Falso Credita et Ementita Constantini Donatione/On the Forgery of the Alleged Donation of Constantine*
1440	First version of *Elegantiae Linguae*

Latinae/The Elegance of the Latin Language circulated

1446 *Gesta Ferdinandi Regis Aragonum/Deeds of Ferdinand, King of Aragon*

1447 *Antidotum in Facium,* an attack on Bartolomeo Fazio (and Panormita) for his criticisms of his *Gesta Ferdinandi Regis*

1452–53 Dispute with Poggio, with each writing invectives (*Antidotum*)

1452 Translation of Thucydides' *History*

1453 Revised version of *Annotations* dedicated to Nicholas V

1457 *Encomium Sancti Thomae Aquinatis/Praise of S Thomas Aquinas*

While other early humanists most admired the example of Cicero, Valla's role model was Quintilian. Both Classical authors wrote on rhetoric but Valla found in Quintilian an introduction to the role of eloquence which assisted the development of his own philosophical outlook. An argument can not be won by force of argument alone; it must also be persuasive, which requires rhetoric. The recognition of this did not, however, make Valla a sceptic who doubted certainty of knowledge; indeed, works like his tract on the *Donation of Constantine* combine rhetoric with philological insights to prove a fact – that the *Donation* was a forgery.

Valla's life was dogged by controversy and dispute, perhaps more so than many other humanists. At the same time, some of his works proved enduringly popular. In particular, his *Elegentiae*, a guidebook to what he considered good Latin usage, circulated widely in manuscript and a paraphrase of it was produced by ◊Erasmus in 1488. Erasmus was also influenced by another of Valla's works: his *Annotations on the New Testament*. Erasmus discovered a copy of this and printed it in 1505; it provided a starting point for his own work on revising the Latin translation of the New Testament.

Vanni, Andrea (1332–1414)

Italian painter. He was a follower of Simone Martini. Employed on ambassadorial missions, he visited and worked in Rome, Naples, and Avignon. He corresponded with the religious mystic Catherine of Siena and painted her portrait. Works by him are in Siena and a triptych by him is in the Corcoran Gallery, Washington, DC.

Vargas, Luis de (1502–1568)

Castilian painter. He spent almost 30 years in Italy, where he was deeply influenced by the work of Giorgio ◊Vasari. On returning to Spain about 1550, he introduced the art of fresco painting to Seville. His finest work is the *Nativity Altar* in Seville Cathedral.

Vargas was born in Seville and trained in Rome.

Vasari, Giorgio (1511–1574)

Tuscan painter, architect, and art historian. Born of a humble family of potters in Arezzo, Vasari rose to become the premier artist of his day in Italy. Although hugely prolific as an artist who enjoyed the patronage of the dukes of Florence and numerous popes, he is today best known for *Le vite de' più eccelenti architetti, pittori, et sculteri italiani/The Lives of the Most Excellent Italian Architects, Painters, and Sculptors* (1550; revised and enlarged in 1568), which became the crucial defining discussion of the history of art in the Renaissance (see feature).

Although best known for his decoration in fresco and oil painting of the Palazzo Vecchio in Florence, throughout his career Vasari executed numerous religious paintings for a wide-ranging group of erudite ecclesiastical patrons from Venice in the north to Naples in the south. His graceful and sophisticated paintings were developed from a career of continuous study and a passionate concern for ◊*disegno*, qualities which he repeatedly stresses in the *Lives*. As an architect Vasari worked in Tuscany, executing projects largely in conjunction with the Medici and was deeply influenced by the work of ◊Michelangelo.

Based on his experiences as a journeyman painter travelling throughout Italy, the *Lives* was a hugely popular publication which for the first time contained a history of art. The second edition of the *Lives*, published in 1568, supplied further details to particular biographies, added others and generally provided a more comprehensive account of Italian art with an eye to greater accuracy and readability. While modern scholarship has corrected particulars, the *Lives* still provide invaluable anecdotal information on those artists of the Renaissance Vasari cared to mention; the book also defines Vasari's experiences as an artist, summed up in the autobiography he appended to the 1568 edition.

Vasari trained as a painter in Arezzo and Florence,

where he studied in the workshops of Baccio ◊Bandinelli and ◊Andrea del Sarto, before coming under the influence of ◊Rosso Fiorentino. Studies in Rome with Francesco ◊Salviati brought Vasari into contact with the art of ◊Raphael and ◊Michelangelo. Vasari developed a style which stressed the use of complex allegorical imagery to convey meaning and expression, as can be seen in the *Allegory of the Immaculate Conception* (copy in the Ashmolean Museum, Oxford). His paintings demonstrate his assimilation of Florentine and Roman motifs, which he developed over decades of travel, executing paintings throughout Italy. With the publication of the *Lives*, Vasari's career turned increasingly to massive decorative and architectural projects for the dukes of Florence and a succession of popes, including the construction of the Uffizi Palace, Florence, and the De Monte chapel in the Church of San Pietro in Montorio, Rome. Unique to artists of his day, he dramatically renovated the Gothic Church of the Pieve, Arezzo, and constructed a gigantic high altarpiece replete with paintings and a family tomb as a memorial, and was buried there upon his death.

Vauquelin de la Fresnaye, Jean, Sieur des Yveteaux (1536–c. 1608)

French poet. He wrote *Satyres françaises*, the earliest collection of regular satires in France; these were largely borrowed from Italian writers.

He also wrote *Art poétique* (1575, published 1605) in support of the ideals of the ◊*Pléiade* poets, and *Idylles*, a collection of sonnets and epigrams.

Vázquez, Juan (c. 1510–c. 1560)

Spanish composer. He was maestro de capilla at Badajoz Cathedral 1545–50, and was later in the service of Don Antonio de Zuñiga. He was an important exponent of the Spanish song form known as the *villancico*, and also wrote church music.

Vecchi, Orazio (Tiberio) (1550–1605)

Italian composer. As well as sacred music, he wrote canzonettes and madrigals, and was celebrated as a composer of entertainments.

Vecchi was born in Modena. He was maestro di cappella at Salò Cathedral from 1581, at Modena from 1584, and at Reggio Emilia in 1586, then became a canon at Correggio and an archdeacon in 1591. Wishing to devote himself to music, he returned to Modena as maestro di cappella in 1593, and then became maestro di cappella at the d'Este court in 1598. He became famous, being summoned to the court of the Emperor Rudolf II at one time and invited to compose music for the king of Poland. In 1604 his pupil Geminiano Capi-Lupi intrigued successfully against him and supplanted him in his post.

His works include *L'Amfiparnaso* comprising 14 madrigals for five voices, with a dramatic plot set to a *commedia dell'arte* text. The characters' parts are not acted, but are sung by concerted voices in the madrigal style.

Works include:
Madrigal comedy *L'Amfiparnaso* (1597); Masses, motets, Lamentations, and other church music; madrigals, canzonets.

Vecchietta, Lorenzo di Pietro (1413–1480)

Italian painter and sculptor. In painting he followed Stefano di Sassetta and had considerable influence on the development of the art of Siena, where he was active. He was a pupil of Jacopo della Quercia and Donatello.

Vecellio, Francesco (1483–1560)

Italian painter. He worked at first as an assistant and later alone in the provinces. His works include a Nativity in the Church of S Guiseppe in Belluno, *Ecce Homo* (Gemäldegalerie Alter Meister, Dresden), and *The Annunciation* (Accademia, Venice). He was the brother of ◊Titian.

Veen (VENIUS), Otto van (1558–1629)

Flemish painter. Producing historical and religious subjects and portraits, he worked in Liège, Brussels, and Antwerp. He also worked in Italy in the studio of Federigo ◊Zuccaro, becoming Italianate in style. He settled in Antwerp in 1593 but left the city for Brussels in 1620.

Vega, Lope Felix de (Carpio) (1562–1635)

Spanish poet and dramatist. He was one of the

founders of modern Spanish drama. He wrote epics, pastorals, odes, sonnets, novels, and over 500 plays (of which 426 are still in existence), mostly tragicomedies. He set out his views on drama in *Arte nuevo de hacer comedias/The New Art of Writing Plays* (1609), in which he defended his innovations while reaffirming the Classical forms. *Fuenteovejuna* (*c.* 1614) has been acclaimed as the first proletarian drama.

life His early years are obscure, but many of his love affairs are well documented. He was born in Madrid but banished in 1588 for eight years for insulting his lover's family; he then married another woman and days later set sail from Lisbon as a sailor in Philip II's Armada. He returned, pardoned, to Madrid in 1590. His marriages and love affairs continued; in 1614, however, he became a priest. Celibacy did not last, as in 1617 he fell passionately in love with a married woman of 26, Marta de Nevares. Despite his vows, they lived together, and she apparently encouraged him to write the *Novelas a Marcia Leonardo* (the title was a thinly disguised reference to Nevares herself). But she gradually descended into blindness and madness, dying in 1632. Her death, which inspired Lope's eclogue 'Amarilis' (1633), was shortly followed by his own. He was buried with much pomp in the church of St Sebastian, Madrid, but his remains are untraceable, as they were later removed to a common grave.

poetry Vega was a lyric poet who wrote sonnets, eclogues, and ballads, many of which were inspired by his love affairs. Of his sonnets, 200 were published in 1602; another 100 appeared in 1614, and an anthology of his poetry, *La Vega del Parnaso/The Parnassian Valley* (a play on his surname) was printed shortly after his death in 1637. In 1634 his comic poem 'La Gatomaquia', on the deeds of a wicked cat, was published in another anthology of his works, *Rimas divinas y humanas/Verses Divine and Human*.

novels Lope wrote the obligatory ◊pastoral novel, *La Arcadia/Arcadia* in 1598 (with the added interest that it was a *roman à clef*, closely based on real persons). In 1604 he produced a work in another fashionable genre, the ◊byzantine novel, *El Peregrino en su patria/The Pilgrim in His Own Country*, which had a useful (for modern scholars) appendix listing Lope's 219 plays to date. He responded to

Miguel de Cervantes's *Novelas ejemplares* with a series of *Novelas a Marcia Leonardo/Novels for Marcia Leonardo*, which appeared at intervals, published in different collections: the first, *Las fortunas de Diana/Diana's Adventures*, was included in *La Filomena/Filomena* (1621), and he published three more in *La Circe/Circe* (1624). Finally, the lengthy prose dialogues of *La Dorotea/Dorotea* (1632) recall *La ◊Celestina*, although Vega's tale of his early loves is also interspersed with lyric poems.

plays Ironically for one who was such a prolific playwright (Lope wrote some 501 dramatic works), there exists no completely reliable text of any of his plays. It was not until 1619 that he authorized publication of a selection of these; by then, however, there were numerous unauthorized editions in circulation. His plays drew their inspiration from earlier Castilian literature (ballads, chronicles) or historical events; from Classical dramatists – particularly Plautus – from the Bible, or simply from popular sayings. Thus the tragic *Caballero de Olmedo/The Gentleman of Olmedo* (*c.* 1615–26, published 1641) alludes heavily to *La ◊Celestina*, while *Fuenteovejuna* merges a line from a chronicle with 15th-century Castilian history. *Perro del hortelano/Dog in the Manger* (literally, 'the gardener's dog'), written 1613–15, is a comedy of aristocratic intrigue and false identity which, in the style of Classical comedy, is ultimately and ingeniously resolved to the satisfaction of the characters.

Vegetius

Ancient Roman military theorist. Very little is known about his life, but he seems to have held a senior position in the imperial bureaucracy of the late empire, late 4th–early 5th centuries. He wrote two works, one on equine and bovine veterinary practices and his *Epitome of Military Science*.

Vegetius is an example of an author whose popularity merely continued through the 15th and 16th centuries. Earlier, his work had circulated widely and been translated into French (several times) and Italian (by Bono Giamboni (*c.* 1230–*c.* 1300)). In the 15th century, there was an English version (John of Trevisa), as well as a German (Ludwig Hohenwang, printed 1475), Castilian (anonymous), and perhaps a Portuguese (by Dom Pedro, Duke of

Coimbra). Further vernacular translations were made in the 16th century, mainly in German and Italian; an English version by Thomas Marshe was printed in 1572 with a translation of Niccolò ◊Machiavelli's *Arte della guerra/The Art of War*, a work which used Vegetius as a major source. The Latin original often appeared in 15th-century manuscript collections – ◊Frederigo da Montefeltre, for example, owned several copies. From 1474/75, it was regularly printed; in this period, its editors included Guillaume ◊Budé (1524) and Josse ◊Bade (1533).

Venegas de Henestrosa, Luis (*c.* 1510– *c.* 1557 OR LATER)

Spanish composer. He published a book of variations and transcriptions in a special tablature suitable for keyboard instruments, harp, vihuela, or guitar (*Libro de cifra nueva*, 1557). The notation was later used by Antonio de Cabezón (1510–1566) and Francisco Correa de Arauxo (1576–1654).

Veneziano, Agostino (LIVED 16TH CENTURY)

Italian engraver. He was a pupil and assistant of Marcantonio ◊Raimondi, and engraved many works, chiefly after ◊Raphael.

A collection of his works is in the British Museum, London.

Verdelot, Philippe (*c.* 1470–*c.* 1552)

French composer. His sacred music includes two Masses, about 57 motets, and a Magnificat, and was popular throughout Europe, but he was admired chiefly for his nine volumes of madrigals. He was one of the first composers to write madrigals (he was writing them as early as the 1520s), and influenced other madrigalists.

Verdelot was born in northern France. He went to Italy, probably at an early age, and was maestro at the baptistry in Florence 1523–25 and at Florence Cathedral 1523–27.

His motets were parodied by other composers, including Roland de Lassus and Palestrina.

Works include:
Two Masses, about 57 motets; about 100 madrigals, three chansons.

Verdonck, Cornelis (1563–1625)

Flemish singer and composer. He was in the service of Cornelius Pruenen, treasurer and later sheriff of Antwerp, until 1598, then on the death of his patron he served two of his nephews. He was singer at the royal chapel in Madrid 1584–98.

Works include:
Magnificat, *Ave Gratia Plena*, four motets; 21 chansons, 42 madrigals.

Vergerio, Pier Paolo (1370–1444)

Italian educationalist and scholar. He was born in Venice and linked to Coluccio ◊Salutati's Florentine humanist circle. He spent much of his early career in Padua, though for a while (1397–1400) he gave up teaching to become a pupil again: he learned Greek from ◊Chrysoloras, then in Florence. On his return to Padua, Vergerio dedicated to his Carrara patron *De Ingenuis Moribus* (*c.* 1401), an educational treatise which proved highly influential. He later attended the Council of ◊Constance and there secured a position at the court of Emperor Sigismund, where he remained for the next decades.

During his time in Florence, Vergerio became friends with Florentine scholars like Leonardo ◊Bruni, who later dedicated to him his *Dialogi*. The two men were colleagues again when they were both in the papal curia (which Vergerio joined in 1405), but, during the ◊Great Schism, this provided a precarious existence. Vergerio later gained the patronage of Cardinal ◊Zabarella, and it was with him that he travelled to Constance.

Apart from *De Ingenuis Moribus*, Vergerio's writings included a *Life of Petrarch*, an unfinished tract in praise of Venice (*De Republica Veneta*, *c.* 1400) and several sermons and epistles. In style and interests, these works are similar to – indeed, often anticipate – those of early 15th-century Florentine humanists, but Vergerio's commitment to the active life and to republicanism was even less constant than that of his Florentine colleagues.

Vergil

As ◊Politian showed, most of the ancient manuscripts provide this spelling for the Classical poet usually and less properly known as ◊Virgil.

Vergil, Polydore (*c.* 1470–1555)

Italian humanist author from Urbino. Sent to England in 1502 as a papal tax collector, Vergil found time to begin writing his *Anglica Historia/English History*; for his efforts he received Henry VII's patronage. Royal favour continued in the next reign, albeit fitfully: at one point, Vergil was imprisoned for allegedly slandering cardinal Wolsey to the pope in 1515. Despite this upset, Vergil continued to live in England, and completed his *Anglica Historia* in 1532. He acquiesced to the religious changes imposed by Henry VIII and Edward VI; he finally returned to his homeland in 1553.

Vergil wrote in a range of genres, including dialogues and translation (Chrysostom's *De Perfecto Monacho*, 1528). His most popular works were his earliest: *Proverbiorum Libellus/A Little Book of Proverbs* (1498), an early set of adages, and *De Inventoribus Rerum/On Inventors of Things* (1499, revised 1521), which, though mocked by the French novelist ◊Rabelais, was translated into most vernaculars (English version 1546). In England, his *Anglica Historia* was very influential, being a major source for the chroniclers Raphael ◊Holinshed and Edward ◊Hall.

Veronese, Paolo (PAOLO CALIARI) (*c.* 1528–1588)

Italian painter, born in Verona. He was the pupil of Antonio Badile, but also learned from the study of ◊Titian and ◊Tintoretto. Some part of his youth was spent in the shop of his brother Antonio, who dealt in the embroidery and rich stuffs that were to play an important decorative part in his painting. From 1555 he lived in Venice, producing those huge decorative compositions with their representation of splendid architecture and crowds of luxuriously dressed figures for which he is famous. He was active mainly in Venice. He specialized in grand decorative schemes, such as his ceilings in the Doge's Palace, noted for their rich colouring, broad composition, *trompe l'oeil* effects, and inventive detail. Religious, mythological, historical, or allegorical, his paintings – usually of banquets and scenes of pageantry – celebrated the power and splendour of Venice.

Many of his finest works are *in situ* – in the Doge's Palace, the church of San Sebastiano, the Accademia, and the Villa Masiera – but elsewhere paintings now held include *Marriage at Cana* (1562–63, Louvre, Paris), the *Family of Darius before Alexander* (*c.* 1570, National Gallery, London), and the *Finding of Moses* (Mellon Collection, Washington, DC).

The *Marriage at Cana* is typical in its pomp and luxury, containing more than 130 figures, including portraits of many leading figures – Charles V, Francis I, Sultan Suleiman II, the painters Titian, Bassano, and Tintoretto, and the writer Pietro Aretino – together with an assortment of fools, dwarfs, pages, and dogs, in a grandiose architectural setting.

The *Feast in the House of Levi* (1573, Accademia, Venice), conceived as a version of the *Last Supper* but subsequently renamed, was considered irreverent in its treatment of a religious theme and caused Veronese to be questioned by the Inquisition in 1573. The Inquisitors pointed out that in Michelangelo's *Last Judgement* there were no such 'drunkards nor dogs nor similar buffooneries' as Veronese had painted. He answered: 'Mine is no art of thought; my art is joyous and praises God in light and colour.'

Veronese was assisted in his huge undertakings by his brother **Benedetto** and his sons **Carlo** and **Gabriel**, who carried on the work of his studio after his death.

Verrocchio, Andrea del (ANDREA DI CIONE) (*c.* 1435–1488)

Florentine sculptor, painter, and goldsmith. He ran a large workshop in Florence and received commissions from the Medici family. His works include the vigorous equestrian statue of *Bartolommeo Colleoni* begun about 1480 (Campo SS Giovanni e Paolo, Venice) and the painting *The Baptism of Christ* (*c.* 1470, Uffizi, Florence).

He studied as a goldsmith under Giuliano Verrocchi and was probably also a pupil of Donatello. He is famous principally as a sculptor, his bronze equestrian statue of Colleoni being one of the great masterpieces of Renaissance sculpture. As a painter he is less eminent; the only painting that can be attributed to him with certainty is *The Baptism of Christ*. However, his studio-workshop, in which painting was only one of many activities, was an important Florentine training ground, and Verrocchio has a secondary reputation as the master of ◊Leonardo da

Vinci, ◊Perugino, and Lorenzo di Credi. A well-grounded tradition has it that Leonardo painted the angel (on the left) in *The Baptism of Christ*.

Vertue, Robert (DIED 1506)

English mason, probable architect of Henry VII's palace at Greenwich (subsequently destroyed). He was Henry's master mason and also worked on a new tower at the Tower of London, as well as designing the king's chapel at Westminster Abbey.

Vesalius, Andreas (1514–1564)

Anatomist from Brabant. He taught in Padua and then became physician to Philip II. He completed his education in Paris, where he assisted in producing an edition of ◊Galen. His own textbook of human anatomy, *De Humani Corporis Fabrica/On the Construction of the Human Body* (1543), added to and (particularly in the revised edition, 1555) in some respects challenged the writings of Galen.

At Padua, Vesalius became famous for using human dissections for research and teaching. It was this practice that raised questions about some of Galen's assumptions. It also provided the knowledge that informs the 250 anatomical drawings by Jan Steven van ◊Calcar which were a valued part of *De Fabrica*. His work at Padua was continued by Realdus Columbus and Gabriele Falloppio. Vesalius died in a shipwreck off Greece while returning from pilgrimage to Jerusalem.

Vespasiano da Bisticci (1422–1498)

Florentine book-dealer and author. Setting up shop near the centre of Florence (just on the far side of the Arno), Vespasiano became bookseller to princes and humanists. He specialized in manuscripts, written in the fashionable ◊*littera antiqua*, of Classical, patristic, and humanist texts. In the last years of his life, he compiled a record of some of his customers by writing *Vite d'uomini illustri/Lives of Illustrious Men*.

Vespasiano supplied some of the leading magnates of his day with books, including Cosimo de' ◊Medici, for whom he claims to have employed 45 scribes to produce 200 volumes in 22 months. He was also the book supplier of choice to ◊Federigo da Montefeltro, Duke of Urbino, whom, he claimed, shared his dis-taste for the late-15th-century fad for printed books (Vespasiano was deceived, however, if he thought Frederigo's library included no books made with the new technology). As well as being highly regarded by scholars and rulers, Vespasiano was an astute businessman. For example, when the Congress of Mantua convened, he seems to have travelled there taking with him manuscripts to sell – setting up the Renaissance equivalent of a publishers' stall at an international conference. The disadvantage of this exercise was that the speed with which some manuscripts had to be produced led to a slipping in the quality of transcription. Usually, however, humanists seem to have regarded copies from his workshop as of high quality.

The *Vite* provides short biographies, based on (sometimes wayward) recollections, of a wide range of Vespasiano's customers: from popes (◊Eugenius IV and ◊Nicholas V) to writers (like ◊Poggio Bracciolini or Flavio ◊Biondo) via princes, cardinals and bishops (including ◊Alfonso V, ◊Bessarion, and ◊Nicholas of Cusa). He was also proud of the cosmopolitan nature of his clientele – as well as Greeks and Germans, there were Englishmen (like John ◊Tiptoft and William ◊Gray), Castilians (Núñez de Guzman) and Portuguese (for instance, Vasco da Lucena).

Vespucci, Amerigo (1454–1512)

Florentine merchant. The Americas were named after him as a result of the widespread circulation of his accounts of his explorations. His accounts of the voyage 1499–1501 include descriptions of places he could not possibly have reached (the Pacific Ocean, British Columbia, Antarctica).

Viadana, Lodovico (REAL NAME GROSSI DA VIADANA) (*c.* 1560–1627)

Italian composer. He was a prolific composer, writing mostly vocal church music. His works include 100 *Concerti ecclesiastici* (1602), for one to four voices with organ continuo.

Viadana studied with Costanzo Porta and before 1590 was appointed maestro di cappella at Mantua Cathedral. In 1596 he joined the Franciscan order, in 1609 became maestro di cappella at Concordia, and in 1612 at Fano Cathedral. In 1615 he went to live at Piacenza, whence he retired to the Franciscan monastery at Gualtieri.

Works include:
Masses, psalms, and other church music; 100 *Concerti ecclesiastici* for one to four voices with organ continuo (1602); madrigals, canzonets.

Vicente (VINCENTE), Gil (*c.* 1465–1536)
Portuguese dramatist, who wrote also in Spanish. Over 40 of his works survive, including moralities, farces, romantic comedies, and allegorical spectacles devised for the Portuguese court.

Vicentino, Nicola (1511–*c.* 1576)
Italian composer and theorist. He sought to revive the Greek modes in his madrigals, and invented an instrument he called the archicembalo, which could play various microtones.

Vicentino studied with Adrian Willaert at Venice, then entered the service of Ippolito d'Este, cardinal of Ferrara, with whom he went to live in Rome. His treatise *L'antica musica ridotta alla prattica moderna* (1555) involved him in a controversy with Vicente Lusitano in which he was defeated. He returned to Ferrara with his patron and became his maestro di cappella. He wrote madrigals and motets.

Victoria, Tomás Luis de (1548–1611)
Spanish composer. He wrote only sacred music, including 20 Masses, 52 motets, and many other liturgical pieces, and is noted for his expressive settings of the Mass (for example, *Ave Regina Caelorum*) and other Latin texts.

Victoria sang as a boy at the cathedral of his native Ávila. In 1565 he received a grant from Philip II and went to Rome, where he became a priest and singer at the German College. From 1569 he was employed at the Roman Church of Sta Maria di Monserrato; from 1571 he taught music at the German College, and was choirmaster there from 1573 to about 1577. He was a chaplain at San Girolamo della Carità 1578–85. From 1587 to 1603 he was chaplain to the dowager empress María, Philip II's sister and the widow of Maximilian II, at the convent of the Descalzas Reales in Madrid, where the empress lived and her daughter, the Infanta Margaret, became a nun. On the death of the empress in 1603 he wrote an *Officium Defunctorum* (Requiem Mass) for six voices.

Victoria is as great a master of polyphony in the Spanish school as his contemporaries Palestrina, Lassus, and Byrd were in the Italian, Flemish, and English.

Works include:
Twenty Masses (including two Requiems), 18 Magnificats, one *Nunc Dimittis*, nine Lamentations, 25 responsories, 13 antiphons, eight polychoral psalms, 52 motets, 36 hymns, one Litany, two Passions, three Sequences.

Vienna, Battle of
During the Ottoman Wars, unsuccessful siege of Vienna in September–October 1529 by the Turks, commanded by Suleiman the Magnificent. Vienna marked the furthest extent of the Ottoman invasion of the West.

Vienna was held by a garrison of about 16,000 soldiers when an army of 120,000 Turks besieged it. Several desperate assaults were made and repulsed, and Turkish artillery bombarded the walls and eventually breached them. A final attempt by the Turks to storm this breach and enter the city was beaten off with heavy casualties among the Turks. Suleiman therefore raised the siege and retired east.

Viète, François (1540–1603)
French mathematician who developed algebra and its notation. He was the first mathematician to use letters of the alphabet to denote both known and unknown quantities, and is credited with introducing the term 'coefficient' into algebra.

Viète was born in Fontenay-le-Comte in the Poitou region and studied law at Poitiers. In 1570 he moved to Paris and was employed by Charles IX until 1584, when persecution of the Huguenots forced him to flee to Beauvoir-sur-Mer. It was in these years that his most fruitful algebraic research was carried out. On the accession of Henry IV in 1589, Viète returned to the royal service, and deciphered coded messages captured during war with Spain. He was dismissed from the court in 1602.

Viète's mathematical achievements were the result of his interest in cosmology; for example, a table giving the values of six trigonometrical lines based on a method originally used by Egyptian astronomer Ptolemy. Viète was the first person to use the cosine law for plane triangles and he also published the law of tangents.

His works include *Canon Mathematicus seu ad Tiangula* (1579), *In Artem Analytica Isogoge* (1591), and *De Aequationum Recognitione et Emandatione* (1615).

Vigarny, Felipe (*c.* 1475–1542)

Burgundian sculptor who, from 1498, worked in Spain. He employed a style full of Italianate motifs and styling. An early patron was cardinal ◊Ximénes de Cisneros, of whom he carved an alabaster medallion. Vigarny's main commissions, for tombs, altarpieces, and choir stalls, were in Toledo and Burgos; he collaborated with other sculptors, in particular Alonso ◊Berruguete.

Vignola, Giacomo Barozzi da (1507–1573)

Italian architect, the leading architect in Rome after the death of Michelangelo. He is largely remembered for his architectural textbook *Regole delle cinque ordini/On the Five Orders* (1562). He appears to have designed much of the complex plan for the Villa di Papa Giulio, Rome (1551–55). In 1567 he succeeded ◊Michelangelo, whose work he followed meticulously, as architect to St Peter's, Rome.

His first important work was the completion of Palazzo Farnese Capravola (1550), from designs by Baldassare ◊Peruzzi. He worked in France 1541–43. He collaborated on the Villa di Papa Giulio, with Bartolommeo ◊Ammanati and Giorgio ◊Vasari. The Gesù church in Rome, another of Vignola's highly influential designs, was built 1568–75 for the Jesuits.

The *Regole delle cinque ordini/On the Five Orders* became an architect's handbook and is considered one of the most important books ever written on architecture.

Villena, Enrique de (1384–1434)

Self-taught Spanish translator, astrologer, and cook. He was friends with Iñigo ◊Santillana and his colourful life would be dramatized by Lope de ◊Vega. On Santillana's request, he produced the first complete Castilian translation of Virgil's *Aeneid* and in 1428

translated Dante's *Divine Comedy*. He also composed an *Arte cisoria o tratado del arte de cortar con el cuchillo/The Art of Cutting with a Knife* (1423), on culinary matters.

He rose to become the Master of the Order of Calatrava, but even this supremely orthodox position could not save his library, most of which was burned on his death because of his reputation as a magician.

Villon, François (1431–*c.* 1465)

French poet. He used satiric humour, pathos, and irony in works like *Petit Testament* or *Louis* (1456) and *Grand Testament* (1461) (the latter includes the 'Ballade des dames du temps jadis/Ballad of the Ladies of Former Times'), both of which are mock wills bequeathing absurd or obscene possessions. His *Ballades en jargon* are written in lowlife argot.

He was born in Paris and dropped his surname (Montcorbier or de Logos) to assume that of one of his relatives, a canon, who sent him to study at the Sorbonne, where he graduated in 1449 and 1452. In 1455 he stabbed a priest in a street fight and had to flee the city. Pardoned the next year, he returned to Paris but was soon in flight again after robbing the College of Navarre. He stayed briefly at the court of the Duke of Orléans until sentenced to death for an unknown offence, from which he was saved by the amnesty of a public holiday. Theft and public brawling continued to occupy his time, in addition to the production of the *Grand Testament* (1461). A sentence of death in Paris, commuted to ten-year banishment in 1463, is the last that is known of his life.

Vincentius, Caspar (*c.* 1580–1624)

Flemish composer and organist. He provided a *bassus generalis* to the three volumes of Abraham Schadaeus's *Promptuarium Musicum*, and in 1617 added a fourth volume of his own. He also wrote a continuo part for Lassus's *Magnum Opus Musicum*.

Vincentius was a choirboy at the Imperial chapel in Vienna 1595–97. While serving as town organist at Speyer, about 1602–15, he met Schadaeus. He later held appointments at Worms and, from 1618 until his death, at Würzburg.

Virgil (PUBLIUS VERGILIUS MARO) (70–19 BC)

Ancient Roman poet. He wrote the *Eclogues* (37 BC),

a series of pastoral poems; the *Georgics* (30 BC), four books on the art of farming; and his epic masterpiece, the *Aeneid* (30–19 BC). He was patronized by Maecenas on behalf of Octavian (later the emperor Augustus).

Dante's choice of Virgil as his guide through the inferno and purgatory was a symptom of the medieval popularity of the ancient epic poet. His status as guide to the ambitious poet was one that he retained through the 15th and 16th centuries. His writings were not completely unproblematic – the adultery in *Aeneid* IV and the homosexuality of *Eclogue II* made some readers uncomfortable. But, unlike some other Classical poets, his works did not need to be 'rediscovered' in the Renaissance and the same level of textual emendation was unnecessary, although some did occur (affecting even the spelling of his name which, ◊Politian demonstrated, should be Vergil). Like other Classical authors, the late 15th century saw a series of commentaries by the likes of Domizio ◊Calderini; into this category perhaps falls the moralizing discussion of Cristoforo ◊Landino. More unusually, in the early quattrocento, Maffeo Vegio, dissatisfied with Virgil's ending to the *Aeneid*, decided to augment the epic with a 13th book (1427), detailing the hero's final achievement of happiness; this addition enjoyed a popularity in early printed editions and was translated, with the original *Aeneid*, by both Gavin ◊Douglas and Thomas Phaer.

The *Aeneid* was repeatedly translated into various vernaculars: there were, for example, eleven translations of parts of the work into French in the 16th century – including one by Joachim ◊du Bellay, even though he had expressed doubts about the efficacy of such translations. Virgil's other works did not lack similar attention; particularly popular was *Eclogue IV* which provided the *locus classicus* of the returning Golden Age. Interest in Virgil was not confined to editors and translators; the *Aeneid* provided the prototype of the epic influencing vernacular attempts from Ludovico ◊Ariosto to Edmund ◊Spenser via, for example, Luis de ◊Camões's *Lusiads*. The subject matter of the original epic could also provide the theme for vernacular works like Christopher ◊Marlowe's *Dido Queen of Carthage*, as well as for works of art from fresco cycles (for example by Dosso Dossi and by Niccolò dell' ◊Abbate) to cassone panels.

> Of arms and the man I sing…
>
> VIRGIL, *Aeneid*, opening line
>
> ～
>
> Of the women, the knights, the arms, the lovers,
> the courtliness, the brave deeds I sing…
>
> ～
>
> ARIOSTO, *Orlando Furioso*, opening line

Visconti

Dukes and rulers of Milan 1277–1447. They originated as north Italian feudal lords who attained dominance over the city as a result of alliance with the Holy Roman Emperors. Despite papal opposition, by the mid-14th century they ruled 15 other major towns in northern Italy. The duchy was claimed by the ◊Sforzas in 1450.

They had no formal title until Giangaleazzo bought the title of duke from Emperor Wenceslas IV (1361–1419). On the death of the last male Visconti, Filippo Maria, 1447, the duchy passed into the hands of the Sforzas in 1450, after the short-lived ◊Ambrosian Republic.

Visconti, Giangaleazzo (1351–1402)

Ruler, styled the Count of Vertu, and, from 1395, Duke of Milan. Giangaleazzo came to power in Milan by ousting his own uncle Bernabò in 1385. The leading Italian warlord of his generation, his expansionist policies saw him take control of city after city, including Pisa in 1399, Siena in 1399, and Perugia in 1400, and threaten Florence. The threat was removed, not by Florentine military success, but by Giangaleazzo's own death.

From 1385, Milan Cathedral was rebuilt – a large undertaking which was certainly not Giangaleazzo's brainchild but which he did support by, for example, providing privileges in 1387 to ensure a supply of marble. In some ways, though, the cultural centre of Visconti rule was not Milan but nearby Pavia. It was there that the ducal library was held, which by the death of Giangaleazzo numbered over a thousand volumes.

However, whatever the level of learning and patronage in Giangaleazzo's domain, the cultural reaction to Giangaleazzo's expansionism was undeniably significant: the Florentines – in particular, their chancellor, Coluccio ◊Salutati – developed further their rhetoric of defending Italian liberty against tyranny. Salutati's eloquent letters (worth, Giangaleazzo is said to have claimed, a thousand horsemen) were echoed by the early work of one of his pupils: the *Laudatio Florentinae Urbis* of Leonardo ◊Bruni.

Vitelli, Cornelio (*c.* 1440–*c.* 1500)

Italian humanist teacher and writer, born in Cortona. His early career was in Padua and Venice but, after quarrelling (like so many others) with Giorgio ◊Merula, he left Italy and travelled north. He taught at Oxford from perhaps from 1482 to 1486 (where Thomas ◊Linacre may have learned Greek from him), in Louvain from 1487–88, and Paris in 1489. He returned to England in 1490 and attempted (like his compatriot Pietro ◊Carmeliano) to gain royal patronage. He failed, and retreated to Oxford and teaching.

Viti, Timoteo (1467–1523)

Italian painter. He settled in Urbino, where he was Raphael Sanzio's first master. Paintings by him include *St Mary Magdalene* (Pinacoteca Nazionale, Bologna) and *Annunciation* (Brera, Milan).

He served an apprenticeship as a goldsmith with Francesco ◊Francia, who also taught him painting.

Vitruvius, Marcus Pollio (LIVED 1ST CENTURY BC)

Ancient Roman architect. He wrote a ten-book discussion of the discipline, *De Architectura*.

In the Middle Ages, Vitruvius (like Suetonius) was one of the Classical authors better known in northern Europe than in Italy. However, in the mid-14th century, ◊Petrarch – and, via him, ◊Boccaccio – came by a manuscript of *De Architectura*. The circulation of the work was further stimulated by ◊Poggio's discovery of another manuscript in St Gall in 1416. It was, however, by no means immediately taken as the gospel for classical architecture; L B ◊Alberti, in his *De Re Aedificatoria*, was influenced by Vitruvius but he also criticized aspects of his work. Attempts to design on Vitruvian lines were not made until the 1480s; in part, the difficulty of applying Vitruvius was

that his text survived without the original illustrations, making it difficult to follow. This omission was rectified by the illustrated edition by Giovanni ◊Giocondo printed in 1511. Meanwhile, several Italians also undertook the fairly thankless task of translating the whole text, and the first commentary, by Cesare ◊Cesariano, was also in Italian; among other commentaries was that by Daniele ◊Barbaro, first printed in 1556, repeatedly reprinted and including illustrations by the quintessentially classicizing architect ◊Palladio.

Alberti and Lorenzo ◊Ghiberti (who quoted Vitruvius in his *Commentaries*) were exceptions among early 15th-century architects in being conversant with *De Architectura*. However, practical Vitruvian influence appeared in several of Giuliano da Sangallo's designs. Then, in 1502, Donato ◊Bramante designed the round ◊Tempietto (small temple) in Rome, following Vitruvius' description of the Doric order.

Other Italian architects were not as convinced of Vitruvius' authority. Baldassare ◊Peruzzi commented that surviving ancient buildings provided greater inspiration than did *De Architectura*. Works like Palladio's *I quattro libri dell'architettura/Four Books on Architecture* (1570) attempted to supplement and update Vitruvius; in so doing, they both reflected his influence and replaced his text as the architectural handbook.

Vitry, Philippe de (1291–1361)

French composer, poet, and theorist. One of the masters of ◊ars nova, his works are characterized by contrapuntal intricacy. He wrote four treatises on *ars nova* and some of his motets survive today.

Vittorino da Feltre (1378–1446)

Teacher from Feltre (near Venice). Educated at Padua, he remained at the university to teach, where one of his colleagues was Gasparino ◊Barzizza. He came to know ◊Guarino da Verona, while the latter had a school in Venice; it is said that Guarino taught Vittorino Greek in return for Vittorino improving Guarino's Latin. In the early 1420s, Vittorino moved to Mantua where he became schoolmaster to the Gonzaga dynasty.

His pupils also included ◊Federigo da Montefeltro and, of the lesser-born, Lorenzo ◊Valla, for example, and Antonio ◊Beccaria. Though, unlike Barzizza or

Guarino, he was not an author, he was remembered as someone who promoted *studia humanitatis* in his teaching.

Vivarini

Family of Venetian painters. They were Antonio (1420–1476), his younger brother Bartolommeo (active 1450–1499), and Alvise (1447–1504), the son of Antonio.

Antonio Vivarini collaborated with his brother-in-law Giovanni d'Allemagna on religious paintings of a Gothic character. Some German admixture of style may have been due to Giovanni d'Allemagna, though the two painters are not distinguishable one from another.

Bartolommeo Vivarini at first collaborated with Antonio but developed a style influenced by Andrea Mantegna.

Alvise Vivarini conducted a school on the island of Murano rivalling that of the Bellini family. He painted altarpieces for a number of churches in Venice, and portraits influenced by Antonello da Messina.

Vives, Juan Luis (1492–1540)

Aragonese humanist writer and teacher, born in Valencia. Educated in his home town and in Paris, he settled in 1512 in Bruges, Flanders. He found income rarely secure; he courted Henry VIII, dedicating to him in 1522 his commentary on St Augustine's *De civitate Dei/City of God*, which he had undertaken at the behest of the humanist scholar Erasmus. English patronage came primarily from Henry VIII's wife Catherine of Aragon and from cardinal Wolsey, who paid Vives to lecture at Oxford in 1523. In this period, Vives also produced a range of works: commentaries on Classical texts, educational treatises, and political works.

volgare (ITALIAN FOR VULGAR)

Italian vernacular or vernaculars. To complement the politically fragmented nature of the peninsula, the various regions each had its own dialect. Of these Tuscan had, thanks to Florence's *tre corone* (three crowns) of Dante, Petrarch, and Boccaccio, the strongest tradition of being used as a literary language. In the early 16th century, however, the best dialect to use for *volgare* writings became a debated issue – the ◊*questione della lingua*.

Vos, Marten de (*c.* 1531–1603)

Flemish painter. He spent some years in Italy, in Rome, Florence, and Venice, where he worked in the studio of ◊Tintoretto). On his return to Antwerp in 1588 he was much in demand as a painter of church altarpieces executed in the Venetian manner.

Vos (Voz), Laurent de (1533–1580)

Flemish composer. He worked at Antwerp Cathedral and was appointed music director and choirmaster at Cambrai Cathedral by the archbishop Louis de Berlaymont. When the latter's place was usurped by Baron d'Inchy, Voz composed a motet compiled from words from the Psalms in such a way as to attack Inchy, who had Voz hanged without trial. He was the brother of the painter Marten de Vos.

Works include:
Motets, chansons.

Walch, Jacob

See Jacupo de' ◊Barbari.

Wannenmacher, Johannes (c. 1485–1551)

Swiss priest and composer. He wrote vocal pieces, of which 26 survive.

Wannenmacher was appointed cantor of the collegiate foundation of St Vincent at Bern in 1510, but left in 1514 after a dispute and went to Germany as canon and cantor at Freiburg, Baden. After a brief return to Switzerland in 1519, when he went to Sion (Valais), he went back to Freiburg, but having come under the influence of the Swiss religious reformer ◊Zwingli, he embraced Protestantism in 1530, was tortured and banished, returned to Bern and, finding no employment there, became town clerk at Interlaken.

Works include:

Psalm cxxxvii for three to six voices, motets; German sacred and secular songs.

Wassenhove, Joos van

Probable identity of the painter ◊Justus of Ghent.

Watson, Thomas (c. 1557–1592)

English scholar and amateur musician. He published in 1590 *The First Sett of Italian Madrigalls Englished*, the successor of Nicholas Yonge's *Musica Transalpina* (1588), and with it the foundation of the native English school of madrigalists.

Waynflete, William (c. 1400–1486)

English cleric and schoolteacher. Headmaster of Winchester College from 1430, he moved in 1441 to the new royal foundation of ◊Eton College, of which he became provost. Royal favour secured his next, and most prestigious, appointments as bishop of Winchester from 1447 and chancellor 1456–60. He used his episcopal position to endow a foundation at his old university, Oxford: first established as a Hall in 1448, Magdalen College was founded in 1458.

He later added to this foundation a school to prepare boys for college; its grammar teaching, under its headmaster John ◊Anwykyll, introduced elements of the *studia humanitatis*.

Webster, John (c. 1580–c. 1625)

English dramatist. His reputation rests on two tragedies, *The White Devil* (1612) and *The Duchess of Malfi* (c. 1613). Though both show the preoccupation with melodramatic violence and horror typical of the Jacobean ◊revenge tragedy, they are also remarkable for their poetry and psychological insight. He collaborated with a number of other dramatists, notably with Thomas ◊Dekker on the comedy *Westward Ho* (c. 1606).

Born in London, he was the son of a tailor and was apprenticed to the same trade, becoming a freeman of the Merchant Taylors' Company in 1603. But he was also active in the theatre by 1602, working on collaborations and perhaps also acting. His first independent work was *The White Devil*, printed (and probably first performed) in 1612.

Little is known of his life, and the details and dates of his various collaborations are still unclear. Among those usually credited to him (apart from the two major tragedies) are the following:

comedies Northward Ho (c. 1605) and *Westward Ho* c. 1606 (both with Dekker), *Any Thing for a Quiet Life* (c. 1621) (with Thomas ◊Middleton), and *A Cure for a Cuckold* (c. 1624) (with William Rowley)

tragedies The Famous History of Sir Thomas Wyatt (c. 1606) (with Dekker) and *Appius and Virginia* (c. 1608) (probably with John ◊Heywood)

tragicomedy The Devil's Law Case (c. 1610).

Weelkes, Thomas (c. 1576–1623)

English composer. He wrote ten Anglican services and around 40 anthems, including 'When David heard'. He was also one of the most significant madrigalists of his time, contributing *As Vesta was from Latmos Hill Descending* to the *Triumphs of Oriana* (1601).

409

Weelkes was in the service of George Phillpot at Compton near Winchester in his early years and then that of Edward Darcye, Groom of the Privy Chamber. In 1598 he was appointed organist at Winchester College, in 1601 he became organist and choirmaster at Chichester Cathedral, and in 1602 was awarded a degree in music at Oxford University. His career at Chichester was turbulent: he received repeated reprimands for unruliness, drunkenness, and neglect of duty, and was dismissed in 1617. He later resumed the post, but died during a visit to London.

Weelkes published almost 100 madrigals, often for four, five, and six voices; they demonstrate his intricate style, fine counterpoint, and brilliant imagery.

Works include:
Services and numerous anthems; three books of madrigals, *Ayeres or Phantasticke Spirites* for three voices (1608), two vocal pieces contributed to Leighton's *Teares or Lamentacions*; three In Nomines for four to five viols and other pieces for five viols.

Weerbeke, Gaspar van (*c.* 1445–*c.* 1517)
Flemish composer and singer. Of his works, about eight Masses, 28 motets, and several other liturgical works survive. Five of his Masses were published by the Venetian printer and publisher Ottaviano Petrucci.

Weerbeke took holy orders at Tournai and went to Italy in the 1470s, becoming maestro di cappella at Milan Cathedral and a singer in the service of the Sforza family at the ducal court. He was in Rome as a singer at the papal chapel 1481–89, but in 1488 produced music for allegorical plays given at the marriage of Galeazzo Sforza, Duke of Milan, to Isabella of Aragon. He returned to the Sforza court in 1489. From 1495 he spent two years as a singer in the court choir of Philip the Handsome, Archduke of Austria and Duke of Burgundy. He returned to Rome in 1500, where he again sang in the papal choir. He is last heard of as a canon at St Maria ad Gradus in Mainz.

Works include:
Eight Masses, 28 motets, *Stabat Mater*, and other church music.

Wert, Giaches de (1535–1596)
Flemish composer. He was music director at the ducal court of Mantua from the early 1560s until 1595. He was a prolific composer, and wrote over 150 sacred vocal pieces, but his most celebrated compositions are his madrigals. He published 16 books of madrigals and other secular works, and had a great influence on his successors, especially Monteverdi.

Wert was sent to Italy as a choirboy when a small child, to sing at the court of the Marchese della Padulla at Avellino near Naples. At age nine he entered the service of Count Alfonso Gonzaga as a member of the choir of the Novellara at Reggio. He began to publish madrigals towards the end of the 1550s and about 1560 went into service at the ducal court of Mantua under Guglielmo Gonzaga. He was also attached to the Church of Santa Barbara, where he succeeded Giovanni Contina as maestro di cappella in 1565. In 1566 he accompanied the duke to Augsburg and there declined an offer from the Emperor Maximilian II. In 1567 he visited Venice with the court and later Ferrara under Alfonso (II) d'Este. About that time he suffered much from the intrigues of the Italian musicians, who disliked him as a foreigner, and in 1570 one of them, Agostino Bonvicino, was dismissed for a love affair with Wert's wife. In 1580 he and his family were given the freedom of the city of Mantua in perpetuity.

His madrigals often had high-quality texts, and were declamatory in style and with the three upper voices frequently emphasized; they were written for virtuoso court singers, particularly the *concerto delle donne* or 'singing ladies' of Ferrara.

Works include:
Motets, 11 books of madrigals for five voices (1558–95), one for four voices, canzonets, villanelle.

Weston, Elizabeth Jane (ALSO KNOWN AS WESTONIA) (1582–1612)
English poet. Her Catholic family emigrated from England while she was still a child and settled in Prague in 1598. Despite her youth she impressed her humanist correspondents from across Europe, including Joseph Justus Scaliger and Justus Lipsius, with her learning. She published *Carmina/Poems* (1602); she married the following year but died when she was 30.

Weyden, Rogier van der (*c.* 1399–1464)
Netherlandish artist. He was the official painter to the city of Brussels from 1436. He produced portraits and

religious paintings like *The Last Judgement* (*c.* 1450, Hôtel-Dieu, Beaune) in a refined and elegant realist style.

He visited Italy (where his works were greatly admired) in 1450, and had a busy workshop in Brussels until his death. Though he signed no paintings, his work is as distinctive as that of Jan van ◊Eyck, and the products of his studio exerted an important influence not only in northern Europe, but also in Spain and, to some extent, in Italy.

Lucid and graceful composition, a feeling for relief (suggesting that he made use of effects observed in Gothic sculpture), and a warm humanity and mastery of emotional expression characterize his work. These qualities can be seen in his *Deposition* before 1443 (Prado, Madrid).

Among his religious works are the *Pietà*

(Mauritshuis, The Hague), the polyptych of the *Last Judgement*, the *Seven Sacraments* (Musée Royal des Beaux-Arts, Antwerp), and the *Adoration of the Magi* (Gemäldegalerie, Berlin). His portraits include the lucid *Portrait of a Lady* (National Gallery, Washington).

White (WHYTE), Robert (*c.* 1538–1574)

English composer. He was choirmaster at Ely, Chester, and Westminster Abbey, and wrote church music including psalm motets, anthems, and Lamentations.

White was probably the son of a London organ builder, also named Robert White, and took a degree in music at Cambridge University in 1560. In 1561 he succeeded Tye as choirmaster at Ely Cathedral. He married Tye's daughter Ellen in 1565 and left Ely in 1566 (he was succeeded by John Farrant) to become choirmaster of Chester Cathedral until about 1570, when he went to London to take up a similar post at Westminster Abbey. Along with nearly all his family, he succumbed to the plague of 1574.

Works include:
Nineteen Latin motets; English anthems; In Nomines for viols; hexachord fantasia for keyboard.

Whitgift, John (*c.* 1530–1604)

English prelate, archbishop of Canterbury 1583–1604. He founded his almshouses in 1569 and the Whitgift School in 1599 in Croydon.

Although doctrinally a Calvinist, he strongly defended the liturgy and discipline of the Church of England against the Puritans, notably in a lengthy controversy with the leader of the early Puritans, Thomas Cartwright, and in his administrative capacity as archbishop. In his primacy, the High

Weyden Roger van der Weyden, *The Nativity*, 1576 (Royal Chapel, Granada), one of the northern works of art which came from the collection of Isabella of Castile. *e.t. archive*

Commission court was permanently established.

Born in Grimsby, England, Whitgift was educated at St Anthony's College, London, and at Cambridge. He became a fellow of Peterhouse in 1555, and was Lady Margaret professor of divinity at Cambridge 1563–67, master of Pembroke Hall and of Trinity College, Cambridge, during 1567–77, dean of Lincoln in 1571, and bishop of Worcester in 1577.

Whythorne, Thomas (1528–1596)

English composer. He travelled in Italy and elsewhere in Europe, and published his first book of music, *Songes* for several voices, in 1571, and his second, a book of duets, in 1590; the second volume contains the earlier printed English instrumental music. His autobiography, written around 1576, was published in 1961.

Works include:

Psalms and secular songs for two to five voices or solo voice with instruments.

Wilbye, John (1574–1638)

English composer. He was not only one of the first English composers to write madrigals, but also one of the finest. Among his most characteristic works are the popular madrigals 'Draw on Sweet Night' and 'Sweet honey sucking bees' (both 1609).

Wilbye was born at Diss, Norfolk, where his father was a tanner and landowner. Wilbye was patronized by the Cornwallis family at Brome Hall near Diss. In about 1595 he went into the service of their son-in-law, Sir Thomas Kytson, at Hengrave Hall near Bury St Edmunds, and was frequently in London with the family. After the death of his patron he remained in the service of Kytson's widow, Lady Elizabeth Kytson, who died in 1628, whereupon he went to Colchester to join the household of her daughter, Lady Rivers. He never married and was well-to-do, having been granted the lease of a sheep farm by Kyston and gradually acquiring property at Diss, Bury St Edmunds, and elsewhere.

Wilbye was influenced by Morley and Ferrabosco. He published two books of madrigals (1598 and 1609), the second of which is generally regarded as one of the greatest English madrigal collections. It contains 'Draw on sweet Night', which uses major and minor tonalities to depict deep melancholy.

Works include:

Two sacred vocal pieces contributed to Leighton's *Teares or Lamentacions*; two books of 64 madrigals (1598, 1609), madrigal 'The Lady Oriana' contributed to *The Triumphes of Oriana*; five sacred works; three fantasies for viols (incomplete), lute lessons (lost).

Willaert, Adrian (c. 1490–1562)

Flemish composer. One of the most prolific and influential musicians of the mid-16th century, he was one of the earliest composers of madrigals, though his most important works are his motets. He also had a great influence on church music, broadening its character and achieving effect by a wide use of chromatic scales.

Willaert was trained in law but studied music with Jean Mouton in Paris. In 1515 he became a singer in the household of Cardinal Ippolito d'Este, his extensive travels with the cardinal included visits to Rome, Ferrara, and Esztergom, and a two-year stay in Hungary. On the cardinal's death in 1520 Willaert transferred to the service of Duke Alfonso I d'Este. In 1527 he became maestro di cappella at St Mark's, Venice, where his pupils included Cipriano de Rore, Nicola Vicentino, Andrea Gabrieli, Gioseffe Zarlino, and Costanzo Porta. He revisited Flanders in 1542 and 1556–57.

Willaert's works include a large quantity of church music, as well as many madrigals, chansons, villanelles, and some instrumental pieces. *Salmi spezzati* (1550) contains music for double choirs and set a tradition for polychoral music in St Mark's. His most important work is the collection of motets and madrigals, *Musica nova*, published in 1559, though probably written much earlier.

Works include:

Masses, hymns, psalms, motets, madrigals, chansons, and instrumental ensemble pieces.

William the Silent (1533–1584)

Prince of Orange from 1544. Leading a revolt against Spanish rule in the Netherlands from 1573, he briefly succeeded in uniting the Catholic south and Protestant northern provinces, but the former provinces submitted to Spain while the latter formed a federation in 1579 (Union of Utrecht) which repudiated Spanish suzerainty in 1581.

William, brought up at the court of Charles V, was appointed governor of Holland by Philip II of Spain in 1559, but joined the revolt of 1572 against Spain's oppressive rule and, as a Protestant from 1573, became the national leader and first stadholder (the chief magistrate of the United Provinces of the Netherlands). He was known as 'the Silent' because of his absolute discretion. He was assassinated by a Spanish agent.

Witz, Konrad (c. 1400–c. 1445)

German-born Swiss painter. His sharply observed realism suggests that he was familiar with the work of contemporary Flemish artists such as Jan van ◊Eyck. Lake Geneva is the setting for a biblical story in his *The Miraculous Draught of Fishes* (1444, Musée d'Art et d'Histoire, Geneva), one of the earliest recognizable landscapes in European art.

Witz was the son of a painter who worked for Philip the Bold, Duke of Burgundy. He went with his father to Burgundy and the Netherlands, and was influenced by the art of both. He worked mainly in Basel, developing a strength and sureness of design which can be seen in the *Annunciation* of about 1445 (Germanisches Nationalmuseum, Nuremberg).

Wolgemut, Michael (1434–1519)

German painter and engraver. As the head of a large workshop in Nuremberg, he produced many carved and painted altarpieces. He also made woodcut book illustrations. He was the master of Albrecht ◊Dürer.

Among his altarpieces are those in Zwickau, southern Saxony, 1479 and Schwabach, just south of Nuremberg, 1508. He illustrated with woodcuts the *Schatzkammer der wahren Reichthümer des Heils* (1491) and the *Weltchronik* (1493–94) by Hartman Schedel, more commonly known as the *Nuremberg Chronicle*.

Wolsey, Thomas (c. 1475–1530)

English cleric and politician. In Henry VIII's service from 1509, he became archbishop of York in 1514, cardinal and lord chancellor in 1515, and began the dissolution of the monasteries.

His reluctance to further Henry's divorce from Catherine of Aragon led to his downfall in 1529. He was charged with high treason in 1530 but died before being tried.

Wotton, Henry (1568–1639)

English poet and diplomat under James I. He was provost of Eton College public school 1624–39. His tastes in art and architecture were influenced by his years of service in Venice, and he published *The Elements of Architecture* (1624).

Wotton was born near Maidstone, Kent, and studied at Oxford. He defined an ambassador as 'an honest man sent to lie abroad for the good of his country'. The *Reliquiae Wottonianae* (1651), a collection of his writings, is prefixed with Izaak Walton's life of Wotton, and includes his lyric 'You meaner beauties of the night'.

Wtewael, Joachim Anthonisz. (1566–1638)

Dutch painter. He studied in Italy and France before settling in Utrecht, and produced works reflecting the influence of his travels, such as *The Adoration of the Shepherds* (Ashmolean Museum, Oxford).

Wyatt, Thomas (c. 1503–1542)

English courtier and poet. He was employed on diplomatic missions by Henry VIII, but in 1536 was imprisoned for a time in the Tower of London, suspected of having been the lover of Henry's second wife, Anne ◊Boleyn. Knighted in 1537 and sent on an embassy to Spain, Wyatt was again arrested in 1541 on charges of treason. Like the Earl of ◊Surrey, Wyatt experimented with Petrarchan verse forms and thus introduced the sonnet into the English language.

Whatever the truth of the accusations of his relations with Anne Boleyn (and much has been read into several poems), Wyatt was well acquainted with the evangelicals at Henry's court; one of his patrons was Thomas ◊Cromwell. His poetry was originally written to be passed from hand to hand among the courtiers – and so probably tells us more about courtly fashions than Wyatt's personal outlook. His first literary work was, in fact, a prose translation of a Plutarch text (from the Latin version of Budé); it was dedicated to Catherine of Aragon and printed by Richard Pynson in c. 1528. His poems show a similar interest in humanist fashions: apart from his debt to Petrarch, he certainly also knew, for example, Pietro ◊Aretino's version of the penitential psalms, and Castiglione's recently published *The* ◊*Courtier*. Some of his verses are also paraphrases of Classical sources like Seneca.

Only a very few of his poems were printed in his lifetime; like Surrey (who wrote an epitaph upon Wyatt), his works were first collected together in *Totell's Miscellany* (1557).

Wycliffe (Wycliffe), John (*c.* 1320–1384)

English religious reformer. Allying himself with the party of John of Gaunt, which was opposed to ecclesiastical influence at court, he attacked abuses in the church, maintaining that the Bible rather than the church was the supreme authority. He criticized such fundamental doctrines as priestly absolution, confession, and indulgences, and set disciples to work on translating the Bible into English.

Having studied at Oxford University, he became Master of Balliol College there, and sent out bands of travelling preachers. He was denounced as a heretic, but died peacefully at Lutterworth, Leicestershire.

Wyntoun, Andrew of (*c.* 1350–1420)

Scottish chronicler. He was prior of the monastery of St Serf on Loch Leven from about 1395 and wrote *The Orygynale Cronykil of Scotland* about 1420, a metrical record from the creation of the world to 1408. It contains the first appearance of the story of Macbeth.

Xavier, St Francis (1506–1552)

Spanish Jesuit missionary. He went to the Portuguese colonies in the East Indies, arriving at Goa in 1542. He was in Japan 1549–51, establishing a Christian mission that lasted for 100 years. He returned to Goa in 1552, and sailed for China, but died of fever there. He was canonized in 1622.

Xenophon (c. 428 BC–c. 354 BC)

Ancient Athenian soldier and writer. He was a follower of Socrates, whom he commemorated in his *Memorabilia*. Unhappy with Athenian democratic politics, he joined the army of Cyrus; after the king's death, Xenophon was made general and led the troops' retreat. His contact with Cyrus inspired *Cyropedia*, a work which later gained the praise of the Roman politician Cicero. Other works include *Hiero* (c. 403 BC), a discussion of the tribulations faced by a tyrant.

Xenophon's work was unknown in Western Europe before the 15th century; his earliest translator was Leonardo ◊Bruni. His version of the *Hiero*, which might be called a 'mirror for tyrants', was certainly the most popular of Xenophon's works in the 15th century, but the *Cyropedia* – an idealized 'mirror for princes' text – also enjoyed a wide circulation. It was translated (in an abridged form) into Latin by ◊Poggio in 1446; his version was, in turn, translated into French by Vasco de Lucena (1470) and Italian by both Poggio's son Jacopo (c. 1476) and ◊Boiardo (c. 1470). Poggio's translation received criticism from an unsurprising quarter: Francesco ◊Filelfo, who produced his own version in 1467. While Poggio's proved successful in manuscript circulation, his rival's became the standard printed version, until revised by Henri ◊Estienne in 1561.

The interest in Xenophon, then, can be characterized as mainly political, although other works, like his discussions of hunting, were rendered into Latin (by, among others, Lapo da ◊Castiglionchio); the *Memorabilia* was translated by Cardinal ◊Bessarion and part of this work – the tale of Heracles at the crossroads where he chooses between virtue and vice – became standard reading in the 16th century, with several Latin versions, including one by Philip ◊Melanchthon.

Ximénes de Cisneros, Francisco (1436–1517)

Spanish churchman, politician, and scholar. He was an energetic church reformer, seeking a return to more austere standards of Christian life, and he encouraged the conversion of the Moors of Granada. In 1507 he became inquisitor-general. A noted scholar and patron of the arts, he patronized the project to produce the ◊Complutensian Polyglot Bible; the work on this was carried out at the university of Alcalá which he founded in 1500.

A Castilian by birth, he studied at Salamanca, becoming doctor in both canon and civil law. In 1492 Isabella of Castile chose him as her confessor and in 1495 he became archbishop of Toledo. From January 1516 until his death in November 1517 at Valladolid, he was governor of Castile and consolidated the unification of Spain achieved by Ferdinand and Isabella.

Zabarella, Francesco (c. 1339–1417)

Italian canon lawyer. Zabarella taught at Padua and wrote a series of influential commentaries on canon law texts; but he was also a theorist of ◊conciliarism, producing *De Schismate* (1408), which methodically demonstrated how a council, convened by the emperor, was the legitimate means by which to end the ◊Great Schism. Created a cardinal in 1411 (alongside Pierre d'Ailly), he attended the Council of ◊Constance and died there. His funeral sermon was written, in classicizing style, by ◊Poggio Bracciolini.

By Eternal God (of whom he was the sharpest defender), who – unless they have exceptional genius and nearly god-like eloquence – could list the praises of his whole life, let alone elaborate on them? Many I have seen, many I myself have known, excellent men of today who have been endowed with a single singular virtue; but of those who exhibit all the virtues in all their strength, I have known – apart from this man – none.

POGGIO BRACCIOLINI, *Funeral Oration on Cardinal Zabarella*, 1417

Zarlino, Gioseffo (1517–1590)

Italian music theorist and composer. He wrote two large treatises, the three-volume *Istitutioni armoniche* (1558) and *Dimostrationi armoniche* (1571). He was attacked for these by Vincenzo Galilei, whereupon he issued another volume, *Sopplimenti musicali* (1588); a fourth, non-musical volume, was added to the complete edition later. In his theories he discussed modes and intervals, and also looked back to Classical models, seeking to summarize and develop the musical theory of the Greeks.

Born in Chioggia, Zarlino was educated by Franciscan monks, and joined the order in 1521. In 1536 he was a singer at Chioggia Cathedral. He studied theology and received minor orders in 1539 (when he became organist at the cathedral), but was learned also in philosophy, sciences, and languages. He settled in Venice in 1541, became a fellow student with Cipriano de Rore under Adrian Willaert, and in 1565 became first maestro di cappella at St Mark's. In 1583 he was offered the bishopric of Chioggia, but declined it, preferring to remain at St Mark's.

Zarlino wrote motets and madrigals, but was chiefly a theorist. *Le istitutioni harmoniche* caused Willaert's methods of contrapuntal writing to become models of the style.

Works include:

Mass for the foundation of the Church of Santa Maria della Salute and other church music; pageant for the victory of Lepanto.

Zenale, Bernardino (1436–1526)

Italian painter. He was a friend of Leonardo da Vinci, whose influence appears in some of his work. On the polyptych in the Church of S Martino, Treviglio, he collaborated with Bernardino ◊Butinone.

Zeuxis (LIVED LATE 5TH CENTURY – EARLY 4TH CENTURY BC)

Ancient Greek painter, who, like ◊Apelles, was invoked in the Renaissance as a symbol of artistic achievement, despite the lack of surviving paintings. ◊Pliny the Elder's story, for example, that Zeuxis, when asked to paint a picture of Helen of Troy, took five women and constructed the portrait from the finest features of each, was the subject of frescoes by Domenico Beccafumi and Giorgio ◊Vasari, and was also said to have inspired ◊Raphael. Likewise, Lucian's ◊ekphrasis of Zeuxis' *Centaur Family* inspired a drawing in imitation by Albrecht Dürer in 1505.

Zieleński, Mikołaj (1550–1615)

Polish organist and composer. He composed offertories and communions for the service of the whole year. He was in the service of the archbishop of

Gniezno 1608–15 and studied with Andrea Gabrieli in Italy.

Zoppo, Marco (1423–1478)

Italian painter. He was trained in the studio of Francesco Squarcione in Padua about 1453, and worked mainly in Venice. His style shows the influence of Cosimo Tura.

Zsamboky, János

Hungarian name of the historian better known as Johannes ◊Sambucus.

Zuccaro

Two Italian painter brothers. **Federigo Zuccaro** (1542–1609) was the younger of the two; **Taddeo Zuccaro** (1529–1569) was the principal partner in the decorative works in which he collaborated with his brother.

The brothers worked together on the decoration of the Sala Regia in the Vatican, Rome, and in the Villa Farnese at Caprarola, Federigo completing the work when his brother died. Federigo, who studied under Taddeo, also finished frescoes in Florence Cathedral begun by Giorgio Vasari, and worked in Rome for Pope Gregory XIII. He travelled in Italy, France, and the Netherlands and visited England in 1574, drawing portraits of Elizabeth I and the Earl of Leicester (British Museum, London). He also worked for a time in Madrid for Philip II. He was a founder of the Academy of St Luke in Rome and also wrote on the theory of art.

Zurara, Gomes Eanes de (OR AZURARA) (1410/20–1473/74)

Portuguese chronicler, librarian, and archivist. The illegitimate son of a priest, educated at ◊Afonso V's court, he became keeper of the royal library in 1451, succeeding Fernão Lopes as royal archivist in 1454 (a post he held until his death). Like Lopes, he was also appointed royal chronicler, and the first evidence of his literary activity is his *Crónica da tomada de Ceuta/Chronicle of the Capture of Ceuta* (1449). His last surviving work is the *Crónica do Conde Dom Duarte de Meneses/Chronicle of Dom Duarte de Meneses*, completed in 1467–68.

The *Crónica da tomada de Ceuta*, which came to be considered the third part of Lopes's *Chronicle of João I*, was translated into Latin as *De Bello Septensi* by Afonso's former tutor Mateus Pisano, at the king's behest. Zurara's three other chronicles also concern particular people and incidents. The first of these was *Crónica do Infante Dom Henrique/Chronicle of Prince Henry*, initially completed in 1452–53, but a lengthy panegyric was added after his death in 1460 and the expanded version became known as the *Crónica dos feitos da Guiné/Chronicle of the Deeds in Guinea* (probably 1468/73). Zurara's other two chronicles concentrated on members of the Meneses family. The first, composed in about 1458–63, relates the life of Pedro, first governor of Ceuta, while the second (composed in about 1464–68) concerns his son Duarte, captain of Alcaçer-Ceguer. These successive royal commissions were not entirely welcome to Zurara: as he complained constantly in the prologues to these works, their composition left him little chance to work on his own project: a general history of Portugal.

As keeper of the royal archive, Zurara, like Lopes before him, had unrestricted access to primary historical sources. However, since the events he chronicled were mostly still within living memory, he preferred eyewitness accounts, and at one stage travelled to Africa to conduct interviews and to gain an appreciation of the terrain. Despite this practical approach, he was content to rely on 13th-century scientific and geographical information elsewhere in his chronicles.

Zurita, Jerónimo de (1512–1580)

Spanish historian from Aragon. He studied at Alcalá and in 1548 he was appointed Aragon's first chronicler. He took a more scientific and investigative approach to historical narrative than had his predecessors elsewhere in the peninsula: Zurita pursued sources in different archives, and eliminated from his accounts the more fantastic elements present in earlier chronicles. The result of his labours was the six-volume *Anales de la Corona de Aragón/Annals of the Crown of Aragon*, an account of the kingdom from the 711 Arab invasion to 1516. It was published between 1562 and 1580.

An index was added to *Anales de la Corona de Aragón* in 1604 and the third edition appeared 1610–21.

Zwingli, Ulrich (1484–1531)

Swiss church reformer. A contemporary of Luther's, Zwingli moved away from the Catholic church at the same time: it is unclear whether he was influenced by Luther's actions, though he insisted his theology had developed independently. Zwingli introduced his religion to the city of Zürich in the early 1520s and his ideas proved popular in other German-speaking cities.

In 1529, an attempt was made to create a common front between Luther and Zwingli at the Colloquy of Marburg but this broke down over the question of the Mass, Zwingli denying that it had anything more than a symbolic value. Two years later, however, Zwingli was dead, killed in a skirmish at Kappel which was caused by the attempt to impose Zwinglianism on that area.

THEMATIC INDEX

RULERS OF CHRISTENDOM

POPES

Clement VI (Pierre Roger)	1342-52
Innocent VI	1352-62

at Rome:

Urban VI (Bartolomeo Prignani)	1378-89
Boniface IX (Pietro Tomacelli)	1389-1404
Innocent VII (Cosimo Migliorati)	1404-06
Gregory XII (Angelo Correr)	1406-15
Martin V (Otto Colonna)	1417-31
Eugenius IV (Gabriele Condulmer)	1431-47
Nicholas V (Tommaso Parentucelli)	1447-55
Calixtus III (Alfonso Borgia)	1455-58
Pius II (Aeneas Sylvius Piccolomini)	1458-64
Paul II (Pietro Barbo)	1464-71
Sixtus IV (Francesco della Rovere)	1471-84
Innocent VIII (Giovanni Battista Cibò)	1484-92
Alexander VI (Roderigo Borgia)	1492-1503
Pius III (Franceso Piccolomini)	1503
Julius II (Giuliano della Rovere)	1503-13
Leo X (Giovanni de' Medici)	1513-21
Adrian VI (Adrian of Utrecht)	1522-23
Clement VII (Giulio de' Medici)	1523-34
Paul III (Alessandro Farnese)	1534-49
Julius III (Giovanni Maria Ciocchi del Monte)	1550-55
Marcellus II (Marcello Cervini)	1555
Paul IV (Gian Pietro Carafa)	1555-59
Pius IV (Giovanni Angelo de' Medici)	1559-65
Pius V (Antonio Ghislieri)	1566-72
Gregory XIII (Ugo Boncompagni)	1572-85
Sixtus V (Felice Peretti)	1585-90
Urban VII (Gian Battista Castagna)	1590
Gregory XIV (Niccolò Sfondrati)	1590-91

Urban V	1362-70
Gregory XI (Pierre Roger)	1370-78

at Avignon

Clement VII	1378-94
Benedict XIII	1394-1417

(after deposition, lived in Spain continuing to claim himself pope; on death in 1424, a successor, Clement VIII, elected, who resigned 1429)

at Pisa:

Alexander V (Pietro Filagro)	1409-10
John XXIII (Baldassare Cossa)	1410-15

at Basel:

Felix V	1439-49

Innocent IX (Giovanni Antonio
    Facchinetti)   1591
Clement VIII (Ippolito Aldobrandini)   1592-1605

HOLY ROMAN EMPERORS

(see also **Holy Roman Emperor** and **King of the Romans;** also **Habsburg**)

Wenceslas of Bohemia	1378-1400	**Maximilian**	1493-1519
Robert of Bavaria	1400-10	**Charles V**	1519-56
Sigismund	1410-37	**Ferdinand**	1556-64
Albert II of Habsburg (King		Maximilian II	1564-72
of the Romans)	1438-39	**Rudolf II**	1576-1612
Frederick III	1440-93		

Note: Those marked in bold have entries in the A-Z text.

ISSUES OF THE CHURCH OF CHRISTENDOM
(including the Reformations)

THEMES AND EVENTS

Anabaptist
antipope
Augsburg, Confession of
Augsburg, Peace of
Basel, Confessions of
Basel, Council of
Belgic Confession
Bologna, Concord(at) of
Bourges, Pragmatic Sanction of
Common Life, Brothers of
conciliarism

Concord, Formula of
Constance, Council of
devotio moderna
Erastianism
Family of Love
Feuillants
Florence, Council of
Gallican Confession
General Council
General Council of the Church
Great Schism

Heidelberg Catechism
Helvetic Confessions
Huguenot
Inquisition
Lutheranism
Marburg, Colloquy
papalism
Pisa, Council of
Puritan
reform and Reformation
Trent, Council of

CHARACTERS

Aquaviva, Claudius
Bellarmine, Roberto Francesco
    Romolo
Beza, Théodore
Borromeo, St Carlo
Bucer, Martin
Bullinger, Johann Heinrich

Cajetan, Jacopo
Calvin, John (see also *Institutes*)
Gerson, Jean
Huss, John
Loyola, St Ignatius
Luther, Martin
Melanchthon, Philip

Reuchlin, Johannes
Thomas à Kempis
Traversari, Ambrogio
Zabarella, Francesco
Zwingli, Ulrich

BRITISH ISLES

KINGS OF ENGLAND

Richard II	1377-99	**Henry VII** (see **Tudor dynasty**)	1485-1509
Henry IV	1399-1413	**Henry VIII**	1509-47
Henry V	1413-22	**Edward VI**	1547-53
Henry VI	1422-61; 1470-71	**Mary**	1553-58
Edward IV	1461-70; 1471-83	**Elizabeth**	1558-1603
Edward V	1483	**James I**	1603-25
Richard III	1483-85		

KINGS OF SCOTLAND

Robert II	1371-90	**James IV**	1488-1513
Robert III	1390-1406	**James V**	1513-42
James I	1406-37	**Mary**	1542-67
James II	1437-60	James VI (**James I** of England)	1567-1625
James III	1460-86		

Note: Those marked in bold have entries in the A-Z text.

THEMES AND EVENTS

Common Prayer, Book of
Dissolution of the Monasteries
Hampton Court Conference
Marprelate controversy

Roses, Wars of
Thirty-Nine Articles
Tudor dynasty
Tudor Rose

POLITICAL AND RELIGIOUS FIGURES

Anne of Denmark
Audley, Thomas
Beaufort, Lady Margaret
Bedford, John, Duke of Bedford
Bekynton, Thomas
Bodley, Thomas
Boleyn, Anne
Burghley, William Cecil,
    1st Baron Burghley
Cecil, Robert
Cotton, Robert Bruce
Cranmer, Thomas
Cromwell, Thomas
Drake, Francis

Essex, Robert Devereux, 2nd Earl
    of Essex
Fisher, John
Foxe, Richard
Gardiner, Stephen
Gloucester, Humfrey, Duke of
Grindal, Edmund
Hatton, Sir Christopher
Hooker, Richard
Knox, John
Latimer, Hugh
Leicester, Robert Dudley, Earl of
Leicester
Norfolk, Thomas Howard, 3rd
    Duke of

Northumberland, John Dudley,
    Duke of
Parker, Matthew
Pole, Reginald
Raleigh, Walter
Ridley, Nicholas
Somerset, Edward Seymour,
    1st Duke of Somerset
Tiptoft, John, 1st Earl of
    Worcester
Waynflete, William
Whitgift, John
Wolsey, Thomas
Wycliffe, John

Artists and Architects

Eworth, Hans
Hilliard, Nicholas
Holbein, Hans

Janyns, Henry
Jones, Inigo
Oliver, Isaac

Smythson, Robert
Teerlinc, Levina
Vertue, Robert

Literature

Adlington, William
Alleyn, Edward
André, Bernard
Anwykyll, John
Armin, Robert
Ascham, Roger
Aytoun, Robert
Bacon, Francis
Bale, John
Barclay, Alexander
Barnes, Barnabe
Barnfield, Richard
Bourchier, John, Lord Berners
Boyd, Mark Alexander
Breton, Nicholas
Burbage, Richard Chapman,
    George
Camden, William
Chaucer, Geoffrey
Cheke, John
Chettle, Henry
Churchyard, Thomas
Clanvowe, John
Colet, John
Constable, Henry
Coverdale, Miles
Daniel, Samuel
Davies, John
Day, John
Dekker, Thomas
Deloney, Thomas
Donne, John
Douglas, Gavin
Drayton, Michael
Dunbar, William
Dyer, Edward
Edwards, Richard
Elyot, Thomas
Everyman
Fletcher, Giles

Fletcher, John
Florio, John
Foxe, John
Fraunce, Abraham
Free, John
Gascoigne, George
Googe, Barnabe
Gosson, Stephen
Gower, John
Gray, William
Greene, Robert
Greville, Fulke
Grimald, Nicholas
Hall, Edward
Hardyng, John
Harington, John
Harvey, Gabriel
Haughton, William
Heminge, John
Henslowe, Philip
Heywood, John
Heywood, Thomas Hawes,
    Stephen
Hoby, Sir Thomas
Holinshed, Raphael
Holland, Philemon
Jonson, Ben(jamin)
Keating, Geoffrey
Kemp, Will
Kyd, Thomas
Leland, John
Lily, William
Lindsay, David
Lodge, Thomas
Lydgate, John
Lyly, John
Maitland, Richard
Malory, Thomas
Markham, Gervase
Marlowe, Christopher

Marston, John
Middleton, Thomas
Mirror for Magistrates
Montgomerie, Alexander
More, Thomas (see also *Utopia*)
Munday, Anthony
Nashe, Thomas
North, Thomas
Norton, Thomas
Owen, John
Oxford, Edward de Vere, 17th
    Earl of Oxford
Painter, William
Peele, George
Pembroke, Mary, Countess of
    Pembroke
Rich, Barnabe
Sackville, Thomas
Savile, Henry
Scott, Alexander
Sempill, Robert
Shakespeare, William
Sidney, Philip
Skelton, John
Southampton, Henry Wriothesley,
    3rd Earl of Southampton
Spenser, Edmund (see also *The
    Faerie Queene*)
Stanyhurst, Richard
Surrey, Henry Howard, Earl of
    Surrey
Tarleton, Richard
Tourneur, Cyril
Tyndale, William
Udall, Nicholas
Vergil, Polydore
Webster, John
Wotton, Henry
Wyatt, Thomas
Wyntoun, Andrew of

EASTERN EUROPE

POLITICAL EVENTS

Czech Brethren
Mohács, Battle of

Tannenberg, Battle of
Vienna, Battle of

POLITICAL AND LITERARY FIGURES

Báthory, Stephen
Chelčický, Petr
Hunyadi, János Corvinus
Ivan III

Ivan IV (the Terrible)
Kochanowski, Jan
Matthias Corvinus
Pontan, Jiri

Rej, Mikołaj
Zsamboky, János

FRENCH LANDS AND LOW COUNTRIES

KINGS OF FRANCE

Charles VI	1380-1422	Louis XII	1498-1515	Charles IX	1560-74
Charles VII	1422-61	**Francis I**	1515-47	Henry III	1574-89
Louis XI	1461-83	**Henry II**	1547-59	**Henry IV**	
Charles VIII	1483-98	**Francis II**	1559-60	of Bourbon	1589-1610

Note: Those marked in bold have entries in the A-Z text.

VALOIS DUKES OF BURGUNDY

Philip the Bold	1363-1404	Philip the Good	1419-67
John the Fearless	1404-19	Charles the Bold	1467-77

THEMES AND EVENTS

Cambrai, League of
Nantes, Edict of

Placards, Day of
Religion, Wars of

St Bartholomew, Massacre of

POLITICAL FIGURES

Amboise, Georges d'
Bourbon, Charles, 8th Duke of
   Bourbon
Brantôme, Pierre de Bourdeille
Catherine de' Medici
Coligny, Gaspard de
Condé, Louis I de Bourbon

Condé, Henri I de Bourbon
Coeur, Jacques
Crillon, Louis des Balbes de
   Berton de
Diane de Poitiers
Marguerite of Navarre
Mary, Duchess of Burgundy

Montluc, Blaise de Lasseran-
   Massencôme
Montmorency, Anne de
René the Good
Sully, Maximilien de Béthune,
   duc de Sully

ARTISTS AND ARCHITECTS

AUTHORS

GERMAN-SPEAKING LANDS

ARTISTS

LITERATURE

IBERIAN PENINSULA

MONARCHS

CASTILE AND ARAGON

João III	1521-57	Charles I (**Charles V**)	1516-56
Sebastião	1557-78	**Philip II** (King of Portugal from 1580)	1556-98
Henrique	1578-80		

PORTUGAL, CASTILE, AND ARAGON

Philip II	1580-98
Philip III	1598-1621

Note: Those marked in bold have entries in the A-Z text.

THEMES AND EVENTS

converso
Escorial, El

Maneuline style
marrano

plateresque
Spanish Armada

POLITICAL FIGURES

Albuquerque, Afonso de, the
  Younger
Alva, Ferdinand Alvarez
Luna, Alvaro de

Menéndez de Avilés, Pedro
Pedro, Constable of Portugal
Pedro, Prince and Duke of
  Coimbra

Ximénes de Cisneros, Cardinal
  Francisco

ARTISTS AND ARCHITECTS

Bermejo, Bartolomé
Berruguete, Alonso
Berruguete, Pedro
Coello, Alonso Sánchez
Covarrubias, Alonso de

Egas, Enrique de
Gonçalves, Nuno
Greco, El
Herrera, Juan de
Huguet, Jaime

Morales, Luis de
Pantoja de la Cruz, Juan
Roelas, Juan de las
Vargas, Luis de

LITERATURE

Abravanel, Isaac
Acosta, José de
Alemán, Mateo (see also *Guzmán
  de Alfarache*)
Boscà i Almogàver, Joan
Camões, Luis Vaz de (see also
  The Lusiads)
Castanheda, Fernão Lopes de
Castillejo, Cristóbal de
Castro y Bellvís, Guillén de
Celestina, La
Cervantes Saavedra, Miguel de
  (see also *Don Quixote*)
Complutensian Polyglot
Cueva, Juan de la
Diana, La
Ercilla y Zúñiga, Alonso de (see
  also the *Araucana*)
Fernández de Avellaneda, Alonso
Ferreira, António
Figueroa, Francisco de

Garcilaso de la Vega
Garcilaso de la Vega, el Inca
Góis, Damião de
Góngora y Argote, Luis de
Guevara, Fray Antonio
Hebreo, Leone
Herrera, Fernando de
Hurtado de Mendoza, Diego
Lazarillo de Tormes
Leone Ebreo (see Hebreo,
  Leone)
Lope de Rueda
Lopes, Fernão
López, de Ayala, Pero
Luis de León, Fray
Lusiads, The
Manrique, Jorge
March, Ausiàs
Mena, Juan de
Montemayor, Jorge de (see also
  La Diana)

Morales, Ambrosio de
Nebrija, Elio Antonio Martinez
  de Cala, de
Núñez de Toledo y Guzmán,
  Hernán
Pérez de Guzmán, Fernán
Quixote, Don
Rojas, Fernando de (see also
  Celestina, La)
Sá de Miranda, Francisco
Santillana, Iñigo López de
  Mendoza, Marqués de
Valdés, Alfonso de
Valdés, Juan de
Vega Carpio, Lope Félix de
Villena, Enrique de
Vives, Juan Luis
Zurara, Gomes Eanes de
Zurita, Jerónimo de

ITALIAN PENINSULA

For Ferrara, see **Este dynasty.**
For Florence, see **Medici family,** also **Piero Soderini.**

For Mantua, see **Gonzaga dynasty.**
For Milan, see **Visconti dynasty** and **Sforza dynasty.**

NAPLES

KINGS

Louis II of Anjou (see **Anjou Dynasty**)	1386-1400	Alfonso II	1494-95
Ladislas	1400-14	Ferdinand II (**Ferdinand V** of Aragon)	1495-96
Joanna II	1414-35	Federico	1496-1501
René 'the Good' of Anjou	1435-42	Louis XII of France	1501-03
Alfonso I (**Alfonso V** of Aragon)	1442-58	from 1503 ruled once again by the Kings of Aragon	
Ferrante I	1458-94		

Note: Those marked in bold have entries in the A-Z text.

POLITICAL TERMS

Ambrosian Republic	*gonfaloniere*	*signore*
Arrabbiati	Maggior Consiglio	*signoria*
condottiere	Pavia, Battle of	
Council of Ten	Pazzi conspiracy	

POLITICAL FIGURES

Acciaiuoli family	Colonna, Prospero	Rienzo, Cola di
Albizzi, Rinaldo degli	Cornaro, Caterina	Rucellai, Bernardo di Giovanni
Baglioni family	Cosimo de' Medici	Rucellai, Cosimo
Bardi family	Datini, Francesco di Marco	Rucellai, Giovanni di Paolo
Borgia, Cesare	Doria, Andrea	Savonarola, Girolamo
Borgia, Lucrezia	Federigo da Montefeltro	Scala, Bartolomeo
Cane, Facino	Gattamelata, Il	Sforza, Ludovico
Chigi, Agostino	Grimani, Cardinal Domenico	Visconti, Giangaleazzo
Colleoni, Bartolommeo	Medici, Cosimo de'	
Colonna, Pompeo	Medici, Lorenzo de'	

ARTISTIC PRODUCTIONS

Arena Chapel (Padua)	Marciana, Biblioteca (Venice)	Té, Palazzo del
Farnese, Palazzo (Rome)	Pienza	Tempietto (Rome)
Laurenziana, Biblioteca (Florence)	St Peter's Cathedral (Rome)	
Marciana, Biblioteca (Florence)	Sistine Chapel (Rome)	

ARTISTS AND ARCHITECTS

AUTHORS (INCLUDING GREEKS ACTIVE IN ITALY)

ARTISTIC THEMES AND TECHNIQUES

DECORATIVE ARTS

EXPLORATION

Davis, John
de Soto, Hernando
Diaz de Solís, Juan
Diaz, Bartolomeu
Fernandez de Quirós, Pedro
Fernández, Juan
Frobisher, Martin
Gama, Vasco da

Garcilaso de la Vega, el Inca
Gilbert, Humphrey
Gomez, Diego
Hakluyt, Richard
Henry the Navigator
Hudson, Henry
Magellan, Ferdinand
Menéndez de Avilés, Pedro

Núñez de Balbea, Vasco
Orellana, Francisco de
Pizarro, Francisco
Ponce de León, Juan
Valdivia, Pedro de
Vespucci, Amerigo

LITERATURE

THEMES

academy
auto
bowdlerization
Byzantine novel
cancionero
chambers of rhetoric
commedia erudita

concetto
dedications
diphthongs
culteranismo
euphuism
facetiae

humanism (see feature on *Studia Humanitatis*)
pastoral novel
picaresque
poet laureate
terza rima

CLASSICAL AND PATRISTIC INFLUENCES

Apuleius
Athanasius, St
Basil of Caesarea, St
Galen
Horace
Juvenal

Lucretius
Martial
Plautus
Pliny the Elder
Pliny the Younger
Plotinus

Suetonius
Tacitus
Vegetius
Virgil
Vitruvius
Xenophon

MANUSCRIPTS, PRINTED BOOKS, AND ENGRAVING

Aldine Press
Amman, Jobst
Bade, Josse
bianchi girari
Book of Hours
Caxton, William
Elzevir Press
Estienne Press

Froben, Johann
Giunti (Junta) Press
Gutenberg, Johannes
Hopfer, Daniel
italic script
Jenson, Nicolas
littera antiqua
Manutius, Aldus (see also

Neakademia)
Ortelius, Abraham
Pannartz, Arnold
Petit, Jean
print
Raimondi, Marcantonio
Sweynheym, Conrad
Vespasiano da Bisticci

MUSIC

COMPOSERS AND MUSICIANS

Agricola, Alexander
Agricola, Martin
Alberti, Gasparo
Amat, Juan Carlos
Ammerbach, Elias Nikolaus
Ana, Francesco d'
Antico, Andrea de
Apel, Nikolas
Appenzeller, Benedictus
Appleby, Thomas
Arbeau, Thoinot
Arcadelt, Jacob
Ashwell, Thomas
Asola, Giammateo
Aston, Hugh
Bakfark, Balint Valentin
Banchieri, Adriano
Barbé, Anton
Bassano, Giovanni
Bateson, Thomas
Batten, Adrian
Bauldeweyn, Noel
Bedyngham, John
Belli, Girolamo
Berchem, Jachet de
Bermudo, Juan
Bertrand, Antoine de
Besard, Jean-Baptiste
Binchois, Gilles de Bins
Brumel, Antoine
Buchner, Johann (Hans von
    Constantz)
Buonamente, Giovanni Battista
Burmeister, Joachim
Burton, Avery
Busnois, Antoine
Buus, Jacques
Byrd, William
Cabezón, Antonio de
Caccini, Giulio
Calvisius, Seth
Canis, Corneille
Carlton, Richard

Carver, Robert
Caserta, Anthonello (Marotus) da
Caserta, Philipottus da
Cavalieri, Emilio de'
Cavazzoni, Marco Antonio
Certon, Pierre
Clemens non Papa
Cobbold, William
Coclico (Coclicus), Adrianus Petit
Compenius, Heinrich
Compère, Loyset
Coperario, John
Cornyshe, William
Corsi, Jacopo
Corteccia, (Pier) Francesco di
    Bernardo
Cowper, Robert
Damett, Thomas
Davy, Richard
Decius, Nikolaus
Dering, Richard
Dowland, John
Dufay, Guillaume
Dunstable, John
East, Michael
Eccard, Johann
Encina, Juan del
Escobar, Pedro
Esquivel Barahona, Juan de
Faber, Heinrich
Farnaby, Giles
Farrant, Richard
Fayrfax, Robert
Fedé, Jehen
Feragut, Beltrame
Ferrabosco, Alfonso
Finck, Hermann
Flecha, Mateo, the Elder
Flecha, Mateo, the Younger
Fogliano, Ludovico
Formé, Nicolas
Forster, Georg
Fossa, Johannes de

Francesco Canova da Milano
Frescobaldi, Girolamo
Fulda, Adam of
Gabrieli, Andrea
Gabrieli, Giovanni
Gafori, Franchino
Gagliano, Marco da
Galilei, Vincenzo
Genet, Elzéar (Carpentras)
Gese, Bartholomäus
Gesualdo, Carlo
Gherardello da Firenze
Ghiselin, Jean
Gibbons, Orlando
Giles, Nathaniel
Gintzler, Simon
Giovannelli, Ruggiero
Glareanus, Henricus
Gombert, Nicolas
Gorzanis, Giacomo
Goudimel, Claude
Grandi, Alessandro
Grenon, Nicolas
Guerrero, Francisco
Hacomblene, Robert
Hampton, John
Handl, Jacob
Hassler, Hans Leo
Hayne van Ghizeghem
Hemmel, Sigmund
Heroldt, Johannes
Holborne, Anthony
Horwood, William
India, Sigismondo d'
Isaac, Henricus
Jachet da Mantova
Janequin, Clément
Johnson, John
Johnson, Robert
Johnson, Robert
Jones, Robert
Jones, Robert
Josquin Desprez

THEMES

ars nova	counterpoint	oratorio
ballet de cour	*intermedii*	
cantus firmus	madrigal	

SCIENCE

THEMES

anatomy	Galen	syphilis
astrology	humours, theory of	

CHARACTERS

Achillini, Alessandro	Croll, Oswald	Lippershey, Hans
Aldrovandi, Ulisse	Dee, John	Mästlin, Michael
Alpini, Prospero	Dodoens, Rembert	Mattioli, Pierandrea
Apian, Peter	Eustachio, Bartolommeo	Napier, John
Bayer, Johann	Fabricius, David	Nostradamus
Belon, Pierre	Fabricius, Geronimo	Orta, Garcia da
Blaeu, Willem Janszoon	Fallopius, Gabriel	Paracelsus
Bombelli, Raffaele	Fernel, Jean François	Paré, Ambroise
Brahe, Tycho	Fracastoro, Girolamo	Porta, Giambattista della
Brunfels, Otto	Galileo	Regiomontanus
Bürgi, Jost	Gemma Frisius	Sanctorius, Sanctorius
Caius, John	Gerard, John	Stevinus, Simon
Cardano, Girolamo	Gilbert, William	Tagliacozzi, Gaspare
Cesalpino, Andrea	Harvey, William	Tartaglia
Clavius, Christopher	Kepler, Johannes	Tradescant, John
Colombo, Matteo Realdo	L'Ecluse, Charles de	Vesalius, Andreas
Copernicus, Nicolaus	Libavius, Andreas	Viète, François
Cornaro, Luigi	Linacre, Thomas	